THE FILM BOOK
BIBLIOGRAPHY
1940-1975

by
Jack C. Ellis
Charles Derry
Sharon Kern

with research assistance from
Stephen E. Bowles

The Scarecrow Press, Inc.
Metuchen, N.J. & London
1979

Library of Congress Cataloging in Publication Data

Ellis, Jack C   , 1922-
  The film book bibliography, 1940-1975.

  Includes indexes.
  1. Moving-pictures--Bibliography. I. Derry,
Charles, 1951-   joint author. II. Kern, Sharon,
joint author. III. Title.
Z5784.M9E44   [PN1994]   016.79143   78-4055
ISBN 0-8108-1127-8

HOW TO USE
THE FILM BOOK BIBLIOGRAPHY

This bibliography is a subject-organized listing of books published in English between 1940 and 1975 which deal with the various aspects of the motion picture. It also includes monographs and unpublished doctoral dissertations.

The body of film literature has been divided into ten major classifications: I-Reference, II-Film Technique and Technology, III-Film Industry, IV-Film History, V-Film Classifications, VI-Biography, Analysis, and Interview, VII-Individual Films, VIII-Film Theory and Criticism, IX-Film and Society, and X-Film and Education. Each of these classifications has been further subdivided into more specific categories. Definitions and explanations of the contents of the various classifications, as well as of the problems inherent in categorization, appear after each major classification and at various places within the body of the bibliography. Some books, because of the scope of their content, inevitably escape simple categorization; as an aid to the reader, works such as these have been classified in several categories. With the exceptions of classifications VI and VII, which have been organized alphabetically by subject person and film title, respectively, the entries within the various categories have been arranged chronologically, in order to present the evolution of film literature within each area.

Each citation is composed of an author listing, title, publication information, and page or leaf numbers. As a rule, annotations have been included only 1) to provide a reference for the name index by listing the persons a book is about or the contributors to it, 2) to clarify the content of a book whose title is misleading or nondescriptive or whose classification does not sufficiently characterize it.

To find material on a given topic, the reader should first consult the Table of Contents and then refer to the appropriate sections for a listing of relevant books. The reader may also consult the two indexes: 1) the name index, which lists all individuals cited in the bibliography, as authors or as subjects; and 2) the title index. The indexes utilize entry numbers rather than page numbers to direct the reader more easily to the appropriate citations.

TABLE OF CONTENTS

vi

INTRODUCTION

The Film Book Bibliography developed from our seminar in film historiography at Northwestern University in 1976. After familiarizing ourselves with the available film reference literature, we realized that a large-scale classified bibliography of books on film would be a useful addition to the field. The first major film bibliography, The Film Index, edited by Harold Leonard and published in 1941, provided bibliographic information on both books and periodicals. The New Film Index, edited by Richard Dyer MacCann and Edward S. Perry and published in 1975, attempted to bring The Film Index partially up to date by indexing film periodical material published between 1930 and 1970. From the outset we have regarded our project as essentially complementary to these two works, in that it attempts to list comprehensively books and monographs on film published in English between 1940 and 1975.

We began our research with a core of bibliographic citations accumulated by Jack Ellis over the past twenty-five years; these were supplemented by a number of entries collected by Stephen Bowles at various libraries in the United States. This initial core represented approximately 1500 entries. We then spent several weeks devising a workable classification scheme and tentatively classifying some of the original entries. Utilizing this basic structure, Charles Derry and Sharon Kern proceeded to seek out additional film book titles, to verify all entries, to make final classification decisions, and to guide the manuscript to its final form. With this additional research, plus the compilation of selected unpublished dissertation titles by Stephen Bowles, The Film Book Bibliography now contains more than 5400 classified entries.

Classification, being an ex post facto process, is understandably an undertaking fraught with difficulties. With dismaying frequency the classifier discovers new and different kinds of works which require that established classifications be re-defined, modified, or expanded. Occasionally he must discard classification categories which, although containing like books, cannot be accurately and succinctly labeled. Or, perhaps most frustrating of all, he encounters works which seem unclassifiable, either because they fit into no category or because they overlap many categories. Admitting these inherent difficulties, we have attempted to maintain throughout the project as consistent a classification as possible. Each book has been classified according to its dominant subject; books equally appropriate to more than one category have received multiple classification. Thus, desire for consistency tempered by concern for reader convenience informed our general methodology. Explanations of the various categories and classification distinctions can be found at the beginning of the sections within this bibliography.

We hope that this work will achieve two primary goals. First, that it will provide a reliable record of books on film in English published between 1940 and 1975. We were finally forced to realize that absolute comprehensiveness was an impossible goal, but we do believe that our bibliography provides accurate information for the large number of works that are recorded. Every book was verified by actually seeking it out or by corroborating secondhand information with unimpeachable sources like the National Union Catalog or the British National Bibliography. To aid accurate classification of books that could not actually be seen, we have consulted multiple sources, including other film bibliographies and book reviews in various periodicals.

Our second and equally important goal for this bibliography is to facilitate research in the various aspects of film by the film scholar and student. It is this goal that determined the subject-organized format. As was already briefly explained, we have arranged entries in chronological order so that the historical evolution as well as the scope of the literature on a given aspect of film can be readily perceived. Because of the size of this project, extensive descriptive annotations were simply impossible. Instead, we have attempted to communicate the nature of a book's content through its title plus its classification. We have departed from this rule in cases where the title was misleading, where it insufficiently suggested content, where we wished to annotate contributors or subjects of discussion for purpose of the indexes, or where we judged that additional information would be particularly helpful to the researcher. Our annotations are never intended to be evaluative, mainly because we feel that we cannot presume to know what the researcher is looking for. A book which is primarily photographic may be useful for one type of project and not another; a book which covers its topic somewhat superficially with no academic rigor (as, admittedly, many of the books in the genre section, for example, do) may be useful later as a document of popular interests; a book dealing with some now forgotten performer may eventually turn out to be a crucial source should that performer be rediscovered; and so forth. For those who want evaluations of a book's content, we suggest the very useful volumes by George Rehrauer, Cinema Booklist and Cinema Booklist: Supplement One and Supplement Two.

In deciding what publication information to include we have adhered to the following rules:

1) The primary publication entry for any work is the first American edition (or the British edition if the work has not been published in the United States).

2) In the case of dual British/American publication, we have

included the British edition as well as the American edition only if it precedes the American by two years or more.

3) The original publication year determines the position of the work's entry in the listings, although revised and reprinted editions are noted in parentheses. If a book published before 1940 has been revised or reprinted after 1940, the original date of publication has been given in parentheses before the first post-1940 edition.

4) In general, we have not listed reprints unless the reprint date follows the original date of publication by ten years or more.

5) The term "republished" has been used whenever we have been unable to ascertain whether a book has been revised or just reprinted. Often, however, even reprints may have updated prefaces or introductions.

6) Translated material tends to be entered chronologically according to its first English-language publication, rather than its original publication.

7) Whenever possible, we have tried to cite a book's original hardbound edition rather than its paperback edition.

8) Although the editors of anthologies generally contribute essays to their own books, we have as a rule not repeated the editor's name in the annotation as a contributor.

The reader should note that this bibliography specifically excludes program books, festival catalogs, and foreign publications, primarily because we believe that these areas deserve full-scale research projects of their own rather than a cursory treatment on our part. We have also excluded publicity material issued by studios and agencies, unpublished works (except for dissertations), and film distributors' catalogs. Although many exclusively British publications have been included, the bias of this bibliography is on material most readily available in the United States. For additional works the reader should consult the Catalogue of the Book Library of the British Film Institute.

The reader should also be aware of certain stylistic choices that we have made. Book and magazine titles are always underscored, primarily for easy readability. Movie titles, however, have been capitalized. Supplementary authorship credits such as "with the assistance of," "with material by," "with," and "as told to," have all been standardized as "with." Abbreviations used throughout this book include "pp." for page numbers, "ℓ." for number of leaves, "ca." for circa, "c." for copyright (used especially in cases when a book's publication and copyright dates differ), "approx." for approximately, "n.p." for no publisher listed, "ed." for editor, "comp." for compiler, and various standard abbreviations for American states. In general the state or country of publication has not been listed unless the city of publication is not commonly familiar.

We would like to acknowledge the assistance on this project of Gretchen Bisplinghoff and Barbara Warnke, who helped with some of the early checking processes, and Merle Kaminsky, who helped with the late indexing process. We would also like to thank the many individuals who allowed us to consult their personal libraries, including Russell Campbell, Bill Horrigan, Stuart Kaminsky, and Paddy Whannel; Richard Olson and the many librarians of Northwestern University who encouraged us and provided us with assistance over the past eighteen months; as well as all those friends who never lost patience with us as we queried them about the existence or whereabouts of obscure and perhaps irrelevant publications and who supported us with good wishes and encouragement during this long process. Finally, we would like to invite the users of this volume to point out any errors they may find so that these can be corrected in subsequent revisions.

Jack C. Ellis
Charles Derry
Sharon Kern

PART I

REFERENCE

A. GENERAL REFERENCE WORKS

The term reference refers mainly to those books not intended to be read from cover to cover, but rather to be consulted in order to find particular information. Organizing this section has proven to be especially difficult because various types of film reference provide much the same kinds of information; consequently, the works have been classified according to the basic format in which that material is organized.

The general reference works have been divided into four categories: encyclopedias, glossaries, annuals, and directories. Our definition of encyclopedia has been relatively strict. Ideally, a film encyclopedia would contain material on filmmakers, significant films, film subjects (genres, movements), national cinemas, film technique, and film institutions. Most encyclopedias contain information on some but not all of these aspects, and by their very nature their information is directed toward breadth rather than depth. For information on film credits, production data, as well as biographical material, the reader is especially advised to consult section I-B, filmographies, as well. Finally, since many reference books tend to be continually revised, the reader is cautioned to search for the most recent revision of any book he consults.

1. Encyclopedias

1 Cameron, James Ross and Cifre, Joseph S. Cameron's Encyclopedia: Sound Motion Pictures. (Originally published as Cameron's Encyclopedia on Sound Motion Pictures, 1930.) Sixth edition. Coral Gables, Florida: Cameron Publishing, 1959. 375 pp.
    Largely technical.

2 Miller, Maud M. (ed.) Winchester's Screen Encyclopedia. London: Winchester, 1948. 404 pp.
    An international encyclopedia, with much material on Great Britain.

3 The Focal Encyclopedia of Photography. New York: Macmillan, 1957. 1298 pp. (Revised New York, London: Focal, 1965, 1699 pp.)
    Includes material on cinematography.

4 Halliwell, Leslie. The Filmgoer's Companion. New York:
   Hill and Wang, 1965. 469 pp. (Revised 1967, 847 pp. Revised again London: MacGibbon, 1970, 1072 pp. Fourth
   edition, revised New York: Hill and Wang, 1974, 873 pp.)
      Thousands of entries on individuals, significant films,
   subject and themes, and film terms.

5 Michael, Paul (ed.) The American Movies Reference Book:
   The Sound Era. Englewood Cliffs, N.J.: Prentice-Hall,
   1969. 629 pp. (A portion reprinted as The American Movies: The History, Films, Awards: A Pictorial Encyclopedia,
   New York: Galahad, 1974, 387 pp. Another portion reprinted as Movie Greats: The Players, Directors, Producers,
   New York: Garland, 1974, 239 pp.)

6 Spottiswoode, Raymond and others (eds.) The Focal Encyclopedia of Film and Television Techniques. New York: Hastings, 1969. 1100 pp.

7 Levitan, Eli L. An Alphabetical Guide to Motion Picture, Television and Videotape Production. New York: McGraw-Hill,
   1970. 797 pp.

8 Manvell, Roger (general editor). The International Encyclopedia
   of Film. New York: Crown, 1972. 574 pp.
      Comprehensive reference material on individuals, coun-
   tries, and terminology.

9 Smith, John and Cawkwell, Tim. The World Encyclopedia of
   the Film. New York: World, 1972. 442 pp.
      Biographical entries on over 1500 people, plus a film
   title list with abbreviated credits.

10 Worth, Fred L. The Trivia Encyclopedia. Los Angeles:
   Brooke, 1974. 303 pp.
      Much material on film.

11 Bawden, Liz-Anne (ed.) The Oxford Companion to Film. New
   York: Oxford University Press, 1976. 767 pp.

2. Glossaries

12 Johnstone, A. Betty Lloyd (comp.) Dictionary of Motion Picture
   and Sound Recording Terms. Washington, D.C.: n.p.,
   194-. Various pagings.

13 Alvey, Glenn H., Jr. Dictionary of Terms for the Cinema:
   English--Italian. Rome: Mediterranea, 1952. 183 pp.

14 Clason, W. E. (comp.) Elsevier's Dictionary of Cinema, Sound
   and Music in Six Languages. Amsterdam: Elsevier, 1956.

948 pp.
British and American terms defined in English with their
French, Spanish, Italian, Dutch, and German equivalents.

15 Photo Dictionary and Quick Reference Guide: Photographic
   Terms, Abbreviations, Nomenclature for Motion Picture
   Films and Illumination, and a Descriptive Listing of Chem-
   icals Used in Photography. New York: Morgan and Morgan,
   1957. 128 pp.

16 Grau, Wolfgang. Dictionary of Photography and Motion Picture
   Engineering and Related Topics. Berlin: Verlag für Radio-
   Foto-Kinotechnik, 1958. 633 pp.
   Includes English terms along with German and French
   equivalents.

17 Sharps, Wallace Samuel. Dictionary of Cinematography and
   Sound Recording. London: Fountain, 1959. 144 pp.
   Includes detailed explanations of film production processes.

18 Sakharov, Aleksandr A. English-Russian Dictionary of Photography and Cinematography. Moscow: Foreign-Language Scientific and Technical Dictionaries, 1960. 395 pp.

19 Skilbeck, Oswald. ABC of Film and TV Working Terms. London: Focal, 1960. 157 pp.

20 Jacobson, Howard Boone (ed.) A Mass Communications Dictionary: A Reference Work of Common Terminologies for
   Press, Print, Broadcast, Film, Advertising, and Communications Research. New York: Philosophical Library, 1959.
   553 pp.

21 Telberg, Val. Russian-English Dictionary of Science, Technology, and Art of Cinematography. New York: Telberg, 1961.
   103 ℓ.

22 Shinde, Madhavrao Krishanji. Dictionary of Cine Art and Film
   Craft (for Students, Educational Institutions and People in
   Profession). Bombay: Popular Prakashan, 1962. 180 pp.
   With an emphasis on Indian cinema.

23 Nooten, S. I. van (ed.) Vocabulaire du Cinema/Film Vocabu-
   lary. 's-Gravenhage: Staatsdrukkerij-en Uitgeverijbedeijf,
   1964. 224 pp.
   Contains hundreds of film terms in French, English,
   Dutch, Italian, German, Spanish, and Danish.

24 Townsend, Derek. Photography and Cinematography: A Four-
   Language Illustrated Dictionary and Glossary of Terms. London: Redman, 1964. 178 pp.
   Terms defined in English, with their French, German,
   and Spanish equivalents.

25 Jordan, Thurston C., Jr. (ed.) Glossary of Motion Picture
      Terminology. Menlo Park, Cal.: Pacific Coast, 1968. 64 pp.

26 Barnet, Sylvan; Berman, Morton; and Burto, William. A Dic-
      tionary of Literary, Dramatic and Cinematic Terms. Boston:
      Little, Brown, 1971. 124 pp.

27 Miller, Tony and Miller, Patricia George. "Cut! Print!" the
      Language and Structure of Filmmaking. Los Angeles: Ohara,
      1972. 188 pp.

28 Geduld, Harry M. and Gottesman, Ronald. An Illustrated Glos-
      sary of Film Terms. New York: Holt, Rinehart and Win-
      ston, 1973. 179 pp.

29 Monaco, James. A Standard Glossary for Film Criticism. New
      York: New York Zoetrope, 1973. 30 pp.

30 Sergel, Sherman Louis. The Language of Show Biz: A Diction-
      ary. Chicago: Dramatic Publishing Company, 1973. 254 pp.
      Although primarily theatre jargon, includes film terms.

3. Annuals

        For this section on annuals, we have departed from our
standard format as explained in the introduction. Because many annuals have long publication histories with many editorial and publication changes, a complete entry for every edition would constitute an
excessive amount of detail. Therefore, each annual has one citation
prepared in a format which indicates as clearly as possible some of
its publication history. Rather than listing the annuals by their editors, we have listed them by their titles, which are arranged chronologically according to their earliest publication.
        The citations for annuals can be decoded as follows. The
first date appearing after the annual's title signifies the earliest
date for which we have verified the annual's existence. The hyphen
after this date signifies that the annual continued publication for a
certain period of time. If another date immediately follows the hyphen, it should be assumed that this is the last date the annual was
published (and that it subsequently discontinued publication). For instance, the notation "1918-1944" signifies that the annual appeared
as early as 1918 and suspended publication as of 1944. If, however,
as is usually the case, the hyphen is followed by a comma, the next
date indicates the most recent date for which we have confidently
verified the annual's continued existence. Thus, the notation "1916-,
1945" signifies that the annual appeared as early as 1916 and continued at least until 1945 (and, indeed, may have continued beyond).
Information given after this initial dating notation is not necessarily
inclusive. For instance, "1920-, 1960. Edited by John Smith" need
not imply that John Smith edited the annual each year from 1920 to
1960; rather that during that period he was at one time credited as
editor. Information separated by a semicolon implies exclusivity.

In other words, "1933-, 1966. Edited by Terry Ramsaye; edited by James D. Ivers" means that both Ramsaye and Ivers worked separately as editor sometime during the period between 1933 and 1966. In many cases the information after the initial dated notation will be followed by more specific information for particular years of the annual's publication. Alternate titles have been listed as consistently as possible. Since, however, page numbers in annuals tend to change every year, they are not listed.

The reference information which is contained in any particular annual is not annotated. Annuals consist of many kinds of information, including credits, casts, and synopses, especially (although not exclusively) in relationship to the particular year's films. Many annuals also include essays by people who were prominent during the year, as well as photographs, listings of awards, production data, historical essays, industry statistics, and directories of various professional services. The annuals which have been consistently published over long periods of time, such as Film Daily Year Book, International Motion Picture Almanac, Film Review, Screen World, and others, tend, of course, to be the most useful and the most accessible.

31 Writers' and Artists' Year Book: A Directory for Writers, Artists, Playwrights, Film Writers, Photographers, and Composers. 1906-, 1968. London: Black; New York. Subtitle varies.

32 Kinematograph Year Book. 1914-, 1961. London: Longacre. Also published as Kinematograph and Television Year Book.

33 Film Daily Year Book of Motion Pictures. 1918-, 1970. New York: Alicoate; New York: Film TV Daily. Also published as Film TV Daily Yearbook of Motion Pictures and Television. From 1918 to 1969: Reprinted New York: Arno, 1972, 1973. From 1918 to 1920: Published as Wid's Year Book. From 1920 to 1926: Published as Film Year Book. Edited by Joseph Darmenberg. 1927: Published as Film Year Book. Edited by M. D. Kann. From 1928 to 1929: Published as Film Daily Yearbook. Edited by M. D. Kann.

34 The Blue Book of Audio-Visual Materials. 1920-, 1953/54. Chicago: Educational Screen. Title varies. Also published as The Blue Book of 16mm Films.

35 The Best Moving Pictures of 1922-23; also Who's Who in the Movies and the Yearbook of the American Screen. 1923. Edited by Robert E. Sherwood. Boston: Small, Maynard. Reprinted New York: Revisionist, 1974.

36 International Motion Picture Almanac. 1929-, 1975. New York: Quigley. From 1929 to 1935/36: Published as The Motion Picture Almanac. From 1933 to 1949/50: Edited by Terry Ramsaye. From 1952/53 to 1955: Published as Motion Picture and Television Almanac. 1965: Edited by Charles B. Aaronson. 1975: Edited by Richard Gertner.

37 Picture Show Annual. 1929-, 1961. London: Amalgamated
     Press.

38 Fame: Annual Audit of Personalities of Screen, Radio and
     Television. 1933-, 1966. Edited by Terry Ramsaye; edited
     by James D. Ivers. New York: Quigley. Subtitle varies.
     From 1933 to 1935: Published as The Box Office Check-Up.

39 Music and Dance in California and the West. 1933, 1940, 1948.
     Hollywood: Bureau of Musical Research. Irregular. Title
     varies. 1933: Published as Who's Who in Music and Dance
     in Southern California. Edited by Bruno Ussher. 1940:
     Published as Music and Dance in California. Edited by Jose
     Rodriguez. 1948: Edited by Richard Drake Saunders.
     With material on film music.

40 Educational Film Guide. 1936-, 1958. New York: H. W.
     Wilson. Irregular. Title varies. From 1936 to 1944:
     Published as Educational Film Catalog. From 1936 to 1949:
     Edited by Dorothy Elizabeth Cook and K. M. Holden. From
     1950 to 1953: Edited by Frederic A. Krahn. From 1954 to
     1958: Edited by Josephine S. Antonini.

41 Film Facts. 1938-. New York: Motion Picture Producers and
     Distributors of America.

42 Best Pictures, and the Year Book of Motion Pictures in America.
     1939/40. Edited by Jerry Wald and Richard Macauley. New
     York: Dodd, Mead.

43 Educators Guide to Free Films. 1941-. 1975. Edited by Mary
     Foley Horkheimer and John W. Diffor. Randolph, Wisc.:
     Educators' Progress Service.

44 Hollywood Studio Blu-Book. 1941-, 1966. Hollywood.

45 Dipali Year-Book of Motion Pictures. 1943-. Edited by Bankim
     Chandra Chatterjea. Calcutta: Dipali Granthashala.

46 Film Review. 1944-, 1974/75. Edited by F. Maurice Speed.
     London: Macdonald; London: W. H. Allen.

47 Filmgoer's Review: A Pictorial Survey of the Year's Films.
     1944/45-. Edited by Forsyth Hardy. Edinburgh: Albyn.

48 Film Fun Annual. 1945. London: Amalgamated Press.

49 British Film Yearbook. 1946-, 1975/76. Edited by Peter
     Noble. London: British and American Press. From 1955/
     56: Published as British Film and Television Year Book.

50 Junior Film Annual. 1946/47-, 1949. Edited by Eric Gillett.
     London: Collins; London: Low, Marston. Also published

as Collins Film Book, Film Book, and Eric Gillett's Film
Book.

51 Preview Film Album: Hollywood-London. 1946-, 1962. Edited
    by Eric Warman. London: Golden Pleasure Books. Title
    varies.

52 This Year of Films: What the Critics Said. 1946-. Edited by
    Ion Hammond. London: Dewynters.

53 Film Portraits. 1947-, 1949. London: MacDonald.

54 Hollywood Album: The Wonderful City and Its Famous Inhabi-
    tants. 1947-, 1960. Edited by Ivy Crane Wilson. London:
    Low.

55 Informational Film Year Book. 1947-. Edinburgh: Albyn.
    Also published as Informational Film and Television Yearbook.

56 Motion Pictures and Books. 1947-. Edited by John L. Andriot
    with M. J. Andriot. Cincinnati. Also published as Motion
    Picture Index.

57 British Film Annual. 1948-. London: Daily Mail. Also
    published as Film Award Annual.

58 British Film Industry Yearbook. 1948. Edited by John Sullivan.
    London.

59 Film Monthly Review Annual. 1948-. London: Precinct.

60 Film, Radio, Television Sponsor. 1948-, 1951. Edited by R.
    Strode. London: Press Center. Also published as Film
    Sponsor and Film Sponsor and Viewers' Guide.

61 Film World. 1948-, 1951/52. Edited by Syd Cassyd. Holly-
    wood: Ver Halen. Also published as Film and Industry
    Directory.

62 Motion Picture Production Encyclopedia. 1948-. Hollywood:
    Hollywood Reporter.

63 Movie Review. 1948, 1949. Edited by Albert Edward Wilson.
    1948: London: Hammond. 1949: London: Dewynters.

64 Science in Films: A World Review and Reference Book. 1948-.
    Edited by Blodwen Lloyd. London: S. Low.

65 Film Parade. 1948-, 1951. Edited by Douglas Crane and
    Harold Myers. London: Marks and Spencer. Also published
    as Introducing the Hollywood-London Film Parade: The Two
    Film Cities in One Book.

66   Film Stars and Their Pictures.   ca. 1949-.   Edited by M. P.
     Reuben.   Worcester, England.

67   Film User Year Book.   1949-.   Edited by Bernard Dolman.
     London: Current Affairs.

68   Picture Parade.   1949-, 1952.   Edited by Peter Noble.   Lon-
     don: Burke.

69   Picturegoer Film Annual.   1949/50-, 1961/62.   Edited by
     Connery Chappell.   London: Odhams.   From 1959/60 to
     1960/61:   Edited by Robert Ottaway.   1961/62:   Edited by
     Guy Wall.

70   Screen World.   1949-, 1976.   New York: Biblo and Tannen;
     Philadelphia: Chilton; New York: Crown.   Also published
     as Daniel Blum's Screen World and John Willis' Screen
     World.   From 1949 to 1966:   Edited by Daniel Blum.   From
     1967 to 1976:   Edited by John Willis.

71   The Year's 16mm Films.   1950-, 1957.   London: Current
     Affairs.

72   Western Film and T.V. Annual.   1951-.   Edited by F. Maurice
     Speed.   London: Macdonald.   Also published as Western
     Film Annual.

73   Yearbook of the Canadian Motion Picture Industry.   1951-,
     1964/65.   Edited by Ed Hocura.   Toronto: Publications of
     Canada.   Also published as Yearbook of the Canadian Enter-
     tainment Industry.

74   Indian Motion Picture Almanac and Who's Who.   1953.   Bombay.

75   Movie Screen Yearbook.   1954-.   New York: Star Guidance.

76   Films of the Year.   1955/56-.   Edited by Peter Noble.   Lon-
     don: Express.

77   Hollywood Diaries Annual.   1955-.   New York: Affiliated
     Magazines.

78   Hollywood Love Life Annual.   1955-.   New York: Affiliated
     Magazines.

79   Girl Television and Film Annual.   1957-, 1964.   London: Od-
     hams.   Title varies.

80   International Film Annual.   1957-.   Edited by William White-
     bait.   London: Calder.

81   Japan Motion Picture Almanac.   1957-.   Edited by Jiri

Tsushinsha. Tokyo: Promotion Council of Motion Picture
Industry of Japan.

82 Annuaire de L'Industrie Cinematographique Internationale/Year-
    book of the International Motion Picture Industry. 1958-.
    Edited under the auspices of the International Federation of
    Film Producers Associations. Rome: Edizioni Cinematogra-
    fiche Internazionali.

83 Italian Production. 1958-, 1963. Rome: Unitalia Film. Also
    published as Italian Film Production.

84 Japanese Films. 1958-. Tokyo: Association for the Diffusion
    of Japanese Films Abroad.

85 Screen Education Yearbook. 1960-, 1969. London: Society
    for Education in Film and Television.

86 Film World. 1964-, 1967. Madras, India: Ranganathan.

87 International Federation of Film Archives Yearbook. 1964-.
    Paris: International Federation of Film Archives.

88 International Film Guide. 1964-, 1976. Edited by Peter Cowie.
    New York: A. S. Barnes.

89 Films: A Comprehensive Review of the Year in Motion Pictures.
    1965-, 1969/70. New York: National Catholic Office for
    Motion Pictures.

90 International Cinema Advertising Yearbook. 1965-. London:
    Admark.

91 Film Canadiana. 1970-1975/76. Ottawa: Canadian Film Insti-
    tute. 1972/73: Edited by Piers Handling and Louis Valen-
    zuela. 1973/74: Edited by Piers Handling, Louis Valenzuela,
    and Maynard Collins. 1974/75: Edited by Dave Goldfield
    and Piers Handling. 1975/76: Edited by Piers Handling and
    Dave Goldfield.

92 Multi Media Reviews Index. 1970-, 1975/76. Edited by C.
    Edward Wall. Ann Arbor, Mich.: Pierian. From 1973/74:
    Published as Media Review Digest.

93 Academy Awards Oscar Annual. 1971-, 1975. Edited by
    Robert A. Osborne. La Habra, Cal.: ESE California.

94 Film "Sneaks" Annual. 1972-. Edited by James L. Limbacher.
    Ann Arbor, Mich.: Pierian.
    Guide to non-theatrical 16mm films.

95 Indian Films. 1972-. Edited by B. V. Dharap. Poona, India:
    Motion Picture Enterprises.

96   Educational Media Yearbook.   ca. 1973-.   Edited by James
      W. Brown.   New York: Bowker.

                         4.   Directories

      The directories section includes those books which serve as
directories to film services, associations, people, and sometimes
even films.   "Who's whos" are also classified here.   Since most of
these directories are published yearly, all the books in this section
use the special format already created for annuals and explained in
the text before the previous section.   Note, however, that the absence of a hyphen after the first date in a citation implies that the
book was not issued as an annual.   Only for these "non-annual"
directories have we tried to include page numbers.   The reader
interested in audio-visual directories should also consult Part X,
Sections B-2 and B-3.

97   Academy Players Directory.   1937-. 1972.   Hollywood: Acade-
      my of Motion Picture Arts and Sciences.   From 1937 to
      1942:   Published as Players Directory Bulletin.   From 1939:
      Published with cover title, The Players Directory.   From
      1960:   Published in two volumes, Men and Women.

98   Hollywood Who's Who.   1941, 1942.   New York.

99   Players' Guide: A Pictorial Directory of Legitimate Theatre
      People.   1944-, 1966.   Edited by Terese Hayden with Paul
      L. Ross.   New York: Actor's Equity Association.   Subtitle
      varies.

100   Writers' Information and Hollywood Directory.   ca. 1945.
      Hollywood.

101   A Directory of ... 16mm Film Libraries.   1949, 1951, 1953,
      1956, 1959.   Compiled by Seerley Reid and Anita Carpenter.
      Washington, D.C.:   Office of Education.   Title varies.
      Comprehensive 1959 volume supersedes others.   1949: 32 pp.
      1951: 113 pp.   1953: 172 pp.   1956: 196 pp.   1959:
      236 pp.

102   Madras Film Diary (Directory).   1949.   Madras, India: V.
      Rama Rao.

103   Who's Who in Los Angeles County.   1950/51-.   Edited by Alice
      Catt Armstrong.   Los Angeles: Who's Who Historical So-
      ciety.

104   Asian Film Directory and Who's Who.   1952-, 1956.   Edited by
      V. Doraiswamy.   New Delhi.

105 Mike and Screen Press Directory. 1954/55-, 1957. Edited
    by Chester Burger. New York: Radio-Newsreel-Television
    Working Press Association of New York.

106 Feature Film Buyers Directory. 1955. Scarsdale, N.Y.:
    Film Directories Publishing.

107 Simon's Directory of Theatrical Materials, Services, and In-
    formation. 1955, ..., 1970, 1975. Edited by Bernard
    Simon. New York: Bernard Simon. 1975: 388 pp.

108 Kemp's International Film and Television Directory. 1957-,
    1972/73. London: Kemp's Commercial Guides. Title
    varies.

109 Cinema Laboratories. 1959. New York: Association of
    Cinema Laboratories. 59 pp.

110 International Celebrity Register (U.S. Edition). 1959. Edited
    by Cleveland Amory. New York: Celebrity Register.
    864 pp.
       Includes biographical material on film stars.

111 Professional Association in the Mass Media: Handbook of
    Press, Film, Radio, Television Organizations. 1959.
    Paris: UNESCO, Division of Free Flow of Information.
    206 pp.

112 Directory of Directors. 1960/61-. New York: Screen Di-
    rectors International Guild.

113 Palm Springs Personages. 1961-. 1964. Edited by Hildy
    Crawford. Palm Springs.

114 World Film Directory: Agencies Concerned with Educational,
    Scientific, and Cultural Films. 1962. Paris: UNESCO,
    Department of Mass Communication. 66 pp.

115 The IFTC Directory of International Film and TV Organiza-
    tions and Their National Branches. 1963. International
    Film and Television Council. 211 pp.

116 Feature Films on 8mm and 16mm: A Directory of Feature
    Films Available for Rental, Sale and Lease in the United
    States. 1966, 1969, 1971, 1974. Compiled by James L.
    Limbacher. Subtitle varies. 1974: New York: Bowker.
    368 pp.

117 Theatrical Variety Guide. 1966-. Los Angeles: Theatrical
    Variety Publications on behalf of the American Guild of
    Variety Artists.

118 Directory of Members. 1967/68-, 1975/76. Hollywood:
    Directors Guild of America.

119   Who's Who in Show Business: The International Directory of
       the Entertainment World. 1967/68-. Edited by Ken Hecht.
       New York.

120   Audio-Visual Market Place. 1969-, 1977. New York: Bowker.

121   Guide to College Film Courses. 1969/70-, 1975. Washington,
       D.C.: American Film Institute. Title varies. 1975:
       286 pp.

122   World Directory of Stockshot and Film Production Libraries.
       1969. Edited by John Chittock. Elmsford, N.Y.: Perga-
       mon.

123   Film and TV Festival Directory. 1970. Edited by Shirley
       Zwerdling. New York: Back Stage. 174 pp.

124   West Coast Theatrical Directory. 1970-. Los Angeles:
       Tarcher/Gousha Guides. 1974: Edited by Frank A.
       Joergler.

125   Directory of Film Libraries in North America. 1971. New
       York: Film Library Information Council.

126   Index to Producers and Distributors. 1971-. Los Angeles:
       National Information Center for Educational Media.

127   Canadian Professional Film Directory. ca. 1973/74-, 1975/76.
       Edited by Phil Auguste. Toronto: Filmcraft. Irregular.

128   Directory of American Film Scholars. 1975. Compiled by
       Leona and Jill Phillips. New York: Gordon. 120 pp.

129   Production Directory: 500 TV-Film Producers. 1975. New
       York: Show Business. 48 pp.

B. FILMOGRAPHIES

Filmographies are defined at their simplest level as lists of films. These lists may be heavily annotated and include synopses, credits, production information, and reviews, or may be limited to titles alone. This section of filmographic information has been divided into four categories: international filmographies; national filmographies; filmographies of persons; and filmographies of subjects. These books provide similar kinds of information; they merely organize their material in different ways.

The section of international filmographies is composed of those books which list films of all countries and, generally speaking, do not limit their inclusion on any grounds more specific than, occasionally, dates of release.

The section of national filmographies is composed of those books which limit the films they list to a particular country of origin. It is here that material can be found on American films, Swedish films, Soviet films, etc.

The section of personal filmographies is composed of those books which list films according to the people who participated in their making. It is these books which provide filmographies of performers, screenwriters, directors, et al.

The final section, subject filmographies, is composed of those books which limit the films listed according to a particular subject or genre. It is here that material can be found on the horror film, the documentary, films about women, etc.

The user of this bibliography is advised, however, to look through all four categories in search of the particular kind of information he needs. Since many of these reference books have name, title, or subject indexes, one might very easily find material on a certain director, for instance, who has worked in the horror genre, by looking up his name in the index of a book whose main organization is by nationality. With this inherent overlapping of function in mind, we have listed only a few filmographies in more than one category.

In general, all these film lists are limited to the concept of film as art. For lists of films on subjects relevant to classroom studies or films to be used in an instructional context, the user is referred to the 16mm and audio-visual catalogs in Part X, Section B-3.

1. International Filmographies

130 National Legion of Decency. Motion Pictures Classified. New
     York: National Legion of Decency, 1951. 184 pp.
         Catholic moral classifications of films from 1936 to
     1950.

131 Scheuer, Steven H. (ed.) TV Movie Almanac and Ratings.
     New York: Bantam, 1958. 244 pp. (Second revised edi-
     tion published as TV Key Movie Reviews and Ratings, 1961.
     Third revised edition published as TV Key Movie Guide,
     1966, 403 pp. Fourth revised edition published as Movies
     on TV, 1968, 393 pp. Fifth revised edition published as
     Movies on TV, 1969, 404 pp. Sixth revised edition pub-
     lished as Movies on TV, 1971. Seventh revised "1975-76"
     edition published as Movies on TV, 1974, 621 pp.
         Brief synopsis, cast, and rating for almost 10,000
     films, primarily American.

132 Dimmitt, Richard B. A Title Guide to the Talkies: A Com-
     prehensive Listing of 16,000 Feature-Length Films from
     October, 1927, until December, 1963 [In Two Volumes].
     New York: Scarecrow, 1965. 2133 pp.
         Provides limited production data and publication infor-
     mation on each film's literary source.

133 National Catholic Office for Motion Pictures. Film Classifica-
     tion Catalog: 1936-65. New York: National Catholic Office
     for Motion Pictures, 1966.
         Classifications and ratings of the Legion of Decency.

134 Dimmitt, Richard B. An Actor Guide to the Talkies: A Com-
     prehensive Listing of 8000 Feature-Length Films from
     January, 1949, until December, 1964 [In Two Volumes].
     Volume I. Metuchen, N.J.: Scarecrow, 1967. 1167 pp.
     Volume II. 1968. Pagination continues to 1555 pp.
         Volume I lists the acting credits of each film title;
     Volume II indexes performers by name.

135 Consumers Union. Movies for TV, 21 Years of Ratings: The
     Results of Consumer Reports' Continuing Movie Poll, 1947-
     1968, Covering more than 5600 Films. Mount Vernon,
     N.Y.: Consumers Union, 1968. 48 pp. (Revised as
     Movies for TV, 6900 Ratings: 25 Years of Consumer Re-
     ports' Continuing Movie Poll, 1947-1972, published 1972,
     58 pp. Revised again as Movies for TV, 7393 Ratings:
     The Results of Consumer Reports' Continuing Movie Poll,
     April 1947-January 1974, published 1974, 60 pp.)
         The compiled movie ratings of Consumer Reports'
     readers on motion pictures, primarily American.

136 Maltin, Leonard (ed.). TV Movies. New York: New

American Library, 1969. 536 pp. (Revised "1975 Edition"
published 1974, 669 pp.)

137 The New York Times Film Reviews, 1913-1968 [In Six Volumes].
     Volume I, 1913-1931; Volume II, 1932-1938; Volume III,
     1939-1948; Volume IV, 1949-1958; Volume V, 1959-1968;
     Volume VI, Appendix, Index. New York: The New York
     Times and Arno, 1970. 4961 pp. (Supplements published
     biennially. The New York Times Film Reviews, 1969-1970
     published 1971, 333 pp. The New York Times Film Re-
     views, 1971-1972 published 1973, 435 pp. The New York
     Times Film Reviews, 1973-1974 published 1975, 383 pp.)
          First six volumes are reprinted reviews from the New
     York Times. Volume VI includes a comprehensive name
     index, a title index, a corporate index to all studios, pro-
     duction companies, and distributors whose names appear in
     the reviews, as well as a portrait gallery and awards
     listings. Reviews and indexes are continued in the supple-
     ments.

138 Thompson, Howard (ed.) The New York Times Guide to
     Movies on TV. Chicago: Quadrangle, 1970. 223 pp.
          Provides credit information and short critique of over
     2000 films.

139 Pickard, R. A. E. Dictionary of 1,000 Best Films. New
     York: Association Press, 1971. 496 pp.
          Provides credits and brief synopses.

140 Baer, D. Richard (ed.) The Film Buff's Bible of Motion
     Pictures (1915-1972). Hollywood: Hollywood Film Archive,
     1972. 171 pp.
          13,000 films given numerical critical ratings.

141 London Film Society. Programmes, 1st-108th Performance:
     October 25, 1925-April 23, 1939. New York: Arno, 1972.
          Reprinting of original program notes on hundreds of
     films.

142 Pedler, Garth. The Encyclopaedia of 9.5mm Silent Film Re-
     leases. South Croydon, England: Garth Pedler, 1972.
     52 pp.
          Credits and synopses on over 400 9.5mm films from
     1921-1953.

143 Sadoul, Georges. Dictionary of Films. Edited, translated,
     and updated by Peter Morris. Berkeley: University of
     California Press, 1972. 432 pp.
          Includes credits, synopsis, and critical comments on
     1200 films.

144 Crist, Judith. Judith Crist's TV Guide to the Movies. New

York: Popular Library, 1974.   415 pp.
Includes credits and criticism.

145   Garbicz, Adam and Klinowski, Jacek. Cinema, The Magic
      Vehicle: A Guide to Its Achievement. Journey One: The
      Cinema Through 1949. Metuchen, N.J.: Scarecrow, 1975.
      551 pp.
            Credits, synopsis, and critique on over 400 films.

146   American Film Institute. The American Film Institute Catalog of
      Motion Pictures: Feature Films 1961-1970 [In Two Volumes].
      Richard P. Krafsur, executive editor. Volume I; Volume II,
      Indexes. New York: Bowker, 1976. 1268 and 976 pp.
            Volume I includes detailed credit information and synop-
      ses of thousands of films, both American and foreign.
      Volume II offers a credit index, a literary and dramatic
      source index, a subject index, and a national production
      index to the listed foreign films.

                   2.   National Filmographies

147   National Film Archive. National Film Library Catalogue [In
      Three Volumes].   Volume I, Silent News Films 1895-1933.
      London: British Film Institute, 1951.   208 pp.   (Revised
      1965, 308 pp.)   Volume II, Silent Non-Fiction Films 1895-
      1934.   1960.   195 pp.   Volume III, Silent Fiction Films
      1895-1930.   1966.   326 pp.

148   U.S. Copyright Office. Motion Pictures, 1912-1939: Catalog
      of Copyright Entries.   Washington, D.C.: U.S. Library of
      Congress, 1951.   1256 pp.
            A cumulative listing of all film titles registered with
      the U.S. Copyright Office; indexes individual names and
      corporate organizations.

149   U.S. Copyright Office. Motion Pictures, 1894-1912: Catalog
      of Copyright Entries.   Washington, D.C.: U.S. Library of
      Congress, 1953.
            A cumulative listing of all film titles registered with
      the U.S. Copyright Office; indexes individual names and
      corporate organizations.

150   U.S. Copyright Office. Motion Pictures, 1940-1949: Catalog
      of Copyright Entries.   Washington, D.C.: U.S. Library
      of Congress, 1953.   599 pp.
            A cumulative listing of all film titles registered with
      the U.S. Copyright Office; indexes individual names and
      corporate organizations.

151   Raborn, George. How Hollywood Rates: 27 Years of Rating,

700 Stars and 1500 Movies.   Los Altos, Cal.:   Nelson,
1955.   64 pp.

152   Cavender, Kenneth and others (comps.) British Feature Di-
      rectors: An Index to Their Work.   London: British Film
      Institute, 1958.

153   Ghana Film Unit.   Films from Ghana.   Accra: Government
      Printer, ca. 1958.   20 pp.

154   Italian Directors.   Rome: Unitalia Film, 1958.   203 pp.
            Biographies and filmographies on over 80 Italian di-
      rectors.

155   Holmes, Winifred, for the British Film Institute.   Orient: A
      Survey of Films Produced in Countries of Arab and Asian
      Culture.   London: UNESCO, 1959.   Unpaged.

156   U.S. Copyright Office.   Motion Pictures, 1950-1959: Catalog
      of Copyright Entries.   Washington, D.C.: U.S. Library of
      Congress, 1960.   494 pp.
            A cumulative listing of all film titles registered with
      the U.S. Copyright Office; indexes individual names and
      corporate organizations.

157   Morris, Peter and Kardish, Larry (eds.) Canadian Feature
      Films 1914-1964.   Ottawa: Canadian Film Institute, 1965.
      57 pp.

158   Rigdon, Walter (ed.) The Biographical Encyclopaedia and
      Who's Who of the American Theatre.   New York: Heine-
      man, 1966.   1101 pp.
            Over 3000 entries; includes both theatre and film work.

159   Niver, Kemp R.   Motion Pictures from the Library of Congress
      Paper Print Collection 1894-1912.   Edited by Bebe Bergsten.
      Berkeley: University of California Press, 1967.   402 pp.
            Descriptions and credits of 3,000 films, primarily
      American.

160   Niver, Kemp R.   The First Twenty Years: A Segment of Film
      History.   Edited by Bebe Bergsten.   Los Angeles: Locare
      Research Group, 1968.   176 pp.
            Material on 100 American films from 1894 to 1913.

161   Winquist, Sven G.   Swedish Silent Pictures, 1896-1931, and
      their Directors: A Checklist.   Stockholm: Proprius,
      1967.   182 pp.

162   Winquist, Sven G.   Swedish Sound Pictures, 1929-66, and
      their Directors: A Checklist.   Stockholm: Proprius,
      1967.   158 pp. (Revised as Swedish Sound Pictures, 1929-
      69, and their Directors: A Checklist, 1969, 156 pp.)

163 Gifford, Denis. British Cinema: An Illustrated Guide. New York: A. S. Barnes, 1968. 176 pp.
   Filmographies of over 500 British performers and directors; includes a title index.

164 Rangoonwalla, Firoze. Indian Films Index: 1912-1967. Bombay: Udeshi, 1968. 130 pp.

165 Zalman, Jan. Films and Film-Makers in Czechoslovakia. Prague: Orbis, 1968. 99 pp.
   Includes career information and filmographies on 17 Czech directors.

166 Boost, Charles. Dutch Film '66/'68. The Hague: Government Publishing Office, 1969. Unpaged.

167 Hibbin, Nina. Eastern Europe: An Illustrated Guide. New York: A. S. Barnes, 1969. 239 pp.

168 Michael, Paul (ed.) The American Movies Reference Book: The Sound Era. Englewood Cliffs, N.J.: Prentice-Hall, 1969. 629 pp. (A portion reprinted as The American Movies: The History, Films, Awards: A Pictorial Encyclopedia, New York: Galahad, 1974, 387 pp.)

169 Winquist, Sven G. Authors of Swedish Feature Films and Swedish TV Theatre: A Checklist. Stockholm: Proprius, 1969. 333 pp.

170 Bucher, Felix with Gmür, Leonhard H. Germany. New York: A. S. Barnes, 1970. 298 pp.
   Filmographies for over 400 individuals and an index to cover 6,000 films.

171 Canadian Film Institute. Canadian Feature Films 1913-1969 [In Three Volumes]. Volume I, 1913-1940. Edited by Peter Morris. Ottawa: Canadian Film Institute, 1970. 20 pp. Volume II, 1941-1963. Edited by Peter Morris. 1974. 44 pp. Volume III, 1964-1969. Edited by Piers Handling. 1975. 64 pp.

172 Cowie, Peter. Sweden 1. New York: A. S. Barnes, 1970. 224 pp.
   A guide to the work of 170 directors, players, technicians, and other figures in the Swedish cinema, with credits and plot outlines of more than 70 important films, and an index to 1,000 titles.

173 Rangoonwalla, Firoze. Indian Filmography: Silent and Hindi Films, 1897-1969. Bombay: Udeshi, 1970. 471 pp.

174 American Film Institute. The American Film Institute Catalog

of Motion Pictures Produced in the United States: Feature
Films 1921-1930. [In Two Volumes]. Kenneth W. Munden,
executive editor. Volume I; Volume II, Credit and Subject
Indexes. New York: Bowker, 1971. 1653 pp.
    Volume I includes detailed credit information and synop-
ses of thousands of American films. Volume II offers a
complete name index and film subject classification index.

175   Billings, Pat and Eyles, Allen. Hollywood Today. New York:
    A. S. Barnes, 1971. 192 pp.
    Post-1960 filmographies of 370 individuals, plus a film
title index.

176   Martin, Marcel. France. New York: A. S. Barnes, 1971.
    191 pp.
    Filmographies on 400 individuals, plus a film title
index.

177   Niver, Kemp R. Biograph Bulletins 1896-1908. Edited by
    Bebe Bergsten. Los Angeles: Locare Research Group,
    1971. 464 pp.
    Handbills and bulletins, providing credit and synopsis
information on films produced by the American Mutoscope
and Biograph Company.

178   Svensson, Arne. Japan. New York: A. S. Barnes, 1971.
    189 pp.
    Filmographies of Japanese directors, players, and
technicians, with credits and outlines of important films,
plus a film title index.

179   U.S. Copyright Office. Motion Pictures, 1960-1969: Catalog
    of Copyright Entries. Washington, D.C.: U.S. Library of
    Congress, 1971. 744 pp.
    A cumulative listing of all film titles registered with
the U.S. Copyright Office; indexes individual names and
corporate organizations.

180   Beattie, Eleanor. A Handbook of Canadian Film. Toronto:
    Peter Martin, 1973. 280 pp.
    Includes filmographies, biographies, and bibliographies
on over 80 Canadian filmmakers.

181   Bowser, Eileen (ed.) Biograph Bulletins 1908-1912. New
    York: Octagon, 1973. 471 pp.
    Handbills and bulletins, providing credit and synopsis
information on films produced by the American Mutoscope
and Biograph Company.

182   Fuksiewicz, Jacek. Polish Cinema. Warsaw: Interpress,
    1973. 166 pp.
    Includes filmographies of 55 directors, screenwriters,
and cameramen.

183 Gifford, Denis. The British Film Catalogue, 1895-1970: A
     Reference Guide. New York: McGraw-Hill, 1973. Approx.
     1100 pp.
          Credit information and content notations for thousands
     of British films.

184 Wilson, Arthur (ed.)   The Warner Bros. Golden Anniversary
     Book: The First Complete Feature Filmography. New
     York: Film and Venture, 1973. 192 pp.

185 Parish, James Robert. Film Directors Guide: Western
     Europe. Metuchen, N.J.: Scarecrow, 1976. 292 pp.
          Filmographies of hundreds of directors of Western
     Europe.

                    3.   Person Filmographies

     This section includes only those books which provide refer-
ence material for 50 or more individuals. We have somewhat arbi-
trarily arrived at this number as an aid to classification, since
most of the books in Part VI, Sections A and B (individual and collective biography, analysis, and interview) do contain filmographic
reference as well. Indeed, the filmographies there may often be
more extensively annotated and complete than those to be found here.
The books in Part V, Section B edited by James Robert Parish, for
example, contain much reference material of a hard-to-find nature
and may be found particularly useful. For a general discussion of
filmographic reference books, see the extended explanation before
section B-1 of Part I.

186 Huntley, John. British Film Music. London: Robinson, 1947.
     247 pp. (Reprinted New York: Arno, 1972.)
          Biographies and filmographies on 170 composers, music
     directors, sound track stars, and film music writers.

187 Enser, A. G. S. Filmed Books and Plays: A List of Books
     and Plays from which Films Have Been Made. London:
     Deutsch, 1951. 218 pp. (Revised and updated 1968, 448
     pp. Revised again 1971, 509 pp. Revised again 1975,
     549 pp.)
          Includes listing of playwrights and novelists with the
     films derived from their work; 1975 revision indexes film
     titles from 1928 to 1974.

188 McCarty, Clifford (comp.) Film Composers in America: A
     Checklist of Their Work. Glendale, Cal.: John Valentine,
     1953. 193 pp. (Reprinted with minor additions New York:
     Da Capo, 1972.)

189 Smith, Frederick Y. (ed.)   American Cinema Editors First

Decade Anniversary Book. Hollywood: American Cinema
Editors, 1961. 224 pp.
 Includes a listing of members and their screen credits.

190   Graham, Peter. A Dictionary of the Cinema. New York: A.
S. Barnes, 1964. 158 pp. (Revised 1968, 175 pp.)
 Primarily filmographies for over 600 individuals of all
nationalities; includes film title index.

191   Rigdon, Walter (ed.)   The Biographical Encyclopaedia and
Who's Who of the American Theatre. New York: Heine-
man, 1966. 1101 pp.
 Over 3000 entries; includes both theatre and film work.

192   Meyers, Warren B. Who Is That? The Late Late Viewers
Guide to the Old Old Movie Players. New York: Personality Posters, 1967. 63 pp.
 Photographs of over 600 Hollywood character actors,
organized by type.

193   Sarris, Andrew. The American Cinema: Directors and Directions 1929-1968. New York: Dutton, 1968. 383 pp.
 Filmographies, evaluations, and analysis of 200 directors.

194   Twomey, Alfred E. and McClure, Arthur F. The Versatiles:
A Study of Supporting Actors and Actresses in American
Motion Pictures, 1930-1955. South Brunswick, N.J.: A.
S. Barnes, 1969. 304 pp.
 Biographical material and limited filmographies on over
500 character performers.

195   Academy of Motion Picture Arts and Sciences and the Writers
Guild of America, West (comps.). Who Wrote the Movie
and What Else Did He Write? An Index of Screenwriters
and Their Film Works, 1936-1969. Los Angeles: Academy
of Motion Picture Arts and Sciences and the Writers Guild
of America, West, 1970. 491 pp.
 Provides filmographies for 2,000 writers, writing
credits for 13,000 films, and a listing of awards, including
those given by the Writers Guild.

196   The New York Times Film Reviews, 1913-1968 [In Six Volumes].
Volume VI, Appendix, Index. New York: The New York
Times and Arno, 1970.
 Includes filmographies for all individuals whose names
appear in New York Times reviews. For supplemental
post-1968 filmographies, see entry 137.

197   Shipman, David. The Great Movie Stars: The Golden Years.
New York: Crown, 1970. 576 pp.
 Career information on over 150 pre-1945 stars.

198   Weaver, John T. (ed.)   Forty Years of Screen Credits 1929-
      1969 [In Two Volumes].   Metuchen, N.J.: Scarecrow,
      1970.   1458 pp.
            Filmographies for over 4000 players, primarily Ameri-
      can.

199   American Film Institute.   The American Film Institute Catalog
      of Motion Pictures Produced in the United States: Feature
      Films 1921-1930.   [In Two Volumes].   Kenneth W. Munden,
      executive editor.   Volume II, Credit and Subject Indexes.
      New York: Bowker, 1971.
            Provides filmographies (1921-1930) of thousands of indi-
      viduals in American films; see complete entry 174.

200   Daisne, Johan.   Filmographic Dictionary of World Literature
      [In Two Volumes].   Volume I, A to K.   New York: Hu-
      manities Press, 1971.   681 pp.
            Filmographies of authors whose work has been adapted
      to film; multi-lingual format.

201   Weaver, John T. (comp.)   Twenty Years of Silents 1908-1928.
      Metuchen, N.J.: Scarecrow, 1971.   514 pp.
            Filmographies of performers, directors, and producers;
      also lists studios and distributors of the era.

202   Corliss, Richard (ed.)   The Hollywood Screenwriters.   New
      York: Avon, 1972.   328 pp.
            Includes filmographies of 50 screenwriters.

203   Meeker, David.   Jazz in the Movies: A Tentative Index to
      the Work of Jazz Musicians for the Cinema.   London:
      British Film Institute, 1972.   89 pp.

204   Pickard, Roy.   A Companion to the Movies, from 1903 to the
      Present Day: A Guide to the Leading Players, Directors,
      Screenwriters, Composers, Cameramen and Other Artistes
      Who Have Worked in the English-Speaking Cinema Over the
      Last Seventy Years.   New York: Hippocrene, 1972.   287 pp.
            Selective filmographies, organized according to the
      genres in which the individuals work.

205   Reid, Alison (comp.)   Canadian Women Film-Makers: An
      Interim Filmography.   Ottawa: Canadian Film Institute,
      1972.   14 pp.
            Filmographies of 70 directors.

206   Sadoul, Georges.   Dictionary of Film Makers.   Edited, trans-
      lated and updated by Peter Morris.   Berkeley: University
      of California Press, 1972.   288 pp.
            Includes material on directors, screenwriters, cinema-
      tographers, art directors, composers, producers, editors,
      animators, choreographers, and inventors.

207 Parish, James Robert. Actors' Television Credits 1950-1972.
     Metuchen, N.J.: Scarecrow, 1973. 869 pp.

208 Parish, James Robert and Bowers, Ronald L. The MGM
     Stock Company: The Golden Era. New Rochelle, N.Y.:
     Arlington, 1973. 862 pp.
        Material, including filmographies, on 147 MGM actors
     and actresses.

209 Shipman, David. The Great Movie Stars: The International
     Years. New York: St. Martin's, 1973. 568 pp.
        Career information on over 150 post-1945 stars.

[210-299 no entries]

300 Ash, Rene L. The Motion Picture Film Editor. Metuchen,
     N.J.: Scarecrow, 1974. 171 pp.
        Credits of over 600 film editors in the United States
     and abroad.

301 Chaneles, Sol and Wolsky, Albert (eds.) The Movie Makers.
     Secaucus, N.J.: Derbibooks, 1974. 544 pp.
        Material on over 2000 performers and directors.

302 Limbacher, James L. (ed.) Film Music: From Violins to
     Video. Metuchen, N.J.: Scarecrow, 1974. 835 pp.
        Includes a film composers' filmography.

303 Michael, Paul. Movie Greats: The Players, Directors, Pro-
     ducers. New York: Garland, 1974. 239 pp. (Originally
     published as a portion of The American Movies Reference
     Book, 1969; see entry 5.)

304 The New York Times Directory of the Film. Introduction by
     Arthur Knight. New York: Arno, 1974. 961 pp.
        Abridged version of Volume VI of The New York Times
     Film Reviews, 1913-1968; designed for individual purchase;
     includes the personal name index--which provides filmogra-
     phies, awards lists, and portrait gallery of the stars.

305 Parish, James R. and Pitts, Michael R. Film Directors: A
     Guide to Their American Films. Metuchen, N.J.: Scare-
     crow, 1974. 436 pp.
        Filmographies on hundreds of directors.

306 Truitt, Evelyn Mack. Who Was Who on Screen. New York:
     Bowker, 1974. 363 pp.
        Filmographies of over 6000 deceased performers, pri-
     marily American, British, and French.

307 Dawson, Bonnie. Women's Films in Print: An Annotated Guide
     to 800 16mm Films by Women. San Francisco: Booklegger
     Press, 1975. 165 pp.

308 Guiles, Fred Lawrence. Hanging On in Paradise. New York:
     McGraw-Hill, 1975. 412 pp.
        Includes a lengthy section of selected filmographies of
     American screenwriters, compiled by John E. Schultheiss.

309 McCarthy, Todd and Flynn, Charles. Kings of the Bs: Work-
     ing Within the Hollywood System; An Anthology of Film
     History and Criticism. New York: Dutton, 1975. 561 pp.
        Includes filmographies of 325 less well known American
     directors.

310 Smith, Sharon. Women Who Make Movies. New York: Hop-
     kinson and Blake, 1975. 307 pp.
        Contains information on over 600 women filmmakers in
     the United States.

311 Stewart, John (comp.) Filmarama. Volume I: The Formidable
     Years, 1893-1919. Metuchen, N.J.: Scarecrow, 1975.
     394 pp.
        Primarily filmographies of American performers, plus
     a film title index.

312 Thomson, David. A Biographical Dictionary of the Cinema.
     London: Secker and Warburg, 1975. 629 pp.
        Contains material on 800 directors, producers, and
     performers.

313 American Film Institute. The American Film Institute Catalog
     of Motion Pictures: Feature Films 1961-1970 [In Two
     Volumes]. Richard P. Krafsur, executive editor. Volume
     II, Indexes. New York: Bowker, 1976.
        Provides filmographies (1961-1970) of thousands of indi-
     viduals working in film; see complete entry 146.

314 Parish, James Robert. Film Directors Guide: Western
     Europe. Metuchen, N.J.: Scarecrow, 1976. 292 pp.
        Filmographies of hundreds of directors of Western
     Europe.

315 Parish, James Robert and Leonard, William T. Hollywood
     Players: The Thirties. New Rochelle, N.Y.: Arlington,
     1976. 576 pp.
        Includes filmographies on over 70 individuals.

                    4. Subject Filmographies

        For a general discussion of filmographic reference books,
see the extended explanation before Part I, section B-1. For lists
of 16mm films on subjects relevant to classroom studies and films
on art, see Part X, section B-3.

316   British Film Institute. British Documentary Films Selected as
      Especially Suitable for Programmes of Film Societies and
      Clubs Interested in the Art of this Branch of the Film.
      London: British Film Institute, 1946. 15 pp.

317   Neergaard, Ebbe (ed.) Documentary in Denmark: One Hun-
      dred Films of Fact in War, Occupation, Liberation, Peace,
      1940-1948: A Catalogue with Synopses. Copenhagen:
      Statens, 1948. 89 pp.

318   Enser, A. G. S. Filmed Books and Plays: A List of Books
      and Plays from which Films Have Been Made. London:
      Deutsch, 1951. 218 pp. (Revised and updated 1968, 448
      pp. Revised again 1971, 509 pp. Revised again 1975,
      549 pp.)
          1975 revision indexes film titles from 1928 to 1974.

319   Burton, Jack. The Blue Book of Hollywood Musicals: Songs
      from the Sound Tracks and the Stars Who Sang Them Since
      the Birth of the Talkies a Quarter-Century Ago. Watkins
      Glen, N.Y.: Century House, 1953. 296 pp.
          Includes credit information on musicals and other films
      with songs from 1927 to 1952.

320   Geltzer, George. An Index to the Silent American Serial,
      1913-1930. New York: New Theodore Huff Memorial Film
      Society, 1955. 19 ℓ.

321   Jones, Jack Ray. Fantasy Films and Their Fiends. Okla-
      homa City: n.p., 1964. 131 pp.

322   Lahue, Kalton C. Continued Next Week: A History of the
      Moving Picture Serial. Norman: University of Oklahoma
      Press, 1964. 293 pp.
          Contains a lengthy filmography of serials.

323   Limbacher, James L. (comp.) Original Film Sources and
      Titles with Subsequent Remakes. Dearborn, Mich.: Dear-
      born Public Library, 1964. 43 ℓ. (Revised as Remakes,
      Series and Sequels on Film and Television, 1969, 74 pp.
      Revised again 1970, 87 pp.)

324   Morris, Peter. Shakespeare on Film. Ottawa: Canadian
      Film Institute, 1964. (Revised 1972, 39 pp.)
          An index to Shakespeare's plays on film.

325   Eyles, Allen. The Western: An Illustrated Index. New York:
      A. S. Barnes, 1967. 183 pp.
          Filmographies for over 350 individuals associated with
      the western, plus a film title index.

326   Corneau, Ernest N. The Hall of Fame of Western Film Stars.

North Quincy, Mass.: Christopher Publishing, 1969.
307 pp.
Biographies and undated filmographies on over 150
stars.

327 Limbacher, James L. Four Aspects of the Film. New York:
Brussel and Brussel, 1969. 385 pp.
Includes filmographies of natural color and tinted films,
widescreen films, 3-dimensional films, and pioneering sound
films.

328 Baxter, John. The Gangster Film. New York: A. S. Barnes,
1970. 160 pp.
Filmographies for over 200 individuals.

329 Carey, Gary. Lost Films. New York: Museum of Modern
Art, 1970. 91 pp.
Credits, synopses, and stills for 30 lost films.

330 Dougall, Lucy. The War/Peace Film Guide. Berkeley, Cal.:
World Without War Council, 1970. 50 pp. (Revised Chicago: World Without War, 1973, 123 pp.)

331 Vallance, Tom. The American Musical. New York: A. S.
Barnes, 1970. 192 pp.
Filmographies for over 500 individuals.

332 American Film Institute. The American Film Institute Catalog
of Motion Pictures Produced in the United States: Feature
Films 1921-1930. [In Two Volumes]. Kenneth W. Munden,
executive editor. Volume II, Credit and Subject Indexes.
New York: Bowker, 1971.
Provides classifications of films according to their
subject matter; see complete entry 174.

333 Taylor, John Russell and Jackson, Arthur. The Hollywood
Musical. New York: McGraw-Hill, 1971. 234 pp.
Contains career information on individuals and detailed
credits on 275 musicals (including musical numbers and
performers).

334 Lee, Walt (comp.) Reference Guide to Fantastic Films,
Science Fiction, Fantasy and Horror [In Three Volumes].
Volume I, A-F. Los Angeles: Chelsea-Lee Books, 1972.
154 pp. Volume II, G-0, 1973. Pagination continues to
355 pp. Volume III, P-Z, 1974. Pagination continues to
559 pp.
Mainly credit information, with some bibliographic
references.

335 Limbacher, James L. Movies About Movies. New York:
Educational Film Library Association, 1972. 8 pp.

336 Meeker, David. Jazz in the Movies: A Tentative Index to
the Work of Jazz Musicians for the Cinema. London:
British Film Institute, 1972. 89 pp.

337 Pickard, Roy. A Companion to the Movies, from 1903 to the
Present Day: A Guide to the Leading Players, Directors,
Screenwriters, Composers, Cameramen and Other Artistes
Who Have Worked in the English-Speaking Cinema Over the
Last Seventy Years. New York: Hippocrene, 1972. 287 pp.
   Primarily composed of reference sections on comedy,
western, musical, romance, adventure, thrillers and crime,
war, epics, and films based on plays and novels.

338 Weiss, Ken and Goodgold, Ed. To Be Continued.... New
York: Crown, 1972. 341 pp.
   Credit information and synopses on American serials
from 1929 to 1956.

339 Willis, Donald C. Horror and Science Fiction Films: A
Checklist. Metuchen, N.J.: Scarecrow, 1972. 612 pp.
   Credits and brief content notation on over 4000 titles.

340 Women's History Research Center. Films By and/or About
Women 1972: Directory of Filmmakers, Films, and Dis-
tributors, Internationally, Past and Present. Berkeley,
Cal.: Women's History Research Center, 1973. 72 pp.

341 Betancourt, Jeanne. Women in Focus. Dayton, Ohio: Pflaum,
1974. 186 pp.
   Discusses over 80 films about women; includes filmographic and biographic information on the filmmakers.

342 Naha, Ed. Horrors: From Screen to Scream. New York:
Avon, 1975. 306 pp.
   An encyclopedic guide to horror and fantasy films.

343 Parish, James Robert and Pitts, Michael R. The Great Spy
Pictures. Metuchen, N.J.: Scarecrow, 1974. 585 pp.
   Primarily credits and synopses for over 400 spy films.

344 Holman, L. Bruce. Puppet Animation in the Cinema: History
and Technique. South Brunswick, N.J.: A. S. Barnes,
1975. 120 pp.
   Includes filmographic information on puppet films and
puppet film animators.

345 Women's Films: A Critical Guide. Bloomington, Ind.: Audio-
Visual Center, Indiana University, 1975. 121 pp.
   A descriptive guide to 161 films by and about women.

346 American Film Institute. The American Film Institute Catalog of Motion Pictures: Feature Films 1961-1970 [In Two

Volumes]. Richard P. Krafsur, executive editor. Volume II, Indexes. New York: Bowker, 1976.
Provides classifications of films according to their subject matter; see complete entry 146.

347 Parish, James Robert and Pitts, Michael R. The Great Gangster Pictures. Metuchen, N.J.: Scarecrow, 1976. 431 pp.
Credits and discussion of hundreds of gangster films.

348 Parish, James Robert and Pitts, Michael R. The Great Western Pictures. Metuchen, N.J.: Scarecrow, 1976. 457 pp.
Credits and discussion of hundreds of westerns.

C. DISCOGRAPHIES

Discographies are defined as lists of recordings. Such lists may be heavily annotated and include detailed descriptions, credits, and production information, or may be limited to titles alone. All the discographies listed here contain material on the recordings of film performers or film composers.

349 Smolian, Steven. A Handbook of Film, Theatre and Television Music on Record, 1948-1969. New York: Record Undertaker, 1970. 128 pp.

350 American Society of Composers, Authors and Publishers. 30 Years of Motion Picture Music: The Big Hollywood Hits from 1928-1958. New York: A.S.C.A.P., 1958. 122 pp. (Revised as 30 Years of Motion Picture Music: The Big Hollywood Hits Since 1928, ca. 1959, 135 pp.)

351 Rust, Brian with Debus, Allen G. The Complete Entertainment Discography: From the Mid-1890s to 1942. New Rochelle, N.Y.: Arlington, 1973. 677 pp.

352 Limbacher, James L. A Selected List of Recorded Musical Scores from Radio, Television and Motion Pictures. Dearborn, Mich.: Dearborn Public Library, 1962. 31 ℓ. (Revised 1967, 48 ℓ.)

353 Thomas, Tony. Music for the Movies. South Brunswick, N.J.: A. S. Barnes, 1973. 270 pp.
Discographies of over 75 film composers.

354 Limbacher, James L. Film Music: From Violins to Video. Metuchen, N.J.: Scarecrow, 1974. 835 pp.

D. BIBLIOGRAPHIES

355 Lewin, William. What Shall We Read About the Movies? A Guide to the Many Books About Motion Pictures. (Originally published by the Photoplay Appreciation Committee of the National Council of Teachers of English, 1933.) Revision reprinted from Film and Radio Guide (January 1946), 1946. 12 pp.

356 Baden, Anne L. (comp.) Moving Pictures in the United States and Foreign Countries: A Selected List of Recent Writings. Washington, D.C.: U.S. Library of Congress, Division of Bibliography, 1940. 67 pp.

357 U.S. Film Service. Bibliography of Books on Motion Pictures. Washington, D.C.: U.S. Film Service, 1940. 8 numbered ℓ.

358 U.S. Film Service. Bibliography of Magazine Articles and Other Sources. Washington, D.C.: U.S. Film Service, 1940. 7 numbered ℓ.

359 U.S. Film Service. Bibliography of Periodicals and Newspapers. Washington, D.C.: U.S. Film Service, 1940. 3 numbered ℓ.

360 Writer's Program of the Work Projects Administration of New York City. The Film Index: A Bibliography. Volume I, The Film as Art. Edited by Harold Leonard. New York: Museum of Modern Art Film Library and H. W. Wilson, 1941. 723 pp.
    Annotations of 8600 items on film, both book and periodical material.

361 Leyda, Jay (comp.) Selected Bibliography of Current Motion Picture Literature, Sept. 1944/Sept. 1945-. Hollywood: Academy of Motion Picture Arts and Sciences, 1945.

362 U.S. Naval Photographic Science Laboratory, Anacostia, D.C. Selected Bibliography of Volumes Relating to the Creative Aspects of Motion Picture Production. Washington, D.C.: Producers-directors Section, Photographic Science Labora-

tory, Branch, Bureau of Aeronautics, United States Navy, ca. 1945. 23 pp.

363 Barry, Iris; Conover, Helen F.; and Fitz-Richard, Helen. The Motion Picture: A Selected Booklist. Chicago: American Library Association, 1946. 20 pp.

364 Smith, Bruce L.; Lasswell, Harold D.; and Casey, Ralph D. Propaganda, Communication, and Public Opinion: A Comprehensive Reference Guide. Princeton: Princeton University Press, 1946. 435 pp.
     An annotated bibliography.

365 Manvell, Roger. Film: A Reader's Guide. London: Cambridge University Press, 1947. 11 pp.

366 Goodman, Louis S. and Jones, Yvonne. Selected References on Audio-Visual Methods: An Annotated Bibliography Correlated with Edgar Dale's Audio-Visual Methods in Teaching, Dryden Press, 1946. New York: Film Research Associates, 1948. 30 pp.

367 Noble, Peter. The Cinema and the Negro, 1905-1948. London: Sight and Sound, 1948. 21 pp.

368 Zuckerman, John V. Music in Motion Pictures: Review of Literature with Implications for Instructional Films. Port Washington, N.Y.: Office of Naval Research, 1949. 17 pp.

369 Kitching, Jessie B. and Jones, Emily S. Index to Selected Film Lists. New York: Educational Film Library Association, 1950. 40 pp.

370 Dale, Edgar and Morrison, John. Motion Picture Discrimination: An Annotated Bibliography. Columbus, Ohio: Bureau of Educational Research, Ohio State University, ca. 1951. 41 pp.

371 Vincent, Carl; Redi, Riccardo; and Venturini, Franco (comps.) Bibliografia Generale del Cinema/Bibliographie Generale du Cinema/General Bibliography of Motion Pictures. Rome: Edizione del'Ateneo, 1953. 251 pp. (Reprinted New York: Arno, 1971.)
     Bibliography of international film literature, with textual material presented in Italian, French, and English.

372 Bouman, Jan C. (comp.) Bibliography on Filmology as Related to the Social Sciences. Paris: UNESCO, 1954. 42 pp.

373 Cinematheque de Belgique. Repertoire Mondial des Periodiques Cinematographiques/World List of Film Periodicals and Serials. Brussels: Cinematheque de Belgique, 1955. 127

pp. (Revised 1960.)
A listing of over 600 periodicals.

374 MacCann, Richard Dyer and Jorrin, Michael. Good Reading
About Motion Pictures: An Annotated List of Books in
English. Los Angeles: Department of Cinema, University
of Southern California, 1957. 24 ℓ.

375 Melnitz, William W. (comp.) Theatre Arts Publications in
the United States, 1947-1952. Dubuque, Iowa: Brown, for
the American Educational Theatre Association, 1959. 91 pp.
Contains a section on motion pictures and includes both
book and periodical material.

376 UNESCO, Department of Mass Communication. The Influence
of the Cinema on Children and Adolescents: An Annotated
International Bibliography. Paris: UNESCO, 1961. 106 pp.
(Reprinted Westport, Conn.: Greenwood, 1975.)

377 Blum, Eleanor. Reference Books in the Mass Media: An
Annotated, Selected Booklist Covering Book Publishing,
Broadcasting, Films, Newspapers, Magazines, and Advertising. Urbana: University of Illinois Press, 1962. 103
pp. (Revised as Basic Books in the Mass Media, 1972,
252 pp.)

378 Manz, Hans P. (ed.) Internationale Filmbibliographie 1952-62.
Zurich: Hans Rohr, 1963. 262 pp. (1963-65 Supplement
published ca. 1965.)

379 Santaniello, A. E. Theatre Books in Print. New York:
Drama Book Shop, 1963. 266 pp. (Revised with subtitle
An Annotated Guide to the Literature of the Theatre, the
Technical Arts of the Theatre, Motion Pictures, Television,
and Radio, 1966, 509 pp.)

380 Busfield, Roger M., Jr. Theatre Arts Publications Available
in the United States, 1953-1957. New York(?): American
Educational Theatre Association, 1964. 188 pp.
Contains a section on motion pictures and includes both
book and periodical material.

381 International Federation of Film Archives. Bibliography: FIAF
Members Publications, 1966. Ottawa: Canadian Film Ar-
chives for the International Federation of Film Archives
(FIAF), 1967. 48 ℓ.

382 International Federation of Film Archives. Union Catalogue of
Books and Periodicals Published Before 1914, Held by the
Film Archives Members of the International Federation of
Film Archives. Brussels: Royal Film Archive of Belgium
for the International Federation of Film Archives, 1967.
89 ℓ.

383 Jarvie, I. C. Movies and Society. New York: Basic Books,
     1970. 394 pp.
         Includes an extensive annotated bibliography of book and
     periodical material, especially relating to film and society.

384 Luboviski, Git. Cinema Catalog. Hollywood: Larry Edmunds
     Bookshop, ca. 1970. 524 pp.
         A listing of the bookstore's books, periodicals, promo-
     tional materials, and special items related to film.

385 The New York Times Film Reviews, 1913-1968 [In Six Volumes].
     Volume VI, Appendix, Index. New York: The New York
     Times and Arno, 1970.
         Indexes film reviews appearing in the New York Times.

386 Reilly, Adam (comp.) Current Film Periodicals in English:
     An Annotated Bibliography. New York: Adam Reilly, 1970.
     35 ℓ. (Revised New York: Educational Film Library Asso-
     ciation, 1972. 25 pp.)

387 Andrew, Janet. Non-Book Materials and the Librarian: A
     Select Bibliography. London: Aslib (Audio-Visual Group),
     1971. 21 pp.

388 McCarty, Clifford. Published Screenplays: A Checklist.
     Kent, Ohio: Kent State University Press, 1971. 127 pp.

389 Salem, James M. A Guide to Critical Reviews: Part IV,
     The Screenplay From the Jazz Singer to Dr. Strangelove
     [In Two Volumes]. Metuchen, N.J.: Scarecrow, 1971.

390 Samples, Gordon. How to Locate Criticism and Reviews of
     Plays and Films. San Diego: San Diego State University,
     Malcolm A. Love Library, 1971. 23 ℓ. (Revised as How
     to Locate Reviews of Plays and Films: A Bibliography of
     Criticism from the Beginnings to the Present, Metuchen,
     N.J.: Scarecrow, 1976, 114 pp.)

391 Schuster, Mel (comp.) Motion Picture Performers: A Bibliog-
     raphy of Magazine and Periodical Articles, 1900-1969.
     Metuchen, N.J.: Scarecrow, 1971. 702 pp.

392 Bukalski, Peter J. (comp.) Film Research: A Critical Bib-
     liography with Annotations and Essay. Boston: G. K. Hall,
     1972. 215 pp.

393 Cinemabilia Catalogue of Film Literature. New York: Cine-
     mabilia, 1972. 264 pp.
         Bookstore's catalogue of books on film, as well as
     periodicals and special materials.

394 Gottesman, Ronald and Geduld, Harry M. Guidebook to Film:
     An Eleven-in-One Reference. New York: Holt, Rinehart

and Winston, 1972.   230 pp.
Provides information on festivals, awards, archives,
schools, and distributors, as well as film books, periodicals, and bookstores.

395   Jones, Karen (ed.)   International Index to Film Periodicals
      1972.   New York: Bowker, 1973.   344 pp.
      Indexes film material from 60 periodicals.

396   Limbacher, James L.   A Reference Guide to Audiovisual In-
      formation.   New York: Bowker, 1972.   197 pp.
      A bibliography of books and periodicals, with an empha-
      sis on film; includes a glossary of audio-visual terms and
      information for the audio-visual librarian.

397   Rachow, Louis and Hartley, Katherine (comps.)   Guide to the
      Performing Arts, 1968.   Metuchen, N.J.:   Scarecrow,
      1972.   407 pp.
      Annual bibliography since 1957; dealt with film mini-
      mally until this volume, which indexes 7 film periodicals.

398   Rehrauer, George.   Cinema Booklist.   Metuchen, N.J.:
      Scarecrow, 1972.   473 pp.
      Descriptive and evaluative annotations on over 1500
      film books.

399   Theatre Arts Library, University of California at Los Angeles.
      Motion Pictures: A Catalogue of Books, Periodicals,
      Screenplays and Production Stills [In Two Volumes].   Volume
      I, Books and Periodicals, Screenplays; Volume II, Produc-
      tion Stills.   Boston: G. K. Hall, 1972.   662 and 507 pp.

400   Aceto, Vincent J.; Graves, Jane; and Silva, Fred (eds.)   Film
      Literature Index: Annual Cumulation of a Quarterly Author-
      Subject Periodical Index to the International Literature of
      Film [Multi-Volumed].   1973 Volume.   Albany: Filmdex,
      1975.   430 pp.   1974 Volume.   1976.   545 pp.   1975
      Volume.   1977.   609 pp.

401   Cohen, Louis Harris.   The Soviet Cinema: Annotated Bibliog-
      raphy on Film Literature.   n. p., 1973.   165 pp.

402   Manchel, Frank.   Film Study: A Resource Guide.   Ruther-
      ford, N.J.:   Fairleigh Dickinson University Press, 1973.
      422 pp.
      An annotated survey of film literature.

403   Monaco, James and Schenker, Susan.   A Selective Bibliography
      of Film Literature.   New York: New York Zoetrope, 1973.
      26 pp.

404   Schoolcraft, Ralph Newman.   Performing Arts Books in Print:

An Annotated Bibliography.   New York: Drama Book
Specialists, 1973.   761 pp.
    Includes a section on motion pictures.

405   Schuster, Mel (comp.)   Motion Picture Directors: A Bibliog-
      raphy of Magazine and Periodical Articles, 1900-1972.
      Metuchen, N.J.:   Scarecrow, 1973.   417 pp.

406   Sheahan, Eileen.   Motion Pictures: A Bibliography of Selected
      Reference Works for the Study of Film (With Emphasis on
      Holdings in the Libraries of Yale University).   New Haven:
      Yale University Library, 1973.   78 pp.

407   Ulrich's International Periodicals Directory: A Classified
      Guide to Current Periodicals, Foreign and Domestic: 15th
      Edition 1973-1974.   New York: Bowker, 1973.   2706 pp.
          With a short section including material on over 300
      film publications.

408   Bowles, Stephen E.   An Approach to Film Study: A Selected
      Booklist.   New York: Revisionist, 1974.   108 pp.

409   Bowles, Stephen E. (comp.)   Index to Critical Film Reviews
      in British and American Periodicals [Three Volumes in Two
      Books].   Volume I, Critical Film Reviews A-M.   New
      York: Burt Franklin, 1974.   345 pp.   Volume II, Critical
      Film Reviews N-Z [and] Volume III, Critical Reviews of
      Books about Film A-Z, and Indexes.   1975.   Pagination
      continues to 782 pp.

410   Gerlach, John and Lana.   The Critical Index: A Bibliography
      of Articles on Film in English, 1946-1973, Arranged by
      Names and Topics.   New York: Teachers College Press,
      1974.   726 pp.
          Indexes film material from 22 film periodicals and
      more than 60 general periodicals.

411   Moulds, Michael (ed.)   International Index to Film Periodicals
      1973.   New York: Bowker, 1974.   395 pp.
          Indexes film material from over 60 periodicals.

412   The New York Times Directory of the Film.   Introduction by
      Arthur Knight.   New York: Arno, 1974.   961 pp.
          Abridged version of Volume VI of The New York Times
      Film Reviews, 1913-1968; designed for individual purchase;
      indexes by performer, director, and other film contributors
      the film reviews appearing in the New York Times.

413   Powers, Anne (comp.)   Blacks in American Movies: A Se-
      lected Bibliography.   Metuchen, N.J.:   Scarecrow, 1974.
      157 pp.

414   Rehrauer, George.   Cinema Booklist: Supplement One.

Metuchen, N.J.: Scarecrow, 1974. 405 pp.
Descriptive and evaluative annotations on over 900 film
books, including many program books.

415 Samples, Gordon. The Drama Scholars' Index to Plays and
Filmscripts: A Guide to Plays and Filmscripts in Selected
Anthologies, Series and Periodicals. Metuchen, N.J.:
Scarecrow, 1974. 448 pp.

416 Batty, Linda. Retrospective Index to Film Periodicals 1930-
1971. New York: Bowker, 1975. 425 pp.
Indexes material from 19 periodicals, including book
review citations.

417 British Film Institute. Catalogue of the Book Library of the
British Film Institute [In Three Volumes]. Volume I,
Author Catalogue; Title Catalogue A-F. Volume II, Title
Catalogue G-Z; Script Catalogue; Subject Catalogue: Per-
sonality Index, Film Index. Volume III, Subject Catalogue:
Alphabetical Subject Index. Boston: G. K. Hall, 1975.
877 and 836 and 827 pp.

418 Dyment, Alan R. The Literature of the Film: A Bibliographic
Guide to the Film as Art and Entertainment, 1936-1970.
London: White Lion, 1975. 398 pp.
Includes over 1300 books on film.

419 Heinzkill, Richard. Film Criticism: An Index to Critics'
Anthologies. Metuchen, N.J.: Scarecrow, 1975. 151 pp.
Indexes the collected works of over 25 film critics,
primarily American.

420 Jones, Karen (ed.) International Index to Film Periodicals
1974. New York: St. Martin's, 1975. 517 pp.
Indexes film material from over 75 periodicals.

421 MacCann, Richard Dyer and Perry, Edward S. with Moisio,
Mikki. The New Film Index: A Bibliography of Magazine
Articles in English, 1930-70. New York: Dutton, 1975.
522 pp.

422 Nachbar, John G. Western Films: An Annotated Critical
Bibliography. New York: Garland, 1975. 98 pp.

423 Poteet, G. Howard. Published Radio, Television, and Film
Scripts: A Bibliography. Troy, N.Y.: Whitston, 1975.
245 pp.

424 Sitney, P. Adams (ed.) The Essential Cinema: Essays on
Films in the Collection of the Anthology Film Archives.
New York: Anthology Film Archives and New York Uni-
versity Press, 1975. 380 pp.

Includes lengthy bibliography of books and articles on the films in the collection.

425 Sive, Mary Robinson. Educators' Guide to Media Lists. Littleton, Co.: Libraries Unlimited, 1975. 234 pp.

426 Kowalski, Rosemary Ribich. Women and Film: A Bibliography. Metuchen, N.J.: Scarecrow, 1976. 278 pp.

427 Thorpe, Frances (ed.) International Index to Film Periodicals 1975: An Annotated Guide. New York: St. Martin's, 1976. 511 pp.
     Indexes film material from over 75 periodicals.

E. AWARDS AND FILM FESTIVALS

This section contains books which deal in whole or in significant part with film awards and film festivals. Other material on film awards (especially for a particular year) can be found in the individual volumes of the film annuals and yearbooks which are listed in Part I, section A-3. For other material on the Academy of Motion Picture Arts and Sciences, see Part I, section F, film institutions. For listings of the awards given by the National Society of Film Critics since 1967, see the organization's annual volume of criticism in Part VIII, section D, anthologies of theory and criticism.

428 Petrucci, Antonio (ed.) Twenty Years of Cinema in Venice. Rome: International Exhibition of Cinematographic Art, distributed by Ateneo, 1952. 698 pp.
   History of the international contributors to the Venice Film Festival, 1932-1952; includes essays by Paul Rotha, Giovanni Calendoli, Carl Vincent, Mario Verdone, Herman Weinberg, Gösta Werner, Gian Luigi Rondi, Andre Bazin, and others.

429 Neusbaum, Frank (comp.) International Calendar of Film Festivals, Contests and Awards. University Film Producers Association, 1957. 20 pp.

430 Clark, Henry. Academy Award Diary, 1928-1955: A Motion Picture History. New York: Pageant, 1959. 188 pp.

431 National Board of Review of Motion Pictures. 30 Years of the "10 Best": The Movies, Players, Directors, etc., Designated as the Best, 1930 through 1959. Compiled and introduced by Henry Hart. New York: National Board of Review of Motion Pictures, 1960. Unpaged.

432 Scherer, Kees (photographs) and Bertina, Bob and others (text). Film Festival. London: Deutsch, 1962. 95 pp. Translated by Karen Sweny.
   A record of the International Film Festival at Cannes.

433 Academy of Motion Picture Arts and Sciences. Academy

Award: A Complete List of Academy Award Winners for the First Thirty-Five Years They Were Conferred. Hollywood: Academy of Motion Picture Arts and Sciences, 1963. 59 pp.

434 Michael, Paul. The Academy Awards: A Pictorial History. Indianapolis: Bobbs-Merrill, 1964. 341 pp. (Revised New York: Crown, 1968, 374 pp. Revised again 1975, 390 pp.)

435 Likeness, George C. The Oscar People: From Wings to My Fair Lady. Mendota, Ill.: Wayside, 1965. 432 pp.

436 Mayer, Michael F. Foreign Films on American Screens. New York: Arno, 1965. 119 pp.
     Includes index of major international film festival awards.

437 Osborne, Robert A. Academy Awards Illustrated: A Complete History of Hollywood's Academy Awards in Words and Pictures. La Habra, Cal.: Schworck, 1966. 297 pp. (Updated yearly: 1967, 301 pp.; 1968, 313 pp.; 1972, 346 pp.)

438 Staples, Donald Edward. A Statistical Study of Award-Winning American Films and Their Makers, 1930-1964. Northwestern University: Ph.D., 1967. 172 pp.

439 Fredrik, Nathalie. Hollywood and the Academy Awards. Los Angeles: Award Publications, 1968. 191 pp. (Updated Beverly Hills, Cal.: Hollywood Awards Publications, 1972, 213 pp. Updated again, with Auriel Douglas, New York: Ace, 1973, 217 pp. Also published as History of the Academy Award Winners.)

440 Academy of Motion Picture Arts and Sciences. Academy Award Nominations and Winners [1927/28-1969]. Hollywood: Academy of Motion Picture Arts and Sciences, ca. 1969. Various pagings.

441 Michael, Paul (ed.) The American Movies Reference Book: The Sound Era. Englewood Cliffs, N.J.: Prentice-Hall, 1969. 629 pp. (A portion reprinted as The American Movies: The History, Films, Awards: A Pictorial Encyclopedia, New York: Galahad, 1974, 387 pp.)
     Includes a major section containing a cumulative list of various film awards, including Academy awards, Photoplay awards, and top grossing films.

442 Osborne, Robert. Academy Awards: Best Actor. La Habra, Cal.: ESE California, 1969. Unpaged. (Another edition 1972, unpaged.)

443 Osborne, Robert. Academy Awards: Best Actress. La
Habra, Cal.: ESE California, 1969. Unpaged.

444 Wasserman, Paul. Awards, Honors, and Prizes: A Directory
and Source Book. Detroit: Gale, 1969. 307 pp. (Revised with a subtitle A Directory of Awards and Their
Donors, 1972, 579 pp. Revised again with subtitle An
International Directory of Awards and Their Donors, 1975,
2 volumes.)
Includes material on motion pictures.

445 Academy of Motion Picture Arts and Sciences and the Writers
Guild of America, West (comps.) Who Wrote the Movie;
And What Else Did He Write? An Index of Screenwriters
and Their Film Works, 1936-1969. Los Angeles: Academy
of Motion Picture Arts and Sciences and the Writers Guild
of America, West, 1970. 491 pp.
Provides filmographies for 200 writers, writing credits
for 13,000 films, as well as a listing of awards, including
those given by the Writers Guild.

446 Eastman Kodak Company. Some Suggestions for Conducting
Film Competitions and Film Festivals. Rochester, N.Y.:
Eastman Kodak Company, 1970. 14 pp.

447 Zwerdling, Shirley (ed.) Film and TV Festival Directory.
New York: Back Stage Publications, 1970. 174 pp.

448 Gottesman, Ronald and Geduld, Harry M. Guidebook to Film:
An Eleven-in-One Reference. New York: Holt, Rinehart
and Winston, 1972. 230 pp.
Includes information on festivals and awards.

449 Osborne, Robert. 40 Years with Oscar at the Academy Awards.
La Habra, Cal.: ESE California, 1972. Unpaged.

450 Osborne, Robert. The Years with Oscar at the Academy
Awards. La Habra, Cal.: ESE California, 1973. Unpaged.

F. FILM INSTITUTIONS:
ARCHIVES, LIBRARIES, MUSEUMS

This section includes both historical and reference material on various film institutions and archives, such as the British Film Institute, the American Film Institute, the National Film Board of Canada, the Library of Congress, the International Federation of Film Archives, etc. It also includes material on film associations and libraries, listings of the book and film holdings of archives, as well as directories of educational institutions which offer film programs. For material on techniques relating to the cataloging, indexing, and preservation of film or the management of film institutions, see Part II, section F, techniques for the film collection and film archive.

451 Academy of Motion Picture Arts and Sciences. Check List of the Motion Picture Still Collection of the Academy of Motion Picture Arts and Sciences Library. Hollywood: Academy of Motion Picture Arts and Sciences, ca. 1941. 32 pp.

452 McDonald, Gerald Doan. Educational Motion Pictures and Libraries. Chicago: American Library Association, 1942. 184 pp.

453 U.S. Library of Congress, Motion Picture Division. Motion Picture Activities of the Library of Congress: An Analysis by John G. Bradley. Washington, D.C.: U.S. Library of Congress, 1948. Various pagings.

454 Waldron, Gloria with Starr, Cecile. The Information Film: A Report of the Public Library Inquiry. New York: Columbia University Press, 1949. 281 pp.
    Deals with the educational use and distribution of the documentary film as well as library film services.

455 Edinburgh Film Guild. Twenty-One Years of Cinema, A Twenty-First Anniversary Retrospect of the Work of the Edinburgh Film Guild. Edinburgh: Film House, ca. 1951. 24 pp.
    Includes essays by Norman Wilson and Forsyth Hardy, and film program lists.

456   Lods, Jean. Professional Training of Film Technicians.
      Paris: UNESCO, 1951. 155 pp.
      Survey of available training institutions.

457   National Film Archive. National Film Library Catalogue
      [In Three Volumes]. Volume I, Silent News Films 1895-
      1933. London: British Film Institute, 1951. 208 pp.
      (Revised 1965, 308 pp.) Volume II, Silent Non-Fiction
      Films 1895-1934. 1960. 195 pp. Volume III, Silent Fic-
      tion Films 1895-1930. 1966. 326 pp.

458   Film Council of America. A Guide to Film Services of Na-
      tional Associations. Evanston, Ill.: Film Council of
      America, 1954. 146 pp.

459   British Film Institute. The British Film Institute, 1954-1955.
      London: British Film Institute, 1955. 40 pp.

460   Cory, Patricia Blair and Myer, Violet F. Cooperative Film
      Services in Public Libraries: A Report of a Survey of
      Public Library Film Cooperatives, Made by the ALA Office
      for Adult Education. Chicago: American Library Associa-
      tion, 1956. 127 pp.

461   National Film Archive. The National Film Archive. London:
      British Film Institute, 1956. 16 pp.
      Explains the institution's purpose and procedures.

462   United Nations, Office of Public Information. United Nations
      Film Footage Library Index. New York: United Nations,
      Office of Public Information, Radio and Visual Services
      Division, 1957. Approx. 80 pp.

463   Ash, Lee. Subject Collections: A Guide to Special Book Col-
      lections and Subject Emphases as Reported by University,
      College, Public, and Special Libraries in the United States,
      [The Territories,] and Canada. New York: Bowker, 1958.
      476 pp. (Second edition 1961, 651 pp. Third edition com-
      piled by Lee Ash and Denis Lorenz, 1967, 1221 pp. Fourth
      edition 1974, 908 pp.)
      With short sections on motion picture and motion picture-
      related material.

464   British Film Institute. The First Twenty-Five Years. London:
      British Film Institute, 1958. 39 pp.

465   Buache, Freddy (ed.) International Federation of Film Archives.
      Paris: International Federation of Film Archives, 1958.
      47 pp.

466   International Federation of Library Associations, Section for
      Theatrical Libraries and Museums. Bibliotheques et Musees

des Artes du Spectacle dans le Monde/Performing Arts
Collections: An International Handbook. Published under
the direction of Andre Veinstein and others. Paris:
Centre National de la Recherche Scientifique, 1960. 761
pp. English translation by George Miller with Seabury
Quinn and Donald Fowle. (Revised as Bibliotheques et
Musees des Arts du Spectacle dans le Monde/Performing
Arts Libraries and Museums of the World, 1967, 803 pp,
translated by Helen A. Gaubert.)
With text in English and French.

467 Ledoux, Jacques. Study of the Establishment of National
     Centres for Cataloguing of Films and Television Programmes.
     Paris: UNESCO, 1963. 34 pp.

468 University Film Foundation. Motion Picture Production Facili-
     ties of Selected Colleges and Universities: A Survey, Re-
     ported by Don G. Williams and Luella V. Snyder. Wash-
     ington, D.C.: U.S. Department of Health, Education, and
     Welfare, Office of Education, 1963. 345 pp.

469 McKay, Marjorie. History of the National Film Board of
     Canada. Montreal: National Film Board of Canada, 1964.
     147 pp.

470 Scottish Central Film Library, Glasgow. Films by the
     Thousand: Story of the Scottish Central Film Library's
     First 25 Years, 1939-1964. Glasgow: Scottish Film Of-
     fice, ca. 1964. 19 pp.

471 Steele, Robert. The National Film Theatre of London, England.
     Boston: Boston University, Communication Arts Division,
     ca. 1964. 12 pp.

472 Morris, Peter (ed.) The National Film Board of Canada: The
     War Years: A Collection of Contemporary Articles and a
     Selected Index of Productions. Ottawa: Canadian Film In-
     stitute, 1965. 32 pp. (Reprinted 1976.)

473 Rockefeller Brothers Fund. The Performing Arts: Problems
     and Prospects: Rockefeller Panel Report on the Future of
     Theatre, Dance, Music in America. New York: McGraw-
     Hill, 1965. 258 pp.
        Includes material on private, corporate, and government
     support of the arts.

474 Swedish Film Institute. The Swedish Film Institute. Stock-
     holm: Svenska Film Institutet, 1965. 20 pp.

475 Great Britain. Committee to Consider the Need for a National
     Film School. National Film School: Report. London: Her
     Majesty's Stationery Office, 1967. 49 pp.

476 Niver, Kemp L. Motion Pictures from the Library of Congress
     Paper Print Collection 1894-1912. Edited by Bebe Bergsten.
     Berkeley: University of California Press, 1967. 402 pp.

477 International Federation of Film Archives. Union Catalogue of
     Books and Periodicals Published Before 1914, Held by the
     Film Archives Members of the International Federation of
     Film Archives. Brussels: Royal Film Archive of Belgium
     for the International Federation of Film Archives, 1967.
     89 ℓ.

478 James, Clifford Rodney. The National Film Board of Canada:
     Its Task of Communication. Ohio State University: Ph.D.,
     1968. 520 pp.

479 Quinn, James. The Film and Television as an Aspect of
     European Culture. Leyden, Netherlands: A. W. Sijthoff,
     1968. 168 pp.
         Includes major sections on the British Film Institute
     and other national film institutions.

480 American Film Institute. A First Year. Washington, D.C.:
     American Film Institute, ca. 1969. 32 pp.

481 American Film Institute. Guide to College Film Courses
     1969-70. Washington, D.C.: American Film Institute,
     1969. 44 pp. (Fifth edition published as Guide to College
     Courses in Film and Television, Washington, D.C.:
     Acropolis, 1975, 286 pp.)
         Includes a section on foreign film programs.

482 New York Public Library. Films: A Catalog of the Film Col-
     lection in the New York Public Library. New York: New
     York Public Library, 1969, 104 pp.

483 U.S. National Archives. The Guide to the Ford Film Collec-
     tion in the National Archives, 1914-1940. Washington,
     D.C.: General Services Administration, 1970. 118 pp.

484 British Film Institute. The B.F.I. in the Regions. London:
     British Film Institute, 1971. 32 pp.

485 Butler, Ivan. "To Encourage the Art of the Film": The Story
     of the British Film Institute. London: Hale, 1971. 208 pp.

486 Directory of Film Libraries in North America. New York:
     Film Library Information Council, 1971. 87 pp.

487 Young, William C. American Theatrical Arts: A Guide to
     Manuscripts and Special Collections in the United States
     and Canada. Chicago: American Library Association, 1971.
     166 pp.
         Includes some material on film items.

488   Gottesman, Ronald and Geduld, Harry M.   Guidebook to Film:
      An Eleven-in-One Reference.   New York: Holt, Rinehart
      and Winston, 1972.   230 pp.
            Includes information on archives, schools, film books
      and periodicals, distributors, and book stores.

489   American Film Institute.   American Film Institute Report.
      Washington, D.C.: American Film Institute, ca. 1972.
      80 pp.
            Report of the first several years of the A.F.I.

490   Theatre Arts Library, University of California at Los Angeles.
      Motion Pictures: A Catalogue of Books, Periodicals,
      Screenplays and Production Stills [In Two Volumes].
      Volume I, Books and Periodicals, Screenplays; Volume II,
      Production Stills.   Boston: G. K. Hall, 1972.   662 and
      507 pp.

491   International Film and Television Council.   Cinematographic
      Institutions: A Report.   Paris: UNESCO, 1973.   98 pp.
            The objectives and roles of film institutions in the
      development of national film industries.

492   Report on the Conference on Regional Development of Film
      Centers and Services.   New York: Museum of Modern
      Art, 1973.   51 pp.

493   Sands, Pierre Norman.   A Historical Study of the Academy of
      Motion Picture Arts and Sciences (1927-1947).   New York:
      Arno, 1973.   262 pp.

494   Backhouse, Charles.   Canadian Government Motion Picture
      Bureau 1917-1941.   Ottawa: Canadian Film Institute, 1974.
      44 pp.
            A history of the bureau which was a forerunner of the
      National Film Board.

495   Rose, Ernest D.   World Film and TV Study Resources: A
      Reference Guide to Major Training Centers and Archives.
      Bonn-Bad Godesberg, Federal Republic of Germany: Fried-
      rich-Ebert-Stiftung, 1974.   421 pp.
            Information on programs and institutions in 75 countries.

496   Barrett, Gillian (ed.) Periodical Holdings 1974.   London:
      British Film Institute, 1975.   80 pp.

497   British Film Institute.   Catalogue of the Book Library of the
      British Film Institute [In Three Volumes].   Volume I,
      Author Catalogue; Title Catalogue A-F.   Volume II, Title
      Catalogue G-Z; Script Catalogue; Subject Catalogue: Per-
      sonality Index, Film Index.   Volume III, Subject Catalogue:
      Alphabetical Subject Index.   Boston: G. K. Hall, 1975.
      877 and 836 and 827 pp.

498 Goldfield, Dave (ed.) A Guide to Film and Television Courses
     in Canada/Un Guide des Cours de Cinema et Television
     Offerts au Canada 1975-76. Ottawa: National Film Board
     of Canada, 1975. 209 pp.

499 Perry, Ted (ed.) Performing Arts Resources. New York:
     Drama Book Specialists, 1975. 231 pp.
          Reports on various research collections, including film
     resources at the Anthology Film Archives, Museum of
     Modern Art, Academy of Motion Picture Arts and Sciences,
     UCLA, American Film Institute, Wisconsin Center for
     Theatre Research, Library of Congress, and others.

500 Phillips, Leona and Jill. Directory of American Film Scholars.
     New York: Gordon, 1975. 120 pp.

501 Sitney, P. Adams (ed.) The Essential Cinema: Essays on
     Films in the Collection of the Anthology Film Archives.
     New York: Anthology Film Archives and New York Uni-
     versity Press, 1975. 380 pp.

502 Wheaton, Christopher D. and Jewell, Richard B. (comps.)
     Primary Cinema Resources: An Index to Screenplays,
     Interviews and Special Collections at the University of
     Southern California. Boston: G. K. Hall, 1975. 312 pp.

PART II

FILM TECHNIQUE AND TECHNOLOGY

A. BASIC AESTHETICS OF TECHNIQUE

Regrettably, filmmaking technique is too often considered a strictly nuts-and-bolts process. As Lee Bobker has suggested in Elements of Film, any film is the combination of two kinds of elements: the technical elements such as camera, lighting, and sound, and those aesthetic elements that transform the craft of filmmaking into an art. This section of the bibliography contains works which attempt to explain and analyze the aesthetic principles of film. Although the books here generally do not explore new areas of film theory, they do elucidate film's aesthetic systems in a fashion that makes them accessible to the filmmaker, film student, and critic. These aesthetics of technique, therefore, may be used in conjunction with the general (and more technical) filmmaking guides of Part II, sections B and C, although the books in those sections do occasionally contain limited aesthetic material as well. For more complex or theoretical analysis of film aesthetics, the reader is directed to the section of individual theorists, Part VIII, section A.

503 Freeburg, Victor Oscar. The Art of Photoplay Making. (Originally published 1918.) New York: Arno, 1970. 283 pp.

504 Freeburg, Victor Oscar. Pictorial Beauty on the Screen. (Originally published 1923.) New York: Arno, 1970. 191 pp.

505 Pudovkin, V. I. Film Technique. (Originally published 1929, enlarged 1933.) Reprinted in Film Technique and Film Acting. New York: Lear, 1949. 204, 153 pp.
See entry 4445.

506 Dale, Edgar. How to Appreciate Motion Pictures. (Originally published with subtitle A Manual of Motion-Picture Criticism Prepared for High School Students, 1933.) New York: Arno, 1970. 243 pp.
Payne Fund Study.

507 Spottiswoode, Raymond. A Grammar of the Film: An Analysis of Film Technique. (Originally published 1935.) Berkeley: University of California Press, 1950. 328 pp. (Reprinted 1969.)

508 Nilsen, Vladimir S. The Cinema as a Graphic Art (On a
     Theory of Representation in the Cinema); with an Apprecia-
     tion by S. M. Eisenstein. (Originally published 1937.)
     New York: Hill and Wang, 1959. 227 pp. Translated by
     Stephen Gary, with editorial advice from Ivor Montagu.
     (Reprinted 1972.)

509 Manvell, Roger. Film. Harmondsworth: Penguin, 1944.
     191 pp. (Revised 1946, 240 pp. Revised again 1950,
     287 pp.)

510 O'Laoghaire, Liam. Invitation to the Film. Tralee, Ireland:
     Kerryman, 1945. 203 pp.

511 Benoit-Levy, Jean Albert. The Art of the Motion Picture.
     New York: Coward-McCann, 1946. 263 pp. Translated
     by Theodore R. Jaeckel. (Reprinted New York: Arno,
     1970.)

512 Lindgren, Ernest. The Art of the Film: An Introduction to
     Film Appreciation. London: Allen and Unwin, 1948.
     242 pp. (Revised without subtitle New York: Macmillan,
     1963. 258 pp.)

513 Schmidt, Georg; Schmalenbach, Werner; and Bachlin, Peter.
     The Film: Its Economic, Social, and Artistic Problems.
     English language version: Hugo Weber and Roger Manvell.
     London: Falcon, 1948. 132 pp.
     Includes a largely visual presentation of film aesthetics.

514 Larsen, Egon. Spotlight on Films: A Primer for Film-
     Lovers. London: Parrish, 1950. 301 pp.

515 Feldman, Joseph and Harry. Dynamics of the Film. New
     York: Hermitage, 1952. 255 pp. (Reprinted New York:
     Arno, 1972.)

516 Livingston, Don. Film and the Director: A Handbook and
     Guide to Film Making. New York: Macmillan, 1953.
     209 pp. (Reprinted New York: Capricorn, 1969.)

517 Fischer, Edward. The Screen Arts: A Guide to Film and
     Television Appreciation. New York: Sheed and Ward,
     1960. 184 pp.

518 Fulton, A. R. Motion Pictures: The Development of an Art
     From Silent Films to the Age of Television. Norman:
     University of Oklahoma Press, 1960. 320 pp.
     Deals with film aesthetics by tracing the artistic de-
     velopment of motion pictures.

519 Montagu, Ivor. Film World: A Guide to Cinema. Baltimore:
     Penguin, 1964. 327 pp.

520 Stephenson, Ralph and Debrix, Jean R. The Cinema as Art.
     Baltimore: Penguin, 1965. 272 pp.

521 Gessner, Robert. The Moving Image: A Guide to Cinematic
     Literacy. New York: Dutton, 1968. 444pp.
           Explicates film aesthetics through analysis of dramatic
     techniques.

522 Huss, Roy and Silverstein, Norman. The Film Experience:
     Elements of Motion Picture Art. New York: Harper and
     Row, 1968. 172 pp.

523 Bobker, Lee R. Elements of Film. New York: Harcourt,
     Brace, 1969. 303 pp. (Revised New York: Harcourt
     Brace Jovanovich, 1974, 272 pp.)

524 Eastman Kodak Company. Elements of Visual Literacy: Se-
     lected Articles from Kodak's Periodical "Visuals are a
     Language." Rochester, N.Y.: Motion Picture and Educa-
     tion Markets Division, Eastman Kodak Company, 1969.
     23 pp.

525 Jacobs, Lewis (comp.) The Movies as Medium. New York:
     Farrar, Straus and Giroux, 1970. 335 pp.
           Essays on elements of image, movement, time and
     space, color, and sound; contributors include Gregg Toland,
     Maya Deren, John Howard Lawson, Ivor Montagu, Carl
     Dreyer, Eisenstein, Bela Balazs, Kurt Weill, Jonas Mekas,
     and others.

526 Whitaker, Rod. The Language of Film. Englewood Cliffs,
     N.J.: Prentice-Hall, 1970. 178 pp.

527 Casty, Alan. The Dramatic Art of the Film. New York:
     Harper and Row, 1971. 192 pp.

528 Fischer, Edward. Film as Insight. Notre Dame, Ind.: Fides
     Press, 1971. 208 pp.

529 Jinks, William. The Celluloid Literature: Film in the Hu-
     manities. Beverly Hills, Cal.: Glencoe Press, 1971.
     164 pp.

530 Coynik, David. Film: Real to Reel. Winona, Minn.: St.
     Mary's College Press, 1972. 274 pp.

531 Giannetti, Louis D. Understanding Movies. Englewood Cliffs,
     N.J.: Prentice-Hall, 1972. 217 pp.

532 Solomon, Stanley J. The Film Idea. New York: Harcourt
     Brace Jovanovich, 1972. 403 pp.

533 Currie, Hector and Staples, Donald. Film Encounter. Dayton,
     Ohio: Pflaum/Standard, 1973. 272 pp.
         Primarily stills accompanied by quotes which raise
     aesthetic questions.

534 Harrington, John. The Rhetoric of Film. New York: Holt,
     Rinehart and Winston, 1973. 175 pp.

535 Madsen, Roy Paul. The Impact of Film: How Ideas are
     Communicated through Cinema and Television. New York:
     Macmillan, 1973. 571 pp.

536 Zettl, Herbert. Sight, Sound, Motion: Applied Media Aes-
     thetics. Belmont, Cal.: Wadsworth, 1973. 401 pp.

537 Johnson, Lincoln F. Film: Space, Time, Light and Sound.
     New York: Holt, Rinehart and Winston, 1974. 340 pp.

538 Kuhns, William with Groetsch, Raymond and McJimsey, Joe.
     The Moving Picture Book. Dayton, Ohio: Pflaum, 1975.
     292 pp.
         Contains detailed pictorial analysis, including a chapter
     on Citizen Kane.

539 Scott, James F. Film, The Medium and the Maker. New
     York: Holt, Rinehart and Winston, 1975. 340 pp.

B. GENERAL FILMMAKING GUIDES:
PROFESSIONAL, INDEPENDENT, AMATEUR

This section contains those books intended as general guides to the complete filmmaking process for the professional, the independent, and the amateur filmmaker. Books on this subject which are organized in reference format, though often useful in explaining filmmaking techniques, have not been included here. For such works the reader is advised to consult Part I, section A-1, encyclopedias, and Part I, section A-2, glossaries. Material on producing films commercially and works which deal with the overall filmmaking process in the context of the studio system can be found in the production category, Part III, section A.

540 Hepworth, Cecil M. Animated Photography: The ABC of the Cinematograph; A Simple and Thorough Guide to the Projection of Living Photographs, with Notes on the Production of Cinematograph Negatives. (Originally published 1897, 108 pp. Revised 1900, 128 pp.) New York: Arno, 1970. 128 pp.

541 Talbot, Frederick A. Moving Pictures: How They Are Made and Worked. (Originally published 1912, 340 pp. Revised 1923, 429 pp.) New York: Arno, 1970. 340 pp.

542 Hulfish, David S. Motion-Picture Work: A General Treatise on Picture Taking, Picture Making, Photo-Plays, and Theatre Management and Operation. (Originally published 1913.) New York: Arno, 1970. 282, 297 pp.

543 Pudovkin, V. I. Film Technique. (Originally published 1929, enlarged 1933.) Reprinted in Film Technique and Film Acting. New York: Lear, 1949. 204, 153 pp.
    See entry 4445.

544 Hall, Hal (ed.) Cinematographic Annual [In Two Volumes]. Volume I, 1930. (Originally published 1930.) New York: Arno, 1972. 606 pp. Volume II, 1931. (Originally published 1931.) New York: Arno, 1972. 425 pp.
    Anthology on technical and aesthetic aspects of filmmaking.

545 Buchanan, Andrew. Film-Making From Script to Screen.
     (Originally published 1937.) Revised London: Phoenix,
     1951. 159 pp.

546 Strasser, Alex. Amateur Movies and How to Make Them.
     (Originally published 1937.) Revised London, New York:
     Studio, 1949. 88 pp.

547 Bau, Nicolas. How to Make 8mm Films as an Amateur.
     (Originally published in French, 1939.) Seventh edition
     London: Focal, 1961. 165 pp. (Eighth edition London,
     New York: Focal, 1966, 182 pp.)

548 McKay, Herbert C. Movie Making for the Beginner. (Origi-
     nally published 1939.) Revised Chicago: Ziff-Davis, 1948.
     143 pp. (Republished New York: Crown, 1953, 142 pp.)

549 Spencer, D. A. and Waley, H. D. The Cinema To-Day.
     (Originally published 1939.) Revised London: Oxford Uni-
     versity Press, 1956. 202 pp.

550 Amateur Cinema League. The ACL Movie Book: A Guide to
     Making Better Movies. New York: Amateur Cinema
     League, 1940. 311 pp.

551 Burnford, Paul. Filming for Amateurs. London: Pitman,
     1940. 108 pp.

552 Crump, Irving. Our Moviemakers. New York: Dodd, Mead,
     1940. 231 pp.

553 Home Movie Gadgets, Compiled by the Editors of Home
     Movies. Hollywood: Ver Halen, 1940. 91 pp.

554 Simon, S. Sylvan. Let's Make Movies. New York, Los
     Angeles: French, 1940. 112 pp.

555 Child, Eleanor D. and Finch, Hardy R. Producing School
     Movies: A Manual for Teachers and Students Interested in
     Producing Amateur Films. Chicago: National Council of
     Teachers of English, 1941. 151 pp.

556 Tuttle, Harris B. Color Movies for the Beginner. Chicago,
     New York: Ziff-Davis, 1941. 143 pp. (Republished 1949,
     144 pp. Reprinted New York: Crown, 1953.)

557 British Film Institute. Film Appreciation and Visual Educa-
     tion: A Summary of Some of the Speeches Delivered at the
     BFI's Summer School at Bangor, August, 1944. London:
     British Film Institute, ca. 1944. 91 pp.
         With contributions by Thorold Dickinson, Sidney Cole,
     Ken Cameron, Edward Carrick, and others.

558   Society of Motion Picture Engineers. The Technique of Motion
      Picture Production: A Symposium of Papers Presented at
      the 51st Semi-Annual Convention of the Society of Motion
      Picture Engineers, Hollywood, California. New York:
      Interscience, 1944. 150 pp.

559   Bendick, Jeanne. Making the Movies. New York: McGraw-
      Hill, 1945. 190 pp.
            Pictorial account of production and industry; for the
      young reader.

560   Cameron, James Ross. Sound Motion Pictures, Recording and
      Reproducing, Cinematography and Talkies [Fifth Edition].
      Coral Gables, Florida: Cameron Publishing, 1945. 322 pp.
      (Revised as Sound Motion Pictures, Recording and Repro-
      ducing: With Chapters on Motion Picture Studio and Film
      Laboratory Practice, 1947, 617 pp. Eighth edition 1959,
      996 pp.)

561   Eastman Kodak Company. How to Make Good Movies: A Non-
      Technical Handbook for Those Considering the Ownership of
      an Amateur Movie Camera and for Those Already Actively
      Engaged in the Making of Home Movies Who Want to Improve
      the Interest and Quality of Their Films. Rochester, N.Y.:
      Eastman Kodak Company, ca. 1946. 232 pp. (Republished
      with slightly different subtitle ca. 1956.)

562   Gaskill, Arthur L. and Englander, David A. Pictorial Conti-
      nuity: How to Shoot a Movie Story. New York: Duell,
      Sloan and Pearce, 1947. 149 pp. (Revised as How to
      Shoot a Movie Story: Techniques of Pictorial Continuity,
      New York: Morgan and Morgan, 1959, 135 pp. Reprinted
      1970.)

563   Bond, Fred. Better Color Movies: Quick, Simple Answers
      to Common Problems of Amateur Movie Makers. San
      Francisco: Camera Craft, 1948. 156 pp. (Republished
      1955, 159 pp. Reprinted New York: Ziff-Davis, 1960.)

564   Spottiswoode, Raymond. Basic Film Techniques. Berkeley:
      University of California Press, 1948. 185 pp.

565   Cook, Canfield. Color Movie Making for Everybody. New
      York: Whittlesey, 1949. 351 pp.

566   Offenhauser, William H. 16-mm Sound Motion Pictures: A
      Manual for the Professional and the Amateur. New York:
      Interscience, 1949. 580 pp.

567   Pereira, Arthur (ed.) Manual of Sub-Standard Cinematography.
      London: Fountain, 1949. 470 pp. (Revised as Manual of
      Narrow-Gauge Cinematography, 1952, 514 pp.)
            Includes 16mm, 8mm, and 9.5mm film information.

568   Wain, G. How to Film as an Amateur. London: Focal,
      1949. 152 pp. (Reprinted 1960.)

569   Battison, John H. Movies for TV. New York: Macmillan,
      1950. 376 pp.
          Discusses the production and use of motion pictures for
      television.

570   Brodbeck, Emil E. Handbook of Basic Motion-Picture Tech-
      niques. New York: McGraw-Hill, 1950. 311 pp. (Re-
      published Philadelphia: Chilton, 1966, 224 pp. Republished
      again New York: Amphoto, 1975, 268 pp.)

571   Maddison, John. Living Pictures. London: Puffin Picture
      Book, 1950. 30 pp.
          For the young reader.

572   Moen, Lars. 28 Basic Steps to Better Movies: Taking Up
      Where the Instruction Book Leaves Off. Los Angeles:
      Ver Halen, 1950. 110 pp.

573   Neale, Denis Manktelow. How to Use 9.5mm. London, New
      York: Focal, 1951. 167 pp.

574   Sewell, George H. Amateur Film-Making. London: Blackie,
      1951. 118 pp.

575   Spottiswoode, Raymond. Film and Its Techniques. Berkeley:
      University of California Press, 1951. 516 pp. (Reprinted
      1963 and 1970.)

576   Baddeley, Hugh. How to Make Holiday Films. New York:
      Focal, 1952. 120 pp.

577   Curran, Charles W. The Handbook of Motion Picture Technique
      for Business Men. New York: Times Square Productions,
      1952. (Republished as The Handbook of TV and Film Tech-
      nique: A Non-Technical Production Guide for Executives,
      New York: Pellegrini and Cudahy, 1953, 120 pp. Revised
      as Screen Writing and Production Techniques: The Non-
      Technical Handbook for TV, Film and Tape, New York:
      Hastings, 1958, 240 pp.)

578   Davis, Denys. Cine Hints, Tips and Gadgets. London:
      Fountain, 1952. 100 pp.

579   Field, Alice Evans. Hollywood, U.S.A.: From Script to
      Screen. New York: Vantage, 1952. 256 pp.

580   Wheeler, Leslie J. Principles of Cinematography: A Hand-
      book of Motion Picture Technology. London: Fountain,
      1953. 472 pp. (Revised 1965, 424 pp. Republished New

York: Morgan and Morgan, 1969, 440 pp.)

581 Sewell, George H. Making and Showing Your Own Films. New York: Pitman, 1955. 311 pp.

582 Tydings, Kenneth S. Bell and Howell Movie Guide. New York: Greenberg, 1955. 80 pp. (Revised Philadelphia: Chilton, 1960, 127 pp.)

583 U.S. Department of Agriculture, Office of Information Motion Picture Service. A Diagnosis of Common Cinematic Troubles: Their Probable Causes and Suggested Methods for Correction. Washington, D.C.: U.S. Department of Agriculture, 1956. 10 pp.

584 Bulleid, Henry Anthony Vaughan. G.B.-Bell & Howell 8mm Cine Manual. London: Fountain, 1957. 257 pp.

585 Gowland, Peter. How to Take Better Home Movies. New York: Arco, 1957. 144 pp.

586 Minter, L. F. and Chard, E. J. How to Film Indoors as an Amateur. London: Focal, 1957. 139 pp.

587 Rose, Tony. The Simple Art of Making Films. London, New York: Focal, 1957. 294 pp.

588 Eastman Kodak Company. How to Make Good Home Movies: A Harvest of Ideas for Shooting Wonderful Color Films with Any Kind of Home Movie Camera. Rochester, N.Y.: Eastman Kodak Company, 1958. 192 pp.

589 Matzkin, Myron A. 8mm and 16mm Movie Equipment Rating Guide. New York: Universal Photo, 1958. 127 pp.

590 Monier, Pierre. The Complete Technique of Making Films. London, New York: Focal, 1958. 304 pp. Translated by Gerald R. Sharp.

591 Postlethwaite, Herbert Almond. Introduction to Cine. London: Fountain, 1958. 125 pp.

592 Salkin, Leo. Story-Telling Home Movies: How to Make Them. New York: McGraw-Hill, 1958. 257 pp.

593 Grosset, Philip. Making 8mm. Movies. London: Fountain, 1959. 232 pp.

594 Matzkin, Myron A. Better Electric Eye Movies. New York: Universal Photo, 1959. 127 pp.

595   Pittaro, Ernest M.   TV and Film Production Data Book.   New
      York: Morgan and Morgan, 1959. 448 pp.

596   Regnier, George with Matzkin, Myron A. Movie Techniques
      for the Advanced Amateur. New York: American Photo-
      graphic, 1959. 160 pp. Translated by Nadine Dormoy
      Savage.

597   Alder, R. H. Movie Making for Everyone. London: Fountain,
      1960. 141 pp.

598   Barleben, Karl August. Earning Money with Your Movie
      Camera. Philadelphia: Chilton, 1960. 127 pp.

599   Bateman, Robert. Movie-Making as a Pastime. London:
      Souvenir, 1960. 128 pp.

600   Cooke, David Coxe. Behind the Scenes in Motion Pictures.
      New York: Dodd, Mead, 1960. 64 pp.
          For the young reader; uses Paramount Studio as
      example.

601   Davis, Denys. Filming with 16mm. London: Iliffe, 1960.
      167 pp.

602   Duitz, Murray. Better 8mm Home Movie Guide. Philadelphia:
      Chilton, 1960. 107 pp.

603   Eastman Kodak Company. The Kodak Home Movie Camera
      Guide. New York: Pocket Books, 1960. 200 pp.

604   Pollock, Norman. Basic 8mm Movie Reference Guide. Phila-
      delphia: Chilton, 1960. 127 pp.

605   Rose, Tony. Tackle Movie-Making This Way. London: Paul,
      1960. 119 pp.

606   Tydings, Kenneth S. Guide to 8mm Kodak Brownie Movie
      Camera. Philadelphia: Chilton, 1960. 119 pp.

607   Grosset, Philip. How to Use 8mm. London: Fountain, 1961.
      94 pp.

608   Townsend, Derek. How to Use 16mm. London: Fountain,
      1961. 96 pp.

609   Tydings, Kenneth S. Basic All-8mm Movie Shooting Guide.
      Philadelphia: Chilton, 1961. 126 pp.

610   Wallace, Carlton. Cine Photography for Amateurs. London:
      Evans, 1961.

611   Ankersmit, K. S.   Beginner's Guide to Cine-Photography.
      New York: McBride, 1962. 139 pp.

612   Bardwell, Michael.   Amateur Cinematography.   London: Old-
      bourne, 1962. 168 pp.

613   Larson, Egon.   Film Making.   London: Frederick Muller,
      1962. 142 pp.
            A survey of film history and filmmaking methods, in-
      tended for the novice.

614   Tydings, Kenneth S.   New Bolex 8/16mm Movie Guide.
      Philadelphia: Chilton, c. 1962. 126 pp.

615   Wain, George.   Filming the Family.   London: Fountain,
      1962. 96 pp.

616   Wigens, Anthony.   Successful Movie Making.   London, New
      York: Focal, 1962. 148 pp.

617   Gilmour, E. A.   Photographer's Guide to Movie Making.
      New York: Barnes, 1963. 68 pp.

618   Grosset, Philip.   Planning and Scripting Amateur Movies.
      London: Fountain, 1963. 127 pp.

619   Horn, Donald R.   Scenarios! Scenarios! Scenarios! Stories,
      Incidents, Gimmicks, Tricks for Interesting Home Movies.
      Philadelphia: Chilton, 1963. 94 pp.

620   Tydings, Kenneth S.   Dejur Movie Guide.   Philadelphia:
      Chilton, c. 1963, 95 pp.

621   Bateman, Robert.   Ideas for Amateur Movies.   London:
      Fountain, c. 1964. 114 pp.

622   Catling, Gordon and Serjeant, Richard.   Movie Making for the
      Young Cameraman.   London: Kaye, 1964. 128 pp.

623   Freytag, Heinrich.   Reinhold's Photo and Movie Book.   New
      York: Reinhold, 1964. 416 pp.

624   Matzkin, Myron A.   Family Movie Fun for All.   New York:
      Amphoto, c. 1964. 96 pp.

625   Townsend, Derek.   The Practical Guide to Holiday and Family
      Movies.   London: Paul, 1964. 174 pp.

626   Willson, C. V.   How to Plan Your 8mm. Films.   London:
      Focal, 1964. 122 pp. (Revised as How to Plan Your
      Super 8mm. Movies, Garden City, New York: Amphoto,
      1973, 130 pp.)

627 Eastman Kodak Company. Better Movies in Color. Rochester,
     N.Y.: Eastman Kodak Company, 1965. 25 pp.

628 Hewitt, Michael. Starting Cine. London: Fountain, 1965.
     56 pp.

629 Knight, Bob. Making Home Movies: A Self Instruction Guide
     to Technique and Equipment in Family Films. New York:
     Collier, 1965. 98 pp.

630 Mascelli, Joseph V. The Five C's of Cinematography: Motion
     Picture Filming Techniques Simplified. Hollywood: Cine /
     Grafic, 1965. 251 pp.
     Camera angles, continuity, cutting, close-ups, and
     composition.

631 Wallace, Carlton. Making Movies. London: Evans, 1965.
     143 pp.

632 Bateman, Robert. Instructions in Filming. London: Museum
     Press, 1967. 124 pp.

633 Branston, Brian. A Film Maker's Guide to Planning, Directing
     and Shooting Films for Pleasure and Profit. London: Allen
     and Unwin, 1967. 205 pp.

634 Grosset, Philip. The Complete Book of Amateur Film Making.
     London: Evans, 1967. 220 pp.

635 Matzkin, Myron A. Better Super 8 Movie Making. Phila-
     delphia: Chilton, 1967. 128 pp.

636 Mercer, John. An Introduction to Cinematography. Champaign,
     Ill: Stipes, 1967. 198 pp. (Revised 1971, 181 pp.)

637 Bateman, Robert. Hints and Tips for the Movie Maker. Lon-
     don: Fountain, 1968. 83 pp.

638 Beal, J. D. How to Make Films at School. London: Focal,
     1968. 147 pp.

639 Eastman Kodak Company. Better Movies in Minutes. Roches-
     ter, N.Y.: Eastman Kodak Company, 1968. 40 pp. (Re-
     published 1972, 48 pp.)

640 Eastman Kodak Company. Movies With a Purpose: A Teacher's
     Guide to Planning and Producing Super 8 Movies for Class-
     room Use. Rochester, N.Y.: Eastman Kodak Company, ca.
     1968. 27 pp.

641 Manchel, Frank. Movies and How They Are Made. Englewood
     Cliffs, N.J.: Prentice-Hall, 1968. 70 pp.
     For the young reader.

642 Colman, Hila. Making Movies: Student Films to Features.
New York: World, 1969. 192 pp.
Oriented toward young people interested in film-related
careers; includes interviews with crew members of Alice's
Restaurant.

643 Ferguson, Robert. How to Make Movies: A Practical Guide
to Group Film Making. New York: Viking, 1969. 88 pp.

644 Larson, Rodger with Meade, Ellen. Young Filmmakers.
New York: Dutton, 1969. 190 pp.
General filmmaking guide for the novice.

645 Matzkin, Myron A. GAF Guide to Better Home Movies. New
York: American Photographic, 1969. 128 pp.

646 Petzold, Paul. All-In-One Movie Book. Garden City, N.Y.:
Amphoto, 1969. 222 pp.
A guide to super-8.

647 Pincus, Edward with Lincoln, Jairus. Guide to Filmmaking.
New York: New American Library, 1969. 256 pp.

648 Smallman, Kirk. Creative Film-Making. New York: Macmillan, 1969. 245 pp.

649 Eastman Kodak Company. Home Movies Made Easy. Rochester, N.Y.: Eastman Kodak Company, Consumer Markets
Division, 1970. 128 pp. (Revised 1974, 148 pp.)

650 Bendick, Jeanne and Robert. Filming Works Like This. New
York: McGraw-Hill, 1970. 95 pp.
For the young reader.

651 Cappello, Patrick H. Life in a Movie Club. New York:
Vantage, 1970. 127 pp.

652 Helfman, Harry C. Making Your Own Movies. New York:
Morrow, 1970. 95 pp.
For the young reader.

653 Hill, Roger. Teach Yourself Film-Making. London: English
Universities Press, 1970. 149 pp.

654 Kuhns, William and Giardino, Thomas P. Behind the Camera.
Dayton, Ohio: Pflaum, 1970. 178 pp.
Directed to the student filmmaker.

655 Provisor, Henry. 8mm/16mm Movie-Making. Philadelphia:
Chilton, 1970. 272 pp.

656 Rilla, Wolf. A-Z of Movie Making. New York: Viking,
1970. 128 pp.

657   Society of Motion Picture and Television Engineers. Sympo-
      sium on Super 8 Film Production Techniques. New York(?):
      Society of Motion Picture and Television Engineers, 1970.
      126 pp.

658   Brakhage, Stan. A Moving Picture Giving and Taking Book.
      West Newbury, Mass.: Frontier, 1971. 65 pp.

659   Brown, William. Low Budget Features. Hollywood: W. O.
      Brown, 1971. 231 pp.

660   Butler, Ivan. The Making of Feature Films--A Guide. Balti-
      more: Penguin, 1971. 191 pp.

661   Cushman, George W. Movie Making in 18 Lessons. Phila-
      delphia: Chilton, 1971. 122 pp.

662   Eastman Kodak Company. Basic Production Techniques for
      Motion Pictures. Rochester, New York: Eastman Kodak
      Company, 1971. 60 pp.

663   Goodwin, Nancy and Manilla, James N. Make Your Own Pro-
      fessional Movies. New York: Macmillan, 1971. 209 pp.

664   Happe, L. Bernard. Basic Motion Picture Technology. New
      York: Hastings, 1971. 362 pp. (Revised London: Focal,
      1975, 371 pp.)

665   Lewis, Jerry. The Total Film-Maker. New York: Random,
      1971. 208 pp.
           Derived from informal and non-technical lectures given
      by Lewis.

666   Roberts, Kenneth H. and Sharples, Win, Jr. A Primer for
      Film-Making: A Complete Guide to 16mm and 35mm Film
      Production. New York: Pegasus, 1971. 546 pp.

667   Rynew, Arden. Filmmaking for Children; Including Motion
      Picture Production Handbook. Dayton, Ohio: Pflaum/
      Standard, 1971. 85, 59 pp.

668   Carrier, Rick and Carroll, David. Action! Camera! Super 8
      Cassette Film Making for Beginners. New York: Scrib-
      ner's, 1972. 78 pp.

669   Lipton, Lenny. Independent Filmmaking. San Francisco:
      Straight Arrow, 1972. 431 pp.
           Explains both super-8 and 16mm filmmaking procedures;
      includes introduction by Stan Brakhage.

670   Murray, John and Janette. In Focus. Melbourne: Georgian,
      1972. 74 pp.

671 Quick, John and LaBau, Tom. Handbook of Film Production.
     New York: Macmillan, 1972. 304 pp.

672 Rose, Tony. The Complete Book of Movie Making. New York:
     Morgan and Morgan, 1972. 109 pp.

673 Schultz, Ed and Dodi. How to Make Exciting Home Movies &
     Stop Boring Your Friends and Relatives. Garden City,
     N.Y.: Doubleday, 1972. 152 pp.

674 Yulsman, Jerry. The Complete Book of 8mm (Super-8, Single-
     8, Standard-8) Movie Making. New York: Coward-McCann
     and Geoghegan, 1972. 224 pp.

675 Bobker, Lee R. with Marinis, Louise. Making Movies: From
     Script to Screen. New York: Harcourt Brace Jovanovich,
     1973. 304 pp.

676 Burch, Noel. Theory of Film Practice. New York: Praeger,
     1973. 172 pp. Translated by Helen R. Lane.
     Emphasizes spatial and temporal elements.

677 Costa, Sylvia Allen. How to Prepare a Production Budget for
     Film and Video Tape. Blue Ridge Summit, Pa.: TAB
     Books, 1973. 192 pp.

678 Eastman Kodak Company. How to Make Good Sound Movies.
     Rochester, N.Y.: Eastman Kodak Company, Consumer
     Markets Division, 1973. 98 pp.

679 Ewing, Sam with Abolin, R. W. (Ozzie). Don't Look at the
     Camera! Shortcuts to Television Photography & Film-
     making. Blue Ridge Summit, Pa.: TAB Books, 1973.
     224 pp.

680 MacLoud, David. Petersen's Guide to Movie Making. Los
     Angeles: Petersen, 1973. 80 pp.

681 Malkiewicz, J. Kris with Rogers, Robert E. Cinematography:
     A Guide for Film Makers and Film Teachers. New York:
     Van Nostrand Reinhold, 1973. 216 pp.

682 Morrow, James and Suid, Murray. Moviemaking Illustrated:
     The Comicbook Filmbook. New Rochelle Park, N.J.:
     Hayden, 1973. 150 pp.

683 Satariano, Cecil. Canon-Fire! The Art of Making Award-
     Winning Amateur Movies. London: Bachman and Turner,
     1973. 74 pp.

684 Weiss, Harvey. How to Make Your Own Movies: An Introduc-
     tion to Filmmaking. New York: Young Scott, 1973. 96 pp.
     For the young reader.

685   Wildi, Ernst. Petersen's Bolex Guide to 16mm Movie Making.
       Los Angeles: Petersen, 1973. 80 pp.

686   Wyckoff, Robert and Alvarez, Felipe. Anatomy of Movie
       Making. Visual Publications, 1973. 37 pp.

687   Beal, J. David. Cine Craft. London: Focal, 1974. 255 pp.

688   Callaghan, Barry. Van Nostrand Reinhold Manual of Film-
       Making. New York: Van Nostrand Reinhold, 1974. 164 pp.
       (Also published as The Thames and Hudson Manual of Film-
       Making.)

689   Coynik, David. Moviemaking: A Worktext for Super 8 Film
       Production. Chicago: Loyola University Press, 1974.
       240 pp.

690   Ewing, Sam and Abolin, R. W. (Ozzie). Professional Film-
       making. Blue Ridge Summit, Pa.: TAB Books, 1974.
       251 pp.

691   Fellows, Malcolm Stuart. Home Movies. New York: Drake,
       1974. 144 pp.

692   Glenn, George D. and Scholz, Charles B. Super 8 Handbook.
       Indianapolis: Howard W. Sams, 1974. 240 pp.

693   Gulliver, Ann W. and William C. A Guide to Creative Film-
       making. West Haven, Conn.: Pendulum, 1974. 137 pp.

694   Horvath, Joan. Filmmaking for Beginners. Nashville: Nelson,
       1974. 162 pp.
       For the young reader.

695   Johnson, Lincoln F. Film: Space, Time, Light and Sound.
       New York: Holt, Rinehart and Winston, 1974. 340 pp.

696   Lafrance, Andre. 8/Super 8/16. Montreal: Habitex, 1974.
       237 pp.

697   Parker, Ben and Drabik, Patricia. Creative Intention: About
       Audiovisual Communication, From Hollywood to John Doe.
       New York: Law-Arts, 1974. 292 pp.
       Describes basic production principles and skills for
       film and television.

698   Priest, Christopher. Your Book of Film-Making. London:
       Faber and Faber, 1974. 80 pp.
       For the young reader.

699   Chase, Donald (for the American Film Institute). Filmmaking:
       The Collaborative Art. Boston: Little, Brown, 1975.
       314 pp.

Interviews with Hollywood professionals about their respective functions; for list of names, see entry 3802.

700 Glimcher, Sumner and Johnson, Warren. Movie Making: A Guide to Film Production. New York: Washington Square, distributed by Simon and Schuster, 1975. 288 pp. (Also published as Making Movies.)

701 Lipton, Lenny. The Super 8 Book. San Francisco: Straight Arrow, 1975. 308 pp.

702 Matzkin, Myron A. Super 8 mm Movie Making Simplified: A Modern Photoguide. Garden City, N.Y.: Amphoto, 1975. 96 pp.

703 Piper, James. Personal Filmmaking. Reston, Va.: Reston, 1975. 269 pp.

704 Resch, George T. Super 8 Filmmaking. New York: Watts, 1975. 61 pp.
     For the young reader.

705 Yerian, Cameron and Margaret (eds.) Radio & Movie Productions. Chicago: Children's Press, 1975. 45 pp.
     For the young reader.

C. SPECIFIC TECHNIQUES

The cinema has often been called an eclectic art because so many of its techniques are derived from previously existing disciplines. Acting derives from the theatre, animation from the visual arts, screenwriting from storytelling and literature, sound technique from radio and recording processes, and, of course, cinematography from photography. In general (with the major exception of acting, section C-1), we have included only books which deal directly with the filmic aspect of the technique, and have omitted those books which deal with the technique's source in other disciplines. Thus, books dealing with general stereo sound systems have been excluded from section C-11, sound; books dealing with general composition of music have been excluded from section C-8, music; books dealing with the general techniques of photography have been excluded from section C-4, cinematography. Any exceptions to this rule are explained in the text prior to the specific technique section. It should, however, be clear that much valuable and relevant material can be gleaned from these "peripheral books," and the reader is urged to consult bibliographies in other disciplines for more information.

1. Acting

The acting section below does selectively include many theatre-grounded works, especially those dealing with Stanislavsky and his method, not just because there are few books specifically on film acting, but because we recognize the important influence of "method" acting on Hollywood and the relevance of many general acting books to film. For more material on theatre acting, the reader should consult a theatre bibliography such as Ralph Newman Schoolcraft's Performing Arts Books in Print. For advice to the actor trying to make a career in Hollywood, see Part III, section D, occupations.

706 Pudovkin, V. I. Film Acting. (Originally published 1933.)
     Reprinted in Film Technique and Film Acting, New York:
     Lear, 1949. 204, 153 pp.
          See entry 4445.

707 Stanislavski, Constantin. An Actor Prepares. (Originally
   published 1936.) New York: Theatre Arts, 1948. 295 pp.
   Translated by Elizabeth Reynolds Hapgood. (Reprinted New
   York: Macgregor, 1959, 295 pp. Reprinted again Harmondsworth: Penguin, 1967, 284 pp.)

708 Eustis, Morton. Players at Work: Actors According to Actors.
   (Originally published 1937.) New York: Blom, 1969.
   127 pp.
   For names, see entry 3620.

709 Gable, Josephine (Dillon). Modern Acting: A Guide for Stage,
   Screen and Radio. New York: Prentice-Hall, 1940. 313 pp.

710 Herman, Lewis and Marguerite S. Manual of Foreign Dialects
   for Radio, Stage and Screen. Chicago, New York: Ziff-
   Davis, 1943. 416 pp. (Reprinted as Foreign Dialects: A
   Manual for Actors, Directors, and Writers, New York:
   Theatre Arts, ca. 1958.)

711 Seyler, Athene and Haggard, Stephen. The Craft of Comedy:
   Correspondence Between Athene Seyler and Stephen Haggard.
   London: Muller, 1943. 86 pp. (Republished without subtitle New York: Theatre Arts, 1946, 104 pp. Republished
   again 1957.)

712 Klaw, Irving. How to Become a Movie Star. New York:
   Klaw, 1946. 126 pp.

713 Albertson, Lillian. Motion Picture Acting. New York: Funk
   and Wagnalls, 1947. 135 pp.

714 Cole, Toby. Acting: A Handbook of the Stanislavski Method.
   New York: Lear, 1947. 223 pp. (Republished New York:
   Crown, 1957. Republished again 1971, 223 pp.)

715 Dunn, Emma. You Can Do It. Agoura, Cal.: n.p., 1947.
   190 pp.

716 Herman, Lewis and Marguerite S. Manual of American Dia-
   lects for Radio, Stage, Screen and Television. Chicago,
   New York: Ziff-Davis, 1947. 326 pp. (Reprinted as
   American Dialects: A Manual for Actors, Directors, and
   Writers, New York: Theatre Arts, 1959, 328 pp.)

717 Cole, Toby and Chinoy, Helen Krich (eds.) Actors On Acting:
   The Theories, Techniques and Practices of the Great Actors
   of All Time as Told in Their Own Words. New York:
   Crown, 1949. 596 pp. (Reprinted 1965. Revised 1970,
   715 pp.)

718 Stanislavski, Constantin. Building a Character. New York:

Theatre Arts, 1949. 292 pp. Translated by Elizabeth
Reynolds Hapgood. (Reprinted 1962.)

719 Rose, Tony and Benson, Martin. How to Act for Amateur
Films. London, New York: Focal, 1951. 117 pp.

720 Chekhov, Michael. To the Actor: On the Technique of Acting.
New York: Harper and Row, 1953. 201 pp.

721 Redgrave, Michael. The Actor's Ways and Means. New York:
Theatre Arts, 1953. 90 pp. (Reprinted 1966.)

722 Cole, Toby (comp.) Acting: A Handbook of the Stanislavsky
Method. New York: Lear, 1947. 223 pp. (Reprinted
New York: Crown, 1955, 223 pp.)

723 Joels, Merrill E. Acting Is a Business: How to Get Into
Television and Radio. New York: Hastings, 1955. 96 pp.
(Revised as How to Get Into Show Business, 1969, 157 pp.)

724 McGaw, Charles J. Acting Is Believing: A Basic Method for
Beginners. New York: Rinehart, 1955. 177 pp.

725 Hodapp, William C. Face Your Audience: Audition Readings
for Actors. New York: Hastings, 1956. 130 pp.

726 Strickland, Francis Cowles. The Technique of Acting. New
York: McGraw-Hill, 1956. 306 pp.

727 Chenoweth, Stuart Curran. A Study of the Adaptation of Acting
Technique From Stage to Film, Radio and Television in the
United States, 1900-1951. Northwestern University: Ph.D.,
1957. 393 pp.

728 Lewis, Robert. Method--Or Madness? New York: French,
1958. 165 pp.
Lectures on the method school of acting.

729 Redgrave, Michael. Mask or Face: Reflections in an Actor's
Mirror. New York: Theatre Arts, 1958. 188 pp.

730 Albright, Harry D. Working Up a Part: A Manual for the
Beginning Actor. Boston: Houghton Mifflin, 1947. 224 pp.
(Republished 1959, 246 pp.)

731 Lane, Yoti. The Psychology of the Actor. New York: Day,
1960. 224 pp.

732 Dorcy, Jean. The Mime. New York: Speller, 1961. 116 pp.
Translated by Robert Speller, Jr. and Pierre de Fontnouvelle.

733 Funke, Lewis and Booth, John E. (eds.) Actors Talk About

Acting: Fourteen Intimate Interviews. New York: Random, 1961. 469 pp.
For list, see entry 3663.

734 Marowitz, Charles. The Method as Means: An Acting Survey. London: Jenkins, 1961. 174 pp.

735 Stanislavski, Constantin. Creating a Role. Edited by Hermione I. Popper. New York: Theatre Arts, 1961. 271 pp. Translated by Elizabeth Reynolds Hapgood.

736 Duerr, Edwin. The Length and Depth of Acting. New York: Holt, Rinehart and Winston, 1962. 590 pp.
A history of acting.

737 Kahan, Stanley. Introduction to Acting. New York: Harcourt, Brace, 1962. 312 pp.

738 Stanislavski, Constantin. An Actor's Handbook: An Alphabetical Arrangement of Concise Statements on Aspects of Acting. New York: Theatre Arts, 1963. 160 pp.

739 Benner, Ralph and Clements, Mary Jo. The Young Actors' Guide to Hollywood. New York: Coward-McCann, 1964. 185 pp.

740 Moore, Sonia. The Stanislavski Method: The Professional Training of an Actor. New York: Viking, 1960. 78 pp. (Also published as An Actor's Training: The Stanislavsky Method. Revised as The Stanislavky System: The Professional Training of an Actor, New York: Viking, 1965, 112 pp.)

741 Strasberg, Lee. Strasberg at the Actors Studio: Tape-Recorded Sessions. Edited by Robert H. Hethmon. New York: Viking, 1965. 428 pp.

742 Blunt, Jerry. The Composite Art of Acting. New York: Macmillan, 1966. 450 pp.

743 Easty, Edward Dwight. On Method Acting. New York: Allograph, 1966. 191 pp.

744 Burton, Hal (ed.) Great Acting: Laurence Olivier, Sybil Thorndike, Ralph Richardson, Peggy Ashcroft, Edith Evans, Michael Redgrave, John Gielgud, Noel Coward. New York: Hill and Wang, 1967. 192 pp.
Interviews.

745 Munk, Erika (ed.) Stanislavski and America: An Anthology from the Tulane Drama Review. New York: Hill and Wang, 1966. 279 pp.

With contributions from Stella Adler, Eric Bentley,
Bertolt Brecht, Robert Lewis, Sanford Meisner, Lee Strasberg, Geraldine Page, and others.

746   Moore, Sonia. Training an Actor: The Stanislavsky System
      in Class. New York: Viking, 1968. 260 pp.

747   Nicholson, Dianne. Turn on to Stardom. New York: Corner-
      stone, 1968. 192 pp.

748   Hayman, Ronald. Techniques of Acting. London: Methuen,
      1969. 188 pp. (Reprinted New York: Holt, Rinehart and
      Winston, 1971.)

749   Lewis, Mary Kane. Acting for Children: A Primer. New
      York: Day, 1969. 176 pp.

750   Burton, Hal (ed.) Acting in the Sixties: Richard Burton, Harry
      H. Corbett, Albert Finney, John Neville, Eric Porter,
      Vanessa Redgrave, Maggie Smith, Robert Stephens, Dorothy
      Tutin. London: British Broadcasting Corporation, 1970.
      256 pp.
      Interviews.

751   Pate, Michael. The Film Actor: Acting for Motion Pictures
      and Television. South Brunswick, N.J.: A. S. Barnes,
      1970. 245 pp.

752   Schreck, Everett M. with McGraw, William R. and DeChaine,
      Faber B. Principles and Styles of Acting. Reading, Mass.:
      Addison-Wesley, 1970. 354 pp.

753   Harris, Julie with Tarshis, Barry. Julie Harris Talks to
      Young Actors. New York: Lothrop, Lee and Shepard,
      1971. 192 pp.

754   Cohen, Robert. Acting Professionally: Raw Facts About Acting
      and the Acting Industries. Palo Alto, Cal.: National Press
      Books, 1972. 101 pp.

755   Penrod, James. Movement for the Performing Artist. Palo
      Alto, Cal.: National Press Books, 1974. 189 pp.

2.   Animation

This section contains those books dealing with the techniques
of animation. For historical or analytical material on the animated
film, see Part V, section D, animated films.

756 Turney, Harold. Film Guide's Handbook: Cartoon Production.
Hollywood: Film Guide, 1940. 96 pp.

757 Falk, Nat. How to Make Animated Cartoons: The History and
Technique. New York: Foundation Books, 1941. 79 pp.

758 Feild, Robert D. The Art of Walt Disney. New York: Macmillan, 1942. 290 pp.
Study of animation studio procedures.

759 Foster, Walter T. Animated Cartoons: Problems Given by
Leading Studios. Hollywood: n.p., ca. 1942. 36 pp.

760 Epstein, Alvin. How to Draw Animated Cartoons. New York:
Greenberg, 1945. 64 pp.

761 Blair, Preston. Advanced Animation. Laguna Beach, Cal.:
Walter T. Foster, 1949. 40 pp.

762 Halas, John and Privett, Bob. How to Cartoon for Amateur
Films. London: Focal, 1951. 132 pp. (Reprinted 1970.)

763 Barton, C. H. How to Animate Cut-Outs. London: Focal,
1955. 116 pp.

764 Barton, Jack. Animating for Fun, and Analysis of the Species.
London: Stockbook, 1957. 150 pp.

765 The Art of Animation. Los Angeles(?): Disney Productions,
1958. 24 pp.

766 National Film Board of Canada. Cameraless Animation: A
Technique Developed at the National Film Board of Canada.
Montreal: Information and Promotion Division, National
Film Board of Canada, 1958. 11 pp.

767 Thomas, Bob. Walt Disney, The Art of Animation: The
Story of the Disney Studio Contribution to a New Art.
New York: Simon and Schuster, 1958. 181 pp.

768 Halas, John and Manvell, Roger. The Technique of Film Animation. New York: Hastings, 1959. 348 pp. (Revised
1968, 360 pp.)

769 Levitan, Eli L. Animation Art in the Commercial Film. New
York: Reinhold, 1960. 128 pp.

770 Eastman Kodak Company. Basic Titling and Animation.
Rochester, N.Y.: Eastman Kodak Company, 1961. 64 pp.
(Republished as Basic Titling and Animation for Motion
Pictures, 1970, 56 pp.)

771   Levitan, Eli L. Animation Techniques and Commercial Film
      Production. New York: Reinhold, 1962. 192 pp.

772   Helfman, Harry. Making Pictures Move. New York: Mor-
      row, 1969. 48 pp.
          Nine animation projects for children, including peep
      shows, flip books, and moving shadows.

773   Madsen, Roy P. Animated Film: Concepts, Methods, Uses.
      New York: Interland, distributed by Pitman, 1969. 234 pp.

774   Andersen, Yvonne. Make Your Own Animated Movies: Yellow
      Ball Workshop Film Techniques. Boston: Little, Brown,
      1970. 101 pp.
          For the young reader.

775   Andersen, Yvonne. Teaching Film Animation to Children.
      New York: Van Nostrand Reinhold, 1970. 112 pp.

776   Bryne-Daniel, J. Grafilm: An Approach to a New Medium.
      New York: Van Nostrand Reinhold, 1970. 96 pp.
          Material on the production of "grafilms," films which
      combine graphic and illustrative techniques with film tech-
      niques.

777   Halas, John with Manvell, Roger. Art in Movement: New
      Directions in Animation. New York: Hastings, 1970.
      192 pp.

778   Kinsey, Anthony. How to Make Animated Movies. New York:
      Viking, 1970. 95 pp. (Also published as Animated Film
      Making, London: Studio Vista, 1970.)

779   Reiniger, Lotte. Shadow Theatres and Shadow Films. New
      York: Watson-Guptill, 1970. 128 pp.

780   Heath, Robert. Animation in 12 Hard Lessons. West Islip,
      N.Y.: R. P. Heath Productions, 1972. 142 pp.

781   Cleave, Alan. Cartoon Animation for Everyone. New York:
      Morgan and Morgan, 1973. 132 pp.

782   Larson, Rodger; Hofer, Lynne; and Barrios, Jaime. Young
      Animators and Their Discoveries: A Report From Young
      Filmmakers Foundation. New York: Praeger, 1973.
      159 pp.
          Interviews with 12 young filmmakers.

783   Trojanski, John and Rockwood, Louis. Making It Move. Day-
      ton, Ohio: Pflaum/Standard, 1973. 148 pp.
          For the young reader; instructor's manual available.

784 Bourgeois, Jacques. Animating Films Without a Camera.
     New York: Sterling, 1974. 48 pp. Translated by Anne
     E. Kallem.

785 Godfrey, Bob and Jackson, Anna. The Do-It-Yourself Film
     Animation. London: British Broadcasting Corporation,
     1974. 95 pp.

786 Halas, John (ed.) Computer Animation. New York: Hastings,
     1974. 176 pp.
          With contributions by Bruce Cornwell, Frank E.
     Taylor, Paul M. Nelson, Kenneth C. Knowlton, Stan
     Hayward, Lillian Schwartz, Malcolm LeGrice, and
     others.

787 Heraldson, Donald. Creators of Life: A History of Animation.
     New York: Drake, 1975. 298 pp.

788 Hobson, Andrew and Mark. Film Animation as a Hobby. New
     York: Sterling, 1975. 46 pp.
          For the young reader.

789 Holman, L. Bruce. Puppet Animation in the Cinema: History
     and Technique. South Brunswick, N.J.: A. S. Barnes,
     1975. 120 pp.

               3. Art Direction and Set Design

     Although there are few books specifically on art direction
and set design, material on these techniques can be found in the
biographies, analyses, and interviews of people who have had careers
in these fields.

790 Gorelick, Mordecai. New Theatres for Old. New York:
     French, 1940. 553 pp. (Reprinted 1952 and 1962.)
          Includes material on theatre set design relevant to mo-
     tion pictures.

791 Myerscough-Walker, R. Stage and Film Decor. London:
     Pitman, 1940. 192 pp.
          Includes material on Vincent Korda, Edward Carrick,
     and Laurence Irving.

792 Carrick, Edward. Designing for Moving Pictures. London:
     Studio, 1941. 104 pp. (Revised as Designing for Films,
     1949, 128 pp.)

793 Koenig, John. Scenery for Cinema. Baltimore: Baltimore
     Museum of Art, 1942. 94 pp.
          A record of the exhibition "Scenery for Cinema"

held at the Baltimore Museum of Art, January through March, 1942.

794   Carrick, Edward (comp.) Art and Design in the British Film: A Pictorial Directory of British Art Directors and Their Work. London: Dobson, 1948. 133 pp. (Reprinted New York: Arno, 1972.)
        For list of names, see entry 3635.

795   Larson, Orville K. (ed.) Scene Design for Stage and Screen: Readings on the Aesthetics and Methodology of Scene Design for Drama, Opera, Musical Comedy, Ballet, Motion Pictures, Television and Arena Theatre. East Lansing: Michigan State University Press, 1961. 334 pp.
        With contributions by Harry Horner, Oliver Smith, and others.

796   Silantieva, T. A. (ed.) Khudozhniki Sovetskogo Kino/Designers of Soviet Films. Moscow: Imported Publications, 1972. 58 pp.
        Text in Russian and English; many illustrations.

797   Bay, Howard. Stage Design. New York: Drama Book Shop Specialists, 1974. 218 pp.
        Includes limited material on film design.

798   Marner, Terence St. John with Stringer, Michael. Film Design. New York: A. S. Barnes, 1974. 165 pp.

4. Cinematography, Lighting, Color

        This section contains books which deal with cinematography, lighting, color, film laboratories, and film processing. We have not included books on photographic technique or photographic theory, even though such books have an obvious relevance to cinematography. The only books non-specific to cinematography included here are those dealing specifically with the concepts of color, color reproduction, and color perception. For other material on cinematography, see the technical encyclopedias in Part I, section A-1 and the many glossaries in Part I, section A-2.

799   Freeburg, Victor Oscar. Pictorial Beauty on the Screen. (Originally published 1923.) New York: Arno, 1970. 191 pp.

800   Lutz, Edwin George. The Motion-Picture Cameraman. (Originally published 1927.) New York: Arno, 1972. 248 pp.

801   Hall, Hal (ed.) Cinematographic Annual [In Two Volumes].

Volume I, 1930. (Originally published 1930.) New York: Arno, 1972. 606 pp. Volume II, 1931. (Originally published 1931.) New York: Arno, 1972. 425 pp.
Anthology on technical and aesthetic aspects of film-making.

802 Cornwell-Clyne, Adrian. Colour Cinematography. (Originally published 1936.) London: Chapman and Hall, 1951. 780 pp.
Historical survey of color development.

803 Eastman Kodak Company. Motion Picture Films for Professional Use. Rochester, N.Y.: Eastman Kodak Company, 1942. 80 pp. (Fourth revised edition 1968, 48 pp.)

804 Boucher, Paul Edward. Fundamentals of Photography, With Laboratory Experiments. New York: Van Nostrand, 1947. (Republished 1955, 473 pp.)

805 Evans, Ralph M. An Introduction to Color. New York: Wiley, 1948. 340 pp. (Reprinted 1959.)
A detailed discussion of color, relevant to its use in motion pictures.

806 Alton, John. Painting With Light. New York: Macmillan, 1949. 191 pp.

807 Huntley, John. British Technicolor Films. London: Skelton Robinson, ca. 1949. 224 pp.
Includes production notes on 25 films from 1936 to 1948.

808 Bomback, R. H. (comp.) Cine Data Book: The Comprehensive Reference Book for All Cine Workers. London: Fountain, 1950. 286 pp.

809 Eastman Kodak Company. Kodachrome Films for Miniature and Movie Cameras. Rochester, N.Y.: Eastman Kodak Company, 1950. 48 pp.

810 Greenleaf, Allen R. Photographic Optics. New York: Macmillan, 1950. 214 pp.

811 Rudatis, Domenico. The Integral Solution of the Problem of the Color Motion Picture. Venice: n.p., ca. 1950. 40 ℓ.

812 Wheeler, Leslie J. How to Process Substandard Films. London, New York: Focal, 1950. 120 pp.

813 Cricks, R. Howard. Illumination: The Technique of Light. London, New York: Focal, 1951. 320 pp.

814 Kingslake, Rudolf. Lenses in Photography: The Practical

Guide to Optics for Photographers.   Garden City, N.Y.:
Garden City Books, 1951.   246 pp.

815   Sipley, Louis Walton.   A Half Century of Color.   New York:
Macmillan, 1951.   216 pp.
Historical account of the growth of color photography
with material relevant to film.

816   Bomback, R. H. (ed.)   Handbook of Amateur Cinematography
[In Two Volumes].   Volume I.   London: Fountain, 1953.
Volume II.   1958.

817   Evans, Ralph M.; Hanson, W. T., Jr.; and Brewer, W. Lyle.
Principles of Color Photography.   New York: Wiley, 1953.
709 pp.
With material relevant to motion pictures.

818   Tydings, Kenneth S.   The Bolex Movie Guide.   New York:
Greenberg, 1953.   127 pp.

819   Wheeler, Leslie J.   Principles of Cinematography: A Handbook of Motion Picture Technology.   London: Fountain,
1953.   472 pp.   (Revised 1965, 424 pp.)

820   Schenck, Hilbert, Jr. and Kendall, Henry W.   Underwater
Photography.   Cambridge, Md.:   Cornell Maritime, 1954.
110 pp.   (Republished 1957, 126 pp.)
With material relevant to motion pictures.

821   Trimble, Lyne S.   Color in Motion Pictures and Television.
North Hollywood: Optical Standards, 1954.   270 pp.   Revised 1969, 267 pp.

822   Tydings, Kenneth S.   The Keystone Movie Guide.   New York:
Greenberg, 1954.   128 pp.

823   Abramson, Albert.   Electronic Motion Pictures: A History of
the Television Camera.   Berkeley: University of California
Press, 1955.   212 pp.

824   Clairmont, Leonard.   The Professional Cine Photographer.
Edited by Henry Provisor.   Hollywood: Ver Halen, 1956.
154 pp.

825   Bomback, R. H.   Basic Leica Technique.   London: Fountain;
Philadelphia: Rayelle, 1957, c. 1954.   254 pp.

826   The Focal Encyclopedia of Photography.   New York: Macmillan,
1957.   1298 pp.   (Revised in two volumes New York, London: Focal, 1965, 1699 pp.)

827   Rebikoff, Dimitri and Cherney, Paul.   A Guide to Underwater

Photography. New York: Greenberg, 1957. 113 pp.
With material relevant to motion pictures.

828 Society of Motion Picture and Television Engineers, Special
Committee; Wilton R. Holm, Chairman. Elements of Color
in Professional Motion Pictures. New York: Society of
Motion Picture and Television Engineers, 1957. 104 pp.

829 Larmore, Lewis. Introduction to Photographic Principles.
Englewood Cliffs, N.J.: Prentice-Hall, 1958. 229 pp.

830 Turner, Glen H. Lens Techniques for Color Movie Magic.
San Francisco: Camera Craft, 1958. 96 pp.

831 Evans, Ralph M. Eye, Film, and Camera in Color Photography.
New York: Wiley, 1959. 410 pp.
With material relevant to motion pictures.

832 Ham, Dick. Camera Techniques for the Color Movie Maker.
San Francisco: Camera Craft, 1959. 96 pp.

833 Walden, Harry. How to Make Cine Gadgets for Amateur
Camerawork. London, New York: Focal, 1959. 120 pp.

834 American Cinematographer Manual. Edited by Joseph V. Mascelli. Hollywood: American Society of Cinematographers,
1960. 482 pp. (Second edition edited by Joseph V. Mascelli,
1966, 626 pp. Third edition edited by Arthur C. Miller and
Walter Strenge, 1969, 650 pp. Fourth edition edited by
Charles G. Clarke and Walter Strenge, 1973, 655 pp.)

835 Eastman Kodak Company. The Kodak Home Movie Camera
Guide. New York: Pocket Books, 1960. 200 pp.

836 Gibson, Brian. Exposing Cine Film. London: Fountain, 1960.
126 pp.

837 Gilmour, Edwyn. Choosing and Using a Cine Camera. London:
Fountain, 1960. 124 pp.

838 Society of Motion Picture and Television Engineers, Special
Subcommittee; Walter I. Kisner, Chairman. Control Tech-
niques in Film Processing. New York: Society of Motion
Picture and Television Engineers, 1960. 181 pp.

839 Townsend, Derek. Filming in Colour. London: Fountain,
1960. 121 pp.

840 Wheeler, Leslie J. Film Processing and After-Processing
Treatment of 16 mm Films. London: British Broadcasting
Corporation, 1960. 19 pp.

841 Wheeler, Leslie J. Sensitometric Control in Film Making.

London: British Broadcasting Corporation, 1960.   23 pp.

842   Current, Ira B.   Electric Eye Movie Manual.   New York:
Amphoto, 1961.   123 pp.

843   Gibson, Brian.   Lighting for Cine--Indoors and Out.   London:
Fountain, 1962.   93 pp.

844   Surgenor, Alexander John.   Bolex Guide: Filming with the
Bolex H.16 and H.8 Cine Cameras.   Revision by Edwyn
Gilmour.   London: Focal, 1962.   112 pp.   (Revised by
Paul Petzold 1967, 127 pp.)

845   Association of Cinema Laboratories, Product Specifications
Committee.   Handbook: Recommended Standards and Procedures for Motion Picture Laboratory Services.   Washington, D.C.:   Association of Cinema Laboratories, 1963.
Unpaged.   (Republished 1966, 50 pp.)

846   Limbacher, James L.   A Historical Study of the Color Motion
Picture.   Dearborn, Mich.: n.p., 1963   30 ℓ.

847   Society of Motion Picture and Television Engineers, Color
Committee.   Principles of Color Sensitometry.   New York:
Society of Motion Picture and Television Engineers, 1963.
102 pp.

848   Clarke, Clarles G.   Professional Cinematography.   Hollywood:
American Society of Cinematographers, 1964.   183 pp.
(Revised 1968, 192 pp.)

849   Townsend, Derek.   Underwater Photography: Movies and Still.
London: Paul, 1964.   160 pp.

850   Mascelli, Joseph V.   The Five C's of Cinematography: Motion
Picture Filming Techniques Simplified.   Hollywood: Cine /
Grafic, 1965.   251 pp.
Camera angles, continuity, cutting, composition, and
close-ups.

851   Paul, Norman.   Cine-Photography.   London: Foyle, 1965.
92 pp.

852   Wallace, Carlton.   Cine Photography All the Year Round.
London: Evans, 1965.   128 pp.

853   Ryan, Roderick Thomas.   A Study of the Technology of Color
Motion Picture Processes Developed in the United States.
University of Southern California: Ph.D., 1966.   456 pp.

854   Sharp, Gerald Reynolds.   Bolex-8 Guide: How to Make Films
with Bolex B.8, C.8, D.8, L.8, and Zoom Reflex P.1,

P. 2, P. 3, P. 4, S. 1, K. 1, K. 2 Cameras.   London, New
York: Focal, 1966.   120 pp.

855   Warham, John.   The Technique of Wildlife Cinematography.
London: Focal, 1966.   222 pp.

856   Fielding, Raymond.   A Technological History of Motion Pictures
and Television: An Anthology from the Pages of the Journal
of the Society of Motion Picture and Television Engineers.
Berkeley: University of California Press, 1967.   255 pp.
See entry 1425.

857   Souto, Mario Raimondo.   The Technique of the Motion Picture
Camera.   Edited by Raymond Spottiswoode.   New York:
Hastings, 1967.   263 pp.

858   Corbett, D. J.   Motion Picture and Television Film: Image
Control and Processing Techniques.   London, New York:
Focal, 1968.   231 pp.

859   Thomas, D. B.   The First Colour Motion Pictures.   London:
Her Majesty's Stationery Office, 1969.   44 pp.
An account of pre-1917 motion picture color.

860   Campbell, Russell (comp.)   Photographic Theory for the Motion
Picture Cameraman.   New York: A. S. Barnes, 1970.
160 pp.

861   Campbell, Russell (comp.)   Practical Motion Picture Photography.   New York: A. S. Barnes, 1970.   192 pp.
Interview material; for list of names, see entry 3715.

862   Carlson, Verne and Sylvia.   Professional 16/35mm Cameraman's Handbook.   New York: Hastings, 1970.   383 pp.
(Republished New York: Amphoto, 1974, 429 pp.)

863   Fisher, J. David (ed.)   The Craft of Film.   London: Attic,
1970.   Loose-leaf.

864   Higham, Charles.   Hollywood Cameramen: Sources of Light.
Bloomington: Indiana University Press, 1970.   176 pp.

865   National Camera, Inc., Technical Training Division.   Camera
Repairman's Handbook.   Englewood, Co.: National Camera,
1970.   (Revised as Photo Technology Data Book, 1973,
385 pp.)

866   Ross, Rodger J.   Color Film for Color Television.   New York:
Hastings, 1970.   165 pp.

867   Clark, Frank P. (ed.)   Technologies in the Laboratory Handling
of Motion Picture and Other Long Films.   New York(?):

Society of Motion Picture and Television Engineers, 1971.
223 pp.

868 Maltin, Leonard. Behind the Camera: The Cinematographer's
     Art. New York: New American Library, 1971. 240 pp.

869 Tölke, Arnim and Ingeborg. Macrophoto and Cine Methods.
     London, New York: Focal, 1971. 270 pp.

870 Eastman Kodak Company. Selection and Use of Kodak and
     Eastman Motion Picture Films. Rochester, N.Y.: East-
     man Kodak Company, 1972. 47 pp.

871 Carroll, John S. Amphoto Color Film and Color Processing
     Data Book. New York: Amphoto, 1972. 168 pp.

872 Millerson, Gerald. The Technique of Lighting for Television
     and Motion Pictures. New York: Hastings, 1972.
     366 pp.

873 Young, Freddie and Petzold, Paul. The Work of the Motion
     Picture Cameraman. New York: Hastings, 1972. 245 pp.

874 American Cinematographer (ed.) The American Cinematogra-
     pher Special Reprint. Hollywood(?): American Cinema-
     tographer, 1973. 98 pp.
         Includes material on super-8, super-16, videotape, and
     the filming of 2001: A SPACE ODYSSEY.

875 Malkiewicz, J. Kris with Rogers, Robert E. Cinematography:
     A Guide for Film Makers and Film Teachers. New York:
     Van Nostrand Reinhold, 1973. 216 pp.

876 Mascelli, Joseph V. Mascelli's Cine Workbook [In Two Vol-
     umes]. Volume I, Text; Volume II, Tools. Hollywood:
     Cine/Grafic, 1973.

877 Happe, L. Bernard. Your Film and the Lab. New York:
     Hastings, 1974. 208 pp.

5. Costume and Makeup

     Although there are few books specifically on costume and
makeup, material on these techniques can be found in the biographies, analyses, and interviews of people who have had careers in
these areas.

878 Strenkovsky, Serge. The Art of Make-Up for Stage, Screen
     and Everyday Life. (Originally published as The Art of

Make-Up, 1937.)   Edited by Elizabeth S. Taber.   New York:
Dutton, 1943.   350 pp.

879   Kehoe, Vincent J. R.   The Technique of Film and Television
Make-Up.   New York: Hastings, 1958.   263 pp.   (Revised
1969, 280 pp.)

880   Emerald, Jack.   Make-Up in Amateur Movies, Drama and
Photography.   London: Fountain, 1966.   93 pp.

881   Lee, Sarah T. (ed.)   American Fashion: The Life and Lines
of Adrian, Mainbocher, McCardell, Norell, and Trigere.
New York: Quadrangle, 1975.   509 pp.

882   Buchman, Herman.   Film and Television Make-Up.   New York:
Watson-Guptill, 1973.   223 pp.

883   Westmore, Michael G.   The Art of Theatrical Makeup for
Stage and Screen.   New York: McGraw-Hill, 1973.   155 pp.

6.   Directing

884   Eisenstein, Sergei.   Programme for Teaching the Theory and
Practice of Film Direction.   Hollywood: Larry Edmunds
Bookshop, 1944.   20 pp.   Translated by Stephen Gary with
Ivor Montagu.

885   Rose, Tony.   How to Direct as an Amateur.   London, New
York: Focal, 1949.   152 pp.   (Reprinted 1958.)

886   Livingston, Don.   Film and the Director: A Handbook and
Guide to Film Making.   New York: Macmillan, 1953.
209 pp.   (Reprinted New York: Capricorn, 1969.)

887   Rider, Richard.   A Comparative Analysis of Directing Television and Film Drama.   University of Illinois, Urbana-
Champaign: Ph.D., 1958.   192 pp.

888   Nizhny, Vladimir.   Lessons With Eisenstein.   Edited and
translated by Ivor Montagu and Jay Leyda.   New York:
Hill and Wang, 1962.   182 pp.
A reconstruction of Eisenstein's lectures at the State
Institute of Cinematography in Moscow.

889   Geduld, Harry M.   Film Makers on Filmmaking: Statements
on Their Art by Thirty Directors.   Bloomington: Indiana
University Press, 1967.   302 pp.
For list of names, see entry 3685.

890   Sarris, Andrew (comp.)   Interviews with Film Directors.

Indianapolis: Bobbs-Merrill, 1967. 476 pp.
For list of names, see entry 3693.

891   Higham, Charles and Greenberg, Joel. The Celluloid Muse:
Hollywood Directors Speak. Chicago: Regnery, 1969.
268 pp.
For list of names, see entry 3705.

892   Gelmis, Joseph. The Film Director as Superstar. Garden
City, N.Y.: Doubleday, 1970. 316 pp.
Interviews; for list of names, see entry 3718.

893   Kantor, Bernard R.; Blacker, Irwin R.; and Kramer, Anne
(eds.) Directors at Work: Interviews with American
Film-Makers. New York: Funk and Wagnalls, 1970. 442 pp.
For list of names, see entry 3720.

894   Reynertson, A. J. The Work of the Film Director. New
York: Communication Arts Books, 1970. 259 pp.

895   Bare, Richard L. The Film Director: A Practical Guide to
Motion Picture and Television Techniques. New York:
Macmillan, 1971. 243 pp.

896   Lewis, Jerry. The Total Film-Maker. New York: Random,
1971. 208 pp.
Derived from non-technical lectures given by Lewis.

897   Sarris, Andrew (comp.) Hollywood Voices: Interviews with
Film Directors. Indianapolis: Bobbs-Merrill, 1971.
180 pp. (An abridged version of Interviews with Film
Directors, 1967.)
For list of names, see entry 3744.

898   Marner, Terence St. John (comp.) Directing Motion Pictures.
New York: A. S. Barnes, 1972. 158 pp.

899   Samuels, Charles. Encountering Directors. New York: Putnam, 1972. 255 pp.
Interviews; for list of names, see entry 3757.

900   Vidor, King. King Vidor on Filmmaking. New York: McKay,
1972. 239 pp.

901   Kazan, Elia. On What Makes a Director. Los Angeles: Directors Guild of America, 1973. 22 pp.

902   Thomas, Bob (ed.) Directors in Action: Selections from
Action, the Official Magazine of the Directors Guild of
America. Indianapolis: Bobbs-Merrill, 1973. 283 pp.
Interviews and articles; for list of names, see entry
3776.

903   Schickel, Richard. The Men Who Made the Movies: Inter-
      views with Frank Capra, George Cukor, Howard Hawks,
      Alfred Hitchcock, Vincente Minnelli, King Vidor, Raoul
      Walsh, and William A. Wellman. New York: Atheneum,
      1975. 308 pp.

                          7. Editing

      For additional material, see also the works of Sergei
Eisenstein and V. I. Pudovkin in Part VIII, section A, individual
theorists.

904   Cole, Sydney. Film Editing: A Speech Delivered at the BFI's
      Summer School at Bangor. London: British Film Institute,
      1944. 15 pp.

905   Sprungman, Ormal I. Editing and Titling Movies. Chicago:
      Ziff-Davis, 1947. 144 pp.

906   Baddeley, W. Hugh. How to Edit Amateur Films. New York:
      Focal, 1951. 136 pp. (Republished 1958 and 1968, 144 pp.)

907   Reisz, Karel. The Technique of Film Editing. Introduced by
      Thorold Dickinson. London, New York: Focal, 1953.
      288 pp. (Revised by Karel Reisz and Gavin Miller, New
      York: Hastings, 1968, 411 pp.)

908   Cushman, George W. Editing Your Color Movies. San Fran-
      cisco: Camera Craft, 1959. 96 pp.

909   Gregory, John Robert. Some Psychological Aspects of Motion
      Picture Montage. University of Illinois, Urbana-Champaign:
      Ph.D., 1961. 138 pp.

910   Smith, Frederick Y. (ed.) American Cinema Editors First
      Decade Anniversary Book. Hollywood: American Cinema
      Editors, 1961. 224 pp.
          With contributions from Walter M. Mirisch, Mark
      Robson, John Sturges, David Weisbart, Robert Wise, and
      others.

911   Underhill, Frederic. Post-Literate Man and Film Editing:
      An Application of the Theories of Marshall McLuhan.
      Boston: Boston University, School of Public Communica-
      tion, 1964. 42 pp.

912   Penn, Roger. An Experimental Study of the Meaning of Cutting-
      Rate Variables in Motion Pictures. University of Iowa:
      Ph.D., 1967. 138 pp.

913 Burder, John. The Technique of Editing 16mm Films. New
     York: Hastings, 1968. 152 pp.

914 Eastman Kodak Company, Consumer Markets Division. Editing
     Your Movies. Rochester: Eastman Kodak Company, ca.
     1968. 11 pp.

915 Walter, Ernest. The Technique of the Film Cutting Room.
     New York: Hastings, 1969. 282 pp. (Revised London:
     Focal, 1973, 316 pp.)

916 Smith, Federick Y. (ed.) American Cinema Editors Second
     Decade Anniversary Book. Los Angeles: American Cinema
     Editors, 1971. 301 pp.

917 Churchill, Hugh B. Film Editing Handbook: Technique of
     16mm Film Cutting. Belmont, Cal. : Wadsworth, 1972.
     198 pp.

                          8. Music

918 Lang, Edith and West, George. Musical Accompaniment of
     Moving Pictures: A Practical Manual for Pianists and
     Organists and an Exposition of the Principles Underlying
     the Musical Interpretation of Moving Pictures. (Originally
     published 1920.) New York: Arno, 1970. 64 pp.

919 Rapee, Erno. Motion Picture Moods for Pianists and Organists:
     A Rapid-Reference Collection of Selected Pieces. (Origi-
     nally published 1924.) New York: Arno, 1974. 678 pp.

920 Rapee, Erno. Encyclopaedia of Music for Pictures. (Origi-
     nally published 1925.) New York: Arno, 1970. 510 pp.
     Guide to selection of silent film accompaniment.

921 Foort, Reginald. The Cinema Organ: A Description in Non-
     Technical Language of a Fascinating Instrument and How It
     Is Played. (Originally published 1932.) Vestal, N. Y. :
     Vestal, 1970. 199 pp.

922 London, Kurt. Film Music: A Summary of the Characteristic
     Features of Its History, Aesthetics, Technique; and Possible
     Developments. (Originally published 1936.) New York:
     Arno, 1970. 280 pp. Translated by Eric S. Bensinger.

923 Rodriguez, Jose (ed.) Music and Dance in California. Holly-
     wood: Bureau of Musical Research, 1940. 467 pp.

924 Cockshott, Gerald. Incidental Music in the Sound Films. Lon-
     don: British Film Institute, 1946. 7 pp.

925 Courtney, Jack. Theatre Organ World: Cinema Organists and Their Instruments "Spotted" for Your Information and Entertainment by Famous Writers, Artists and Musicians. London(?): Theatre Organ World Publications, 1946. 200 pp.

926 Eisler, Hanns. Composing for the Films. New York: Oxford University Press, 1947. 165 pp.

927 Heinsheimer, H. W. Menagerie in F Sharp. Garden City, N.Y.: Doubleday, 1947. 275 pp.
    Includes chapters on film music.

928 Huntley, John. British Film Music. London: Robinson, 1947. 247 pp. (Reprinted New York: Arno, 1972.)

929 Levy, Louis. Music for the Movies. London: Low, Marston, 1948. 182 pp.

930 Saunders, Richard Drake (ed.) Music and Dance in California and the West. Hollywood: Bureau of Musical Research, 1948. 311 pp.

931 Rubsamen, Walter Howard. Descriptive Music for Stage and Screen. Los Angeles: U.C.L.A. Students' Store, 1949. 14 pp.

931a Zuckerman, John V. Music in Motion Pictures: Review of Literature with Implications for Instructional Films. Port Washington, N.Y.: Office of Naval Research, 1949. 17 pp.

932 Skinner, Frank. Underscore. Los Angeles: Skinner Music, 1950. 291 pp. (Revised New York: Criterion Music, 1960, 239 pp.)
    Includes reproduction of passages from film scores as well as material on the composing and arranging of music for motion pictures.

933 Rawlings, F. How to Choose Music for Amateur Films. London, New York: Focal, 1955. 128 pp.

934 Copland, Aaron. What to Listen for in Music. New York: McGraw-Hill, 1957. 307 pp.
    Includes one chapter on film music.

935 Manvell, Roger and Huntley, John. The Technique of Film Music. London, New York: Focal, 1957. 299 pp.

936 Mancini, Henry. Sounds and Scores: A Practical Guide to Professional Orchestration. New York(?): Northridge Music, 1962. 245 pp.

937 Dolan, Robert E. Music in Modern Media: Techniques in Tape,

Disc and Film Recording, Motion Picture and Television
Scoring and Electronic Music. New York: Schirmer, 1967.
181 pp.
   Includes samples from the scores of Aaron Copland, Alfred Newman, and Alex North.

938 Gerrero, Richard Henry. Music as a Film Variable. Michi-
     gan State University: Ph.D., 1969. 110 pp.

939 Hofmann, Charles. Sounds for Silents. New York: Drama
     Book Shop Publications, 1970. 90 pp.
     The history and technique of silent film music.

940 Faulkner, Robert R. Hollywood Studio Musicians: Their Work
     and Careers in the Recording Industry. Chicago: Aldine,
     Atherton, 1971. 218 pp.
     A sociological study of the musician's role within the
     Hollywood work structure.

941 Hagen, Earle. Scoring for Films: A Complete Text. New
     York: Criterion Music, 1971. 253 pp.

942 Berg, Charles. An Investigation of the Motives for and Reali-
     zation of Music to Accompany the American Silent Film,
     1896-1927. University of Iowa: Ph.D., 1973. 311 pp.

943 Thomas, Tony. Music for the Movies. South Brunswick, N.J.:
     A. S. Barnes, 1973. 270 pp.
     A study of the techniques and careers of Hollywood film
     composers; for list of names, see entry 3778.

944 Collins, W. H. The Amateur Filmmaker's Handbook of Sound,
     Sync & Scoring. Blue Ridge Summit, Pa.: TAB Books,
     1974. 210 pp.

945 Limbacher, James L. (ed.) Film Music: From Violins to
     Video. Metuchen, N.J.: Scarecrow, 1974. 835 pp.
     With contributions by Gordon Hendricks, Dimitri Tiom-
     kin, Louis Applebaum, John Huntley, William Hamilton,
     David Raskin, Leonard Rosenman, George Duning, Elmer
     Bernstein, Page Cook, Leith Stevens, Arthur Bliss, Jack
     Shaindlin, Miklos Rozsa, William Walton, Muir Mathieson,
     John Green, Sergei Eisenstein, Mary Ellen Bute, and
     others.

946 Bazelon, Irwin. Knowing the Score: Notes on Film Music.
     New York: Van Nostrand, 1975. 352 pp.
     Techniques and aesthetics of film music, plus inter-
     views; for list of names, see entry 3799.

947 Evans, Mark. Soundtrack: The Music of the Movies. New
     York: Hopkinson and Blake, 1975. 303 pp.
     Primarily an historical approach.

9. Projection

948 Richardson, Frank Herbert. **F. H. Richardson's Bluebook of Projection.** (Originally published as Motion Picture Handbook: A Guide for Managers and Operators of Motion Picture Theatres, 1910.) Edited by Aaron Nadell. New York, Chicago: Quigley, 1942. 706 pp. (Eighth edition published as Bluebook of Projection, New York: Quigley, 1953, 662 pp.)

949 Cameron, James Ross. **Motion Picture Projection and Sound Pictures.** (Originally published as Motion Picture Projection, 1918.) Revised Woodmont, Conn.: Cameron Publishing, 1944. 586 pp. (Fifteenth edition Coral Gables, Florida: Cameron Publishing, 1969, 310 pp.)

950 Cameron, James Ross. **Examination Questions and Answers on Sound Motion Picture Projection.** (Originally published 1922.) Revised Coral Gables, Florida: Cameron Publishing, 1953. Examination questions for projectionist's operating license.

951 Cricks, R. Howard. **The Complete Projectionist: A Textbook for All Who Handle Sound and Pictures in the Kinema.** (Originally published 1937.) Revised London: Kinematograph, 1943. 326 pp. (Revised again London: Odhams, 1949, 335 pp.)

952 Noel, Francis W. **Projecting Motion Pictures in the Classroom.** Washington, D.C.: American Council on Education, 1940. 53 pp.

953 Molloy, Edward (ed.) **Sound-Film Projection: Dealing With the Installation, Operation and Maintenance of the Leading Types of Sound-Projection Equipment, and Public-Address Systems.** London: Newnes, 1945. 232 pp. (Revised 1949, 260 pp. Revised again 1951, 343 pp.)

954 Cameron, James Ross. **Motors and Motor-Generators for the Projectionist; Care, Operation and Maintenance of Motors and Generators.** Coral Gables, Florida: Cameron Publishing, 1946. 98 pp.

955 Mannino, Philip. **ABC's of Visual Aids and Projectionist's Manual.** Ypsilanti, Mich.: n.p., 1946. 83 pp. (Revised 1948, 110 pp. Revised again as ABC's of Audio-Visual Equipment and the School Projectionist's Manual, State College, Pa., 1958, 80 pp.)

956 Atkinson, N. J. **Practical Projection for Teachers.** London: Current Affairs, 1948. 119 pp.

957 Hill, Cecil A. Cine-Film Projection: A Practical Manual for
    Users of All Types of 16-mm. and Sub-Standard Film Pro-
    jectors. London: Fountain, 1948. 180 pp. (Revised with
    subtitle A Practical Manual for Users of All Types of 16-
    mm. and Narrow Gauge Film Projectors, 1952, 192 pp.)

958 Jenkins, Norman. How to Project Substandard Films. Lon-
    don, New York: Focal, 1949. 152 pp.

959 Schreiber, Robert Edwin. The EFLA Redbook of Audio-Visual
    Equipment: A Handbook of Information on Film and Film-
    strip Projectors, Recording and Public Address Equipment.
    New York: Educational Film Library Association, 1949.
    37 pp.

960 Cameron, James Ross. Trouble-Shooting and Maintenance
    Guide; Complete Easy to Understand Instructions for Main-
    tenance and Trouble-Shooting of All Commercial Sound Pic-
    ture Equipment. Coral Gables, Florida: Cameron Pub-
    lishing, 1950. 224 pp.
       Portions originally published in many earlier editions
    under varying titles.

961 Reid, Seerley. Movie Projectors in Public High Schools.
    Washington, D.C.: Federal Security Agency, Office of
    Education, 1950. 16 pp.

962 Mitchell, Robert A. Manual of Practical Projection. New
    York: International Projectionists Publishing, 1956. 450 pp.

963 Cameron, James Ross. Projection Room Guide: Servicing
    Sound Equipment. Coral Gables, Florida: Cameron Pub-
    lishing, 1957. Unpaged.

964 Gilmour, Edwyn A. Choosing and Using a Cine Projector.
    London: Fountain, 1960. 127 pp.

965 Simpson, Margaret. Film Projecting Without Tears or Techni-
    calities. London: National Committee for Audio-Visual
    Aids in Education, 1960. (Revised 1966, 51 pp.)

966 Kloepfel, Don V. (ed.) Motion-Picture Projection and Theatre
    Presentation Manual. New York: Society of Motion Picture
    and Television Engineers, 1969. 178 pp.

10. Screenwriting

    This section is primarily comprised of books which specifi-
cally discuss the techniques of screenwriting. We have, however,
included a few books on playwriting or storytelling in general which

might be found particularly useful. For material on copyrights and
legal concepts of interest to the writer, the reader should consult
the production category, Part III, section C. Since screenwriting
often involves the process of adaptation, the reader may also find
relevant some of the works in Part VIII, section F-1, film and
literature, and section F-2, film and theatre.

967 Phillips, Henry Albert. The Photodrama: The Philosophy of
    Its Principles, the Nature of Its Plot, Its Dramatic Con-
    struction and Technique, Illumined by Copious Examples,
    Together with a Complete Photoplay and a Glossary, Making
    the Work a Practical Treatise. (Originally published 1914.)
    New York: Arno, 1970. 221 pp.
    Includes script of Salt of Vengeance.

968 Polti, Georges. The Thirty-Six Dramatic Situations. (Origi-
    nally published 1916.) Boston: The Writer, 1940. 181 pp.
    Translated by Lucille Ray. (Reprinted 1954.)

969 Freeburg, Victor Oscar. The Art of Photoplay Making. (Origi-
    nally published 1918.) New York: Arno, 1970. 283 pp.

970 Strasser, Alex. Ideas for Short Films: Simple Scripts for
    Amateurs. (Originally published 1937.) London: Link,
    1944. 80 pp. Translated by P. C. Smethurst.

971 Kennedy, Margaret. The Mechanized Muse. London: Allen
    and Unwin, 1942. 52 pp.
    Includes discussion of adaptation, dialogue, and original
    scripts.

972 Kanigher, Robert. How to Make Money Writing for the Movies.
    New York: Cambridge House, 1943. 64 pp.

973 Vale, Eugene. The Technique of Screenplay Writing: A Book
    About the Dramatic Structure of Motion Pictures. New
    York: De Vorss, distributed by Crown, 1944. 274 pp.
    (Revised as The Technique of Screenplay Writing: An
    Analysis of the Dramatic Structure of Motion Pictures,
    New York: Grosset and Dunlap, 1972, 306 pp.)

974 Egri, Lajos. The Art of Dramatic Writing: Its Basis in the
    Creative Interpretation of Human Motives. New York:
    Simon and Schuster, 1946. 294 pp. (Revised 1960, 304 pp.)

975 Brunel, Adrian. Film Script: The Technique of Writing for
    the Screen. London: Burke, 1948. 192 pp.

976 White, Moresby and Stock, Freda. The Right Way to Write
    for the Films. Kingswood, England: Elliot, 1948. 117
    pp.

977 Blakeston, Oswell. How to Script Amateur Films. London:
   Focal, 1949. 152 pp.

978 Lawson, John Howard. Theory and Technique of Playwriting
   and Screenwriting. New York: Putnam, 1949. 464 pp.

979 Beranger, Clara. Writing for the Screen (With Story, Picture
   Treatment, and Shooting Script.) Dubuque, Iowa: Brown,
   1950. 199 pp.

980 Herman, Lewis. A Practical Manual of Screen Playwriting
   for Theater and Television Films. Cleveland: World,
   1952. 294 pp. (Reprinted 1963.)

981 Harrison, Richard M. How to Write Film Stories for Amateur
   Films. London, New York: Focal, 1954. 144 pp.

982 Busfield, Roger M., Jr. The Playwright's Art: Stage, Radio,
   Television, Motion Pictures. New York: Harper, 1958.
   260 pp.

983 Yoakem, Lola Goelet (ed.) TV and Screen Writing. Berkeley:
   University of California Press, 1958. 124 pp.
       With contributions from 16 members of the Writers
   Guild of America, including Frank Nugent, Jesse L. Lasky,
   Jr., Hal Kanter, Ivan Tors, Reuven Frank, and Erik
   Barnouw.

984 Thompson, Charles Victor. The Film Script. London: Fountain, 1962. 93 pp.

985 Horn, Donald R. Scenarios! Scenarios! Scenarios! Stories,
   Incidents, Gimmicks, Tricks, for Interesting Home Movies.
   Philadelphia: Chilton, 1963. 94 pp.

986 Gessner, Robert. The Moving Image: A Guide to Cinematic
   Literacy. New York: Dutton, 1968. 444 pp.
       A detailed examination of dramatic techniques in screen-
   writing.

987 Parker, Norton S. Audiovisual Script Writing. New Brunswick, N.J.: Rutgers University Press, 1968. 330 pp.
   Concentrates on non-theatrical films.

988 Beveridge, James A. Script Writing for Short Films. Paris:
   UNESCO, 1969. 45 pp.

989 Capote, Truman; Perry, Eleanor; and Perry, Frank. Trilogy:
   An Experiment in Multi-Media. New York: Macmillan,
   1969. 276 pp.
       Includes detailed account of story-to-script adaptation.

990 Froug, William. The Screenwriter Looks at the Screenwriter.

New York: Macmillan, 1972. 352 pp.
Interviews; for list of names, see entry 3750.

991 Rilla, Wolf. The Writer and the Screen: On Writing for
     Film and Television. London, New York: W. H. Allen,
     1973. 191 pp.

992 Rockwell, F. A. How to Write Plots that Sell. Chicago:
     Regnery, 1975. 279 pp.

11. Sound

993 Olson, Harry F. Elements of Acoustical Engineering. New
     York: Van Nostrand, 1940. 344 pp. (Revised 1947,
     539 pp. Revised again as Acoustical Engineering, Prince-
     ton, N.J.: Van Nostrand, 1957, 718 pp.)

994 Cameron, Ken. Sound in Films. London: British Film
     Institute, 1944. 8 pp.
     Focuses on sound and music in documentary.

995 Kellogg, Edward W. The ABC of Photographic Sound Recording.
     New York: Society of Motion Picture Engineers, 1945.
     44 pp.

996 Cameron, Ken. Sound and the Documentary Film. London:
     Pitman, 1947. 157 pp.

997 Frayne, John G. and Wolfe, Halley. Elements of Sound Re-
     cording. New York: Wiley, 1949. 686 pp.

998 Read, Oliver. The Recording and Reproduction of Sound.
     Indianapolis: Sams, 1949. 364 pp. (Revised 1952, 790 pp.)

999 Neale, Denis M. How to Add Sound to Amateur Films. Lon-
     don, New York: Focal, 1954. 160 pp. (Revised by R. A.
     Hole as How to Do Sound Films, 1969, 155 pp.)

1000 Cushman, George W. Sound for Your Color Movies. San
     Francisco: Camera Craft, 1958. 95 pp.

1001 Tall, Joel. Techniques of Magnetic Recording. New York:
     Macmillan, 1958. 472 pp.
     Discusses film along with other sound mediums.

1002 Lewin, Frank. The Soundtrack in Nontheatrical Motion Pic-
     tures. Easton, Pa.: Reprinted from the Journal of the
     Society of Motion Picture and Television Engineers, 1959.
     20 pp.

1003   Chittock, John. How to Produce Magnetic Sound for Films.
          London: Focal, 1962. 152 pp.

1004   Murphy, Burt. Home Movies in Sound. New York: Uni-
          versal Photo, 1962. 127 pp.

1005   Nisbett, Alec. The Technique of the Sound Studio. New
          York: Hastings, 1962. 288 pp. (Revised 1970, 559 pp.)

1006   Dolan, Robert. Music in Modern Media: Techniques in
          Tape, Disc and Film Recording, Motion Picture and Tele-
          vision Scoring and Electronic Music. New York: Schir-
          mer, 1967. 181 pp.

1007   Eastman Kodak Company. Basic Magnetic Sound Recording
          for Motion Pictures. Rochester, N.Y.: Eastman Kodak
          Company, 1969. 41 pp.

1008   Wysotsky, Michael Z. Wide-Screen Cinema and Stereophonic
          Sound. Edited and introduced by Raymond Spottiswoode.
          Translated by A. E. C. York. New York: Hastings,
          1971. 282 pp.

1009   Olson, Harry F. Modern Sound Reproduction. New York:
          Van Nostrand Reinhold, 1972. 335 pp.

1010   Alkin, E. G. M. Sound With Vision: Sound Techniques for
          Television and Film. New York: Crane, Russak, 1973.
          283 pp.

1011   Collins, W. H. The Amateur Filmmaker's Handbook of
          Sound, Sync & Scoring. Blue Ridge Summit, Pa.: TAB
          Books, 1974. 210 pp.

1012   Nisbett, Alec. The Use of Microphones. New York: Hast-
          ings, 1974. 168 pp.

12.   Special Effects and Stunting

This section contains books which deal with special effects
(both laboratory and studio) and stunting. In addition to the material
on stunting cited below, there are a number of stuntmen biographies
which contain information particularly pertinent to this category (see
Joe Bonomo, Harry Froboess, Dick Grace, John Hagner, Reginald
Kanavagh, Paul Mantz, Audrey Scott and others in Section VI-A,
Biography, Analysis and Interview).

1013   Society of Motion Picture and Television Engineers. Instru-
          mentation and High-Speed Photography. New York: So-
          ciety of Motion Picture and Television Engineers, ca. 1949.

1014   Chesterman, William Deryck. The Photographic Study of
       Rapid Events. Oxford: Clarendon, 1951. 167 pp.

1015   Bulleid, H. A. V. Special Effects in Cinematography. Lon-
       don: Fountain, 1954. 264 pp.

1016   Caunter, Julien. How To Do Tricks in Amateur Films. Lon-
       don, New York: Focal, 1956. 175 pp. (Republished in
       How To Make Movie Magic in Amateur Films, New York:
       Amphoto, 1970, 348 pp.)

1017   Ott, John. My Ivory Cellar. Chicago: Twentieth Century,
       1958. 157 pp.
           Discusses time-lapse photography in still and motion
       pictures.

1018   Caunter, Julien. How To Do the Simpler Tricks in Amateur
       Films. London: Focal, 1961. 184 pp. (Republished in
       How To Make Movie Magic in Amateur Films, New York:
       Amphoto, 1970, 348 pp.)

1019   Duckworth, Paul. Experimental and Trick Photography. New
       York: Universal Photo, 1961. 127 pp.

1020   Fielding, Raymond. The Technique of Special-Effects Cine-
       matography. New York: Hastings, 1965. 396 pp. (Re-
       vised London, New York: Focal, 1972. 425 pp.)

1021   Clark, Frank P. Special Effects in Motion Pictures: Some
       Methods for Producing Mechanical Special Effects. New
       York: Society of Motion Picture and Television Engineers,
       1966. 238 pp.

1022   Hagner, John G. The Greatest Stunts Ever. Hollywood: El
       Jon, 1967. 30 pp.

1023   Brodbeck, Emil E. Movie and Videotape Special Effects.
       Philadelphia: Chilton, 1968. 192 pp.

1024   Caunter, Julien. How To Make Movie Magic in Amateur
       Films. New York: Amphoto, 1970. 348 pp. (Revised
       and combined edition of How To Do Tricks in Amateur
       Films, 1956, and How To Do the Simpler Tricks in Ama-
       teur Films, 1961.)

1025   Eastman Kodak Company. Cinephotomicrography. Rochester,
       N. Y.: Eastman Kodak Company, 1970. 40 pp.

1026   Harryhausen, Ray. Film Fantasy Scrapbook. South Bruns-
       wick, N. J.: A. S. Barnes, 1972. 117 pp. (Revised
       1974, 142 pp.)
           With material on Harryhausen's special effects and
       animation techniques.

1027 Azarmi, Mehrdad. Optical Effects Cinematography: Its Development, Methods and Techniques. University of Southern
California: Ph.D., 1973. 231 pp.

1028 Wise, Arthur and Ware, Derek. Stunting in the Cinema.
New York: St. Martin's, 1973. 248 pp.

1029 Baxter, John. Stunt: The Story of the Great Movie Stunt
Men. Garden City, N.Y.: Doubleday, 1974. 320 pp.
For list of names, see entry 3782.

1030 Brosnan, John. Movie Magic: The Story of Special Effects
in the Cinema. New York: St. Martin's, 1974. 285 pp.

13.   Theatre and Studio Design and Management

1031 Hulfish, David S. Motion-Picture Work: A General Treatise
on Picture Taking, Picture Making, Photo-Plays, and
Theatre Management and Operation. (Originally published
1913.) New York: Arno, 1970. 282, 297 pp.

1032 Alexander, Edward. Become a Theatre Manager. New York:
Theatrical Publication, 1943. 64 pp.

1033 Stote, Helen M. (ed.) The Motion Picture Theater: Planning,
Upkeep: 38 Articles on the Technical Aspects of Motion
Picture Theater Planning, Construction, Maintenance,
Modernization, and Theater Television. New York: So-
ciety of Motion Picture Engineers, 1948. 428 pp.

1034 Motiograph, Inc. The Design, Construction, and Equipment
of a Drive-In Theatre. Chicago: Motiograph, 1949. 20 pp.

1035 Chambers, Robert W. Problems in Motion Picture Theatre
Management. Harvard University: Ph.D., 1950.

1036 Worthington, Clifford. The Influence of the Cinema on Contemporary Auditoria Design. London: Pitman, 1952. 123 pp.

1037 Hall, Ben M. The Best Remaining Seats: The Story of the
Golden Age of the Movie Palace. New York: Clarkson
Potter, 1961. 266 pp. (Reprinted as The Golden Age of
the Movie Palace: The Best Remaining Seats, 1975,
distributed by Crown.)

1038 Kloepfel, Don V. (ed.) Motion-Picture Projection and Theatre
Presentation Manual. New York: Society of Motion Picture and Television Engineers, 1969. 178 pp.

1039 Sharp, Dennis. The Picture Palace and Other Buildings for
the Movies. New York: Praeger, 1969. 224 pp.

With much material on British theatres.

1040 Mankovsky, V. S. Acoustics of Studios and Auditoria. New
      York: Communication Arts, 1971. 395 pp. Translated
      by Gordon Clough.

1040a Ingham, Gordon. Everyone's Gone to the Movies: The Sixty
      Cinemas of Auckland and Some Others. Auckland: Minerva,
      1973. 46 pp.

1041 Headley, Robert Kirk. Exit: A History of Movies in Balti-
      more. University Park, Md.: Headley, 1974. 162 pp.
      With material on the theatres in Baltimore.

   14. 3-D and Special Projection and Production Systems

1042 McKay, Herbert C. Principles of Stereoscopy. Boston:
      American Photographic, 1948. 191 pp. (Revised as
      Three-Dimension Photography: Principles of Stereoscopy,
      Minneapolis: American Photography, 1951. 334 pp.)
      Includes one chapter on amateur 3-D movies.

1043 Judge, Arthur William. Stereoscopic Photography: Its Appli-
      cation to Science, Industry, and Education. London:
      Chapman and Hall, 1950. 480 pp.
      Discusses both still and motion pictures.

1044 Cameron, James Ross. Third Dimension and E-X-P-A-N-D-E-D
      Screen. Coral Gables, Florida: Cameron Publishing, 1953.
      188 pp.

1045 Quigley, Martin Jr. (ed.) New Screen Techniques. New York:
      Quigley, 1953. 208 pp.
      Essays on 3-D and wide screen techniques.

1046 Spottiswoode, Raymond and Nigel. The Theory of Stereoscopic
      Transmission and Its Application to the Motion Picture.
      Berkeley: University of California Press, 1953. 177 pp.

1047 Cornwell-Clyne, Adrian. 3-D Kinematography and New Screen
      Techniques. London: Hutchinson's Scientific and Technical
      Publications, 1954. 266 pp.

1048 Dewhurst, H. Introduction to 3-D: Three Dimensional Photog-
      raphy in Motion Pictures, with Chapters on Wide-Screen
      Cinemascope, Cinerama, and Stereo Television. London:
      Chapman and Hall, 1954. 152 pp.

1049 Limbacher, James L. Movies are Wider Than Ever. Dear-
      born, Mich.: n.p., 1964. 33 ℓ.

1050 Limbacher James L. A Perspective on the Third-Dimensional

Film. Dearborn, Mich.: Public Library, 1964. 23 ℓ.

1051 Eastman Kodak Company. Wide-Screen and Multiple-Screen
      Presentations. Rochester, N.Y.: Eastman Kodak Com-
      pany, Motion Picture and Educational Markets Division,
      1970. 15 pp.

1052 Wysotsky, Michael Z. Wide-Screen Cinema and Stereophonic
      Sound. Edited and introduced by Raymond Spottiswoode.
      New York: Hastings, 1971. 282 pp. Translated by
      A. E. C. York.

1053 Brennan, William B., Jr. The Development of Special Forms
      of Film at World Expositions (1900-1970). Northwestern
      University: Ph.D., 1972. 349 pp.

15. Titling

        This section contains books which deal almost exclusively
with titling. For supplementary material, the reader should consult
books in the animation category, Part II, section C-2, many of
which discuss graphic and titling techniques.

1054 Cushman, George W. How to Title Home Movies. Hollywood:
      Ver Halen, 1943, c. 1940. 85 pp.

1055 Sprungman, Ormal I. Editing and Titling Movies. Chicago:
      Ziff-Davis, 1947. 144 pp.

1056 Minter, L. F. How to Title Amateur Films. London, New
      York: Focal, 1949. 128 pp. (Reprinted 1957 and 1970.)

1057 Moore, James Whitney. Titling Your Color Movies. San
      Francisco: Camera Craft, 1958. 96 pp.

1058 Daborn, John. Cine Titling. London: Fountain, 1960. 112 pp.

1059 Eastman Kodak Company. Basic Titling and Animation.
      Rochester, N.Y.: Eastman Kodak Company, 1961. 64 pp.
      (Republished as Basic Titling and Animation for Motion Pic-
      tures, 1970, 56 pp.)

1060 Bomback, Edward S. Table-Tops and Titles in Color. Lon-
      don: Fountain, 1962. 94 pp.

16. Miscellaneous Techniques

1061 Hamilton, G. E. How to Make Handmade Lantern Slides.

Meadville, Penn.: Keystone View Company, 1940.   23 pp.
(Reprinted 1950.)

1062   Robinson, Martha.   Continuity Girl: A Story of Film Produc-
       tion. London: Oxford University Press, 1946.   181 pp.

1063   Ballantine, William.   Wild Tigers and Tame Fleas.   New
       York: Rinehart, 1958.   344 pp.
       With material on animal training.

1064   Bernstein, Irving.   The Position of the Story Analyst in the
       Motion Picture Industry.   Hollywood(?):   Story Analyst's
       Guild, 1958.   25 ℓ.

1065   Amaral, Anthony.   Movie Horses: Their Treatment and
       Training.   Indianapolis: Bobbs-Merrill, 1967.   152 pp.

1066   Hunt, Todd.   Reviewing for the Mass Media.   Philadelphia:
       Chilton, 1972.   190 pp.

1067   Levenson, Jordan.   The Back Lot: Motion Picture Studio
       Laborer's Craft Described by a Hollywood Laborer.
       Hollywood(?): Levenson Press, 1972.   Various pagings.

1068   Trent, Paul.   The Image Makers: 60 Years of Hollywood
       Glamour.   Designed by Richard Lawton.   New York:
       McGraw-Hill, 1972.   327 pp.
       Includes an essay on Hollywood portrait photographers
       and samples of their work.

1069   Holman, L. Bruce.   Cinema Equipment You Can Build.
       Tully, N.Y.: Walnut, 1975.   90 pp.

D. FILMMAKING FOR BUSINESS AND INDUSTRY

1070 Gipson, Henry Clay. Films in Business and Industry. New York: McGraw-Hill, 1947. 291 pp.

1071 Wilson, William H. and Haas, Kenneth B. The Film Book for Business, Education and Industry. New York: Prentice-Hall, 1950. 259 pp.

1072 Eastman Kodak Company. Industrial Motion Pictures. Rochester, N.Y.: Eastman Kodak Company, 1957. 76 pp. (Reprinted 1966.)

1073 Spooner, Peter. Business Films: How to Make and Use Them. London: Business Publications, 1959. 360 pp.

1074 Gordon, Jay E. Motion Picture Production for Industry. New York: Macmillan, 1961. 352 pp.

1075 Magnan, George. Visual Art for Industry. New York: Reinhold, 1961. 176 pp.
      Includes material on film.

1076 Association of National Advertisers, Audio-Visual Committee. Steps in Producing and Costing a Business Film. New York: Association of National Advertisers, c. 1962. 21 pp.

1077 Stork, Leopold. Industrial and Business Films: A Modern Means of Communication. London: Phoenix, 1962. 180 pp.

1078 Wigens, Anthony. How to Use 8mm at Work. London, New York: Focal, 1964. 160 pp.
      Material on sales and demonstration films.

1079 Herman, Lewis. Educational Films: Writing, Directing and Producing for Classroom, Television, and Industry. New York: Crown, 1965. 338 pp.

1080 DeWitt, Jack. Producing Industrial Films: From Fade-In to Fade-Out. South Brunswick, N.J.: A. S. Barnes, 1968. 148 pp.

1081   Burder, John.   The Work of the Industrial Film Maker.
          New York: Hastings, 1973.   255 pp.

E. SPECIAL FILMMAKING APPROACHES

This section of specialized approaches is composed of filmmaking guides aimed toward the making of certain kinds of films. There are books here on the making of documentary films, educational films, wildlife films, and so forth. Works intended as filmmaking texts for children or students, however, have been classified in Part II, section B, general guides.

1082 Rotha, Paul. Documentary Film. (Originally published 1936. Revised 1939.) Third revised edition London: Faber and Faber, 1952. 412 pp. (Reprinted 1970.)
Includes a section detailing documentary filmmaking techniques.

1083 Buchanan, Andrew. Film-Making from Script to Screen. (Originally published 1937.) Revised London: Phoenix, 1951. 159 pp.
Includes chapters on the filming of villages, towns, factories, farms, foreign cities, and hospitals.

1084 Cameron, Ken. Sound and the Documentary Film. London: Pitman, 1947. 157 pp.

1085 Association of National Advertisers, Films Committee. Check List for Producer and Sponsor Responsibilities in the Production of Motion Pictures. New York: Association of National Advertisers, 1948. 14 ℓ. (Revised as Responsibilities of the Film Producer and Sponsor, 1957, 35 pp.)

1086 Battison, John H. Movies for TV. New York: Macmillan, 1950. 376 pp.
A guide to the various uses of film in television.

1087 Franks, Arthur H. Ballet for Film and Television. London: Pitman, 1950. 85 pp.
With material on the problems of recording ballet.

1088 Storck, Henri. The Entertainment Film for Juvenile Audiences. Paris: UNESCO, distributed by Columbia University Press, 1950. 240 pp.

Includes a section on filmmaking with children and making children's films.

1089   Association of National Advertisers, Films Steering Committee. Criteria for Business-Sponsored Educational Films. New York: Association of National Advertisers, c. 1955. 16 pp.

1090   Michaelis, Anthony R. Research Films in Biology, Anthropology, Psychology and Medicine. New York: Academic Press, 1955. 490 pp.
Includes history, technique and special problems of the research film.

1091   Natkin, M. How to Film Children. London: Focal, 1955. 136 pp. Translated by G. R. Sharp.

1092   Densham, D. H. Construction of Research Films. New York: Pergamon, 1959. 104 pp.

1093   Steele, Robert Scott. An Experimental Approach to the Production of a Motion Picture Surveying the Sarvodaya Movement in India. Ohio State University: Ph.D., 1959. 397 pp.

1094   Winter, Myrtle and Spurr, Norman. Film-Making on a Low Budget: The UNESCO-UNRWA Pilot Project. Paris: UNESCO, 1960. 31 pp.

1095   UNESCO, Mass Communication Techniques Division. Film and Television in the Service of Opera and Ballet and of Museum: Reports on Two International Meetings. Paris: UNESCO, 1961. 55 pp.

1096   Baddeley, W. Hugh. The Technique of Documentary Film Production. New York: Hastings, 1963. 268 pp. (Revised 1973, 282 pp.)

1097   Kemp, Jerrold E. and others. Planning and Producing Audiovisual Materials. San Francisco: Chandler, 1963. 169 pp. (Revised Scranton, Pa.: Chandler, 1968, 251 pp.)

1098   Ruspoli, Mario. Towards a New Film Technique in the Developing Countries; The Light-Weight Synchronized Cinematographic Unit. Paris: UNESCO, 1964. 38 pp.

1099   Atkins, Jim, Jr. and Willette, Leo. Filming TV News and Documentaries. Philadelphia: Chilton, 1965. 158 pp.

1100   Herman, Lewis. Educational Films: Writing, Directing and Producing for Classroom, Television, and Industry. New York: Crown, 1965. 338 pp.

1101   Warham, John. The Technique of Wildlife Cinematography. London: Focal, 1966. 222 pp.

1102   Ferguson, Robert. How to Make Movies: A Practical Guide to Group Film Making. New York: Viking, 1969. 88 pp.

1103   Cappello, Patrick H. Life in a Movie Club. New York: Vantage, 1970. 127 pp.

1104   Burton, Alexis L. (ed.) Cinematographic Techniques in Biology and Medicine. New York: Academic Press, 1971. 394 pp.

1105   Parsons, Christopher. Making Wildlife Movies: A Beginner's Guide. Harrisburg, Pa.: Stackpole, 1971. 224 pp.

1106   Strasser, Alex. The Work of the Science Film Maker. New York: Hastings, 1972. 308 pp.

1107   Hockings, Paul (ed.) Principles of Visual Anthropology. The Hague: Mouton, distributed by Chicago: Aldine, 1975. 521 pp.
        Includes material on making anthropological films.

F. TECHNIQUES FOR THE FILM COLLECTION AND FILM ARCHIVE

This section includes books on various archival techniques, including film cataloging, film collecting, film preservation, film research, film evaluation and reviewing, the administration of film archives and film libraries, and audio-visual librarianship. For material on particular archives and institutions, see Part I, section F, film institutions. For material surveying criticism and techniques of criticism, see also Part VIII, section E.

1108   Brown, H. G.   Problems of Storing Film for Archive Purposes. London: National Film Library, 1952. 14 pp.

1109   Collison, Robert L.   Indexes and Indexing: A Guide to the Indexing of Books, and Collections of Books, Periodicals, Music, Gramophone Records, Films, and Other Material, with a Reference Section and Suggestions for Further Reading. New York: J. De Graff, 1953. (Revised 1959, 200 pp.)

1110   British Film Institute.   Rules for Use in the Cataloguing Department of the National Film Archive. London: British Film Institute, 1956. 40 pp. (Revised 1960, 46 pp.)

1111   Allison, Mary L. and others.   Manual for Evaluators of Films and Filmstrips. Paris: Educational Film Library Association, 1956. 23 pp.

1112   UNESCO, Department of Mass Communications.   International Rules for the Cataloguing of Educational, Scientific, and Cultural Films and Filmstrips on 3" x 5" Cards. Paris: Clearing House, Department of Mass Communications, UNESCO, 1956. 53 pp.

1113   Scientific Film Association.   The Evaluation of Scientific, Industrial and Medical Films. London: Scientific Film Association, c. 1958. 15 pp.

1114   Eastman Kodak Company.   The Handling, Repair, and Storage of 16mm Films. Rochester, N.Y.: Eastman Kodak Company, 1960. 11 pp.

1115 Film Production Librarians Group. Film Cataloguing Rules.
      London: Aslib, 1963. 71 pp.

1116 Ledoux, Jacques. Study of the Establishment of National
      Centres for Cataloguing of Films and Television Pro-
      grammes. Paris: UNESCO, 1963. 34 pp.

1117 Volkmann, Herbert (comp.) Film Preservation: Preservation
      and Restoration of Cinematograph Film. Berlin: Inter-
      national Federation of Film Archives, Preservation Com-
      mittee, 1963. 148 ℓ. (Republished as Film Preservation:
      A Report by Herbert Volkmann, London: British Film
      Institute, 1966, 60 pp.)

1118 Hollywood Museum. The Preservation of Motion Picture Film:
      Handling, Storage, Identification. Los Angeles(?): Holly-
      wood Museum, 1964. Unpaged.

1119 U.S. Library of Congress, Descriptive Cataloging Division.
      Rules for Descriptive Cataloging in the Library of Con-
      gress: Motion Pictures and Filmstrips. Washington,
      D.C.: U.S. Library of Congress, 1965. 20 pp.

1120 Jones, Emily S. Manual on Film Evaluation. New York:
      Educational Film Library Association, 1967. 32 pp.
          Guide to committee evaluation of films by institutions
      and festivals.

1121 Steele, Robert. The Cataloguing and Classification of Cinema
      Literature. Metuchen, N.J.: Scarecrow, 1967. 133 pp.

1122 Kujoth, Jean Spealman (comp.) Readings in Nonbook Librian-
      ship. Metuchen, N.J.: Scarecrow, 1968. 463 pp.

1123 Lahue, Kalton C. Collecting Classic Films. New York:
      Amphoto, 1970. 159 pp.

1124 Reiss, Alvin H. The Arts Management Handbook: A Guide
      for those Interested in or Involved with the Administration
      of Cultural Institutions. New York: Law-Arts, 1970.
      655 pp.

1125 Lahue, Kalton C. and Bailey, Joseph A. Collecting Vintage
      Cameras: Volume I, The American 35mm. New York:
      Amphoto, 1972.

1126 Muro, Fred F., Jr. Collecting and Enjoying Old Movies.
      Bellmore, N.Y.: Impact Promotion and Publishing, 1972.
      57 pp.

1127 Pearce, S. Grove and Clement, Evelyn G. (eds.) Biblio-
      graphic Control of Nonprint Media. Chicago: American
      Library Association, 1972. 415 pp.

1128 Harrison, Helen P. Film Library Techniques: Principles of
      Administration. New York: Hastings, 1973. 277 pp.
      Discusses operation of stock-shot libraries.

1129 Asheim, Lester and Fenwick, Sara I. (eds.) Differentiating
      the Media: Proceedings of the Thirty-Seventh Annual
      Conference of the Graduate Library School, August 5-6,
      1974. Chicago: University of Chicago Press, 1975.
      74 pp.

1130 Rehrauer, George. The Film User's Handbook: A Basic
      Manual for Managing Library Film Services. New York:
      Bowker, 1975. 301 pp.

PART III

FILM INDUSTRY

A. ORGANIZATIONAL STRUCTURE, PRODUCTION, AND ECONOMICS

The books dealing with the film industry have been divided into four sections. This first section (organizational structure, production, and economics) contains those books which deal with the overall structure of the film studio system, techniques of film producing, economic analyses or histories of particular film industries, and works which are primarily statistical and deal with film as commodity rather than with film as art. For works dealing with the monopolistic structure of industry or with any of the unions or guilds in Hollywood, see Part III, section C. For other material on aspects of the film industry, the reader should consult works in the history classification--especially the studio history section, Part IV, section D-2. Material on the film industry and production practices can also be found in the biographies of many Hollywood moguls (see Section VI-A, Biography, Analysis and Interview).

1131 Grau, Robert. The Business Man in the Amusement World: A Volume of Progress in the Field of the Theatre. (Originally published 1910.) New York: Ozer, 1972. 362 pp.
Includes material on the rise of the film industry.

1132 Grau, Robert. The Theatre of Science: A Volume of Progress and Achievement in the Motion Picture Industry. (Originally published 1914.) New York: Blom, 1969. 378 pp.

1133 King, Clyde L. and Tichenor, Frank A. (eds.) The Motion Picture in its Economic and Social Aspects. (Originally published 1926, 195 pp.) Reprinted in The Motion Picture in its Economic and Social Aspects [and] The Motion Picture Industry. New York: Arno, 1970. 195, 236 pp.

1134 Seabury, William Marston. The Public and the Motion Picture Industry. (Originally published 1926.) New York: Ozer, 1971. 340 pp.
Describes industry practices and argues for its conversion to a public utility.

1135 Kennedy, Joseph P. (ed.) The Story of the Films: As Told by Leaders of the Industry to the Students of the Graduate

School of Business Administration, George F. Baker
Foundation, Harvard University. (Originally published
1927.) New York: Ozer, 1971. 377 pp.
Includes contributions by Jesse Lasky, Marcus Loew,
William Fox, Jack Warner, Will Hays, Adolph Zukor,
Sam Katz, Cecil B. De Mille, and others.

1136 Hampton, Benjamin B. History of the American Film Industry
from its Beginnings to 1931. (Originally published 1931
as A History of the Movies.) New York: Dover, 1970.
456 pp.

1137 Thorp, Margaret Farrand. America at the Movies. (Originally published 1939, 313 pp.) London: Faber and Faber,
1946. 184 pp. (Reprinted New York: Arno, 1970, 313 pp.)

1138 Rosten, Leo C. Hollywood: The Movie Colony, The Movie
Makers. New York: Harcourt, Brace, 1941. 436 pp.
(Reprinted New York: Arno, 1970.)

1139 Jester, Ralph. Talking Shadows: The Way of Life in Hollywood. Evanston, Ill.: Row, Peterson, 1942. 64 pp.

1140 Motion Picture Producers and Distributors of America. Film
Facts 1942: 20 Years of Self Government, 1922-1942.
New York: Motion Picture Producers and Distributors of
America, 1942. 65 pp.
Industry statistics, the motion picture production code,
and a summary of war-related activities.

1141 Moss, Louis and Box, Kathleen. The Cinema Audience: An
Inquiry Made by the Wartime Social Survey for the Ministry
of Information. London: Wartime Social Survey, 1943.
24 pp.

1142 Lee, Norman. A Film Is Born: How 40 Film Fathers Bring
a Modern Talking Picture into Being. London: Jordan,
1945. 127 pp.

1143 Bond, Ralph. Monopoly: The Future of British Films. Lon-
don: Association of Cine Technicians, 1946. 31 pp.
A study of British film industry with emphasis on J.
Arthur Rank and Hollywood influence.

1144 Indian Film Industry's Mission to Europe and America. Report of the Mission, Sent by the Indian Film Industry,
with the Approval and Support of the Government of India,
to Study the Latest Developments in the Application and
Manufacturing Sides of the Film Industry Abroad, July-
December, 1945. Bombay: Hirlekar, ca. 1946. 84 pp.

1145 Bird, John H. Cinema Parade: 50 Years of Film Shows.

Birmingham: Cornish Brothers, 1947. 107 pp.
Primarily about the early British film industry, particularly focusing on exhibitor Walter Jeffs.

1146 Czechoslovak Ministry of Information. The Czechoslovak
Nationalized Film Industry. Prague: Czechoslovak Ministry of Information, 1947. 63 pp.

1147 Minney, R. J. Talking of Films. London: Home and Van
Thal, 1947. 82 pp.
British film production.

1148 UNESCO. Press, Film, Radio. Paris: UNESCO, 1947.
(Reprinted in Press, Film, Radio, V. 1-5 (1947-1951),
New York: Arno, 1972.)

1149 Watkins, Gordon S. (ed.) The Motion Picture Industry.
Philadelphia: American Academy of Political and Social
Science, 1947. 236 pp. (Reprinted in The Motion Pic-
ture in its Economic and Social Aspects [and] The Motion
Picture Industry, New York: Arno, 1970, 195, 236 pp.)

1150 Box, Kathleen. The Cinema and the Public: An Inquiry into
Cinema Going Habits and Expenditure Made in 1946. London: Central Office of Information, Social Service Division,
ca. 1948. 17 pp.

1151 Losey, Mary. A Report on the Outlook for the Profitable
Production of Documentary Films for the Non-Theatrical
Market, for the Sugar Research Foundation. New York:
Film Program Services, 1948. 50 pp.

1152 Neergaard, Ebbe. Motion Pictures in Denmark: An Account
of the Cinema Act of 1938 and Its Effects, up to 1948.
Copenhagen: Central Film Library of the Danish Government, 1948. 20 pp.

1153 Pitts, Dick. What's Right with Hollywood? A Look at the
Motion Picture Industry. Washington, D. C.: Motion
Picture Association of America, 1948. 30 pp.

1154 UNESCO. Press, Film, Radio: Report of the Commission
on Technical Needs. Paris: UNESCO, 1948. 307 pp.
(Reprinted in Press, Film, Radio, V. 1-5 (1947-1951),
New York: Arno, 1972.)
Surveys facilities in Austria, Hungary, Italy, Cuba,
Dominican Republic, Ecuador, Haiti, Honduras, Mexico,
Peru, Uruguay, Venezuela, Burma, India, Malaya, Pakis-
tan, and Singapore.

1155 Woodhouse, Bruce. From Script to Screen. London: Winchester, 1948. 192 pp.

1156   Great Britain Board of Trade.   Report of the Working Party
       on Film Production Costs.   London: His Majesty's
       Stationery Office, 1949.   32 pp.

1157   UNESCO.   Press, Film, Radio: Report of the Commission
       on Technical Needs.   Paris: UNESCO, 1949.   296 pp.
       (Reprinted in Press, Film, Radio, V. 1-5 (1947-1951),
       New York: Arno, 1972.)
           Surveys facilities in Finland, Sweden, Switzerland,
       Algeria, Egypt, Morocco, Tunisia, Lebanon, Turkey,
       Argentina, Bolivia, Brazil, Chile, and Paraguay.

1158   Walker, James Blaine.   The Epic of American Industry.
       New York: Harper, 1949.   513 pp.
           Includes a chapter on the motion picture industry.

1159   Adams, Walter.   The Structure of American Industry: Some
       Case Studies.   New York: Macmillan, 1950.   588 pp.
       (Second edition 1961, 603 pp.   Fourth edition 1971, 502 pp.)

1160   Balcon, Michael.   Film Production and Management.   London:
       British Institute of Management, 1950.   20 pp.

1161   Booch, S. H.   Film Industry in India.   New Delhi: India
       Information Services, ca. 1950.   32 pp.

1162   British Film Academy.   The Film Industry in Great Britain:
       Some Facts and Figures.   London: British Film Academy,
       1950.   40 pp.

1163   Film Centre, London.   The Film Industry in Six European
       Countries: A Detailed Study of the Film Industry in Den-
       mark as Compared with that in Norway, Sweden, Italy,
       France and the United Kingdom.   Paris: UNESCO, 1950.
       156 pp.

1164   Greenwald, William I.   The Motion Picture Industry: An
       Economic Study of the History and Practices of a Business.
       New York University: Ph. D. , 1950.

1165   Handel, Leo A.   Hollywood Looks at Its Audience: A Report
       of Film Audience Research.   Urbana: University of Illinois
       Press, 1950.   240 pp.

1166   Luther, Rodney.   The Motion Picture Industry.   University of
       Minnesota: Ph. D. , 1950.

1167   Shah, Pauna.   The Indian Film.   Bombay: Motion Picture
       Society of India, 1950.   290 pp.

1168   UNESCO.   Press, Film, Radio.   Paris: UNESCO, 1950.
       606 pp.   (Reprinted in Press, Film, Radio, V. 1-5 (1947-

1951), New York: Arno, 1972.)
Surveys facilities in over 40 countries, including Union
of South Africa, Canada, United States, Israel, Ireland,
Great Britain, and Australia.

1169 UNESCO, Division of Free Flow of Information. World Com-
munications: Press, Radio, Film. Paris: UNESCO,
1950. 220 pp. (Revised as World Communications: Press,
Radio, Film, Television, 1951, 223 pp. Revised again New
York: UNESCO, 1964, 380 pp.)
International survey of facilities.

1170 Conrad, Bernadette. Financial Policies of the Motion Picture
Industry. New York University: Ph.D. , 1951.

1171 UNESCO. Press, Film, Radio. Paris: UNESCO, 1951.
583 pp. (Reprinted in Press, Film, Radio, V.1-5 (1947-
1951), New York: Arno, 1972.)
Surveys facilities in over 60 countries, including
Japan, Germany, Portugal, and New Zealand.

1172 Field, Alice Evans. Hollywood, U.S.A.: From Script to
Screen. New York: Vantage, 1952. 256 pp.

1173 Political and Economic Planning. The British Film Industry:
A Report on Its History and Present Organization, with
Special Reference to the Economic Problems of British
Feature Film Production. London: Political and Economic
Planning, 1952. 307 pp. (Supplement published 1958; see
entry 1185.)

1174 Rodker, Francis. A Day with the Film Makers. London:
Pitman, 1952. 68 pp.
Account of a visit to a film studio; for the young
reader.

1175 Association of National Advertisers, Film Steering Committee.
The Dollars and Sense of Business Films, Study of 157
Business Films: A Report on the Production and Distribu-
tion Costs of Representative Advertising and Public Rela-
tions Motion Pictures. New York: Association of National
Advertisers, 1954. 128 pp.

1176 Film Council of America. Sixty Years of 16mm Film, 1923-
1983. Evanston, Ill.: Film Council of America, 1954.
220 pp.
Anthology providing overview of 16mm production,
distribution, and usage.

1177 Hollywood Film Production Manual. Burbank: Arejay Sales,
1954. Loose-leaf. (Republished 1972.)

1178 James, Marquis and Bessie R. Biography of a Bank: The

Story of Bank of America. New York: Harper, 1954.
566 pp.
    Includes material on motion picture financing.

1179 Babitsky, Paul and Rimberg, John. The Soviet Film Industry.
      New York: Praeger, 1955. 377 pp.

1180 Reed, Stanley and Huntley, John. How Films Are Made.
      London: Educational Supply Association, 1955. 90 pp.
      For the young reader.

1181 UNESCO. Film and Cinema Statistics: A Preliminary Report
      on Methodology with Tables Giving Current Statistics.
      Paris: UNESCO, 1955. 111 pp.
          International survey of production, importation, exhi-
      bition facilities, and box office.

1182 Fenderson, Julia K. Let's Visit a Movie Lot. Culver City,
      Cal.: Board of Education, Culver City Unified School
      District, 1956. 47 pp.
      For the young reader.

1183 Bernstein, Irving. Hollywood at the Crossroads: An Economic
      Study of the Motion Picture Industry. Hollywood: n. p.,
      prepared for the Hollywood A. F. of L. Film Council, 1957.
      78 pp.

1184 Bernstein, Irving. The Position of the Story Analyst in the
      Motion Picture Industry. Hollywood(?): Story Analyst
      Guild, 1958. 25 ℓ.

1185 Political and Economic Planning. The British Film Industry
      1958. London: Political and Economic Planning, 1958.
      40 pp.
          Updating of the 1952 report entitled The British Film
      Industry; see entry 1173.

1186 Anderson, Joseph L. and Richie, Donald. The Japanese
      Film: Art and Industry. Rutland, Vt.: Charles Tuttle,
      1959. 456 pp. (Also New York: Grove, 1960.)

1187 Jain, Rikhab Dass. The Economic Aspects of the Film
      Industry in India. Delhi: Atma Ram, 1960. 28, 327 pp.

1188 Gordon, Jay E. Motion Picture Production for Industry.
      New York: Macmillan, 1961. 352 pp.

1189 Jongbloed, H. J. L. (ed.) Film Production by International
      Co-operation: A Report on Various Methods of Co-pro-
      duction in the Field of Educational and Cultural Films.
      Paris: UNESCO, 1961. 35 pp.

1190 Film Fact Finding Committee of Pakistan. Report of the Film

Fact Finding Committee, Govt. of Pakistan, Ministry of
Industries, April 1960-April 1961. Karachi: Manager of
Publications, 1962. 410 pp.
Describes Pakistan's film industry.

1191 MacCann, Richard Dyer. Hollywood in Transition. Boston:
Houghton Mifflin, 1962. 208 pp.
Study of changes in Hollywood production since the
advent of television.

1192 Spraos, John. The Decline of the Cinema: An Economist's
Report. London: Allen and Unwin, 1962. 168 pp.
Discusses the implications of cinema-going trends in
Great Britain.

1193 Barnouw, Erik and Krishnaswamy, S. Indian Film. New
York: Columbia University Press, 1963. 301 pp.

1194 Guback, Thomas Henry. The Film Industry in Post-War
Western Europe: The Role of Euro-American Interaction
in the Shaping of Economic Structures and Operations.
University of Illinois, Urbana-Champaign: Ph.D., 1964.
405 pp.

1195 Oakley, C. A. Where We Came In: Seventy Years of the
British Film Industry. London: Allen and Unwin, 1964.
245 pp.

1196 Goyal, Trishla. The Marketing of Films. Calcutta: Inter-
trade, ca. 1966. 545 pp.

1197 Jobes, Gertrude. Motion Picture Empire. Hamden, Conn.:
Archon, 1966. 398 pp.
An economic history of the American film industry.

1198 Kelly, Terrence with Norton, Graham and Perry, George.
A Competitive Cinema. London: Institute of Economic
Affairs, 1966. 204 pp.
Analysis of British film industry.

1199 Perry, Donald. An Analysis of the Financial Plans of the Motion Picture Industry for the Period 1929 to 1962. University of Illinois, Urbana-Champaign: Ph.D., 1966.
236 pp.

1200 Grey, Elizabeth. Behind the Scenes in a Film Studio. New
York: Roy, 1967. 102 pp.

1201 Taylor, Theodore. People Who Make Movies. Garden City,
N.Y.: Doubleday, 1967. 158 pp.
For the young reader.

1202 Dunne, John Gregory. The Studio. New York: Farrar,

Straus and Giroux, 1968. 255 pp.
Deals with Twentieth-Century Fox in 1967-68.

1203   Ireland, Film Industry Committee. <u>Report of the Film Indus-
       try Committee.</u> Dublin: Stationery Office, 1968. 61 pp.

1204   Russell-Cobb, Trevor. <u>Paying the Piper: The Theory and
       Practice of Industrial Patronage.</u> London: Queen Anne
       Press, 1968. 111 pp.
       Includes limited material on film.

1205   Williams, Henry. <u>Economic Changes in the Motion Picture
       Industry as Affected by Television and Other Factors.</u>
       Indiana University: Ph.D., 1968. 170 pp.

1206   Basti, Abdul Zaher. <u>The Impact of the American Motion
       Picture Industry on the United States Balance of Payments.</u>
       University of Colorado: Ph.D., 1969. 256 pp.

1207   Guback, Thomas H. <u>The International Film Industry: Western
       Europe and America Since 1945.</u> Bloomington: Indiana
       University Press, 1969. 244 pp.

1208   <u>The Cinema in Denmark.</u> Copenhagen: Danish Government
       Film Foundation, 1970. 37 pp.

1209   Minus, Johnny and Hale, William Storm. <u>The Movie Industry
       Book (How Others Made and Lost Money in the Movie In-
       dustry).</u> Hollywood: 7 Arts Press, 1970. 601 pp.

1210   Butler, Ivan. <u>The Making of Feature Films: A Guide.</u> Bal-
       timore: Penguin, 1971. 171 pp.
       Various participants in the filmmaking process, from
       the producer to the continuity girl, discuss their respec-
       tive functions; for list of names, see entry 3733.

1211   Minus, Johnny and Hale, William Storm. <u>The Managers', En-
       tertainers', and Agents' Book: How to Plan, Plot, Scheme,
       Learn, Perform, Avoid Dangers, and Enjoy Your Career
       in the Entertainment Industry.</u> Hollywood: 7 Arts Press,
       1971. 732 pp.

1212   Bluem, A. William and Squire, Jason E. (eds.) <u>The Movie
       Business: American Film Industry Practice.</u> New York:
       Hastings, 1972. 368 pp.
       With contributions by William Goldman, David Picker,
       Gordon Stulberg, Saul Rittenberg, Charlton Heston, Fouad
       Said, Stanley Kramer, Sydney Pollack, Bud Yorkin and
       Norman Lear, Stirling Silliphant, Russ Meyer, Walter
       Reade, Jr., Peter Guber, and others.

1213   Fadiman, William. <u>Hollywood Now.</u> New York: Liveright,

1972. 174 pp.
Analysis of the various collaborative functions.

1214 Baker, Fred with Firestone, Ross. Movie People: At Work in the Business of Film. New York: Lancer, 1973. 242 pp.
Interviews with various film professionals about their respective functions, including an exhibitor, a distributor, and a critic; for list of names, see entry 3762.

1215 Baumgarten, Paul A. and Farber, Donald C. Producing, Financing and Distributing Film. New York: Drama Book Specialists, 1973. 198 pp.

1216 Costa, Sylvia Allen. How to Prepare a Production Budget for Film & Video Tape. Blue Ridge Summit, Pa.: TAB Books, 1973. 192 pp.

1217 International Film and Television Council. Cinematographic Institutions: A Report. Paris: UNESCO, 1973. 98 pp.
The objectives and roles of film institutions in the development of national film industries.

1218 Mayer, Michael F. The Film Industries: Practical Business/ Legal Problems in Production, Distribution and Exhibition. New York: Hastings, 1973. 212 pp.

1219 Nationalising the Film Industry: Report of the ACTT Nationali- sation Forum, August 1973. London: Association of Cinematograph, Television and Allied Technicians, 1973. 59 pp.
Survey of British film industry and demands for its public ownership.

1220 Reische, Diana (ed.) The Performing Arts in America. New York: Wilson, 1973. 252 pp.
Material on the current state of the performing arts, particularly economic aspects; essays on film include "Cashing In on Vintage Flicks," "The Hollywood Come- back," and Roger Ebert's "Black Box Office Is Beautiful."

1221 Lyons, Timothy J. The Silent Partner: The History of the American Film Manufacturing Company 1910-1921. New York: Arno, 1974. 256 pp.

1222 McLaughlin, Robert. Broadway and Hollywood: A History of Economic Interaction. New York: Arno, 1974. 302 pp.

1223 Steen, Mike (ed.) Hollywood Speaks: An Oral History. New York: Putnam, 1974. 379 pp.
Interviews with members of the various Hollywood pro- fessions; for list of names, see entry 3795.

1224 Walker, Alexander. Hollywood UK: The British Film Indus-
      try in the Sixties. New York: Stein and Day, 1974.
      493 pp. (Also published as Hollywood, England: The
      British Film Industry in the Sixties.)

1225 Atkins, Dick and others. Method to the Madness (Hollywood
      Explained). Livingston, N.J.: Prince, 1975. 207 pp.
           Includes articles by Arthur Knight and Stephen Farber.

1226 Jenkins, Reese V. Images and Enterprise: Technology and
      the American Photographic Industry 1839 to 1925. Balti-
      more: Johns Hopkins University Press, 1975. 371 pp.

1227 Toeplitz, Jerzy. Hollywood and After: The Changing Face
      of Movies in America. Chicago: Regnery, 1975. 288 pp.
      Translated by Boleslaw Sulik. (Also published as Holly-
      wood and After: The Changing Face of American Cinema.)
           Includes discussion of changes in the Hollywood studio
      system of the last two decades.

B.   DISTRIBUTION, ADVERTISING, AND EXHIBITION

This section contains books which deal with the distribution, advertising, and exhibition of motion pictures--in short, with the process by which a film is brought to the public.   For related material on theatre management, see Part II, section C-13.   The reader may also find useful many of the books by Alan G. Barbour which, although not included in this section, reproduce many of the original advertisements used by studios in the promotion of their films; see the name index under Barbour for his book entries.

1228   Goode, Kenneth and Kaufman, Zenn.   Profitable Showman-
           ship.   (Originally published 1939.)   New York: Prentice-
           Hall, 1946.   180 pp.   (Reprinted 1955.)

1229   Hendricks, Bill and Waugh, Howard.   Charles "Chick" Lewis
           Presents the Encyclopedia of Exploitation.   New York:
           Showmen's Trade Review, 1940.   432 pp.
                An encyclopedic account of show-business merchan-
           dising and advertising.

1230   U.S. House Committee on Interstate and Foreign Commerce.
           Motion-Picture Films (Compulsory Block Booking and
           Blind Selling):   Hearings Before the Committee on Inter-
           state and Foreign Commerce, House of Representatives,
           Seventy-Sixth Congress, Third Session, on S. 280, A Bill
           to Prohibit and to Prevent the Trade Practices Known as
           Compulsory Block Booking and Blind Selling in the Leasing
           of Motion-Picture Films in Interstate and Foreign Com-
           merce.   Washington, D.C.:   U.S. Government Printing
           Office, 1940.   688 pp.

1231   Hollywood Reporter.   How to Win Hollywood Sales and In-
           fluence National Buying Habits.   Hollywood: Hollywood
           Reporter, 1947.   41 pp.

1232   Movie Advertising Bureau, Kansas City, Mo.   The $100,000
           Study of Theatres for Movie Advertising;   Rates and Data.
           Kansas City: Movie Advertising Bureau, 1947.   Unpaged.

1233   Great Britain Board of Trade.   Distribution and Exhibition of

Cinematograph Films. London: His Majesty's Stationery
Office, 1949. 63 pp.

1234 Hendricks, Bill and Orr, Montgomery. Showmanship in Ad-
vertising: The Fundamentals of Salesmanship in Print.
New York: Showmen's Trade Review, 1949. 220 pp.
With material relevant to motion pictures.

1235 Momand, A. B. Help Wanted, Male and Female; or, The
Great Motion Picture Conspiracy, Condensed ... An Ex-
hibitor's Story. Shawnee: Printed by Oklahoma Baptist
University Press, 1949. 52, 21 pp.

1236 Wilson, William H. and Haas, Kenneth B. The Film Book
for Business, Education and Industry. New York: Prentice-Hall, 1950. 259 pp.
Includes discussion of theatrical and non-theatrical
distribution.

1237 U. S. Senate Committee on Small Business. Motion Picture
Distribution Trade Practices: Hearings Before a Subcommittee of the Select Committee on Small Business,
United States Senate, Eighty-Third Congress, First Session, on Problems of Independent Motion Picture Exhibi-
tors Relating to Distribution Trade Practices. Washington,
D. C.: U. S. Government Printing Office, 1953. 952 pp.

1238 UNESCO. Agreement for Facilitating the International Circu-
lation of Visual and Auditory Material of an Educational,
Scientific, and Cultural Character: A Guide to Its Operation. Paris: UNESCO, 1954. 26 pp.

1239 Association of National Advertisers. Export and Import of
Business Films, Time and Cost Procedures. New York:
Association of National Advertisers, 1956. (Revised
1963, 44 pp.)

1240 Leglise, Paul. Methods of Encouraging the Production and
Distribution of Short Films for Theatrical Use; Documentaries and Films on Science and Culture for Commercial Exhibition. Paris: UNESCO, 1962. 48 pp.

1241 Brodsky, Jack and Weiss, Nathan. The Cleopatra Papers:
A Private Correspondence. New York: Simon and
Schuster, 1963. 175 pp.
Correspondence of the film's publicity managers.

1242 Association of National Advertisers, Audio-Visual Committee.
Advertiser Practices in the Production and Distribution
of Business Films. New York: Association of National
Advertisers, 1965. 61 pp.

1243   Barbour, Alan G. Movie Ads of the Past. Kew Gardens,
        N.Y.: Screen Facts, 1966. Unpaged.

1244   Monopolies Commission. Films: A Report on the Supply of
        Films for Exhibition in Cinemas. London: Her Majesty's
        Stationery Office, 1966. 113 pp.

1245   Leglise, Paul. The Theatrical Distribution of Cultural Films.
        Strasbourg: Council for Cultural Co-operation, 1967.
        137 pp.
            Concerns national and international distribution of short
        films, documentaries, and films for children.

1246   Musun, Chris. The Marketing of Motion Pictures: Both
        Sides of the Coin: Art--Business. Los Angeles: Musun,
        1969. 336 pp.

1247   Morella, Joe; Epstein, Edward Z.; and Clark, Eleanor.
        Those Great Movie Ads. New Rochelle, N.Y.: Arlington,
        1972. 320 pp.
            Primarily reproductions of ads.

1248   Kobal, John (ed.) 50 Years of Movie Posters. New York:
        Bounty, 1973. 175 pp.

1249   Sweeney, Russell C. Coming Next Week: A Pictorial History
        of Film Advertising. South Brunswick, N.J.: A. S.
        Barnes, 1973. 303 pp.
            Motion picture newspaper and magazine advertising of
        the twenties and thirties.

1250   Hurst, Walter E. and Hale, William Storm. Motion Picture
        Distribution (Business and/or Racket?!?). Hollywood:
        7 Arts, 1975. 158 pp.

C. LEGAL ASPECTS, MONOPOLY, AND WORK ORGANIZATIONS

This section contains books which deal with film monopolies, work organizations such as unions and guilds, and all legal aspects of film, including copyrights. Although material on obscenity law and particular censorship cases is included here, the reader is also referred to the section on censorship, Part IX, section D-1.

1251 Nizer, Louis. New Courts of Industry: Self-Regulation Under the Motion Picture Code; Including an Analysis of the Code. (Originally published 1935.) New York: Ozer, 1971. 344 pp.
Details production, distribution, and exhibition legalities of the Motion Picture Production Code.

1252 U.S. House Committee on Interstate and Foreign Commerce. Motion-Picture Films (Compulsory Block Booking and Blind Selling): Hearings Before the Committee on Interstate and Foreign Commerce, House of Representatives, Seventy-Sixth Congress, Third Session, on S. 280, A Bill to Prohibit and to Prevent the Trade Practices Known as Compulsory Block Booking and Blind Selling in the Leasing of Motion-Picture Films in Interstate and Foreign Commerce. Washington, D.C.: U.S. Government Printing Office, 1940. 688 pp.

1253 American Society of Composers, Authors, and Publishers. An American Institution. New York: ASCAP, ca. 1941. 15 pp. (Also published as The Story of ASCAP: An American Institution, 1944.)

1254 Bertrand, Daniel; Evans, W. Duane; and Blanchard, E. L. The Motion Picture Industry: A Pattern of Control. Washington, D.C.: Government Printing Office, 1941. 92 pp.

1255 Ross, Murray. Stars and Strikes: Unionization of Hollywood. New York: Columbia University Press, 1941. 233 pp.

1256 U.S. Senate Committee on Interstate Commerce. Propaganda in Motion Pictures: Hearings Before a Subcommittee of the Committee on Interstate Commerce, United States Senate, Seventy-Seventh Congress, First Session, on S. Res. 152, A Resolution Authorizing an Investigation of War Propaganda Disseminated by the Motion-Picture Industry and of any Monopoly in the Production, Distribution, or Exhibition of Motion Pictures. Washington, D.C.: U.S. Government Printing Office, 1942. 449 pp.

1257 Huettig, Mae D. Economic Control of the Motion Picture Industry: A Study in Industrial Organization. Philadelphia: University of Pennsylvania Press, 1944. 163 pp.

1258 Great Britain, Board of Trade. Tendencies to Monopoly in the Cinematograph Film Industry: Report of a Committee Appointed by the Cinematographic Films Council. London: Her Majesty's Stationery Office, 1944. 41 pp.

1259 Ernst, Morris L. The First Freedom. New York: Macmillan, 1946. 316 pp.
One section on film and monopolistic practices.

1260 Hartman, Dennis. Motion Picture Law Digest: Including All Court Decisions From 1900 to June 1947. Los Angeles: Motion Picture Law Review, 1947. 265 pp.

1261 Lindey, Alexander. Motion Picture Agreements Annotated: A Manual of Contract Forms Covering Every Phase of the Motion Picture Industry ... With Digests of Cases Applicable Thereto. Albany: Bender, 1947. 1039 pp.

1262 Kaufman, Thomas. Movie Tickets and Monopoly: A Study of Effective Competition in a Service Industry. Harvard University: Ph.D., 1949.

1263 Dahn, Maurice. Unionism and Labor Problems in the Motion Pictury Industry. University of Iowa: Ph.D., 1950.

1264 Dunne, George Harold. Hollywood Labor Dispute: A Study in Immorality. Los Angeles: Conference Publishing, ca. 1950. 44 pp.

1265 Pugliese, Peter F. Kill or Cure: Application of the Anti-Trust Laws to the Motion Picture Industry. New York University: Ph.D., 1951. 114 pp.

1266 Terrou, Fernand and Solal, Lucien. Legislation for Press, Film and Radio: Comparative Study of the Main Types of Regulations Governing the Information Media. Paris: UNESCO, 1951. 420 pp.

1267 Lindey, Alexander. Plagiarism and Originality. New York:

Harper, 1952.   366 pp.
Discusses plagiarism in writing, including motion
pictures.

1268   Spring, Samuel.   Risks and Rights in Publishing, Television,
Radio, Motion Pictures, Advertising, and the Theatre.
New York: Norton, 1952.   385 pp.   (Revised 1956, 365
pp.)

1269   Ivamy, Edward R. H.   Show Business and the Law.   London:
Stevens, 1955.   188 pp.
With material on British show business law.

1270   Lovell, Hugh and Carter, Tasile.   Collective Bargaining in
the Motion Picture Industry: A Struggle for Stability.
Berkeley: Institute of Industrial Relations, University of
California, 1955.   54 pp.

1271   Knopp, Leslie.   The Cinematograph Regulations, 1955.   London: Cinema Press, 1956.   185 pp.
British law and regulations, especially pertaining to
theatres.

1272   Wittenberg, Philip.   The Law of Literary Property.   Cleveland: World, 1957.   284 pp.

1273   Whitney, Simon N.   Antitrust Policies: American Experience
in Twenty Industries.   New York: Twentieth Century
Fund, 1958.   1101 pp.
Includes material on the motion picture industry and
the theatre divorcement decree.

1274   Cassady, Ralph, Jr.   Monopoly in Motion Picture Production
and Distribution: 1908-1915.   Los Angeles: Bureau of
Business and Economic Research, University of California,
1959.   66 pp.
Includes material on the Motion Picture Patents Company and the General Film Company.

1275   Conant, Michael.   Antitrust in the Motion Picture Industry:
Economic and Legal Analysis.   Berkeley: University of
California Press, 1960.   240 pp.

1276   Pilpel, Harriet F. and Zavin, Theodora S.   Rights and
Writers: A Handbook of Literary and Entertainment Law.
New York: Dutton, 1960.   384 pp.

1277   Nizer, Louis.   My Life in Court.   Garden City, N. Y. :
Doubleday, 1961.   524 pp.
Includes a lengthy section on the proxy struggle over
Loew's Incorporated.

1278   Smith, Frederick Y. (ed.)   American Cinema Editors First

Decade Anniversary Book.   Hollywood: American Cinema
Editors, 1961.   224 pp.
   Discusses the organization's background and aims as
well as listing its members.

1279 U.S. Copyright Office.   Copyright Law Revision: Report of
      the Register of Copyrights on the General Revision of the
      U.S. Copyright Law [In Two Volumes].   Volume I.   Wash-
      ington, D.C.:   U.S. Government Printing Office, 1961.
      Volume II.   1963.

1280 Lindey, Alexander.   Entertainment, Publishing, and the Arts;
      Agreements and the Law: Books, Magazines, Newspapers,
      Plays, Motion Pictures, Radio and Television, Music,
      Phonograph Records, Art Work, Photographs, Advertising
      and Publicity, and Commercial Exploitation.   New York:
      Boardman, 1963.   Loose-leaf.

1281 Perry, Louis B. and Richard S.   A History of the Los Ange-
      les Labor Movement 1911-1941.   Berkeley: University of
      California Press, 1963.   622 pp.
         Includes material on the movie industry.

1282 Ringer, Barbara A. and Gitlin, Paul.   Copyrights.   New
      York: Practicing Law Institute, 1963.   162 pp.   (Re-
      vised 1965, 187 pp.)

1283 Walls, Howard Lamarr.   The Copyright Handbook for Fine
      and Applied Arts.   New York: Watson-Guptill, 1963.
      125 pp.

1284 Cassady, Ralph, Jr. and Ralph III.   The Private Antitrust
      Suit in American Business Competition: A Motion Picture
      Industry Case Analysis.   Los Angeles: Bureau of Busi-
      ness and Economic Research, University of California,
      1964.   66 pp.

1285 Screen Actors Guild.   The Story of the Screen Actors Guild.
      Hollywood: Public Relations Department, 1966.   23 pp.

1286 Hunnings, Neville March.   Film Censors and the Law.   Lon-
      don: Allen and Unwin, 1967.   474 pp.
         Discusses legal variations in England, United States,
      India, Canada, Australia, Denmark, France, and Soviet
      Russia.

1287 Wincor, Richard.   Literary Property.   New York: Potter,
      distributed by Crown, 1967.   154 pp.

1288 Federal Bar Association of New York, New Jersey, and
      Conn., Committee on the Law of the Theatre.   Subsidiary
      Rights and Residuals: A Symposium.   Edited by Joseph

Taubman. New York: Federal Legal Publications, 1968.
199 pp.

1289 Moskow, Michael H. Labor Relations in the Performing
Arts: An Introductory Survey. New York: Associated
Council of the Arts, 1969. 218 pp.

1290 Friedman, Leon (ed.) Obscenity: The Complete Oral Argu-
ments Before the Supreme Court in the Major Obscenity
Cases. New York: Chelsea, 1970. 342 pp.
     Includes several film cases.

1291 Devol, Kenneth S. (ed.) Mass Media and the Supreme Court:
The Legacy of the Warren Years. New York: Hastings,
1971. 369 pp.
     Includes material on film censorship.

1292 Farber, Donald C. Actor's Guide: What You Should Know
About the Contracts You Sign. New York: Drama Book
Specialists, 1971. 134 pp.

1293 Practising Law Institute. Motion Picture Industry: Business
and Legal Problems. New York: Practising Law Institute, 1972. 424 pp.

1294 Baumgarten, Paul A. (comp.) Legal and Business Problems
of Motion Picture Industry. New York: Practising Law
Institute, 1973. 616 pp.
     With material on patents, copyrights, trademarks,
literary properties, etc.

1295 Mayer, Michael F. The Film Industries: Practical Business/
Legal Problems in Production, Distribution and Exhibition.
New York: Hastings, 1973. 212 pp.

1296 Minus, Johnny and Hale, William Storm. Your Introduction
to Film-TV Copyright, Contracts, and Other Law. Hollywood: 7 Arts Press, 1973. 232 pp.

1297 Nationalising the Film Industry: Report of the ACTT Na-
tionalisation Forum, August 1973. London: Association
of Cinematograph, Television and Allied Technicians,
1973. 59 pp.
     Survey of British film industry and demands for its
public ownership.

1298 Wheaton, Christopher. A History of the Screen Writers'
Guild (1920-1942): The Writer's Quest for a Freely-
Negotiated Basic Agreement. University of Southern
California: Ph. D., 1974. 189 pp.

1299 Patterns of Discrimination Against Women in the Film and

Television Industries. London: Association of Cinematograph, Television and Allied Technicians, 1975.

D. OCCUPATIONS

This section contains books which are intended to offer guidance to the individual who seeks a career in the film industry.

1300 Photoplay Research Society. Opportunities in the Motion Picture Industry--And How to Qualify for Positions in Its Many Branches. (Originally published 1922.) New York: Arno, 1970. 117 pp.

1301 Shapiro, Clarence M. I Scout for Movie Talent: A Guide to the Requirements for an Artist's Entry into Motion Pictures, with Practical Suggestions Applicable to Any Line of Dramatic Endeavour. Chicago: Kroch, 1940. 84 pp.

1302 Robertson, Marian. One in a Thousand: The Way of Life on the Road to Hollywood. Evanston, Ill.: Row, Peterson, 1941. 64 pp.

1303 Alexander, Edward. Become a Theater Manager. New York: Theatrical Publications, 1943. 64 pp.

1304 Klaw, Irving. How to Become a Movie Star. New York: Klaw, 1946. 126 pp.

1305 Ramsaye, Terry. Vocational and Professional Monographs: The Motion Picture Industry. Boston: Bellman, ca. 1946. 24 pp.
Briefly surveys the various occupations within the film industry.

1306 Blakeston, Oswell (ed.) Working for the Films. London, New York: Focal, 1947. 207 pp.
Essays on various careers in filmmaking; contributors include Gerbrand Schürmann, Sidney Cole, John Halas, Roger Burford, David Lean, J. B. Holmes, Eric Portman, Alberto Cavalcanti, David Rawnsley, Frederick Young, and others.

1307 Denis, Paul. Your Career in Show Business. New York: Dutton, 1948. 240 pp.

1308 Jones, Charles Reed (ed.) <u>Your Career in Motion Pictures,</u>
      <u>Radio, Television</u>. New York: Sheridan, 1949. 255 pp.
           With essays by Bob Hope, Frank Sinatra, Loretta
      Young, Veronica Lake, Alan Ladd, Jerry Wald, Sam Wood,
      Ward Bond, Gene Autry, Leo McCarey, Betty Hutton,
      Betty Grable, Dimitri Tiomkin, Linda Darnell, Dana An-
      drews, Edith Head, and others.

1309 Tell, Pincus W. <u>Opportunities in Motion Pictures</u>. New
      York: Vocational Guidance Manuals, 1949. 68 pp.

1310 Wood, Robert. <u>Crashing Hollywood: As Compiled From Inter-</u>
      <u>views with More than 500 Actors, Producers, and Direc-</u>
      <u>tors in the Fields of Motion Pictures, Television, Radio,</u>
      <u>and the Stage</u>. Los Angeles: Hollywood Imprint, 1952.
      72 pp.

1311 LeRoy, Mervyn with Canfield, Alyce. <u>It Takes More Than</u>
      <u>Talent</u>. New York: Knopf, 1953. 300 pp.

1312 Joels, Merrill E. <u>Acting Is a Business: How to Get Into</u>
      <u>Television and Radio</u>. New York: Hastings, 1955. 96 pp.
      (Revised as <u>How to Get Into Show Business</u>, 1969, 157 pp.)
      Revised edition has material specifically on film.

1313 Moore, Dick. <u>Opportunities in Acting: Stage, Motion Pic-</u>
      <u>tures, Television</u>. New York: Vocational Guidance Manu-
      als, 1963. 128 pp.

1314 Zugsmith, Albert. <u>How to Break Into the Movies</u>. New York:
      Macfadden, 1963. 173 pp.

1315 Benner, Ralph and Clements, Mary Jo. <u>The Young Actors'</u>
      <u>Guide to Hollywood</u>. New York: Coward-McCann, 1964.
      185 pp.

1316 Nicholson, Dianne. <u>Turn On to Stardom</u>. New York: Corner-
      stone, 1968. 192 pp.

1317 Gordon, George N. and Falk, Irving A. <u>Your Career in Film</u>
      <u>Making</u>. New York: Messner, 1969. 224 pp.

1318 Izay, Victor. <u>For Actors--While Waiting in the Unemployment</u>
      <u>Line</u>. Toluca Lake, Cal.: Pacifica, 1970. 88 pp.

1319 Bayer, William S. <u>Breaking Through, Selling Out, Dropping</u>
      <u>Dead</u>. New York: Macmillan, 1971. 227 pp.
           Diverse notes on the industry addressed to the young
      filmmaker trying to develop his career.

1320 Farber, Donald C. <u>Actor's Guide: What You Should Know</u>
      <u>About the Contracts You Sign</u>. New York: Drama Book
      Specialists, 1971. 134 pp.

1321   Minus, Johnny and Hale, William Storm. The Managers',
       Entertainers', and Agents' Book: How to Plan, Plot,
       Scheme, Learn, Perform, Avoid Dangers, and Enjoy
       Your Career in the Entertainment Industry. Hollywood:
       7 Arts Press, 1971. 732 pp.

1322   Cohen, Robert. Acting Professionally: Raw Facts About
       Acting and the Acting Industries. Palo Alto, Cal.: Na-
       tional Press, 1972. 101 pp.

1323   Hyland, Wende and Haynes, Roberta. How to Make It in
       Hollywood. Chicago: Nelson-Hall, 1975. 237 pp.
          Interviews; for list of names, see entry 3809.

PART IV

FILM HISTORY

INTRODUCTION

The film history classification contains a variety of works including those which are coherent historical texts, those which are composed of collected historical/critical essays--often on individual films, and those which are predominantly pictorial. Most of the books in this classification approach film history primarily from the concept of film's potential as an art. Statistical or primarily economic works, as well as those books which approach film strictly from the concept of film as a business and a commodity, can be found in Part III, film industry. For historical material on the documentary film, the animated film, the experimental film, various film genres, and other types of film, the reader should refer to Part V, sections A through H. Historical material can also be found in many of the anthologies of theory and criticism in Part VIII, section D. For detailed filmographic information (data on the films and filmmakers of a given country), the reader should consult the reference classification, Part I, particularly sections B-1 and B-2, the international and national filmographies.

It should be noted that we have not included in the history classification books such as James Ross Cameron's 1922 book Examination Questions and Answers on Sound Motion Picture Projection --that is, books which are now useful primarily as historical documents. These books have been filed instead in the category appropriate to their original intended purpose; many can be found in the early chronological listings in the various technique sections in Part II. In a sense, all the books in this bibliography can be seen as historical documents of their time.

A. PRE-HISTORY AND EARLY INVENTION PERIOD

      This first history section contains those books which deal in whole or in significant part with the pre-history and early invention period of the cinema. The archaeology of the movies can be traced back almost as far as one wishes: all the way back to cave painting or, at least, to the invention of photography and the work of William Talbot and Louis Daguerre. The reader should be aware, however, that we have not included in this section general histories of photography, because most of them do not deal substantially with photography's relationship to cinematography; yet, obviously, the history of photography occupies an important place in cinema pre-history. For these books the reader should consult a bibliography of photography. For our film bibliography we have found it most reasonable and appropriate to begin this section with the work of Eadweard Muybridge, whose photographic study of motion published in 1887 can be seen as a pioneering achievement in the evolution of the moving image.

      There is, of course, no clear demarcation between the end of the pre-history and early invention period and the beginning of the silent period, although Georges Melies' A TRIP TO THE MOON is generally considered the first narrative movie in the popular sense of the term. This first section, therefore, can be seen as extending through the various simultaneous inventions of the camera throughout the world in 1895 and 1896 and ending roughly at the turn of the century, when the concept of "the movies," more or less as we understand it today, became established. Other material on pre-history can be found within many of the works in other of the history sections, especially section B, the silent period, and section C, surveys of world cinema.

1324 Muybridge, Eadweard. Animal Locomotion. (Originally published in 1887 with subtitle An Electro-Photographic Investigation of Consecutive Phases of Animal Movements, 1872-1885.) New York: Da Capo, 1969. Multiple volumes.

1325 Muybridge, Eadweard. Animals in Motion. (Abridged from Animal Locomotion, 1887.) Edited and introduced by Lewis S. Brown. New York: Dover, 1957. 74 pp., 183 plates.

1326 Muybridge, Eadweard. The Human Figure in Motion. (Abridged

from Animal Locomotion, 1887.) Introduced by Robert
Taft. New York: Dover, 1955. 17 pp., 195 plates.

1327   Dickson, W. K. L. and Antonia. History of the Kinetograph,
       Kinetoscope, & Kinetophonograph. (Originally published
       1895.) New York: Arno, 1970. 55 pp.

1328   Marey, Etienne Jules. Movement. (Originally published
       1895.) New York: Arno, 1972. 323 pp. Translated by
       Eric Pritchard.
          Summary of experiments in photographing movement.

1329   Hepworth, Cecil M. Animated Photography: The ABC of the
       Cinematograph; A Simple and Thorough Guide to the Pro-
       jection of Living Photographs, with Notes on the Production
       of Cinematograph Negatives. (Originally published 1897,
       108 pp. Revised 1900, 128 pp.) New York: Arno, 1970.
       128 pp.
          Includes a review of pre-history and early silent
       period developments.

1330   Jenkins, Charles Francis. Animated Pictures: An Exposition
       of the Historical Development of Chronophotography, Its
       Present Scientific Applications and Future Possibilities,
       and of the Methods and Apparatus Employed in the Enter-
       tainment of Large Audiences by Means of Projecting
       Lanterns to Give the Appearance of Objects in Motion.
       (Originally published 1898.) New York: Arno, 1970.
       118 pp.

1331   Hopwood, Henry V. Living Pictures: Their History, Photo-
       Production, and Practical Workings. (Originally published
       1899.) New York: Arno, 1970. 275 pp.
          Includes a digest of British patents.

1332   Hammer, Mina Fisher. History of the Kodak and Its Continu-
       ations; The First Folding and Panoramic Cameras; Magic
       Lantern--Kodak--Movie; Closeup of the Inventor and the
       Kodak State. New York: Pioneer, 1940. 95 pp.

1333   Quigley, Martin, Jr. Magic Shadows: The Story of the
       Origin of Motion Pictures. Washington, D.C.: George-
       town University Press, 1948. 191 pp. (Reprinted New
       York: Quigley Publishing, 1960.)

1334   Hogben, Lancelot. From Cave Painting to Comic Strip: A
       Kaleidoscope of Human Communication. New York:
       Chanticleer, 1949. 288 pp.
          Includes some material on pre-cinema inventions.

1335   North, Joseph H. The Early Development of the Motion Pic-
       ture, 1887-1909. (Originally published Cornell University:
       Ph.D., 1949.) New York: Arno, 1973. 313 pp.

1336 Hendricks, Gordon. The Edison Motion Picture Myth.
Berkeley: University of California Press, 1961. 216 pp.
(Reprinted in Origins of the American Film, New York:
Arno, 1972.)
Account of the collaboration of W. K. L. Dickson
and Edison.

1337 Cook, Olive. Movement in Two Dimensions: A Study of the
Animated and Projected Pictures Which Preceded the Invention of Cinematography. London: Hutchinson, 1963.
143 pp.

1338 Hendricks, Gordon. Beginnings of the Biograph: The Story
of the Invention of the Mutoscope and the Biograph and
Their Supplying Camera. New York: Beginnings of the
American Film, 1964. 78 pp. (Reprinted in Origins of
the American Film, New York: Arno, 1972.)

1339 Pfragner, Julius. The Eye of History: The Motion Picture
From Magic Lantern to Sound Film. Chicago: Rand
McNally, 1964. 240 pp. Translated by Theodore Mc-
Clintock.
Historical presentation in a novelized format.

1340 Thomas, David B. The Origins of the Motion Picture: An
Introductory Booklet on the Pre-History of the Cinema.
London: Her Majesty's Stationery Office, 1964. 32 pp.

1341 Ceram, C. W. (pseudonym for Marek, Kurt W.) Archaeology
of the Cinema. New York: Harcourt, Brace, 1965. 264
pp. Translated by Richard Winston.

1342 Fay, Arthur. Bioscope Shows and Their Engines. Lingfield,
England: Oakwood, 1966. 36 pp.

1343 Hendricks, Gordon. The Kinetoscope: America's First Commercially Successful Motion Picture Exhibitor. New York:
Beginnings of the American Film, 1966. 182 pp. (Reprinted in Origins of the American Film, New York: Arno,
1972.)

1344 Barnes, John. Precursors of the Cinema: Shadowgraphy,
Panoramas, Dioramas and Peepshows Considered in Their
Relation to the History of the Cinema. St. Ives, England:
Barnes Museum of Cinematography. 1967. 69 pp.
Catalogues the John and William Barnes collection.

1345 The Origins of the Cinema: A Mid-Summer 1968 Exhibition
[at] Dynevor Castle, Llandilo, Wales. Cardiff: E. Roberts,
1968. 24 pp.
Details the items in an exhibition of pre-cinema arti-
facts.

1346 Hendricks, Gordon. Origins of the American Film. New
York: Arno, 1972.
Compiles three previously published works: The
Edison Motion Picture Myth, The Kinetoscope, and Be-
ginnings of the Biograph.

1347 Jenkins, Reese V. Images and Enterprise: Technology and
the American Photographic Industry, 1839 to 1925. Baltimore: Johns Hopkins University Press, 1975. 371 pp.
Includes chapter entitled "The Emergence of the
Cinematographic Industry."

B. SILENT PERIOD

This section contains those books which deal predominantly with the silent film period between the turn of the century and the coming of sound in 1928. These books may be general international surveys or limited to a particular national silent cinema. As with the previous section, the demarcation between the silent and sound periods cannot ultimately be fixed on a definite date; nor can the literature dealing with these two periods be perfectly divided. In general, most of the books here end with a discussion of the coming of sound. For more information the reader should refer to the books in Part IV, section C, surveys of world cinema, as well as to the books on the various national cinemas, since most of these volumes incorporate material on silent film as well.

1348   Grau, Robert. The Theatre of Science: A Volume of Progress and Achievement in the Motion Picture Industry. (Originally published 1914.) New York: Blom, 1969. 378 pp.

1349   Sherwood, Robert E. (ed.) The Best Moving Pictures of 1922-23; Also Who's Who in the Movies and the Yearbook of the American Screen. (Originally published 1923.) New York: Revisionist, 1974. 346 pp.
        Includes essays by Sherwood on 16 films of that year.

1350   Carter, Huntly. The New Theatre and Cinema of Soviet Russia. (Originally published 1924.) New York: Arno, 1970. 277 pp.

1351   Ramsaye, Terry. A Million and One Nights: A History of the Motion Picture. (Originally published 1926.) New York: Simon and Schuster, 1964. 868 pp.

1352   Carter, Huntly. The New Spirit in the Russian Theatre, 1917-1928; and a Sketch of the Russian Kinema and Radio, 1919-1928, Showing the New Communal Relationship Between the Three. (Originally published 1929.) New York: Blom, 1970. 348 pp. (Also published with abridged title, The New Spirit in the Russian Theatre, 1917-1928, New York: Arno, 1970.)

1353 Green, Fitzhugh. The Film Finds Its Tongue. (Originally
        published 1929.) New York: Putnam, 1971. 316 pp.

1354 Seldes, Gilbert. An Hour With the Movies and the Talkies.
        (Originally published 1929.) New York: Arno, 1973.
        156 pp.

1355 Hampton, Benjamin B. History of the American Film Industry
        From Its Beginnings to 1931. (Originally published 1931.)
        New York: Dover, 1970. 456 pp.
            New edition includes introduction by Richard Griffith.

1356 Foort, Reginald. The Cinema Organ: A Description in Non-
        Technical Language of a Fascinating Instrument and How
        It Is Played. (Originally published 1932.) Vestal, N.Y.:
        Vestal Press, 1970. 199 pp.

1357 Low, Rachael and Manvell, Roger. The History of the British
        Film, 1896-1906. London: Allen and Unwin, 1948. 136
        pp. (Reprinted 1973, distributed in U.S. by Bowker.)

1358 Low, Rachel. The History of the British Film, 1906-1914.
        London: Allen and Unwin, 1949. 309 pp. (Reprinted
        1973, distributed in U.S. by Bowker.)

1359 Morris, Lloyd. Not So Long Ago. New York: Random,
        1949. 504 pp.
            A social history of silent motion pictures, radio, and
        the automobile.

1360 North, Joseph H. The Early Development of the Motion Pic-
        ture, 1887-1909. (Originally published Cornell University:
        Ph.D., 1949.) New York: Arno, 1973. 313 pp.

1361 Vardac, A. Nicholas. Stage to Screen: Theatrical Method
        From Garrick to Griffith. Cambridge: Harvard Uni-
        versity Press, 1949. 283 pp. (Reprinted New York:
        Blom, 1968.)

1362 Low, Rachael. The History of the British Film, 1914-1918.
        London: Allen and Unwin, 1950. 332 pp. (Reprinted
        1973, distributed in U.S. by Bowker.)

1363 Idestam-Almquist, Bengt. Classics of the Swedish Cinema:
        The Stiller and Sjostrom Period. Stockholm: Swedish
        Institute, 1952. 48 pp.

1364 Blum, Daniel. A Pictorial History of the Silent Screen.
        New York: Putnam, 1953. 334 pp. (Reprinted 1972.)
            Primarily about American cinema.

1365 Bachmann, Gideon (ed.) Dawn of the American Screen,

1893-1916. New York: Group for Film Study, 1955.
48 pp.

1366 Lee, Raymond. M. Encino, Cal.: Defilee, 1958. 64 pp.
Author's experiences as a child actor in silent films,
with material on the era and prominent film personalities.

1367 Cassady, Ralph, Jr. Monopoly in Motion Picture Production
and Distribution: 1908-1915. Los Angeles: Bureau of
Business and Economic Research, University of California,
1959. 66 pp.
Includes material on the Motion Picture Patents Company and the General Film Company.

1368 Franklin, Joe. Classics of the Silent Screen: A Pictorial
Treasury. New York: Citadel, 1959. 255 pp.
Brief synopsis and discussion of 50 silent films and
biographical material on 75 stars; primarily on American
film.

1369 Sanderson, Richard Arlo. A Historical Study of the Development of American Motion Picture Content and Techniques
Prior to 1904. University of Southern California: Ph.D.,
1961. 251 pp.

1370 Byrne, Richard Burdick. German Cinematic Expressionism:
1919-1924. University of Iowa: Ph.D., 1962. 560 pp.

1371 Wagenknecht, Edward. The Movies in the Age of Innocence.
Norman: University of Oklahoma Press, 1962. 280 pp.
(Reprinted New York: Ballantine, 1971, 270 pp.)
Personal and selective view of silent films and per-
sonalities, primarily American.

1372 Pfragner, Julius. The Eye of History: The Motion Picture
From Magic Lantern to Sound Film. Chicago: Rand
McNally, 1964. 240 pp. Translated by Theodore Mc-
Clintock.
Historical presentation in a novelized format.

1373 O'Leary, Liam. The Silent Cinema. New York: Dutton,
1965. 160 pp.

1374 Lennig, Arthur. The Silent Voice. Albany: Faculty-Student
Association of the State University of New York, 1966.
176 pp.
Concentrates on American, German, and Soviet cinema.

1375 Pratt, George C. (ed.) Spellbound in Darkness: A History
of the Silent Film. Rochester, N.Y.: University of
Rochester, 1966. 452 pp. (Revised Greenwich, Conn.:
New York Graphic Society, 1973, 548 pp.)

Compilation of historical and critical articles on silent
film from contemporary sources; see entry 4579.

1376   Lennig, Arthur.   The Silent Voice: A Sequel.   Troy, N.Y.:
       Printed by W. Snyder, 1967.   158 pp.

1377   Niver, Kemp R.   In the Beginning: Program Notes to Ac-
       company One Hundred Early Motion Pictures.   New York:
       Brandon, 1967.   60 pp.

1378   Brownlow, Kevin.   The Parade's Gone By.   New York: Knopf,
       1968.   577 pp.
       Essay and interview material, primarily on American
       film figures; for list of names see entry 3695.

1379   Niver, Kemp R.   The First Twenty Years: A Segment of
       Film History.   Edited by Bebe Bergsten.   Los Angeles:
       Locare Research Group, 1968.   176 pp.
       Material on 100 American films between 1894 and
       1913.

1380   Lennig, Arthur.   The Silent Voice: A Text.   Troy, N.Y.:
       Printed by W. Snyder, 1969.   367 pp.

1381   Manchel, Frank.   When Pictures Began to Move.   Englewood
       Cliffs, N.J.:   Prentice-Hall, 1969.   76 pp.
       For the young reader.

1382   Thomas, D. B.   The First Colour Motion Pictures.   London:
       Her Majesty's Stationery Office, 1969.   44 pp.
       Account of pre-1917 color in motion pictures.

1383   Hofmann, Charles.   Sounds for Silents.   New York: Drama
       Book Shop, 1970.   90 pp.
       History of silent film music.

1384   Reade, Eric.   Australian Silent Films: A Pictorial History
       of Silent Films From 1896 to 1929.   Melbourne: Lans-
       downe, 1970.   192 pp.

1385   Slide, Anthony with O'Dell, Paul.   Early American Cinema.
       New York: A. S. Barnes, 1970.   192 pp.
       Account of the pre-1920 period.

1386   Low, Rachael.   The History of the British Film, 1918-1929.
       London: Allen and Unwin, 1971.   544 pp.   (Reprinted
       1973, distributed in U.S. by Bowker.)

1387   Berg, Charles.   An Investigation of the Motives for and
       Realization of Music to Accompany the American Silent
       Film, 1896-1927.   University of Iowa: Ph.D., 1973.
       311 pp.

1388   Lahue, Kalton C. (ed.) Motion Picture Pioneer: The Selig
       Polyscope Company. South Brunswick, N.J.: A. S.
       Barnes, 1973. 224 pp.

1389   Lyons, Timothy J. The Silent Partner: The History of the
       American Film Manufacturing Company, 1910-1921. New
       York: Arno, 1974. 256 pp.

1390   Wenden, D. J. The Birth of the Movies. New York: Dut-
       ton, 1975. 192 pp.

1391   Geduld, Harry M. The Birth of the Talkies: From Edison
       to Jolson. Bloomington: Indiana University Press, 1975.
       337 pp.

1392   Jenkins, Reese V. Images and Enterprise: Technology and
       the American Photographic Industry, 1839 to 1925. Balti-
       more: Johns Hopkins University Press, 1975. 371 pp.
          Includes a lengthy section on the silent cinematographic
       industry.

C. WORLD CINEMA

This section is composed of general surveys of world cinema. For books dealing primarily with the silent period, see Part IV, section B. The reader might also consult many of the general introductions to film in the education category, Part X, section A-2, since these books often contain an overview of world cinema history.

1393 Carter, Huntly. <u>The New Spirit in the Cinema.</u> (Originally published 1930 with the subtitle <u>An Analysis and Interpretation of the Parallel Paths of the Cinema, Which Have Led to the Present Revolutionary Crisis Forming a Study of the Cinema as an Instrument of Sociological Humanism.</u>) New York: Arno, 1970. 403 pp.

1394 Rotha, Paul. <u>The Film Till Now: A Survey of World Cinema.</u> (Originally published 1930.) Revised, with an additional section by Richard Griffith, New York: Funk and Wagnalls, 1949. 755 pp. (Revised with an epilogue, New York: Twayne, 1960, 820 pp. Republished 1967.)

1395 Spottiswoode, Raymond. <u>A Grammar of the Film: An Analysis of Film Technique.</u> (Originally published 1935.) Berkeley: University of California Press, 1950. 328 pp. (Reprinted 1969.)
       Includes a lengthy chapter on pre-1935 film history.

1396 Bardeche, Maurice and Brasillach, Robert. <u>The History of Motion Pictures.</u> Edited and translated by Iris Barry. (Originally published 1938.) London: Allen and Unwin, 1945. 412 pp. (Reprinted New York: Arno, 1970.)

1397 Kennedy, Margaret. <u>The Mechanized Muse.</u> London: Allen and Unwin, 1942. 52 pp.
       Discusses the advent of sound and the development of the art of screenwriting.

1398 Strong, Harry Hotchkiss. <u>Then and Now: The Story of the Motion Picture.</u> Toledo, Ohio: Strong Electric Corporation, 1943. 45 pp.

1399   Speed, F. Maurice. Movie Cavalcade: The Story of the
       Cinema, Its Stars, Studios and Producers. London:
       Raven, 1944. 112 pp.

1400   Wood, Leslie. The Miracle of the Movies. London: Burke,
       1947. 352 pp.
          Emphasis on British film history.

1401   Cross, John E. and Rattenbury, Arnold (eds.) Film Today
       Books: Screen and Audience, An Occasional Miscellany
       Devoted to the Contemporary Cinema. London: Saturn,
       ca. 1949. 90 pp.
          Material on international trends and practices, with
       emphasis on Great Britain.

1402   Manvell, Roger (ed.) Experiment in the Film. London:
       Grey Walls, 1949. 285 pp. (Reprinted New York: Arno,
       1970.)
          Discusses experiment within various national main-
       stream cinemas as well as the avant-garde.

1403   Larsen, Egon. Spotlight on Films: A Primer for Film-
       Lovers. London: Parrish, 1950. 301 pp.
          Includes a lengthy section on the historical develop-
       ment of film.

1404   Rotha, Paul and Manvell, Roger. Movie Parade 1888-1949:
       A Pictorial Survey of World Cinema. London: Studio,
       1950. 160 pp. (Based on Movie Parade by Paul Rotha,
       1936, 142 pp.)

1405   Waldekranz, Rune. Modern Film. Stockholm: Wahlstrom
       and Widstrand, 1951. 286 pp.

1406   Hauser, Arnold. The Social History of Art [In Two Volumes].
       New York: Knopf, 1952. 1022 pp.
          Includes a chapter entitled "The Film Age."

1407   National Film Library. Forty Years of Film History, 1895-
       1935. London: British Film Institute, ca. 1952. 108 pp.

1408   Reed, Stanley. The Cinema. London: Educational Supply
       Association, 1952. 122 pp.
          General survey with a concentration on the silent era;
       written for the film novice.

1409   Manvell, Roger. The Film and the Public. Harmondsworth:
       Penguin, 1955. 352 pp.
          Includes lengthy survey of film history and discussions
       of 23 classic films.

1410   Knight, Arthur. The Liveliest Art: A Panoramic History of

the Movies. New York: Macmillan, 1957. 383 pp.
(Numerous reprintings New York: New American Library,
352 pp.)

1411   Blum, Daniel. A Pictorial History of the Talkies. New
       York: Putnam, 1958. 318 pp. (Revised by John Kobal
       as A New Pictorial History of the Talkies, 1968, 352 pp.
       Revised again 1973, 392 pp.)

1412   Fulton, A. R. Motion Pictures: The Development of an Art
       From Silent Films to the Age of Television. Norman:
       University of Oklahoma Press, 1960. 320 pp.

1413   Lennig, Arthur (ed.) Film Notes of Wisconsin Film Society.
       Madison: Wisconsin Film Society, 1960. 139 pp.
            Discusses numerous films, primarily from the German,
       Soviet, Scandinavian, and American cinemas.

1414   Lindgren, Ernest. A Picture History of the Cinema. New
       York: Macmillan, 1960. 160 pp.

1415   National Film Theatre: Fifty Famous Films, 1915-1945.
       London: British Film Institute, 1960. 106 pp.
            Notes on 50 films, primarily foreign and silent clas-
       sics.

1416   Limbacher, James L. A Short History of the Sound Motion
       Picture. Dearborn, Mich.: Dearborn Public Library,
       1962. 8 ℓ.

1417   Tyler, Parker. Classics of the Foreign Film: A Pictorial
       Treasury. New York: Citadel, 1962. 253 pp.

1418   Houston, Penelope. The Contemporary Cinema. Baltimore:
       Penguin, 1963. 222 pp.
            Surveys post-World War II cinema, primarily Ameri-
       can and European.

1419   Limbacher, James L. A Historical Study of the Color Motion
       Picture. Dearborn, Mich.: n.p., 1963. 30 ℓ.

1420   Schickel, Richard. Movies: The History of an Art and an
       Institution. New York: Basic, 1964. 208 pp.

1421   Mayer, Michael F. Foreign Films on American Screens.
       New York: Arco, 1965. 119 pp.
            Discusses post-war foreign films, primarily European;
       includes index of major festival winners.

1422   Macgowan, Kenneth. Behind the Screen: The History and
       Techniques of the Motion Picture. New York: Delacorte,
       1965. 528 pp.

1423 Wiseman, Thomas. Cinema. New York: A. S. Barnes,
      1965. 181 pp.

1424 Crowther, Bosley. The Great Films: Fifty Golden Years
      of Motion Pictures. New York: Putnam, 1967. 258 pp.
          Credits and historical/critical discussion on 50 films.

1425 Fielding, Raymond (ed.) A Technological History of Motion
      Pictures and Television: An Anthology from the Pages
      of the Journal of the Society of Motion Picture and Tele-
      vision Engineers. Berkeley: University of California
      Press, 1967. 255 pp.
          Includes articles by W. K. L. Dickson, Thomas Ar-
      mat, Robert Paul, Louis Lumiere, H. T. Kalmus, Oscar
      B. Depue, and Leon Gaumont, and articles about Eugene
      Lauste, L. A. A. LePrince, Edison, Oskar Messter,
      Norman O. Dawn, and Joseph T. Tykociner.

1426 Lewis, Leon and Sherman, William David. The Landscape
      of Contemporary Cinema. Buffalo, N. Y. : Buffalo Spec-
      trum, 1967. 97 pp.
          Brief essays on films, filmmakers, and performers,
      primarily of the sixties.

1427 Gregg, Eugene Stuart. The Shadow of Sound. New York:
      Vantage, 1968. 174 pp.
          Discusses problems of the advent of sound.

1428 Cowie, Peter. Seventy Years of Cinema. South Brunswick,
      N. J. : A. S. Barnes, 1969. 287 pp.
          Primarily a year-by-year discussion of significant
      films, from 1895 to 1967.

1429 Guback, Thomas H. The International Film Industry:
      Western Europe and America Since 1945. Bloomington:
      Indiana University Press, 1969. 244 pp.

1430 Lennig, Arthur (ed.) The Sound Film: An Introduction.
      Troy, N. Y. : Printed by W. Snyder, 1969. 339 pp.

1431 Limbacher, James L. Four Aspects of the Film. New York:
      Brussel and Brussel, 1969. 386 pp.
          Historical study of technical innovations in sound,
      color, width, and depth.

1432 Manchel, Frank. When Movies Began to Speak. Englewood
      Cliffs, N. J. : Prentice-Hall, 1969. 76 pp.
          For the young reader.

1433 Roth, William David. Technology, Film and the Body Politic.
      University of California, Berkeley: Ph. D. , 1970. 321 pp.
          In part, discusses Soviet, German, American, and
      French film between the two world wars.

1434 Zinman, David. 50 Classic Motion Pictures: The Stuff That
      Dreams Are Made Of. New York: Crown, 1970. 311 pp.
      Films arranged generically.

1435 Cowie, Peter (ed.) A Concise History of the Cinema [In
      Two Volumes]. Volume I: Before 1940. Volume II:
      Since 1940. New York: A. S. Barnes, 1971. 212 and
      261 pp.

1436 Dickinson, Thorold. A Discovery of Cinema. London, New
      York: Oxford University Press, 1971. 164 pp.

1437 Malone, Peter. The Film. Sydney: Chevalier, 1971.
      182 pp.

1438 Mast, Gerald. A Short History of the Movies. New York:
      Pegasus, 1971. 463 pp.

1439 Bayer, William. The Great Movies. New York: Grosset
      and Dunlap, 1973. 252 pp.
      Primarily photographs, with brief essays on 60 films.

1440 Casty, Alan. Development of the Film: An Interpretive
      History. New York: Harcourt Brace Jovanovich, 1973.
      425 pp.

1441 Robinson, David. The History of World Cinema. New York:
      Stein and Day, 1973. 440 pp.

1442 Armes, Roy. Film and Reality: An Historical Survey.
      Baltimore: Penguin, 1974. 254 pp.

1443 Leish, Kenneth W. Cinema. New York: Newsweek Press,
      1974. 192 pp.

1444 Manvell, Roger. Films and the Second World War. South
      Brunswick, N.J.: A. S. Barnes, 1974. 388 pp.

1445 Scheuer, Steven H. The Movie Book. Chicago: Playboy
      Press, 1974. 384 pp.

1446 Wright, Basil. The Long View. New York: Knopf, 1974.
      709 pp.
      An admittedly personal history of world cinema.

1447 Bohn, Thomas W. and Stromgren, Richard L. with Johnson,
      Daniel H. Light and Shadows: A History of Motion
      Pictures. Port Washington, N.Y.: Alfred, 1975. 537 pp.

1448 Davies, Mary; Anderson, Janice; and Arnold, Peter. The
      Hamlyn History of the Movies. London: Hamlyn, 1975.
      224 pp.

1449 Evans, Mark. Soundtrack: The Music of the Movies.
      New York: Hopkinson and Blake, 1975.   303 pp.

1450 Finler, Joel W. All-Time Movie Favourites: Comedies,
      Thrillers, Epics, Musicals, Love Stories, Westerns,
      War Films and Others. London: Sundial, 1975.   189 pp.

1451 Garbicz, Adam and Klinowski, Jacek. Cinema, The Magic
      Vehicle: A Guide to Its Achievement. Journey One:
      The Cinema Through 1949. Metuchen, N.J.: Scarecrow,
      1975.   551 pp.
          Utilizes a film-by-film approach.

1452 Smith, Sharon. Women Who Make Movies. New York:
      Hopkinson and Blake, 1975.   307 pp.
          Surveys women filmmakers since 1896.

D. NORTH AMERICA

1. United States

     This category is composed of books on the history of the American film. Although many books on the silent film deal primarily or exclusively with the American film, these books have not been included here; for books on the American pre-history or silent periods, the reader is directed to Part IV, sections A and B. Some titles which may seem to be world film histories have been included in this section because of their predominantly American content. For historical material on various American film genres, see Part V, sections C-1 through C-10. For anecdotal, historical, and sociological material on the Hollywood community, see Part IX, section F. For histories of particular American studios, see Part IV, section D-2. For statistical or primarily economic works, as well as those books which approach film strictly as a business and a commodity, see Part III, film industry. For filmographic information on the American film, see the reference classification, Part I, particularly section B-2, national filmographies, and section A-3, annuals.

1453 Green, Fitzhugh. The Film Finds Its Tongue. (Originally
       published 1929.) New York: Putnam, 1971. 316 pp.

1454 Seldes, Gilbert. An Hour With the Movies and the Talkies.
       (Originally published 1929.) New York: Arno, 1973.
       156 pp.

1455 Hampton, Benjamin B. History of the American Film Industry
       From Its Beginnings to 1931. (Originally published 1931
       as A History of the Movies.) New York: Dover, 1970.
       456 pp.
          New edition includes introduction by Richard Griffith.

1456 Anderson, John and Fülöp-Miller, Rene. The American
       Theatre by John Anderson [and] The Motion Picture in

America by Rene Fülöp-Miller. (Originally published
1938.) New York: Johnson Reprint, 1970. 430 pp.

1457 Jacobs, Lewis. The Rise of the American Film: A Critical
History. (Originally published 1939.) Revised and en-
larged New York: Teachers College Press, 1968. 631 pp.
Revised edition includes essay entitled "Experimental
Cinema in America, 1921-1947. "

1458 Taylor, Deems; Peterson, Marcelene; and Hale, Bryant. A
Pictorial History of the Movies. New York: Simon and
Schuster, 1943. 350 pp. (Revised 1949, 375 pp.)

1459 Huettig, Mae D. Economic Control of the Motion Picture Industry: A Study in Industrial Organization. Philadelphia:
University of Pennsylvania Press, 1944. 163 pp.

1460 Writers' Congress, University of California at Los Angeles.
Writers' Congress: The Proceedings of the Conference
Held in October 1943 Under the Sponsorship of the Holly-
wood Writers' Mobilization and the University of California.
Berkeley: University of California Press, 1944. 663 pp.
Includes material on the role of the writer and of
Hollywood in aiding the war effort; for list of contributors,
see entry 4798.

1461 Editors of Look. Movie Lot to Beachhead: The Motion Picture Goes to War and Prepares for the Future. Garden
City, N. Y. : Doubleday, Doran, 1945. 291 pp.

1462 Thrasher, Frederic M. (ed.) Okay for Sound: How the
Screen Found Its Voice. New York: Duell, Sloan and
Pearce, 1946. 303 pp.

1463 War Activities Committee, Motion Picture Industry. Movies
At War: Reports of War Activities Committee, Motion
Picture Industry, 1942-1945. New York: War Activities
Committee, ca. 1946. 172 pp.

1464 Green, Abel and Laurie, Joe, Jr. Show Biz From Vaude to
Video. New York: Henry Holt, 1951. 613 pp. (Re-
printed Port Washington, New York: Kennikat, 1972.)
Based on material culled from Variety.

1465 Geis, Gilbert. American Motion Pictures in Norway: A
Study in International Mass Communications. University
of Wisconsin: Ph. D. , 1954. 182 pp.

1466 Griffith, Richard and Mayer, Arthur. The Movies: The
Sixty-Year History of the World of Hollywood and Its Ef-
fect on America, From Pre-Nickelodeon Days to the
Present. New York: Simon and Schuster, 1957. 442 pp.
(Revised 1970, 495 pp.)

1467 Stuart, Frederic. The Effects of Television on the Motion
       Picture and Radio Industries. Columbia University: Ph.D.,
       1960. 228 pp.

1468 Goodman, Ezra. The Fifty-Year Decline and Fall of Holly-
       wood. New York: Simon and Schuster, 1961. 465 pp.

1469 Hall, Ben M. The Best Remaining Seats: The Story of the
       Golden Age of the Movie Palace. New York: Clarkson
       N. Potter, 1961. 266 pp. (Reprinted as The Golden Age
       of the Movie Palace: The Best Remaining Seats, 1975,
       distributed by Crown.)

1470 MacCann, Richard Dyer. Hollywood in Transition. Boston:
       Houghton Mifflin, 1962. 208 pp.
          Account of Hollywood production changes since World
       War II and the advent of television.

1471 Everson, William K. The American Movie. New York:
       Atheneum, 1963. 149 pp.

1472 Jobes, Gertrude. Motion Picture Empire. Hamden, Conn.:
       Archon, 1966. 398 pp.
          Primarily an economic history.

1473 Baxter, John. Hollywood in the Thirties. New York: A. S.
       Barnes, 1968. 160 pp.

1474 Higham, Charles and Greenberg, Joel. Hollywood in the
       Forties. New York: A. S. Barnes, 1968. 192 pp.

1475 Manvell, Roger. New Cinema in the USA: The Feature Film
       Since 1946. New York: Dutton, 1968. 160 pp.

1476 Robinson, David. Hollywood in the Twenties. New York:
       A. S. Barnes, 1968. 176 pp.

1477 Williams, Henry. Economic Changes in the Motion Picture
       Industry as Affected by Television and Other Factors.
       Indiana University: Ph.D., 1968. 170 pp.

1478 Quigley, Martin, Jr. and Gertner, Richard. Films in America,
       1929-1969. New York: Golden Press, 1970. 379 pp.
          Discussion and credits for almost 400 representative
       films.

1479 Walker, Alexander. Stardom: The Hollywood Phenomenon.
       New York: Stein and Day, 1970. 392 pp.

1480 Barbour, Alan G. A Thousand and One Delights. New York:
       Macmillan, 1971. 164 pp.
          Material on the films of the forties; largely pictorial.

1481 Bergman, Andrew. We're in the Money: Depression America
      and Its Films. New York: New York University Press,
      1971. 200 pp.

1482 Freulich, Roman and Abramson, Joan. Forty Years in Holly-
      wood: Portraits of a Golden Age. South Brunswick, N.J.:
      A. S. Barnes, 1971. 201 pp.
          Primarily photographs, including many of Universal
      and Republic studios, their films, and their stars.

1483 Gow, Gordon. Hollywood in the Fifties. New York: A. S.
      Barnes, 1971. 208 pp.

1484 Griffith, Richard (comp.) The Talkies: Articles and Illustra-
      tions From Photoplay Magazine, 1928-1940. New York:
      Dover, 1971. 360 pp.

1485 Paine, Jeffrey Morton. The Simplification of American Life:
      Hollywood Films of the 1930's. Princeton University:
      Ph.D., 1971. 311 pp.

1486 Spears, Jack. Hollywood: The Golden Era. South Bruns-
      wick, N.J.: A. S. Barnes, 1971. 440 pp.
          Collection of articles from Films In Review. Includes
      material on various subjects in American films (World
      War I, comic strips, doctors, Indians, and others) and on
      individual film figures; for list of names, see entry 3745.

1487 Thomas, Bob. The Heart of Hollywood: A 50-Year Pictorial
      History of the Film Capital and the Famed Motion Picture
      and Television Relief Fund. Los Angeles: Price, Stern,
      Sloan, 1971. 110 pp.

1488 Baxter, John, Hollywood in the Sixties. New York: A. S.
      Barnes, 1972. 172 pp.

1489 Gartley, Linda Jo Blood. The American Film Industry in
      Transition: 1946-1956. University of Michigan: Ph.D.,
      1972. 204 pp.

1490 Gelman, Barbara (comp.) Photoplay Treasury. New York:
      Crown, 1972. 373 pp.
          Articles and photographs from Photoplay magazine.

1491 Higham, Charles. Hollywood at Sunset. New York: Saturday
      Review Press, 1972. 181 pp.
          Account of post-war Hollywood.

1492 Jowett, Garth Samuel. Media Power and Social Control: The
      Motion Picture in America, 1894-1936. University of
      Pennsylvania: Ph.D., 1972. 499 pp.

1493 Kardish, Laurence. Reel Plastic Magic: A History of Films

and Filmmaking in America. Boston: Little, Brown,
1972. 297 pp.

1494 Kuhns, William. Movies in America. Dayton, Ohio: Pflaum/
Standard, 1972. 248 pp.

1495 Shales, Tom; Brownlow, Kevin; and others. American Film
Heritage: Impressions From the American Film Institute
Archives. Edited by Kathleen Karr. Washington, D.C.:
Acropolis, 1972. 184 pp.
Essays on various films, genres, and individuals in
American film, primarily the pre-1940 years; for list of
individuals, see entry 3759.

1496 Baxter, John. Sixty Years of Hollywood. South Brunswick,
N.J.: A. S. Barnes, 1973. 254 pp.

1497 Dowdy, Andrew. Movies Are Better Than Ever: Wide-Screen
Memories of the Fifties. New York: Morrow, 1973.
242 pp. (Reprinted as The Films of the Fifties, 1975.)

1498 Higham, Charles. The Art of the American Film, 1900-1971.
Garden City, N.Y.: Doubleday, 1973. 322 pp.

1499 Jones, Ken D. and McClure, Arthur F. Hollywood At War:
The American Motion Picture and World War II. South
Brunswick, N.J.: A. S. Barnes, 1973. 320 pp.

1500 Kobal, John (ed.) 50 Years of Movie Posters. New York:
Bounty, 1973. 175 pp.

1501 Lawton, Richard. Grand Illusions. Text by Hugo Leckey.
New York: McGraw-Hill, 1973. 254 pp.
Chronologically arranged photographs of stars and
films; includes an essay on Hollywood.

1502 Lawton, Richard. A World of Movies: 70 Years of Film
History. Introduction by Ella Smith. New York: Dela-
corte, 1974. 383 pp.
Primarily photographs from American films.

1503 McLaughlin, Robert. Broadway and Hollywood: A History of
Economic Interaction. New York: Arno, 1974. 302 pp.

1504 Willoughby, Bob (photographs) and Schickel, Richard (text).
The Platinum Years. New York: Random, 1974. 268 pp.
Photographs, credits, and discussion of 22 films from
1953 to 1971.

1505 Geduld, Harry M. The Birth of the Talkies: From Edison
to Jolson. Bloomington: Indiana University Press, 1975.
337 pp.

1506 Life Goes to the Movies. New York: Time-Life, c. 1975.
304 pp.
Photographs, culled from Life magazine, on movies,
stars, and filmmaking.

1507 Madsen, Axel. The New Hollywood: American Movies in
the '70s. New York: Crowell, 1975. 183 pp.

1508 Sklar, Robert. Movie-Made America: A Social History of
American Movies. New York: Random, 1975. 340 pp.
(Also published as Movie Made America: A Cultural
History of American Movies.)

1509 Thomas, Tony. The Films of the Forties. Secaucus, N.J.:
Citadel, 1975. 278 pp.

1510 Toeplitz, Jerzy. Hollywood and After: The Changing Face
of Movies in America. Chicago: Regnery, 1975.
288 pp. Translated by Boleslaw Sulik. (Also published
as Hollywood and After: The Changing Face of American
Cinema.)
Discusses both Hollywood and underground film activities, primarily of the sixties and seventies.

1511 Trent, Paul. Those Fabulous Movie Years: The 30's.
Barre, Mass.: Barre, distributed by Crown, 1975.
192 pp.

2. Specific Studio Histories

This section contains those books which deal with specific
American studios.

1512 Green, Fitzhugh. The Film Finds Its Tongue. (Originally
published 1929.) New York: Blom, 1971. 316 pp.
Emphasis on Warner Brothers sound pioneering.

1513 Huettig, Mae D. Economic Control of the Motion Picture
Industry: A Study in Industrial Organization. Philadelphia:
University of Pennsylvania Press, 1944. 163 pp.
Includes discussion of how the major studios achieved
their monopolies.

1514 Crowther, Bosley. The Lion's Share: The Story of an
Entertainment Empire. New York: Dutton, 1957.
320 pp.
History of Metro-Goldwyn-Mayer.

1515 Thomas, Bob. Walt Disney, The Art of Animation: The

Story of the Disney Studio Contribution to a New Art.
New York: Simon and Schuster, 1958. 181 pp.

1516 Dunne, John Gregory. The Studio. New York: Farrar,
      Straus, Giroux, 1968. 255 pp.
          An examination of Twentieth Century-Fox and its prac-
      tices over the course of one year (1967-68).

1517 Fernett, Gene. Next Time Drive Off the Cliff! Cocoa,
      Florida: Cinememories, 1968. 205 pp.
          An account of Mascot Pictures and its president, Nat
      Levine.

1518 Lahue, Kalton C. and Brewer, Terry. Kops and Custards:
      The Legend of Keystone Films. Norman: University of
      Oklahoma Press, 1967. 177 pp.
          Includes a filmography of the Keystone Film Company
      from 1912-1917.

1519 French, Philip. The Movie Moguls: An Informal History of
      the Hollywood Tycoons. Chicago: Regnery, 1969. 170 pp.

1520 Zierold, Norman. The Moguls. New York: Coward-McCann,
      1969. 354 pp.

1521 Catalog of the Public Auction of the Countless Treasures Ac-
      quired from Metro-Goldwyn-Mayer [In Five Volumes].
      David Weisz Co., 1970.
          Catalog from the auction of MGM's sets, props, and
      costumes, held at MGM Studio, Culver City, California
      from May 3 to May 20, 1970.

1522 Lahue, Kalton C. Dreams For Sale: The Rise and Fall of
      the Triangle Film Corporation. South Brunswick, N.J.:
      A. S. Barnes, 1971. 216 pp.

1523 Lahue, Kalton C. Mack Sennett's Keystone: The Man, The
      Myth and The Comedies. South Brunswick, N.J.: A. S.
      Barnes, 1971. 315 pp.

1524 Movie Memorabilia: Inactive Properties Including Furniture,
      Decorative Items, Paintings, Posters, Set Sketches &
      Other Decorations, Full Size & Model Boats and Ships,
      Airplanes, Model Trains; The Property of Twentieth Cen-
      tury-Fox Film Corporation. Los Angeles: Sotheby, Parke-
      Bernet, 1971. 275 pp.
          Catalog from the auction of Twentieth Century-
      Fox's property, held from February 25 to February
      28, 1971.

1525 Niver, Kemp R. Biograph Bulletins 1896-1908. Edited by
      Bebe Bergsten. Los Angeles: Locare Research Group,

1971.   464 pp.
Handbills and bulletins providing credit and synopsis
information on films produced by the American Mutoscope
and Biograph Company.

1526   Sennett, Ted. Warner Brothers Presents: The Most Exciting
Years, From The Jazz Singer to White Heat. New Ro-
chelle, N.Y.: Arlington, 1971.   428 pp.
Includes a studio filmography from 1930-1949.

1527   Parish, James Robert. The Paramount Pretties. Edited by
T. Allan Taylor. New Rochelle, N.Y.: Arlington, 1972.
587 pp.
Material on 16 female stars; for list of names, see
entry 3756.

1528   Thomas, Lawrence B. The MGM Years. New York: Columbia, 1972.   138 pp.
Primarily deals with MGM musicals.

1529   Bowser, Eileen (ed.) Biograph Bulletins 1908-1912. New
York: Octagon, 1973.   471 pp.
Handbills and bulletins, providing synopsis and credits
information of films produced by the American Mutoscope
and Biograph Company.

1530   Fernett, Gene. Poverty Row. Satellite Beach, Florida:
Coral Reef, 1973.   163 pp.
Material on the minor film studios which produced
numerous B-films and serials in the thirties and forties.

1531   Lahue, Kalton C. (ed.) Motion Picture Pioneer: The Selig
Polyscope Company. South Brunswick, N.J.: A. S.
Barnes, 1973.   224 pp.

1532   Maltin, Leonard. The Disney Films. New York: Crown,
1973.   312 pp.
Credits, synopsis, and discussion of over 75 films
from the Disney studios.

1533   Parish, James Robert and Bowers, Ronald L. The MGM
Stock Company: The Golden Era. New Rochelle, N.Y.:
Arlington, 1973.   862 pp.
Primarily biographical material on MGM stars.

1534   Wilson, Arthur (ed.) The Warner Bros. Golden Anniversary
Book: The First Complete Feature Filmography. New
York: Film and Venture, 1973.   192 pp.
Includes a critical essay by Arthur Knight.

1535   Parish, James Robert. The RKO Gals. Edited by T. Allan
Taylor. New Rochelle, N.Y.: Arlington, 1974.   896 pp.

Material on RKO producers as well as actresses; for
list of names, see entry 3792.

1536   Eames, John Douglas. The MGM Story: The Complete
       History of Fifty Roaring Years. New York: Crown, 1975.
       400 pp.

1537   Fordin, Hugh. The World of Entertainment: Hollywood's
       Greatest Musicals. Garden City, N. Y.: Doubleday, 1975.
       566 pp.
            An account of Arthur Freed and the MGM musical
       unit.

1538   Higham, Charles. The Warner Brothers. New York: Scrib-
       ner's, 1975. 232 pp.

1539   Larkin, Rochelle. Hail Columbia. New Rochelle, N. Y.:
       Arlington, 1975. 445 pp.
            History of Columbia studio, including listing of feature
       films since 1922.

1540   Balio, Tino. United Artists: The Company Built by the Stars.
       Madison: University of Wisconsin Press, 1976. 323 pp.

                         3. Canada

            This section is composed of those books dealing with the
       history of Canadian film. For books dealing with the National Film
       Board of Canada or the Canadian Film Institute, see Part I, section
       F, film institutions. For a general discussion of the history sec-
       tions, see the extended explanation at the beginning of Part IV.

1541   Buchanan, Donald William. Documentary and Educational
       Films in Canada 1935-1950: A Survey of Problems and
       Achievements. Ottawa: Canadian Film Institute, 1952.
       24 pp.
            Includes material on National Film Board, Canadian
       Film Institute, and other film organizations.

1542   Irving, John A. (ed.) Mass Media in Canada. Toronto:
       Ryerson, 1962. 236 pp.
            Includes a chapter on film by J. R. Kidd.

1543   Paquet, Andre (ed.) How To Make or Not To Make a
       Canadian Film. Montreal: La Cinémathèque Canadienne,
       1967. Unpaged.

1544   Beattie, Eleanor. A Handbook of Canadian Film. Toronto:
       Peter Martin, 1973. 280 pp.

1545 Hofsess, John. <u>Inner Views: Ten Canadian Film-Makers.</u>
      Toronto, New York: McGraw-Hill Ryerson, 1975. 171 pp.
      For list of names, see entry 3808.

E. EUROPE

1546 Film Centre, London. The Film Industry in Six European
Countries: A Detailed Study of the Film Industry in Denmark as Compared With That in Norway, Sweden, Italy,
France and the United Kingdom. Paris: UNESCO, 1950.
156 pp.

1547 Manvell, Roger. New Cinema in Europe. New York: Dutton, 1966. 160 pp.

1548 Lovell, Alan (ed.) Art of the Cinema in Ten European Countries. Strasbourg: Council of Europe, 1967. 265 pp.

1. Great Britain and Ireland

This section is composed of those works dealing with the
history of film in Great Britain (including Wales and Scotland) or
Ireland. For statistical or primarily economic works, as well as
those books which approach British film as a business and a commodity, see Part III, film industry. For filmographic information
on the British film, see the reference classification, Part I, particularly sections B, filmographies, and A-3, annuals. And finally,
because of the strength of the documentary movement in Britain,
the reader should also see Part V, section A, documentary.

1549 Ripley, A. Crooks. Vaudeville Pattern. London: Brownlee,
1942. 123 pp.
Includes material on British film and theatre.

1550 Great Britain, Board of Trade. Tendencies to Monopoly in
the Cinematographic Film Industry: Report of a Committee Appointed by the Cinematograph Films Council. London: Her Majesty's Stationery Office, 1944. 41 pp.
Includes material on the Rank organization.

1551 Junge, Helmut. Plan for Film Studios: A Plea for Reform.
London, New York: Focal, 1945. 64 pp.

1552 O'Laoghaire, Liam. Invitation to the Film. Tralee, Ireland:
      Kerryman, 1945. 203 pp.
          Includes material on Irish Cinema.

1553 Wilson, Norman. Presenting Scotland: A Film Survey.
      Edinburgh: Edinburgh Film Guild, 1945. 36 pp.
          Concentrates on documentary film.

1554 Alexander, Donald. Facts About Films. London: Bureau of
      Current Affairs, 1946. 20 pp.
          Survey of film history, British film industry, and
      future prospects.

1555 Bond, Ralph. Monopoly: The Future of British Films. Lon-
      don: Association of Cine-Technicians, 1946. 31 pp.
          Study of British film industry, with emphasis on J.
      Arthur Rank and the Hollywood influence.

1556 Fifty Years at the Pictures. Glasgow: Scottish Film Council,
      1946. 16 pp.

1557 Andrews, Cyril Bruyn. The Theatre, The Cinema and Our-
      selves. London: Clarence House, 1947. 52 pp.
          Primarily on British theatre and films of the forties.

1558 The Arts Enquiry. The Factual Film: A Survey Sponsored
      by the Dartington Hall Trustees, Published on Behalf of
      the Arts Enquiry by PEP (Political and Economic Planning).
      London, New York: Oxford University Press, 1947.
      260 pp.
          Primarily about British documentary, but includes ma-
      terial on Canadian, Scottish, and international production.

1559 Balcon, Michael; Lindgren, Ernest; Hardy, Forsyth; and Man-
      vell, Roger. Twenty Years of British Film: 1925-1945.
      London: Falcon, 1947. 116 pp.

1560 Bird, John H. Cinema Parade: 50 Years of Film Shows.
      Birmingham: Cornish, 1947. 107 pp.
          Primarily about early British film days, with empha-
      sis on exhibitor Waller Jeffs.

1561 Huntley, John. British Film Music. London: Robinson,
      1947. 247 pp. (Reprinted New York: Arno, 1972.)

1562 Minney, R. J. Talking of Films. London: Home and Van
      Thal, 1947. 82 pp.
          General survey of industry, with concentration on
      British production.

1563 Powell, Dilys. Films Since 1939. London: Longmans
      Green, 1947. 40 pp.

1564   Discusses British features and documentaries made
            during World War II.

1564   Towers, Harry Alan and Mitchell, Leslie. The March of the
        Movies. London: Low, Marston, 1947. 88 pp.

1565   British Film Institute. The Film in Colonial Development:
        A Report of a Conference. London: British Film Insti-
        tute, 1948. 53 pp.
            Articles on the work and aims of the Colonial Film
        Unit; contributions by John Grierson, George Pearson, and
        others.

1566   Carrick, Edward (comp.) Art and Design in the British Film:
        A Pictorial Directory of British Art Directors and Their
        Work. London: Dobson, 1948. 133 pp. (Reprinted New
        York: Arno, 1972.)

1567   The Elstree Story: Twenty-One Years of Film-Making. Lon-
            don: Clerke and Cockeran, in cooperation with the Asso-
            ciated British Picture Corporation, ca. 1948. 95 pp.
                Contributions by Leslie Banks, Anna Neagle, John
            Mills, Ray Milland, Charles Laughton, Alfred Hitchcock,
            Margaret Lockwood, and others.

1568   Haskell, Arnold L.; Powell, Dilys; and others. Since 1939.
        London: Phoenix, 1948. 184 pp.
            Material on the various arts, including a section on
        film by Dilys Powell.

1569   Low, Rachael and Manvell, Roger. The History of the British
        Film, 1896-1906. London: Allen and Unwin, 1948. 136 pp.
        (Reprinted 1973, distributed in U. S. by Bowker.)

1570   Morgan, Guy. Red Roses Every Night: An Account of London
        Cinemas Under Fire. London: Quality, 1948. 127 pp.

1571   Sadoul, Georges. British Creators of Film Technique; British
        Scenario Writers, the Creators of the Language of D. W.
        Griffith, G. A. Smith, Alfred Collins and Some Others.
        London: British Film Institute, 1948. 10 pp.

1572   Huntley, John. British Technicolour Films. London: Robin-
        son, ca. 1949. 224 pp.
            Production notes on 25 technicolor films from 1936
        to 1948.

1573   Low, Rachael. The History of the British Film, 1906-1914.
        London: Allen and Unwin, 1949. 309 pp. (Reprinted
        1973, distributed in U. S. by Bowker.)

1574   British Film Academy. The Film Industry in Great Britain:

Some Facts and Figures. London: British Film Academy,
1950. 40 pp.

1575 Low, Rachael. The History of the British Film, 1914-1918.
      London: Allen and Unwin, 1950. 332 pp. (Reprinted
      1973, distributed in U.S. by Bowker.)

1576 Manvell, Roger (ed.) The Year's Work in Film 1949. Lon-
      don: Published for the British Council by Longmans Green,
      1950. 104 pp.
         Contributions by Basil Wright, Denis Forman, Edgar
      Anstey, Jean George Auriol, Eric Newton, Paul Rotha,
      John Huntley, and others.

1577 British Film Institute. Films in Britain 1951, Festival of
      Britain. London: British Film Institute, 1951. 72 pp.
         Material on J. Arthur Rank, Alexander Korda, Michael
      Balcon, Carol Reed, T. E. B. Clarke, Jack Cardiff, Jack
      Harris, Laurence Olivier, John Grierson and other topics;
      contributions by Forsyth Hardy, Mary Field, Norman Wil-
      son, Karel Reisz, Ernest Lindgren, Basil Wright, and
      others.

1578 The Crisis of British Films. Foreword by Laurence Olivier.
      London: Film Industry Employees' Council, 1951. 12 pp.

1579 Political and Economic Planning. The British Film Industry:
      A Report on Its History and Present Organization, with
      Special Reference to the Economic Problems of British
      Feature Film Production. London: Political and Economic
      Planning, 1952. 307 pp. (Supplement published 1958; see
      citation below.)

1580 Forman, Denis. Films 1945-1950. London, New York:
      Published for the British Council by Longmans Green,
      1952. 64 pp.

1581 Chadwick, Stanley. The Mighty Screen: The Rise of the
      Cinema in Huddersfield. Huddersfield, England: Ven-
      turers, 1953. 128 pp.

1582 Political and Economic Planning. The British Film Industry
      1958. London: Political and Economic Planning, 1958.
      40 pp.
         Updating of the 1952 report entitled The British Film
      Industry; see citation above.

1583 Spraos, John. The Decline of the Cinema: An Economist's
      Report. London: Allen and Unwin, 1962. 168 pp.

1584 Oakley, Charles. Where We Came In: Seventy Years of the
      British Film Industry. London: Allen and Unwin, 1964.
      245 pp.

1585 Kelly, Terrence with Norton, Graham and Perry, George. A Competitive Cinema. London: Institute of Economic Affairs, 1966. 204 pp.

1586 Knight, Derrick and Porter, Vincent. A Long Look at Short Films: An A.C.T.T. Report on the Short Entertainment and Factual Film. New York: Association of Cinematograph, Television and Allied Technicians in association with Pergamon, 1967. 185 pp.

1587 The Rank Organization. No Case for Compulsion. London: n.p., 1967. 20 pp.
     Rank Organization's comment on the A.C.T.T. report, A Long Look at Short Films.

1588 Ireland, Film Industry Committee. Report of the Film Industry Committee. Dublin: Stationery Office, 1968. 61 pp.

1589 Manvell, Roger. New Cinema in Britain. New York: Dutton, 1969. 160 pp.
     Concentrates on post-war cinema; mainly photographs.

1590 Durgnat, Raymond. A Mirror for England: British Movies From Austerity to Affluence. New York: Praeger, 1971. 336 pp.

1591 Low, Rachael. The History of the British Film, 1918-1929. London: Allen and Unwin, 1971. 544 pp. (Reprinted 1973, distributed in U.S. by Bowker.)

1592 Mellor, G. J. Picture Pioneers: The Story of the Northern Cinema 1896-1971. Newcastle-upon-Tyne: Frank Graham, 1971. 96 pp.

1593 Betts, Ernest. The Film Business: A History of British Cinema, 1896-1972. New York: Pitman, 1973. 349 pp.

1594 Butler, Ivan. Cinema in Britain: An Illustrated Survey. South Brunswick, N.J.: A. S. Barnes, 1973. 307 pp.
     Discussion and credits of over 300 British films, 1895-1971, chronologically arranged.

1595 Nationalizing the Film Industry: Report of the A.C.T.T. Nationalization Forum, August 1973. London: Association of Cinematograph, Television and Allied Technicians, 1973. 59 pp.
     Surveys British film industry and discusses demands for public ownership.

1596 Eyles, Allen; Adkinson, Robert; and Fry, Nicholas. The House of Horror: The Story of Hammer Films. New York: Third Press, 1974. 126 pp.

1597 Field, Audrey. The Picture Palace: A Social History of the
      Cinema. London: Gentry, 1974. 160 pp.

1598 Perry, George. The Great British Picture Show from the
      90s to the 70s. New York: Hill and Wang, 1974.
      367 pp.

1599 Walker, Alexander. Hollywood UK: The British Film Indus-
      try in the Sixties. New York: Stein and Day, 1974.
      493 pp. (Also published as Hollywood, England: The
      British Film Industry in the Sixties.)

                      2.   France

           For material on the new wave, see also Part VIII, section
      C, film movements, styles, and special critical approaches. For a
      general discussion of the history sections, see the extended explana-
      tion at the beginning of Part IV.

1600 Fowler, Roy. The Film in France. London: Pendulum,
      1946. 56 pp.
           Concentrates on French film of the early forties.

1601 Sadoul, Georges. French Film. London: Falcon, 1953.
      130 pp. (Reprinted New York: Arno, 1972.)

1602 Durgnat, Raymond. Nouvelle Vague: The First Decade.
      Loughton, England: Motion, 1963. 90 pp. (Also pub-
      lished as French Cinema: The A-Z Guide to the "New
      Wave. ")

1603 Reif, Tony. Innovators of the French Cinema. Ottawa:
      Canadian Film Institute, 1965. 25 pp.
           Primarily discussions of French directors.

1604 Armes, Roy. French Cinema Since 1946: Volume 1, The
      Great Tradition. Cranbury, N. J. : A. S. Barnes, 1966.
      176 pp. (Revised 1970, 208 pp.)
           Includes chapters on René Clair, Jean Renoir, Marcel
      Carné, Max Ophuls, Jean Cocteau, Henri-Georges Clouzot,
      René Clement, Jacques Becker, Claude Autant-Lara,
      Robert Bresson, Jacques Tati, Jean Gremillon, Georges
      Rouquier, and Roger Leenhardt.

1605 Armes, Roy. French Cinema Since 1946: Volume 2, The
      Personal Style. Cranbury, N. J. : A. S. Barnes, 1966.
      176 pp. (Revised 1970, 228 pp.)
           Includes chapters on Georges Franju, Jean-Pierre

Melville, Claude Chabrol, François Truffaut, Jean-Luc
Godard, Jacques Rivette, Agnes Varda, Alain Resnais,
Chris Marker, Alexandre Astruc, Roger Vadim, Louis
Malle, Jean Rouch, Alain Robbe-Grillet, Jacques Demy,
Pierre Etaix, and Claude Lelouch.

1606   Gollub, Judith Podselver. Nouveau Roman et Nouveau Cinema/
       New Novel and New Cinema. University of California, Los
       Angeles: Ph.D., 1966. 174 pp.

1607   Armes, Roy. French Film. New York: Dutton, 1970.
       160 pp.

1608   Strebel, Elizabeth Grottle. French Social Cinema of the Nine-
       teen-Thirties: A Cinematographic Expression of Popular
       Front Consciousness. Princeton University: Ph.D., 1974.
       299 pp.

                          3. Soviet Union

1609   Carter, Huntly. The New Theatre and Cinema of Soviet Rus-
       sia. (Originally published 1924.) New York: Arno, 1970.
       277 pp.

1610   Carter, Huntly. The New Spirit in the Russian Theatre, 1917-
       1928; and a Sketch of the Russian Kinema and Radio, 1919-
       1928, Showing the New Communal Relationship Between the
       Three. (Originally published 1929.) New York: Blom,
       1970. 348 pp. (Also published with abridged title, The
       New Spirit in the Russian Theatre, 1917-1928, New York:
       Arno, 1970.)

1611   Marshall, Herbert. Soviet Cinema. London: Russia Today
       Society, 1945. 40 pp.

1612   Dickinson, Thorold and De La Roche, Catherine. Soviet
       Cinema. London: Falcon, 1948. 136 pp. (Reprinted
       New York: Arno, 1972.)

1613   The Soviet Cinematography. Bombay: People's Publishing,
       1950. 244 pp.
       Discusses various aspects of Soviet cinema.

1614   Pudovkin, V.; Alexandrov, G.; and Piryev, I. Soviet Films:
       Principal States of Development. Bombay: People's
       Publishing, 1951. 58 pp.

1615   Babitsky, Paul and Rimberg, John. The Soviet Film Industry.
       New York: Praeger, 1955. 377 pp.

1616 Leyda, Jay. <u>Kino: A History of the Russian and Soviet Film</u>.
      New York: Macmillan, 1960. 525 pp. (Reprinted New
      York: Collier, 1973, 501 pp.)

1617 Baskakov, Vladimir. <u>Soviet Cinema: A Brief Essay</u>. Mos-
      cow: Novosti Press Agency, ca. 1967. 22 pp.

1618 National Film Theatre. <u>Fifty Years of Soviet Cinema, 1917-
      1967; Prepared by the British Film Institute and Sovex-
      port Film on the Occasion of the 50th Anniversary of the
      October Revolution</u>. London: British Film Institute, 1967.
      29 pp.
          Exclusively photographs.

1619 Hibbin, Nina. <u>Eastern Europe: An Illustrated Guide</u>. New
      York: A. S. Barnes, 1969. 239 pp.

1620 London Arts Council. <u>Art in Revolution: Soviet Art and De-
      sign Since 1917</u>. London: Hayward Gallery, 1971.
      112 pp.
          Exhibition catalog; includes essays on film by Dziga
      Vertov, Sergei Eisenstein, Lenin, and others.

1621 Silantieva, T. A. (ed.) <u>Khudozhniki Sovetskogo Kino/De-
      signers of Soviet Films</u>. Moscow: Imported Publications,
      1972. 58 pp.
          Text in Russian and English; mainly illustrations.

1622 Vronskaya, Jeanne. <u>Young Soviet Film Makers</u>. London:
      Allen and Unwin, 1972. 127 pp.
          Emphasizes 1955-1970 period.

1623 Cohen, Louis Harris. <u>The Soviet Cinema: Annotated Bibliog-
      raphy on Film Literature</u>. n.p., 1973. 165 pp.

1624 Rimberg, John David. <u>The Motion Picture in the Soviet
      Union, 1918-1952: A Sociological Analysis</u>. New York:
      Arno, 1973. 238 pp.

1625 Schnitzer, Luda; Schnitzer, Jean; and Martin, Marcel (eds.)
      <u>Cinema in Revolution: The Heroic Era of the Soviet
      Film</u>. Translated and with additional material by
      David Robinson. New York: Hill and Wang, 1973.
      208 pp.
          For list of names, see entry 3773.

1626 Cohen, Louis H. <u>The Cultural-Political Traditions and De-
      velopments of the Soviet Cinema: 1917-1972</u>. New York:
      Arno, 1974. 724 pp.

1627 Constantine, Mildred and Fern, Alan. <u>Revolutionary Soviet</u>

Film Posters. Baltimore: Johns Hopkins University
Press, 1974. 97 pp.

1628 Stoil, Michael Jon. Cinema Beyond the Danube: The Camera
and Politics. Metuchen, N.J.: Scarecrow, 1974.
198 pp.

4. Germany

For works on East German cinema, see Part IV, section
E-8, Eastern Europe. For books on German expressionism, see
also Part VIII, section C, film movements, styles, and special
critical approaches. For a general discussion of the history section, see the extended explanation at the beginning of Part IV.

1629 Kracauer, Siegfried. Propaganda and the Nazi War Film.
New York: Museum of Modern Art Film Library, 1942.
90 pp. (Reprinted as a supplement in From Caligari to
Hitler: A Psychological History of the German Film.
See entry 1631.)

1630 Kracauer, Siegfried. The Conquest of Europe on the Screen:
The Nazi Newsreel, 1939-1940. Washington, D.C.: Li-
brary of Congress, Experimental Division for the Study of
War Time Communications, 1943. 33 pp.

1631 Kracauer, Siegfried. From Caligari to Hitler: A Psychological History of the German Film. Princeton: Princeton
University Press, 1947. 361 pp. (Reprinted 1969.)

1632 Wollenberg, H. H. Fifty Years of German Film. London:
Falcon, 1948. 80 pp. Translated by Ernst Sigler. (Reprinted New York: Arno, 1972.)

1633 Byrne, Richard Burdick. German Cinematic Expressionism:
1919-1924. University of Iowa: Ph.D., 1962.
560 pp.

1634 Eisner, Lotte H. The Haunted Screen: Expressionism in
the German Cinema and the Influence of Max Reinhardt.
Berkeley: University of California Press, 1969. 360 pp.
Translated by Roger Greaves.

1635 Hull, David Stewart. Film in the Third Reich: A Study of
the German Cinema from 1933-1945. Berkeley: University of California Press, 1969. 291 pp. (Reprinted
as Film in the Third Reich: Art and Propaganda in Nazi
Germany, New York: Simon and Schuster, 1973.)

1636   Manvell, Roger and Fraenkel, Heinrich.   The German Cinema.
       New York: Praeger, 1971. 159 pp.

1637   Leiser, Erwin. Nazi Cinema. New York: Macmillan,
       1975. 179 pp. Translated by Gertrud Mander and
       David Wilson.

5. Italy

       For material on neo-realism, see also Part VIII, section
C, film movements, styles, and special critical approaches. For a
general discussion of the history sections, see the extended explanation at the beginning of Part IV.

1638   Jarratt, Vernon. The Italian Cinema. New York: Mac-
       millan, 1951. 115 pp. (Reprinted New York: Arno,
       1972.)

1639   Malerba, Luigi (ed.) Italian Cinema 1945-1951. Rome:
       Edizioni d'Arte, Bestetti, 1951. 99 pp.

1640   Malerba, Luigi and Siniscalco, Carmine (eds.) Fifty Years
       of Italian Cinema. American edition edited by Herman
       G. Weinberg. Rome: Carlo Bestetti, Edizioni d'Arte,
       1954. 208 pp.
            Essays by E. Ferdinando Palmieri, Ettore M. Marga-
       donna, and Mario Gromo.

1641   Unitalia Film. Italian Directors. Rome: Unitalia Film,
       1958. 203 pp.

1642   McCraw, William. Political Sponsorship of the Arts: Sub-
       sidization and Censorship of Motion Pictures and the Per-
       forming Arts by the Italian National Government, 1943-
       1962. Stanford University: Ph.D., 1966. 398 pp.

1643   Rondi, Gian Luigi. Italian Cinema Today, 1952-1965. New
       York: Hill and Wang, 1966. 279 pp.

1644   Armes, Roy. Patterns of Realism. South Brunswick, N.J.:
       A. S. Barnes, 1971. 226 pp.
       A study of Italian neo-realism.

1645   Leprohon, Pierre. The Italian Cinema. New York: Praeger,
       1972. 256 pp. Translated by Roger Greaves and Oliver
       Stallybrass.

6. Spain, Holland, and Belgium

1646 Boost, Charles. Dutch Art Today: Film. Amsterdam: Con-
       tact, ca. 1958. 100 pp.

1647 Vizcaino Casas, Fernando. Spanish Films. Madrid: Spanish
       Publications, 1965. 29 pp.

1648 Jerrems, Kay Green. The Idea Is Forbidden! A Report on
       the Motion Picture Art and Industry in Spain, With Empha-
       sis on the 1955-65 Period. Los Angeles: University of
       Southern California, 1967. 46 ℓ.
       Includes an interview with José Luis Font.

1649 Maelstaf, R. The Animated Cartoon Film in Belgium. Brus-
       sels: Ministry of Foreign Affairs and External Trade,
       1970. 100 pp.

1650 Bolen, Francis. Several Aspects of Belgian Cinema. Brus-
       sels: Ministeries van Cultuur, 1971. 22 pp.

7. Scandinavia

1651 Neergaard, Ebbe (ed.) Documentary in Denmark: One Hun-
       dred Films of Fact in War, Occupation, Liberation, Peace
       (1940-1948): A Catalog With Synopses. Copenhagen:
       Statens, 1948. 89 pp.

1652 Neergaard, Ebbe. Motion Pictures in Denmark: An Account
       of the Cinema Act of 1938 and Its Effects, up to 1948.
       Copenhagen: Central Film Library, 1948. 20 pp.

1653 Film Centre, London. The Film Industry in Six European
       Countries: A Detailed Study of the Film Industry in Den-
       mark as Compared with that in Norway, Sweden, Italy,
       France and the United Kingdom. Paris: UNESCO, 1950.
       156 pp.

1654 Hardy, Forsyth. Scandinavian Film. London: Falcon, 1952.
       62 pp. (Reprinted New York: Arno, 1972.)
       Material on Swedish, Danish, and Norwegian film.

1655 Idestam-Almquist, Bengt. Classics of the Swedish Cinema:
       The Stiller and Sjostrom Period. Stockholm: Swedish
       Institute, 1952. 48 pp.

1656 Waldekranz, Rune. Swedish Cinema. Stockholm: Swedish
       Institute, 1959. Unpaged. English version by Steve
       Hopkins.

1657   Lauritzen, Einar. Swedish Films. New York: Museum of
       Modern Art Film Library, 1962. 32 pp.

1658   Waldekranz, Rune. Modern Swedish Film. Stockholm:
       Swedish Institute for Cultural Relations with Foreign
       Countries, 1962. 19 pp.

1659   Neergaard, Ebbe. The Story of Danish Film. Copenhagen:
       Danish Institute, ca. 1963. 119 pp. Translated by Elsa
       Gress.

1660   Waldekranz, Rune. Psychological Realism: A Literary Tra-
       dition in Swedish Films. Stockholm: Swedish Institute
       for Cultural Relations with Foreign Countries, 1965. 15 pp.

1661   Cowie, Peter. Swedish Cinema. New York: A. S. Barnes,
       1966. 224 pp. (Revised as Sweden I and Sweden II, 1970,
       224 and 256 pp.)

1662   Furhammar, Leif and Lauritzen, Bertil. Film in Sweden.
       Stockholm: Swedish Institute, 1967. 36 pp.

1663   The Cinema in Denmark. Copenhagen: Danish Government
       Film Foundation, 1970. 37 pp.

1664   Sundgren, Nils Petter. The New Swedish Cinema. Stockholm:
       Swedish Institute for Cultural Relations with Foreign Coun-
       tries, 1970. 57 pp. Translated by Keith Bradfield.
       Concentrates on Swedish cinema of the sixties.

1665   Hillier, Jim (ed.) New Cinema in Finland. London: British
       Film Institute, 1972. 43 pp.

1666   Bergsten, Bebe. The Great Dane and the Great Northern Film
       Company. Los Angeles: Locare Research Group, 1973.
       116 pp.
       Material on Ole Olsen and the Nordisk Film Company.

1667   Hillier, Jim (ed.) Cinema in Finland: An Introduction. Lon-
       don: British Film Institute, 1975. 67 pp.

                    8. Eastern Europe

1668   Czechoslovak Ministry of Information. The Czechoslovak
       Nationalized Film Industry. Prague: Czechoslovak Minis-
       try of Information, 1947. 63 pp.

1669   Hungarian Film Producing Company. The Hungarian Film in
       Pictures. Budapest: Hungarian Film Producing Company,
       ca. 1949. 55 pp.

1670   Komitet za Kinematografia. Bulgarian Cinematography.
       Edited by Nikola Spirov. Sofia: Bulgarian National Com-
       mittee for Cinematography, 1953. Unpaged. Translated
       by Alexander Rizov.
       Primarily photographs.

1671   Grodzicki, August and Merz, Irena. Ten Years of People's
       Poland: Theatre, Film. Warsaw: Polonia, 1955. 61 pp.

1672   Kowalski, Tadeusz (ed.) Polski Plakat Filmowy/The Polish
       Film Poster. Warsaw: Filmowa Agencja Wydawnicza,
       1957. 141 pp.
       Primarily illustrations, with multi-lingual introduction.

1673   Yugoslav Institute of Journalism. Press, Radio, Television,
       Film in Yugoslavia. Belgrad: Yugoslav Institute of
       Journalism, 1961. 131 pp.

1674   Banaszkiewicz, Wladyslaw and others. Contemporary Polish
       Cinematography. Edited by Jerzy Chocilowski. Warsaw:
       Polonia, 1962. 173 pp.
       Surveys post-war Polish cinema.

1675   Popescu Gopo, Ion. All About Films. Bucharest: Meridiane,
       1963. 73 pp.
       Includes material on Rumanian cinema.

1676   Zvonicek, Stanislav (ed.) Modern Czechoslovak Film, 1945-
       1965. Prague: Artia, 1965. Unpaged. Translated by
       Alice Denesova.
       Contributions by Jaroslav Bocek and others.

1677   Canadian Film Archives. New Face of the Czechoslovak
       Cinema. Ottawa: Canadian Film Institute, 1966. 20 pp.

1678   Haller, Robert. Film Against the State: Polish Motion Pic-
       tures From 1956 to 1961. Cambridge Springs, Pa.:
       Alliance College Polish Club, ca. 1966. Unpaged.

1679   Broz, Jaroslav. The Path of Fame of the Czechoslovak Film:
       A Short Outline of Its History From the Early Beginning
       to the Stream of Recent International Successes. Prague:
       Ceskoslovensky Filmexport, 1967. 111 pp.

1680   Nemeskurty, Istvan. Word and Image: History of the Hun-
       garian Cinema. Budapest: Corvina, 1968. 246 pp.

1681   Zalman, Jan. Films and Film-Makers in Czechoslovakia.
       Prague: Orbis, 1968. 99 pp.

1682   Grzelecki, Stanislaw. Twenty Years of Polish Cinema, Film
       1947-1967. Warsaw: Art and Film, 1969. 152 pp.

1683 Racheva, Maria. Present Day Bulgarian Cinema. Sofia: Sofia Press, 1969. 153 pp. Translated by Liliana Vesselinova.

1684 Zvonicek, Stanislav. 25 Years of Czechoslovak Socialist Cinematography and Its Prospects, 1945-1970. Prague: Czech Film Institute, 1970. 58 pp. Translated by Milena Kingham and Eva Stichova.

1685 Dewey, Langdon. Outline of Czechoslovakian Cinema. London: Informatics, 1971. 122 pp.

1686 Skvorecky, Josef. All the Bright Young Men and Women: A Personal History of the Czech Cinema. Toronto: Peter Martin, 1971. 280 pp. Translated by Michael Schonberg.

1687 Whyte, Alistair. New Cinema in Eastern Europe. New York: Dutton, 1971. 159 pp.

1688 Holloway, Ronald. Z Is for Zagreb. South Brunswick, N.J.: A. S. Barnes, 1972. 127 pp.
Yugoslavian cartoon production.

1689 Wittek, Jerzy (ed.) Polish Film. Warsaw: Ministry of Culture and Art, 1972. 107 pp.
Essay by Stanislaw Grzelecki plus credits, synopsis and discussion of over 30 films.

1690 Fuksiewicz, Jacek. Polish Cinema. Warsaw: Interpress, 1973. 166 pp.

1691 Liehm, Antonin J. Closely Watched Films: The Czechoslovak Experience. White Plains, N.Y.: International Arts and Sciences, 1974. 485 pp.
Primarily background and interviews of Czechoslovak producers and directors; for a list of names, see entry 3789.

1692 Stoil, Michael Jon. Cinema Beyond the Danube: The Camera and Politics. Metuchen, N.J.: Scarecrow, 1974. 198 pp.

F. ASIA

1. Japan

1693 U. S. Office of Strategic Services, Research and Analysis
      Branch. Japanese Films: A Phase of Psychological War-
      fare; An Analysis of the Themes, Psychological Content,
      Technical Quality, and Propaganda Value of Twenty Recent
      Japanese Films. Washington, D. C.: U. S. Office of Stra-
      tegic Services, 1944. 19 pp.

1694 Anderson, Joseph L. and Richie, Donald. The Japanese Film:
      Art and Industry. Rutland, Vermont: Charles Tuttle,
      1959. 456 pp. (Also New York: Grove, 1960.)

1695 Richie, Donald. Japanese Movies. Tokyo: Japan Travel
      Bureau, 1961. 198 pp. (Revised as Japanese Cinema:
      Film Style and National Character, Garden City, N. Y. :
      Doubleday, 1971, 261 pp.)

1696 Richie, Donald. The Japanese Movie: An Illustrated History.
      Tokyo: Kodansha International, distributed Rutland, Ver-
      mont: Japan Publications, 1966. 200 pp.

1697 Small, Edward. Japanese Animated Film: A Study of Nar-
      rative, Intellectual Montage and Metamorphosis Structures
      for Semiotic Unit Sequencing. University of Iowa: Ph. D. ,
      1972. 407 pp.

1698 Tucker, Richard N. Japan: Film Image. London: Studio
      Vista, 1973. 144 pp.

1699 Mellen, Joan. Voices From the Japanese Cinema. New York:
      Liveright, 1975. 295 pp.
          Interviews with filmmakers; for list of names, see
      entry 3811.

2. India and Pakistan

1700   Patel, Jagannath J.   Possibilities of Manufacture of Talkie
       Equipment in India.   Bombay: n.p., 1945.   8 pp.

1701   Indian Film Industry's Mission to Europe and America.   Re-
       port of the Mission, Sent by the Indian Film Industry,
       with the Approval and Support of the Government of India,
       to Study the Latest Developments in the Application and
       Manufacturing Sides of the Film Industry Abroad, July-
       December, 1945.   Bombay: Hirlekar, ca. 1946.   84 pp.

1702   Booch, S. H.   Film Industry in India.   New Delhi: India
       Information Services, ca. 1950.   32 pp.

1703   Shah, Pauna.   The Indian Film.   Bombay: Motion Picture
       Society of India, 1950.   290 pp.

1704   Honigmann, John J. and Van Doorslaer, Marguerite.   Some
       Themes from Indian Film Reviews.   Chapel Hill: Uni-
       versity of North Carolina, Institute for Research in Social
       Science, 1955.   28 ℓ.

1705   Ray, Ram Mohan (ed.)   Film Seminar Report, 1955.   New
       Delhi: Sangeet Natak Akadami, 1956.   271 pp.

1706   Jain, Rikhab Dass.   The Economic Aspects of the Film In-
       dustry in India.   Delhi: Atma Ram, 1960.   28, 327 pp.

1707   Film Fact Finding Committee of Pakistan.   Report of the
       Film Fact Finding Committee, Govt. of Pakistan, Ministry
       of Industries, April 1960-April 1961.   Karachi: Manager
       of Publications, 1962.   410 pp.
       Detailed description of Pakistan film industry.

1708   Barnouw, Erik and Krishnaswamy, S.   Indian Film.   New
       York: Columbia University Press, 1963.   301 pp.

1709   Goyal, Trishla.   The Marketing of Films.   Calcutta: Inter-
       trade, ca. 1966.   545 pp.

1710   Kabir, Alamgir.   The Cinema in Pakistan.   Dacca: Sandhani,
       1969.   194 pp.

1711   Gaur, Madan.   Other Side of the Coin: An Intimate Study
       of Indian Film Industry.   Bombay: Trimurti Prakashan,
       distributed Delhi: Universal Book Service, 1973.   347 pp.

1712   Roberge, Gaston.   Chitra Bani: A Book on Film Appreciation.
       Calcutta: Chitra Bani, 1974.   274 pp.

1713   Rangoonwalla, Firoze.   75 Years of Indian Cinema.   New
       Delhi: Indian Book Company, 1975.   168 pp.

1714   Sarkar, Kobita.   Indian Cinema To-Day: An Analysis.   New
       Delhi: Sterling, 1975.   167 pp.

3.   China and Southeast Asia

1715   Salumbides, Vicente.   Motion Pictures in the Philippines.
       Manila: n. p. , 1952.   144, 31, 62 pp.

1716   Eberhard, Wolfram.   The Chinese Silver Screen: Hong Kong
       and Taiwanese Motion Pictures in the 1960's.   Taipei:
       Orient Cultural Service, 1972.   241 pp.

1717   Leyda, Jay.   Dianying: Electric Shadows, An Account of
       Films and the Film Audience in China.   Cambridge,
       Mass. : M. I. T. Press, 1972.   515 pp.

G. AFRICA AND THE MIDDLE EAST

1718 Gutsche, Thelma. The History and Social Significance of Mo-
      tion Pictures in South Africa, 1895-1940. (Originally Uni-
      versity of Cape Town: Dissertation, 1946.) Cape Town:
      Timmins, 1972. 404 pp.

1719 Morton-Williams, P. Cinema in Rural Nigeria: A Field
      Study of the Impact of Fundamental-Education Films on
      Rural Audiences in Nigeria. Lagos(?): Federal Informa-
      tion Service, ca. 1955. 195 pp.

1720 Arab Cinema and Culture: Round Table Conferences Under
      the Auspices and with the Participation of the UNESCO,
      Beirut, October 1963. Beirut: Arab Film and Television
      Centre, 1965. 178 pp.

1721 Arab Cinema and Culture: Round Table Conferences Under
      the Auspices and with the Participation of the UNESCO,
      Beirut, October 1964. Beirut: Arab Film and Television
      Centre, 1965. 188 pp.

1722 Landau, Jacob M. Studies in the Arab Theater and Cinema.
      Philadelphia: University of Pennsylvania Press, 1958.
      290 pp.

1723 Sadoul, Georges (ed.) The Cinema in the Arab Countries:
      Anthology Prepared for UNESCO. Beirut: Inter-Arab
      Centre of Cinema and Television, 1966. 291 pp.

1724 Kahn, M. An Introduction to the Egyptian Cinema. London:
      Informatics, 1969. 93 pp.
            General survey, with emphasis on the work of Salah
      Abu Saif, Youssef Shahin, Hussein Kamal, and Omar
      Sharif.

H. LATIN AMERICA

1725 Botting, David C. , Jr. History of the Motion Picture in
      Latin America. University of Chicago: Ph. D. , 1950.
      227 pp.

1726 Koenigil, Mark. Movies in Society: Sex, Crime and Censor-
      ship. New York: Speller, 1962. 214 pp.
      Includes an appendix on Brazilian cinema.

1727 Nubila, Domingo di. History of the Argentine Cinema: A
      Summary. Olivos: Cruz de Malta, ca. 1962. 16 pp.

1728 Cinema of the Third World. Auckland: Auckland University
      Students' Association, 1972. 76 pp.
      Includes material on films from Argentina, Chile,
      and Cuba.

1729 Myerson, Michael (ed.) Memories of Underdevelopment: The
      Revolutionary Films of Cuba. New York: Grossman, 1973.
      214 pp.

1730 Burns, E. Bradford (ed.) The Visual Dimensions of Latin
      American Social History: Student Critiques of Eight
      Major Latin American Films. Los Angeles: n. p. , ca.
      1974.

1731 Burns, E. Bradford. Latin American Cinema: Film and
      History. Los Angeles: UCLA Latin American Center,
      1975. 137 pp.

I.   AUSTRALIA AND NEW ZEALAND

1732   Mirams, Gordon.   Speaking Candidly: Films and People in
       New Zealand.   Hamilton: Paul's Book Arcade, 1945.
       241 pp.

1733   Porter, Hal.   Stars of the Australian Stage and Screen.
       Adelaide: Rigby, 1965.   304 pp.
           Also includes a title listing of Australian films.

1734   Baxter, John.   The Australian Cinema.   Sydney: Pacific
       Books, 1970.   118 pp.

1735   Reade, Eric.   Australian Silent Films: A Pictorial History
       of Silent Films from 1896 to 1929.   Melbourne: Lans-
       downe, 1970.   192 pp.

1736   Cinema of the Third World.   Auckland: Auckland University
       Students' Association, 1972.   76 pp.
           Includes material on cinema in New Zealand.

1737   Reade, Eric.   The Talkies Era: A Pictorial History of
       Australian Sound Film Making, 1930-1960.   Melbourne:
       Lansdowne, 1972.   127 pp.

PART V

FILM CLASSIFICATIONS

INTRODUCTION

This major category of film classifications contains all
those books whose material is organized according to a particular
type of film such as the documentary, the animated film, the western, etc. The concept of film classification is a problematic one
since often books dealing with the same kind of film do not share
methodologies. For instance, some books on the western may be
historical surveys, some may propose a western aesthetic or analyze the sociological meaning of the western myth, while others
may do no more than present a series of western movie stills. In
an important sense this classification category can be seen as a
bridge between history, on one hand, and theory and criticism, on
the other. Even an historical or pictorial work dealing with a film
classification implicitly transforms itself, by its very classification
organization, into a work of criticism.

The reader should note that the classification categories
herein are not mutually exclusive, and should consult all the sections which seem to have a relevance. For instance, many of the
"B" films of the forties are westerns; many of the most famous
serials are science-fiction; many documentaries were in their time
considered experimental, etc. In general, books have been classified only in the one section we have judged to be the most appropriate.

For other material relating to genres and film classifications, the reader should also consult many of the texts in the history
category, Part IV, particularly section C, the world cinema surveys;
section D-1, United States film history; and section D-2, histories
of American studios. A book on Warner Brothers, for example,
would have much material on gangster films; a book on MGM would
likewise have material on musicals; and almost every general history
text has sections on documentary and experimental film. The reader
should also consult Part VIII, section D, anthologies of theory and
criticism, and Part IX, section B, reflection and influence, for other
works which include discussion relevant to genre concepts.

A. DOCUMENTARY

This category contains specifically those film books which deal with the various documentary movements. The reader should also consult books in the experimental section, Part V, section B, for information on recent documentary trends in new American cinema. For books dealing with the war film genre (which includes some documentary), see Part V, section C-7. For books dealing with the technique of documentary film production, see Part II, section E, special filmmaking approaches. Finally, since the documentary movement has been particularly strong in Great Britain, consult many of the works in Part IV, section E-1, British history.

1738 Rotha, Paul. Documentary Film. (Originally published 1936. Revised 1939.) Third revised edition published as Documentary Film: The Use of the Film Medium to Interpret Creatively and in Social Terms the Life of the People as It Exists in Reality, by Paul Rotha with Sinclair Road and Richard Griffith. London: Faber and Faber, 1952. 412 pp. (Reprinted New York: Hastings, 1970.)

1739 Kracauer, Siegfried. The Conquest of Europe on the Screen: The Nazi Newsreel, 1939-1940. Washington, D.C.: Library of Congress, Experimental Division for the Study of War-Time Communications, 1943. 33 pp.

1740 Writers' Congress, University of California at Los Angeles. Writers' Congress: The Proceedings of the Conference Held in October 1943 Under the Sponsorship of the Hollywood Writers' Mobilization and the University of California. Berkeley: University of California Press, 1944. 663 pp.
        Includes material on the documentary film, with contributions by Arthur Mayer, Joris Ivens, Kenneth Macgowan, James Wong Howe, and others.

1741 Alexander, Donald. The Documentary Film. London: British Film Institute, 1945. 9 pp.

1742 Editors of Look. Movie Lot to Beachhead: The Motion Pic-

ture Goes to War and Prepares for the Future. Garden
City, N. Y.: Doubleday, Doran, 1945. 291 pp.
    Includes material on newsreel films, training films,
combat cinematographers, and post-war possibilities for
information films; many photographs.

1743 Wilson, Norman. Presenting Scotland: A Film Survey.
      Edinburgh: Edinburgh Film Guild, 1945. 36 pp.
          Includes an account of the Scottish documentary film
      movement.

1744 Benoit-Levy, Jean. The Art of the Motion Picture. New
      York: Coward-McCann, 1946. 263 pp. Translated by
      Theodore R. Jaeckel. (Reprinted New York: Arno,
      1970.)
          Includes material on documentary and information
      films, particularly their use in education.

1745 The Arts Inquiry. The Factual Film: A Survey Sponsored
      by the Dartington Hall Trustees, Published on Behalf of
      the Arts Enquiry by PEP (Political and Economic Plan-
      ning). London, New York: Oxford University Press,
      1947. 260 pp.
          Primarily about British documentary.

1746 Grierson, John. Grierson on Documentary. Edited by For-
      syth Hardy. New York: Harcourt, Brace, 1947. 324 pp.
      (Revised Berkeley: University of California Press, 1966.
      411 pp.)
          Revised edition includes new material by Grierson.

1747 The Public's Progress. London: Contact, 1947. 104 pp.
          Includes brief essays on Grierson and the British docu-
      mentary by Basil Wright and Paul Rotha.

1748 Wilson, Norman (ed.) Documentary 47. Edinburgh: Albyn,
      1947. 36 pp.
          With contributions by John Grierson, Forsyth Hardy,
      Basil Wright, and others; published on the occasion of the
      First International Festival of Documentary.

1749 Losey, Mary. A Report on the Outlook for the Profitable
      Production of Documentary Films for the Non-Theatrical
      Market, for the Sugar Research Foundation. New York:
      Film Program Services, 1948. 50 pp.

1750 Wilson, Norman (ed.) Documentary 48. Edinburgh; Albyn,
      1948. 36 pp.
          With contributions by Basil Wright, Roger Manvell,
      Forsyth Hardy, Catherine De La Roche, George W.
      Stoney, and others; published on the occasion of the
      Second International Festival of Documentary Films.

1751 Documentary 49, Film Festival. Edinburgh: Albyn, 1949.
36 pp.
With contributions by John Grierson, Roger Manvell,
Lotte Eisner, Forsyth Hardy, Paul Rotha; published on
the occasion of the Third International Festival of Documentary Films.

1752 Greenhill, Leslie P. and Tyo, John. Instructional Film Production, Utilization, and Research in Great Britain,
Canada, and Australia. Port Washington, N. Y.: Office
of Naval Research, Special Devices Center, 1949. 27 ℓ.

1753 Waldron, Gloria with Starr, Cecile. The Information Film:
A Report of the Public Library Inquiry. New York:
Columbia University Press, 1949. 281 pp.
Discusses the educational use and distribution of the
documentary film.

1754 Starr, Cecile (ed.) Ideas on Film: A Handbook for the
16mm Film User. New York: Funk and Wagnalls, 1951.
251 pp. (Reprinted Freeport, N. Y.: Books for Libraries,
1971.)
Contains material relating to documentary; contributors
include Julien Bryan, Willard Van Dyke, Mary Losey,
Kurtz Myers, Pearl S. Buck, Arthur L. Mayer, among
others.

1755 Baechlin, Peter and Muller-Strauss, Maurice. Newsreels
Across the World. Paris: UNESCO, 1952. 100 pp.

1756 Buchanan, Donald William. Documentary and Educational
Films in Canada, 1935-1950: A Survey of Problems and
Achievements. Ottawa: Canadian Film Institute, 1952.
24 pp.

1757 International Edinburgh Film Festival. New Directions in
Documentary: Report of the International Conference Held
at Edinburgh, August 25-26, 1952. Edinburgh: Film
House, 1952. 41 pp.

1758 Wagner, Robert Walter. Design in the Educational Film: An
Analysis of the Production Elements in Twenty-One Widely
Used Non-Theatrical Motion Pictures. Ohio State Uni-
versity: Ph. D., 1953. 294 pp.

1759 Rotha, Paul. Rotha on the Film: A Selection of Writings
About the Cinema. Fairlawn, N. J.: Essential Books,
1958. 338 pp.
Material on the British film industry, documentary
film, and various individual films.

1760 Wisconsin Film Society. Toward an Understanding of

<u>Documentary</u>.   Madison, Wisc.:   Wisconsin Film Society,
1958.   23 pp.
    Anthology of brief essays on documentary, plus notes
on 23 films.

1761   Couffer, Jack.   <u>Song of Wild Laughter</u>.   New York: Simon
and Schuster, 1963.   190 pp.
    Material on the making of Disney wildlife films.

1762   Leyda, Jay.   <u>Films Beget Films</u>.   New York: Hill and Wang,
1964.   176 pp.
    Study of the compilation film.

1763   Bluem, A. William.   <u>Documentary in American Television:
Form, Function, Method</u>.   New York: Hastings, 1965.
311 pp.

1764   Swallow, Norman.   <u>Factual Television</u>.   New York: Hastings,
1966.   228 pp.
    Includes sections discussing the current affairs docu-
mentary and the personal documentary.

1765   Knight, Derrick and Porter, Vincent.   <u>A Long Look at Short
Films: An A. C. T. T. Report on the Short Entertainment
and Factual Film</u>.   New York: Association of Cinematograph, Television and Allied Technicians in association
with Pergamon, 1967.   185 pp.

1766   The Rank Organization.   <u>No Case for Compulsion</u>.   London:
n. p., 1967.   20 pp.
    Rank Organization's comment on the A. C. T. T. re-
port, <u>A Long Look at Short Films</u>; see citation above.

1767   British Universities' Film Council.   <u>Film and the Historian</u>.
London: British Universities' Film Council, 1968.   50 pp.
    Record of a conference about the use of film as his-
torical document.

1768   Snyder, Robert L.   <u>Pare Lorentz and the Documentary Film</u>.
Norman: University of Oklahoma Press, 1968.   232 pp.
    Includes material on the establishment of the U. S.
Film Service.

1769   Issari, Mohammad Ali.   <u>Cinema Verité</u>.   East Lansing:
Michigan State University, 1971.   208 pp.

1770   Jacobs, Lewis (ed.)   <u>The Documentary Tradition: From
Nanook to Woodstock</u>.   New York: Hopkinson and Blake,
1971.   530 pp.
    Essays by over 90 critics and major figures in the
documentary movement.

1771   Levin, G. Roy.   <u>Documentary Explorations: 15 Interviews</u>

With Film-Makers. Garden City, N.Y.: Doubleday, 1971.
420 pp.
For list of names, see entry 3738.

1772 Rosenthal, Alan. The New Documentary in Action: A Casebook in Film-Making. Berkeley: University of California
Press, 1971. 287 pp.
Interviews with contemporary filmmakers; for list of
names, see entry 3743.

1773 Fielding, Raymond. The American Newsreel, 1911-1967.
Norman: University of Oklahoma Press, 1972. 392 pp.

1774 Lovell, Alan and Hillier, Jim. Studies in Documentary.
New York: Viking, 1972. 176 pp.
Primarily about British documentary, with sections
on John Grierson, Humphrey Jennings, and Free Cinema.

1775 Barsam, Richard Meran. Nonfiction Film: A Critical History.
New York: Dutton, 1973. 332 pp.

1776 MacCann, Richard Dyer. The People's Films: A Political
History of U.S. Government Motion Pictures. New York:
Hastings, 1973. 238 pp.

1777 Marcorelles, Louis with Rouzet-Albagli, Nicole. Living
Cinema: New Directions in Contemporary Film-Making.
New York: Praeger, 1973. 155 pp. Translated by Isa-
bel Quigley.
Discusses direct cinema, Brazil's cinema novo, the
American underground, and "concrete cinema."

1778 Rotha, Paul. Documentary Diary: An Informal History of
the British Documentary Film, 1928-1939. New York:
Hill and Wang, 1973. 305 pp.

1779 Barnouw, Erik. Documentary: A History of the Non-Fiction
Film. New York: Oxford University Press, 1974. 332 pp.

1780 Edmonds, Robert. About Documentary: Anthropology on
Film, A Philosophy of People and Art. Dayton, Ohio:
Pflaum, 1974. 115 pp.

1781 Mamber, Stephen. Cinema Verite in America: Studies in Un-
controlled Documentary. Cambridge, Mass.: M.I.T.
Press, 1974. 288 pp.
Includes studies of Robert Drew Associates, the Mays-
les Brothers, D. A. Pennebaker, Richard Leacock, and
Frederick Wiseman.

1782 Hockings, Paul (ed.) Principles of Visual Anthropology. The
Hague: Mouton, distributed by Aldine, Chicago, 1975.
521 pp.

Material on the history, techniques, and uses of the ethnographic film; contributions by Jean-Dominique Lajoux, Richard Leacock, John Marshall and Emilie de Brigard, Jean Rouch, Colin Young, and others.

1783 Sussex, Elizabeth. The Rise and Fall of British Documentary: The Story of the Film Movement Founded by John Grierson. Berkeley: University of California Press, 1975. 219 pp.

Selectively edited interviews; for list of names, see entry 3818.

B. EXPERIMENTAL

1784 Jacobs, Lewis. The Rise of the American Film: A Critical
      History. (Originally published 1939.) Revised and en-
      larged New York: Teachers College Press, 1968.   631 pp.
      Revised edition includes essay entitled "Experimental
      Cinema in America, 1921-1947. "

1785 Stauffacher, Frank (ed.) Art In Cinema: A Symposium on
      the Avant-Garde Film, Together With Program Notes and
      References for Series One of Art In Cinema. San Fran-
      cisco: Art in Cinema Society, San Francisco Museum of
      Art, 1947.   104 pp.   (Reprinted New York: Arno, 1968.)
      Contributions by Henry Miller, Hans Richter, Elie
      Faure, Man Ray, Luis Buñuel, John and James Whitney,
      Erich Pommer, Oskar Fischinger, Maya Deren, George
      Leite, and Paul Velguth.

1786 Manvell, Roger (ed.) Experiment In the Film. London:
      Grey Walls, 1949.   285 pp.   (Reprinted New York: Arno,
      1970.)
      Discusses experiment within various national main-
      stream cinemas as well as the avant-garde; contributions
      by Lewis Jacobs, Hans Richter, Edgar Anstey, and others.

1787 Young, Colin. The American Experimental Film in the Last
      Decade. Paris: UNESCO, 1964.   33 pp.

1788 Gruen, John. The New Bohemia: The Combine Generation.
      New York: Shorecrest, 1966.   183 pp.
      Includes a chapter on the work of underground film-
      makers in New York's East Village.

1789 Barrios, Gregg (ed.) Harbinger. Austin, Texas: Cassandra,
      1967.   38 pp.
      The first and apparently only issue of a periodical
      focusing on the avant-garde; includes articles on Bruce
      Baillie, a letter from Stan Brakhage, and an interview
      with Andy Warhol.

1790 Battcock, Gregory (ed.) The New American Cinema: A
      Critical Anthology. New York: Dutton, 1967.   256 pp.

Articles by or about Jonas Mekas, Ken Kelman, Tay-
lor Mead, Andrew Sarris, Rudolf Arnheim, Parker Tyler,
Annette Michelson, Amos Vogel, Marcel Duchamp, P.
Adams Sitney, Harry Smith, Stan Vanderbeek, Gregory
Markopoulos, Dwight MacDonald, Susan Sontag, Jack Smith,
Bruce Baillie, Andy Warhol, and others.

1791 Lawder, Standish Dyer. Structuralism and Movement in Experimental Film and Modern Art, 1896-1925. Yale University: Ph.D., 1967. 419 pp.

1792 Renan, Sheldon. An Introduction to the American Underground
Film. New York: Dutton, 1967. 318 pp.

1793 Currie, Hector and Porte, Michael (eds.) Cinema Now: Stan
Brakhage, John Cage, Jonas Mekas, Stan Vanderbeek.
Cincinnati, Ohio: University of Cincinnati, Perspectives
on American Underground Film, 1968. 28 pp.
Transcript of a symposium.

1794 Tyler, Parker. The Underground Film: A Critical History.
New York: Grove, 1969. 249 pp.

1795 Cox, William. American Limited Audience Cinema as an Art
Form. Ohio University: Ph.D., 1970. 429 pp.
Concentrates on American independent films of the
sixties.

1796 Sitney, P. Adams (ed.) Film Culture Reader. New York:
Praeger, 1970. 438 pp.
Selection of articles, primarily about experimental
film, from magazine titled Film Culture; see entry 4600.

1797 Youngblood, Gene. Expanded Cinema. Introduction by R.
Buckminster Fuller. New York: Dutton, 1970. 432 pp.
Explores the theoretical ramifications of film's new
technological possibilities.

1798 Curtis, David. Experimental Cinema. New York: Universe,
1971. 168 pp.

1799 Mekas, Jonas. Movie Journal: The Rise of the New American Cinema, 1959-1971. New York: Macmillan, 1972.
434 pp.

1800 Wheeler, Dennis (ed.) Form and Structure in Recent Film.
Vancouver: Vancouver Art Gallery/Talonbooks, 1972.
Approx. 100 pp.
Articles by and about Annette Michelson, Hollis Framp-
ton, Stan Brakhage, Barry Gerson, Ken Jacobs, George
Landow, David Rimmer, Paul Sharits, Michael Snow, Joyce
Wieland, and others.

1801 Weightman, John. The Concept of the Avant-Garde: Explora-
       tions in Modernism. LaSalle, Ill.: Library Press, 1973.
       323 pp.
            Includes articles on Don Levy's HEROSTRATUS,
       Pasolini's THEOREM, and Andy Warhol's FLESH and
       TRASH, as well as several mainstream films of the late
       sixties and early seventies.

1802 Michelson, Annette (ed.) New Forms in Film. Montreux,
       Switzerland: n.p., 1974. 117 pp.
            Material by and about Stan Brakhage, Bruce Baillie,
       P. Adams Sitney, Robert Breer, Hollis Frampton, Michael
       Snow, Ernie Gehr, Ken Jacobs, Bill Simon, Peter Kubelka,
       George Landow, Jonas Mekas, Yvonne Rainer, Paul Sharits,
       Harry Smith, Joyce Wieland, and others.

1803 Sitney, P. Adams. Visionary Film: The American Avant-
       Garde. New York: Oxford University Press, 1974.
       452 pp.

1804 Vogel, Amos. Film as a Subversive Art. New York: Ran-
       dom, 1974. 336 pp.
            Discusses aesthetic, sexual, and ideological forms of
       subversion in both mainstream and experimental films.

1805 Dwoskin, Stephen. Film Is: The International Free Cinema.
       Woodstock, N.Y.: Overlook, 1975. 268 pp.
            Historical background of the avant-garde, plus exten-
       sive material on individual films and filmmakers.

1806 Lawder, Standish D. The Cubist Cinema. New York: New
       York University Press, 1975. 265 pp.
            Includes material on Hans Richter, Viking Eggeling,
       Fernand Leger, Walter Ruttmann, Blaise Cendrars, Abel
       Gance, Marcel L'Herbier, and others.

C. GENRES

This classification includes those books which deal primarily with popular American genres. There are currently few books dealing explicitly with genre as a theoretical and critical concept, the main exception being Stuart Kaminsky's American Film Genres, which can be found both in Part VIII, section A, individual theorists, and in Part V, section C-10. The reader might also consult the bibliography in John G. Cawelti's Adventure, Mystery, and Romance: Formula Stories as Art and Popular Culture (Chicago: University of Chicago Press, 1976). The final generic subcategory, Part V, section C-10, includes those books about miscellaneous genres such as the religious film, the kung-fu film, the romantic film, etc., as well as those books which organize their material according to a particular concept or image such as film violence or film in which automobiles or trains are prominent. For filmographic information on various genres, see Section I-B-4, Subject Filmographies.

1. Comedy

1807 Treadwell, Bill. 50 Years of American Comedy. New York: Exposition, 1951. 241 pp.

1808 Montgomery, John. Comedy Films, 1894-1954. London: Allen and Unwin, 1954. 337 pp. (Revised 1968, 286 pp.)

1809 Allen, Steve. The Funny Men. New York: Simon and Schuster, 1956. 280 pp.
Discusses the nature of comedy, plus chapters on 15 comedians; for list of names, see entry 3652.

1810 Cahn, William. The Laugh Makers: A Pictorial History of American Comedians. New York: Putnam, 1957. 192 pp. (Revised as A Pictorial History of the Great Comedians, New York: Grosset and Dunlap, 1970, 221 pp.)

1811 Blistein, Elmer M. Comedy in Action. Durham, N.C.: Duke University Press, 1964. 146 pp.
Study of comedy in various media, including film.

1812 Lahue, Kalton C. World of Laughter: The Motion Picture
      Comedy Short, 1910-1930. Norman: University of Okla-
      homa Press, 1966. 240 pp. (Reprinted 1972.)

1813 Lahue, Kalton C. and Brewer, Terry. Kops and Custards:
      The Legend of Keystone Films. Norman: University of
      Oklahoma Press, 1968. 177 pp.

1814 McCaffrey, Donald W. Four Great Comedians: Chaplin, Lloyd,
      Keaton, Langdon. New York: A. S. Barnes, 1968. 175
      pp.

1815 Robinson, David. The Great Funnies: A History of Film
      Comedy. New York: Dutton, 1969. 160 pp.

1816 Wilde, Larry. The Great Comedians Talk About Comedy.
      New York: Citadel, 1969. 382 pp.
      Interview material; for list of names, see entry 3711.

1817 Durgnat, Raymond. The Crazy Mirror: Hollywood Comedy
      and the American Image. New York: Horizon, 1970.
      280 pp.

1818 Lahue, Kalton C. Clown Princes and Court Jesters: Some
      Great Comics of the Silent Screen. South Brunswick,
      N.J.: A. S. Barnes, 1970. 406 pp.
      Material on careers of 50 comedians of the twenties.

1819 Maltin, Leonard. Movie Comedy Teams. New York: New
      American Library, 1970. 352 pp.
      For list of teams discussed, see entry 3726.

1820 Lewis, Jerry. The Total Film-Maker. New York: Random,
      1971. 208 pp.
      Includes a short section on comedians and comic
      techniques.

1821 Maltin, Leonard. The Great Movie Shorts. New York:
      Crown, 1972. 236 pp.
      Includes material on many comedy figures; for list of
      names, see entry 3755.

1822 McCaffrey, Donald W. The Golden Age of Sound Comedy:
      Comic Figures and Comedians of the Thirties. South
      Brunswick, N.J.: A. S. Barnes, 1973. 208 pp.

1823 Manchel, Frank. Yesterday's Clowns: The Rise of Film
      Comedy. New York: Watts, 1973. 154 pp.

1824 Mast, Gerald. The Comic Mind: Comedy and the Movies.
      Indianapolis: Bobbs-Merill, 1973. 353 pp.

1825 Sennett, Ted. Lunatics and Lovers: A Tribute to the Giddy

and Glittering Era of the Screen's "Screwball" and Romantic Comedies. New Rochelle, N.Y.: Arlington, 1973.
368 pp.

1826 Jordon, Thomas H. The Anatomy of Cinematic Humor: With
      an Essay on the Marx Brothers. New York: Revisionist,
      1975. 164 pp.

1827 Kerr, Walter. The Silent Clowns. New York: Knopf, 1975.
      373 pp.

1828 Madden, David. Harlequin's Stick--Charlie's Cane: A Com-
      parative Study of Commedia Dell'Arte and Silent Slapstick
      Comedy. Bowling Green, Ohio: Bowling Green University
      Popular Press, 1975. 174 pp.

                        2. Western

1829 Adler, Bill with Reisner, Bob. Western on Wry. New York:
      Citadel, 1960. Unpaged.
          Primarily photographs of western films with humorous
      captions.

1830 Fenin, George N. and Everson, William K. The Western:
      From Silents to Cinerama. New York: Crown, 1962.
      362 pp. (Revised as The Western, From Silents to the
      Seventies, New York: Grossman, 1973. 396 pp.)

1831 Warshow, Robert. The Immediate Experience: Movies,
      Comics, Theatre, and Other Aspects of Popular Culture.
      Garden City, N.Y.: Doubleday, 1962. 282 pp. (Re-
      printed New York: Atheneum, 1970.)
          Includes a seminal essay on the western.

1832 Warman, Eric and Vallance, Tom (eds.) Westerns: A Pre-
      view Special. London: Golden Pleasure Books, 1964.
      152 pp.

1833 Barbour, Alan G. (ed.) The "B" Western. Kew Gardens,
      N.Y.: Screen Facts, 1966. 64 pp.
          Largely photographs.

1834 Carter, Donald. The Western. Ottawa: Ottawa Film So-
      ciety, 1966. 14 pp.

1835 Eyles, Allen. The Western: An Illustrated Guide. New
      York: A. S. Barnes, 1967. 183 pp. (Revised 1975,
      207 pp.)

1836 Everson, William K. A Pictorial History of the Western
      Film. New York: Citadel, 1969. 246 pp.

1837 Cawelti, John. The Six-Gun Mystique. Bowling Green, Ohio:
      Bowling Green University Popular Press, ca. 1970. 138
      pp.
           An interdisciplinary interpretation of popular artistic
      forms, utilizing the western in literature and film as
      primary example.

1838 Kitses, Jim. Horizons West: Anthony Mann, Budd Boetti-
      cher, Sam Peckinpah: Studies of Authorship Within the
      Western. Bloomington: Indiana University Press, 1970.
      176 pp.

1839 Lahue, Kalton C. Winners of the West: The Sagebrush
      Heroes of the Silent Screen. New York: A. S. Barnes,
      1970.   353 pp.

1840 Barbour, Alan G. The Thrill of It All. New York: Mac-
      millan, 1971.   201 pp.
           A pictorial history of the "B" western.

1841 Eyles, Allen. Westerns Film Album. London: Ian Allen,
      1971.   52 pp.

1842 Manchel, Frank. Cameras West. Englewood Cliffs, N. J.:
      Prentice-Hall, 1971.   150 pp.
           For the high school audience.

1843 Parkinson, Michael and Jeavons, Clyde. A Pictorial History
      of Westerns. London, New York: Hamlyn, 1972.   218 pp.

1844 Clapham, Walter C. Western Movies: The Story of the West
      on Screen. London: Octopus, 1974.   160 pp.

1845 French, Philip. Westerns: Aspects of a Movie Genre. New
      York: Viking, 1974.   176 pp.

1846 Maynard, Richard A. (ed.) The American West on Film:
      Myth and Reality. Rochelle Park, N. J.: Hayden, 1974.
      130 pp.

1847 Nachbar, Jack (ed.) Focus on the Western. Englewood
      Cliffs, N. J.: Prentice-Hall, 1974.   150 pp.
           Contributions by Robert Warshow, John Cawelti, Jim
      Kitses, and others.

1848 Place, J. A. The Western Films of John Ford. Secaucus,
      N. J.: Citadel, 1974.   246 pp.

1849 Calder, Jenni. There Must Be a Lone Ranger: The Ameri-
      can West in Film and in Reality. New York: Taplinger,
      1975.   241 pp.

1850 Cary, Diana Serra. The Hollywood Posse: The Story of a

Gallant Band of Horsemen Who Made Movie History.
Boston: Houghton Mifflin, 1975.   268 pp.
  Focuses on the lives of cowboy stuntmen and bit
players.

1851   Eyles, Allen. The Western. South Brunswick, N.J.: A. S.
Barnes, 1975.   207 pp.

1852   Simmons, Louis Garner. The Cinema of Sam Peckinpah and
the American Western: A Study of the Interrelationship
Between an Auteur/Director and the Genre in Which He
Works. Northwestern University: Ph.D. , 1975.   449 pp.

1853   Wright, Will. Sixguns and Society: A Structural Study of
the Western. Berkeley: University of California Press,
1975.   217 pp.

3.   Fantasy, Horror, and Science-Fiction

1854   Reisner, Robert George. The Brave Ghouls. Indianapolis:
Bobbs-Merill, 1960.   64 pp.
  Photographs from horror films with humorous captions.

1855   Ackerman, Forrest J. (ed.) The Best From Famous Monsters of Filmland. New York: Paperback Library, 1964.
162 pp.

1856   Ackerman, Forrest J. (ed.) Famous Monsters of Filmland
Strike Back. New York: Paperback Library, 1965.
162 pp.

1857   Ackerman, Forrest (ed.) Son of Famous Monsters of Filmland. New York: Paperback Library, 1965.   162 pp.

1858   Drake, Douglas. Horror! New York: Macmillan, 1966.
309 pp.

1859   Butler, Ivan. The Horror Film. New York: A. S. Barnes,
1967.   176 pp.   (Revised as Horror in the Cinema, 1970,
208 pp.)

1860   Clarens, Carlos. An Illustrated History of the Horror Films.
New York: Putnam, 1967.   256 pp.   (Also published as
Horror Movies: An Illustrated Survey, London: Secker
and Warburg, 1968, 264 pp.)

1861   Gifford, Denis. Movie Monsters. New York: Dutton, 1969.
159 pp.

1862   Baxter, John. Science Fiction in the Cinema. New York:
A. S. Barnes, 1970.   240 pp.

1863   Manchel, Frank. Terrors of the Screen. Englewood Cliffs,
          N.J.: Prentice-Hall, 1970. 122 pp.
          For the young reader.

1864   Eyles, Allen (ed.) Horror Film Album. London: Ian Allen,
          1971. 52 pp.

1865   Gifford, Denis. A Pictorial History of Horror Movies. New
          York: Hamlyn, 1973. 216 pp.

1866   Gifford, Denis. Science Fiction Film. New York: Dutton,
          1971. 160 pp.

1867   Haining, Peter (ed.) The Ghouls. New York: Stein and
          Day, 1971. 383 pp.
          Brief commentaries on 18 horror films followed by
          the original stories on which they were based.

1868   Aylesworth, Thomas G. Monsters From the Movies. Phila-
          delphia: Lippincott, 1972. 160 pp.

1869   Harryhausen, Ray. Film Fantasy Scrapbook. South Bruns-
          wick, N.J.: A. S. Barnes, 1972. 117 pp. (Revised
          1974, 142 pp.)
          Includes photographs and commentary on the author's
          special effects work in horror and fantasy films.

1870   McNally, Raymond and Florescu, Radu. In Search of Dracula:
          A True History of Dracula and Vampire Legends. Green-
          wich, Conn.: New York Graphic Society, 1972. 225 pp.

1871   Huss, Roy and Ross, T. J. (eds.) Focus on the Horror Film.
          Englewood Cliffs, N.J.: Prentice-Hall, 1972. 186 pp.
          Contributions by Curtis Harrington, Jack Kerouac,
          Raymond Durgnat, Stephen Farber, Manny Farber, Ray
          Bradbury, Brian Henderson, and others.

1872   Johnson, William (ed.) Focus on the Science Fiction Film.
          Englewood Cliffs, N.J.: Prentice-Hall, 1972. 182 pp.
          Contributions by Terry Ramsaye, Maurice Bessy,
          Thea von Harbou, Francois Truffaut, Robert Heinlein,
          Ado Kyrou, Herb A. Lightman, and others.

1873   Steinbrunner, Chris and Goldblatt, Burt. Cinema of the
          Fantastic. New York: Saturday Review Press, 1972.
          282 pp.
          Studies of 15 classic fantasy films from A TRIP TO
          THE MOON (1902) to FORBIDDEN PLANET (1956).

1874   Wolf, Leonard. A Dream of Dracula: In Search of the
          Living Dead. Boston: Little, Brown, 1972. 327 pp.
          Discussion of the vampire legend in various media,
          including film.

1875 Edelson, Edward. Great Monsters of the Movies.   Garden
      City, N.Y.: Doubleday, 1973. 101 pp.
      For the young reader.

1876 Glut, Donald F.   The Frankenstein Legend: A Tribute to
      Mary Shelley and Boris Karloff.   Metuchen, N.J.:
      Scarecrow, 1973.   372 pp.

1877 Pirie, David.   A Heritage of Horror: The English Gothic
      Cinema, 1946-1972.   London: Gordon Fraser, 1973.
      192 pp.
      Includes material on Hammer and Amicus studios,
      Terence Fisher, Don Sharp, John Gilling, Vernon Sewell,
      and Michael Reeves.

1878 Amelio, Ralph J. (ed.) Hal in the Classroom: Science Fic-
      tion Films. Dayton, Ohio: Pflaum, 1974.   153 pp.
      Contributions by William Johnson, Susan Sontag,
      William MacPherson, Stuart Kaminsky, Bernard Beck,
      R. C. Dale, and others.

1879 Barber, Dulan.   The Horrific World of Monsters.   London:
      Cavendish, 1974.   121 pp.

1880 Everson, William K.   Classics of the Horror Film.   Secau-
      cus, N.J.: Citadel, 1974.   247 pp.

1881 Eyles, Allen; Adkinson, Robert; and Fry, Nicholas.   The
      House of Horror: The Story of Hammer Films.   New
      York: Third Press, 1974.   126 pp.

1882 Frank, Alan G.   Horror Movies: Tales of Terror in the
      Cinema.   London: Octopus, 1974.   160 pp.

1883 Hutchinson, Tom.   Horror and Fantasy in the Cinema.   Lon-
      don: Studio Vista, 1974.   160 pp.

1884 Moss, Robert F.   Karloff and Company: The Horror Film.
      New York: Pyramid, 1974.   158 pp.

1885 Wolf, Leonard.   Monsters: Twenty Terrible and Wonderful
      Beasts From the Classic Dragon and Colossal Minotaur to
      King Kong and the Great Godzilla.   San Francisco: Straight
      Arrow, 1974.   127 pp.
      Also discusses Dracula and the Golem.

1886 Annan, David.   Ape: The Kingdom of Kong.   London: Lorri-
      mer, 1975.   95 pp.
      A study of apes in horror films.

1887 Annan, David.   Catastrophe: The End of the Cinema?   New
      York: Crown, 1975.   111 pp.

1888 Annan, David. Movie Fantastic: Beyond the Dream Machine.
      New York: Bounty, 1975. 132 pp. (Also published as
      Cinefantastic: Beyond the Dream Machine.)

1889 Aylesworth, Thomas G. Movie Monsters. Philadelphia: Lip-
      pincott, 1975. 79 pp.
          For the young reader.

1890 Beck, Calvin Thomas. Heroes of the Horrors. New York:
      Macmillan, 1975. 353 pp.
          Material on the careers of several horror film stars.

1891 Edelson, Edward. Visions of Tomorrow: Great Science
      Fiction From the Movies. Garden City, N.Y.: Double-
      day, 1975. 117 pp.
          For the young reader.

1892 Florescu, Radu with Barbour, Alan and Cazacu, Matei. In
      Search of Frankenstein. Boston: New York Graphic So-
      ciety, 1975. 244 pp.
          Includes material on the Frankenstein films.

1893 Glut, Donald F. The Dracula Book. Metuchen, N.J.:
      Scarecrow, 1975. 388 pp.
          A survey of the Dracula legend in several media, in-
      cluding film.

1894 Menville, Douglas. A Historical and Critical Survey of the
      Science Fiction Film. New York: Arno, 1975. 185 pp.

1895 Pattison, Barrie. The Seal of Dracula. New York: Bounty,
      1975. 136 pp.
          Survey of the many varieties of vampires in film.

1896 Rovin, Jeff. A Pictorial History of Science Fiction Films.
      Secaucus, N.J.: Citadel, 1975. 240 pp.

1897 Ursini, James and Silver, Alain. The Vampire Film. South
      Brunswick, N.J.: A. S. Barnes, 1975. 238 pp.

1898 Welsh, Paul. The Spine Chillers: Chaney, Jr., Cushing,
      Lee and Price. Ilfracombe: Stockwell, 1975. 68 pp.

                    4. Musical and Dance

1899 Franks, Arthur H. Ballet for Film and Television. London:
      Pitman, 1950. 85 pp.

1900 Hungerford, Mary J. Dancing in Commercial Motion Pictures.
      Columbia University: Ph.D., 1951. 82 pp.

1901 Burton, Jack. The Blue Book of Hollywood Musicals: Songs
      from the Sound Tracks and the Stars Who Sang Them
      Since the Birth of the Talkies a Quarter-Century Ago.
      Watkins Glen, N.Y.: Century, 1953. 296 pp.
           Includes year-by-year account of the Hollywood musical.

1902 UNESCO, Mass Communication Techniques Division. Film and
      Television in the Service of Opera and Ballet and of Mu-
      seums: Reports on Two International Meetings. Paris:
      UNESCO, 1961. 55 pp.

1903 Springer, John. All Talking! All Singing! All Dancing! A
      Pictorial History of the Movie Musical. New York: Cita-
      del, 1966. 256 pp.

1904 McVay, Douglas. The Musical Film. New York: A. S.
      Barnes, 1967. 175 pp.

1905 Bebb, Richard (ed.) Opera and the Cinema: Some of the
      Films. London: National Film Theatre, 1969. 6 pp.

1906 Minton, Eric (ed.) American Musicals, 1929-1933. Ottawa:
      n.p., 1969. 75 pp.
           Compilation of selected film reviews from the New
      York Times.

1907 Kobal, John. Gotta Sing, Gotta Dance! A Pictorial History
      of Film Musicals. London, New York: Hamlyn, 1970.
      320 pp.

1908 Vallance, Tom. The American Musical. New York: A. S.
      Barnes, 1970. 192 pp.
           Material on individuals associated with film musicals.

1909 Taylor, John Russell and Jackson, Arthur. The Hollywood
      Musical. New York: McGraw-Hill, 1971. 234 pp.
           Primarily reference material, but also includes a
      lengthy essay on the Hollywood musical by Taylor.

1910 Thomas, Lawrence B. The MGM Years. New York: Colum-
      bia House, 1972. 138 pp.
           Primarily about the MGM musicals.

1911 Cine-Dance. New York: Johnson Reprint, 1973. 52 pp.
           Reprint of a 1967 issue of Dance Perspectives; con-
      tributions by Arthur Knight, Maya Deren, Parker Tyler,
      Sidney Peterson, Shirley Clarke, Ed Emshwiller, Stan
      Vanderbeek, Jonas Mekas, Stan Brakhage, Slavko Vorka-
      pitch, Len Lye, Hilary Harris, and Allegra Fuller Snyder.

1912 Jenkinson, Philip and Warner, Alan. Celluloid Rock: Twenty
      Years of Movie Rock. London: Lorrimer, 1974. 136 pp.

1913   Stern, Lee Edward. The Movie Musical. New York: Pyra-
        mid, 1974. 160 pp.

1914   Dyer, Richard. The Musical: Notes. London: British Film
        Institute, Educational Advisory Service, 1975. 56 pp.

1915   Fordin, Hugh. The World of Entertainment: Hollywood's
        Greatest Musicals. Garden City, N.Y.: Doubleday, 1975.
        566 pp.
            Account of Arthur Freed and the MGM musical unit.

1916   Kreuger, Miles (ed.) The Movie Musical From Vitaphone to
        42nd Street: As Reported in a Great Fan Magazine. New
        York: Dover, 1975. 367 pp.
            Articles and illustrations from Photoplay, 1926-1933.

1917   Thomas, Tony. Harry Warren and the Hollywood Musical.
        Secaucus, N.J.: Citadel, 1975. 344 pp.

                5. Gangster and Detective

1918   Warshow, Robert. The Immediate Experience: Movies,
        Comics, Theatre and Other Aspects of Popular Culture.
        Garden City, N.Y.: Doubleday, 1962. 282 pp. (Re-
        printed New York: Atheneum, 1970.)
            Includes a seminal essay on the gangster film.

1919   Chertok, Harvey and Torge, Martha (eds.) Quotations From
        Charlie Chan. New York: Golden Press, 1968. 51 pp.
            Primarily photographs, credits, and captions.

1920   Baxter, John. The Gangster Film. New York: A. S.
        Barnes, 1970. 160 pp.
            Material on individuals associated with the gangster
        film.

1921   Lee, Raymond and Van Hecke, B. C. Gangsters and Hood-
        lums: The Underworld in the Cinema. South Brunswick,
        N.J.: A. S. Barnes, 1971. 264 pp.
            Primarily photographs.

1922   Everson, William K. The Detective in Film. Secaucus,
        N.J.: Citadel, 1972. 247 pp.

1923   McArthur, Colin. Underworld USA. New York: Viking,
        1972. 176 pp.
            Analysis of the "gangster film/thriller," including
        material on individual directors; for list of names, see
        entry 3753.

1924 Gabree, John. Gangsters From Little Caesar to the God-
      father. New York: Pyramid, 1973. 160 pp.

1925 Karpf, Stephen L. The Gangster Film: Emergence, Varia-
      tion, and Decay of a Genre, 1930-1940. New York: Arno,
      1973. 299 pp.

1926 Hossent, Harry. Gangster Movies: Gangsters, Hoodlums and
      Tough Guys of the Screen. London: Octopus, 1974.
      160 pp.

1927 Cameron, Ian. A Pictorial History of Crime Films. London:
      Hamlyn, 1975. 221 pp.

              6. Thriller, Suspense, and Spy

1928 Gow, Gordon. Suspense in the Cinema. New York: A. S.
      Barnes, 1968. 167 pp.

1929 Brosnan, John. James Bond in the Cinema. South Bruns-
      wick, N.J.: A. S. Barnes, 1972. 176 pp.

1930 Cameron, Ian. Adventure in the Movies. New York: Cres-
      cent, 1973. 152 pp. (Also published as Adventure and
      the Cinema.)

1931 Davis, Brian. The Thriller: The Suspense Film From 1946.
      New York: Dutton, 1973. 159 pp.

1932 Hammond, Lawrence. Thriller Movies: Classic Films of
      Suspense and Mystery. London: Octopus, 1974. 160 pp.

1933 Parish, James Robert and Pitts, Michael R. The Great Spy
      Pictures. Metuchen, N.J.: Scarecrow, 1974. 585 pp.
          Primarily reference, but includes a lengthy essay on
      the history of the spy film.

                    7. War

1934 Hughes, Robert (ed.) Film: Book 2, Films of Peace and
      War. New York: Grove, 1962. 255 pp.

1935 Shain, Russell Earl. An Analysis of Motion Pictures About
      War Released by the American Film Industry: 1939-1970.
      University of Illinois, Urbana-Champaign: Ph.D., 1972.
      455 pp.

1936 Jones, Ken D. and McClure, Arthur F. Hollywood at War:

The American Motion Picture and World War II.   South
Brunswick, N.J.:   A. S. Barnes, 1973.   320 pp.

1937   Butler, Ivan.   The War Film.   South Brunswick, N.J.:
       A. S. Barnes, 1974.   191 pp.

1938   Jeavons, Clyde with Unwin, Mary.   A Pictorial History of
       War Films.   London, New York: Hamlyn, 1974.   253 pp.

1939   Kagan, Norman.   The War Film.   New York: Pyramid,
       1974.   160 pp.

1940   Manvell, Roger.   Films and the Second World War.   South
       Brunswick, N.J.:   A. S. Barnes, 1974.   388 pp.

1941   Perlmutter, Tom.   War Movies.   London, New York: Ham-
       lyn, 1974.   156 pp.

1942   Smith, Julian.   Looking Away: Hollywood and Vietnam.   New
       York: Scribner's, 1975.   236 pp.
           Cultural analysis, including consideration of the war
       film.

8.   Tarzan and Jungle

1943   Behlmer, Rudy.   Jungle Tales of the Cinema.   Hollywood:
       n.p., 1960.   37 ℓ.
           Includes material on King Kong, Tarzan, and others.

1944   Lee, Raymond and Coriell, Vernell.   A Pictorial History of
       the Tarzan Movies: 50 Years of the Jungle Superman and
       All-Time Box Office Film Champion.   Los Angeles:
       Golden State News, 1966.   82 pp.

1945   Fenton, Robert W.   The Big Swingers.   Englewood Cliffs,
       N.J.:   Prentice-Hall, 1967.   258 pp.
           Includes material on the Tarzan character in various
       media.

1946   Essoe, Gabe.   Tarzan of the Movies: A Pictorial History of
       More than Fifty Years of Edgar Rice Burroughs' Legendary
       Hero.   Secaucus, N.J.:   Citadel, 1968.   208 pp.

9.   Shakespeare

1947   Nicoll, Allardyce.   Film and Theatre.   (Originally published
       1936.)   New York: Arno, 1972.   255 pp.
           Includes a chapter on Shakespeare and cinema.

1948   Garrett, John (ed.) Talking of Shakespeare. New York:
          Theatre Arts Books, 1954. 264 pp.
              Includes a chapter on Shakespeare and cinema by Paul
          Dehn.

1949   Morris, Peter. Shakespeare on Film: An Index to William
          Shakespeare's Plays on Film. Ottawa: Canadian Film
          Institute, 1964. 30 pp. (Revised without subtitle 1972,
          39 pp.)

1950   Whitehead, Peter and Bean, Robin (eds.) Olivier: Shakes-
          peare. London: Lorrimer, 1966. 40 pp.
              Primarily a photographic record of Olivier's Shakes-
          pearean films.

1951   Ball, Robert Hamilton. Shakespeare on Silent Film: A
          Strange Eventful History. New York: Theater Arts
          Books, 1968. 403 pp.

1952   Skoller, Donald S. Problems of Transformation in the Adapta-
          tions of Shakespeare's Tragedies From Playscript to
          Cinema. New York University: Ph.D., 1968. 459 pp.

1953   Manvell, Roger. Shakespeare and the Film. New York:
          Praeger, 1971. 172 pp.

1954   Eckert, Charles W. (ed.) Focus on Shakespearean Films.
          Englewood Cliffs, N.J.: Prentice-Hall, 1972. 184 pp.
              Brief critical essays on specific films by many promi-
          nent critics, including Andre Bazin.

1955   Silber, Joan Ellyn Frager. Cinematic Techniques and Inter-
          pretations in Film and Television Adaptations of Shakes-
          peare's "Hamlet." University of Michigan: Ph.D., 1973.
          379 pp.

                    10. Miscellaneous Genres and Recurrent
                            Themes and Iconography

1956   UNESCO. Films on Art: A Specialized Study. Paris:
          UNESCO, 1949. 72 pp.
              Includes eight essays as well as a listing of films
          on art.

1957. Chapman, William McKissack (ed.) Films on Art 1952.
          New York: American Federation of Arts, 1952. 160 pp.
              Essays on the history and use of the art film; in-
          cludes contributions by Iris Barry and Arthur Knight.

1958   Worden, James William. The Portrayal of the Protestant

Minister in American Motion Pictures, 1951-1960, and Its
Implications for the Church Today. Boston University:
Ph.D., 1962. 400 pp.

1959 Schwartz, Jack. The Portrayal of Education in American Motion Pictures, 1931-1961. University of Illinois, Urbana-
Champaign: Ph.D., 1963. 178 pp.

1960 Coulteray, George de. Sadism in the Movies. New York:
Medical Press, 1965. 191 pp. Translated by Steve Hult.

1961 Lanier, Vincent. The Image of the Artist in Fictional Cinema.
Eugene: University of Oregon, 1968. 46 ℓ.

1962 Butler, Ivan. Religion in the Cinema. New York: A. S.
Barnes, 1969. 208 pp.

1963 Huntley, John. Railways in the Cinema. London: Ian Allen,
1969. 168 pp.
Results of research undertaken for a railway film
series presented at the National Film Theatre in London.

1964 Lee, Raymond. Fit for the Chase: Cars and the Movies.
South Brunswick, N.J.: A. S. Barnes, 1969. 237 pp.

1965 Karimi, Amir Massoud. Toward a Definition of the American
Film Noir (1941-1949). University of Southern California:
Ph.D., 1970. 261 pp.

1966 Alloway, Lawrence. Violent America: The Movies, 1946-
1964. New York: Museum of Modern Art, 1971. 95 pp.
Critical/historical discussion of formulaic elements,
including violence, in various film genres; prepared in
coordination with a Museum of Modern Art series entitled
"The American Action Movie, 1946-1964."

1967 Callahan, Michael Anthony. A Critical Study of the Image of
Marriage in the Contemporary Cinema. University of
Southern California: Ph.D., 1971. 319 pp.
Primarily discusses films of the sixties.

1968 Furhammar, Leif and Isaksson, Folke. Politics and Film.
New York: Praeger, 1971. 257 pp. Translated by Kersti
French.
Discusses films which have a clear political purpose,
particularly their propagandistic aspects.

1969 Schweitzer, Robert Fred. The Biblical Christ in Cinema.
University of Missouri: Ph.D., 1971. 212 pp.

1970 Mitchell, George. The Image of the City in the American
Film, 1896-1928. University of Chicago: Ph.D., 1972.
295 pp.

1971   Schuth, Howard W. The College Milieu in the American Film
        with Emphasis on the Work of Mike Nichols: A Study in
        Belief Systems. Ohio State University: Ph.D., 1972.
        234 pp.

1972   White, David Manning and Averson, Richard. The Celluloid
        Weapon: Social Comment in the American Film. Boston:
        Beacon, 1972. 271 pp.
            History of the social problem film.

1973   Faure, William. Images of Violence. London: Studio Vista,
        1973. 128 pp.
            Photographs and discussion of the use of violence in
        various types of films since cinema's beginnings.

1974   Kobal, John. Gods and Goddesses of the Movies. New York:
        Crescent, 1973. 152 pp. (Also published as Romance
        and the Cinema.)
            Discusses various films, stars, and directors in rela-
        tion to the concept of romance.

1975   Mason, John Lenard. The Identity Crisis Theme in American
        Feature Films, 1960-1969. Ohio State University: Ph.D.,
        1973. 396 pp.
            Primarily uses youth-oriented films of the sixties.

1976   Cary, John. Spectacular! The Story of Epic Films. Edited
        by John Kobal. London, New York: Hamlyn, 1974.
        160 pp.

1977   Fraser, John. Violence in the Arts. London: Cambridge
        University Press, 1974. 192 pp.
            A study of aesthetics of violence in the arts, with
        frequent discussion of films.

1978   Glaessner, Verina. Kung Fu: Cinema of Vengeance. New
        York: Bounty, 1974. 134 pp.
            Includes chapters on Angela Mao, Bruce Lee, Wang
        Yu, Ti Lung, and others.

1979   Kaminsky, Stuart M. American Film Genres: Approaches to
        a Critical Theory of Popular Film. Dayton, Ohio: Pflaum,
        1974. 232 pp.
            Includes chapters on film noir, films of white-hot
        violence, big caper films, and genre directors Don Siegel
        and John Ford, as well as material on the conventionally
        recognized genres.

1980   Quirk, Lawrence J. The Great Romantic Films. Secaucus,
        N.J.: Citadel, 1974. 224 pp.

1981   Annan, David. Catastrophe: The End of the Cinema? New

York: Crown, 1975. 111 pp.
Material on various genres, including the disaster
film.

1982 Behlmer, Rudy and Thomas, Tony. Hollywood's Hollywood:
The Movies About the Movies. Secaucus, N.J.: Citadel,
1975. 345 pp.

1983 Scagnetti, Jack. Movie Stars in Bathtubs. Middle Village,
N.Y.: Jonathan David, 1975. 160 pp.
Primarily photographs of movie bathtubs.

1984 Witcombe, Rick Trader. Savage Cinema. New York: Crown,
1975. 95 pp.
Discusses violence in films.

D. ANIMATED FILMS

This section contains books dealing with animated films as a genre. For books dealing with the techniques of film animation, see Part II, section C-2. For material on the animated work of Walt Disney, see Part VI, section A, individual biography, analysis, and interview. Since there is much animation work being done in the Eastern European countries, the reader might also consult the history section, Part IV, section E-8.

1985 Falk, Nat. How to Make Animated Cartoons: The History and Technique. New York: Foundation, 1941. 79 pp.

1986 Manvell, Roger. The Animated Film: With Pictures From the Film "Animal Farm" by Halas and Batchelor. London: Sylvan, 1954. 63 pp.
      History of animation, plus discussion of ANIMAL FARM.

1987 Halas, John and Manvell, Roger. Design in Motion. New York: Hastings, 1962. 160 pp.
      Surveys various styles of animation around the world.

1988 Herdeg, Walter (ed.) Film and TV Graphics: An International Survey of Film and Television Graphics. Texts by John Halas. Zurich: Herdeg, Graphis Press, distributed by Hastings, 1967. 199 pp.
      Discusses animation and graphic design in entertainment films, sponsored films, advertising, titling, and television; text in English, German, and French.

1989 Stephenson, Ralph. Animation in the Cinema. New York: A. S. Barnes, 1967. 176 pp. (Revised as The Animated Film, 1973, 206 pp.)

1990 Madsen, Roy P. Animated Film: Concepts, Methods, Uses. New York: Interland, distributed by Pitman, 1969. 234 pp.

1991 Halas, John with Manvell, Roger. Art in Movement: New Direction in Animation. New York: Hastings, 1970. 192 pp.

1992 Maelstaf, R. The Animated Cartoon Film in Belgium. Brussels: Ministry of Foreign Affairs and External Trade, 1970. 100 pp.

1993 Holloway, Ronald. Z Is for Zagreb. South Brunswick, N.J.: A. S. Barnes, 1972. 127 pp.
      Material on Yugoslavian cartoon production.

1994 Small, Edward. Japanese Animated Film: A Study of Narrative, Intellectual Montage and Metamorphosis Structures for Semiotic Unit Sequencing. University of Iowa: Ph.D., 1972. 407 pp.

1995 Heraldson, Donald. Creators of Life: A History of Animation. New York: Drake, 1975. 298 pp.

1996 Holman, L. Bruce. Puppet Animation in the Cinema: History and Technique. South Brunswick, N.J.: A. S. Barnes, 1975. 120 pp.

E.   CHILDREN'S FILMS

This category contains those books which discuss (and sometimes list) films for children, primarily entertainment films. For further information on films for children, particularly educational films, see Part X, section B-3, 16mm film and audio-visual catalogs. For books dealing with the effect of films on children, see Part IX, section C-2.

1997 Advisory Council on Children's Entertainment Films. Annual Report of the Advisory Council on Children's Entertainment Films. London, 1946. Unpaged.

1998 Storck, Henri. The Entertainment Film for Juvenile Audiences. Paris: UNESCO, 1950. 240 pp.

1999 Bauchard, Philippe. The Child Audience: A Report on Press, Film and Radio for Children. Paris: UNESCO, 1952. 198 pp.

2000 Field, Mary. Good Company: The Story of the Children's Entertainment Film Movement in Great Britain, 1943-1950. London: Longmans Green, 1952. 192 pp.

2001 Barclay, John Bruce. Children's Film Tastes: Report of an Experimental Series of Film Programmes for Children at the Gateway Theatre, Edinburgh. Edinburgh: Scottish Educational Film Association, 1956. 63 pp.

2002 Barrot, Jean-Pierre with Billard, Ginette (eds.) Films for Children and Adolescents: Selections Made in 22 Countries. Paris: UNESCO, Department of Mass Communications, 1956. 118 pp.

2003 UNESCO, Department of Mass Communications. Film Programmes for the Young: Report on a Presentation of Children's Films Organized by the International Centre of Films for Children, Brussels, 19-23 September 1958. Paris: UNESCO, 1959. 30 pp.

2004 Educational Film Library Association. Films for Children.

New York: Educational Film Library Association, 1961.
59 pp.

2005   Children's Film Foundation. Saturday Morning Cinema.   London: Children's Film Foundation, 1969.   52 pp.

2006   Rice, Susan with Ludlum, Barbara (eds.)   Films Kids Like:
A Catalogue of Short Films for Children.   Chicago:
American Library Association, 1973.   150 pp.

2007   Zornow, Edith and Goldstein, Ruth M.   Movies for Kids: A
Guide for Parents and Teachers on the Entertainment Film
for Children 9 to 13.   New York: Avon, 1973.   224 pp.

F. SEXUAL FILMS AND SEXUAL THEMES

This section contains those books which deal with eroticism, nudity, sex, and pornography in the cinema, as well as those which analyze sexual themes. For related material, the reader should also consult Part IX, section A-3, men and women, as well as Part IX, section D-1, censorship, obscenity, self-regulation, and pressure groups.

2008 Brusendorff, Ove and Henningsen, Poul. Erotica for the
       Millions: Love in the Movies. Los Angeles: Book Mart,
       1960. 147 pp.

2009 Lo Duca, Giuseppe. Technique of Eroticism. London: Eros
       Library, 1963. 230 pp. Translated by Alan Hull Walton.

2010 Lee, Raymond. A Pictorial History of Hollywood Nudity.
       Chicago: Camerarts, 1964. 127 pp.

2011 Milner, Michael. Sex on Celluloid. New York: McFadden,
       1964. 224 pp.

2012 De Coulteray, George. Sadism in the Movies. New York:
       Medical Press, 1965. 191 pp. Translated by Steve Hult.

2013 Durgnat, Raymond. Eros in the Cinema. London: Calder
       and Boyars, 1966. 207 pp.

2014 Walker, Alexander. The Celluloid Sacrifice: Aspects of Sex
       in the Movies. New York: Hawthorn, 1967. 241 pp.
       For list of individuals discussed, see entry 3694.

2015 Tyler, Parker. Sex, Psyche, Etcetera in the Film. New
       York: Horizon, 1969. 240 pp.

2016 Hanson, Gillian. Original Skin: Nudity and Sex in Cinema
       and Theatre. London: Tom Stacey, 1970. 192 pp.

2017 Grove, Martin A. and Ruben, William S. The Celluloid Love
       Feast: The Story of Erotic Movies. New York: Lancer,
       1971. 174 pp.

2018   Knight, Arthur and Alpert, Hollis. Playboy's Sex in Cinema,
       1970. Chicago: Playboy Press, 1971. 144 pp. (Also
       published as Playboy's Sex in Cinema 1.)

2019   Durgnat, Raymond. Sexual Alienation in the Cinema. London:
       Studio Vista, 1972. 320 pp.

2020   Knight, Arthur and Alpert, Hollis. Playboy's Sex in Cinema 2.
       Chicago: Playboy Press, 1972. 144 pp.

2021   Tyler, Parker. Screening the Sexes: Homosexuality in the
       Movies. New York: Holt, Rinehart, and Winston, 1972.
       367 pp.

2022   Knight, Arthur and Alpert, Hollis. Playboy's Sex in Cinema 3.
       Chicago: Playboy Press, 1973. 144 pp.

2023   Rotsler, William. Contemporary Erotic Cinema. New York:
       Ballantine, 1973. 280 pp.

2024   Knight, Arthur. Playboy's Sex in Cinema 4. Chicago: Play-
       boy Press, 1974. 144 pp.

2025   Turan, Kenneth and Zito, Stephen F. Sinema: American
       Pornographic Films and the People Who Make Them. New
       York: Praeger, 1974. 244 pp.

2026   Tyler, Parker. Pictorial History of Sex in Films. Secaucus,
       N.J.: Citadel, 1974. 256 pp.

2027   Wells, John Warren. Different Strokes or, How I (Gulp)
       Wrote, Directed, and Starred in an X-Rated Movie. New
       York: Dell, 1974. 252 pp.

2028   Atkins, Thomas R. (ed.) Sexuality in the Movies. Blooming-
       ton: Indiana University Press, 1975. 244 pp.
          With contributions by John Baxter, Arthur Lennig,
       Evelyn Renold, Gene D. Phillips, and others.

2029   Hurwood, Bernhardt J. (ed.) The Whole Sex Catalogue. New
       York: Pinnacle, 1975. 319 pp.
          Includes a chapter on sex in movies.

2030   Knight, Arthur. Playboy's Sex in Cinema 5. Chicago: Play-
       boy Press, 1975. 144 pp.

2031   Kronhausen, Phyllis and Eberhard. The Sex People: Erotic
       Performers and Their Bold New Worlds. Chicago: Play-
       boy Press, 1975. 265 pp.

2032   Pascall, Jeremy and Jeavons, Clyde. A Pictorial History of
       Sex in the Movies. London, New York: Hamlyn, 1975.
       219 pp.

2033 Strick, Marv and Lethe, Robert. The Sexy Cinema. Los
        Angeles: Sherbourne, 1975. 160 pp.

2034 Wortley, Richard. Erotic Movies. London: Studio Vista,
        1975. 140 pp.

G. "B" FILMS

2035 Barbour, Alan G. (comp.) The "B" Western. Kew Gardens, N.Y.: Screen Facts, 1966. 64 pp.

2036 Barbour, Alan G. (comp.) The Wonderful World of B-Films. Kew Gardens, N.Y.: Screen Facts, 1968. Approx. 60 pp. Reproductions of "B"-movie ads.

2037 Barbour, Alan G. The Thrill of It All. New York: Macmillan, 1971. 204 pp.
Pictorial history of the "B" western.

2038 Miller, Don. "B" Movies: An Informal Survey of the American Low-Budget Film, 1933-1945. New York: Curtis, 1973. 350 pp.

2039 McCarthy, Todd and Flynn, Charles (eds.) Kings of the Bs: Working Within the Hollywood System: An Anthology of Film History and Criticism. New York: Dutton, 1975. 561 pp.
Articles on less well known Hollywood directors; for list of names, see entry 3812. Contributions by Manny Farber, Andrew Sarris, Roger Ebert, Douglas Gomery, Peter Bogdanovich, and others.

H. SERIES, SHORTS, SERIALS, AND REMAKES

This section contains those books dealing with film series, shorts, serials, and remakes. Although Alan G. Barbour has published numerous pictorial and reference books on the American serial, only a few of these books could be verified for inclusion in this bibliography. An unverified listing of these books can be found in Git Luboviski's Cinema Catalog or in the Cinemabilia Catalogue of Film Literature.

2040 Lahue, Kalton C. Continued Next Week: A History of the Moving Picture Serial. Norman: University of Oklahoma Press, 1964. 293 pp.

2041 Barbour, Alan G. (comp.) Great Serial Ads. Kew Gardens, N.Y.: Screen Facts, 1965. Unpaged.

2042 Barbour, Alan G. (comp.) The Serials of Republic. Kew Gardens, N.Y.: Screen Facts, 1965. approx. 66 pp.

2043 Lahue, Kalton C. World of Laughter: The Motion Picture Comedy Short, 1910-1930. Norman: University of Oklahoma Press, 1966. 240 pp. (Reprinted 1972.)

2044 Barbour, Alan G. (comp.) The Serial. Kew Gardens, N.Y.: Screen Facts, 1967. Unpaged.

2045 Barbour, Alan G. (comp.) The Serials of Columbia. Kew Gardens, N.Y.: Screen Facts, 1967. approx. 64 pp.

2046 Barbour, Alan G. (comp.) Days of Thrills and Adventure. Kew Gardens, N.Y.: Screen Facts, 1968. 64 pp. (Revised New York: Macmillan, 1970. 168 pp.)
Reproductions of serial ads.

2047 Barbour, Alan G. (comp.) Serial Showcase. Kew Gardens, N.Y.: Screen Facts, 1968. Unpaged.

2048 Chertok, Harvey and Torge, Martha (eds.) Quotations From Charlie Chan. New York: Golden Press, 1968. 51 pp.
Primarily photographs, credits, and captions.

2049   Lahue, Kalton. Bound and Gagged: The Story of the Silent
        Serials. South Brunswick, N.J.: A. S. Barnes, 1968.
        352 pp.

2050   Barbour, Alan G. (comp.) Thrill After Thrill: Another Col-
        lection of Original Serial Ads. Kew Gardens, N.Y.:
        Screen Facts, 1971. Unpaged.

2051   Parish, James Robert, and others (eds.) The Great Movie
        Series. South Brunswick, N.J.: A. S. Barnes, 1971.
        333 pp.
        Material on 25 movie series, such as Bomba, Boston
        Blackie, Bowery Boys, Dr. Kildare, Ellery Queen, The
        Falcon, Philo Vance, Francis--The Talking Mule, James
        Bond, Jungle Jim, Maisie, Matt Helm, and others.

2052   Stedman, Raymond William. The Serials: Suspense and
        Drama by Installment. Norman: University of Oklahoma
        Press, 1971. 514 pp.
        History of serials in radio, television, and film.

2053   Harmon, Jim and Glut, Donald F. The Great Movie Serials:
        Their Sound and Fury. Garden City, N.Y.: Doubleday,
        1972. 384 pp.

2054   Maltin, Leonard. The Great Movie Shorts. New York:
        Crown, 1972. 236 pp.
        For list of individuals discussed, see entry 3755.

2055   Weiss, Ken and Goodgold, Ed. To Be Continued.... New
        York: Crown, 1972. 341 pp.
        Survey of American serials from 1929-1956.

2056   Zinman, David. Saturday Afternoon at the Bijou. New Ro-
        chelle, N.Y.: Arlington, 1973. 511 pp.
        Material on series of the thirties and forties, in-
        cluding Tarzan, The Wolf Man, The Invisible Man, The
        Mummy, Gene Autry, The Cisco Kid, Hopalong Cassidy,
        Sherlock Holmes, The Saint, The Thin Man, Crime Doc-
        tor, Charlie Chan, Mr. Moto, Fu Manchu, Dr. Christian,
        Andy Hardy, Henry Aldrich, Blondie, Nancy Drew, The
        Dead End Kids, Our Gang, and others.

2057   Druxman, Michael B. Make It Again, Sam: A Survey of
        Movie Remakes. South Brunswick, N.J.: A. S. Barnes,
        1975. 285 pp.

2058   Mathis, Jack. Valley of the Cliffhangers. Northbrook, Ill.:
        Jack Mathis Advertising, 1975. 448 pp.
        Material on Republic's serials.

PART VI

BIOGRAPHY, ANALYSIS AND INTERVIEW

A. INDIVIDUAL BIOGRAPHY, ANALYSIS, AND INTERVIEW

This section contains books which deal in whole or in significant part with one person associated with the filmmaking community. The books listed here may be composed of biography, analysis, interview, or a combination of all three. In general, there are no annotations identifying the individuals. The user of this volume looking for more information on a particular individual is instructed to look in at least four other places. First, consult the name index, which will indicate all the places the person is cited as an author or as a subject. Second, consult the section of collective biography, analysis, and interview, Part VI, section B. There are no books, for instance, devoted completely to a single child star like Patty McCormack or a single character actor like Ed Begley, yet there are many books with material on numerous child stars and character actors, including McCormack and Begley. Third, look in Part VII, individual films, under the specific films with which the individual is associated. For instance, although there is no full-length biography of Charlton Heston, some material on him can be found in the case history of EARTHQUAKE. And finally, consult other sections of this bibliography--especially the history section--which have a relationship to the individual. While there may be few books on Alexander Dovzhenko, for instance, almost any international or Soviet film history will contain material on him. This bibliography tends inevitably to be more complete for individuals who are clearly at the center of the film world, like Alfred Hitchcock or Judy Garland, and less complete for those at the periphery, like F. Scott Fitzgerald or Aaron Copland. For these peripheral figures, readers should also consult bibliographies in other disciplines.

ABBOTT, BUD

2059 Anobile, Richard J. (ed.) Who's On First? Verbal and Visual Gems From the Films of Abbott and Costello. New York: Darien, 1972. 256 pp.

2060 Mulholland, Jim. The Abbott and Costello Book. New York: Popular Library, 1975. 254 pp.

ABBOTT, GEORGE

2061   Abbott, George. Mister Abbott. New York: Random, 1963.
       279 pp.

ACKLAND, RODNEY

2062   Ackland, Rodney and Grant, Elspeth. The Celluloid Mistress:
       Or the Custard Pie of Dr. Caligari. London: Allan Win-
       gate, 1954. 264 pp.

ADRIAN

2063   Lee, Sarah T. (ed.) American Fashion: The Life and Times
       of Adrian, Mainbocher, McCardell, Norell, and Trigere.
       New York: Quadrangle, 1975. 509 pp.

AGATE, JAMES

2064   Agate, James. Ego 4: Yet More of the Autobiography of
       James Agate. London: Harrap, 1940. 272 pp.

2065   Agate, James. Ego 5: Again More of the Autobiography of
       James Agate. London: Harrap, 1942. 283 pp.

2066   Agate, James. Ego 6: Once More the Autobiography of
       James Agate. London: Harrap, 1944. 307 pp.

2067   Agate, James. Ego 7: Even More of the Autobiography of
       James Agate. London: Harrap, 1945. 822 pp.

2068   Agate, James. Ego 8: Continuing the Autobiography of
       James Agate. London: Harrap, 1946. 269 pp.

2069   Agate, James. Ego 9: Concluding the Autobiography of
       James Agate. London: Harrap, 1949. 351 pp.

2070   Agate, James. The Later Ego, Consisting of Ego 8 and
       Ego 9. New York: Crown, 1951. 625 pp.

AGEE, JAMES

2071   Agee, James. Letters of James Agee to Father Flye. New
       York: Braziller, 1962. 235 pp. (Republished Boston:
       Houghton Mifflin, 1971, 267 pp.)

2072   Ohlin, Peter H. Agee. New York: Obolensky, 1966. 247 pp.

2073   Seib, Kenneth. James Agee: Promise and Fulfillment.
       Pittsburgh: University of Pittsburgh Press, 1968. 175 pp.

2074   Snyder, John J. James Agee: A Study of His Film Criti-
       cism. St. John's University: Ph.D., 1969. 174 pp.

2075   Flanders, Mark. Film Theory of James Agee. University
       of Iowa: Ph.D., 1971. 272 pp.

2076   Larsen, Erling. James Agee. Minneapolis: University of
       Minnesota Press, 1971. 47 pp.

2077   Barson, Alfred T. A Way of Seeing: A Critical Study of
       James Agee. Amherst: University of Massachusetts
       Press, 1972. 217 pp.

2078   Madden, David (comp.) Remembering James Agee. Baton
       Rouge: Louisiana State University Press, 1974. 172 pp.

2079   Kramer, Victor A. James Agee. Boston: Twayne, 1975.
       182 pp.

AHERNE, BRIAN

2080   Aherne, Brian. A Proper Job. Boston: Houghton Mifflin,
       1969. 355 pp.

ALGREN, NELSON

2081   Donohue, H. E. F. Conversations with Nelson Algren. New
       York: Hill and Wang, 1964. 333 pp.
            Includes material on Algren's dealings with Hollywood.

ALLEN, FRED

2082   Allen, Fred. Treadmill to Oblivion. Boston: Little, Brown,
       1954. 240 pp.

2083   Allen, Fred. Much Ado About Me. Boston: Little, Brown,
       1956. 380 pp.

2084   Allen, Fred. Fred Allen's Letters. Edited by Joe McCarthy.
       Garden City, N.Y.: Doubleday, 1965. 359 pp.

ALLEN, STEVE

2085   Allen, Steve. Mark It and Strike It: An Autobiography. New
       York: Holt, Rinehart and Winston, 1960. 432 pp.

ALLEN, WOODY

2086   Adler, Bill and Feinman, Jeffrey. Woody Allen: Clown
       Prince of American Humor. New York: Pinnacle, 1975.
       178 pp.

2087   Lax, Eric. On Being Funny: Woody Allen and Comedy. New
       York: Charterhouse, 1975. 243 pp.

ALLEY, NORMAN

2088   Alley, Norman. I Witness. New York: Funk, 1941. 370 pp.
        The experiences of a news cameraman.

ALMOND, PAUL

2089   Edsforth, Janet. Paul Almond: The Flame Within. Ottawa:
        Canadian Film Institute, 1972. 56 pp.

ANDERSON, JOHN MURRAY

2090   Anderson, John Murray with Anderson, Hugh Abercrombie.
        Out Without My Rubbers: The Memoirs of John Murray
        Anderson. New York: Library Publishers, 1954. 253 pp.

ANDERSON, LINDSAY

2091   Sussex, Elizabeth. Lindsay Anderson. New York: Praeger,
        1970. 96 pp.

ANDRESS, URSULA

2092   Laborderie, Renaud de. Ursula Andress. Manchester, Eng-
        land: World Distributors, 1965.

ANDREWS, JULIE

2093   Cottrell, John. Julie Andrews: The Unauthorized Life Story
        of a Super-Star. New York: Dell, 1968. 212 pp. (Also
        published as Julie Andrews: The Story of a Star.)

2094   Windeler, Robert. Julie Andrews: A Biography. New York:
        Putnam, 1970. 253 pp.

ANTHEIL, GEORGE

2095   Antheil, George. Bad Boy of Music. Garden City, N.Y.:
        Doubleday, Doran, 1945. 378 pp.

ANTONIONI, MICHELANGELO

2096   Leprohon, Pierre. Michelangelo Antonioni: An Introduction.
        New York: Simon and Schuster, 1963. 205 pp. Trans-
        lated by Scott Sullivan.
            Essays by and about Antonioni as well as script ex-
        cerpts from various films.

2097   Strick, Philip. Michelangelo Antonioni. Loughton, England:
        Motion, 1963. 58 pp.

2098   Cowie, Peter. Antonioni, Bergman, Resnais. New York:
        A. S. Barnes, 1964. 160 pp.

2099 Taylor, John Russell. Cinema Eye, Cinema Ear: Some Key
      Film-Makers of the Sixties. New York: Hill and Wang,
      1964. 294 pp.

2100 Cameron, Ian and Wood, Robin. Antonioni. New York:
      Praeger, 1968. 144 pp.

ARBUCKLE, FATTY

2101 Guild, Leo. The Fatty Arbuckle Case. New York: Paper-
      back Library, 1962. 156 pp.
      Includes account of the Virginia Rappe incident.

ARDEN, EVE

2102 Parish, James Robert. Good Dames. South Brunswick, N.J.:
      A. S. Barnes, 1974. 277 pp.

ARLEN, HAROLD

2103 Jablonski, Edward. Harold Arlen: Happy with the Blues.
      Garden City, N.Y.: Doubleday, 1961. 286 pp.

ARLEN, MICHAEL J.

2104 Arlen, Michael J. Exiles. New York: Farrar, Straus and
      Giroux, 1970. 226 pp.

ARLISS, GEORGE

2105 Arliss, George. My Ten Years in the Studios. Boston:
      Little, Brown, 1940. 349 pp. (Also published as George
      Arliss, By Himself.)

ARMSTRONG, LOUIS

2106 Armstrong, Louis. Satchmo: My Life in New Orleans. New
      York: Prentice-Hall, 1954. 240 pp.

ARNOLD, EDWARD

2107 Arnold, Edward with Dubuc, Frances Fisher. Lorenzo Goes
      to Hollywood: The Autobiography of Edward Arnold. New
      York: Liveright, 1940. 282 pp.

ARTAUD, ANTONIN

2108 Knapp, Bettina L. Antonin Artaud, Man of Vision. New
      York: David Lewis, 1969. 233 pp.
      Includes one chapter on Artaud's film work.

ARZNER, DOROTHY

2109 Johnston, Claire (ed.) The Work of Dorothy Arzner: Towards

a Feminist Cinema. London: British Film Institute,
1975. 34 pp.
Includes essays and an interview with Arzner.

ASHCROFT, PEGGY

2110   Keown, Eric. Peggy Ashcroft: An Illustrated Study of Her
Work, With a List of Her Appearances on Stage and
Screen. London: Rockliff, 1955. 102 pp.

ASKEY, ARTHUR

2111   Hirst, Robert. Three Men and a Gimmick. Kingswood,
England: The World's Work, 1957. 125 pp.

2112   Askey, Arthur. Before Your Very Eyes. London: Woburn,
1975. 191 pp.

ASQUITH, ANTHONY

2113   Noble, Peter (comp.) Anthony Asquith. London: British
Film Institute, 1952. 44 pp.

2114   Minney, R. J. "Puffin" Asquith: A Biography of the Hon.
Anthony Asquith, Aesthete, Aristocrat, Prime Minister's
Son, and Film Maker. London: Frewin, 1973. 273 pp.

ASTAIRE, FRED

2115   Astaire, Fred. Steps in Time. New York: Harper, 1959.
338 pp.

2116   Hackl, Alfons. Fred Astaire and His Work. Vienna: Edition
Austria International, 1970. 120 pp.

2117   Thompson, Howard. Fred Astaire: A Pictorial Treasury of
His Films. New York: Falcon, 1970. 154 pp.

2118   Croce, Arlene. The Fred Astaire and Ginger Rogers Book.
New York: Outerbridge and Lazard, 1972. 191 pp.

2119   Smith, Milburn (ed.) Astaire and Rogers. New York:
Barven, 1972. 66 pp.

2120   Green, Stanley and Goldblatt, Burt. Starring Fred Astaire.
New York: Dodd, Mead, 1973. 501 pp.

2121   Harvey, Stephen. Fred Astaire. New York: Pyramid, 1975.
158 pp.

ASTOR, MARY

2122   Astor, Mary. My Story: An Autobiography. Garden City,
N.Y.: Doubleday, 1959. 332 pp.

2123 Astor, Mary. A Life on Film. New York: Delacorte, 1967.
      245 pp.

AVERY, TEX

2124 Adamson, Joe. Tex Avery: King of Cartoons. New York:
      Popular Library, c. 1975. 237 pp.

BABY PEGGY (see CARY, DIANA SERRA)

BACALL, LAUREN

2125 Hyams, Joe. Bogart and Bacall: A Love Story. New York:
      McKay, 1975. 245 pp.

BACKUS, JIM

2126 Backus, Jim. Rocks on the Roof. New York: Putnam,
      1958. 190 pp.

BAILEY, PEARL

2127 Bailey, Pearl. The Raw Pearl. New York: Harcourt Brace
      Jovanovich, 1968. 206 pp.

2128 Bailey, Pearl. Pearl: Talking to Myself. New York: Har-
      court Brace Jovanovich, 1971. 233 pp.

BALABAN, BARNEY (ABE J.)

2129 Balaban, Carrie. Continuous Performance: The Story of
      A. J. Balaban. New York: Putnam, 1942. 240 pp.
      (Republished New York: A. J. Balaban Foundation, 1964.
      176 pp.)
          Includes history of the Balaban and (Sam) Katz movie
      theatres of Chicago.

BALCON, MICHAEL

2130 Danischewsky, Monja (ed.) Michael Balcon's 25 Years in
      Films. London: World Film Publications, 1947. 112 pp.
          Contributors include G. Campbell Dixon, Michael Red-
      grave, Françoise Rosay, and Alberto Cavalcanti.

2131 Balcon, Michael. Michael Balcon Presents ... A Lifetime
      of Films. London: Hutchinson, 1969. 239 pp.

2132 Slide, Anthony (comp.) Michael Balcon: Producer. London:
      National Film Theatre, 1969. 14 pp.

BALL, LUCILLE

2133 Harris, Eleanor. The Real Story of Lucille Ball. New

York: Farrar, Straus and Young, 1954. 119 pp.

2134 Morella, Joe and Epstein, Edward Z. Lucy: The Bitter-sweet Life of Lucille Ball. Secaucus, N.J.: Lyle Stuart, 1973. 281 pp.

2135 Gregory, James. Lucille Ball. New York: New American Library, 1974.

BALLARD, LUCIEN

2136 Maltin, Leonard. Behind the Camera: The Cinematographer's Art. New York: New American Library, 1971. 240 pp. Includes a lengthy interview with Ballard.

BALSHOFER, FRED J.

2137 Balshofer, Fred J. and Miller, Arthur C. with Bergsten, Bebe. One Reel a Week. Berkeley: University of California Press, 1967. 218 pp.

BANKHEAD, TALLULAH

2138 Bankhead, Tallulah. Tallulah: My Autobiography. New York: Harper, 1952. 335 pp.

2139 Brian, Denis. Tallulah, Darling: A Biography of Tallulah Bankhead. New York: Pyramid, 1972. 285 pp.

2140 Gill, Brendan. Tallulah. New York: Holt, Rinehart and Winston, 1972. 287 pp.

2141 Israel, Lee. Miss Tallulah Bankhead. New York: Putnam, 1972. 384 pp.

2142 Tunney, Kieran. Tallulah: Darling of the Gods; An Intimate Portrait. New York: Dutton, 1973. 228 pp.

BARA, THEDA

2143 Zierold, Norman. Sex Goddesses of the Silent Screen. Chicago: Regnery, 1973. 207 pp.

BARDOT, BRIGITTE

2144 Reid, Gordon. Brigitte: The Story of Brigitte Bardot. London: Eurap, 1958. 35 pp.

2145 Beauvoir, Simone de. Brigitte Bardot and the Lolita Syndrome. New York: Reynal, 1960. 37 pp. Translated by Bernard Fretchman. (Reprinted New York: Arno, 1972.)

2146   Carpozi, George. The Brigitte Bardot Story. New York:
       Belmont, 1961. 157 pp.

2147   Laborderie, Renaud de. Brigitte Bardot: Renaud de Laborde-
       rie Spotlights in Words and Pictures the Career of the Re-
       markable Brigitte Bardot. Manchester, England: World
       Distributors, 1964. 48 pp.

2148   Evans, Peter. Bardot: Eternal Sex Goddess. New York:
       Drake, 1973. 186 pp.

2149   Crawley, Tony. Bebe: The Films of Brigitte Bardot. Lon-
       don: LSP Books, 1975. 256 pp.

BARRAULT, JEAN-LOUIS

2150   Barrault, Jean-Louis. Memories for Tomorrow: The
       Memoirs of Jean-Louis Barrault. New York: Dutton,
       1974. 336 pp. Translated by Jonathan Griffin.

BARRETT, RONA

2151   Barrett, Rona. Miss Rona: An Autobiography. Los Ange-
       les: Nash, 1974. 281 pp.

BARRYMORE, BLANCHE OELRICHS

2152   Strange, Michael. Who Tells Me True. New York: Scrib-
       ner's, 1940. 396 pp.
           Autobiography of Michael Strange, pseudonym for
       Blanche Oelrichs Barrymore; contains material on John
       Barrymore.

BARRYMORE, DIANA

2153   Barrymore, Diana and Frank, Gerold. Too Much, Too Soon.
       New York: Holt, 1957. 380 pp.

BARRYMORE, ETHEL

2154   Barrymore, Ethel. Memories: An Autobiography. New
       York: Harper, 1955. 310 pp. (Reprinted New York:
       Kraus Reprints, 1968.)

2155   Alpert, Hollis. The Barrymores. New York: Dial, 1964.
       397 pp.

2156   Newman, Shirlee. Ethel Barrymore, Girl Actress. Indianapo-
       lis: Bobbs-Merrill, 1966. 200 pp.
           For the young reader.

2157   Fox, Mary Virginia. Ethel Barrymore: A Portrait. Chi-
       cago: Reilly and Lee, 1970. 133 pp.

BARRYMORE, JOHN

2158 Barrymore, John. Confessions of an Actor. (Originally published 1926.) New York: Blom, 1971. Unpaged.

2159 Power-Waters, Alma. John Barrymore: The Legend and the Man. New York: Messner, 1941. 282 pp. (Also published as John Barrymore: The Authorized Life.)

2160 Fowler, Gene. Good Night, Sweet Prince: The Life and Times of John Barrymore. New York: Viking, 1944. 477 pp. (Reprinted New York: Ballantine, 1971.)

2161 Alpert, Hollis. The Barrymores. New York: Dial, 1964. 397 pp.

2162 Barrymore, Elaine and Dody, Sanford. All My Sins Remembered. New York: Appleton-Century, 1964. 274 pp.

BARRYMORE, LIONEL

2163 Barrymore, Lionel with Shipp, Cameron. We Barrymores. New York: Appleton-Century-Crofts, 1951. 311 pp. (Reprinted Westport, Conn.: Greenwood, 1974.)

2164 Alpert, Hollis. The Barrymores. New York: Dial, 1964. 397 pp.

BARTOK, EVA

2165 Bartok, Eva. Worth Living For. London: Putnam, 1959. 181 pp.

BAZIN, ANDRE

2166 Andrew, James Dudley. Realism and Reality in Cinema: The Film Theory of Andre Bazin and Its Source in Recent French Thought. University of Iowa: Ph.D., 1972. 273 ℓ.

THE BEATLES

2167 De Blasio, Edward. All About the Beatles. New York: Macfadden-Bartell, 1964. 96 pp.

2168 Epstein, Brian. A Cellarful of Noise. Garden City, N.Y.: Doubleday, 1964. 120 pp.

2169 Hamblett, Charles. Here Are the Beatles. London: New English Library, 1964. Unpaged.

2170 Leaf, Earl. The Original Beatles Book: Delicious Insanity,

Where Will It End? Los Angeles: Petersen, 1964. Unpaged.

2171 Parkinson, Norman and Cleave, Maureen. The Beatles Book.
      London: Hutchinson, 1964. 32 pp.

2172 Davies, Hunter. The Beatles: The Authorized Biography.
      New York: McGraw-Hill, 1968. 357 pp.

2173 Fast, Julius. The Beatles: The Real Story. New York:
      Putnam, 1968. 252 pp.

2174 Davis, Edward E. (ed.) The Beatles Book. New York:
      Cowles, 1969. 213 pp.

2175 McCabe, Peter and Schonfeld, Robert D. Apple to the Core:
      The Unmaking of the Beatles. New York: Pocket Books,
      1972. 200 pp.

BEATON, CECIL

2176 Beaton, Cecil. Photobiography. London: Odhams, 1951.
      191 pp.

2177 Beaton, Cecil. The Wandering Years: Diaries 1922-1939.
      Boston: Little, Brown, 1962. 387 pp.

2178 Beaton, Cecil. Cecil Beaton: Memoirs of the Forties. New
      York: McGraw-Hill, 1972. 310 pp. (Also published as
      The Happy Years.)

2179 Spencer, Charles. Cecil Beaton: Stage and Film Designs.
      New York: St. Martin's, 1975. 115 pp.

BEAUCHAMP, ANTHONY

2180 Beauchamp, Anthony. Focus on Fame. London: Odhams,
      1958. 208 pp.
          Autobiography of photographer; includes material on
      many stars.

BEAVERS, ROBERT

2181 Markopoulos, Gregory J. Erb. Rome: Temenos, 1975. 53 pp.

BEHRMAN, S. N.

2182 Behrman, S. N. People in a Diary: A Memoir. Boston:
      Little, Brown, 1972. 338 pp.

BELAFONTE, HARRY

2183 Steirman, Hy (ed.) Harry Belafonte: His Complete Life

Story. Dunellen, N.J.: Hillman, 1957. 74 pp.

2184 Shaw, Arnold. Belafonte: An Unauthorized Biography.
Philadelphia: Chilton, 1960. 338 pp.

BELL, MARY HAYLEY

2185 Bell, Mary Hayley. What Shall We Do Tomorrow? New
York: Lippincott, 1969. 235 pp.
Story of the Mills family, including material on John
Mills, daughters Juliet and Hayley, as well as mother,
Mary Hayley Bell.

BENCHLEY, ROBERT

2186 Benchley, Nathaniel. Robert Benchley: A Biography. New
York: McGraw-Hill, 1955. 258 pp.

2187 Redding, Robert. A Humorist in Hollywood: Robert Benchley
and His Comedy Films. University of New Mexico: Ph.D.,
1968. 338 pp.

2188 Rosmond, Babette. Robert Benchley: His Life and Good
Times. Garden City, N.Y.: Doubleday, 1970. 239 pp.

2189 Redding, Robert. Starring Robert Benchley: Those Magnificent Movie Shorts. Albuquerque: University of New
Mexico Press, 1973. 209 pp.

BENNETT, JOAN

2190 Bennett, Joan and Kibbee, Lois. The Bennett Playbill. New
York: Holt, Rinehart and Winston, 1970. 332 pp.

BERG, GERTRUDE

2191 Berg, Gertrude with Berg, Cherney. Molly and Me. New
York: McGraw-Hill, 1961. 278 pp.

BERGMAN, INGMAR

2192 Cowie, Peter. Ingmar Bergman. Loughton, England: Motion, 1962. 42 pp.

2193 Cowie, Peter. Antonioni, Bergman, Resnais. New York:
A. S. Barnes, 1964. 160 pp.

2194 Donner, Jorn. The Personal Vision of Ingmar Bergman.
Bloomington: Indiana University Press, c. 1964. 276 pp.
Translated by Holger Lundberg. (Reprinted as The Films
of Ingmar Bergman: From Torment to All These Women,
New York: Dover, 1972.)

2195   Taylor, John Russell. Cinema Eye, Cinema Ear: Some Key
       Film-Makers of the Sixties. New York: Hill and Wang,
       1964. 294 pp.

2196   Steene, Birgitta. Ingmar Bergman. New York: Twayne,
       1968. 158 pp.

2197   Gibson, Arthur. The Silence of God: Creative Response
       to the Films of Ingmar Bergman. New York: Harper
       and Row, 1969. 171 pp.

2198   Gill, Jerry. Ingmar Bergman and the Search for Meaning.
       Grand Rapids, Mich.: Eerdmans, 1969. 45 pp.

2199   Wood, Robin. Ingmar Bergman. New York: Praeger, 1969.
       191 pp.

2200   Young, Vernon. Cinema Borealis: Ingmar Bergman and
       the Swedish Ethos. New York: David Lewis, 1971.
       331 pp.

2201   Blake, Richard. The Lutheran Milieu of the Films of Ingmar
       Bergman. Northwestern University: Ph.D., 1972.
       340 pp.

2202   Simon, John. Ingmar Bergman Directs. New York: Har-
       court Brace Jovanovich, 1972. 315 pp.

2203   Bergman, Ingmar. Bergman on Bergman: Interviews with
       Ingmar Bergman by Stig Bjorkman, Torsten Manns, and
       Jonas Sima. New York: Simon and Schuster, 1974,
       c. 1973. 288 pp. Translated by Paul Britten Austin.

2204   Harcourt, Peter. Six European Directors: Essays on the
       Meaning of Film Style. Baltimore: Penguin, 1974.
       287 pp.

2205   Kaminsky, Stuart M. with Hill, Joseph F. (eds.) Ingmar
       Bergman: Essays in Criticism. New York: Oxford
       University Press, 1975. 340 pp.

BERGMAN, INGRID

2206   Steele, Joseph Henry. Ingrid Bergman: An Intimate Portrait.
       New York: McKay, 1959. 365 pp.

2207   Quirk, Lawrence J. The Films of Ingrid Bergman. New
       York: Citadel, 1970. 224 pp.

2208   Brown, Curtis F. Ingrid Bergman. New York: Pyramid,
       1973. 157 pp.

BERKELEY, BUSBY

2209 Martin, David. The Films of Busby Berkeley. San Fran-
      cisco: n.p., 1965. 28 ℓ.

2210 Rohauer, Raymond. A Tribute to Busby Berkeley: The
      Master Builder of the American Musical Film. New York:
      Gallery of Modern Art Monograph, ca. 1966. 12 pp.

2211 Pike, Bob and Martin, Dave. The Genius of Busby Berkeley.
      Reseda, Cal.: Creative Film Society, 1973. 194 pp.
      Includes extensive interview with Berkeley.

2212 Thomas, Tony and Terry, Jim with Berkeley, Busby. The
      Busby Berkeley Book. Greenwich, Conn.: New York
      Graphic Society, 1973. 192 pp.

BERLE, MILTON

2213 Berle, Milton with Frankel, Haskel. Milton Berle: An Auto-
      biography. New York: Delacorte, 1974. 337 pp.

BERLIN, IRVING

2214 Ewen, David. The Story of Irving Berlin. New York: Holt,
      1950. 179 pp.

BERNHARDT, SARAH

2215 Verneuil, Louis. The Fabulous Life of Sarah Bernhardt.
      (Originally published 1942.) Westport, Conn.: Green-
      wood, 1972. 312 pp. Translated by Ernest Boyd.

2216 Skinner, Cornelia Otis. Madame Sarah. Boston: Houghton
      Mifflin, 1967. 356 pp.

2217 Taranow, Gerda. Sarah Bernhardt: The Art Within the
      Legend. Princeton, N.J.: Princeton University Press,
      1972. 287 pp.

BESSIE, ALVAH

2218 Bessie, Alvah. Inquisition in Eden. New York: Macmillan,
      1965. 278 pp.

BETTS, ERNEST

2219 Betts, Ernest. Inside Pictures. London: Cresset, 1960.
      161 pp.

BICKFORD, CHARLES

2220 Bickford, Charles. Bulls, Balls, Bicycles and Actors. New
      York: Eriksson, 1965. 336 pp.

BITZER, G. W. (BILLY)

2221 Bitzer, Billy. Billy Bitzer: His Story. New York: Farrar,
      Straus and Giroux, 1973. 266 pp.

BOETTICHER, BUDD

2222 Kitses, Jim (ed.) Budd Boetticher: The Western. London:
      British Film Institute, ca. 1969. 50 pp.
          Includes an interview with Boetticher and articles by
      Burt Kennedy, Andre Bazin, Andrew Sarris, Peter Wol-
      len and Jim Kitses.

2223 Kitses, Jim. Horizons West: Anthony Mann, Budd Boetticher,
      Sam Peckinpah: Studies of Authorship Within the Western.
      Bloomington: Indiana University Press, 1970. 176 pp.

2224 Sherman, Eric and Rubin, Martin. The Director's Event:
      Interviews with Five American Film-Makers. New York:
      Atheneum, 1970. 200 pp.

BOGARDE, DIRK

2225 Hinxman, Margaret and d'Arcy, Susan. The Cinema of Dirk
      Bogarde. South Brunswick, N.J.: A. S. Barnes, 1975.
      200 pp. (Also published as The Films of Dirk Bogarde.)

BOGART, HUMPHREY

2226 Gelman, Richard. Bogart. Greenwich, Conn.: Fawcett,
      1965. 159 pp.

2227 Goodman, Ezra. Bogey: The Good-Bad Guy. New York:
      Lyle Stuart, 1965. 223 pp.

2228 McCarty, Clifford. Bogey: The Films of Humphrey Bogart.
      New York: Citadel, c. 1965. 191 pp.

2229 Michael, Paul. Humphrey Bogart: The Man and His Films.
      Indianapolis: Bobbs-Merrill, 1965. 190 pp.

2230 Ruddy, Jonah and Hill, Jonathan. Bogey. New York: Tower,
      1965. 248 pp. (Also published as The Bogey Man.)

2231 Hyams, Joe. Bogie: The Biography of Humphrey Bogart.
      New York: New American Library, 1966. 210 pp.

2232 Bogart's Face. Los Angeles: Stanyan, 1970. 58 pp.
          Fifty photographs of Bogart.

2233 Barbour, Alan G. Humphrey Bogart. New York: Pyramid,
      1973. 160 pp.

2234 Benchley, Nathaniel. Humphrey Bogart. Boston: Little,
      Brown, 1975. 242 pp.

2235 Eyles, Allen. Bogart. Garden City, N.Y.: Doubleday,
      1975. 128 pp.

2236 Hyams, Joe. Bogart and Bacall: A Love Story. New York:
      McKay, 1975. 245 pp.

BOGDANOVICH, PETER

2237 Sherman, Eric and Rubin, Martin. The Director's Event:
      Interviews with Five American Film-Makers. New York:
      Atheneum, 1970. 200 pp.

BOLESLAVSKY, RICHARD

2238 Hardy, Michael Carrington. The Theatre Art of Richard
      Boleslavsky. University of Michigan: Ph.D., 1971.
      216 pp.

BOLTON, GUY

2239 Wodehouse, P. G. and Bolton, Guy. Bring On the Girls!
      The Improbable Story of Our Life in Musical Comedy,
      with Pictures to Prove It. New York: Simon and
      Schuster, 1953. 278 pp.

BONOMO, JOE

2240 Bonomo, Joe. The Strongman: A True Life Pictorial Auto-
      biography of the Hercules of the Screen, Joe Bonomo.
      New York: Bonomo Studios, 1968. 352 pp.

BORZAGE, FRANK

2241 Belton, John. The Hollywood Professionals, Vol. III: Howard
      Hawks, Frank Borzage, Edgar G. Ulmer. New York:
      A. S. Barnes, 1974. 182 pp.

BOW, CLARA

2242 Zierold, Norman. Sex Goddesses of the Silent Screen. Chi-
      cago: Regnery, 1973. 207 pp.

BOX, MURIEL

2243 Box, Muriel. Odd Woman Out: An Autobiography. London:
      Frewin, 1974. 272 pp.

BRAKHAGE, STAN

2244 Clark, Dan. Brakhage. New York: Film-Maker's Cinema-
      theque, 1966. 82 pp.

2245 Brakhage, Stan. The Seen: Remarks Following a Screening
      of "The Text of Light" at the San Francisco Art Institute,
      November 18, 1974. San Francisco: Paspeurize, 1975.
      Approx. 31 pp.

BRAND, MAX, pseudonym (see FAUST, FREDERICK)

BRANDO, MARLON

2246 Hamblett, Charles. Brando. New York: May Fair, 1962.
      160 pp.

2247 Carey, Gary. Brando! New York: Pocket Books, 1973.
      278 pp.

2248 Jordan, Rene. Marlon Brando. New York: Pyramid, 1973.
      157 pp.

2249 Morella, Joe and Epstein, Edward Z. Brando: The Un-
      authorized Biography. New York: Crown, 1973. 248 pp.

2250 Offen, Ron. Brando. Chicago: Regnery, 1973. 222 pp.

2251 Thomas, Bob. Marlon: Portrait of the Rebel as an Artist.
      New York: Random, 1973. 276 pp.

2252 Thomas, Tony. The Films of Marlon Brando. Secaucus,
      N.J.: Citadel, 1973. 246 pp.

2253 Fiore, Carlo. Bud: The Brando I Knew; The Untold Story
      of Brando's Private Life. New York: Delacorte, 1974.
      294 pp.

2254 Shipman, David. Brando. Garden City, N.Y.: Doubleday,
      1974. 127 pp.

BRENT, GEORGE

2255 Parish, James Robert and Stanke, Don E. The Debonairs.
      New Rochelle, N.Y.: Arlington, 1975. 511 pp.
          Contains a lengthy chapter on George Brent, including
      complete filmography.

BRESSON, ROBERT

2256 Taylor, John Russell. Cinema Eye, Cinema Ear: Some Key
      Film-Makers of the Sixties. New York: Hill and Wang,
      1964. 294 pp.

2257 Cameron, Ian (series ed.) The Films of Robert Bresson.
      New York: Praeger, 1970. 144 pp.
          Contributors include Amedee Ayfre, Charles Barr,

Andre Bazin, Raymond Durgnat, Phil Hardy, Daniel Millar
and Leo Murray.

2258 Schrader, Paul. Transcendental Style in Film: Ozu, Bresson,
Dreyer. Berkeley: University of California Press, 1972.
194 pp.

BRICE, FANNY

2259 Katkov, Norman. The Fabulous Fanny. New York: Knopf,
1953. 337 pp.

BRONSON, CHARLES

2260 Harbinson, W. A. Bronson! A Biographical Portrait. New
York: Pinnacle, 1975. 164 pp.

2261 Whitney, Steven. Charles Bronson: Superstar. New York:
Dell, 1975. 284 pp.

BROWN, JIM

2262 Toback, James. Jim: The Author's Self-Centered Memoir
on the Great Jim Brown. Garden City, N.Y.: Doubleday,
1971. 133 pp.

BROWN, JOE E.

2263 Brown, Joe E. with Hancock, Ralph. Laughter is a Wonderful Thing. New York: A. S. Barnes, 1956. 312 pp.

BROWN, JOHN MASON

2264 Stevens, George. Speak for Yourself, John: The Life of
John Mason Brown, with Some of His Letters and Many
of His Opinions. New York: Viking, 1974. 308 pp.

BROWN, KARL

2265 Brown, Karl. Adventures with D. W. Griffith. New York:
Farrar, Straus and Giroux, 1973. 252 pp.

BRUNEL, ADRIAN

2266 Brunel, Adrian. Nice Work: The Story of Thirty Years in
British Film Production. London: Forbes Robertson,
1949. 217 pp.

BRYAN, JULIEN

2267 Julien Bryan and His Documentary Motion Pictures. New
York: International Film Foundation, ca. 1951. 22 pp.

BUCK, FRANK

2268   Buck, Frank with Fraser, Ferrin. All In a Lifetime. New
       York: McBride, 1941. 277 pp.

BULL, CLARENCE SINCLAIR

2269   Bull, Clarence Sinclair with Lee, Raymond. The Faces of
       Hollywood. South Brunswick, N.J.: A. S. Barnes,
       1968. 256 pp.
          Includes material on Bull's career as a Hollywood
       portrait photographer, as well as examples of his work.

BULL, PETER

2270   Bull, Peter. I Say, Look Here! The Rather Random Remi-
       niscenses of a Round Actor in the Square. London:
       Peter Davies, 1965. 200 pp.

BUÑUEL, LUIS

2271   Kyro, Ado. Luis Buñuel: An Introduction. New York: Simon
       and Schuster, 1963. 208 pp. Translated by Adrienne
       Foulke.

2272   Taylor, John Russell. Cinema Eye, Cinema Ear: Some Key
       Film-Makers of the Sixties. New York: Hill and Wang,
       1964. 294 pp.

2273   Durgnat, Raymond. Luis Buñuel. Berkeley: University of
       California Press, 1968. 152 pp.

2274   Matthews, J. H. Surrealism and Film. Ann Arbor: Uni-
       versity of Michigan Press, 1971. 198 pp.
          With an emphasis on the work of Buñuel.

2275   Buache, Freddy. The Cinema of Luis Buñuel. New York:
       A. S. Barnes, 1973. 207 pp. Translated by Peter
       Graham.

2276   Wall, James M. (ed.) Three European Directors. Grand
       Rapids, Mich.: Eerdmans, 1973. 224 pp.
          Section on Buñuel by Peter Schillaci.

2277   Harcourt, Peter. Six European Directors: Essays on the
       Meaning of Film Style. Baltimore: Penguin, 1974.
       287 pp.

2278   Sandro, Paul Denney. Assault and Disruption in the Cinema:
       Four Films by Luis Buñuel. Cornell University: Ph.D.,
       1974. 163 pp.
          Discusses UN CHIEN ANDALOU, L'AGE D'OR, THE

EXTERMINATING ANGEL, and THE DISCREET CHARM
OF THE BOURGEOISIE.

2279   Aranda, Francisco. Luis Buñuel: A Critical Biography.
London: Secker and Warburg, 1975. 327 pp. Translated
and edited by David Robinson.

BURKE, BILLIE

2280   Burke, Billie with Shipp, Cameron. With a Feather on My
Nose. New York: Appleton-Century-Crofts, 1949. 272 pp.

2281   Burke, Billie with Shipp, Cameron. With Powder on My
Nose. New York: Coward-McCann, 1959. 249 pp.

BURNETT, CAROL

2282   Carpozi, George, Jr. The Carol Burnett Story. New York:
Warner Paperback Library, 1975. 206 pp.

BURNS, GEORGE

2283   Burns, George with Lindsay, Cynthia Hobart. I Love Her,
That's Why. New York: Simon and Schuster, 1955.
267 pp.

BURROUGHS, EDGAR RICE

2284   Fenton, Robert W. The Big Swingers. Englewood Cliffs,
N.J.: Prentice-Hall, 1967. 258 pp.

BURTON, RICHARD

2285   Waterbury, Ruth. Richard Burton. New York: Pyramid,
1965. 171 pp.

2286   Cottrell, John and Cashin, Fergus. Richard Burton: Very
Close Up. Englewood Cliffs, N.J.: Prentice-Hall, 1972.
385 pp. (Also published as Richard Burton: A Biography.)

CAGNEY, JAMES

2287   Dickens, Homer. The Films of James Cagney. Secaucus,
N.J.: Citadel, 1972. 249 pp.

2288   Offen, Ron. Cagney. Chicago: Regnery, 1972. 217 pp.

2289   Bergman, Andrew. James Cagney. New York: Pyramid,
1973. 156 pp.

2290   Freedland, Michael. Cagney: A Biography. New York:
Stein and Day, 1975. 255 pp.

2291 McGilligan, Patrick. Cagney: The Actor as Auteur. South
     Brunswick, N. J.: A. S. Barnes, 1975. 240 pp.

CANOVA, JUDY

2292 Parish, James Robert. The Slapstick Queens. South Bruns-
     wick, N. J.: A. S. Barnes, 1973. 297 pp.

CANTOR, EDDIE

2293 Cantor, Eddie and Freedman, David. (Originally published
     1929, 1931.) Yoo-Hoo Prosperity [and] Caught Short.
     Reprinted New York: Greenwood, 1969. 56, 45 pp.

2294 Cantor, Eddie with Ardmore, Jane Kesner. Take My Life.
     Garden City, N. Y.: Doubleday, 1957. 288 pp.

2295 Cantor, Eddie. The Way I See It. Englewood Cliffs, N. J.:
     Prentice-Hall, 1959. 204 pp.

2296 Cantor, Eddie. As I Remember Them. New York: Duell,
     Sloan and Pearce, 1963. 144 pp.

CAPRA, FRANK

2297 Griffith, Richard. Frank Capra. London: British Film In-
     stitute, ca. 1950. 38 pp.

2298 Capra, Frank. The Name Above the Title: An Autobiography.
     New York: Macmillan, 1971. 513 pp.

2299 Silke, James R. (ed.) Frank Capra: "One Man--One Film."
     Washington, D. C.: American Film Institute, 1971. 27 pp.
     Transcript of an AFI discussion with Capra.

2300 Willis, Donald C. The Films of Frank Capra. Metuchen,
     N. J.: Scarecrow, 1974. 214 pp.

2301 Glatzer, Richard and Raeburn, John (eds.) Frank Capra:
     The Man and His Films. Ann Arbor: University of
     Michigan Press, 1975. 190 pp.

2302 Poague, Leland. The Cinema of Frank Capra: An Approach
     to Film Comedy. South Brunswick, N. J.: A. S. Barnes,
     1975. 252 pp.

CARMICHAEL, HOAGY

2303 Carmichael, Hoagy. The Stardust Road. New York, Toronto:
     Rinehart, 1946. 156 pp.

2304 Carmichael, Hoagy with Longstreet, Stephen. The Story of

Hoagy Carmichael. New York: Farrar, Straus and Giroux, 1965. 313 pp.

CARNE, MARCEL

2305 Queval, Jean. Marcel Carné. London: British Film Institute, 1950. 27 pp.

CARRILLO, LEO

2306 Carrillo, Leo. The California I Love. Englewood Cliffs, N.J.: Prentice-Hall, 1961. 280 pp.

CARROLL, NANCY

2307 Nemcek, Paul L. The Films of Nancy Carroll. New York: Lyle Stuart, 1969. 223 pp.

CARSTAIRS, JOHN PADDY

2308 Carstairs, John Paddy. Honest Injun! A Light-Hearted Autobiography. London: Hurst and Blackett, 1942. 168 pp.

2309 Carstairs, John Paddy. Hadn't We the Gaiety? London: Hurst and Blackett, 1945. 107 pp.

CARUSO, ENRICO

2310 Caruso, Dorothy. Enrico Caruso: His Life and Death. New York: Simon and Schuster, 1945. 303 pp.

CARY, DIANA SERRA

2311 Cary, Diana Serra. The Hollywood Posse: The Story of a Gallant Band of Horsemen Who Made Movie History. Boston: Houghton Mifflin, 1975. 268 pp.

CASSAVETES, JOHN

2312 Loeb, Anthony (ed.) A Conversation with John Cassavetes. Chicago: Film Department, Columbia College, 1975. 16 pp.

CASTLE, IRENE and VERNON

2313 Castle, Irene with Duncan, Bob and Wanda. Castles in the Air. Garden City, N.Y.: Doubleday, 1958. 264 pp.

CHABROL, CLAUDE

2314 Wood, Robin and Walker, Michael. Claude Chabrol. New York: Praeger, 1970. 144 pp.

CHAMBERS, MARILYN

2315   Chambers, Marilyn. Marilyn Chambers: My Story. New
       York: Warner Paperback Library, 1975. 206 pp.

CHANDLER, RAYMOND

2316   Chandler, Raymond. Raymond Chandler Speaking. Edited by
       Dorothy Gardiner and Kathrine Sorley Walker. Boston:
       Houghton Mifflin, 1962. 271 pp.

2317   Durham, Philip. Down These Mean Streets a Man Must Go:
       Raymond Chandler's Knight. Chapel Hill: University of
       North Carolina Press, 1963. 173 pp.

CHANEY, LON

2318   Anderson, Robert. Faces, Forms, Films: The Artistry of
       Lon Chaney. South Brunswick, N.J.: A. S. Barnes,
       1971. 216 pp.

2319   Beck, Calvin Thomas. Heroes of the Horrors. New York:
       Macmillan, 1975. 353 pp.

CHANEY, LON, JR.

2320   Beck, Calvin Thomas. Heroes of the Horrors. New York:
       Macmillan, 1975. 353 pp.

CHAPLIN, CHARLES

2321   Bowman, William Dodgson. Charlie Chaplin: His Life and
       Art. (Originally published 1931.) Reprinted New York:
       Haskell, 1974. 142 pp.

2322   Ulm, Gerith von. Charlie Chaplin: King of Tragedy. Cald-
       well, Idaho: Claxton, 1940. 403 pp.

2323   Huff, Theodore. An Index to the Films of Charlie Chaplin.
       London: Sight and Sound, 1945. 35 pp.

2324   Tyler, Parker. A Little Boy Lost: Marcel Proust and
       Charlie Chaplin. New York: Prospero Pamphlets, 1947.
       12 pp.

2325   Tyler, Parker. Chaplin: Last of the Clowns. New York:
       Vanguard, 1948. 180 pp. (Republished New York:
       Horizon, 1972, 249 pp.)

2326   Cotes, Peter and Niklaus, Thelma. The Little Fellow: The
       Life and Work of Charlie Spencer Chaplin. New York:
       Philosophical Library, 1951. 160 pp. (Republished New
       York: Citadel, 1965, 181 pp.)

2327   Huff, Theodore. Charlie Chaplin. New York: Schuman,
       1951. 354 pp. (Reprinted New York: Arno, 1972.)

2328   Payne, Robert. The Great God Pan: A Biography of the
       Tramp Played by Charles Chaplin. New York: Hermi-
       tage, 1952. 301 pp. (Also published as The Great
       Charlie and as Charlie Chaplin.)

2329   Minney, R. J. Chaplin, The Immortal Tramp: The Life
       and Work of Charles Chaplin. London: Newnes, 1954.
       170 pp.

2330   Eastman, Max. Great Companions: Critical Memoirs of
       Some Famous Friends. New York: Farrar, Straus and
       Cudahy, 1959. 312 pp.
       One chapter on Chaplin.

2331   Chaplin, Charles, Jr. with Rau, N. and M. My Father,
       Charlie Chaplin. New York: Random, 1960. 369 pp.

2332   Huff, Theodore. The Early Works of Charles Chaplin. Lon-
       don: British Film Institute, 1961. 24 pp.
       Details on Chaplin films from 1914 to 1917.

2333   Chaplin, Charles. My Autobiography. New York: Simon
       and Schuster, 1964. 512 pp.

2334   McDonald, Gerald; Conway, Michael; and Ricci, Mark. The
       Films of Charlie Chaplin. New York: Citadel, 1965.
       224 pp.

2335   McDonald, Gerald. The Picture History of Charles Chaplin.
       Franklin Square, New York: Nostalgia, 1965. 64 pp.

2336   Sullivan, Ed. Chaplin vs. Chaplin. Los Angeles: Marvin
       Miller Enterprises, 1965. 225 pp.
       About the Lita Grey divorce case.

2337   Chaplin, Lita Grey with Cooper, Morton. My Life with
       Chaplin: An Intimate Memoir. New York: Bernard
       Geis, 1966. 325 pp.

2338   Chaplin, Michael. I Couldn't Smoke the Grass on My Father's
       Lawn. New York: Putnam, 1966. 171 pp.

2339   McCaffrey, Donald W. Four Great Comedians: Chaplin,
       Lloyd, Keaton, Langdon. New York: A. S. Barnes,
       1968. 175 pp.

2340   Quigly, Isabel. Charlie Chaplin: Early Comedies. New
       York: Dutton, 1968. 159 pp.

2341   McCaffrey, Donald W. (ed.) Focus on Chaplin. Englewood

Cliffs, N.J.: Prentice-Hall, 1971.   174 pp.
   Contributors include Chaplin, Louis Delluc, Winston
Churchill, and others.

2342   Asplund, Uno.   Chaplin's Films: A Filmography.   London:
       David and Charles, 1973.   204 pp.   Translated by Paul
       Britten Austin.
          Includes some biography and analysis as well as
       filmographic information.

2343   Chaplin, Charles.   My Life in Pictures.   Designed by David
       King.   London: Bodley Head, 1974.   320 pp.

2344   Gifford, Denis.   Chaplin.   Garden City, N.Y.: Doubleday,
       1974.   128 pp.

2345   Manvell, Roger.   Chaplin.   Boston: Little, Brown, 1974.
       240 pp.

2346   Jacobs, David.   Chaplin, The Movies, and Charlie.   New
       York: Harper and Row, 1975.   143 pp.
          For the young reader.

2347   Madden, David.   Harlequin's Stick--Charlie's Cane: A Com-
       parative Study of Commedia Dell'Arte and Silent Slapstick
       Comedy.   Bowling Green, Ohio: Bowling Green University
       Popular Press, 1975.   174 pp.

2348   Moss, Robert F.   Charlie Chaplin.   New York: Pyramid,
       1975.   158 pp.

CHASE, CHRIS

2349   Chase, Chris.   How to be a Movie Star: Or A Terrible
       Beauty Is Born.   New York: Harper and Row, 1974.
       208 pp.

CHASE, ILKA

2350   Chase, Ilka.   Past Imperfect.   Garden City, N.Y.: Double-
       day, 1945.   278 pp.

2351   Chase, Ilka.   Free Admission.   Garden City, N.Y.: Double-
       day, 1948.   319 pp.

2352   Chase, Ilka.   Elephants Arrive at Half-Past Five.   London:
       W. H. Allen, 1964.   269 pp.

2353   Chase, Ilka.   The Varied Airs of Spring.   Garden City, N.Y.:
       Doubleday, 1969.   262 pp.

2354   Chase, Ilka.   Around the World and Other Places.   Garden
       City, N.Y.: Doubleday, 1970.   300 pp.

2355   Chase, Ilka. Worlds Apart. Garden City, N.Y.: Doubleday,
        1972. 273 pp.

CHAUVEL, ELSA and CHARLES

2356   Chauvel, Elsa. My Life with Charles Chauvel. Sydney:
        Shakespeare Head, 1973. 191 pp.

CHERKASOV, NIKOLAI

2357   Cherkasov, Nikolai. Notes of a Soviet Actor. Moscow:
        Foreign Languages Publishing House, 1957. 227 pp.

CHEVALIER, MAURICE

2358   Chevalier, Maurice. The Man in the Straw Hat: My Story.
        New York: Crowell, 1949. 245 pp. Translated by
        Caroline Clark.

2359   Chevalier, Maurice with Pollock, Eileen and Robert. With
        Love. Boston: Little, Brown, 1960. 424 pp.

2360   Chevalier, Maurice. I Remember It Well. New York: Mac-
        millan, 1970. 221 pp. Translated by Cornelia Higginson.

2361   Ringgold, Gene and Bodeen, DeWitt. Chevalier: The Films
        and Career of Maurice Chevalier. Secaucus, N.J.:
        Citadel, 1973. 242 pp.

CHRISTIAN, LINDA

2362   Christian, Linda. Linda: My Own Story. New York: Crown,
        1962. 280 pp.
            Autobiography of the actress-wife of Tyrone Power.

CHUKHRAI, GRIGORI

2363   Chang, Kuang-nien. An Example of Modern Revisionism in
        Art: A Critique of the Films and Statements of Grigori
        Chukhrai. Peking: Foreign Languages Press, 1965. 53 pp.

CLAIR, RENE

2364   Clair, René. Reflections on the Cinema. London: William
        Kimber, 1953. 160 pp. Translated by Vera Traill.

2365   De La Roche, Catherine. René Clair: An Index. London:
        British Film Institute, 1958. 44 pp.

2366   Clair, René. Cinema Yesterday and Today. Edited and intro-
        duced by R. C. Dale. New York: Dover, 1972. 260 pp.
        Translated by Stanley Appelbaum.

CLUNES, ALEC

2367   Trewin, John Courtenay. Alec Clunes: An Illustrated Study
       of His Work, with a List of His Appearances on Stage and
       Screen. London: Rockliff, 1958. 134 pp.

COCTEAU, JEAN

2368   Cocteau, Jean. Cocteau on the Film: A Conversation Re-
       corded by Andre Fraigneau. New York: Roy, 1954.
       140 pp. Translated by Vera Traill. (Reprinted New
       York: Dover, 1972.)

2369   Crosland, Margaret. Jean Cocteau. London: Nevill, 1955.
       206 pp.

2370   Cocteau, Jean. The Journals of Jean Cocteau. Edited and
       translated by Wallace Fowlie. New York: Criterion,
       1956. 250 pp.

2371   Oxenhandler, Neal. Scandal and Parade: The Theater of
       Jean Cocteau. New Brunswick, N.J.: Rutgers University
       Press, 1957. 284 pp.
       Includes some analysis of Cocteau's films.

2372   Fraigneau, Andre. Cocteau. New York: Grove, 1961.
       192 pp. Translated by Donald Lehmkuhl.

2373   Fowlie, Wallace. Jean Cocteau: The History of a Poet's Age.
       Bloomington: Indiana University Press, 1966. 181 pp.

2374   Cocteau, Jean. The Difficulty of Being. New York: Coward-
       McCann, 1967. 160 pp. Translated by Elizabeth Sprigge.

2375   Brown, Frederick. An Impersonation of Angels: A Biography
       of Jean Cocteau. New York: Viking, 1968. 438 pp.

2376   Sprigge, Elizabeth and Kihm, Jean-Jacques. Jean Cocteau:
       The Man and the Mirror. New York: Coward-McCann,
       1968. 286 pp.

2377   Gilson, Rene. Jean Cocteau. New York: Crown, 1969.
       192 pp. Translated by Ciba Vaughan.

2378   Cocteau, Jean. Professional Secrets: An Autobiography of
       Jean Cocteau, Drawn from His Lifetime Writings by
       Robert Phelps. New York: Farrar, Straus and Giroux,
       1970. 331 pp. Translated by Richard Howard.

2379   Steegmuller, Francis. Cocteau: A Biography. Boston:
       Little, Brown, 1970. 583 pp.

COFFEE, LENORE

2380 Coffee, Lenore. Storyline: Recollections of a Hollywood Screenwriter. London: Cassell, 1973. 212 pp.

COHAN, GEORGE M.

2381 Morehouse, Ward. George M. Cohan: Prince of the American Theater. Philadelphia: Lippincott, 1943. 240 pp.

COHN, HARRY

2382 Thomas, Bob. King Cohn: The Life and Times of Harry Cohn. New York: Putnam, 1967. 381 pp.

COLE, NAT KING

2383 Cole, Maria with Robinson, Louie. Nat King Cole: An Intimate Biography. New York: Morrow, 1971. 184 pp.

COLMAN, RONALD

2384 Colman, Juliet Benita. Ronald Colman, A Very Private Person: A Biography. New York: Morrow, 1975. 294 pp.

COLONNA, JERRY

2385 Colonna, Jerry. Who Threw That Coconut! Garden City, N.Y.: McCombs, distributed by Garden City Publishing, 1946. 94 pp.

CONLON, PAUL HUBERT (SCOOP)

2386 McCallum, John Dennis. Scooper: Authorized Story of Scoop Conlon's Motion Picture World. Seattle: Wood and Reber, 1960. 274 pp.
Biography of Conlon, newspaperman and friend of many Hollywood stars.

CONNERY, SEAN

2387 Gant, Richard. Sean Connery: Gilt-Edged Bond. London: Mayflower, 1967. 109 pp.

COOPER, GLADYS

2388 Stokes, Sewell. Without Veils: The Intimate Biography of Gladys Cooper. London: Peter Davies, 1953. 243 pp.

COOPER, GARY

2389 Gehman, Richard. The Tall American: The Story of Gary

Cooper. New York: Hawthorn, 1963. 187 pp.
For the young reader.

2390 Carpozi, George. The Gary Cooper Story. New Rochelle,
N.Y.: Arlington, 1970. 263 pp.

2391 Dickens, Homer. The Films of Gary Cooper. New York:
Citadel, 1970. 281 pp.

2392 Smith, Milburn (ed.) Gary Cooper. New York: Barven,
1972. 66 pp.

COOPER, MIRIAM

2393 Cooper, Miriam with Herndon, Bonnie. Dark Lady of the
Silents: My Life in Early Hollywood. Indianapolis:
Bobbs-Merrill, 1973. 256 pp.

COPLAND, AARON

2394 Smith, Julia. Aaron Copland: His Work and Contribution to
American Music. New York: Dutton, 1955. 336 pp.

CORMAN, ROGER

2395 Willemen, Paul; Pirie, David; Will, David; and Myles,
Linda. Roger Corman: The Millenic Vision. Cambridge,
England: Edinburgh Film Festival, 1970. 102 pp.

CORTEZ, STANLEY

2396 Higham, Charles. Hollywood Cameramen: Sources of Light.
Bloomington: Indiana University Press, 1970. 176 pp.

COSGRAVE, LUKE

2397 Cosgrave, Luke. Theatre Tonight. Hollywood: House-
Warven, 1952. 245 pp.

COSTELLO, LOU (see ABBOTT, BUD)

COTES, PETER

2398 Cotes, Peter. No Star Nonsense. London: Rockliff, 1949.
198 pp.

COURTNEIDGE, CICELY

2399 Courtneidge, Cicely. Cicely. London: Hutchinson, 1953.
224 pp.

COWARD, NOEL

2400   Coward, Noel. Future Indefinite. Garden City, N.Y.:
       Doubleday, 1954. 352 pp.

2401   Levin, Milton. Noel Coward. New York: Twayne, 1968.
       158 pp.

2402   Morley, Sheridan. A Talent to Amuse: A Biography of
       Noel Coward. Garden City, N.Y.: Doubleday, 1969.
       453 pp.

2403   Castle, Charles. Noel. London: W. H. Allen, 1972. 272 pp.

2404   Marchant, William. The Privilege of His Company: Noel
       Coward Remembered. Indianapolis: Bobbs-Merrill,
       c. 1975. 276 pp.

COX, WALLY

2405   Cox, Wally. My Life as a Small Boy. New York: Simon and
       Schuster, 1961. 128 pp.

CRAWFORD, JOAN

2406   Crawford, Joan with Ardmore, Jane Kesner. A Portrait of
       Joan: The Autobiography of Joan Crawford. Garden City,
       N.Y.: Doubleday, 1962. 239 pp.

2407   Quirk, Lawrence J. The Films of Joan Crawford. New York:
       Citadel, 1968. 222 pp.

2408   Carr, Larry. Four Fabulous Faces: The Evolution and Meta-
       morphosis of Garbo, Swanson, Crawford, and Dietrich.
       New Rochelle, New York: Arlington, 1970. 492 pp.
       Primarily photographs.

2409   Crawford, Joan. My Way of Life. New York: Simon and
       Schuster, 1971. 224 pp.

2410   Harvey, Stephen. Joan Crawford. New York: Pyramid, 1974.
       159 pp.

CROMWELL, JOHN

2411   Davies, Brenda. John Cromwell. London: British Film In-
       stitute, 1974. 40 pp.

CROSBY, BING

2412   Crosby, Ted. The Story of Bing Crosby. (Originally published
       1937.) Cleveland: World, 1946. 239 pp.

2413 Ulanov, Barry. The Incredible Crosby. New York: Whittle-
      sey, 1948. 336 pp.

2414 Crosby, Bing with Martin, Pete. Call Me Lucky. New York:
      Simon and Schuster, 1953. 334 pp.

2415 Crosby, Kathryn. Bing and Other Things. New York: Mere-
      dith, 1967. 214 pp.

2416 Thompson, Charles. Bing: The Authorised Biography. Lon-
      don: W. H. Allen, 1975. 249 pp.

CROWTHER, BOSLEY

2417 Beaver, Frank Eugene. Bosley Crowther: Social Critic of
      the Film, 1940-1967. New York: Arno, 1974. 187 pp.

CUGAT, XAVIER

2418 Cugat, Xavier. Rumba Is My Life. New York: Didier, 1948.
      210 pp.

CUKOR, GEORGE

2419 Battle, Barbara Helen. George Cukor and the American
      Theatrical Film. Columbia University: Ph.D., 1969.
      304 pp.

2420 Carey, Gary. Cukor & Co.: The Films of George Cukor
      and His Collaborators. New York: Museum of Modern
      Art, 1971. 167 pp.

2421 Lambert, Gavin. On Cukor. New York: Putnam, 1972.
      276 pp.
      Interviews.

CURTIZ, MICHAEL

2422 Canham, Kingsley. The Hollywood Professionals, Vol. I:
      Michael Curtiz, Raoul Walsh, Henry Hathaway. New
      York: A. S. Barnes, 1973. 200 pp.

CUSHING, PETER

2423 Hirst, Robert. Three Men and a Gimmick. Kingswood,
      England: The World's Work, 1957. 125 pp.

CUSSLER, MARGRET

2424 Cussler, Margret. Not By a Long Shot: Adventures of a
      Documentary Film Producer. New York: Exposition,
      1951. 200 pp.

DACHE, LILLY

2425 Dache, Lilly with Lewis, Dorothy Roe. Talking Througy My
      Hats. New York: Coward-McCann, 1946. 265 pp.
           Reminiscences of a hatmaker to the stars.

DAGUERRE, L. J. M.

2426 Gernsheim, Helmut and Alison. L. J. M. Daguerre (1787-
      1851): The World's First Photographer. Cleveland:
      World, 1956. 216 pp. (Also published with the subtitle
      The History of the Diorama and the Daguerreotype.)

DANDRIDGE, DOROTHY

2427 Dandridge, Dorothy and Conrad, Earl. Everything and Nothing:
      The Dorothy Dandridge Tragedy. New York: Abelard-
      Schuman, 1970. 215 pp.

2428 Mills, Earl. Dorothy Dandridge: A Portrait in Black. Los
      Angeles: Holloway, 1970. 248 pp.

DANIELS, BEBE

2429 Daniels, Bebe and Lyon, Ben. Life with the Lyons: The
      Autobiography of Bebe Daniels & Ben Lyon. London:
      Odhams, 1953. 256 pp.

DANIELS, WILLIAM

2430 Higham, Charles. Hollywood Cameramen: Sources of Light.
      Bloomington: Indiana University Press, 1970. 176 pp.

DANISCHEWSKY, MONJA

2431 Danischewsky, Monja. White Russian--Red Face. London:
      Gollancz, 1966. 192 pp.

DAVIES, MARION

2432 Guiles, Fred Lawrence. Marion Davies: A Biography. New
      York: McGraw-Hill, 1972. 419 pp.

2433 Davies, Marion. The Times We Had: Life with William
      Randolph Hearst. Edited by Pamela Pfau and Kenneth S.
      Marx. Introduced by Orson Welles. Indianapolis: Bobbs-
      Merrill, 1975. 276 pp.

DAVIS, BETTE

2434 Noble, Peter. Bette Davis: A Biography. London: Robin-
      son, 1948. 232 pp.

2435 Davis, Bette. The Lonely Life. New York: Putnam, 1962.
315 pp.

2436 Ringgold, Gene. The Films of Bette Davis. New York:
Citadel, 1966. 191 pp.

2437 Vermilye, Jerry. Bette Davis. New York: Pyramid, 1973.
159 pp.

2438 Stine, Whitney with a running commentary by Bette Davis.
Mother Goddam: The Story of the Career of Bette Davis.
New York: Hawthorn, 1974. 374 pp.

DAVIS, JOAN

2439 Parish, James Robert. The Slapstick Queens. South Brunswick, N.J.: A. S. Barnes, 1973. 297 pp.

DAVIS, OWEN

2440 Davis, Owen. My First Fifty Years in the Theatre. Boston:
Baker, 1950. 157 pp.

DAVIS, SAMMY, JR.

2441 Davis, Sammy, Jr. and Boyar, Jane and Burt. Yes, I Can:
The Story of Sammy Davis, Jr. New York: Farrar,
Straus and Giroux, 1965. 612 pp.

DAY, DORIS

2442 Day, Doris with Hotchner, A. E. Doris Day: Her Own
Story. New York: Morrow, c. 1975. 313 pp.

DEACOSTA, MERCEDES

2443 Deacosta, Mercedes. Here Lies the Heart. New York:
Reynal, 1960. 372 pp.

DEAN, JAMES

2444 Bast, William. James Dean: A Biography. New York:
Ballantine, 1956. 153 pp.

2445 Meyerson, Peter (ed.) The Official James Dean Anniversary
Book. New York: Dell, 1956. 74 pp.

2446 Thomas, T. T. I, James Dean: The Real Story Behind
America's Most Popular Idol. New York: Popular Library, 1957. 128 pp.

2447 Ellis, Royston. Rebel. London: World, 1962. 157 pp.

2448 Dalton, David. James Dean, The Mutant King: A Biography.
      San Francisco: Straight Arrow, 1974. 356 pp.

2449 Herndon, Venable. James Dean: A Short Life. Garden City,
      N.Y.: Doubleday, 1974. 288 pp.

2450 Whitman, Mark. The Films of James Dean. London: Barn-
      den Castell Williams, 1974. 47 pp.

2451 Gilmore, John. The Real James Dean. New York: Pyramid,
      1975. 160 pp.

2452 Howlett, John. James Dean: A Biography. New York:
      Simon and Schuster, 1975. 190 pp.

2453 Martinetti, Ronald. The James Dean Story. New York:
      Pinnacle, 1975. 185 pp.

DE HAVILLAND, OLIVIA

2454 De Havilland, Olivia. Every Frenchman Has One. New York:
      Random, 1962. 202 pp.

DE MILLE, AGNES

2455 De Mille, Agnes. Dance to the Piper. Boston: Little,
      Brown, 1952. 342 pp.
      Includes material on William and Cecil B. De Mille.

DE MILLE, CECIL B.

2456 De Mille, Cecil B. The Autobiography of Cecil B. De Mille.
      Edited by Donald Hayne. Englewood Cliffs, N.J.: Pren-
      tice-Hall, 1959. 465 pp.

2457 Koury, Phil A. Yes, Mr. De Mille. New York: Putnam,
      1959. 319 pp.

2458 Myers, Hortense and Burnett, Ruth. Cecil B. De Mille:
      Young Dramatist. Indianapolis: Bobbs-Merrill, 1963.
      200 pp.
      For the young reader.

2459 Ringgold, Gene and Bodeen, DeWitt. The Films of Cecil B.
      De Mille. New York: Citadel, 1969. 377 pp.

2460 Essoe, Gabe and Lee, Raymond. De Mille: The Man and
      His Pictures. South Brunswick, N.J.: A. S. Barnes,
      1970. 319 pp.

2461 Higham, Charles. Cecil B. De Mille. New York: Scrib-
      ner's, 1973. 335 pp.

DENHAM, REGINALD

2462 Denham, Reginald. Stars in My Hair: Being Certain Indis-
     creet Memoirs. New York: Crown, 1958. 256 pp.

DENIS, ARMAND

2463 Denis, Armand. On Safari: The Story of My Life. New
     York: Dutton, 1963. 320 pp.

DESMOND, FLORENCE

2464 Desmond, Florence. Florence Desmond. London: Harrap,
     1953. 303 pp.

DICKSON, W. K. L.

2465 Hendricks, Gordon. The Edison Motion Picture Myth. Berke-
     ley: University of California Press, 1961. 216 pp. (Re-
     printed in Origins of the American Film, New York: Arno,
     1972.)
          Discusses the collaboration of W. K. L. Dickson and
     Edison.

DIETRICH, MARLENE

2466 Frewin, Leslie. Blond Venus: A Life of Marlene Dietrich.
     New York: Roy, 1956. 159 pp. (Revised as Dietrich:
     The Story of a Star, New York: Stein and Day, 1967,
     192 pp.)

2467 Griffith, Richard. Marlene Dietrich: Image and Legend.
     Garden City, N.Y.: Doubleday, for the Museum of Modern
     Art Film Library, 1959. 32 pp.

2468 Dietrich, Marlene. Marlene Dietrich's A B C. New York:
     Avon, 1962. 160 pp.
          Dietrich's personal comments on a wide variety of
     topics.

2469 Dickens, Homer. The Films of Marlene Dietrich. New York:
     Citadel, 1968. 223 pp.

2470 Kobal, John. Marlene Dietrich. New York: Dutton, 1968.
     160 pp.

2471 Carr, Larry. Four Fabulous Faces: The Evolution and Meta-
     morphosis of Garbo, Swanson, Crawford and Dietrich.
     New Rochelle, N.Y.: Arlington, 1970. 492 pp.
          Primarily photographs.

2472 Silver, Charles. Marlene Dietrich. New York: Pyramid,
     1974. 160 pp.

DIETZ, HOWARD

2473 Dietz, Howard. Dancing in the Dark: Words by Howard
     Dietz. New York: Quadrangle, 1974. 370 pp.

DILLER, PHYLLIS

2474 Parish, James Robert. The Slapstick Queens. South Bruns-
     wick, N.J.: A. S. Barnes, 1973. 297 pp.

DISNEY, WALT

2475 Feild, Robert D. The Art of Walt Disney. New York: Mac-
     millan, 1942. 290 pp.

2476 Miller, Diane Disney with Martin, Pete. The Story of Walt
     Disney. New York: Holt, 1957. 247 pp.

2477 Thomas, Bob. Walt Disney, The Art of Animation: The
     Story of the Disney Studio Contribution to a New Art.
     New York: Simon and Schuster, 1958. 181 pp.

2478 Thomas, Bob. Walt Disney: Magician of the Movies. New
     York: Grosset and Dunlap, 1966. 176 pp.

2479 Schickel, Richard. The Disney Version: The Life, Times,
     Art, and Commerce of Walt Disney. New York: Simon
     and Schuster, 1968. 384 pp.

2480 Hammontree, Marie. Walt Disney, Young Movie Maker.
     Indianapolis: Bobbs-Merrill, 1969. 200 pp.
     For the young reader.

2481 Kurland, Gerald. Walt Disney, The Master of Animation.
     Charlotteville, N.Y.: SamHar Press, 1971. 31 pp.

2482 Montgomery, Elizabeth R. Walt Disney: Master of Make-
     Believe. Champaign, Ill.: Garrard, 1971. 96 pp.
     For the young reader.

2483 Arseni, Ercole; Bosi, Leone; and Marconi, Massimo. Magic
     Moments: Walt Disney. Milan: Mondadori, 1973. 191 pp.

2484 Finch, Christopher. The Art of Walt Disney: From Mickey
     Mouse to the Magic Kingdoms. New York: Abrams,
     1973. 458 pp. (Published in a shorter version 1975,
     160 pp.)

2485 Maltin, Leonard. The Disney Films. New York: Crown,
     1973. 312 pp.

2486 Larson, Norita. Walt Disney: An American Original.

Mankato, Minn.: Creative Education, 1974. 31 pp.
For the young reader.

2487 Munsey, Cecil. Disneyana: Walt Disney Collectibles. New
York: Hawthorn, 1974. 385 pp.

2488 Dorfman, Ariel and Mattelart, Armand. How to Read Donald
Duck: Imperialist Ideology in the Disney Comic. Introduction and translation by David Kunzle. New York: International General, 1975. 112 pp.
A Marxist study of the Disney comic and cultural imperialism.

DIX, BEULAH MARIE

2489 Scott, Evelyn F. Hollywood When Silents Were Golden. New
York: McGraw-Hill, 1972. 223 pp.
Reminiscence of early Hollywood life with emphasis on
the author's mother, scenarist Beulah Marie Dix, and the
DeMille family.

DONAT, ROBERT

2490 Trewin, J. C. Robert Donat: A Biography. London: Heinemann, 1968. 252 pp.

DONEN, STANLEY

2491 Davies, Brenda (comp.) Stanley Donen: Director. London:
British Film Institute, 1969. 8 pp.

DOUGLAS, KIRK

2492 Thomas, Tony. The Films of Kirk Douglas. Secaucus, N.J.:
Citadel, 1972. 255 pp.

DOUGLAS, MELVYN

2493 Parish, James Robert and Stanke, Don E. The Debonairs.
New Rochelle, N.Y.: Arlington, 1975. 511 pp.
Contains a lengthy chapter on Melvyn Douglas, including
complete filmography.

DOVZHENKO, ALEXANDER

2494 Leyda, Jay (comp.) An Index to the Creative Work of Alexander Dovzhenko. London: Sight and Sound, 1947.
7 pp.

2495 Dovzhenko, Alexander. Alexander Dovzhenko: The Poet as
Filmmaker; Selected Writings. Edited and translated by
Marco Carynnyk. Cambridge, Mass.: M.I.T. Press,
1973. 323 pp.

DRAGONETTE, JESSICA

2496   Dragonette, Jessica. Faith Is a Song: The Odyssey of an
       American Artist. New York: McKay, 1951. 322 pp.

DRESSLER, MARIE

2497   Raider, Roberta Ann. A Descriptive Study of the Acting of
       Marie Dressler. University of Michigan: Ph.D., 1970.
       295 pp.

DREYER, CARL

2498   Neergaard, Ebbe. Carl Dreyer: A Film Director's Work.
       London: British Film Institute, 1950. 42 pp. Trans-
       lated by Marianne Helweg.

2499   Bowser, Eileen. The Films of Carl Dreyer. New York:
       Museum of Modern Art Film Library, ca. 1964. 7 pp.

2500   Monty, Ib. Portrait of Carl Th. Dreyer. Copenhagen:
       Danish Government Film Foundation, 1967. 16 pp.

2501   Dyssegaard, Soren (ed.) Carl Th. Dreyer: Danish Film
       Director, 1889-1968. Copenhagen: Ministry of Foreign
       Affairs, ca. 1969. 51 pp. Translated by Reginald Spink.
       Includes articles on Dreyer and scenes from the
       script for JESUS.

2502   Milne, Tom. The Cinema of Carl Dreyer. New York: A.
       S. Barnes, 1971. 192 pp.

2503   Brakhage, Stan. The Brakhage Lectures. Chicago: The
       Good Lion, School of the Art Institute of Chicago, 1972.
       106 pp.

2504   Schrader, Paul. Transcendental Style in Film: Ozu, Bresson,
       Dreyer. Berkeley: University of California Press, 1972.
       194 pp.

2505   Dreyer, Carl. Dreyer in Double Reflection: Translation of
       Carl Th. Dreyer's Writings "About the Film" (Om Filmen).
       Edited and with accompanying commentary and essays by
       Donald Skoller. New York: Dutton, 1973. 205 pp.

DUKE, VERNON (DUKELSKY, VLADIMIR)

2506   Duke, Vernon. Passport to Paris. Boston: Little, Brown,
       1955. 502 pp.

DUNCAN, SANDY

2507   Reed, Rochelle. The Sandy Duncan Story. New York: Pyra-
       mid, 1973.

DURANTE, JIMMY

2508 Fowler, Gene. Schnozzola, The Story of Jimmy Durante.
      New York: Viking, 1951. 261 pp.

2509 Halsman, Philippe and others. The Candidate: A Photo-
      graphic Interview with The Honorable James Durante.
      New York: Simon and Schuster, 1952. 119 pp.

2510 Cahn, William. Good Night, Mrs. Calabash: The Secret of
      Jimmy Durante. New York: Duell, Sloan and Pearce,
      1963. 191 pp.

DUTT, GURU

2511 Rangoonwalla, Firoze. Guru Dutt, 1925-1965: A Monograph.
      Poona: National Film Archive of India, 1973. 133 pp.

DWAN, ALLAN

2512 Bogdanovich, Peter. Allan Dwan: The Last Pioneer. New
      York: Praeger, 1971. 200 pp.
            Primarily interview.

EAST, JOHN M.

2513 East, John M. 'Neath the Mask: The Story of the East
      Family. London: Allen and Unwin, 1967. 356 pp.

EASTWOOD, CLINT

2514 Douglas, Peter. Clint Eastwood: Movin' On. Chicago:
      Regnery, 1974. 147 pp.

2515 Kaminsky, Stuart M. Clint Eastwood. New York: New
      American Library, 1974. 150 pp.

2516 Agan, Patrick. Clint Eastwood: The Man Behind the Myth.
      New York: Pyramid, 1975. 188 pp.

EDDY, NELSON

2517 Knowles, Eleanor. The Films of Jeanette MacDonald and
      Nelson Eddy. South Brunswick, N.J.: A. S. Barnes,
      1975. 469 pp.

EDISON, THOMAS ALVA

2518 Edison, Thomas Alva. The Diary and Sundry Observations of
      Thomas A. Edison. Edited by Dagobert D. Runes. New
      York: Philosophical Library, 1948. 247 pp. (Republished
      New York: Greenwood, 1968, 181 pp.)

2519 Josephson, Matthew. Edison: A Biography. New York:
McGraw-Hill, 1959. 511 pp.

2520 Hendricks, Gordon. The Edison Motion Picture Myth.
Berkeley: University of California Press, 1961. 216 pp.
(Reprinted in Origins of the American Film, New York:
Arno, 1972.)
Discusses the collaboration of W. K. L. Dickson and
Edison.

2521 Beasley, Rex. Edison: A Biography. Philadelphia: Chilton,
1964. 176 pp.

2522 Hutchings, David W. Edison at Work: The Thomas A. Edison
Laboratory at West Orange, N.J. New York: Hastings,
1969. 94 pp.

EGGELING, VIKING

2523 O'Konor, Louise. Viking Eggeling, 1880-1925: Artist and
Filmmaker, Life and Work. Stockholm: Almquist and
Wiksell, 1971. 300 pp.

EHRLICH, JACOB W.

2524 Ehrlich, Jacob W. A Life in My Hands: An Autobiography.
New York: Putnam, 1965. 379 pp.
Life story of a lawyer who worked on Hollywood cases.

EICHHORN, FRANZ

2525 Eichhorn, Franz. The Lost World of the Amazon. London:
Souvenir, 1955. 188 pp.

EISENSTEIN, SERGEI

2526 Seton, Marie. Sergei M. Eisenstein: A Biography. New
York: Wyn, 1952. 533 pp. (Reprinted New York: Grove,
1960.)

2527 Eisenstein, Sergei. Notes of a Film Director. London:
Lawrence and Wishart, 1959. 207 pp. Translated by X.
Danko. (Reprinted New York: Dover, 1970.)

2528 Eisenstein, Drawings: Catalogue of an Exhibition at the Vic-
toria and Albert Museum, Sept. 26th-Nov. 10th. Ipswich:
Cowell, 1963. 18 pp.
Brief essays by Eisenstein, Ivor Montagu and David
Robinson; no drawings included.

2529 Montagu, Ivor. With Eisenstein in Hollywood: A Chapter of
Autobiography. New York: International Publishers, 1969.
356 pp.

2530 Wollen, Peter. Signs and Meaning in the Cinema. Bloom-
        ington: Indiana University Press, 1969. 168 pp. (Re-
        vised 1972, 175 pp.)
        Contains a lengthy chapter on Eisenstein.

2531 Moussinac, Leon. Sergei Eisenstein: An Investigation Into
        His Films and Philosophy. New York: Crown, 1970.
        226 pp. Translated by D. Sandy Petrey.
        Contains writings by Eisenstein and film treatment
        excerpts as well as critical analysis by Moussinac and
        others.

2532 Brakhage, Stan. The Brakhage Lectures. Chicago: The
        Good Lion, School of the Art Institute of Chicago, 1972.
        106 pp.

2533 Barna, Yon. Eisenstein. Introduction by Jay Leyda.
        Bloomington: Indiana University Press, 1973. 287 pp.
        Translated by Lise Hunter.

2534 Harcourt, Peter. Six European Directors: Essays on the
        Meaning of Film Style. Baltimore: Penguin, 1974.
        287 pp.

EKBERG, ANITA

2535 Laborderie, Renaud de. Anita Ekberg. Manchester, England:
        World Distributors, 1965.

ELKINS, HILLARD

2536 Davis, Christopher. The Producer. New York: Harper
        and Row, 1972. 321 pp.
        Includes material on the production of ALICE'S RES-
        TAURANT and A NEW LEAF.

ENTERS, ANGNA

2537 Enters, Angna. Artist's Life. New York: Coward-McCann,
        1958. 447 pp.

EPSTEIN, JEAN

2538 Bachmann, Gideon with Benoit-Levy, Jean (eds.) The First
        Comprehensive Presentation of the Work of Jean Epstein
        in the United States. New York: Group for Film Study,
        ca. 1955. 54 pp.

EVANS, DALE (see ROGERS, ROY)

EVANS, EDITH

2539 Trewin, John Courtenay. Edith Evans: An Illustrated Study

of Dame Edith's Work, with a List of Her Appearances
on Stage and Screen. London: Rockliff, 1954. 116 pp.

FAIRBANKS, DOUGLAS

2540 Cooke, Alistair. Douglas Fairbanks: The Making of a Screen
Character. New York: Museum of Modern Art, 1940.
36 pp.

2541 Hancock, Ralph and Fairbanks, Letitia. Douglas Fairbanks:
The Fourth Musketeer. New York: Holt, 1953. 276 pp.

2542 Schickel, Richard. His Picture in the Papers: A Specula-
tion on Celebrity in America Based on the Life of Douglas
Fairbanks, Sr. New York: Charterhouse, c. 1973.
171 pp.

2543 Fairbanks, Douglas, Jr. and Schickel, Richard. The Fairbanks Album. Boston: New York Graphic Society, 1975.
286 pp.

FAIRBANKS, DOUGLAS, JR.

2544 Connell, Brian. Knight Errant: A Biography of Douglas
Fairbanks, Jr. Garden City, N.Y.: Doubleday, 1955.
255 pp.

2545 Fairbanks, Douglas, Jr. and Schickel, Richard. The Fairbanks Album. Boston: New York Graphic Society, 1975.
286 pp.

FALKENBURG, JINX

2546 Falkenburg, Jinx. Jinx. New York: Duell, Sloan and Pearce,
1951. 273 pp.

FARMER, FRANCES

2547 Farmer, Frances. Will There Really Be a Morning? An
Autobiography. New York: Putnam, 1972. 318 pp.

FAULK, JOHN HENRY

2548 Faulk, John Henry. Fear on Trial. New York: Simon and
Schuster, 1964. 398 pp.

FAULKNER, WILLIAM

2549 Savarese, Paul. Cinematic Techniques in the Novels of
William Faulkner. St. Louis University: Ph.D., 1972.
162 pp.

FAUST, FREDERICK

2550 Easton, Robert. Max Brand: The Big Westerner. Norman:
         University of Oklahoma Press, 1970. 330 pp.
         Biography of Max Brand, one of the many pseudonyms
         for Frederick Faust.

FAY, FRANK

2551 Fay, Frank. How to be Poor. New York: Prentice-Hall,
         1945. 172 pp.

FAYE, ALICE

2552 Moshier, W. Franklyn. The Films of Alice Faye. San Fran-
         cisco: W. Franklyn Moshier, 1971. 194 pp. (Reprinted
         as The Alice Fay Movie Book, Harrisburg, Pa.: Stack-
         pole, 1974.)

FEHER DE VERNET, CAMILLE

2553 Harding, Bertita. Hungarian Rhapsody: The Portrait of an
         Actress. Indianapolis: Bobbs-Merrill, 1940. 344 pp.

FELLINI, FEDERICO

2554 Taylor, John Russell. Cinema Eye, Cinema Ear: Some Key
         Film-Makers of the Sixties. New York: Hill and Wang,
         1964. 294 pp.

2555 Budgen, Suzanne. Fellini. London: British Film Institute,
         1966. 128 pp.
         Includes analysis, interviews and script extract from
         LA STRADA.

2556 Solmi, Angelo. Fellini. New York: Humanities Press,
         1968. 183 pp. Translated by Elizabeth Greenwood.

2557 Salachas, Gilbert. Federico Fellini: An Investigation Into
         His Films and Philosophy. New York: Crown, 1969.
         224 pp. Translated by Rosalie Siegel.

2558 Silke, James R. (ed.) Federico Fellini. Washington, D.C.:
         American Film Institute, 1970. 15 pp.

2559 Wall, James M. (ed.) Three European Directors. Grand
         Rapids, Mich.: Eerdmans, 1973. 224 pp.
         Section on Fellini by Roger Ortmayer.

2560 Harcourt, Peter. Six European Directors: Essays on the
         Meaning of Film Style. Baltimore: Penguin, 1974.
         287 pp.

FERNANDEL

2561   Halsman, Philippe. The Frenchman: A Photographic Inter-
       view with Fernandel. New York: Simon and Schuster,
       1949. 24 ℓ.

FIELDS, GRACIE

2562   Fields, Gracie. Sing As We Go: The Autobiography of Gracie
       Fields. Garden City, N.Y.: Doubleday, 1961. 216 pp.

FIELDS, W. C.

2563   Fields, W. C. Fields For President. (Originally published
       1939.) New York: Dodd, Mead, 1971. 163 pp. Intro-
       duction and commentary by Michael M. Taylor.
       Fields' comic views on a variety of topics.

2564   Taylor, Robert Lewis. W. C. Fields: His Follies and For-
       tunes. Garden City, N.Y.: Doubleday, 1949. 341 pp.

2565   Deschner, Donald. The Films of W. C. Fields. New York:
       Citadel, 1966. 192 pp.

2566   Hansen, Alfred. Incomplete Requiem for W. C. Fields. New
       York: Distributed by Something Else Press, 1966. 14 pp.

2567   Everson, William K. The Art of W. C. Fields. Indianapolis:
       Bobbs-Merrill, 1967. 232 pp.

2568   Fields, W. C., Jr. and Rohauer, Raymond. A Tribute to
       W. C. Fields. New York: Gallery of Modern Art Mono-
       graph, 1967. 6 pp.

2569   Fields, W. C. Drat! Being the Encapsulated View of Life
       by W. C. Fields in His Own Words. Edited by Richard
       J. Anobile. New York: New American Library (World),
       1968. 128 pp.

2570   Fields, W. C. I Never Met a Kid I Liked. Edited by Paul
       Mason. Hollywood: Stanyan, 1970. 58 pp.

2571   Fields, W. C. Never Trust a Man Who Doesn't Drink.
       Edited by Paul Mason. Hollywood: Stanyan, 1971. 55 pp.

2572   Monti, Carlotta with Rice, Cy. W. C. Fields and Me.
       Englewood Cliffs, N.J.: Prentice-Hall, 1971. 227 pp.

2573   Anobile, Richard J. (comp.) A Flask of Fields: Verbal and
       Visual Gems from the Films of W. C. Fields. New York:
       Darien, 1972. 272 pp.

2574   Fields, W. C. Fields' Day: The Best of W. C. Fields.
       Kansas City, Mo.: Hallmark Cards, 1972. 26 pp.

2575   Fields, **W. C.** W. C. Fields By Himself: His Intended
       Autobiography. Commentary by Ronald Fields. Engle-
       wood Cliffs, N.J.: Prentice-Hall, 1973. 510 pp.

2576   Yanni, Nicholas. W. C. Fields. New York: Pyramid,
       1974. 157 pp.

2577   Anobile, Richard (ed.) "Godfrey Daniels!" Verbal and Visual
       Gems From the Short Films of W. C. Fields. New York:
       Darien, 1975. 224 pp.

       FITZGERALD, F. SCOTT

2578   Mizener, Arthur. The Far Side of Paradise: A Biography
       of F. Scott Fitzgerald. Boston: Houghton Mifflin, 1951.
       362 pp. (Republished 1965, 416 pp.)

2579   Graham, Sheilah. The Beloved Infidel: The Education of a
       Woman. New York: Holt, 1958. 338 pp.

2580   Turnbull, Andrew. Scott Fitzgerald. New York: Scribner's,
       1962. 364 pp.

2581   Cross, K. G. W. F. Scott Fitzgerald. Edinburgh: Oliver
       and Boyd, 1964. 120 pp.

2582   Graham, Sheilah. College of One. New York: Viking, 1967.
       245 pp.

2583   Margolies, Alan. The Impact of Theatre and Film on F. Scott
       Fitzgerald. New York University: Ph.D., 1969. 286 pp.

2584   Milford, Nancy. Zelda: A Biography. New York: Harper
       and Row, 1970. 424 pp.
       With material on Fitzgerald as well.

2585   Bruccoli, Matthew J. and Bryer, Jackson R. (comps.) F.
       Scott Fitzgerald in His Own Time: A Miscellany. Kent,
       Ohio: Kent State University Press, 1971. 481 pp.

2586   Bruccoli, Matthew J. (comp.) Profile of F. Scott Fitzgerald.
       Columbus, Ohio: Merrill, 1971. 122 pp.

2587   Latham, Aaron. Crazy Sundays: F. Scott Fitzgerald in
       Hollywood. New York: Viking, 1971. 306 pp.

2588   Mayfield, Sara. Exiles From Paradise: Zelda and Scott
       Fitzgerald. New York: Delacorte, 1971. 309 pp.

2589   Reiter, Joan Govan. F. Scott Fitzgerald: Hollywood as
       Literary Material. Northwestern University: Ph.D., 1972.

2590   Bruccoli, Matthew J.; Smith, Scottie Fitzgerald; and Kerr,

Joan P. The Romantic Egoists: Scott and Zelda Fitzgerald. New York: Scribner's, 1974. 246 pp.

FLAGG, JAMES MONTGOMERY

2591 Flagg, James Montgomery. Roses and Buckshot. New York:
Putnam, 1946. 224 pp.

FLAHERTY, ROBERT

2592 Weinberg, Herman G. An Index to the Creative Work of
Two Pioneers: I. Robert J. Flaherty, II. Hans Richter.
London: British Film Institute, 1946. 15 pp.

2593 Griffith, Richard. The World of Robert Flaherty. New York:
Duell, Sloan and Pearce, 1953. 165 pp.

2594 Mainwaring, Mary Louise. Robert Flaherty's Films and
Their Critics. Indiana University: Ed.D., 1954. 224 pp.

2595 Flaherty, Frances Hubbard. The Odyssey of a Film-Maker:
Robert Flaherty's Story. Urbana, Ill: Beta Phi Mu, 1960.
45 pp. (Reprinted New York: Arno, 1972.)

2596 Calder-Marshall, Arthur. The Innocent Eye: The Life of
Robert J. Flaherty. Based on research material by Paul
Rotha and Basil Wright. London: W. H. Allen, 1963.
304 pp. (Also published New York: Harcourt Brace, 1966.)

2597 Morris, Peter. The Flaherty Tradition: Notes on the Film-
making Methods of Robert Flaherty and the Influence of
These Methods on Other Filmmakers. Ottawa: Canadian
Federation of Film Societies, 1965. 14 pp.

2598 Rouse, John Thomas, Jr. A Descriptive Analysis of the
Major Films of Robert J. Flaherty. University of Michigan: Ph.D., 1968. 241 pp.

FLIPPER

2599 Gray, William B. Flipper the Star. Miami: Seemann, 1973.
37 pp.

FLYNN, ERROL

2600 Flynn, Errol. My Wicked, Wicked Ways. New York: Putnam, 1959. 438 pp. (Reprinted New York: Berkeley,
1974, 383 pp.)

2601 Haymes, Nora Eddington Flynn with Rice, Cy. Errol and Me.
New York: New American Library, 1960. 176 pp.

2602 Aadland, Florence with Thomey, Tedd. The Big Love. New

York: Lancer, 1961. 158 pp.
On Flynn's relationship with Beverly Aadland.

2603 Thomey, Tedd. The Loves of Errol Flynn: The Tempestuous
Life Story of One of Hollywood's Most Flamboyant Screen
Stars. Derby, Conn.: Monarch, 1962. 139 pp.

2604 Parish, James Robert; Barbour, Alan G.; and Marill, Alvin
H. Errol Flynn. Kew Gardens, N.Y.: Cinefax, 1969.
Primarily photographs.

2605 Thomas, Tony; Behlmer, Rudy; McCarty, Clifford. The
Films of Errol Flynn. New York: Citadel, 1969. 223 pp.

2606 Morris, George. Errol Flynn. New York: Pyramid, 1975.
160 pp.

THE FONDAS, HENRY, JANE, and PETER

2607 Springer, John. The Fondas: The Films and Careers of
Henry, Jane, and Peter Fonda. New York: Citadel,
1970. 279 pp.

2608 Playboy Interview: Peter Fonda. Chicago: Playboy, c. 1971.
47 pp.

2609 Brough, James. The Fabulous Fondas. New York: McKay,
1973. 296 pp.

2610 Kiernan, Thomas. Jane: An Intimate Biography of Jane
Fonda. New York: Putnam, 1973. 358 pp.

2611 Kerbel, Michael. Henry Fonda. New York: Pyramid, 1975.
160 pp.

FONTANNE, LYNN (see LUNT, ALFRED)

FORBES, BRYAN

2612 Forbes, Bryan. Notes for a Life. London: Collins, 1974.
384 pp.

FORD, GLENN

2613 Ford, Glenn and Redfield, Margaret. Glenn Ford: R.F.D.
Beverly Hills. Old Tappan, N.J.: Hewitt, 1970.
185 pp.

FORD, JOHN

2614 Wootten, William Patrick. An Index to the Films of John
Ford. London: British Film Institute, 1948. 36 pp.

2615   Bogdanovich, Peter. John Ford. Berkeley: University of
        California Press, 1968. 144 pp.
            An extended interview with Ford.

2616   Stavig, Mark. John Ford and the Traditional Moral Order.
        Madison: University of Wisconsin Press, 1968. 225 pp.

2617   Burrows, Michael. John Ford and Andrew V. McLaglen.
        Cromwell, England: Primestyle, 1970. 32 pp.

2618   Baxter, John. The Cinema of John Ford. New York: A. S.
        Barnes, 1971. 176 pp.

2619   Bogdanovich, Peter. John Ford. San Francisco: California
        Arts Commission, 1971. 31 pp.
            Primarily photographs.

2620   Place, J. A. The Western Films of John Ford. Secaucus,
        N. J.: Citadel, 1974. 246 pp.

2621   McBride, Joseph and Wilmington, Michael. John Ford. New
        York: Da Capo, 1975. 234 pp.

FORMAN, HARRISON

2622   Forman, Harrison. Horizon Hunter: The Adventures of a
        Modern Marco Polo. New York: McBride, 1940. 314 pp.

FORMAN, MILOS

2623   Lipton, Leonard. A Critical Study of the Filmmaking Style
        of Milos Forman, with Special Emphasis on His Contribu-
        tions to Film Comedy. University of Southern California:
        Ph. D., 1974. 356 pp.

2624   Liehm, Antonin J. The Milos Forman Stories. White Plains,
        N. Y.: International Arts and Sciences Press, 1975.
        191 pp.
            Biographical material and analysis of Forman's major
        films.

FORMBY, GEORGE

2625   Randall, Alan and Seaton, Ray. George Formby: A Biography.
        London: Allen, 1974. 192 pp.

FOWLER, GENE

2626   Fowler, Gene. ... A Solo in Tom-Toms. New York: Viking,
        1946. 390 pp.

2627   Fowler, Gene. Minutes of the Last Meeting. New York:
        Viking, 1954. 277 pp.

An account of Fowler's attempt to write a biography of Sadakichi Hartmann, with the help of John Barrymore, W. C. Fields, and John Decker.

2628   Fowler, Gene. Skyline: A Reporter's Reminiscence of the 1920s. New York: Viking, 1961. 314 pp.

2629   Fowler, Will. The Young Man From Denver. Garden City, N.Y.: Doubleday, 1962. 310 pp.

FOX, ROY

2630   Fox, Roy. Hollywood, Mayfair and All That Jazz: The Roy Fox Story. London: Frewin, 1975. 248 pp.

FOX, WILLIAM

2631   Sinclair, Upton. Upton Sinclair Presents William Fox. (Originally 1933.) New York: Arno, 1970. 377 pp.

2632   Allvine, Glendon. The Greatest Fox of Them All. New York: Lyle Stuart, 1969. 244 pp.

FRANJU, GEORGES

2633   Durgnat, Raymond. Franju. Berkeley: University of California Press, 1968. 144 pp.

FRANKENHEIMER, JOHN

2634   Pratley, Gerald. The Cinema of John Frankenheimer. New York: A. S. Barnes, 1969. 240 pp.

FREDERICK, PAULINE

2635   Elwood, Muriel. Pauline Frederick: On and Off the Stage. Chicago: Kroch, 1940. 225 pp.

FREED, ARTHUR

2636   Rohauer, Raymond. A Tribute to Arthur Freed. New York: Gallery of Modern Art Monograph, 1967. 12 pp.

2637   Fordin, Hugh. The World of Entertainment: Hollywood's Greatest Musicals. Garden City, N.Y.: Doubleday, 1975. 566 pp.
        Deals with the films of producer Arthur Freed.

FREED, FRED

2638   Yellin, David G. Special: Fred Freed and the Television Documentary. New York: Macmillan, 1973. 289 pp.

FRIESE-GREENE, WILLIAM

2639   Allister, Ray. Friese-Greene: Close-Up of an Inventor.
       London: Marsland, 1948. 192 pp.

FROBOESS, HARRY

2640   Froboess, Harry. The Reminiscing Champ: A World-Famous
       Stunt Man Tells His Story. New York: Pageant, 1953.
       141 pp.

FULLER, SAMUEL

2641   Will, David and Wollen, Peter (eds.) Samuel Fuller. Essex:
       Edinburgh International Film Festival, 1969. 127 pp.

2642   Hardy, Phil. Samuel Fuller. New York: Praeger, 1970.
       144 pp.

2643   Sherman, Eric and Rubin, Martin. The Director's Event:
       Interviews with Five American Film-Makers. New York:
       Atheneum, 1970. 200 pp.

2644   Garnham, Nicholas. Samuel Fuller. New York: Viking,
       1972. 176 pp.

FUNT, ALLEN

2645   Funt, Allen. Eavesdropper At Large: Adventures in Human
       Nature with "Candid Mike" and "Candid Camera." New
       York: Vanguard, 1952. 257 pp.

GABLE, CLARK

2646   Carpozi, George, Jr. Clark Gable. New York: Pyramid,
       1961. 160 pp.

2647   Gable, Kathleen. Clark Gable: A Personal Portrait. Engle-
       wood Cliffs, N.J.: Prentice-Hall, 1961. 153 pp.

2648   Garceau, Jean. Dear Mr. Gable: The Biography of Clark
       Gable. Boston: Little, Brown, 1961. 297 pp.

2649   Samuels, Charles. The King: A Biography of Clark Gable.
       New York: Coward-McCann, 1961. 315 pp.

2650   Essoe, Gabe and Lee, Ray. Gable: A Complete Gallery of
       His Screen Portraits. Los Angeles: Price, Stern, Sloan,
       1967. Unpaged.

2651   Williams, Chester. Gable. New York: Fleet, 1968. 154 pp.

2652   Essoe, Gabe. The Films of Clark Gable. New York: Citadel,
       1970. 255 pp.

2653   Smith, Milburn (ed.) Gable. New York: Barven, 1971.
       66 pp.

2654   Jordan, Rene. Clark Gable. New York: Pyramid, 1973.
       159 pp.

2655   Harris, Warren G. Gable and Lombard. New York: Simon
       and Schuster, 1974. 189 pp.

2656   Morella, Joe and Epstein, Edward Z. Gable & Lombard &
       Powell & Harlow. New York: Dell, 1975. 272 pp.

GABOR, EVA

2657   Gabor, Eva. Orchids and Salami. Garden City, N.Y.:
       Doubleday, 1954. 219 pp.

GABOR, JOLIE

2658   Gabor, Jolie with Adams, Cindy. Jolie Gabor. New York:
       Mason/Charter, 1975. 315 pp.

GABOR, ZSA ZSA

2659   Gabor, Zsa Zsa and Frank, Gerold. Zsa Zsa Gabor: My
       Story. Cleveland: World, 1960. 308 pp.

GARBO, GRETA

2660   Laing, E. E. Greta Garbo: The Story of a Specialist.
       London: Gifford, 1946. 244 pp.

2661   Bainbridge, John. Garbo. Garden City, New York: Double-
       day, 1955. 256 pp. (Republished as Garbo: The Famous
       Biography Lavishly Illustrated, New York: Holt, Rine-
       hart and Winston, 1971. 320 pp.)

2662   Billquist, Fritiof. Garbo: A Biography. New York: Put-
       nam, 1960. 255 pp. Translated by Maurice Michael.

2663   Conway, Michael; McGregor, Dion; and Ricci, Mark (comps.)
       The Films of Greta Garbo. New York: Citadel, 1963.
       155 pp.
            With an introductory essay, "The Garbo Image," by
       Parker Tyler.

2664   Durgnat, Raymond and Kobal, John. Greta Garbo. New
       York: Dutton, 1965. 160 pp.

2665   Zierold, Norman. Garbo. New York: Stein and Day, 1969.
       196 pp.

2666   Carr, Larry. Four Fabulous Faces: The Evolution and

Metamorphosis of Garbo, Swanson, Crawford and Dietrich.
New Rochelle, N.Y.: Arlington, 1970. 492 pp.
Primarily photographs.

2667 Sjölander, Ture. Garbo. New York: Harper and Row, 1971.
135 pp.
Primarily photographs.

2668 Smith, Milburn (ed.) Garbo. New York: Barven, 1972.
66 pp.

2669 Corliss, Richard. Greta Garbo. New York: Pyramid, 1974.
157 pp.

GARDEN, MARY

2670 Garden, Mary and Biancolli, Louis. Mary Garden's Story.
New York: Simon and Schuster, 1951. 302 pp.

GARDNER, AVA

2671 Epstein, Florence. That Girl Ava: The Life and Loves of a
Fabulous Female. New York (?): Literary Enterprises,
1955. 66 pp.

2672 Hanna, David. Ava: A Portrait of a Star. New York: Putnam, 1960. 256 pp.

2673 Higham, Charles. Ava: A Life Story. New York: Delacorte, 1974. 267 pp.

GARFIELD, JOHN

2674 Gelman, Howard. The Films of John Garfield. Secaucus,
N.J.: Citadel, 1975. 222 pp.

2675 Swindell, Larry. Body and Soul: The Story of John Garfield.
New York: Morrow, 1975. 288 pp.

GARGAN, WILLIAM

2676 Gargan, William. Why Me? An Autobiography. Garden
City, N.Y.: Doubleday, 1969. 311 pp.

GARLAND, JUDY

2677 Morella, Joe and Epstein, Edward Z. Judy: The Films and
Career of Judy Garland. New York: Citadel, 1969.
217 pp.

2678 Steiger, Brad. Judy Garland. New York: Ace, 1969.
150 pp.

2679   Torme, Mel. The Other Side of the Rainbow with Judy Gar-
       land on the Dawn Patrol. New York: Morrow, 1970.
       241 pp.

2680   Deans, Mickey and Pinchot, Ann. Weep No More, My Lady.
       New York: Hawthorn, 1972. 247 pp.

2681   Melton, David. Judy: A Remembrance. Hollywood: Stanyan,
       1972. 58 pp.

2682   Smith, Milburn (ed.) Judy Garland and Mickey Rooney. New
       York: Barven, 1972. 66 pp.

2683   DiOrio, Al. Little Girl Lost: The Life and Hard Times of
       Judy Garland. New Rochelle, N.Y.: Arlington, 1974.
       298 pp.

2684   Juneau, James. Judy Garland. New York: Pyramid, 1974.
       159 pp.

2685   Dahl, David and Kehoe, Barry. Young Judy. New York:
       Mason/Charter, 1975. 250 pp.

2686   Edwards, Anne. Judy Garland: A Biography. New York:
       Simon and Schuster, 1975. 349 pp.

2687   Finch, Christopher. Rainbow: The Stormy Life of Judy
       Garland. New York: Grosset and Dunlap, 1975. 255 pp.

2688   Frank, Gerold. Judy. New York: Harper and Row, 1975.
       654 pp.

2689   Smith, Lorna. Judy, With Love: The Story of Miss Show
       Business. London: Hale, 1975. 208 pp.

GARMES, LEE

2690   Higham, Charles. Hollywood Cameramen: Sources of Light.
       Bloomington: Indiana University Press, 1970. 176 pp.

GARNETT, TAY

2691   Garnett, Tay with Balling, Fredda Dudley. Light Your
       Torches and Pull Up Your Tights. New Rochelle, N.Y.:
       Arlington, 1973. 347 pp.

GERSHWIN, GEORGE

2692   Ewen, David. The Story of George Gershwin. New York:
       Holt, 1943. 211 pp.

2693   Ewen, David. A Journey to Greatness: The Life and Music
       of George Gershwin. New York: Holt, 1956. 384 pp.

2694   Goldberg, Isaac and Garson, Edith. George Gershwin: A
       Study in American Music. (Originally published by Gold-
       berg alone, 1931.) Revised New York: Ungar, 1958.
       387 pp.

2695   Jablonski, Edward and Stewart, Lawrence D. The Gershwin
       Years. Garden City, N.Y.: Doubleday, 1958. 313 pp.

2696   Jablonski, Edward. George Gershwin. New York: Putnam,
       1962. 190 pp.

GIELGUD, JOHN

2697   Hayman, John. John Gielgud: A Biography. New York:
       Random, 1971. 276 pp.

GIELGUD, VAL

2698   Gielgud, Val. One Year of Grace: A Fragment of Auto-
       biography. London, New York: Longmans, Green, 1950.
       168 pp.

GIESLER, JERRY

2699   Giesler, Jerry with Martin, Pete. The Jerry Giesler Story.
       New York: Simon and Schuster, 1960. 341 pp.
       A lawyer discusses his life and many of his cele-
       brated cases; includes material on Chaplin, Berkeley,
       Mitchum, Edward G. Robinson, Jr., Ruth Etting and
       others.

2700   Roeburt, John. Get Me Giesler. New York: Belmont, 1962.
       191 pp.
       Includes material on Errol Flynn, Mitchum, Chaplin,
       Cheryl Crane and others.

GILBERT, LOUIS WOLFE

2701   Gilbert, Louis Wolfe. Without Rhyme or Reason. New York:
       Vantage, 1956. 240 pp.

GINGOLD, HERMIONE

2702   Gingold, Hermione. The World Is Square. New York:
       Athene, 1958. 66 pp.

2703   Gingold, Hermione. Sirens Should Be Seen and Not Heard.
       Philadelphia: Lippincott, 1963. 176 pp.

GIROUD, FRANCOISE

2704   Giroud, Francoise. I Give You My Word. Boston: Houghton
       Mifflin, 1974. 275 pp.

GISH, DOROTHY

2705 Gish, Lillian. Dorothy and Lillian Gish. Edited by James
      E. Frasher. New York: Scribner's, 1973. 311 pp.

GISH, LILLIAN

2706 Gish, Lillian with Pinchot, Ann. The Movies, Mr. Griffith,
      and Me. Englewood Cliffs, N.J.: Prentice-Hall, 1969.
      388 pp.

2707 Slide, Anthony (comp.) Lillian Gish: Actress. London:
      National Film Theatre, 1969. 14 pp.

2708 Gish, Lillian. Dorothy and Lillian Gish. Edited by James
      E. Frasher. New York: Scribner's, 1973. 311 pp.

GLEASON, JACKIE

2709 Bishop, Jim. The Golden Ham: A Candid Biography of
      Jackie Gleason. New York: Simon and Schuster, 1956.
      298 pp.

GLYN, ELINOR

2710 Glyn, Anthony. Elinor Glyn: A Biography. Garden City,
      N.Y.: Doubleday, 1955. 348 pp.

GODARD, JEAN-LUC

2711 Barr, Charles and others. The Films of Jean-Luc Godard.
      London: Studio Vista, 1967. 144 pp. (Revised 1969,
      192 pp. Revision reprinted New York: Praeger, 1970.)
      Critics examine individual films; contributors include
      Charles Barr, Stig Björkman, Jacques Bontemps, Barry
      Boys, Ian Cameron, Jean-Louis Comolli, Edgardo Coza-
      rinsky, Raymond Durgnat, Philip French, Jose Luis
      Guarner, Jim Hillier, Paul Mayersberg, V. F. Perkins,
      Michael Walker, Richard Winkler, and Robin Wood.

2712 Mussman, Toby (comp.) Jean-Luc Godard: A Critical An-
      thology. New York: Dutton, 1968. 319 pp.

2713 Roud, Richard. Jean-Luc Godard. Garden City, N.Y.:
      Doubleday, 1968. 176 pp. (Revised Bloomington: Indiana
      University Press, 1970, 192 pp.)

2714 Darling, Brian. Jean-Luc Godard: Politics and Humanism.
      London: British Film Institute, 1969. 4 pp.

2715 Collet, Jean. Jean-Luc Godard: An Investigation Into His
      Films and His Philosophy. New York: Crown, 1970.
      218 pp. Translated by Ciba Vaughan.

2716 Brown, Royal S. (ed.) Focus on Godard. Englewood Cliffs, N.J.: Prentice-Hall, 1972. 190 pp.
Includes many interviews with Godard plus contributions by Jean Collet, Roger Greenspun, Penelope Gilliat, Tom Milne, Aragon, Georges Sadoul and others.

2717 [No entry.]

2718 Crofts, Stephen (ed.) Jean-Luc Godard. London: British Film Institute, 1972. 80 pp.

2719 Godard, Jean-Luc. Godard on Godard: Critical Writings. Edited by Jean Narboni and Tom Milne. New York: Viking, 1972. 292 pp.

2720 Goodwin, Michael and Marcus, Greil. Double Feature: Movies and Politics. New York: Outerbridge and Lazard, 1972. 128 pp.
Includes an extended interview with Godard and Jean-Pierre Gorin.

2721 Harcourt, Peter. Six European Directors: Essays on the Meaning of Film Style. Baltimore: Penguin, 1974. 287 pp.

2722 MacBean, James Roy. Film and Revolution. Bloomington: Indiana University Press, 1975. 339 pp.
Includes many chapters on Godard's work alone and his work with Jean-Pierre Gorin.

GODOWSKY, DAGMAR

2723 Godowsky, Dagmar. First Person Plural: The Lives of Dagmar Godowsky. New York: Viking, 1958. 249 pp.

GOLDWYN, SAMUEL

2724 Griffith, Richard. Samuel Goldwyn: The Producer and His Films. New York: Museum of Modern Art Film Library, 1956. 48 pp.

2725 Easton, Carol. The Search for Sam Goldwyn. New York: Morrow, c. 1975. 304 pp.

GORCEY, LEO B.

2726 Gorcey, Leo B. An Original Dead End Kid Presents: Dead End Yells, Wedding Bells, Cockle Shells, and Dizzy Spells. New York: Vantage, 1967. 111 pp.

GORDON, MAX

2727   Gordon, Max with Funke, Lewis. Max Gordon Presents.
       New York: Bernard Geis, 1963. 314 pp.
            Includes a chapter on his experience producing Abe
       Lincoln in Illinois.

GORDON, RUTH

2728   Gordon, Ruth. Myself Among Others. New York: Atheneum,
       1971. 389 pp.

GORIN, JEAN-PIERRE (see GODARD, JEAN-LUC)

GORTNER, MARJOE

2729   Gaines, Steven S. Marjoe: The Life of Marjoe Gortner.
       New York: Harper and Row, 1973. 238 pp.

GRACE, DICK

2730   Grace, Dick. Visibility Unlimited. New York: Longmans
       Green, 1950. 276 pp. (Reprinted as Crash Pilot, 1956.)
            Autobiography of a stunt pilot who worked in films.

GRADY, BILLY

2731   Grady, Billy. The Irish Peacock: The Confessions of a
       Legendary Talent Agent. New Rochelle, N.Y.: Arlington,
       1972. 288 pp.

GRAHAM, SHEILAH

2732   Graham, Sheilah. The Beloved Infidel: The Education of a
       Woman. New York: Holt, 1958. 338 pp.

2733   Graham, Sheilah. The Rest of the Story. New York: Coward-
       McCann, 1964. 317 pp.

2734   Graham, Sheilah. College of One. New York: Viking, 1967.
       245 pp.

GRANACH, ALEXANDER

2735   Granach, Alexander. There Goes an Actor. Garden City,
       N.Y.: Doubleday, Doran, 1945. 279 pp. Translated by
       Willard Trask.

GRANLUND, NILS THOR

2736   Granlund, Nils Thor with Feder, Sid and Hancock, Ralph.
       Blondes, Brunettes and Bullets. New York: McKay,

1957.   300 pp.
Autobiography of Loew's publicist in early days of Hollywood.

GRANT, CARY

2737   Eyles, Allen. Cary Grant Film Album. London: Allen, 1971.   51 pp.
Primarily illustrations.

2738   Govoni, Albert. Cary Grant: An Unauthorized Biography. Chicago: Regnery, 1971.   233 pp.

2739   Deschner, Donald. The Films of Cary Grant. Secaucus, N.J.: Citadel, 1973.   276 pp.

2740   Vermilye, Jerry. Cary Grant. New York: Pyramid, 1973. 160 pp.

2741   Parish, James Robert and Stanke, Don E. The Debonairs. New Rochelle, N.Y.: Arlington, 1975.   511 pp.
Contains a lengthy chapter on Cary Grant, including complete filmography.

GRANTLEY, RICHARD (LORD GRANTLEY)

2742   Lord Grantley. Silver Spoon: Being Extracts from the Random Reminiscences of Lord Grantley. Edited by Mary and Alan Wood. London: Hutchinson, 1954.   239 pp.

GREEN, MARTYN

2743   Green, Martyn. Here's a How-De-Do: My Life in Gilbert and Sullivan. New York: Norton, 1952.   283 pp.

GREENE, GRAHAM

2744   Phillips, Gene D. Graham Greene: The Films of His Fiction. New York: Teachers College Press, Columbia University, 1974.   204 pp.

GREER, HOWARD

2745   Greer, Howard. Designing Male. New York: Putnam, 1951. 310 pp.
Autobiography of a Hollywood dress designer.

GRIERSON, JOHN

2746   Hardy, Forsyth (ed.) Grierson on Documentary. New York: Harcourt, Brace, 1947.   324 pp. (Revised Berkeley: University of California Press, 1966, 411 pp.)

2747 Lovell, Alan and Hillier, Jim. Studies in Documentary.
      New York: Viking, 1972. 176 pp.
      Includes a chapter on Grierson.

GRIFFITH, CORINNE

2748 Griffith, Corinne. My Life with the Red Skins. New York:
      A. S. Barnes, 1947. 238 pp.

2749 Griffith, Corinne. Papa's Delicate Condition. Boston:
      Houghton Mifflin, 1952. 178 pp.

2750 Griffith, Corinne. I'm Lucky--At Cards. New York: Fell,
      1974. 101 pp.

GRIFFITH, D. W.

2751 Arvidson, Linda (Mrs. D. W. Griffith). When the Movies
      Were Young. (Originally published 1925.) New York:
      Benjamin Blom, 1968. 256 pp.

2752 Barry, Iris. D. W. Griffith, American Film Master. New
      York: Museum of Modern Art, 1940. 40 pp. (Revised
      with an annotated list of films by Eileen Bowser, 1965,
      88 pp.)

2753 Stern, Seymour. An Index to the Creative Work of David
      Wark Griffith. London: Sight and Sound, 1944--.

2754 Croy, Homer. Star Maker: The Story of D. W. Griffith.
      New York: Duell, Sloan and Pearce, 1959. 210 pp.

2755 Henderson, Robert Morton. The Role of David Wark Griffith
      in the Development of the Dramatic Motion Picture, 1908-
      1913. New York University: Ph.D., 1965. 326 pp.

2756 Gish, Lillian with Pinchot, Ann. The Movies, Mr. Griffith,
      and Me. Englewood Cliffs, N.J.: Prentice-Hall, 1969.
      388 pp.

2757 Henderson, Robert M. D. W. Griffith: The Years at Bio-
      graph. New York: Farrar, Straus and Giroux, 1970.
      250 pp.

2758 Merritt, Russell LaMonte. The Impact of D. W. Griffith's
      Motion Pictures From 1908 to 1914 on Contemporary
      American Culture. Harvard University: Ph.D., 1970.
      441 ℓ.

2759 O'Dell, Paul with Slide, Anthony. Griffith and the Rise of
      Hollywood. New York: A. S. Barnes, 1970. 163 pp.

2760 Geduld, Harry M. (ed.) Focus on D. W. Griffith. Englewood

Cliffs, N. J.: Prentice-Hall, 1971. 182 pp.
Contributors include D. W. Griffith, Linda Arvidson,
A. Nicholas Vardac, Lewis Jacobs, Jay Leyda, Richard
Meyer, Lillian Gish, Erich von Stroheim, and others.

2761 Brakhage, Stan. The Brakhage Lectures. Chicago: The
Good Lion, School of the Art Institute of Chicago, 1972.
106 pp.

2762 Griffith, D. W. The Man Who Invented Hollywood: The
Autobiography of D. W. Griffith. Edited by James Hart.
Louisville, Ky.: Touchstone, 1972. 170 pp.

2763 Henderson, Robert M. D. W. Griffith: His Life and Work.
New York: Oxford University Press, 1972. 326 pp.

2764 Brown, Karl. Adventures with D. W. Griffith. New York:
Farrar, Straus and Giroux, 1973. 251 pp.

2765 Niver, Kemp R. D. W. Griffith: His Biograph Films in
Perspective. Edited by Bebe Bergsten. Los Angeles:
Historical Films, 1974. 189 pp.

2766 Wagenknecht, Edward and Slide, Anthony. The Films of
D. W. Griffith. New York: Crown, 1975. 276 pp.

GRUBER, FRANK

2767 Gruber, Frank. The Pulp Jungle. Los Angeles: Sherbourne,
1967. 189 pp.

GUINNESS, ALEC

2768 Tynan, Kenneth. Alec Guinness: An Illustrated Study of His
Work for Stage and Screen, with a List of His Appearances.
London: Rockliff, 1953. 108 pp. (Revised New York:
Macmillan, 1961, 111 pp.)

GUITRY, SACHA

2769 Harding, James. Sacha Guitry: The Last Boulevardier. New
York: Scribner's, 1968. 277 pp.

HAGNER, JOHN G.

2770 Hagner, John G. Falling For Stars. Hollywood: El Jon,
1964. 126 pp.
Autobiography of a stuntman.

HALL, CONRAD

2771 Maltin, Leonard. Behind the Camera: The Cinematographer's

Art. New York: New American Library, 1971. 240 pp.
Includes a lengthy interview with Conrad Hall.

HALL, HENRY

2772 Hall, Henry. Here's to the Next Time: The Autobiography
of Henry Hall. London: Odhams, 1955. 239 pp.

HAMMERSTEIN, OSCAR (see RODGERS, RICHARD)

HARDWICKE, CEDRIC

2773 Hardwicke, Cedric with Brough, James. A Victorian in Orbit:
The Irreverent Memoirs of Sir Cedric Hardwicke. Garden
City, N.Y.: Doubleday, 1961. 311 pp.

HARDY, OLIVER (see LAUREL, STAN)

HARLOW, JEAN

2774 Parsons, Louella. Jean Harlow's Life Story. (Originally
published 1937.) Dunellen, N.J.: Dell, 1964. 48 pp.

2775 Nystedt, Bob (senior ed.) The True Story of Jean Harlow,
Hollywood's All-Time Sex Goddess. Skokie, Ill.: Publishers' Development Corporation, 1964. 66 pp.

2776 Pascal, John. The Jean Harlow Story. New York: Popular
Library, 1964. 158 pp.

2777 Shulman, Irving. Harlow: An Intimate Biography. New
York: Bernard Geis, 1964. 408 pp.

2778 Conway, Michael and Ricci, Mark. The Films of Jean Harlow. New York: Citadel, 1965. 159 pp.

2779 Morella, Joe and Epstein, Edward Z. Gable & Lombard &
Powell & Harlow. New York: Dell, 1975. 272 pp.

HARRIS, RADIE

2780 Harris, Radie. Radie's World. New York: Putnam, 1975.
288 pp.
Autobiography of Hollywood columnist.

HARRISON, REX

2781 Harrison, Rex. Rex: An Autobiography. New York: Morrow, 1975. 256 pp.

2782 Parish, James Robert and Stanke, Don E. The Debonairs.
New Rochelle, N.Y.: Arlington, 1975. 511 pp.

Contains a lengthy chapter on Rex Harrison, including complete filmography.

HARRYHAUSEN, RAY

2783 Harryhausen, Ray. Film Fantasy Scrapbook. South Brunswick, N.J.: A. S. Barnes, 1972. 117 pp. (Revised 1974, 142 pp.)
Discussion and illustration of the work of an animation and special effects expert.

HART, MOSS

2784 Hart, Moss. Act One. New York: Random, 1959. 444 pp.

HART, WILLIAM S.

2785 Hart, William S. My Life East and West. (Originally published 1929.) New York: Benjamin Blom, 1968. 362 pp.

HARVEY, LAURENCE

2786 Hickey, Des and Smith, Gus. The Prince: Being the Public and Private Life of Larushka Mischa Skikne, A Jewish Lithuanian Vagabond Player, Otherwise Known as Laurence Harvey. London: Frewin, 1975. 272 pp.

2787 Stone, Paulene with Evans, Peter. One Tear Is Enough. London: Michael Joseph, 1975. 176 pp.
Wife's account of Harvey's last seven years.

HATHAWAY, HENRY

2788 Canham, Kingsley. The Hollywood Professionals, Vol. I: Michael Curtiz, Raoul Walsh, Henry Hathaway. New York: A. S. Barnes, 1973. 200 pp.

HAVOC, JUNE

2789 Havoc, June. Early Havoc. New York: Simon and Schuster, 1959. 313 pp.

HAWKINS, JACK

2790 Hawkins, Jack. Anything for a Quiet Life: The Autobiography of Jack Hawkins. With a postscript by Doreen Hawkins. New York: Stein and Day, 1974. 180 pp.

HAWKS, HOWARD

2791 Bogdanovich, Peter. The Cinema of Howard Hawks. New York: Museum of Modern Art Film Library, 1962. 38 pp.

2792 Wood, Robin. Howard Hawks. Garden City, N.Y.: Double-
      day, 1968. 200 pp.

2793 McBride, Joseph (ed.) Focus on Howard Hawks. Englewood
      Cliffs, N.J.: Prentice-Hall, 1972. 178 pp.
           Contributors include William Wellman, Jr., Manny
      Farber, Andrew Sarris, Henri Langlois, Jacques Rivette,
      Robin Wood, Molly Haskell, Peter Bogdanovich, and others.

2794 Belton, John. The Hollywood Professionals, Vol. III: Howard
      Hawks, Frank Borzage, Edgar G. Ulmer. New York:
      A. S. Barnes, 1974. 182 pp.

2795 Willis, Don. The Films of Howard Hawks. Metuchen, N.J.:
      Scarecrow, 1975. 235 pp.

HAYAKAWA, SESSUE

2796 Hayakawa, Sessue. Zen Showed Me the Way ... To Peace,
      Happiness, and Tranquility. Indianapolis: Bobbs-Merrill,
      1960. 256 pp.

HAYDEN, STERLING

2797 Hayden, Sterling. Wanderer. New York: Knopf, 1963.
      434 pp.

HAYES, HELEN

2798 Brown, Catherine Hayes. Letters To Mary. New York:
      Random, 1940. 343 pp.
           Biography of Helen Hayes, written by her mother, in
      the form of letters to Mary MacArthur, Helen Hayes's
      daughter.

2799 Hayes, Helen with Funke, Lewis. A Gift of Joy. New York:
      Evans, 1965. 254 pp.

2800 Hayes, Helen with Dody, Sanford. On Reflection: An Auto-
      biography. New York: Evans, 1968. 253 pp.

HAYS, WILL H.

2801 Hays, Will H. The Memoirs of Will H. Hays. Garden City,
      N.Y.: Doubleday, 1955. 600 pp.

HAYWARD, SUSAN

2802 McClelland, Doug. Susan Hayward: The Divine Bitch. 1973.
      (Revised as The Complete Life Story of Susan Hayward ...
      Immortal Screen Star, New York: Pinnacle, 1975,
      213 pp.)

HAYWORTH, RITA

2803 Ringgold, Gene. The Films of Rita Hayworth: The Legend
and Career of a Love Goddess. Secaucus, N.J.: Citadel,
1974. 256 pp.

HEAD, EDITH

2804 Head, Edith and Ardmore, Jane Kesner. The Dress Doctor.
Boston: Little, Brown, 1959. 249 pp.

HEARST, WILLIAM RANDOLPH

2805 Swanberg, W. A. Citizen Hearst: A Biography of William
Randolph Hearst. New York: Scribner's, 1961. 555 pp.
Includes material on CITIZEN KANE.

2806 Murray, Ken. The Golden Days at San Simeon. Garden
City, N.Y.: Doubleday, 1971. 163 pp.
With material on Hearst's relationship to the Holly-
wood community.

2807 Davies, Marion. The Times We Had: Life with William
Randolph Hearst. Edited by Pamela Pfau and Kenneth S.
Marx. Introduced by Orson Welles. Indianapolis: Bobbs-
Merrill, 1975. 276 pp.

HECHT, BEN

2808 Hecht, Ben. A Child of the Century. New York: Simon and
Schuster, 1954. 654 pp.

2809 Hecht, Ben. Gaily, Gaily. Garden City, N.Y.: Doubleday,
1963. 227 pp.

2810 Hecht, Ben. Letters From Bohemia. Garden City, N.Y.:
Doubleday, 1964. 203 pp.

HECKART, EILEEN

2811 Parish, James Robert. Good Dames. South Brunswick, N.J.:
A. S. Barnes, 1974. 277 pp.

HELLINGER, MARK

2812 Bishop, Jim. The Mark Hellinger Story: A Biography of
Broadway and Hollywood. New York: Appleton-Century-
Crofts, 1952. 367 pp.

HELLMAN, LILLIAN

2813 Hellman, Lillian. An Unfinished Woman: A Memoir. Boston:
Little, Brown, 1969. 280 pp.

Includes portraits of Dorothy Parker and Dashiell Hammett.

2814   Moody, Richard. Lillian Hellman, Playwright. New York: Pegasus, 1972. 372 pp.

2815   Hellman, Lillian. Pentimento. Boston: Little, Brown, 1973. 297 pp.

HELPMANN, ROBERT

2816   Walker, Kathrine Sorley. Robert Helpmann. London: Rockliff, 1957. 126 pp.

HEMINGWAY, ERNEST

2817   Laurence, Frank. The Film Adaptations of Hemingway: Hollywood and the Hemingway Myth. University of Pennsylvania: Ph.D., 1970. 418 pp.

HENIE, SONJA

2818   Henie, Sonja. Wings on My Feet. New York: Prentice-Hall, 1940. 177 pp.

HEPBURN, AUDREY

2819   Phillips, Michael Joseph. 7 Poems for Audrey Hepburn. Bloomington: Flower Publishing, 1968. 12 pp.

HEPBURN, KATHARINE

2820   Dickens, Homer. The Films of Katharine Hepburn. New York: Citadel, 1971. 244 pp.

2821   Kanin, Garson. Tracy and Hepburn: An Intimate Memoir. New York: Viking, 1971. 307 pp.

2822   Smith, Milburn (ed.) Tracy and Hepburn. New York: Barven, 1971. 66 pp.

2823   Marill, Alvin H. Katharine Hepburn. New York: Pyramid, 1973. 160 pp.

2824   Carey, Gary. Katharine Hepburn: A Biography. New York: Pocket Books, 1975. 238 pp.

2825   Higham, Charles. Kate: The Life of Katharine Hepburn. New York: Norton, 1975. 244 pp.

HEPWORTH, CECIL

2826   Hepworth, Cecil. Came the Dawn: Memories of a Film Pioneer. London: Phoenix, 1951. 207 pp.

HESTON, CHARLTON

2827 Baxter, Brian; Fischer, Soren; and Dean, Doreen (comps.)
Charlton Heston: Actor. London: National Film Theatre,
1969. 18 pp.

HITCHCOCK, ALFRED

2828 Noble, Peter. Index to the Work of Alfred Hitchcock. London: Sight and Sound, 1949. 42 pp.

2829 Bogdanovich, Peter. The Cinema of Alfred Hitchcock. New
York: Museum of Modern Art, 1963. 48 pp.

2830 Taylor, John Russell. Cinema Eye, Cinema Ear: Some Key
Film-Makers of the Sixties. New York: Hill and Wang,
1964. 294 pp.

2831 Perry, George. The Films of Alfred Hitchcock. New York:
Dutton, 1965. 160 pp. (Republished as Hitchcock, Garden
City, N.Y.: Doubleday, 1975. 126 pp.)

2832 Wood, Robin. Hitchcock's Films. New York: A. S. Barnes,
1965. 193 pp. (Revised 1969, 204 pp.)

2833 Truffaut, François with Scott, Helen G. Hitchcock. New
York: Simon and Schuster, 1967. 256 pp.
An extended interview.

2834 LaValley, Albert J. (ed.) Focus on Hitchcock. Englewood
Cliffs, N.J.: Prentice-Hall, 1972. 186 pp.
Contributors include Lindsay Anderson, Andre Bazin,
Robin Wood, Andrew Sarris, Raymond Durgnat, Eric
Rohmer and Claude Chabrol.

2835 Durgnat, Raymond. The Strange Case of Alfred Hitchcock:
or, The Plain Man's Hitchcock. Cambridge, Mass.:
M.I.T. Press, 1974. 419 pp.

HOLDEN, WILLIAM

2836 Quirk, Lawrence J. The Films of William Holden. Secaucus,
N.J.: Citadel, 1973. 255 pp.

HOLLOWAY, STANLEY

2837 Holloway, Stanley with Richards, Dick. Wiv a Little Bit
O'Luck: The Life Story of Stanley Holloway. London:
Frewin, 1967. 344 pp.

HOPE, BOB

2838 Hope, Bob. They Got Me Covered. Hollywood: n.p., 1941.
95 pp.

2839 Hope, Bob. I Never Left Home. New York: Simon and
      Schuster, 1944. 207 pp.

2840 Hope, Bob. So This Is Peace. Hollywood: Hope Corpora-
      tion, 1946. 208 pp.

2841 Hope, Bob with Martin, Pete. Have Tux, Will Travel: Bob
      Hope's Own Story. New York: Simon and Schuster, 1954.
      308 pp.

2842 Guild, Leo. Where There's Life, There's Bob Hope: The
      Hilarious Life Story of America's Favorite Funny Man.
      Los Angeles: Petersen, 1957. 96 pp.

2843 Hope, Bob. I Owe Russia $1200. Garden City, N.Y.:
      Doubleday, 1963. 272 pp.

2844 Morella, Joe; Epstein, Edward Z.; and Clark, Eleanor. The
      Amazing Careers of Bob Hope: From Gags to Riches.
      New Rochelle, N.Y.: Arlington, 1973. 256 pp.

2845 Hope, Bob with Martin, Pete. The Last Christmas Show.
      Garden City, N.Y.: Doubleday, 1974. 383 pp.

HOPKINSON, PETER

2846 Hopkinson, Peter. Split Focus: An Involvement in Two
      Decades. London: Hart-Davis, 1969. 224 pp.

HOPPER, HEDDA

2847 Hopper, Hedda. From Under My Hat. Garden City, N.Y.:
      Doubleday, 1952. 311 pp.

2848 Eells, George. Hedda and Louella. New York: Putnam,
      1972. 360 pp.

HORNBY, CLIFFORD

2849 Hornby, Clifford. Shooting Without Stars. London: Hutchin-
      son, 1940. 252 pp.

HORNE, LENA

2850 Horne, Lena with Arstein, Helen and Moss, Carlton. In Per-
      son, Lena Horne. New York: Greenberg, 1950. 249 pp.

2851 Horne, Lena and Schickel, Richard. Lena. Garden City,
      N.Y.: Doubleday, 1965. 300 pp.

HOUSE, BOYCE

2852 House, Boyce. How I Took Hollywood By Storm. Dallas:

Banks Upshaw, 1942.   26 pp.
Written by the technical advisor on BOOM TOWN.

HOUSEMAN, JOHN

2853   Houseman, John.   Run-Through: A Memoir.   New York:
Simon and Schuster, 1972.   507 pp.
Includes a section on Herman J. Mankiewicz, Orson
Welles and CITIZEN KANE.

HOWARD, LESLIE

2854   Colvin, Ian Goodhope.   Flight 777.   London: Evans, 1957.
212 pp.
An investigation of Howard's wartime death.

2855   Howard, Leslie Ruth.   A Quite Remarkable Father: The
Biography of Leslie Howard.   New York: Harcourt,
Brace, 1959.   307 pp.

HOWE, JAMES WONG

2856   Higham, Charles.   Hollywood Cameramen: Sources of Light.
Bloomington: Indiana University Press, 1970.   176 pp.

HUGHES, HOWARD

2857   Keats, John.   Howard Hughes.   New York: Random, 1966.
304 pp.

2858   Gerber, Albert B.   Bashful Billionaire: The Story of Howard
Hughes.   New York: Dell, 1968.   352 pp.

2859   Garrison, Omar V.   Howard Hughes in Las Vegas.   New
York: Lyle Stuart, 1970.   293 pp.

2860   Dietrich, Noah and Thomas, Bob.   Howard, The Amazing
Mr. Hughes.   Greenwich, Conn.:   Fawcett, 1972.   303 pp.

HULL, JOSEPHINE

2861   Carson, William.   Dear Josephine: The Theatrical Career of
Josephine Hull.   Norman: University of Oklahoma Press,
1963.   313 pp.

HUSTON, JOHN

2862   Nolan, William F.   John Huston: King Rebel.   Los Angeles:
Sherbourne, 1965.   247 pp.

2863   Tozzi, Romano.   John Huston: A Pictorial Treasury of His
Films.   New York: Falcon, 1971.   148 pp.

HYAMS, JOE

2864   Hyams, Joe. Mislaid in Hollywood. New York: Wyden,
       1973. 224 pp.
       Autobiography of a Hollywood columnist.

IVENS, JORIS

2865   Ivens, Joris. The Camera and I. New York: International
       Publishers, 1969. 280 pp.

IVES, BURL

2866   Ives, Burl. Wayfaring Stranger: An Autobiography. New
       York: Whittlesey, 1948. 253 pp.

JENNINGS, HUMPHREY

2867   Powell, Dilys and others. Humphrey Jennings, 1907-1950:
       A Tribute. London: Humphrey Jennings Memorial Fund
       Committee, ca. 1951. 12 pp.
       Contributors include John Grierson, Kathleen Raine,
       Basil Wright, Ian Dalrymple, John Greenwood and Dilys
       Powell.

2868   Lovell, Alan and Hillier, Jim. Studies in Documentary. New
       York: Viking, 1972. 176 pp.
       Includes a chapter on Jennings.

JESSEL, GEORGE

2869   Jessel, George. So Help Me: The Autobiography of George
       Jessel. New York: Random, 1943. 240 pp.

2870   Jessel, George. This Way, Miss. New York: Holt, 1955.
       228 pp.

2871   Jessel, George with Austin, John. The World I Lived In.
       Chicago: Regnery, 1975. 213 pp.

JOHNSON, MARTIN and OSA

2872   Johnson, Osa. I Married Adventure: The Lives and Adven-
       tures of Martin and Osa Johnson. Philadelphia: Lippin-
       cott, 1940. 376 pp.

JOHNSON, VAN

2873   Beecher, Elizabeth. Van Johnson: The Luckiest Guy in the
       World. Racine, Wisc.: Whitman, 1947. 248 pp.

JOLSON, AL

2874 Abramson, Martin. The Real Story of Al Jolson. New York:
      Spectrolux, 1950. 48 pp.

2875 Jolson, Harry with Emley, Alban. Mistah Jolson. Holly-
      wood: House-Warven, 1951. 257 pp.

2876 Sieben, Pearl. The Immortal Jolson: His Life and Times.
      New York: Fell, 1962. 231 pp.

2877 Freedland, Michael. Jolson. New York: Stein and Day,
      1972. 256 pp. (Also published as Al Jolson.)

JOUVET, LOUIS

2878 Knapp, Bettina Liebowitz. Louis Jouvet: Man of the Theatre.
      New York: Columbia University Press, 1957. 345 pp.
      Includes material on Jouvet's film career.

KAMINSKA, IDA

2879 Kaminska, Ida. My Life, My Theater. Edited and translated
      by Curt Leviant. New York: Macmillan, 1973. 310 pp.

KANIN, GARSON

2880 Kanin, Garson. Hollywood: Stars and Starlets, Tycoons and
      Flesh-Peddlers, Moviemakers and Moneymakers, Frauds
      and Geniuses, Hopefuls and Has-Beens, Great Lovers and
      Sex Symbols. New York: Viking, 1974. 393 pp.

KARLOFF, BORIS

2881 Ackerman, Forrest J. (ed.) The Frankenscience Monster.
      New York: Ace, 1969. 191 pp.

2882 Barbour, Alan; Marill, Alvin H.; and Parish, James Robert.
      Karloff. Kew Gardens, N.Y.: Cinefax, 1969. 64 pp.
      Primarily photographs.

2883 Underwood, Peter. Karloff: The Life of Boris Karloff. New
      York: Drake, 1972. 238 pp.

2884 Gifford, Denis. Karloff: The Man, The Monster, The Movies.
      New York: Curtis, 1973. 350 pp.

2885 Glut, Donald F. The Frankenstein Legend: A Tribute to
      Mary Shelley and Boris Karloff. Metuchen, N.J.: Scare-
      crow, 1973. 372 pp.

2886 Bojarski, Richard and Beale, Kenneth. The Films of Boris
      Karloff. Secaucus, N.J.: Citadel, 1974. 287 pp.

2887 Jensen, Paul M. Boris Karloff and His Films. South Bruns-
      wick, N.J.: A. S. Barnes, 1974. 194 pp.

2888 Moss, Robert F. Karloff and Company: The Horror Film.
      New York: Pyramid, 1974. 158 pp.

2889 Beck, Calvin Thomas. Heroes of the Horrors. New York:
      Macmillan, 1975. 353 pp.

2890 Lindsay, Cynthia. Dear Boris: The Life of William Henry
      Pratt, A.K.A. Boris Karloff. New York: Knopf, 1975.
      274 pp.

KAUFMAN, GEORGE S.

2891 Teichmann, Howard. George S. Kaufman, An Intimate Por-
      trait. New York: Atheneum, 1972. 371 pp.

2892 Meredith, Scott. George S. Kaufman and His Friends.
      Garden City, N.Y.: Doubleday, 1974. 723 pp.

KAVANAGH, REGINALD (CRASH)

2893 Richardson, Anthony. Crash Kavanagh. London: Parrish,
      1953. 256 pp.
          The story of a stunt man.

KAYE, DANNY

2894 Richards, Dick. The Life Story of Danny Kay. London:
      Convoy, 1949. 70 pp.

2895 Singer, Kurt. The Danny Kaye Story. New York: Nelson,
      1958. 241 pp.

KAZAN, ELIA

2896 Basinger, Jeanine; Frazer, John; and Reed, Joseph W., Jr.
      (eds.) Working With Kazan. Middleton, Conn.: Wes-
      leyan University, 1973. 48 pp.
          Published on the occasion of a retrospective; includes
      detailed filmography and tribute essays.

2897 Kazan, Elia. On What Makes a Director. Los Angeles:
      Directors Guild of America, 1973. 22 pp.

2898 Kazan, Elia. Kazan on Kazan. Interviews conducted by
      Michel Ciment. New York: Viking, 1974. 199 pp.

KEATON, BUSTER

2899 Keaton, Buster with Samuels, Charles. My Wonderful World
      of Slapstick. Garden City, N.Y.: Doubleday, 1960. 282 pp.

2900 Blesh, Rudi. Keaton. New York: Macmillan, 1966. 395 pp.

2901 Buster Keaton, 1917-1931. London: British Film Institute,
      1967. 12 pp.

2902 Lebel, Jean-Patrick. Buster Keaton. New York: A. S.
      Barnes, 1967. 179 pp. Trans. by P. D. Stovin.

2903 McCaffrey, Donald W. Four Great Comedians: Chaplin,
      Lloyd, Keaton, Langdon. New York: A. S. Barnes,
      1968. 175 pp.

2904 Robinson, David. Buster Keaton. Bloomington: Indiana Uni-
      versity Press, 1969. 198 pp.

2905 Wead, George Adam. Buster Keaton and the Dynamics of
      Visual Wit. Northwestern University: Ph.D., 1973.
      375 pp.

KELLY, GENE

2906 Griffith, Richard. The Cinema of Gene Kelly. New York:
      Museum of Modern Art Film Library, 1962. 16 pp.

2907 Burrows, Michael. Gene Kelly: Versatility Personified.
      Cornwall, England: Primestyle, 1972. 40 pp.

2908 Thomas, Tony. The Films of Gene Kelly, Song and Dance
      Man. Secaucus, N.J.: Citadel, 1974. 243 pp.

2909 Hirschhorn, Clive. Gene Kelly: A Biography. Chicago:
      Regnery, 1975. 335 pp.

KELLY, GRACE

2910 Gaither, Gant. Princess of Monaco: The Story of Grace
      Kelly. New York: Holt, 1957. 176 pp.

2911 McCallum, John. That Kelly Family. New York: A. S.
      Barnes, 1957. 229 pp.

2912 Newman, Robert. Princess Grace Kelly: The Fascinating
      Life Story of a Girl Who Made the Leap from the Phila-
      delphia Suburb to a Royal Palace. Derby, Conn.:
      Monarch, 1962. 138 pp.

2913 Katz, Marjorie P. Grace Kelly. New York: Coward-Mc-
      Cann, 1970. 96 pp.

KELLY, RON

2914 Gobeil, Charlotte (ed.) The Film and Ron Kelly. Ottawa:

Canadian Film Institute, 1965. 24 pp.
Includes an interview.

KENDALL, HENRY

2915 Kendall, Henry. I Remember Romano's: The Autobiography
      of Henry Kendall. London: Macdonald, 1960. 224 pp.

KENDALL, MESSMORE

2916 Kendall, Messmore. Never Let Weather Interfere. New
      York: Farrar, Straus, 1946. 423 pp.

KERN, JEROME

2917 Ewen, David. The Story of Jerome Kern. New York: Holt,
      1953. 148 pp.

2918 Ewen, David. The World of Jerome Kern: A Biography.
      New York: Holt, 1960. 178 pp.

KEYS, NELSON

2919 Carstairs, John Paddy. "Bunch:" A Biography of Nelson
      Keys. London: Hurst and Blackett, 1941. 255 pp.

KHAN, ALY

2920 Slater, Leonard. Aly: A Biography. New York: Random,
      1965. 303 pp.
          Includes material on Aly Khan's relationship with Rita
      Hayworth, Kim Novak, Gene Tierney, Juliette Greco and
      others.

LORD KILBRACKEN

2921 Lord Kilbracken. Living Like a Lord. Boston: Houghton
      Mifflin, 1956. 243 pp.
          With material on Kilbracken's relationship to John
      Huston and MOBY DICK.·

KIMBROUGH, EMILY

2922 Kimbrough, Emily. We Followed Our Hearts to Hollywood.
      New York: Dodd, Mead, 1943. 210 pp.
          An account of Emily Kimbrough and Cornelia Otis
      Skinner's trip to Hollywood in connection with the filming
      of their book, Our Hearts Were Young and Gay.

KING, ALLAN

2923 Reid, Alison (ed.) Allan King: An Interview with Bruce

Martin and A Filmography. Ottawa: Canadian Film Institute, 1970. 28 pp.

KING, HENRY

2924 Denton, Clive; Canham, Kingsley; and Thomas, Tony. The Hollywood Professionals, Vol. II: Henry King, Lewis Milestone, Sam Wood. New York: A. S. Barnes, 1974. 192 pp.

KITT, EARTHA

2925 Kitt, Eartha. Thursday's Child. New York: Duell, Sloan and Pearce, 1956. 250 pp.

KNEF, HILDEGARD

2926 Knef, Hildegard. The Gift Horse: Report on a Life. New York: McGraw-Hill, 1971. 384 pp. Translated by David Anthony Palastanga.

2927 Knef, Hildegard. The Verdict. New York: Farrar, Straus and Giroux, 1975. 377 pp. Translated by David Anthony Palastanga.

KNIGHT, ERIC

2928 Knight, Eric. Portrait of a Flying Yorkshireman: Letters from Eric Knight in the United States to Paul Rotha in England. Edited by Paul Rotha. London: Chapman and Hall, 1952. 231 pp.

KORDA, ALEXANDER

2929 Tabori, Paul. Alexander Korda. London: Oldbourne, 1959. 324 pp. (Reprinted New York: Living Books, 1966.)

2930 Kulik, Karol. Alexander Korda: The Man Who Could Work Miracles. London: W. H. Allen, 1975. 407 pp.

KOVACS, ERNIE

2931 Walley, David G. Nothing in Moderation: A Biography of Ernie Kovacs. New York: Drake, 1975. 246 pp.

KUBRICK, STANLEY

2932 Walker, Alexander. Stanley Kubrick Directs. New York: Harcourt, Brace, Jovanovich, 1971. 272 pp.

2933 Kagan, Norman. The Cinema of Stanley Kubrick. New York: Holt, Rinehart and Winston, 1972. 204 pp.

2934   De Vries, Daniel. The Films of Stanley Kubrick. Grand
       Rapids, Mich.: Eerdmans, 1973. 75 pp.

2935   Phillips, Gene D. Stanley Kubrick: A Film Odyssey. New
       York: Popular Library, 1975. 189 pp.

KUROSAWA, AKIRA

2936   Richie, Donald. The Films of Akira Kurosawa. Berkeley:
       University of California Press, 1965. 218 pp.

LAHR, BERT

2937   Lahr, John. Notes on a Cowardly Lion: The Biography of
       Bert Lahr. New York: Knopf, 1969. 394 pp.

LAKE, VERONICA

2938   Lake, Veronica with Bain, Donald. Veronica. New York:
       Citadel, 1971. 281 pp.

LAMARR, BARBARA

2939   Zierold, Norman. Sex Goddesses of the Silent Screen.
       Chicago: Regnery, 1973. 207 pp.

LAMARR, HEDY

2940   Lamarr, Hedy. Ecstasy and Me: My Life as a Woman.
       New York: Bartholomew, 1966. 318 pp.

LANCASTER, BURT

2941   Vermilye, Jerry. Burt Lancaster: A Pictorial History of
       His Films. New York: Falcon, 1971. 142 pp.

2942   Thomas, Tony. Burt Lancaster. New York: Pyramid, 1975.
       160 pp.

LANDIS, CAROLE

2943   Landis, Carole. Four Jills in a Jeep. New York: Random,
       1944. 180 pp.
            Account of Landis' role as an overseas wartime enter-
       tainer.

LANDIS, JESSIE ROYCE

2944   Landis, Jessie Royce. You Won't Be So Pretty (But You'll
       Know More). London: Allen, 1954. 256 pp.

LANE, LUPINO

2945   White, James Dillon. Born to Star: The Lupino Lane Story.
       London: Heinemann, 1957. 304 pp.

LANG, FRITZ

2946   Bogdanovich, Peter. Fritz Lang in America. New York:
       Praeger, 1967. 143 pp.
       Interview material.

2947   Jensen, Paul M. The Cinema of Fritz Lang. New York:
       A. S. Barnes, 1969. 223 pp.

LANGDON, HARRY

2948   McCaffrey, Donald W. Four Great Comedians: Chaplin,
       Lloyd, Keaton, Langdon. New York: A. S. Barnes,
       1968. 175 pp.

LANSBURY, ANGELA

2949   Parish, James Robert. Good Dames. South Brunswick,
       N.J.: A. S. Barnes, 1974. 277 pp.

LANZA, MARIO

2950   Bernard, Matt. Mario Lanza. New York: Macfadden-Bar-
       tell, 1971. 224 pp.

2951   Burrows, Michael. Mario Lanza, Max Steiner. Cornwall,
       England: Primestyle, 1971. 44 pp.

LASKY, JESSE L.

2952   Lasky, Jesse L. with Weldon, Don. I Blow My Own Horn.
       Garden City, N.Y.: Doubleday, 1957. 284 pp.

LASKY, JESSE L., JR.

2953   Lasky, Jesse L., Jr. Whatever Happened to Hollywood?
       London: W. H. Allen, 1973. 308 pp. (Reprinted New
       York: Funk and Wagnalls, 1975. 349 pp.)

LASSIE

2954   Weatherwax, Rudd B. and Rothwell, John H. The Story of
       Lassie: His Discovery and Training From Puppyhood to
       Stardom. New York: Duell, Sloan and Pearce, 1950.
       126 pp.

LAUGHTON, CHARLES

2955   Singer, Kurt D. The Laughton Story: An Intimate Story of

Charles Laughton. Philadelphia: Winston, 1954.
308 pp.

2956 Burrows, Michael. Charles Laughton and Fredric March.
      Cornwall, England: Primestyle, 1969. 41 pp.

2957 Brown, William. Charles Laughton: A Pictorial Treasury
      of His Films. New York: Falcon, 1970. 152 pp.

LAUREL, STAN

2958 McCabe, John. Mr. Laurel and Mr. Hardy. Garden City,
      N.Y.: Doubleday, 1961. 240 pp. (Republished New
      York: New American Library, 1966, 175 pp.)

2959 Everson, William K. The Films of Laurel and Hardy. New
      York: Citadel, 1967. 223 pp.

2960 Barr, Charles. Laurel and Hardy. Berkeley: University of
      California Press, 1968. 144 pp.

2961 Maltin, Leonard (ed.) The Laurel and Hardy Book. New
      York: Curtis, 1973. 301 pp.

2962 McCabe, John. The Comedy World of Stan Laurel. Garden
      City, N.Y.: Doubleday, 1974. 221 pp.

2963 Anobile, Richard J. (ed.) A Fine Mess! Verbal and Visual
      Gems from the Crazy World of Laurel and Hardy. New
      York: Darien, 1975. 256 pp.

2964 McCabe, John (text). Laurel and Hardy. Compiled by Al
      Kilgore. Filmography by Richard W. Bann. New York:
      Dutton, 1975. 400 pp.

LAWRENCE, GERTRUDE

2965 Lawrence, Gertrude. A Star Danced. Garden City, N.Y.:
      Garden City Publishing, 1945. 238 pp.

2966 Aldrich, Richard Stoddard. Gertrude Lawrence as Mrs. A:
      An Intimate Biography of the Great Star. New York:
      Greystone, 1954. 414 pp.

LEAN, DAVID

2967 Pratley, Gerald. The Cinema of David Lean. South Bruns-
      wick, N.J.: A. S. Barnes, 1974. 256 pp.

2968 Silver, Alain and Ursini, James. David Lean and His
      Films. London: Frewin, 1974. 255 pp.

LEE, BRUCE

2969 Block, Alex Ben. The Legend of Bruce Lee. New York: Dell, 1974. 171 pp.

2970 Dennis, Felix and Atyeo, Don. Bruce Lee: King of Kung-Fu. London: Wildwood, 1974. 96 pp.

2971 Lee, Linda. Bruce Lee: The Man Only I Knew. New York: Warner Paperback Library, 1975. 207 pp.

LEE, GYPSY ROSE

2972 Lee, Gypsy Rose. Gypsy: A Memoir. New York: Harper, 1957. 337 pp.

LEE, NORMAN

2973 Lee, Norman. My Personal Log of Stars (Mostly Glamorous), People (Famous and Infamous), and Places (of the World) by Norman Lee: The Autobiography of an Amateur Sailor Who Finds the Land More Exciting than the Sea. London: Quality, 1947. 127 pp.

2974 Lee, Norman. Log of a Film Director. London: Quality, 1949. 156 pp.

LEE, RAYMOND

2975 Lee, Raymond. M. Encino, Cal.: Defilee, 1958. 64 pp.

LEIGH, VIVIEN

2976 Barker, Felix. The Oliviers: A Biography. Philadelphia: Lippincott, 1953. 371 pp.

2977 Robyns, Gwen. Light of a Star. London: Frewin, 1968. 256 pp. (Also published South Brunswick, N.J.: A. S. Barnes, 1970.)

2978 Dent, Alan. Vivien Leigh: A Bouquet. London: Hamilton, 1969. 219 pp.

LEISEN, MITCHELL

2979 Chierichetti, David. Hollywood Director: The Career of Mitchell Leisen. New York: Curtis, 1973. 398 pp.

LEJEUNE, C. A.

2980 Lejeune, C. A. Thank You for Having Me. London: Hutchinson, 1964. 255 pp.

LEMMON, JACK

2981 Widener, Don. Lemmon: A Biography. New York: Mac-
      millan, 1975. 247 pp.

LEROY, MERVYN

2982 Rohauer, Raymond. A Tribute to Mervyn LeRoy. New York:
      Gallery of Modern Art Monograph, 1967. 16 pp.

2983 LeRoy, Mervyn with Kleiner, Dick. Mervyn LeRoy: Take
      One. New York: Hawthorn, 1974. 244 pp.

LESTER, MARK

2984 Kidd, Paul. Mark Lester: The Boy, His Life and His Films.
      Elms Court, England: Stockwell, 1975. 81 pp.

LEVANT, OSCAR

2985 Levant, Oscar. The Memoirs of an Amnesiac. New York:
      Putnam, 1965. 320 pp.

2986 Levant, Oscar. The Unimportance of Being Oscar. New
      York: Putnam, 1968. 255 pp.

LEWIN, ALBERT

2987 Rohauer, Raymond. A Tribute to Albert Lewin. New York:
      Gallery of Modern Art Monograph, 1967. 15 pp.

LEWIS, JERRY

2988 Gehman, Richard. That Kid: The Story of Jerry Lewis.
      New York: Avon, 1964. 192 pp.

2989 Marx, Arthur. Everybody Loves Somebody Sometime (Es-
      pecially Himself): The Story of Dean Martin and Jerry
      Lewis. New York: Hawthorn, 1974. 288 pp.

LEWIS, JOE E.

2990 Cohn, Art. The Joker Is Wild: The Story of Joe E. Lewis.
      New York: Random, 1955. 368 pp.

LEWTON, VAL

2991 Siegel, Joel E. Val Lewton: The Reality of Terror. New
      York: Viking, 1973. 176 pp.

LIBERACE

2992 Liberace. Liberace: An Autobiography. New York: Putnam,
      1973. 316 pp.

LILLIE, BEATRICE

2993 Lillie, Beatrice with Philip, John and Brough, James. Every
Other Inch a Lady. Garden City, N.Y.: Doubleday,
1972. 360 pp.

LINDSAY, CYNTHIA

2994 Lindsay, Cynthia. Mother Climbed Trees. New York:
Simon and Schuster, 1958. 236 pp.
Autobiography of a woman who did stunt work and
whose family was involved in the Hollywood community.

LINDSAY, VACHEL

2995 Wolfe, Glenn J. Vachel Lindsay: The Poet as Film Theorist.
New York: Arno, 1973. 191 pp.

LISTER, MOIRA

2996 Lister, Moira. The Very Merry Widow Moira. London:
Hodder and Stoughton, 1969. 189 pp.

LLOYD, HAROLD

2997 Lloyd, Harold with Stout, Wesley W. An American Comedy.
(Originally published 1928.) New York: Dover, 1971.
138 pp.
1971 edition includes a 1966 interview with Lloyd conducted by Hubert I. Cohen.

2998 Cahn, William. Harold Lloyd's World of Comedy. New
York: Duell, Sloan and Pearce, 1964. 208 pp.

2999 McCaffrey, Donald W. Four Great Comedians: Chaplin,
Lloyd, Keaton, Langdon. New York: A. S. Barnes,
1968. 175 pp.

3000 Schickel, Richard. Harold Lloyd: The Shape of Laughter.
Boston: New York Graphic Society, 1974. 218 pp.

LOCKLEAR, ORMER LESLIE

3001 Ronnie, Art. Locklear: The Man Who Walked on Wings.
South Brunswick, N.J.: A. S. Barnes, 1973. 333 pp.
Biography of a stunt man.

LOCKWOOD, MARGARET

3002 Lockwood, Margaret. My Life and Films. Edited by Eric
Warman. London: World Film Publications, 1948.
78 pp.

3003   Lockwood, Margaret. Lucky Star: The Autobiography of
       Margaret Lockwood. London: Odhams, 1955. 191 pp.

LOLLOBRIGIDA, GINA

3004   Reid, Gordon. Gina Lollobrigida: Her Life and Films.
       London: Eurap, 1956. 64 pp.

LOMBARD, CAROLE

3005   Ott, Frederick W. The Films of Carole Lombard. Secaucus,
       N.J.: Citadel, 1972. 192 pp.

3006   Harris, Warren G. Gable and Lombard. New York: Simon
       and Schuster, 1974. 189 pp.

3007   Morella, Joe and Epstein, Edward Z. Gable & Lombard &
       Powell & Harlow. New York: Dell, 1975. 272 pp.

3008   Swindell, Larry. Screwball: The Life of Carole Lombard.
       New York: Morrow, 1975. 324 pp.

LONSDALE, FREDDY

3009   Donaldson, Frances. Freddy Lonsdale. London: Heinemann,
       1957. 257 pp.

LOOS, ANITA

3010   Loos, Anita. A Girl Like I. New York: Viking, 1966.
       275 pp.

3011   Loos, Anita. Kiss Hollywood Good-By. New York: Viking,
       1974. 213 pp.

LOREN, SOPHIA

3012   Reid, Gordon. The Sophia Loren Story. London: Eurap,
       1958. 63 pp.

3013   Laborderie, Renaud de. Sophia Loren: Renaud de Laborderie
       Spotlights in Words and Pictures the Career of the Re-
       markable Sophia Loren. Manchester, England: World
       Distributors, 1964. 48 pp.

3014   Crawley, Tony. The Films of Sophia Loren. London: LSP
       Books, 1974. 256 pp.

3015   Zec, Donald. Sophia. New York: McKay, 1975. 263 pp.

LORENTZ, PARE

3016   Snyder, Robert L. A History of the Early Productions of

Pare Lorentz and the United States Film Service, 1935-1940. University of Iowa: Ph.D., 1965. 375 pp.

3017 Snyder, Robert L. Pare Lorentz and the Documentary Film. Norman: University of Oklahoma Press, 1968. 232 pp.

LORRE, PETER

3018 Beck, Calvin Thomas. Heroes of the Horrors. New York: Macmillan, 1975. 353 pp.

LOSEY, JOSEPH

3019 Leahy, James. The Cinema of Joseph Losey. New York: A. S. Barnes, 1967. 175 pp.

3020 Losey, Joseph. Losey on Losey. Edited and introduced by Tom Milne. Garden City, N.Y.: Doubleday, 1968. 192 pp.
Interview material.

LOVELACE, LINDA

3021 Lovelace, Linda. Inside Linda Lovelace. New York: Pinnacle, 1973. 184 pp.
Includes a discussion of DEEP THROAT.

3022 Lovelace, Linda. The Intimate Diary of Linda Lovelace. New York: Pinnacle, 1974.

LUBITSCH, ERNST

3023 Huff, Theodore. An Index to the Films of Ernst Lubitsch. London: British Film Institute, 1947. 31 pp.

3024 Weinberg, Herman G. The Lubitsch Touch: A Critical Study. New York: Dutton, 1968. 344 pp.

LUGOSI, BELA

3025 Barbour, Alan G. Lugosi. Kew Gardens, N.Y.: Screen Facts Press, 1971. 48 pp.
Primarily illustrations.

3026 Lennig, Arthur. The Count: The Life and Films of Bela "Dracula" Lugosi. New York: Putnam, 1974. 347 pp.

3027 Beck, Calvin Thomas. Heroes of the Horrors. New York: Macmillan, 1975. 353 pp.

LUMIERE, LOUIS

3028 Hepworth, Cecil. Lumière and the Early Days of Film-

Making. London: British Broadcasting Corporation, 1948.
14 pp.

LUNT, ALFRED

3029 Freedley, George. The Lunts: An Illustrated Study of Their
Work, with a List of Their Appearances on Stage and
Screen. New York: Macmillan, 1958. 134 pp.

3030 Zolotow, Maurice. Stagestruck: The Romance of Alfred Lunt
and Lynn Fontanne. New York: Harcourt, Brace, 1965.
278 pp.

LYON, BEN

3031 Daniels, Bebe and Lyon, Ben. Life With the Lyons: The
Autobiography of Bebe Daniels & Ben Lyon. London:
Odhams, 1953. 256 pp.

MACARTHUR, CHARLES

3032 Hecht, Ben. Charles MacArthur: A Eulogy, April 23, 1956.
n.p., 1956. 8 pp.

3033 Hecht, Ben. Charlie: The Improbable Life and Times of
Charles MacArthur. New York: Harper, 1957. 242 pp.

MACARTNEY-FILGATE, TERENCE

3034 Gobeil, Charlotte (ed.) Terence Macartney-Filgate: The
Candid Eye. Ottawa: Canadian Film Institute, 1966. 34 pp.

McCAMBRIDGE, MERCEDES

3035 McCambridge, Mercedes. The Two of Us. London: Peter
Davies, 1960. 182 pp.

MacDONALD, JEANETTE

3036 Rich, Sharon. Jeanette MacDonald: A Pictorial Treasury.
Los Angeles: Times Mirror Press, 1973. 253 pp.

3037 Knowles, Eleanor. The Films of Jeanette MacDonald and
Nelson Eddy. South Brunswick, N.J.: A. S. Barnes,
1975. 469 pp.

McKENNA, VIRGINIA

3038 McKenna, Virginia. Some of My Friends Have Tails. New
York: Harcourt, Brace, 1970. 125 pp.

McLAGLEN, ANDREW V.

3039 Burrows, Michael. John Ford and Andrew V. McLaglen.
Cornwall, England: Primestyle, 1970. 32 pp.

MacLAINE, SHIRLEY

3040 MacLaine, Shirley. Don't Fall Off the Mountain. New York:
Norton, 1970. 270 pp.

3041 MacLaine, Shirley. You Can Get There From Here. New
York: Norton, 1975. 249 pp.

McLAREN, NORMAN

3042 Norman McLaren. Montreal: Cinémathèque Canadienne,
1965. Unpaged.
Catalog of an exhibition at the Journées internationales
du cinéma d'animation, Annecy, 1965.

3043 McLaren, Norman. The Drawings of Norman McLaren. Montreal: Tundra, 1975. 192 pp.
Text in English and French.

MacLIAMMOIR, MICHEAL

3044 MacLiammoir, Micheal. Each Actor on His Ass. London:
Routledge and Paul, 1961. 248 pp.

McLUHAN, MARSHALL

3045 Underhill, Frederic. Post-Literate Man and Film Editing:
An Application of the Theories of Marshall McLuhan.
Boston: Boston University, School of Public Communica-
tion, 1964. 42 pp.

3046 Day, Barry. The Message of Marshall McLuhan. London:
Lintas, 1967. 38 pp.

3047 Stearn, Gerald Emanuel (ed.) McLuhan: Hot and Cool: A
Primer for the Understanding of and A Critical Symposium
with A Rebuttal by McLuhan. New York: Dial, 1967.
312 pp.

3048 Finkelstein, Sidney. Sense and Nonsense of McLuhan. New
York: International Publishers, 1968. 122 pp.

3049 Miller, Jonathan. Marshall McLuhan. New York: Viking,
1971. 133 pp.

MACPHERSON, SANDY

3050 Macpherson, Sandy. Sandy Presents. London: Home and

Van Thal, 1950. 179 pp.
Autobiography of a cinema and radio organist.

McQUEEN, STEVE

3051 Nolan, William. Steve McQueen: Star on Wheels. New
      York: Putnam, 1972. 159 pp.
      For the young reader.

3052 McCoy, Malachy. Steve McQueen: The Unauthorized Biogra-
      phy. Chicago: Regnery, 1974. 233 pp.

MAIN, MARJORIE

3053 Parish, James Robert. The Slapstick Queens. South Bruns-
      wick, N. J.: A. S. Barnes, 1973. 297 pp.

MALTBY, HENRY F.

3054 Maltby, H. F. Ring Up the Curtain: Being the Stage and
      Film Memoirs of H. F. Maltby. London, New York:
      Hutchinson, 1950. 232 pp.

MAMOULIAN, ROUBEN

3055 Rohauer, Raymond. A Fortieth Anniversary Tribute to
      Rouben Mamoulian, 1927-1967. New York: Gallery of
      Modern Art Monograph, 1967. 12 pp.

3056 Milne, Tom. Rouben Mamoulian. Bloomington: Indiana Uni-
      versity Press, 1969. 176 pp.

3057 Mamoulian, Rouben. Style Is the Man. Washington, D.C.:
      American Film Institute, 1971. 34 pp.
      Interview material.

MANEY, RICHARD

3058 Maney, Richard. Fanfare: The Confessions of a Press
      Agent. New York: Harper, 1957. 374 pp.

MANKIEWICZ, JOSEPH L.

3059 Taylor, John Russell (comp.) Joseph L. Mankiewicz: An
      Index to His Work. London: British Film Institute, 1960.
      24 pp.

MANN, ANTHONY

3060 Kitses, Jim. Horizons West: Anthony Mann, Budd Boetticher,
      Sam Peckinpah: Studies of Authorship Within the Western.
      Bloomington, Indiana University Press, 1970. 176 pp.

MANSFIELD, JAYNE

3061 Mansfield, Jayne and Hargitay, Mickey. Jane Mansfield's
     Wild, Wild World. Los Angeles: Holloway, 1963. 128 pp.

3062 Mann, May. Jayne Mansfield: A Biography. New York:
     Drake, 1973. 277 pp.

3063 Strait, Raymond. The Tragic Secret Life of Jayne Mansfield.
     Chicago: Regnery, 1974. 207 pp.

3064 Saxton, Martha. Jayne Mansfield and the American Fifties.
     Boston: Houghton Mifflin, 1975. 223 pp.

MANTZ, PAUL

3065 Dwiggins, Don. Hollywood Pilot: The Biography of Paul
     Mantz. New York: Curtis, 1967. 207 pp.

MARCH, FREDRIC

3066 Burrows, Michael. Charles Laughton and Fredric March.
     Cornwall, England: Primestyle, 1969. 41 pp.

3067 Quirk, Lawrence J. The Films of Fredric March. New
     York: Citadel, 1971. 255 pp.

MARION, FRANCES

3068 Marion, Frances. Off With Their Heads! A Serio-Comic
     Tale of Hollywood. New York: Macmillan, 1972. 356 pp.

MARJOE (see GORTNER, MARJOE)

MARKOPOULOS, GREGORY

3069 Markopoulos, Gregory. Quest for Serenity: Journal of a
     Film-Maker. New York: Film-Makers' Cinematheque,
     ca. 1965. 80 pp.

3070 Markopoulos, Gregory. Chaos Phaos [In Four Volumes].
     Florence: Temenos, 1970.

MARLOWE, DON

3071 Marlowe, Don. The Hollywood That Was. Fort Worth,
     Texas: Branch-Smith, 1969. 189 pp.
        Reminiscences of Hollywood by former member of
     the "Our Gang" comedies.

MARTIN, DEAN

3072 Marx, Arthur. Everybody Loves Somebody Sometime

(Especially Himself): The Story of Dean Martin and Jerry Lewis. New York: Hawthorn, 1974. 288 pp.

THE MARX BROTHERS (GROUCHO, HARPO, CHICO, ZEPPO, and GUMMO)

3073   Crichton, Kyle. The Marx Brothers. Garden City, N.Y.: Doubleday, 1950. 310 pp.

3074   Marx, Arthur. Life with Groucho. New York: Simon and Schuster, 1954. 310 pp.
       Written by Groucho's son.

3075   Marx, Groucho. Groucho and Me. New York: Bernard Geis, 1959. 344 pp.

3076   Marx, Harpo with Barber, Rowland. Harpo Speaks! New York: Bernard Geis, 1961. 475 pp. (Reprinted New York: Freeway, 1974.)

3077   Marx, Groucho. Memoirs of a Mangy Lover. New York: Bernard Geis, 1963. 214 pp.

3078   Eyles, Allen. The Marx Brothers: Their World of Comedy. New York: A. S. Barnes, 1966. 176 pp.

3079   Marx, Groucho. The Groucho Letters: Letters From and To Groucho Marx. New York: Simon and Schuster, 1967. 319 pp.

3080   Rohauer, Raymond. A Tribute to the Marx Brothers. New York: Gallery of Modern Art Monograph, 1967. 8 pp.

3081   Zimmerman, Paul D. and Goldblatt, Burt. The Marx Brothers at the Movies. New York: Putnam, 1968. 224 pp. (Reprinted New York: Berkley, 1975.)

3082   Gardner, Martin Allan. The Marx Brothers: An Investigation of Their Films as Satirical Social Criticism. New York University: Ph.D., 1970. 299 pp.

3083   Anobile, Richard J. (comp.) Why A Duck? Visual and Verbal Gems From the Marx Brothers Movies. New York: Darien, 1971. 288 pp.

3084   Marx, Arthur. Son of Groucho. New York: McKay, 1972. 357 pp.

3085   Adamson, Joe. Groucho, Harpo, Chico, and Sometimes Zeppo: A History of the Marx Brothers and a Satire on the Rest of the World. New York: Simon and Schuster, 1973. 464 pp.

3086 Marx, Groucho and Anobile, Richard J.   The Marx Brothers
      Scrapbook. New York: Grosset and Dunlap, 1973. 256 pp.
      Includes interviews with Jack Benny, Morrie Ryskind,
      Robert Florey, Harry Ruby, Alexander Woollcott, George
      Seaton, Nat Perrin, and the Marx Brothers.

3087 Wolf, William.   The Marx Brothers. New York: Pyramid,
      1975. 157 pp.

MASCHWITZ, ERIC

3088 Maschwitz, Eric.   No Chip on My Shoulder. London: Jenkins,
      1957. 208 pp.

MASON, JAMES

3089 Monaghan, John P.   The Authorised Biography of James
      Mason. London: World Film Publications, 1947. 78 pp.

3090 Hirschhorn, Clive.   The Films of James Mason. London:
      LSP Books, 1975. 256 pp.

MASSINGHAM, RICHARD

3091 Beddington, Jack (and others).   Richard Massingham: A
      Tribute by His Friends and a Record of His Films.
      London: Richard Massingham Memorial Fund, 1955.
      20 pp.

MATTHEWS, A. E.

3092 Matthews, A. E.   Matty: An Autobiography. London:
      Hutchinson, 1952. 232 pp.

MATTHEWS, JESSIE

3093 Thornton, Michael.   Jessie Matthews: A Biography. London:
      Hart-Davis, MacGibbon, 1974. 359 pp.

3094 Matthews, Jessie with Burgess, Muriel.   Over My Shoulder:
      An Autobiography. New Rochelle, N.Y.: Arlington,
      1975. 240 pp.

MAXWELL, ELSA

3095 Maxwell, Elsa.   R.S.V.P.: Elsa Maxwell's Own Story.
      Boston: Little, Brown, 1954. 326 pp. (Also published
      as I Married the World.)

MAYAKOWSKY, VLADIMIR

3096 Rudy, William.   Majakovskij and Film Art. Harvard Uni-
      versity: Ph.D., 1955.

MAYER, ARTHUR

3097 Mayer, Arthur. Merely Colossal. New York: Simon and
      Schuster, 1953. 264 pp.

MAYER, LOUIS B.

3098 Crowther, Bosley. Hollywood Rajah: The Life and Times of
      Louis B. Mayer. New York: Holt, Rinehart and Winston,
      1960. 339 pp.

3099 Marx, Samuel. Mayer and Thalberg: The Make-Believe
      Saints. New York: Random, 1975. 273 pp.

MELIES, GEORGES

3100 Sadoul, Georges. An Index to the Creative Work of Georges
      Méliès, 1896-1912. London: British Film Institute,
      1947. 32 pp.

3101 Brakhage, Stan. The Brakhage Lectures. Chicago: The
      Good Lion, School of the Art Institute of Chicago, 1972.
      106 pp.

3102 Hammond, Paul. Marvellous Méliès. New York: St. Mar-
      tin's, 1975. 159 pp.

MELVILLE, JEAN-PIERRE

3103 Nogueira, Rui (ed.) Melville on Melville. New York: Viking,
      1972. 176 pp.
      Interviews with Melville conducted by Nogueira.

MENJOU, ADOLPHE

3104 Menjou, Adolphe and Musselman, M. M. It Took Nine
      Tailors. New York: Whittlesey, 1948. 238 pp.

MERCOURI, MELINA

3105 Mercouri, Melina. I Was Born Greek. Garden City, N.Y.:
      Doubleday, 1971. 253 pp.

MERMAN, ETHEL

3106 Merman, Ethel with Martin, Pete. Who Could Ask for Any-
      thing More? Garden City, N.Y.: Doubleday, 1955.
      252 pp.

MESTA, PERLE

3107 Mesta, Perle with Cahn, Robert. Perle: My Story. New
      York: McGraw-Hill, 1960. 251 pp.

MIDDLETON, GEORGE

3108 Middleton, George. These Things Are Mine: The Autobiography of a Journeyman Playwright. New York: Macmillan, 1947. 448 pp.

MILESTONE, LEWIS

3109 Shibuk, Charles. An Index to the Films of Lewis Milestone.
New York: Theodore Huff Memorial Film Society, 1958.
31 ℓ.

3110 Denton, Clive; Canham, Kingsley; and Thomas, Tony. The
Hollywood Professionals, Vol. II: Henry King, Lewis
Milestone, Sam Wood. New York: A. S. Barnes, 1974.
192 pp.

MILLAND, RAY

3111 Milland, Ray. Wide-Eyed in Babylon: An Autobiography.
New York: Morrow, 1974. 264 pp.

3112 Parish, James Robert and Stanke, Don E. The Debonairs.
New Rochelle, N.Y.: Arlington, 1975. 511 pp.
Contains a lengthy chapter on Ray Milland, including
complete filmography.

MILLER, ANN

3113 Miller, Ann with Browning, Norma Lee. Miller's High Life.
Garden City, N.Y.: Doubleday, 1972. 283 pp.

MILLER, ARTHUR C.

3114 Balshofer, Fred J. and Miller, Arthur C. with Bergsten,
Bebe. One Reel a Week. Berkeley: University of California Press, 1967. 218 pp.

3115 Higham, Charles. Hollywood Cameramen: Sources of Light.
Bloomington: Indiana University Press, 1970. 176 pp.

3116 Maltin, Leonard. Behind the Camera: The Cinematographer's
Art. New York: New American Library, 1971. 240 pp.
Includes a lengthy interview with Arthur C. Miller.

MILLER, RUBY

3117 Miller, Ruby. Champagne From My Slipper. London:
Jenkins, 1962. 192 pp.

MILLER, VIRGIL E.

3118 Miller, Virgil E. Splinters From Hollywood Tripods:

Memoirs of a Cameraman. New York: Exposition, 1964.
139 pp.

THE MILLS, JOHN, JULIET and HAYLEY (see BELL,
MARY HAYLEY)

MINNELLI, LIZA

3119 Parish, James Robert with Ano, Jack. Liza! An Unauthorized
Biography. New York: Pocket Books, 1975. 176 pp.

MINNELLI, VINCENTE

3120 De la Roche, Catherine. Vincente Minnelli. New Zealand:
New Zealand Film Institute, 1959. 40 pp.

3121 Casper, Joseph Andrew. A Critical Study of the Film Musicals of Vincente Minnelli. University of Southern California: Ph.D., 1973. 522 pp.

3122 Minnelli, Vincente with Arce, Hector. I Remember It Well.
Garden City, N.Y.: Doubleday, 1974. 391 pp.

MITCHELL, GRANT

3123 Dubois, Aaron. The House of Van Du: A Vignette Biography
of the Stage and Screen Actor, Grant Mitchell. New York:
William-Frederick, 1962. 126 pp.

MITCHUM, ROBERT

3124 Tomkies, Mike. The Robert Mitchum Story: "It Sure Beats
Working." Chicago: Regnery, 1972. 271 pp.

MIX, TOM

3125 Mix, Olive Stokes with Heath, Eric. The Fabulous Tom Mix.
Englewood Cliffs, N.J.: Prentice-Hall, 1957. 177 pp.

3126 Mix, Paul E. The Life and Legend of Tom Mix. South
Brunswick, N.J.: A. S. Barnes, 1972. 206 pp.

MIZNER, ADDISON

3127 Johnston, Alva. The Legendary Mizners. New York: Farrar, Straus and Young, 1953. 304 pp.

MIZNER, WILSON

3128 Johnston, Alva. The Legendary Mizners. New York: Farrar, Straus and Young, 1953. 304 pp.

3129 Burke, John. Rogue's Progress: Fabulous Adventures of
Wilson Mizner. New York: Putnam, 1975. 304 pp.

MIZOGUCHI, KENJI

3130 Morris, Peter. Mizoguchi Kenji. Ottawa: Canadian Film
      Institute, 1967. 48 pp.
          Includes letters and statements by Mizoguchi.

MOGER, ART

3131 Moger, Art. Some of My Best Friends Are People. Boston:
      Challenge, 1964. 156 pp.
          Memoirs of a press agent.

MOHOLY-NAGY, LASZLO

3132 Moholy-Nagy, Sibyl. Moholy-Nagy: Experiment in Totality.
      New York: Harper, 1950. 253 pp. (Republished Cam-
      bridge, Mass.: M.I.T. Press, 1969, 259 pp.)

3133 Kostelanetz, Richard (ed.) Moholy-Nagy. New York: Praeger,
      1970. 238 pp.
          Contributions primarily by Laszlo Moholy-Nagy; in-
      cludes some theory as well.

MOHR, HAL

3134 Maltin, Leonard. Behind the Camera: The Cinematographer's
      Art. New York: New American Library, 1971. 240 pp.
          Includes a lengthy interview with Hal Mohr.

MONETT, NEGLEY

3135 Monett, Negley. Hair on a Cue Ball: The Hair-Raising Ad-
      ventures of a Hollywood Writer. New York: Exposition,
      1955. 213 pp.

MONROE, MARILYN

3136 Franklin, Joe and Palmer, Laurie. The Marilyn Monroe
      Story. New York: Field, 1953. 63 pp.

3137 Martin, Pete. Will Acting Spoil Marilyn Monroe? Garden
      City, N.Y.: Doubleday, 1956. 128 pp. (Also published
      as Marilyn Monroe.)

3138 Zolotow, Maurice. Marilyn Monroe. New York: Harcourt,
      Brace, 1960. 340 pp.

3139 Carpozi, George, Jr. Marilyn Monroe: "Her Own Story."
      New York: Belmont, 1961. 222 pp. (Reprinted New
      York: Universal-Award, 1973. Also published as The
      Agony of Marilyn Monroe.)

3140 Her Psychiatrist Friend. Violations of the Child Marilyn
      Monroe. New York: Bridgehead, 1962. 159 pp.

3141   Conway, Michael and Ricci, Mark. The Films of Marilyn
       Monroe. New York: Citadel, 1964. 160 pp.

3142   Hoyt, Edwin Palmer. Marilyn, The Tragic Venus. New
       York: Duell, Sloan and Pearce, 1965. 279 pp.

3143   Capell, Frank A. The Strange Death of Marilyn Monroe.
       Zarephath, N.J.: Herald of Freedom, 1969. 80 pp.

3144   Guiles, Fred Lawrence. Norma Jean: The Life of Marilyn
       Monroe. New York: McGraw-Hill, 1969. 341 pp.

3145   Wagenknecht, Edward (ed.) Marilyn Monroe: A Composite
       View. Philadelphia: Chilton, 1969. 200 pp.
           Contributors include Hollis Alpert, Edith Sitwell,
       Norman Rosten, Cecil Beaton, Lee Strasberg, Diana
       Trilling, David Robinson, Alexander Walker, and Monroe
       herself.

3146   Smith, Milburn and others (eds.) Marilyn. New York:
       Barven, 1971. 66 pp.

3147   Mailer, Norman. Marilyn: A Biography. New York: Gros-
       set and Dunlap, 1973. 271 pp.

3148   Mellen, Joan. Marilyn Monroe. New York: Pyramid, 1973.
       157 pp.

3149   Rosten, Norman. Marilyn: An Untold Story. New York:
       New American Library, 1973. 125 pp. (Also published
       as Monroe: A Very Personal Story.)

3150   Kobal, John (ed.) Marilyn Monroe: A Life on Film. Lon-
       don, New York: Hamlyn, 1974. 176 pp.

3151   Monroe, Marilyn. My Story. New York: Stein and Day,
       1974. 143 pp.

3152   Slatzer, Robert F. The Life and Curious Death of Marilyn
       Monroe. New York: Pinnacle, 1974. 348 pp.

3153   Murray, Eunice with Shade, Rose. Marilyn: The Last
       Months. New York: Pyramid, 1975. 157 pp.

MONTGOMERY, ROBERT

3154   Parish, James Robert and Stanke, Don E. The Debonairs.
       New Rochelle, N.Y.: Arlington, 1975. 511 pp.
           Contains a lengthy chapter on Robert Montgomery,
       including complete filmography.

MOORE, COLLEEN

3155 Moore, Colleen. Silent Star. Garden City, N.Y.: Double-
        day, 1968. 262 pp.

MOORE, GRACE

3156 Moore, Grace. You're Only Human Once. Garden City,
        N.Y.: Doubleday, Doran, 1944. 275 pp.

MOOREHEAD, AGNES

3157 Parish, James Robert. Good Dames. South Brunswick, N.J.:
        A. S. Barnes, 1974. 277 pp.

MORE, KENNETH

3158 More, Kenneth. Happy Go Lucky, My Life. London: Hale,
        1959. 192 pp.

MORLEY, ROBERT

3159 Morley, Robert and Stokes, Sewell. Robert Morley: A Re-
        luctant Autobiography. New York: Simon and Schuster,
        1967. 285 pp.

MOSTEL, ZERO

3160 Mostel, Zero. Zero By Mostel. New York: Horizon, 1965.
        Unpaged.
            Primarily photographs by Max Waldman with some
        commentary and drawings by Mostel.

MÜLLER, RENATE

3161 Clements, R. E. Queen of America? The Case of Renate
        Müller. London: Women's Book Club, 1944. 208 pp.

MULLEN, PAT

3162 Mullen, Pat. Man of Aran. (Originally published 1935.)
        Cambridge, Mass.: M.I.T. Press, 1970. 286 pp.

MUNI, PAUL

3163 Gerlach, Michael Christopher. The Acting of Paul Muni.
        University of Michigan: Ph.D., 1971. 253 pp.

3164 Druxman, Michael B. Paul Muni: His Life and His Films.
        South Brunswick, N.J.: A. S. Barnes, 1974. 227 pp.

3165 Lawrence, Jerome. Actor: The Life and Times of Paul
        Muni. New York: Putnam, 1974. 380 pp.

MUNSTERBERG, HUGO

3166 Fredericksen, Donald Laurence. The Aesthetics of Isolation
       in Film Theory: Hugo Munsterberg. University of Iowa:
       Ph.D., 1973. 366 pp.

MURNAU, F. W.

3167 Huff, Theodore. An Index to the Films of F. W. Murnau.
       London: British Film Institute, 1948. 14 pp.

3168 Eisner, Lotte H. Murnau. (Originally published in France,
       1964.) Revised and translated Berkeley: University of
       California Press, 1973. 287 pp.

MURPHY, GEORGE

3169 Murphy, George with Lasky, Victor. Say ... Didn't You Used
       To Be George Murphy? New York: Bartholomew, 1970.
       438 pp.

MURRAY, KEN

3170 Murray, Ken. Life On a Pogo Stick: Autobiography of a
       Comedian. Philadelphia: Winston, 1960. 180 pp.

MURRAY, MAE

3171 Ardmore, Jane. The Self-Enchanted: Mae Murray, Image
       of an Era. New York: McGraw-Hill, 1959. 262 pp.

3172 Zierold, Norman. Sex Goddesses of the Silent Screen.
       Chicago: Regnery, 1973. 207 pp.

MURROW, EDWARD R.

3173 Kendrick, Alexander. Prime Time: The Life of Edward R.
       Murrow. Boston: Little, Brown, 1969. 548 pp.

MUYBRIDGE, EADWEARD

3174 MacDonnell, Kevin. Eadweard Muybridge: The Man Who In-
       vented the Moving Picture. Boston: Little, Brown, 1972.
       159 pp.

3175 Stanford University Art Department. Eadweard Muybridge:
       The Stanford Years, 1872-1882. Stanford: Stanford Uni-
       versity Art Department, 1972. 135 pp.
           Catalog of an exhibition first held at the Stanford Uni-
       versity Museum of Art, October 7-December 4, 1972.

3176 Hendricks, Gordon. Eadweard Muybridge: The Father of the
       Motion Picture. London: Secker and Warburg, 1975.
       271 pp.

NABOKOV, VLADIMIR

3177 Appel, Alfred, Jr. Nabokov's Dark Cinema. New York:
Oxford University Press, 1974. 324 pp.

NATHAN, ARCHIE

3178 Nathan, Archie. Costumes By Nathan. London: Newnes,
1960. 207 pp.

NAZIMOVA, ALLA

3179 McKerrow, Margaret. A Descriptive Study of the Acting of
Alla Nazimova. University of Michigan: Ph.D., 1974.
321 pp.

NEAGLE, ANNA

3180 Neagle, Anna. Anna Neagle Says "There's Always Tomorrow": An Autobiography. London: Allen, 1974. 236 pp.

NEAL, PATRICIA

3181 Farrell, Barry. Pat and Roald. New York: Random, 1969.
241 pp.

3182 Burrows, Michael. Patricia Neal and Margaret Sullavan.
Cornwall, England: Primestyle, 1971. 42 pp.

NEFF, HILDEGARD (see KNEF, HILDEGARD)

NEGRI, POLA

3183 Negri, Pola. Memoirs of a Star. Garden City, N.Y.:
Doubleday, 1970. 453 pp.

3184 Zierold, Norman. Sex Goddesses of the Silent Screen. Chicago: Regnery, 1973. 207 pp.

NELSON, OZZIE and HARRIET

3185 Nelson, Ozzie. Ozzie. Englewood Cliffs, N.J.: Prentice-
Hall, 1973. 309 pp.

NEVILLE, JOHN

3186 Trewin, John Courtenay. John Neville: An Illustrated Study
of His Work, with a List of His Appearances on Stage
and Screen. London: Barrie and Rockliff, 1961. 136 pp.

NEWMAN, PAUL

3187 Quirk, Lawrence J. The Films of Paul Newman. New York:
Citadel, 1971. 224 pp.

3188 Kerbel, Michael. Paul Newman. New York: Pyramid, 1974.
      158 pp.

3189 Hamblett, Charles. Paul Newman. Chicago: Regnery, 1975.
      232 pp.

NICHOLSON, JACK

3190 Crane, Robert David and Fryer, Christopher. Jack Nicholson:
      Face to Face. New York: Evans, 1975. 192 pp.
      Includes many interviews.

3191 Dickens, Norman. Jack Nicholson: The Search for a Super-
      star. New York: New American Library, 1975. 182 pp.

NIVEN, DAVID

3192 Niven, David. Once Over Lightly. New York: Prentice-
      Hall, 1951. 276 pp.

3193 Niven, David. The Moon's A Balloon. New York: Putnam,
      1971. 380 pp.

3194 Garrett, Gerard. The Films of David Niven. London: LSP
      Books, 1975. 256 pp.

3195 Niven, David. Bring on the Empty Horses. New York: Put-
      nam, 1975. 369 pp.

3196 Parish, James Robert and Stanke, Don E. The Debonairs.
      New Rochelle, N.Y.: Arlington, 1975. 511 pp.
      Contains a lengthy chapter on David Niven, including
      complete filmography.

NOBLE, PETER

3197 Noble, Peter. Reflected Glory: An Autobiographical Sketch.
      London: Jarrolds, 1958. 235 pp.

NOBLE, RONALD

3198 Noble, Ronald. Shoot First! Assignments of a Newsreel
      Cameraman. London: Harrap, 1955. 271 pp.

NOVELLO, IVOR

3199 Macqueen-Pope, Walter. Ivor, The Story of an Achievement:
      A Biography of Ivor Novello. London: W. H. Allen, 1951.
      550 pp.

3200 Noble, Peter. Ivor Novello: Man of the Theatre. London:
      Falcon, 1951. 307 pp. (Reprinted London: White Lion,
      1975.)

3201 Rose, Richard. Perchance to Dream: The World of Ivor
Novello. London: Frewin, 1974. 199 pp.

3202 Wilson, Sandy. Ivor. London: Joseph, 1975. 288 pp.

NUGENT, ELLIOTT

3203 Nugent, Elliott. Events Leading Up to the Comedy: An Autobiography. New York: Trident, 1965. 304 pp.

NUGENT, JOHN CHARLES

3204 Nugent, John Charles. It's A Great Life. New York: Dial,
1940. 331 pp.

O'BRIEN, MARGARET

3205 O'Brien, Margaret. My Diary. Philadelphia: Lippincott,
1948. 117 pp.

O'BRIEN, PAT

3206 O'Brien, Pat. The Wind at My Back: The Life and Times
of Pat O'Brien. Garden City, N.Y.: Doubleday, 1964.
331 pp.

OLIVIER, LAURENCE

3207 Barker, Felix. The Oliviers: A Biography. Philadelphia:
Lippincott, 1953. 371 pp.

3208 Whitehead, Peter and Bean, Robin (comps.) Olivier/Shakes-
peare. London: Lorrimer, 1966. 40 pp.
Primarily photographs.

3209 Darlington, William Aubrey. Laurence Olivier. London:
Grampian, 1968. 92 pp.

3210 Fairweather, Virginia. Olivier: An Informal Portrait. New
York: Coward-McCann, 1969. 183 pp. (Also published
as Cry God for Larry: An Intimate Memoir of Sir Laurence
Olivier.)

3211 Gourlay, Logan (ed.) Olivier. New York: Stein and Day,
1974. 208 pp.
Includes interview material with John Gielgud, Douglas
Fairbanks, Jr., William Wyler, Merle Oberon, Leo Genn,
John Osborne, and Tony Richardson.

3212 Cottrell, John. Laurence Olivier. Englewood Cliffs, N.J.:
Prentice-Hall, 1975. 433 pp.

OLSON, OLE

3213   Bergsten, Bebe. The Great Dane and the Great Northern
       Film Company. Los Angeles: Locare Research Group,
       1973. 116 pp.

OPHULS, MAX

3214   Roud, Richard. Max Ophuls: An Index. London: British
       Film Institute, 1958. 43 pp.

OPPENHEIMER, GEORGE

3215   Oppenheimer, George. The View From the Sixties: Memoirs
       of a Spent Life. New York: McKay, 1966. 273 pp.

ORLANDO, GUIDO

3216   Orlando, Guido with Merwin, Sam. Confessions of a Scoun-
       drel. Philadelphia: Winston, 1954. 275 pp.
             Autobiography of a silent screen actor and press
       agent.

OZU, YASUJIRO

3217   Schrader, Paul. Transcendental Style in Film: Ozu, Bresson,
       Dreyer. Berkeley: University of California Press, 1972.
       194 pp.

3218   Richie, Donald. Ozu. Berkeley: University of California
       Press, 1974. 275 pp.

PABST, G. W.

3219   Bachmann, Gideon (ed.) Six Talks on G. W. Pabst: The
       Man, The Director, The Artist. New York: Group for
       Film Study, ca. 1955. 94 pp.
             Interview material on Pabst.

PAGNOL, MARCEL

3220   Pagnol, Marcel. The Days Were Too Short. Garden City,
       N.Y.: Doubleday, 1960. 335 pp. Translated by Rita
       Barisse.

3221   Pagnol, Marcel. The Time of Secrets. Garden City, N.Y.:
       Doubleday, 1962. 222 pp. Translated by Rita Barisse.

PALMER, LILLI

3222   Palmer, Lilli. Change Lobsters--And Dance: An Autobiogra-
       phy. New York: Macmillan, 1975. 320 pp.

PARKER, DOROTHY

3223 Keats, John. You Might as Well Live: The Life and Times of Dorothy Parker. New York: Simon and Schuster, 1970. 319 pp.

PARKS, GORDON

3224 Turk, Midge. Gordon Parks. New York: Crowell, 1971. 33 pp.
    For the young reader.

PARSONS, LOUELLA

3225 Parsons, Louella. The Gay Illiterate. Garden City, N.Y.: Doubleday, Doran, 1944. 194 pp.

3226 Eells, George. Hedda and Louella. New York: Putnam, 1972. 360 pp.

PARTRIDGE, HELEN AND BELLAMY

3227 Partridge, Helen. A Lady Goes to Hollywood: Being the Casual Adventures of an Author's Wife in the Much Misunderstood Capital of Filmland. New York: Macmillan, 1941. 259 pp.

PASCAL, GABRIEL

3228 Pascal, Valerie. The Disciple and His Devil: Gabriel Pascal [and] Bernard Shaw. New York: McGraw-Hill, 1970. 356 pp.

PASOLINI, PIER PAOLO

3229 Stack, Oswald (ed.) Pasolini on Pasolini: Interviews with Oswald Stack. Bloomington: Indiana University Press, 1970. 176 pp.

PASTERNAK, JOE

3230 Pasternak, Joe with Chandler, David. Easy the Hard Way. New York: Putnam, 1956. 301 pp.

3231 Rohauer, Raymond. A Tribute to Joe Pasternak. New York: Gallery of Modern Art Monograph, 1966. 12 pp.

PAYTON, BARBARA

3232 Payton, Barbara. I Am Not Ashamed. Los Angeles, Holloway, 1963. 190 pp.

PEARSON, GEORGE

3233 Pearson, George. Flashback: The Autobiography of a
      British Film-Maker. London: Allen and Unwin, 1957.
      236 pp.

PECKINPAH, SAM

3234 Kitses, Jim. Horizons West: Anthony Mann, Budd Boetti-
      cher, Sam Peckinpah: Studies of Authorship Within the
      Western. Bloomington: Indiana University Press, 1970.
      176 pp.

PENN, ARTHUR

3235 Wood, Robin. Arthur Penn. London: Studio Vista, 1968.
      96 pp. (Revised New York: Praeger, 1969, 144 pp.)

3236 Sherman, Eric and Rubin, Martin. The Director's Event:
      Interviews with Five American Film-Makers. New York:
      Atheneum, 1970. 200 pp.

PERELMAN, S. J.

3237 Perelman, S. J. The Road to Miltown, or Under the Spread-
      ing Atrophy. New York: Simon and Schuster, 1957.
      273 pp.

PERIES, LESTER JAMES

3238 Coorey, Philip. The Lonely Artist: A Critical Introduction
      to the Films of Lester James Peries. Colombo, Ceylon:
      Lake House Investments, 1970. 118 pp.

PERRELLA, FATHER ROBERT

3239 Perrella, Father Robert. They Call Me the Showbiz Priest.
      New York: Trident, 1973. 287 pp.

PETERS, JEAN

3240 Strait, Raymond. Mrs. Howard Hughes. Los Angeles: Hol-
      loway, 1970. 244 pp.

PETROVA, OLGA

3241 Petrova, Olga. Butter with My Bread: The Memoirs of Olga
      Petrova. Indianapolis, New York: Bobbs-Merrill, 1942.
      371 pp.

PICKFORD, MARY

3242 Pickford, Mary. Sunshine and Shadow. Garden City, N.Y.:
      Doubleday, 1955. 382 pp.

3243 Niver, Kemp. Mary Pickford, Comedienne. Los Angeles: Locare Research Group, 1969. 156 pp. Primarily filmographic information.

3244 Cushman, Robert B. Tribute to Mary Pickford: Appreciation, Critical Notes, and Filmography. Washington, D.C.: American Film Institute, 1970. 16 pp.

3245 Lee, Raymond. The Films of Pickford. South Brunswick, N.J.: A. S. Barnes, 1970. 175 pp.

3246 Windeler, Robert. Sweetheart: The Story of Mary Pickford. New York: Praeger, 1974. 226 pp.

PICON, MOLLY

3247 Picon, Molly with Rosenberg, Eth Clifford. So Laugh a Little. New York: Messner, 1962. 175 pp.

PIRANDELLO, LUIGI

3248 Nulf, Frank Allen, Jr. Luigi Pirandello and the Cinema: A Study of His Relationship to Motion Pictures and the Significance of that Relationship to Selected Examples of His Prose and Drama. Ohio University: Ph.D., 1969. 253 pp.

POITIER, SIDNEY

3249 Ewers, Carolyn H. The Long Journey: A Biography of Sidney Poitier. New York: New American Library, 1969. 126 pp.

3250 Hoffmann, William. Sidney. New York: Lyle Stuart, 1971. 175 pp.

POLANSKI, ROMAN

3251 Butler, Ivan. The Cinema of Roman Polanski. New York: A. S. Barnes, 1970. 191 pp.

POLONSKY, ABRAHAM

3252 Sherman, Eric and Rubin, Martin. The Director's Event: Interviews with Five American Film-Makers. New York: Atheneum, 1970. 200 pp.

PORTER, COLE

3253 Porter, Cole with Hubler, Richard G. The Cole Porter Story. Cleveland: World, 1965. 140 pp.

3254 Eells, George. The Life That Late He Led: A Biography of Cole Porter. New York: Putnam, 1967. 383 pp.

3255   Kimball, Robert (comp.)   Cole.   Designed by Bea Feitler.
       New York: Holt, Rinehart and Winston, 1971.   283 pp.
       Includes a biography essay by Brendan Gill.

POWDERMAKER, HORTENSE

3256   Powdermaker, Hortense.   Stranger and Friend: The Way of
       an Anthropologist.   New York: Norton, 1966.   315 pp.
       Includes material on her work in Hollywood.

POWELL, MICHAEL

3257   Gough-Yates, Kevin with Pressburger, Emeric (eds.)   Michael
       Powell.   London: National Film Theatre, 1971.   16 pp.
       Interviews with Michael Powell and Emeric Press-
       burger.

POWELL, WILLIAM

3258   Morella, Joe and Epstein, Edward Z.   Gable & Lombard &
       Powell & Harlow.   New York: Dell, 1975.   272 pp.

3259   Parish, James Robert and Stanke, Don E.   The Debonairs.
       New Rochelle, N.Y.: Arlington, 1975.   511 pp.
       Contains a lengthy chapter on William Powell, in-
       cluding complete filmography.

PREJEAN, ALBERT

3260   Prejean, Albert.   The Sky and the Stars: The Memoirs of
       Albert Prejean.   London: Harvill, 1956.   216 pp.   Trans-
       lated by Virginia Graham.

PREMINGER, MARION MILL

3261   Preminger, Marion Mill.   All I Want Is Everything.   New
       York: Funk and Wagnalls, 1957.   328 pp.
       Includes material on her husband, Otto Preminger.

PREMINGER, OTTO

3262   Pratley, Gerald.   The Cinema of Otto Preminger.   New York:
       A. S. Barnes, 1971.   191 pp.

3263   Frischauer, Willi.   Behind the Scenes of Otto Preminger.
       New York: Morrow, 1974.   279 pp.

PRESLEY, ELVIS

3264   Levy, Alan.   Operation Elvis.   New York: Holt, 1960.   117 pp.

3265   Hopkins, Jerry.   Elvis: A Biography.   New York: Simon
       and Schuster, 1971.   448 pp.

3266 Lichter, Paul. Elvis in Hollywood. New York: Simon and Schuster, 1975. 188 pp.

3267 Mann, May. Elvis and the Colonel. New York: Drake, 1975. 273 pp.
With material on Presley's relationship with his manager, Colonel Tom Parker.

3268 Parish, James Robert. The Elvis Presley Scrapbook. New York: Ballantine, 1975. 185 pp.

PRICE, VINCENT

3269 Price, Vincent. I Like What I Know: A Visual Autobiography. Garden City, N.Y.: Doubleday, 1959. 313 pp.

3270 Price, Vincent. The Book of Joe: About a Dog and His Man. Garden City, N.Y.: Doubleday, 1961. 144 pp.

3271 Parish, James Robert with Whitney, Steven. Vincent Price Unmasked. New York: Drake, 1974. 266 pp.

3272 Beck, Calvin Thomas. Heroes of the Horrors. New York: Macmillan, 1975. 353 pp.

PUDOVKIN, VSEVOLOD I.

3273 Leyda, Jay. An Index to the Creative Work of Vsevolod I. Pudovkin. London: Sight and Sound, 1948. 12 pp.

3274 Dart, Peter. Pudovkin's Films and Film Theory. New York: Arno, 1974. 237 pp.

QUINN, ANTHONY

3275 Quinn, Anthony. The Original Sin: A Self-Portrait. Boston: Little, Brown, 1972. 311 pp.

3276 Marill, Alvin H. The Films of Anthony Quinn. Secaucus, N.J.: Citadel, 1975. 256 pp.

RAFFLES (THE BIRD)

3277 Wells, Zetta and Carveth. Raff, The Jungle Bird: The Story of Our Talking Mynah. New York: McBride, 1941. 112 pp.

3278 Wells, Zetta and Carveth. Raffles, The Bird Who Thinks He Is a Person. New York: Putnam, 1945. 130 pp.

RAFT, GEORGE

3279 Parish, James Robert with Whitney, Steven. The George Raft

File: The Unauthorized Biography. New York: Drake, 1973. 279 pp.

3280 Yablonsky, Lewis. George Raft. New York: McGraw-Hill, 1974. 289 pp.

RANK, J. ARTHUR

3281 Wood, Alan. Mr. Rank: A Study of J. Arthur Rank and British Films. London: Hodder and Stoughton, 1952. 288 pp.

RAPPE, VIRGINIA (see ARBUCKLE, FATTY)

RATHBONE, BASIL

3282 Rathbone, Basil. In and Out of Character. Garden City, N.Y.: Doubleday, 1962. 278 pp.

3283 Druxman, Michael B. Basil Rathbone: His Life and His Films. South Brunswick, N.J.: A. S. Barnes, 1975. 359 pp.

RAY, MAN

3284 Ray, Man. Self Portrait. London: Deutsch, 1963. 398 pp.

RAY, SATYAJIT

3285 Seton, Marie. Portrait of a Director. Bloomington: Indiana University Press, 1971. 350 pp.

RAYE, MARTHA

3286 Parish, James Robert. The Slapstick Queens. South Brunswick, N.J.: A. S. Barnes, 1973. 297 pp.

REAGAN, RONALD

3287 Reagan, Ronald with Hubler, Richard G. Where's the Rest of Me? New York: Duell, Sloan and Pearce, 1965. 316 pp.

3288 Boyarsky, Bill. The Rise of Ronald Reagan. New York: Random, 1968. 269 pp.

3289 Edwards, Lee. Reagan: A Political Biography. San Diego, Cal.: Viewpoint Books, 1967. 252 pp.

REDFIELD, WILLIAM

3290 Redfield, William. Letters From an Actor. New York: Viking, 1967. 243 pp.

Letters originally written to Robert Mills between
January and August 1964; includes much material on John
Gielgud and Richard Burton.

REDFORD, ROBERT

3291   Hanna, David.   Robert Redford: The Superstar Nobody Knows.
New York: Leisure Books, 1975.   187 pp.

3292   Reed, Donald A.   Robert Redford: A Photographic Portrayal
of the Man and His Films.   New York: Popular Library,
1975.   171 pp.

REDGRAVE, MICHAEL

3293   Findlater, Richard.   Michael Redgrave: Actor.   New York:
Theatre Arts, 1956.   170 pp.

3294   Redgrave, Michael.   Mask or Face: Reflections in an Actor's
Mirror.   New York: Theatre Arts, 1959.   188 pp.

REEMS, HARRY

3295   Reems, Harry.   Here Comes Harry Reems!   New York: Pinnacle, 1975.   209 pp.

REEVE, ADA

3296   Reeve, Ada.   Take It For A Fact.   London: Heinemann,
1954.   263 pp.

REINIGER, LOTTE

3297   Blackham, Olive.   Shadow Puppets.   New York: Harper,
1960.   198 pp.
Includes a chapter on Lotte Reiniger.

RENOIR, JEAN

3298   Renoir, Jean.   Renoir, My Father.   Boston: Little, Brown,
1962.   465 pp.   Translated by Randolph and Dorothy
Weaver.

3299   Bennett, Susan.   Jean Renoir.   London: British Film Institute, ca. 1967.   43 pp.

3300   Leprohon, Pierre.   Jean Renoir: An Investigation Into His
Films and Philosophy.   New York: Crown, 1971.   256 pp.
Translated by Brigid Elson.

3301   Braudy, Leo.   Jean Renoir: The World of His Films.   Garden
City, N.Y.:   Doubleday, 1972.   286 pp.

3302 Bazin, Andre. Jean Renoir. Edited and introduced by
      Francois Truffaut. New York: Simon and Schuster,
      1973. 320 pp. Translated by W. W. Halsey II and
      William H. Simon.

3303 Durgnat, Raymond. Jean Renoir. Berkeley: University of
      California Press, 1974. 429 pp.

3304 Harcourt, Peter. Six European Directors: Essays on the
      Meaning of Film Style. Baltimore: Penguin, 1974.
      287 pp.

3305 Renoir, Jean. My Life and My Films. New York: Athe-
      neum, 1974. 287 pp. Translated by Norman Denny.

3306 Gilliatt, Penelope. Jean Renoir: Essays, Conversations,
      and Reviews. New York: McGraw-Hill, 1975. 136 pp.

RESNAIS, ALAIN

3307 Cowie, Peter. Antonioni, Bergman, Resnais. New York:
      A. S. Barnes, 1964. 160 pp.

3308 Armes, Roy. The Cinema of Alain Resnais. New York:
      A. S. Barnes, 1968. 175 pp.

3309 Ward, John. Alain Resnais; or, The Theme of Time.
      Garden City, N.Y.: Doubleday, 1968. 168 pp.

3310 Blumenberg, Richard Mitchell. The Manipulation of Time
      and Space in the Novels of Alain Robbe-Grillet and in
      the Narrative Films of Alain Resnais, with Particular
      Reference to Last Year at Marienbad. Ohio University:
      Ph. D., 1969. 197 pp.

REYNOLDS, BURT

3311 Reynolds, Burt. Hot Line: The Letters I Get and Write.
      New York: Signet, 1972. 128 pp.

REYNOLDS, DEBBIE

3312 Reynolds, Debbie and Thomas, Bob. If I Knew Then. New
      York: Bernard Geis, 1962. 192 pp.

RICE, ELMER

3313 Rice, Elmer. Minority Report: An Autobiography. New
      York: Simon and Schuster, 1963. 474 pp.

RICHARD, CLIFF

3314 Winter, David. New Singer, New Song: The Cliff Richard
      Story. Waco, Texas: Word Books, 1968. 160 pp.

RICHARDSON, RALPH

3315 Hobson, Harold. Ralph Richardson: An Illustrated Study of
Sir Ralph's Work, with a List of His Appearances on
Stage and Screen. New York: Macmillan, 1958. 98 pp.
(Also published as Ralph Richardson.)

RICHTER, HANS

3316 Weinberg, Herman G. An Index to the Creative Work of
Two Pioneers: I. Robert J. Flaherty, II. Hans Richter.
London: British Film Institute, 1946. 15 pp.

3317 Richter, Hans. Hans Richter. Edited by Cleve Gray. New
York: Holt, Rinehart and Winston, 1971. 191 pp.

RIN TIN TIN

3318 English, James W. The Rin Tin Tin Story. New York:
Dodd, Mead, 1949. 247 pp.

RITT, MARTIN

3319 Whitaker, Sheila. The Films of Martin Ritt. London: British
Film Institute, 1972. 24 pp.

RITTER, THELMA

3320 Parish, James Robert. Good Dames. South Brunswick, N.J.:
A. S. Barnes, 1974. 277 pp.

ROACH, HAL

3321 Everson, William K. The Films of Hal Roach. New York:
Museum of Modern Art, 1971. 96 pp.

3322 Rohauer, Raymond. A Tribute to Hal Roach. New York:
Gallery of Modern Art Monograph, 1971. 96 pp.

ROBBE-GRILLET, ALAIN

3323 Morrissette, Bruce. Alain Robbe-Grillet. New York: Columbia University Press, 1965. 48 pp.

3324 Blumenberg, Richard Mitchell. The Manipulation of Time and
Space in the Novels of Alain Robbe-Grillet and in the Narrative Films of Alain Resnais, with Particular Reference
to Last Year at Marienbad. Ohio University: Ph.D.,
1969. 197 pp.

3325 Gill, June Marian. The Films of Alain Robbe-Grillet. University of California, Berkeley: Ph.D., 1972.

ROBESON, PAUL

3326 Graham, Shirley. Paul Robeson: Citizen of the World.
      New York: Messner, 1946. 264 pp.

3327 Hoyt, Edwin Palmer. Paul Robeson, The American Othello.
      Cleveland: World, 1967. 228 pp.

3328 Schlosser, Anatol I. Paul Robeson: His Career in the
      Theatre, in Motion Pictures, and on the Concert Stage.
      New York University: Ph. D., 1970. 494 pp.

ROBINSON, EDWARD G.

3329 Robinson, Edward G., Jr. with Dufty, William. My Father,
      My Son: An Autobiography. New York: Fell, 1958.
      316 pp.

3330 Parish, James Robert and Marill, Alvin H. The Cinema of
      Edward G. Robinson. South Brunswick, N.J.: A. S.
      Barnes, 1972. 270 pp.

3331 Robinson, Edward G. with Spigelgass, Leonard. All My
      Yesterdays: An Autobiography. New York: Hawthorn,
      1973. 344 pp.

3332 Hirsch, Foster. Edward G. Robinson. New York: Pyramid,
      1975. 160 pp.

ROBSON, FLORA

3333 Dunbar, Janet. Flora Robson. London: Harrap, 1960. 276 pp.

RODGERS, RICHARD

3334 Taylor, Deems. Some Enchanted Evenings: The Story of
      Rodgers and Hammerstein. New York: Harper, 1953.
      244 pp. (Reprinted Westport, Conn.: Greenwood, 1972.)

3335 Ewen, David. Richard Rodgers. New York: Holt, 1957.
      378 pp.

3336 Green, Stanley. The Rodgers and Hammerstein Story. New
      York: Day, 1963. 187 pp.

3337 Richard Rodgers: Fact Book with Supplement. New York:
      Lynn Farnol Group, 1968. 659 pp.
          Includes comprehensive data on composer Rodgers'
      work in theatre, film and television.

ROGERS, GINGER

3338 Richards, Dick. Ginger: Salute To a Star. Brighton: Clifton,
      1969. 192 pp.

3339   Croce, Arlene. The Fred Astaire and Ginger Rogers Book.
        New York: Outerbridge and Lazard, 1972. 191 pp.

3340   Smith, Milburn (ed.) Astaire and Rogers. New York: Bar-
        ven, 1972. 66 pp.

3341   Dickens, Homer. The Films of Ginger Rogers. Secaucus,
        N.J.: Citadel, 1975. 256 pp.

ROGERS, PAUL

3342   Williamson, Audrey. Paul Rogers. London: Rockliff, 1956.
        126 pp.

ROGERS, ROY

3343   Rogers, Dale Evans. Angel Unaware. Westwood, N.J.:
        Revell, 1953. 63 pp.

3344   Davis, Elise Miller. The Answer Is God: The Inspiring
        Personal Story of Dale Evans and Roy Rogers. New York:
        McGraw-Hill, 1955. 242 pp.

3345   Rogers, Dale Evans. My Spiritual Diary. Westwood, N.J.:
        Revell, 1955. 144 pp.

3346   Garrison, Maxine. The Angel Spreads Her Wings. Westwood,
        N.J.: Revell, 1956. 159 pp.

3347   Rogers, Dale Evans. To My Son: Faith at Our Home. West-
        wood, N.J.: Revell, 1957. 142 pp.

3348   Rogers, Dale Evans. The Woman at the Well. Old Tappan,
        N.J.: Revell, 1970. 191 pp.

3349   Rogers, Dale Evans. Dale: My Personal Picture Album.
        Old Tappan, N.J.: Revell, 1971. 127 pp.

3350   Roper, William L. Roy Rogers, King of the Cowboys. Min-
        neapolis: Denison, 1971. 182 pp.
            For the young reader.

ROGERS, WILL

3351   Rogers, Betty. Will Rogers: The Story of His Life Told by
        His Wife, Betty Rogers. Garden City, N.Y.: Garden
        City Publishing, 1943. 312 pp.

3352   Rogers, Will. The Autobiography of Will Rogers. Edited
        by Donald Day. Boston: Houghton Mifflin, 1949. 410 pp.

3353   Day, Donald and Beth. Will Rogers, The Boy Roper. Boston:
        Houghton Mifflin, 1950. 201 pp.

3354   Croy, Homer. <u>Our Will Rogers</u>. New York: Duell, Sloan
        and Pearce, 1953. 377 pp.

3355   Day, Donald. <u>Will Rogers: A Biography</u>. New York: Mc-
        Kay, 1962. 370 pp.

3356   Collings, Ellsworth. <u>The Old Home Ranch: The Will Rogers
        Range in the Indian Territory</u>. Stillwater, Okla.: Red-
        lands, 1964. 177 pp.

3357   Richards, Kenneth G. <u>Will Rogers</u>. Chicago: Childrens
        Press, 1968. 94 pp.
        For the young reader.

3358   Brown, William R. <u>Imagemaker: Will Rogers and the Ameri-
        can Dream</u>. Columbia: University of Missouri Press,
        1970. 304 pp.

3359   Bennett, Cathereen L. <u>Will Rogers: The Cowboy Who
        Walked With Kings</u>. Minneapolis: Lerner, 1971. 71 pp.
        For the young reader.

3360   Ketchum, Richard M. <u>Will Rogers: His Life and Times</u>.
        New York: American Heritage, 1973. 415 pp.

3361   Alworth, E. Paul. <u>Will Rogers</u>. New York: Twayne, 1974.
        140 pp.

ROMBERG, SIGMUND

3362   Arnold, Elliott. <u>Deep in My Heart: A Story Based on the
        Life of Sigmund Romberg</u>. New York: Duell, Sloan and
        Pearce, 1949. 511 pp.

ROONEY, MICKEY

3363   Rooney, Mickey. <u>I. E.: An Autobiography</u>. New York: Put-
        nam, 1965. 249 pp.

3364   Smith, Milburn (ed.) <u>Judy Garland and Mickey Rooney</u>. New
        York: Barven, 1972. 66 pp.

ROSE, BILLY

3365   Rose, Billy. <u>Wine, Women and Words</u>. New York: Simon
        and Schuster, 1948. 295 pp.

3366   Conrad, Earl. <u>Billy Rose: Manhattan Primitive</u>. Cleveland:
        World, 1968. 272 pp.

3367   Gottlieb, Polly Rose. <u>The Nine Lives of Billy Rose</u>. New
        York: New American Library, 1969. 240 pp.

ROSSELLINI, ROBERTO

3368   Guarner, Jose Luis. Roberto Rossellini. New York: Prae-
        ger, 1970. 144 pp. Translated by Elisabeth Cameron.

ROSSEN, ROBERT

3369   Casty, Alan. The Films of Robert Rossen. New York: Mu-
        seum of Modern Art, 1969. 95 pp.

ROSSON, HAROLD (HAL)

3370   Maltin, Leonard. Behind the Camera: The Cinematographer's
        Art. New York: New American Library, 1971. 240 pp.
        Includes a lengthy interview with Hal Rosson.

ROTH, LILLIAN

3371   Roth, Lillian with Connally, Mike and Frank, Gerold. I'll
        Cry Tomorrow. New York: Fell, 1954. 347 pp.

3372   Roth, Lillian. Beyond My Worth. New York: Fell, 1958.
        317 pp.

ROTHA, PAUL

3373   Rotha, Paul. Documentary Diary: An Informal History of
        the British Documentary Film, 1928-1939. New York:
        Hill and Wang, 1973. 305 pp.

RUBY, EDNA

3374   Ruby, Edna. Shorthand With Champagne. Cleveland: World,
        1966. 246 pp.
        Autobiography of a public stenographer in a Beverly
        Hills hotel and her encounters with the stars.

RUNYON, DAMON

3375   Runyon, Damon, Jr. Father's Footsteps. New York: Ran-
        dom, 1954. 180 pp.

RUSSELL, HAROLD

3376   Russell, Harold with Rosen, Victor. Victory in My Hands.
        New York: Creative Age Press, 1949. 279 pp.

RUSSELL, JANE

3377   Russell, Geraldine. Oh, Lord, What Next? New York:
        Vantage, 1960. 174 pp.
        Written by Jane Russell's mother.

RUSSELL, KEN

3378   Baxter, John.   An Appalling Talent--Ken Russell.   London:
           Michael Joseph, 1973.   240 pp.

RUSSELL, ROSALIND

3379   Yanni, Nicholas.   Rosalind Russell.   New York: Pyramid,
           1975.   160 pp.

RUTHERFORD, MARGARET

3380   Keown, Eric.   Margaret Rutherford: An Illustrated Study of
           Her Work for Stage and Screen, with a List of Her Ap-
           pearances.   New York: Macmillan, 1956.   94 pp.

3381   Rutherford, Margaret with Robyns, Gwen.   Margaret Ruther-
           ford: An Autobiography.   London: W. H. Allen, 1972.
           230 pp.

ST. JOHNS, ADELA ROGERS

3382   St. Johns, Adela Rogers.   The Honeycomb.   Garden City,
           N.Y.:   Doubleday, 1969.   598 pp.

SAKALL, S. Z.

3383   Sakall, S. Z.   The Story of Cuddles, My Life Under the
           Emperor Francis Joseph, Adolph Hitler, and the Warner
           Brothers.   London: Cassell, 1954.   231 pp.   Translated
           by Paul Tabori.

SANDERS, GEORGE

3384   Sanders, George.   Memoirs of a Professional Cad.   New York:
           Putnam, 1960.   192 pp.

SASSOON, VIDAL

3385   Sassoon, Vidal.   Sorry I Kept You Waiting, Madam.   New
           York: Putnam, 1968.   251 pp.
               Story of hairdresser to the stars.

SAVALAS, TELLY

3386   Daly, Marsha.   Telly Savalas.   New York: Berkeley, 1975.
           156 pp.

SAVILLE, VICTOR

3387   Victor Saville.   London: British Film Institute, 1972.   24 pp.
           Includes an interview with Saville.

SCHARY, DORE

3388   Schary, Dore. For Special Occasions. New York: Random, 1962. 200 pp.

SCHIAPARELLI, ELSA

3389   Schiaparelli, Elsa. Shocking Life. New York: Dutton, 1954. 254 pp.
        Autobiography of dress designer.

SCHILDKRAUT, JOSEPH

3390   Schildkraut, Joseph with Lania, Leo. My Father and I. New York: Viking, 1959. 246 pp.

SCHILDKRAUT, RUDOLF

3391   Schildkraut, Joseph with Lania, Leo. My Father and I. New York: Viking, 1959. 246 pp.

SCOFIELD, PAUL

3392   Trewin, John Courtenay. Paul Scofield: An Illustrated Study of His Work, with a List of His Appearances on Stage and Screen. London: Rockliff, 1956. 101 pp.

SCOTT, AUDREY

3393   Scott, Audrey. I Was a Hollywood Stunt Girl. Philadelphia: Dorrance, 1969. 119 pp.

SCULLY, FRANK

3394   Scully, Frank. Cross My Heart. New York: Greenberg, 1955. 378 pp.
        Autobiography of studio publicist and columnist.

3395   Scully, Frank. This Gay Knight: An Autobiography of a Modern Chevalier. Philadelphia: Chilton, 1962. 232 pp.

3396   Scully, Frank. In Armour Bright: Cavalier Adventures of My Short Life Out of Bed. Philadelphia: Chilton, 1963. 285 pp.

SEASTROM, VICTOR

3397   Idestam-Almquist, Bengt. Classics of the Swedish Cinema: The Stiller and Sjostrom Period. Stockholm: Swedish Institute, 1952. 48 pp.

3398   Pensel, Hans. Seastrom and Stiller in Hollywood: Two

Swedish Directors in Silent American Films, 1923-1930.
New York: Vantage, 1969. 106 pp.

SELLERS, PETER

3399 Evans, Peter. Peter Sellers: The Mask Behind the Mask.
Englewood Cliffs, N.J.: Prentice-Hall, 1968. 249 pp.

SELZNICK, DAVID O.

3400 Thomas, Bob. Selznick. Garden City, N.Y.: Doubleday,
1970. 381 pp.

3401 Selznick, David O. Memo From David O. Selznick. Edited
by Rudy Behlmer. New York: Viking, 1972. 518 pp.

3402 Bowers, Ronald L. The Selznick Players. South Brunswick,
N.J.: A. S. Barnes, 1976, c. 1975. 255 pp.
A career study of Selznick and the players he worked
with.

SENNETT, MACK

3403 Fowler, Gene. Father Goose: The Story of Mack Sennett.
(Originally published 1934.) New York: Avon, 1974.
288 pp.

3404 Sennett, Mack with Shipp, Cameron. King of Comedy. Garden City, N.Y.: Doubleday, 1954. 284 pp. (Reprinted
New York: Pinnacle, 1975.)

3405 Lahue, Kalton C. and Brewer, Terry. Kops and Custards:
The Legend of Keystone Films. Norman: University of
Oklahoma Press, 1968. 177 pp.

3406 Lahue, Kalton C. Mack Sennett's Keystone: The Man, The
Myth, and The Comedies. South Brunswick, N.J.: A. S.
Barnes, 1971. 315 pp.

SHAMROY, LEON

3407 Higham, Charles. Hollywood Cameramen: Sources of Light.
Bloomington: Indiana University Press, 1970. 176 pp.

SHAW, ARTIE

3408 Shaw, Artie. The Trouble With Cinderella: An Outline of
Identity. New York: Farrar, Straus and Young, 1952.
394 pp.

SHAW, GEORGE BERNARD

3409 Costello, Donald P. The Serpent's Eye: Shaw and the Cinema.

Notre Dame, Ind.: University of Notre Dame Press,
1965. 209 pp.

3410 Pascal, Valerie. The Disciple and His Devil: Gabriel Pascal [and] Bernard Shaw. New York: McGraw-Hill, 1970.
356 pp.

SHERWOOD, ROBERT E.

3411 Brown, John Mason. The Worlds of Robert E. Sherwood:
Mirror to His Times, 1896-1939. New York: Harper
and Row, 1965. 409 pp.
Includes material on his film career.

SIEGEL, DON

3412 Lovell, Alan. Don Siegel: American Cinema. London:
British Film Institute, 1968. 59 pp. (Revised 1975,
81 pp.)
Includes interviews with Siegel.

3413 Kaminsky, Stuart M. Don Siegel: Director. New York:
Curtis, 1974. 319 pp.

SILLMAN, LEONARD

3414 Sillman, Leonard. Here Lies Leonard Sillman--Straightened
Out at Last: An Autobiography. New York: Citadel,
1959. 377 pp.

SILVERS, PHIL

3415 Silvers, Phil with Saffron, Robert. This Laugh Is on Me:
The Phil Silvers Story. Englewood Cliffs, N.J.: Prentice-Hall, 1973. 276 pp.

SINATRA, FRANK

3416 Kahn, E. J., Jr. The Voice: The Story of an American
Phenomenon. New York: Harper, 1947. 125 pp.

3417 Gehman, Richard. Sinatra and His Rat Pack. New York:
Belmont, 1961. 220 pp.

3418 Douglas-Home, Robin. Sinatra. New York: Grosset and
Dunlap, 1962. 64 pp.

3419 Shaw, Arnold. Sinatra: Twentieth-Century Romantic. New
York: Holt, Rinehart and Winston, 1968. 371 pp.

3420 Lonstein, Albert I. and Marino, Vito R. The Compleat
Sinatra: Discography, Filmography, Television Appearances,
Motion Picture Appearances, Radio Appearances, Concert

Appearances, Stage Appearances. Ellenville, N.Y.:
Cameron Publications, 1970. 383 pp.

3421 Ringgold, Gene and McCarty, Clifford. The Films of Frank
Sinatra. New York: Citadel, 1971. 249 pp.

3422 Barnes, Ken with Britt, Stan and others. Sinatra and the
Great Song Stylists. London: Allan, 1972. 192 pp.

SIRK, DOUGLAS

3423 Sirk, Douglas. Sirk on Sirk. Interviews conducted by Jon
Halliday. New York: Viking, 1972. 176 pp.

3424 Mulvey, Laura and Halliday, Jon (eds.) Douglas Sirk. Edin-
burgh: Edinburgh Film Festival, 1972. 120 pp.
With contributions by Paul Willeman, Jean-Loup
Bourget, Fred Camper, R. W. Fassbinder, and others.

SJOSTROM, VICTOR (see SEASTROM, VICTOR)

SKOLSKY, SIDNEY

3425 Skolsky, Sidney. Don't Get Me Wrong--I Love Hollywood.
New York: Putnam, 1975. 258 pp.
Memoirs of a Hollywood columnist.

SKOURAS, SPYROS

3426 Curti, Carlo. Skouras, King of Fox Studios. Los Angeles:
Holloway, 1967. 311 pp.

SLEZAK, WALTER

3427 Slezak, Walter. What Time's the Next Swan? Garden City,
N.Y.: Doubleday, 1962. 227 pp.

SMITH, ALBERT E.

3428 Smith, Albert E. with Koury, Phil A. Two Reels and a
Crank. Garden City, N.Y.: Doubleday, 1952. 285 pp.
Autobiography of one of the founders of Vitagraph.

SNOW, MICHAEL

3429 Snow, Michael. Michael Snow: A Survey. Toronto: Art
Gallery of Ontario, 1970. 124 pp.
Primarily illustrations.

3430 Cornwell, Regina. Ten Years of Snow. Northwestern University: Ph.D., 1975. 177 pp.

SOBEL, BERNARD

3431 Sobel, Bernard. Broadway Heartbeat: Memoirs of a Press Agent. New York: Hermitage, 1953. 352 pp.

SOBOL, LOUIS

3432 Sobol, Louis. The Longest Street: A Memoir. New York: Crown, 1968. 448 pp.
Memoirs of a Broadway/Hollywood columnist.

STANWYCK, BARBARA

3433 Smith, Ella. Starring Miss Barbara Stanwyck. New York: Crown, 1974. 340 pp.

3434 Vermilye, Jerry. Barbara Stanwyck. New York: Pyramid, 1975. 160 pp.

STEEL, TOMMY

3435 Kennedy, John. Tommy Steel: The Facts About a Teenage Idol and an "Inside" Picture of Show Business. London: Souvenir, 1958. 166 pp.

STEINBECK, JOHN

3436 Burrows, Michael. John Steinbeck and His Films. Cornwall, England: Primestyle, 1971. 32 pp.

STEINER, MAX

3437 Burrows, Michael. Mario Lanza, Max Steiner. Cornwall, England: Primestyle, 1971. 44 pp.

STERN, ERNEST JULIAN

3438 Stern, Ernest Julian. My Life, My Stage. London: Gollancz, 1951. 302 pp. Translated by Edward Fitzgerald.
Includes a chapter on film decor and design.

STERNBERG, JOSEPH VON   (see VON STERNBERG, JOSEF)

STEVENS, GEORGE

3439 Richie, Donald. George Stevens: An American Romantic. New York: Museum of Modern Art, 1970. 104 pp.

STEWART, DONALD OGDEN

3440 Stewart, Donald Ogden. By a Stroke of Luck! An Autobiography. New York: Paddington, 1975. 302 pp.

STEWART, JAMES (JIMMY)

3441   Jones, Ken D.; McClure, Arthur F.; and Twomey, Alfred E.
       The Films of James Stewart. South Brunswick, N.J.:
       A. S. Barnes, 1970. 256 pp.

3442   Thompson, Howard. James Stewart. New York: Pyramid,
       1974. 160 pp.

STILLER, MAURITZ

3443   Idestam-Almquist, Bengt. Classics of the Swedish Cinema:
       The Stiller and Sjostrom Period. Stockholm: Swedish
       Institute, 1952. 48 pp.

3444   Pensel, Hans. Seastrom and Stiller in Hollywood: Two
       Swedish Directors in Silent American Films, 1923-1930.
       New York: Vantage, 1969. 106 pp.

STONE, FRED

3445   Stone, Fred. Rolling Stone. New York, London: Whittlesey,
       1945. 246 pp.

STRANGE, MICHAEL, pseudonym (see BARRYMORE,
BLANCHE OELRICHS)

STRAUB, JEAN-MARIE

3446   Roud, Richard. Jean-Marie Straub. New York: Viking, 1972.
       176 pp.
          Includes script of NOT RECONCILED.

STREISAND, BARBRA

3447   Spada, James. Barbra, The First Decade: The Films and
       Career of Barbra Streisand. Secaucus, N.J.: Citadel,
       1974. 224 pp.

3448   Black, Jonathan. Streisand. New York: Leisure Books,
       1975. 187 pp.

3449   Jordan, Rene. The Greatest Star: The Barbra Streisand
       Story, An Unauthorized Biography. New York: Putnam,
       1975. 253 pp.

STROHEIM, ERICH VON (see VON STROHEIM, ERICH)

STRUSS, KARL

3450   Higham, Charles. Hollywood Cameramen: Sources of Light.
       Bloomington: Indiana University Press, 1970. 176 pp.

STUART, JOHN

3451 Stuart, John. Caught in the Act. London: The Silent Picture, 1971. 32 pp.

STURGES, PRESTON

3452 Ursini, James. The Fabulous Life and Times of Preston Sturges: An American Dreamer. New York: Curtis, 1973. 240 pp.

SUCKSDORFF, ARNE

3453 May, Thomas Stephen. An Analysis of Twelve Films by Arne Sucksdorff. University of Wisconsin: Ph. D., 1971. 500 pp.

SULLAVAN, MARGARET

3454 Burrows, Michael. Patricia Neal and Margaret Sullavan. Cornwall, England: Primestyle, 1971. 42 pp.

SWANSON, GLORIA

3455 Carr, Larry. Four Fabulous Faces: The Evolution and Metamorphosis of Garbo, Swanson, Crawford and Dietrich. New Rochelle, N.Y.: Arlington, 1970. 492 pp. Primarily photographs.

3456 Hudson, Richard M. and Lee, Raymond. Gloria Swanson. South Brunswick, N.J.: A. S. Barnes, 1970. 269 pp.

TALBOT, WILLIAM HENRY FOX

3457 Booth, Arthur H. William Henry Fox Talbot: Father of Photography. London: Barker, 1965. 119 pp.

TASHLIN, FRANK

3458 Johnston, Claire and Willeman, Paul (eds.) Frank Tashlin. London: Edinburgh Film Festival, 1973. 149 pp. With contributions by Robert Mundy, Roger Tailleur, Louis Seguin, Peter Bogdanovich, Ian Cameron and others.

TAYLOR, DWIGHT

3459 Taylor, Dwight. Joy Ride. New York: Putnam, 1959. 250 pp.

TAYLOR, ELIZABETH

3460 Allan, John B. Elizabeth Taylor: A Fascinating Story of America's Most Talented Actress and the World's Most

Beautiful Woman. Derby, Conn.: Monarch, 1961.
139 pp.

3461 Levy, Alan. The Elizabeth Taylor Story. New York: Hillman, 1961. 176 pp.

3462 Rice, Cy. Cleopatra in Mink. New York: Paperback Library, 1962. 160 pp.

3463 Waterbury, Ruth. Elizabeth Taylor. New York: Appleton-
Century, 1964. 310 pp.

3464 Taylor, Elizabeth. Elizabeth Taylor: An Informal Memoir.
New York: Harper and Row, 1965. 177 pp.

3465 Burton, Richard. Meeting Mrs. Jenkins. New York: Morrow, 1966. 24 pp.

3466 Hirsch, Foster. Elizabeth Taylor. New York: Pyramid,
1973. 156 pp.

3467 Sheppard, Dick. Elizabeth: The Life and Career of Elizabeth Taylor. Garden City, N.Y.: Doubleday, 1974.
507 pp.

TAYLOR, JACKIE LYNN

3468 Taylor, Jackie Lynn with Fries, Jack. The Turned-On Hollywood 7: Jackie Remembers Our Gang. Toluca Lake,
Cal.: Pacifica, 1970. 76 pp.

TAYLOR, LAURETTE

3469 Courtney, Marguerite. Laurette. New York: Rinehart, 1955.
433 pp. (Reprinted New York: Atheneum, 1968, 445 pp.)

TAYLOR, ROBERT

3470 Wayne, Jane Ellen. The Life of Robert Taylor. New York:
Warner Paperback Library, 1973. 349 pp.

3471 Quirk, Lawrence J. The Films of Robert Taylor. Secaucus,
N.J.: Citadel, 1975. 223 pp.

TEMPLE, SHIRLEY

3472 Temple, Shirley and the editors of Look. My Young Life.
Garden City, N.Y.: Garden City Publishing, 1945.
253 pp.

3473 Eby, Lois. Shirley Temple: The Amazing Story of the Child
Actress Who Grew Up to Be America's Fairy Princess.
Derby, Conn.: Monarch, 1962. 143 pp.

3474 Minott, Rodney G. The Sinking of the Lollipop: Shirley
Temple vs. Pete McCloskey. San Francisco: Diablo,
1968. 269 pp.
Deals with Temple's campaign for the U.S. Congress.

3475 Basinger, Jeanine. Shirley Temple. New York: Pyramid,
1975. 160 pp.

3476 Burdick, Loraine. The Shirley Temple Scrapbook. Middle
Village, N.Y.: Jonathan David, 1975. 160 pp.

TERRY-THOMAS

3477 Hirst, Robert. Three Men and a Gimmick. Kingswood,
England: The World's Work, 1957. 125 pp.

3478 Terry-Thomas. Filling the Gap. London: Parrish, 1959.
168 pp.

TEWKESBURY, JOAN

3479 Loeb, Anthony (ed.) A Conversation with Joan Tewkesbury.
Chicago: Columbia College, 1975. 25 pp.

THALBERG, IRVING

3480 Thomas, Bob. Thalberg: Life and Legend. Garden City,
N.Y.: Doubleday, 1969. 415 pp.

3481 Marx, Samuel. Mayer and Thalberg: The Make-Believe
Saints. New York: Random, 1975. 273 pp.

THEODORAKIS, MIKIS

3482 Giannaris, George. Mikis Theodorakis: Music and Social
Change. New York: Praeger, 1972. 322 pp.

THOMPSON, MORTON

3483 Thompson, Morton. Joe, The Wounded Tennis Player. Garden
City, N.Y.: Doubleday, Doran, 1945. 208 pp.

THORNDIKE, SYBIL

3484 Trewin, John Courtenay. Sybil Thorndike: An Illustrated
Study of Dame Sybil's Work, with a List of Her Appearances on Stage and Screen. London: Rockliff, 1955.
123 pp.

TIOMKIN, DIMITRI

3485 Tiomkin, Dimitri and Buranelli, Prosper. Please Don't Hate
Me. Garden City, N.Y.: Doubleday, 1959. 261 pp.

TODD, MICHAEL

3486 Cohn, Art. The Nine Lives of Michael Todd. New York:
      Random, 1958. 396 pp.

TRACY, SPENCER

3487 Deschner, Donald. The Films of Spencer Tracy. New York:
      Citadel, 1968. 255 pp.

3488 Swindell, Larry. Spencer Tracy: A Biography. New York:
      World, 1969. 319 pp.

3489 Kanin, Garson. Tracy and Hepburn: An Intimate Memoir.
      New York: Viking, 1971. 307 pp.

3490 Smith, Milburn (ed.) Tracy and Hepburn. New York: Bar-
      ven, 1971. 66 pp.

3491 Tozzi, Romano. Spencer Tracy. New York: Pyramid, 1973.
      159 pp.

TRAUBEL, HELEN

3492 Traubel, Helen with Hubler, Richard G. St. Louis Woman.
      New York: Duell, Sloan and Pearce, 1959. 296 pp.

TRAVERS, BEN

3493 Travers, Ben. Vale of Laughter: An Autobiography. London:
      Bles, 1957. 251 pp.

TRAVERS, BILL (see McKENNA, VIRGINIA)

TRENDLE, GEORGE W.

3494 Bickel, Mary E. Geo. W. Trendle, Creator and Producer of:
      The Lone Ranger, The Green Hornet, Sgt. Preston of the
      Yukon, The American Agent, and Other Successes: An
      Authorized Biography. New York: Exposition, 1971.
      193 pp.

TRNKA, JIRI

3495 Bocek, Jaroslav. Jiri Trnka: Artist and Puppet Master.
      Prague: Artia, 1965. 272 pp. Translated by Till
      Gottheiner.

TRUFFAUT, FRANÇOIS

3496 Petrie, Graham. The Cinema of François Truffaut. New
      York: A. S. Barnes, 1970. 240 pp.

3497 Crisp, C. G. François Truffaut. New York: Praeger, 1972. 144 pp.

3498 Wall, James M. (ed.) Three European Directors. Grand Rapids, Mich.: Eerdmans, 1973. 224 pp.

3499 Allen, Don. François Truffaut. New York: Viking, 1974. 176 pp.

TRUMBO, DALTON

3500 Trumbo, Dalton. The Time of the Toad: A Study of the Inquisition in America by One of the Hollywood Ten. Hollywood: n.p., ca. 1950. 38 pp. (Reprinted and revised as The Time of the Toad: A Study of the Inquisition in America, and Two Related Pamphlets, New York: Harper and Row, 1972. 161 pp.) 1972 version includes The Devil in the Book and Honor Bright and All That Jazz.

3501 Trumbo, Dalton. Additional Dialogue: Letters of Dalton Trumbo, 1942-1962. Edited by Helen Manfull. New York: Evans, 1970. 576 pp.

TUCKER, SOPHIE

3502 Tucker, Sophie. Some of These Days: The Autobiography of Sophie Tucker. Garden City, N.Y.: Doubleday, Doran, 1945. 309 pp.

TURNER, LANA

3503 Wright, Jacqueline. The Life and Loves of Lana Turner. New York: Wisdom, 1961. 160 pp.

3504 Morella, Joe and Epstein, Edward Z. Lana: The Public and Private Lives of Miss Turner. New York: Citadel, 1971. 297 pp.

TWIGGY

3505 Twiggy. Twiggy: How I Probably Just Came Along on a White Rabbit at the Right Time, and Met the Smile on the Face of the Tiger. New York: Hawthorn, 1968. 159 pp.

3506 Whiteside, Thomas. Twiggy and Justin. New York: Farrar, Straus and Giroux, 1968. 122 pp.
Includes material on her manager Justin de Villeneuve.

ULMER, EDGAR G.

3507 Belton, John. The Hollywood Professionals, Vol. III: Howard

Hawks, Frank Borzage, Edgar G. Ulmer. New York:
A. S. Barnes, 1974. 182 pp.

USTINOV, PETER

3508   Willans, Geoffrey. Peter Ustinov. London: Peter Owen,
       1957. 180 pp.

3509   Thomas, Tony. Ustinov in Focus. New York: A. S. Barnes,
       1971. 192 pp.

VALENTINO, RUDOLPH

3510   Arnold, Alan. Valentino. London: Hutchinson, 1952.
       165 pp. (Reprinted New York: Library Publishers, 1954.)

3511   McKinstry, Carol. The Return of Rudolph Valentino. Los
       Angeles: Kirby and Gee, 1952. 193 pp.

3512   Oberfirst, Robert. Rudolph Valentino: The Man Behind the
       Myth. New York: Citadel, 1962. 320 pp.

3513   Russell, Lynn. The Voice of Valentino, Through Leslie Flint.
       London: Regency, 1965. 188 pp.
       Reveals Valentino's supposed spiritualistic communica-
       tion from the dead.

3514   Shulman, Irving. Valentino. New York: Trident, 1967.
       499 pp.

3515   MacKenzie, Norman A. The Magic of Rudolph Valentino.
       London: Research Pub., 1974. 210 pp.

3516   Scagnetti, Jack. The Intimate Life of Rudolph Valentino.
       Middle Village, N.Y.: Jonathan David, 1975. 160 pp.

3517   Steiger, Brad and Mank, Chaw. Valentino. New York:
       MacFadden-Bartell, 1966. 192 pp. (Reprinted New York:
       Manor, 1975.)

VALLEE, RUDY

3518   Vallee, Rudy with McKean, Gil. My Time Is Your Time:
       The Story of Rudy Vallee. New York: Obolensky, 1962.
       244 pp.

3519   Vallee, Rudy. Let the Chips Fall. Harrisburg, Pa.: Stack-
       pole, 1975. 320 pp. (Also published as Rudy Vallee
       Kisses and Tells.)

VAN DYKE, W. S.

3520   Cannom, Robert. Van Dyke and the Mythical City,

Hollywood. Culver City, Cal.: Murray and Gee, 1948.
424 pp.

VIDOR, KING

3521 Vidor, King. A Tree Is A Tree. New York: Harcourt,
Brace, 1953. 315 pp.

3522 Vidor, King. King Vidor on Film Making. New York: Mc-
Kay, 1972. 239 pp.

VIERTEL, SALKA

3523 Viertel, Salka. The Kindness of Strangers. New York: Holt,
Rinehart and Winston, 1969. 338 pp.

VIGO, JEAN

3524 Feldman, Joseph and Harry (comps.) Jean Vigo. Edited by
Herman G. Weinberg. London: British Film Institute,
1951. 28 pp.

3525 Gomes, P. E. Salles. Jean Vigo. Berkeley: University of
California Press, 1971. 256 pp.

3526 Smith, John M. Jean Vigo. New York: Praeger, 1972.
144 pp.

VISCONTI, LUCHINO

3527 Nowell-Smith, Geoffrey. Luchino Visconti. Garden City,
N.Y.: Doubleday, 1968. 192 pp. (Revised New York:
Viking, 1974, 220 pp.)

3528 Korte, Walter F., Jr. Marxism and the Scenographic Baroque
in the Films of Luchino Visconti. Northwestern University:
Ph.D., 1970. 138 pp.

VON STERNBERG, JOSEF

3529 Harrington, Curtis. An Index to the Films of Josef von
Sternberg. Edited by Herman G. Weinberg. London:
British Film Institute, 1949. 22 pp.

3530 Milgrom, Al (ed.) A Compendium of Critical Commentary,
Opinion, and Historical Notes on von Sternberg and His
Work. Minneapolis: University Film Society, University
of Minnesota, 1964. 20 pp.

3531 Von Sternberg, Josef. Fun in a Chinese Laundry. New York:
Macmillan, 1965. 348 pp.

3532 Sarris, Andrew. The Films of Josef von Sternberg. New
York: Museum of Modern Art, 1966. 56 pp.

3533 Weinberg, Herman G.   Josef von Sternberg: A Critical Study.
      New York: Dutton, 1967. 254 pp.

3534 Baxter, John.   The Cinema of Josef von Sternberg.   New
      York: A. S. Barnes, 1971. 192 pp.

VON STROHEIM, ERICH

3535 Weinberg, Herman G.   An Index to the Creative Work of
      Erich von Stroheim. London: Sight and Sound, 1943--.

3536 Noble, Peter.   Hollywood Scapegoat: The Biography of
      Erich von Stroheim. London: Fortune, 1950. 246 pp.

3537 Gobeil, Charlotte (ed.)   Hommage à Erich von Stroheim--A
      Tribute: A Compendium of Selected Articles and A
      Filmography. Ottawa: Canadian Film Institute, 1966.
      54 pp.
           With articles by Herman G. Weinberg, Lotte Eisner,
      Gloria Swanson, Karel Reisz, and Iris Barry.

3538 Finler, Joel W.   Stroheim.   Berkeley: University of Cali-
      fornia Press, 1968. 144 pp.

3539 Curtiss, Thomas Quinn.   Von Stroheim.   New York: Farrar,
      Straus and Giroux, 1971. 357 pp.

3540 Weinberg, Herman G.   Stroheim: A Pictorial Record of His
      Nine Films. New York: Dover, 1975. 259 pp.

WAGNER, CHARLES I.

3541 Wagner, Charles I.   Seeing Stars. New York: Putnam, 1940.
      403 pp.
           Autobiography of impresario who worked with many
      stars.

WAJDA, ANDRZEJ

3542 McArthur, Colin (ed.)   Andrzej Wajda: Polish Cinema.   Lon-
      don: British Film Institute, 1970. 60 pp.
           Contributors include Boleslaw Sulik.

3543 Michalek, Boleslaw.   The Cinema of Andrzej Wajda.   South
      Brunswick, N. J.: A. S. Barnes, 1973. 175 pp. Trans-
      lated by Edward Rothert.

WALLIS, HAL B.

3544 Mancia, Adrienne (ed.)   Hal B. Wallis: Film Producer.
      New York: Museum of Modern Art, 1970. 23 pp.

WALSH, RAOUL

3545 Canham, Kingsley. The Hollywood Professionals, Vol. I:
Michael Curtiz, Raoul Walsh, Henry Hathaway. New
York: A. S. Barnes, 1973. 200 pp.

3546 Hardy, Phil (ed.) Raoul Walsh. Edinburgh: Edinburgh Film
Festival, 1974. 155 pp.
Includes essays by Peter Lloyd, Edward Buscombe,
Paul Willemen, Pam Cook, and Lynda Myles, as well as
an interview with Walsh.

3547 Walsh, Raoul. Each Man in His Time: The Life Story of a
Director. New York: Farrar, Straus and Giroux, 1974.
385 pp.

WALTON, WILLIAM

3548 Howes, Frank. The Music of William Walton. New York:
Oxford University Press, 1974. 248 pp.

WARHOL, ANDY

3549 Coplans, John; Mekas, Jonas; and Tomkins, Calvin. Andy
Warhol. Greenwich, Conn.: New York Graphic Society,
1970. 160 pp.

3550 Crone, Rainer. Andy Warhol. New York: Praeger, 1970.
332 pp.

3551 Gidal, Peter. Andy Warhol: Films and Paintings. New York:
Dutton, 1971. 160 pp.

3552 Wilcox, John ("and a cast of thousands"). The Autobiography
and Sex Life of Andy Warhol. New York: Other Scenes,
1971. Unpaged.

3553 Koch, Stephen. Stargazer: Andy Warhol's World and His
Films. New York: Praeger, 1973. 155 pp.

3554 Warhol, Andy. The Philosophy of Andy Warhol. From A to
B and Back Again. New York: Harcourt, Brace, Jovanovich,
1975. 241 pp.

WARNER, JACK L.

3555 Warner, Jack L. with Jennings, Dean. My First Hundred
Years in Hollywood. New York: Random, 1964. 332 pp.

WARREN, HARRY

3556 Thomas, Tony. Harry Warren and the Hollywood Musical.
Secaucus, N.J.: Citadel, 1975. 344 pp.

WATERS, ETHEL

3557   Waters, Ethel with Samuels, Charles. His Eye Is on the
       Sparrow. Garden City, N.Y.: Doubleday, 1951. 278 pp.

WATT, HARRY

3558   Watt, Harry. Don't Look at the Camera. New York: St.
       Martin's, 1974. 197 pp.

WAYNE, JOHN

3559   Fernett, Gene. Starring John Wayne. Cocoa, Florida:
       Cinememories, 1969. 191 pp.

3560   Ricci, Mark; Zmijewsky, Boris; and Zmijewsky, Steve. The
       Films of John Wayne. New York: Citadel, 1970. 288 pp.

3561   Tomkies, Mike. Duke: The Story of John Wayne. Chicago:
       Regnery, 1971. 149 pp.

3562   Carpozi, George. The John Wayne Story. New Rochelle,
       N.Y.: Arlington, 1972. 279 pp.

3563   Barbour, Alan G. John Wayne. New York: Pyramid, 1974.
       160 pp.

3564   Zolotow, Maurice. Shooting Star: A Biography of John
       Wayne. New York: Simon and Schuster, 1974. 416 pp.

3565   Ramer, Jean. Duke: The Real Story of John Wayne. New
       York: Universal Publishing and Distributing, 1975.

WEISSMULLER, JOHNNY

3566   Onyx, Narda. Water, World and Weissmuller: A Biography.
       Los Angeles: VION Publishing, 1964. 330 pp.

WELLES, ORSON

3567   Fowler, Roy Alexander. Orson Welles: A First Biography.
       London: Pendulum, 1946. 100 pp.

3568   Noble, Peter. The Fabulous Orson Welles. London: Hutchin-
       son, 1956. 276 pp.

3569   Bogdanovich, Peter. The Cinema of Orson Welles. New
       York: Museum of Modern Art, 1961. 16 pp.

3570   Cowie, Peter. The Cinema of Orson Welles. New York:
       A. S. Barnes, 1965. 208 pp. (Revised as A Ribbon of
       Dreams: The Cinema of Orson Welles, South Brunswick,
       N.J.: A. S. Barnes, 1973. 262 pp.)

3571   Wollen, Peter.   Orson Welles.   London: British Film Insti-
       tute, 1969.   43 pp.

3572   Higham, Charles.   The Films of Orson Welles.   Berkeley:
       University of California Press, 1970.   210 pp.

3573   Bessy, Maurice.   Orson Welles: An Investigation Into His
       Films and Philosophy.   New York: Crown, 1971.   195 pp.
       Translated by Ciba Vaughan.

3574   McBride, Joseph.   Orson Welles.   New York: Viking, 1972.
       192 pp.

WELLMAN, WILLIAM

3575   Wellman, William.   A Short Time for Insanity: An Auto-
       biography.   New York: Hawthorn, 1974.   276 pp.

WELLS, INGEBORG

3576   Wells, Ingeborg.   Enough, No More.   London: Joseph, 1948.
       294 pp.   Translated by Lord Sudley.

WEST, MAE

3577   West, Mae.   Goodness Had Nothing To Do With It: The Auto-
       biography of Mae West.   Englewood Cliffs, N.J.:   Prentice-
       Hall, 1959.   271 pp.   (Revised New York: Macfadden,
       1970.   288 pp.)

3578   West, Mae.   The Wit and Wisdom of Mae West.   Edited by
       Joseph Weintraub.   New York: Putnam, 1967.   94 pp.

3579   Tuska, Jon.   The Films of Mae West.   Introduction by Parker
       Tyler.   Secaucus, N.J.:   Citadel, 1973.   191 pp.

3580   Bayar, Michael.   Mae West.   New York: Pyramid, 1975.
       160 pp.

WEST, NATHANAEL

3581   Light, James F.   Nathanael West: An Interpretative Study.
       Evanston, Ill.:   Northwestern University Press, 1961.
       220 pp.   (Republished 1971, 236 pp.)

3582   Martin, Jay.   Nathanael West: The Art of His Life.   New
       York: Farrar, Straus and Giroux, 1970.   435 pp.

3583   Martin, Jay (comp.)   Nathanael West: A Collection of Critical
       Essays.   Englewood Cliffs, N.J.:   Prentice-Hall, 1971.
       176 pp.

3584   White, William.   Nathanael West: A Comprehensive

Bibliography. Kent, Ohio: Kent State University Press,
1975. 209 pp.

WHITE, PEARL

3585 Weltman, Manuel and Lee, Raymond. Pearl White: The
Peerless, Fearless Girl. South Brunswick, N.J.: A. S.
Barnes, 1969. 266 pp.

WILCOX, HERBERT

3586 Wilcox, Herbert. Twenty-Five Thousand Sunsets: The Autobiography of Herbert Wilcox. London: Bodley Head,
1967. 233 pp. (Reprinted South Brunswick, N.J.: A. S.
Barnes, 1969.)

WILDER, BILLY

3587 Madsen, Axel. Billy Wilder. Bloomington: Indiana University Press, 1969. 168 pp.

3588 Wood, Tom. The Bright Side of Billy Wilder, Primarily.
Garden City, N.Y.: Doubleday, 1970. 257 pp.

WILK, MAX

3589 Wilk, Max. Every Day's a Matinee: Memoirs Scribbled on
a Dressing Room Door. New York: Norton, 1975.
288 pp.

WILLIAMS, BRANSBY

3590 Williams, Bransby. Bransby Williams, By Himself. London:
Hutchinson, 1954. 240 pp.

WILLIAMS, EMLYN

3591 Findlater, Richard. Emlyn Williams. New York: Macmillan, 1956. 112 pp.

3592 Williams, Emlyn. George: An Early Autobiography. New
York: Random, 1962. 437 pp.

WILLIAMS, TENNESSEE

3593 Warren, Clifton. Tennessee Williams as a Cinematic Writer.
Indiana University: Ph.D., 1963. 313 pp.

3594 Steen, Mike. A Look at Tennessee Williams. New York:
Hawthorn, 1969. 318 pp.
    Recorded interviews with Williams' friends and col-
laborators, including Karl Malden, Irvin Rapper, George
Cukor, William Inge, Jessica Tandy, Geraldine Page, and
Shelley Winters.

3595 Williams, Tennessee. Memoirs. Garden City, N.Y.:
       Doubleday, 1975. 264 pp.

WISE, ROBERT

3596 Zeitlin, David A. The Directors Guild of America Presents
       a Retrospective Showing of Eight Films by Robert Wise,
       Winner of the 1965 DGA Directorial Award. Hollywood:
       Directors Guild of America, 1966. 16 pp.

WODEHOUSE, P. G.

3597 Wodehouse, P. G. and Bolton, Guy. Bring on the Girls!
       The Improbable Story of Our Life in Musical Comedy,
       With Pictures to Prove It. New York: Simon and
       Schuster, 1953. 278 pp.

WOLPER, DAVID L.

3598 Rohauer, Raymond. A Tribute to David L. Wolper. New
       York: Gallery of Modern Art Monograph, 1966. 27 pp.

WOOD, JOAN

3599 Wood, Joan. The Casting Couch and Me: The Uninhibited
       Memoirs of a Young Actress. New York: Walker, 1974.
       216 pp.

WOOD, PEGGY

3600 Wood, Peggy. How Young You Look: Memoirs of a Middle-
       Sized Actress. New York, Toronto: Farrar and Rine-
       hart, 1941. 277 pp.

WOOD, SAM

3601 Denton, Clive; Canham, Kingsley; and Thomas, Tony. The
       Hollywood Professionals, Vol. II: Henry King, Lewis
       Milestone, Sam Wood. New York: A. S. Barnes, 1974.
       192 pp.

WRIGHT, COBINA

3602 Wright, Cobina. I Never Grew Up. New York: Prentice-
       Hall, 1952. 316 pp.

WYLER, WILLIAM

3603 Shibuk, Charles. An Index to the Films of William Wyler.
       New York: Theodore Huff Memorial Film Society, 1957.
       21 pp.

3604 Madsen, Axel. William Wyler: The Authorized Biography.
       New York: Crowell, 1973. 456 pp.

WYNN, ED

3605 Wynn, Keenan with Brough, James. Ed Wynn's Son. Garden
      City, N.Y.: Doubleday, 1959. 236 pp.

WYNN, KEENAN

3606 Wynn, Keenan with Brough, James. Ed Wynn's Son. Garden
      City, N.Y.: Doubleday, 1959. 236 pp.

YOUNG, LORETTA

3607 Young, Loretta with Ferguson, Helen. The Things I Had to
      Learn. Indianapolis: Bobbs-Merrill, 1961. 256 pp.

ZANUCK, DARRYL F.

3608 Zanuck, Darryl F. Tunis Expedition. New York: Random,
      1943. 159 pp.
      Exclusively on Zanuck's war experience.

3609 Guild, Leo. Zanuck: Hollywood's Last Tycoon. Los Angeles:
      Holloway, 1970. 255 pp.

3610 Gussow, Mel. Don't Say Yes Until I Finish Talking: A
      Biography of Darryl F. Zanuck. Garden City, N.Y.:
      Doubleday, 1971. 318 pp.

ZAVATTINI, CESARE

3611 Zavattini, Cesare. Zavattini: Sequences From a Cinematic
      Life. Englewood Cliffs, N.J.: Prentice-Hall, 1970.
      297 pp. Translated by William Weaver.

ZIEGFELD, FLORENZ

3612 Higham, Charles. Ziegfeld. Chicago: Regnery, 1972.
      245 pp.

ZIMMER, JILL SCHARY

3613 Zimmer, Jill Schary. With a Cast of Thousands: A Holly-
      wood Childhood. New York: Stein and Day, 1963. 252 pp.
      Autobiography of Dore Schary's daughter.

ZINNEMANN, FRED

3614 Griffith, Richard. Fred Zinnemann. New York: Museum of
      Modern Art Film Library, 1958. 20 pp.

3615 Rohauer, Raymond. A Tribute to Fred Zinnemann. New
      York: Gallery of Modern Art Monograph, 1968. 10 pp.

ZUKOR, ADOLPH

3616 Irwin, Will. The House That Shadows Built. (Originally
published 1928.) New York: Arno, 1970. 293 pp.
With material on Paramount.

3617 Zukor, Adolph with Kramer, Dale. The Public is Never
Wrong: The Autobiography of Adolph Zukor. New York:
Putnam, 1953. 310 pp.

B. COLLECTIVE BIOGRAPHY, ANALYSIS, AND INTERVIEW

This section includes those works which, in general, have separate sections on a significant number of individuals associated with the filmmaking community. As in Part VI, section A, individual biography, analysis, and interview, these books may be composed of biography, analysis, interview, or a combination of all three. Whenever possible we have listed the names of the subjects so that they can be included in the name index. The reader should not, however, overlook a book's potential value if the names of the individuals it discusses have not been provided; in that case we have tried to characterize by type or time period the individuals discussed so that the reader may at least estimate the book's relevancy to his subject. For anecdotal accounts of Hollywood personalities or gossip-oriented material, see also Part IX, section F-4, anecdotal views of Hollywood and Hollywood personalities.

3618 Hughes, Elinor. Famous Stars of Filmdom--Women. (Originally published 1931.) Freeport, N.Y.: Books for Libraries Press, 1970. 341 pp.
Biographical material on pre-1931 stars.

3619 Hughes, Elinor. Famous Stars of Filmdom--Men. (Originally published 1932.) Freeport, N.Y.: Books for Libraries Press, 1970. 342 pp.
Biographical material on pre-1932 stars.

3620 Eustis, Morton. Players at Work: Acting According to Actors. (Originally published 1937.) New York: Blom, 1969. 127 pp.
With material on Helen Hayes, Lunt and Fontanne, Alla Nazimova, Burgess Meredith, Fred Astaire, Lotte Lehmann, and others.

3621 Levant, Oscar. A Smattering of Ignorance. Garden City, N.Y.: Garden City Publishing, 1940. 267 pp.
With material on film music as well as on Harpo Marx, Max Steiner, George Gershwin, Aaron Copland, and Levant himself.

3622 Cocroft, Thoda. Great Names and How They Are Made. Chicago, New York: Dartnell, 1941. 270 pp.

With material on Katharine Hepburn, Laurence Olivier,
Vivien Leigh, Lillian Gish, Helen Hayes, and others.

3623 Tully, Jim. A Dozen and One. Hollywood: Murray and Gee,
1943. 242 pp.
With material on Charlie Chaplin, Clark Gable, Jim
Cruze, Tod Sloan, Paul Bern, and others.

3624 Bailey, F. E. Film Stars of History. London: MacDonald,
ca. 1944. 167 pp.
With material on Walter Huston, Greta Garbo, Laurence Olivier, Elizabeth Bergner, Charles Laughton, and
others who played historical roles.

3625 Film Star Parade: A Glittering Galaxy of Your Screen
Favourites: Emphasis on Glamour. London: W. H.
Allen, 1944.
Primarily photographs.

3626 Cairn, James. The Heart of Hollywood. London: David
Smith, 1945. 224 pp.
Impressionistic descriptions of 144 Hollywood stars
and their films, including many lesser known personalities.

3627 Paige, Ethel (ed.) Private Lives of Movie Stars: Hedy Lamarr, James Cagney, Barbara Stanwyck, Red Skelton,
Lucille Ball. New York: Arco, 1945. 48 pp.

3628 Beaton, Cecil. Time Exposure. New York: Scribner's,
1946. 134 pp.
Includes photographs of many stars.

3629 Nerman, Einer. Caricature. New York, London: American
Studio Books, 1946. 80 pp.
With caricatures of many stars.

3630 Noble, Peter. British Screen Stars. London: British Yearbooks, 1946. 91 pp.

3631 Noble, Peter. Profiles and Personalities. London: Brown-
lee, 1946. 124 pp.
British personalities, with material on James Agate,
Noel Coward, John Gielgud, Alexander Korda, Vivien
Leigh, James Mason, Laurence Olivier, J. Arthur Rank,
Carol Reed, Peter Ustinov, and others.

3632 Shelley, Frank. Stage and Screen. London: Pendulum, 1946.
55 pp.
With material on John Gielgud, Laurence Olivier,
Vivien Leigh, Paul Muni, Humphrey Bogart, Bette Davis,
Greta Garbo, and others.

3633 Frazier, George. The One with the Mustache is Costello.

New York: Random, 1947. 275 pp.
With material on Humphrey Bogart, Errol Flynn, and
Peter Lorre, as well as on non-film subjects.

3634 Gard, Alex. Stars Off Gard. New York: Scribner's, 1947.
      61 pp.
      Caricatures of many stars.

3635 Carrick, Edward (comp.) Art and Design in the British
      Film: A Pictorial Directory of British Art Directors and
      Their Work. London: Dobson, 1948. 133 pp. (Re-
      printed New York: Arno, 1972.)
           With material on W. C. Andrews, Andre Andrejew,
      Norman Arnold, Wilfred Arnold, Ferdinand Bellan, Ralph
      Brinton, John Bryan, Edward Carrick, Maurice Carter,
      Douglas Daniels, Cedric Dawe, Roger Furse, Hein Heck-
      roth, John Howell, Laurence Irving, Alfred Junge, Vincent
      Korda, Oliver Messel, Tom Morahan, C. P. Norman, Roy
      Oxley, Peter Proud, George Provis, Fred Pusey, David
      Rawnsley, Michael Relph, Paul Sheriff, Wilfrid Shingleton,
      Duncan Sutherland, Alec Vetchinsky, and Lawrence Paul
      Williams.

3636 Hodges, Bart. Life's Little Dramas, As Told to Bart Hodges.
      New York: Duell, Sloan and Pearce, 1948. 173 pp.
           Includes material on Brian Aherne, Gene Autry, Basil
      Rathbone, George Burns and Gracie Allen, Rita Hayworth,
      Mary Pickford, Hal Roach, and others.

3637 Cross, John E. and Rattenbury, Arnold (eds.) Film Today
      Books: Screen and Audience, An Occasional Miscellany
      Devoted to the Contemporary Cinema. London: Saturn,
      ca. 1949. 90 pp.
           With material on David Lean, Carl Dreyer, Louis De-
      Rochemont, Robert Montgomery, Roberto Rossellini, Niko-
      lai Cherkassov, Roger Furse, Laurence Olivier, and
      others.

3638 Lynx, J. J. (ed.) The Film Fan's Bedside Book No. 2.
      London: Co-ordination, 1949. 136 pp.
           A collection of diverse articles on Sid Field, bathing
      beauties, sound technology, television, character players,
      Jean Simmons, Billy Wilder, newsreels, Fred Astaire,
      Fredric March, and other topics.

3639 Sargeant, Winthrop. Geniuses, Goddesses, and People. New
      York: Dutton, 1949. 317 pp.
           Limited film material; includes profiles of Rita Hay-
      worth, Ezio Pinza, and others.

3640 Towers, Harry Alan. Show Business: Stars of the World of
      Show Business. London: Low, Marston, 1949. 110 pp.
           With material on theatre, film, and radio stars.

3641   Barnett, Lincoln. Writing on Life: Sixteen Close-Ups. New
       York: Sloane, 1951. 383 pp.
          With material on Fred and Adele Astaire, Bing Crosby,
       Ingrid Bergman, Tennessee Williams, Richard Rodgers,
       Josh Logan, and others.

3642   Beaton, Cecil. Photobiography. Garden City, N.Y.: Double-
       day, 1951. 255 pp.
          Photographs of many stars.

3643   Zolotow, Maurice. No People Like Show People. New York:
       Random, 1951. 305 pp. (Also published as It Takes All
       Kinds.)
          Includes material on Tallulah Bankhead, Jimmy Durante,
       Oscar Levant, Jack Benny, Frank Fay, Jed Harris, Fred
       Allen, and Ethel Merman.

3644   Berger, Oscar. My Victims. New York: Harper, 1952.
       128 pp.
          Includes caricatures of many stars.

3645   Duncan, Peter. In Hollywood Tonight. London: Laurie,
       1952. 144 pp.
          Interviews with stars.

3646   Green, Abel (ed.) The Spice of Variety. New York: Holt,
       1952. 277 pp.
          Humorous essays selected from Variety's anniversary
       issues; with contributions by Ethel Barrymore, Jack Benny,
       Claude Binyon, Richard Brooks, Jimmy Durante, Groucho
       Marx, Edward G. Robinson, Harry Ruby, Sidney Sheldon,
       Gypsy Rose Lee, Phil Silvers, and others.

3647   Houghton, Norris. But Not Forgotten: The Adventure of the
       University Players. New York: Sloan, 1952. 346 pp.
          History of a Cape Cod theatrical group of the twenties
       and thirties; its members included Henry Fonda, Margaret
       Sullavan, Josh Logan, Myron McCormick, Kent Smith,
       and others.

3648   Myers, Denis. Secrets of the Stars. London: Odhams,
       1952. 143 pp.

3649   Bakeless, Katherine. In the Big Time: Career Stories of
       American Entertainers, Illustrated From Photos. Phila-
       delphia: Lippincott, 1953. 211 pp.
          With material on Fred Astaire, Jimmy Stewart, Bing
       Crosby, and others.

3650   Beaton, Cecil (photographs) and Tynan, Kenneth (text). Per-
       sona Grata. New York: Putnam, 1954. 99 pp.
          Material on 100 celebrities, including many film
       performers.

3651 Haskin, Dorothy C. Twice-Born Stars You Would Like to
Know. Grand Rapids, Mich.: Zondervan, 1955. 89 pp.
Includes material on Roy Rogers, Dale Evans, Col-
leen Evans, and others.

3652 Allen, Steve. The Funny Men. New York: Simon and
Schuster, 1956. 280 pp.
Includes material on Fred Allen, Jack Benny, Milton
Berle, Red Buttons, Sid Caeser, Eddie Cantor, Wally
Cox, Jackie Gleason, George Gobel, Arthur Godfrey, Bob
Hope, Sam Levenson, Jerry Lewis, Groucho Marx, Phil
Silvers, and Red Skelton.

3653 Mankowitz, Wolf. The ABC of Show Business. London:
Oldbourne, 1956. 55 pp.
Anecdotes about international show business personali-
ties.

3654 Vivienne. They Came to My Studio: Famous People of Our
Time, Photographed by Vivienne. London: Hall, 1956.
172 pp.
Includes many film celebrities.

3655 Wiseman, Thomas. The Seven Deadly Sins of Hollywood.
London: Oldbourne, 1957. 222 pp.
Collection of interviews with Hollywood celebrities,
including Liberace, Rossano Brazzi, Susan Hayward,
Orson Welles, Darryl F. Zanuck, Victor Mature, Marilyn
Monroe, Jayne Mansfield, Vera Hruba Ralston, and others.

3656 Bumper Film Book. London: Spring Book, ca. 1958. 160 pp.
With material on Leslie Caron, Cecil Beaton, Jayne
Mansfield, William Wyler, and others.

3657 Wallace, Mike. Mike Wallace Asks: Highlights From 46
Controversial Interviews. Edited by Charles Preston
and Edward A. Hamilton. New York: Simon and Schuster,
1958. 128 pp.
Includes interviews with Jayne Mansfield, Tennessee
Williams, Salvador Dali, Diana Barrymore, Ben Hecht,
Monique van Vooren, Tallulah Bankhead, Zsa Zsa Gabor,
Steve Allen, Rudy Vallee, Oscar Hammerstein II, George
Jessel, Anthony Perkins, Peter Ustinov, Gloria Swanson,
and others.

3658 Franklin, Joe. Classics of the Silent Screen: A Pictorial
Treasury. New York: Citadel, 1959. 255 pp.
Includes biographical material on 75 stars who worked
in American silent films.

3659 Halsman, Philippe. Phillipe Halsman's Jump Book. New
York: Simon and Schuster, 1959. 94 pp.
Photographs of 178 different celebrities jumping in the
air.

3660   Tanner, Louise. Here Today. New York: Crowell, 1959.
        311 pp.
            Limited material on film; includes chapters on James
        Dean, Harold Russell, Shirley Temple, and F. Scott Fitz-
        gerald.

3661   Amory, Cleveland and Bradlee, Frederic (eds.) Vanity Fair:
        Selections From America's Most Memorable Magazine,
        A Cavalcade of the 1920s and 1930s. New York: Viking,
        1960. 372 pp.
            With material on or by Jean Cocteau, Fred Stone,
        W. C. Fields, Charlie Chaplin, Rudolph Valentino, Irving
        Thalberg, George Jean Nathan, and others.

3662   Dorcy, Jean. The Mime. New York: Speller, 1961. 116 pp.
        Translated by Robert Speller, Jr. and Pierre de Fontnou-
        velle.
            Includes material on Jean-Louis Barrault, Charlie
        Chaplin, Marcel Marceau, and others.

3663   Funke, Lewis and Booth, John E. (eds.) Actors Talk About
        Acting: Fourteen Intimate Interviews. New York: Random,
        1961. 469 pp.
            Interviews with Anne Bancroft, Jose Ferrer, John
        Gielgud, Helen Hayes, Bert Lahr, Vivien Leigh, Paul
        Muni, Sidney Poitier, Maureen Stapleton, Shelley Winters,
        and others.

3664   Tynan, Kenneth. Curtains. New York: Atheneum, 1961.
        495 pp.
            With essays on Greta Garbo, W. C. Fields, and James
        Cagney.

3665   Alpert, Hollis. The Dream and the Dreamers. New York:
        Macmillan, 1962. 258 pp.
            Includes material on Marlon Brando, Ingmar Berg-
        man, Ross Hunter, Jean Seberg, Elia Kazan, George
        Stevens, John Huston, Joseph Mankiewicz, Billy Wilder,
        Fred Zinnemann, Marilyn Monroe, and Alfred Hitchcock.

3666   Booch, Harish S. and Doyle, Karing. Star-Portrait: Intimate
        Life Stories of Famous Indian Film Stars. Bombay:
        Lakhani Book Depot, 1962. 152 pp.

3667   Martin, Pete. Pete Martin Calls On.... New York: Simon
        and Schuster, 1962. 510 pp.
            Miscellaneous interviews with celebrities.

3668   Ross, Lillian and Helen. The Player: A Profile of an Art.
        New York: Simon and Schuster, 1962. 459 pp.
            Interview material on 55 players.

3669   Schickel, Richard. The Stars. New York: Dial, 1962. 287 pp.

Biography and persona analysis of over 80 major
Hollywood stars.

3670 Jessel, George. Halo Over Hollywood. Van Nuys, Cal.:
      Toastmaster Publishing, 1963. 176 pp.
      Fictional comic speeches of deceased Hollywood
      personalities.

3671 Wagenknecht, Edward. Seven Daughters of the Theatre:
      Jenny Lind, Sarah Bernhardt, Ellen Terry, Julia Mar-
      lowe, Isadora Duncan, Mary Garden, Marilyn Monroe.
      Norman: University of Oklahoma Press, 1964. 234 pp.

3672 Hirsch, Phil. Hollywood Uncensored. New York: Pyramid,
      1965. 188 pp.
      With material on Rory Calhoun, Tony Curtis, Jimmy
      Durante, Jerry Lewis, George Maharis, Jayne Mansfield,
      Dean Martin, Mickey Rooney, Robert Vaughn, John Wayne,
      Tuesday Weld, Keenan Wynn, and others.

3673 Morgan, Thomas B. Self-Creations: Thirteen Impersonalities.
      New York: Holt, Rinehart and Winston, 1965. 247 pp.
      Interviews with Gary Cooper, Elia Kazan, and John
      Wayne, as well as non-film personalities.

3674 Nolan, William F. Sinners and Supermen. North Hollywood,
      Cal.: All Star, 1965. 192 pp.
      With material on Marlon Brando, Otto Preminger,
      Orson Welles, Peter Sellers, Dean Martin, Howard Hughes,
      Ian Fleming, Raymond Chandler, Ben Hecht, Ray Brad-
      bury, and others.

3675 Stuart, Ray (comp.) Immortals of the Screen. Los Angeles:
      Sherbourne, 1965. 224 pp.
      Stills and brief biographies of over 100 Hollywood
      personalities.

3676 Zierold, Norman J. The Child Stars. New York: Coward-
      McCann, 1965. 250 pp.
      With material on Jackie Coogan, Baby LeRoy, Shirley
      Temple, Jane Withers, Judy Garland, Freddie Bartholo-
      mew, Deanna Durbin, Jackie Cooper, and others.

3677 Dwiggins, Don. The Air Devils: The Story of Balloonists,
      Barnstormers, and Stunt Pilots. Philadelphia: Lippin-
      cott, 1966. 266 pp.
      Includes material on Frank Clarke, Omar Locklear,
      Frank Tomick, Ivan Unger, Art Goebel, Al Johnson,
      Bobby Rose, Ira Reed, Hank Coffin, Paul Mantz, and
      Jimmy Mattern.

3678 Ferguson, Ken and Sylvia (eds.) Western Stars of Television
      and Film. London: Purnell, 1966. Unpaged.

3679 Goldsmith, Warren (ed.) Film Fame. Beverly Hills: Fame,
      1966. 210 pp.

3680 McDowall, Roddy. Double Exposure. New York: Delacorte,
      1966. 251 pp.
          Photographic portraits of celebrities with a commen-
      tary.

3681 Newquist, Roy. Showcase. New York: Morrow, 1966.
      412 pp.
          Includes interviews with Julie Andrews, Hume Cronyn,
      Sammy Davis, Jr., Agnes De Mille, Dame Edith Evans,
      Janet Gaynor, John Gielgud, Julie Harris, Helen Hayes,
      Danny Kaye, Ernest Lehman, Jack Lemmon, Mike Nichols,
      Peter O'Toole, Robert Preston, Harold Prince, Rosalind
      Russell, Jessica Tandy, and others.

3682 Platt, Frank C. (comp.) Great Stars of Hollywood's Golden
      Age. New York: New American Library, 1966. 214 pp.
          Includes material on Rudolph Valentino, Greta Garbo,
      Charlie Chaplin, John Barrymore, Jean Harlow, and
      Carole Lombard; several essays by Adela Rogers St. John.

3683 Rhode, Eric. Tower of Babel: Speculations on the Cinema.
      Philadelphia: Chilton, 1966. 214 pp.
          Analysis of Robert Bresson, Jean Vigo, Sergei Eisen-
      stein, Humphrey Jennings, Fritz Lang, Jacques Rivette,
      Federico Fellini, Alain Resnais, Max Ophuls, Andrzej
      Wajda, and Satyajit Ray.

3684 Cameron, Ian and Elisabeth. The Heavies. London: Studio
      Vista, 1967. 144 pp. (Reprinted New York: Praeger,
      1969.)
          Includes material on Rodolfo Acosta, Wesley Addy,
      Claude Akins, Corey Allen, Pedro Armendariz, Ed Beg-
      ley, William Bendix, Charles Bickford, Richard Boone,
      Ernest Borgnine, Neville Brand, Charles Bronson, Victor
      Buono, Raymond Burr, William Campbell, Timothy Carey,
      Lee J. Cobb, Hans Conreid, Elisha Cook, Jr., Broderick
      Crawford, Michael Dante, Ray Danton, Ted De Corsia,
      John Dehner, Richard Devon, Paul Dubov, Dan Duryea,
      Jack Elam, Robert Emhardt, Peter Falk, Ned Glass, Leo
      Gordon, Frank Gorshin, James Gregory, John Ireland,
      Richard Jaeckel, Henry Jones, Victor Jory, Brian Keith,
      Arthur Kennedy, George Kennedy, Richard Kiley, Jack
      Lambert, Martin Landau, Marc Lawrence, Darren Mc-
      Gavin, Charles McGraw, John McIntire, George Macready,
      Ross Martin, Lee Marvin, Walter Matthau, Ralph Meeker,
      Gary Merrill, Emile Meyer, Robert Middleton, Vic Mor-
      row, Alex Nicol, Simon Oakland, Warren Oates, Frederick
      O'Brady, Edmond O'Brien, Patrick O'Neal, Jack Palance,
      Nehemiah Persoff, Vincent Price, Aldo Ray, Tom Reese,
      Robert Ryan, Frank Silvera, Rod Steiger, Warren Stevens,

Ray Teal, Rip Torn, Ivan Triesault, Lee Van Cleef,
Robert Walker, Eli Wallach, Clifton Webb, Robert Webber,
Jesse White, Richard Widmark, Robert J. Wilke, and
Adam Williams.

3685 Geduld, Harry M. (ed.) Film Makers on Film Making:
      Statements on Their Art by Thirty Directors. Blooming-
      ton: Indiana University Press, 1967. 302 pp.
          Includes Louis Lumière, Cecil Hepworth, Edwin S.
      Porter, Mack Sennett, D. W. Griffith, Robert Flaherty,
      Charlie Chaplin, Eric von Stroheim, Dziga Vertov, Sergei
      Eisenstein, Carl Dreyer, Tony Richardson, Alfred Hitch-
      cock, Jean Cocteau, Alain Resnais, Alain Robbe-Grillet,
      Luis Bunuel, Ingmar Bergman, Federico Fellini, Miche-
      langelo Antonioni, Fritz Lang, Andrzej Wajda, Josef von
      Sternberg, Orson Welles, Satyajit Ray, Akira Kurosawa,
      Lindsay Anderson, Juan-Antonio Bardem, David Lean,
      Jean Renoir, and Kenneth Anger.

3686 Hirsch, Phil (ed.) Hollywood Confidential. New York: Pyra-
      mid, 1967. 222 pp.
          With articles on Robert Mitchum, Lee Marvin, Alan
      Ladd, Jack Palance, Marlon Brando, David Niven, George
      C. Scott, Peter O'Toole, Judy Garland, and Barbara
      Payton.

3687 Lamparski, Richard. Whatever Became of...? [In Five
      Volumes]. Volume 1. New York: Crown, 1967. 207 pp.
      Volume 2. 1968. Volume 3. 1970. Volume 4. 1973.
      Volume 5. 1974.
          Biographical updates of celebrities of the past.

3688 Malanga, Gerard and Warhol, Andy. Screen Tests: A Diary.
      New York: Kulchur, distributed by Citadel, 1967. 216 pp.
          Frame enlargement of Warhol film footage juxtaposed
      with poetic portraits by Gerard Malanga; material on 54
      individuals, including Paul America, Marisa Berenson,
      Salvador Dali, Allen Ginsberg, Jonas Mekas, Ondine,
      Lou Reed, Edie Sedgwick, and others.

3689 Meyers, Warren B. Who Is That? The Late Late Viewer's
      Guide to the Old Old Movie Players. New York: Per-
      sonality Posters, 1967. 63 pp.
          Primarily pictures of character actors, organized by
      type.

3690 Muray, Nickolas (photographs) and Gallico, Paul (text). The
      Revealing Eye: Personalities of the 1920's. New York:
      Atheneum, 1967. 307 pp.
          Portraits and biographical material on Zoë Akins,
      Dame Judith Anderson, Fred and Adele Astaire, Tallulah
      Bankhead, Ethel Barrymore, Richard Barthelmess, Robert
      Benchley, Humphrey Bogart, Clara Bow, Alice Brady, Jack

Buchanan, Billie Burke, Charlie Chaplin, Jean Cocteau,
Claudette Colbert, Jackie Coogan, Noel Coward, Joan
Crawford, Douglas Fairbanks, Jr., Bebe Daniels, Mar-
lene Dietrich, Jeanne Eagels, Douglas Fairbanks, Mary
Pickford, Greta Garbo, Dorothy Gish, Lillian Gish, Hope
Hampton, Jean Harlow, Hedda Hopper, Al Jolson, Anita
Loos, Myrna Loy, Thomas Meighan, Colleen Moore,
Grace Moore, Alla Nazimova, Paul Robeson, Edward G.
Robinson, Fred Stone, Gloria Swanson, Norma Talmadge,
Constance Talmadge, Fannie Ward, Clifton Webb, Johnny
Weissmuller, Louis Wolheim, and others.

3691   Reed, Dena. Success Tips From Young Celebrities. New
       York: Grosset and Dunlap, 1967. 159 pp.
              Character-building advice given by Patty Duke, George
       Maharis, the Lennon Sisters, Ricky Nelson, Connie Fran-
       cis, Brandon De Wilde, Shari Lewis, Perry Como, Annette
       Funicello, Bobby Darin, Sal Mineo, Fabian, Frankie Ava-
       lon, Vince Edwards, David McCallum, Robert Vaughn, and
       Leslie Uggams.

3692   Rollins, Charlemae. Famous Negro Entertainers of Stage,
       Screen and TV. New York: Dodd, Mead, 1967. 122 pp.
              Material on Louis Armstrong, Harry Belafonte, Nat
       King Cole, Sammy Davis, Jr., Lena Horne, Eartha Kitt,
       Sidney Poitier, Paul Robeson, and Bill Robinson; for the
       young reader.

3693   Sarris, Andrew. Interviews With Film Directors. Indianapo-
       lis: Bobbs-Merrill, 1967. 478 pp. (Reprinted New York:
       Avon, 1969, 557 pp.)
              Interviews with Michelangelo Antonioni, Ingmar Berg-
       man, Robert Bresson, Peter Brook, Luis Buñuel, Claude
       Chabrol, Charlie Chaplin, George Cukor, Clive Donner,
       Carl Dreyer, Sergei Eisenstein, Federico Fellini, John
       Ford, Jean-Luc Godard, Howard Hawks, Alfred Hitchcock,
       John Huston, Buster Keaton, Akira Kurosawa, Fritz Lang,
       David Lean, Joseph Losey, Ernst Lubitsch, Rouben Mamou-
       lian, Max Ophuls, Pier Paolo Pasolini, Sam Peckinpah,
       Abraham Polonsky, Nicholas Ray, Satyajit Ray, Jean
       Renoir, Alain Resnais, Leni Riefenstahl, Josef von Stern-
       berg, Erich von Stroheim, Preston Sturges, Francois
       Truffaut, and Orson Welles.

3694   Walker, Alexander. The Celluloid Sacrifice: Aspects of Sex
       in the Movies. New York: Hawthorn, 1967. 241 pp.
              Includes material on Theda Bara, Clara Bow, Cecil
       B. DeMille, Mary Pickford, Mae West, Marlene Dietrich,
       Greta Garbo, Jean Harlow, Marilyn Monroe, Elizabeth
       Taylor, and Marcello Mastroianni.

3695   Brownlow, Kevin (comp.) The Parade's Gone By. New York:
       Knopf, 1968. 577 pp.

Primarily American silent history; includes material
on D. W. Griffith, Allan Dwan, Henry King, Mary Pick-
ford, Clarence Brown, Edward Sloman, William Wellman,
Cecil B. DeMille, Josef von Sternberg, Charles Rosher,
Douglas Fairbanks, Margaret Booth, William Hornbeck,
Geraldine Farrar, Gloria Swanson, Betty Blythe, Louis B.
Mayer, Irving Thalberg, David O. Selznick, Reginald
Denny, Harold Lloyd, Buster Keaton, Charlie Chaplin, and
Abel Gance.

3696 Bull, Clarence Sinclair with Lee, Raymond. The Faces of
      Hollywood. South Brunswick, N.J.: A. S. Barnes, 1968.
      256 pp.
         250 portraits by MGM's chief portrait photographer
      plus some anecdotal material and technical photographic
      data.

3697 Fallaci, Oriana. The Egotists: Sixteen Surprising Interviews.
      Chicago: Regnery, 1968. 256 pp.
         Includes material on Sean Connery, Ingrid Bergman,
      Geraldine Chaplin, Anna Magnani, Jeanne Moreau, Dean
      Martin, Federico Fellini, Sammy Davis, Jr., Alfred
      Hitchcock, and others.

3698 Gruen, John. Close-Up. New York: Viking, 1968. 206 pp.
         Interviews with celebrities; film personalities include
      Federico Fellini, Bette Davis, Judy Garland, Shelley
      Winters, Candice Bergen, Maria Montez, Simone Signoret,
      Vivien Leigh, Busby Berkeley, Joseph Losey, Ruby Keeler,
      and Alain Resnais.

3699 Reed, Rex. Do You Sleep in the Nude? New York: New
      American Library, 1968. 276 pp.
         Interview articles on Michelangelo Antonioni, Barbra
      Streisand, Warren Beatty, Mike Nichols, Lucille Ball,
      Gower Champion, Ava Gardner, Sandy Dennis, Lotte Lenya,
      Shirley Knight, Angela Lansbury, James Mason, Dame
      Edith Evans, Melina Mercouri, Otto Preminger, Michael
      Crawford, Hayley Mills, Lynn Redgrave, Beryl Reid, Jean-
      Paul Belmondo, George Peppard, Gwen Verdon, Geraldine
      Chaplin, Peter Fonda, Marlene Dietrich, and others.

3700 Sarris, Andrew. The American Cinema: Directors and Di-
      rections 1929-1968. New York: Dutton, 1968. 383 pp.
         Filmographies, evaluations, and analysis of 200 di-
      rectors.

3701 Cameron, Ian and Elisabeth. Dames. New York: Praeger,
      1969. 144 pp. (Also published as Broads.)
         Includes material on Lola Albright, Eve Arden, Lynn
      Bari, Joanna Barnes, Francesca Bellini, Joan Bennett,
      Mari Blanchard, Joan Blondell, Veda Ann Borg, Cyd
      Charisse, Barrie Chase, Maxine Cooper, Arlene Dahl,

Linda Darnell, Yvonne De Carlo, Dolores Dorn, Rhonda
Fleming, Dianne Foster, Anne Francis, Valerie French,
Zsa Zsa Gabor, Ava Gardner, Gloria Grahame, Coleen
Gray, Signe Hasso, Susan Hayward, Rita Hayworth, Eileen
Heckart, Charlene Holt, Mary Beth Hughes, Gayle Hunni-
cutt, Carolyn Jones, Jennifer Jones, Shirley Jones, Bea-
trice Kay, Nancy Kovack, Angela Lansbury, Joi Lansing,
Barbara Loden, Barbara Luna, Mercedes McCambridge,
Dorothy Malone, Jayne Mansfield, Marilyn Maxwell,
Dolores Michaels, Vera Miles, Joanna Moore, Rita
Moreno, Barbara Nichols, Kim Novak, Eleanor Parker,
Jean Peters, Dorothy Provine, Lee Remick, Ruth Roman,
Jane Russell, Ann Savage, Lizabeth Scott, Joan Shawlee,
Ann Sothern, Fay Spain, Barbara Stanwyck, Karen Steele,
Stella Stevens, Audrey Totter, Claire Trevor, Lana Turner,
Jo Van Fleet, Tuesday Weld, Jean Willes, Marie Windsor,
and Shelley Winters.

3702   Corneau, Ernest N.   The Hall of Fame of Western Film Stars.
       North Quincy, Mass.:   Christopher Publishing, 1969.
       307 pp.
       Material on over 150 actors.

3703   French, Philip.   The Movie Moguls: An Informal History of
       the Hollywood Tycoons.   Chicago: Regnery, 1969.   170 pp.
       Includes material on Harry Cohn, Cecil B. De Mille,
       William Fox, Samuel Goldwyn, William Randolph Hearst,
       Joseph P. Kennedy, Carl Laemmle, Jesse Lasky, Marcus
       Loew, Louis B. Mayer, Dore Schary, Joseph Schenck,
       David O. Selznick, Spyros Skouras, Irving Thalberg, the
       Warner Brothers, Darryl F. Zanuck, Adolph Zukor, and
       others.

3704   Hallowell, John.   The Truth Game.   New York: Simon and
       Schuster, 1969.   253 pp.
       Includes interview material on Rosemary Harris,
       Angela Lansbury, Melina Mercouri, Rita Hayworth, Raquel
       Welch, Doris Day, Kim Novak, Barbra Streisand, Paul
       Newman and Joanne Woodward, Rona Barrett, and Andy
       Warhol.

3705   Higham, Charles and Greenberg, Joel.   The Celluloid Muse:
       Hollywood Directors Speak.   Chicago: Regnery, 1969.
       268 pp.
       With material on Robert Aldrich, Curtis Bernhardt,
       George Cukor, John Frankenheimer, Alfred Hitchcock,
       Fritz Lang, Rouben Mamoulian, Lewis Milestone, Vincente
       Minnelli, Jean Negulesco, Irving Rapper, Mark Robson,
       Jacques Tourneur, King Vidor, and Billy Wilder.

3706   Kleiner, Dick.   The Ghosts Who Danced With Kim Novak
       and Other True Tales of the Supernatural.   New York:
       Ace, 1969.   160 pp.
       Includes material on Hollywood and Hollywood stars.

3707 Reed, Rex. Conversations in the Raw: Dialogues, Mono-
      logues, and Selected Short Subjects. New York: World,
      1969. 312 pp.
          Interview articles on Bette Davis, Ruth Gordon, Jane
      Wyman, Ingrid Bergman, Myrna Loy, Uta Hagen, Simone
      Signoret, Patricia Neal, Zoe Caldwell, Oskar Werner,
      Colleen Dewhurst, Irene Papas, Paul Newman and Joanne
      Woodward, Joseph Losey, Omar Sharif, Albert Finney,
      Jean Seberg, Mart Crowley, Leslie Caron, Burt Bacha-
      rach, George Sanders, James Earl Jones, China Machado,
      Oliver Reed, Jon Voight, Carol White, Leonard Whiting
      and Olivia Hussey, and Patty Duke.

3708 Phelps, Donald. Covering Ground: Essays for Now. New
      York: Croton, 1969. 290 pp.
          Essays on a variety of subjects; includes material on
      Anthony Mann, Allan Dwan, Spencer Tracy, and Robert
      Warshow.

3709 Shay, Donald. Conversations: Vol. I. Albuquerque, N.M.:
      Kaleidoscope, 1969. Unpaged.
          Interviews with Buster Crabbe, Peter Falk, Henry
      Fonda, Charlton Heston, Karl Malden, Gregory Peck,
      Edward G. Robinson, and Rod Steiger.

3710 Twomey, Alfred E. and McClure, Arthur F. The Versatiles:
      A Study of Supporting Character Actors and Actresses in
      the American Motion Picture, 1930-1955. South Brunswick,
      N.J.: A. S. Barnes, 1969. 304 pp.
          Includes material on over 500 character performers.

3711 Wilde, Larry. The Great Comedians Talk About Comedy.
      New York: Citadel, 1969. 382 pp.
          Interviews with Woody Allen, Milton Berle, Jack
      Benny, George Burns, Maurice Chevalier, Phyllis Diller,
      Jimmy Durante, Bob Hope, George Jessel, Jerry Lewis,
      Ed Wynn, and others.

3712 Zierold, Norman. The Moguls. New York: Coward-McCann,
      1969. 354 pp.
          Material on Adolph Zukor, Carl Laemmle, Sam Gold-
      wyn, Jesse Lasky, the Warner Brothers, William Fox,
      Harry Cohn, Louis B. Mayer, Irving Thalberg, David O.
      Selznick, Darryl F. Zanuck, Cecil B. DeMille, B. P.
      Schulberg, and Joseph and Nicholas Schenck.

3713 Bruno, Michael. Venus in Hollywood: The Continental En-
      chantress From Garbo to Loren. New York: Lyle Stuart,
      1970. 257 pp.
          Includes material on Greta Garbo, Pola Negri, Mar-
      lene Dietrich, Luise Rainer, Hedy Lamarr, Ingrid Berg-
      man, Vilma Banky, and many others.

3714 Cameron, Ian; Chabot, Jean; Ciment, Michel; Daudelin, Robert; Engel, Andi; Walker, Michael; and Wood, Robin. Second Wave. New York: Praeger, 1970. 144 pp.
Essays on Dusan Makavejev, Jerzy Skolimowski, Nagisa Oshima, Ruy Guerra, Glauber Rocha, Gilles Groulx, Jean-Pierre Lefebvre, and Jean-Marie Straub.

3715 Campbell, Russell (comp.) Practical Motion Picture Photography. New York: A. S. Barnes, 1970. 192 pp.
Includes interview material with professional cinematographers, including Paul Beeson, Johnnie Coquillon, Desmond Dickinson, A. A. Englander, Freddie Francis, Stephen Halliday, Peter Hennessy, Norman Johnson, Skeets Kelly, Walter Lassally, Jack Mills, Oswald Morris, C. M. Pennington-Richards, W. B. Pollard, Norman Roundell, and Wolfgang Suschitzky.

3716 Ephron, Nora. Wallflower at the Orgy. New York: Viking, 1970. 179 pp.
General essays; includes material on Jacqueline Susann, Mike Nichols, and CATCH-22.

3717 Frost, David. The Americans. New York: Stein and Day, 1970. 250 pp.
Includes interviews with Orson Welles, Tennessee Williams, Louis Armstrong, Helen Hayes, Jon Voight, Raquel Welch, Dennis Hopper, Peter Fonda, and other non-film personalities.

3718 Gelmis, Joseph. The Film Director as Superstar. Garden City, N.Y.: Doubleday, 1970. 316 pp.
Interviews with Jim McBridge, Brian De Palma, Robert Downey, Norman Mailer, Andy Warhol, John Cassavetes, Lindsay Anderson, Bernardo Bertolucci, Milos Forman, Roman Polanski, Roger Corman, Francis Ford Coppola, Arthur Penn, Richard Lester, Mike Nichols, and Stanley Kubrick.

3719 Griffith, Richard. The Movie Stars. Garden City, N.Y.: Doubleday, 1970. 498 pp.

3720 Kantor, Bernard R.; Blacker, Irwin R.; and Kramer, Anne (eds.) Directors at Work: Interviews with American Film-Makers. New York: Funk and Wagnalls, 1970. 442 pp.
Interviews with Richard Brooks, George Cukor, Norman Jewison, Elia Kazan, Stanley Kramer, Richard Lester, Jerry Lewis, Elliot Silverstein, Robert Wise, and William Wyler.

3721 Kleiner, Dick. ESP and the Stars. New York: Grosset and Dunlap, 1970. 209 pp.
The psychic experiences of over 50 stars.

3722 Lahue, Kalton C. and Gill, Samuel. Clown Princes and
      Court Jesters: Some Great Comics of the Silent Screen.
      South Brunswick, N.J.: A. S. Barnes, 1970. 406 pp.
      The careers of 50 lesser known comedians of the
      twenties.

3723 Lahue, Kalton C. Winners of the West: The Sagebrush
      Heroes of the Silent Screen. South Brunswick, N.J.:
      A. S. Barnes, 1970. 353 pp.
      Includes material on Art Acord, Broncho Billy Ander-
      son, Buzz Barton, Yakima Canutt, Harry Carey, Edmund
      Cobb, Bill Coby, Lester Cuneo, Bob Custer, William
      Desmond, William Duncan, Franklyn Farnum, Hoot Gib-
      son, Texas Guinan, Neal Hart, William S. Hart, Helen
      Holmes, Al Hoxie, Jack Hoxie, Fred Humes, Al Jennings,
      Buck Jones, J. Warren Kerrigan, Leo Maloney, Ken
      Maynard, Tim McCoy, Tom Mix, Pete Morrison, Jack
      Perrin, Buddy Roosevelt, Bob Steele, Roy Stewart, Fred
      Thomson, Tom Tyler, Wally Wales, Ted Wells, Guinn
      "Big Boy" Williams, Jay Wilsey, and others.

3724 Lee, Raymond. Not So Dumb: The Life and Times of the
      Animal Actors. South Brunswick, N.J.: A. S. Barnes,
      1970. 380 pp.

3725 Levin, Martin (comp.) Hollywood and the Great Fan Maga-
      zines. New York: Arbor, 1970. 224 pp.
      A collection of Hollywood fan magazine articles largely
      about the stars; includes much material from the thirties.

3726 Maltin, Leonard. Movie Comedy Teams. New York: New
      American Library, 1970. 352 pp.
      Includes chapters on Laurel and Hardy, Clark and
      McCullough, Wheeler and Woolsey, the Marx Brothers,
      Thelma Todd and ZaSu Pitts, Thelma Todd and Patsy
      Kelly, Burns and Allen, the Three Stooges, the Ritz
      Brothers, Olsen and Johnson, Abbott and Costello, Martin
      and Lewis; briefer material on Moran and Mack, Smith
      and Dale, the Wiere Brothers, Mitchell and Durant, Fibber
      McGee and Molly, Noonan and Marshall, and Rowan and
      Martin.

3727 Miller, Edwin (ed.) Seventeen Interviews: Film Stars and
      Superstars. New York: Macmillan, 1970. 384 pp.
      Interviews with over 50 stars; originally published in
      Seventeen magazine.

3728 Ronan, Margaret. Faces on Film: Newcomers and Oldtimers
      on the Big Screen. New York: Scholastic Book Service,
      1970. 144 pp.
      Material on over 50 stars.

3729 Shipman, David. The Great Movie Stars: The Golden Years.

New York: Crown, 1970. 576 pp.
Career information on over 150 pre-1945 stars.

3730 Talese, Gay. Fame and Obscurity: Portraits. New York:
      World, 1970. 357 pp.
          With material on Frank Sinatra, Josh Logan, and
      Peter O'Toole, as well as on other non-film personalities.

3731 Thomey, Tedd and Wilner, Norman. The Comedians. New
      York: Pyramid, 1970. 208 pp.
          Includes discussion of Red Skelton, Phyllis Diller,
      Oscar Levant, Phil Silvers, Art Carney, Jack Carter,
      Milton Berle, Laurel and Hardy, Joe E. Lewis, Martha
      Raye, and Jackie Gleason.

3732 Best, Marc. Those Endearing Young Charms: Child Per-
      formers of the Screen. South Brunswick, N.J.: A. S.
      Barnes, 1971. 278 pp.
          With material on Freddie Bartholomew, Joan Carroll,
      Ann Carter, Billy Chapin, Cora Sue Collins, Jackie
      Cooper, Donna Corcoran, Kevin "Moochie" Corcoran,
      Philippe DeLacy, Brandon DeWilde, Sandy Descher, Ted
      Donaldson (Pudge), Bobby Driscoll, Edith Fellows, Peggy
      Ann Garner, Ann Gillis, Mitzi Green, Darryl Hickman,
      David Holt, Tim Hovey, Sherry Jackson, Sybil Jason,
      Jackie "Butch" Jenkins, David Ladd, Billy Lee, Carolyn
      Lee, Davey Lee, Baby Leroy, Connie Marshall, Patty
      McCormack, Roddy McDowall, George "Spanky" McFarland,
      Peter Miles, Sharyn Moffett, Dickie Moore, Margaret
      O'Brien, Gigi Perreau, Tommy Rettig, Mickey Rooney,
      Baby Sandy, Jackie Searl, Johnny Sheffield "Boy", Dean
      Stockwell, Carl "Alfalfa" Switzer, Shirley Temple, Bobs
      Watson, Virginia Weidler, George "Foghorn" Winslow,
      Jane Withers, and Natalie Wood.

3733 Butler, Ivan. The Making of Feature Films: A Guide.
      Baltimore: Penguin, 1971. 191 pp.
          Includes interviews with Carl Foreman, Ivan Foxwell,
      Arthur P. Jacobs, Anthony Simmons, Richard Atten-
      borough, Roy Baird, Paul Dehn, Robert Bolt, Graham
      Greene, Ian La Frenais and Dick Clement, John Franken-
      heimer, Sidney Lumet, Jack Clayton, Lindsay Anderson,
      John Huston, George Sidney, Fred Zinnemann, Terence
      Young, Richard Lester, Roman Polanski, John Schlesinger,
      Otto Preminger, J. Lee Thompson, Jack Cardiff, Peter
      Hall, Tony Richardson, James Mason, Jill Bennett, Gregory
      Peck, Sandy Dennis, Alec Guinness, Douglas Slocombe,
      Walter Lassally, Oswald Morris, John Box, Ted
      Marshall, Elliot Scott, Julie Harris (the costume de-
      signer), Cliff Richard.

3734 Greene, Bob. We Didn't Have None of Them Fat Funky Angels
      on the Wall of Heartbreak Hotel and Other Reports From

America. Chicago: Regnery, 1971. 237 pp.
   General essays; includes chapters on Elvis Presley,
   Dustin Hoffman, and Frank Sinatra.

3735 Harman, Bob. Hollywood Panorama. New York: Dutton,
      1971. 95 pp.
      Primarily illustrations of actors and actresses.

3736 Henderson, Ron (ed.) The Image Maker. Richmond, Va.:
      John Knox, 1971. 96 pp.
      Includes interviews with Peter Fonda, Ingmar Berg-
      man, Miklos Jansco, Jaromil Jires, Abraham Polonsky,
      and Jean Renoir, as well as brief essays on film and
      image.

3737 Lahue, Kalton. Ladies in Distress. South Brunswick, N.J.:
      A. S. Barnes, 1971. 334 pp.
      With material on Mary Astor, Theda Bara, Beverly
      Bayne, Clara Bow, Louise Brooks, Grace Cunard, Marion
      Davies, Priscilla Dean, Dolores del Rio, Geraldine Far-
      rar, Pauline Frederick, Greta Garbo, Lillian Gish, Elaine
      Hammerstein, Juanita Hansen, Leatrice Joy, Alice Joyce,
      Barbara La Marr, Lila Lee, Bessie Love, Mae Marsh,
      Mary Miles Minter, Mae Murray, Nita Naldi, Jane Novak,
      Olga Petrova, Mary Pickford, Arline Pretty, Aileen
      Pringle, Allene Ray, Marin Sais, Norma Shearer, Gloria
      Swanson, Blanche Sweet, Norma Talmadge, Alice Terry,
      Florence Vidor, Fannie Ward, Kathlyn Williams, and Clara
      Kimball Young.

3738 Levin, G. Roy. Documentary Explorations: 15 Interviews
      With Film-Makers. Garden City, N.Y.: Doubleday, 1971.
      420 pp.
      Interviews with Basil Wright, Lindsay Anderson,
      Richard Cawston, Tony Garnett and Kenneth Loach,
      Georges Franju, Jean Rouch, Henri Storck, Willard Van
      Dyke, Richard Leacock, D. A. Pennebaker, Albert and
      David Maysles, Arthur Barron, Frederick Wiseman, Ed
      Pincus, Michael Shamberg, and David Cort; includes
      biography and filmography of those interviewed.

3739 McCrindle, Joseph F. (ed.) Behind the Scenes: Theatre and
      Film Interviews From the Transatlantic Review. New
      York: Holt, Rinehart and Winston, 1971. 341 pp.
      Includes material on Federico Fellini, John Schlesinger,
      Philip De Broca, Tony Richardson, Lindsay Anderson,
      Clive Donner, and Harold Pinter.

3740 Parish, James Robert. The Fox Girls. New Rochelle, N.Y.:
      Arlington, 1971. 722 pp.
      Biographical material on Betty Grable, Theda Bara,
      Marilyn Monroe, Carmen Miranda, Linda Darnell, Sonja
      Henie, Raquel Welch, Jeanne Crain, June Haver, Loretta

Young, Sheree North, Alice Faye, Gene Tierney, Shirley
Temple, Anne Baxter, and Janet Gaynor.

3741 Podeschi, John Battista. The Writer in Hollywood. Uni-
versity of Illinois, Urbana-Champaign: Ph.D., 1971.
272 pp.
With material on Robert Sherwood, Clifford Odets,
Preston Sturges, Tennessee Williams, Arthur Miller,
William Inge, Budd Schulberg, F. Scott Fitzgerald, Ray-
mond Chandler, Arch Oboler, Paddy Chayefsky, and Dudley
Nichols.

3742 Rosenberg, Bernard and Silverstein, Harry (comps.) The
Real Tinsel. New York: Macmillan, 1971. 436 pp.
Interview material with Hal Roach, Sr., Sol Lesser,
Joe Rock, Adolph Zukor, Walter Wanger, Albert Lewin,
Dore Schary, Arthur Mayer, Conrad Nagel, Blanche
Sweet, Mae Marsh, Edward Everett Horton, Rod La
Rocque, Dagmar Godowsky, Wini Shaw, Gil Perkins, Billy
Bletcher, William Haddock, Fritz Lang, Hal Mohr, Douglas
Shearer, Max Steiner, Anita Loos, and Arthur Knight.

3743 Rosenthal, Alan. The New Documentary in Action: A Case-
book in Film Making. Berkeley: University of California
Press, 1971. 287 pp.
Interviews with Allan King, Richard Leiterman, Arla
Saare, Frederick Wiseman, Albert Maysles, Charlotte
Zwerin, Jeremy Issacs, Morton Silverstein, Lawrence
Solomon, Jack Willis, Arthur Barron, Peter Watkins,
Jeremy Sandford, Fred Burnley, Don Alan Pennebaker,
Jack Kuney, Richard Crawston, Anthony Jay, George
Stoney, Alan Funt, and Norman McLaren.

3744 Sarris, Andrew. Hollywood Voices: Interviews with Film
Directors. (An abridged version of Interviews with Film
Directors.) Indianapolis: Bobbs-Merrill, 1971. 180 pp.
Interviews with George Cukor, Otto Preminger, John
Huston, Joseph Losey, Orson Welles, Nicholas Ray,
Abraham Polonsky, Rouben Mamoulian, and Preston
Sturges.

3745 Spears, Jack. Hollywood: The Golden Era. South Brunswick,
N.J.: A. S. Barnes, 1971. 440 pp.
With chapters on Max Linder, Norma Talmadge,
Charlie Chaplin's collaborators, Colleen Moore, Marshall
Neilan, Mary Pickford's directors, and Robert Florey.

3746 Town, Harold. Silent Stars, Sound Stars, Film Stars.
Toronto: McClelland and Stewart, 1971. 128 pp.
Primarily illustrations.

3747 Barnes, Ken with Britt, Stan and others. Sinatra and the
Great Song Stylists. London: Allan, 1972. 192 pp.

With material on Al Jolson, Bing Crosby, Louis
Armstrong, Ella Fitzgerald, Judy Garland, Peggy Lee,
Nat King Cole, Doris Day, Tony Bennett, and many
others.

3748 Carroll, David. The Matinee Idols. New York: Arbor,
1972. 160 pp.
Includes a section on film idols with material on
Francis X. Bushman, Lou Tellegen, Douglas Fairbanks,
William S. Hart, Tom Mix, Wallace Reid, Rudolph Valen-
tino, Ramon Novarro, John Gilbert, and John Barrymore.

3749 Corliss, Richard (ed.) The Hollywood Screenwriters. New
York: Avon, 1972. 328 pp.
Includes material on Anita Loos, Jules Furthman,
Ben Hecht, Preston Sturges, Dudley Nichols, Max Ophuls,
Ring Lardner, Jr., Borden Chase, Dalton Trumbo, James
Poe, Eleanor Perry, Penelope Gilliatt, and others.

3750 Froug, William. The Screenwriter Looks at the Screen-
writer. New York: Macmillan, 1972. 352 pp.
Interviews with Lewis Carlino, William Bowers,
Walter Newman, Jonathon Axelrod, Ring Lardner, Jr.,
I. A. L. Diamond, Buck Henry, David Giler, Nunnally
Johnson, Stirling Silliphant, Edward Anhalt, and Fay
Kanin.

3751 Harriman, Margaret. Take Them Up Tenderly: A Collection of Profiles. Freeport, N.Y.: Books for Libraries
Press, 1972. 266 pp.
Profiles, primarily reprinted from The New Yorker,
ca. 1944; with material on Clare Booth (Luce), Moss
Hart, Lillian Hellman, Helen Hayes, Cole Porter, Rodgers
and Hart, Leland Hayward, and Mary Pickford.

3752 Lahue, Kalton C. Gentlemen to the Rescue: The Heroes of
the Silent Screen. South Brunswick, N.J.: A. S. Barnes,
1972. 244 pp.
Biographical sketches of 30 silent screen heroes, including John Barrymore, Francis X. Bushman, John Gilbert, Jack Holt, Elmo Lincoln, Wallace Reid, and Henry
B. Walthall.

3753 McArthur, Colin. Underworld U.S.A. New York: Viking,
1972. 176 pp.
Includes material on Fritz Lang, John Huston, Jules
Dassin, Robert Siodmak, Elia Kazan, Nicholas Ray,
Samuel Fuller, Don Siegel, and Jean-Pierre Melville.

3754 McClure, Arthur F. and Jones, Ken D. Heroes, Heavies and
Sagebrush: A Pictorial History of the "B" Western Players.
South Brunswick, N.J.: A. S. Barnes, 1972. 350 pp.

3755 Maltin, Leonard. The Great Movie Shorts. New York:
      Crown, 1972. 236 pp.
         With material on Our Gang comedies, Laurel and
      Hardy, Charlie Chase, Harry Langdon, the Boy Friends,
      W. C. Fields, Thelma Todd, ZaSu Pitts, Patsy Kelly,
      Andy Clyde, Edgar Kennedy, Leon Errol, the Three
      Stooges, Pete Smith, Buster Keaton, Robert Benchley,
      Ralph Staub, John Nesbitt, George O'Hanlon, and others.

3756 Parish, James Robert. The Paramount Pretties. New
      Rochelle, N.Y.: Arlington, 1972. 587 pp.
         Includes material on Gloria Swanson, Clara Bow,
      Claudette Colbert, Carole Lombard, Marlene Dietrich,
      Miriam Hopkins, Sylvia Sidney, Mae West, Dorothy La-
      mour, Paulette Goddard, Veronica Lake, Diana Lynn,
      Betty Hutton, Joan Caulfield, Lizabeth Scott, and Shirley
      MacLaine.

3757 Samuels, Charles. Encountering Directors. New York:
      Putnam, 1972. 255 pp.
         Includes interviews with Michelangelo Antonioni,
      François Truffaut, Robert Bresson, Rene Clair, Ermanno
      Olmi, Federico Fellini, Vittorio De Sica, Carol Reed,
      Ingmar Bergman, Jean Renoir, and Alfred Hitchcock.

3758 Schulberg, Budd. The Four Seasons of Success. Garden
      City, N.Y.: Doubleday, 1972. 203 pp.
         Studies of Sinclair Lewis, William Saroyan, F. Scott
      Fitzgerald, Nathanael West, Thomas Heggen, and John
      Steinbeck; includes some material on film.

3759 Shales, Tom; Brownlow, Kevin; and others. The American
      Film Heritage: Impressions From the American Film
      Institute. Edited by Kathleen Karr. Washington, D.C.:
      Acropolis, 1972. 184 pp.
         With material on Michael Curtiz, Thomas Ince, William
      Beaudine, Frank Capra, Mary Pickford, Hal Roach, Val
      Lewton, W. C. Fields, Frank Borzage, and others.

3760 Silent Heroes Speak Today: What Yesterday's Stars of the
      Silver Screen Might Say If They Were Here Today.
      Kansas City, Mo.: Hallmark, 1972. 26 pp.

3761 Trent, Paul. The Image Makers: 60 Years of Hollywood
      Glamour. Designed by Richard Lawton. New York:
      McGraw-Hill, 1972. 327 pp.
         Almost exclusively photographs.

3762 Baker, Fred with Firestone, Ross. Movie People: At Work
      in the Business of Film. New York: Lancer, 1973.
      242 pp.
         Interviews with Roger Lewis, David Picker, Sidney
      Lumet, Francis Ford Coppola, Terry Southern, James

Salter, Rod Steiger, Aram Avakian, Quincy Jones, Walter
Reade, Jr., and Andrew Sarris.

3763 Bogdanovich, Peter. Pieces of Time: Peter Bogdanovich on
the Movies. New York: Arbor, 1973. 269 pp. Also
published as Picture Shows: Peter Bogdanovich on the
Movies.
With material on Cary Grant, Humphrey Bogart,
James Cagney, John Wayne, Marlene Dietrich, John Ford,
Leo McCarey, Frank Capra, David O. Selznick, Preston
Sturges, Ernst Lubitsch, Adolph Zukor, and others.

3764 Fleming, Alice. The Moviemakers. New York: St. Martin's
Press, 1973. 184 pp.
With material on Edwin S. Porter, D. W. Griffith,
Mack Sennett, Cecil B. De Mille, Robert Flaherty, Ernst
Lubitsch, Frank Capra, John Ford, Walt Disney, Alfred
Hitchcock, and Stanley Kubrick.

3765 Hudson, Richard M. Sixty Years of Vamps and Camps:
Visual Nostalgia of the Silver Screen. New York: Drake,
1973. Unpaged.
Primarily captioned photographs of performers in
various typed roles.

3766 Lahue, Kalton C. Riders of the Range: The Sagebrush
Heroes of the Sound Screen. South Brunswick, N.J.:
A. S. Barnes, 1973. 259 pp.
With chapters on Bob Allen, Rex Allen, Gene Autry,
Bob Baker, Donald Barry, William Boyd, Johnny Mack
Brown, Sunset Carson, Buster Crabbe, William Elliott,
Kirby Grant, Monte Hale, Russell Hayden, Tim Holt,
George Houston, Tom Keene, Allan Lane, Lash LaRue,
George O'Brien, Jack Randall, Tex Ritter, Roy Rogers,
Reb Russell, Fred Scott, Randolph Scott, Charles Starrett,
Jimmy Wakely, and Whip Wilson.

3767 Landay, Eileen. Black Film Stars. New York: Drake, 1973.
194 pp.
With material on Bert Williams, Stepin Fetchit, Oscar
Micheaux, Paul Robeson, Bill Robinson, Louise Beavers,
Eddie "Rochester" Anderson, Hattie McDaniel, Butterfly
McQueen, Lena Horne, Ethel Waters, Sidney Poitier,
Dorothy Dandridge, Harry Belafonte, Sammy Davis, Diahann
Carroll, Eartha Kitt, Ossie Davis, Ruby Dee, James Earl
Jones, Godfrey Cambridge, Diana Sands, Jim Brown, Ray-
mond St. Jacques, Calvin Lockhart, Gordon Parks, Melvin
Van Peebles, Richard Roundtree, Ron O'Neal, Diana Ross,
and Cicely Tyson.

3768 McCreadie, Marsha (ed.) The American Movie Goddess.
New York: Wiley, 1973. 92 pp.

3769 Maltin, Leonard (ed.) The Real Stars: Articles and Interviews on Hollywood's Great Character Actors. New York: Curtis, 1973. 320 pp.

Includes material on Sara Allgood, Edgar Buchanan, Joyce Compton, Hans Conried, Bess Flowers, Gladys George, Billy Gilbert, Dorothy Granger, Rex Ingram, Rosalind Ivan, Patsy Kelly, Una Merkel, Mabel Paige, Gale Sondergaard, Hope Summers, Grady Sutton, and Blanche Yurka.

3770 Maltin, Leonard (ed.) The Real Stars #2. New York: Curtis, 1973. 287 pp.

With material on Iris Adrian, Lionel Atwill, Roy Barcroft, Cecil Cunningham, Cass Daley, Virginia Field, Sydney Greenstreet, Keye Luke, Barnard Nedell, Virginia O'Brien, Edna May Oliver, Maria Ouspenskaya, Elmira Sessions, Raymond Walburn, and others.

3771 Parish, James Robert and Bowers, Ronald L. The MGM Stock Company: The Golden Era. New Rochelle, N.Y.: Arlington, 1973. 862 pp.

Material on 147 MGM actors and actresses, including June Allyson, Fred Astaire, Fay Bainter, Lionel Barrymore, Joan Crawford, Nelson Eddy, Greta Garbo, Judy Garland, Greer Garson, Van Johnson, Gene Kelly, Hedy Lamarr, Angela Lansbury, Frank Morgan, Margaret O'Brien, William Powell, Mickey Rooney, Norma Shearer, James Stewart, Spencer Tracy, Lana Turner, and Robert Young.

3772 Phillips, Gene D. The Movie Makers: Artists in an Industry. Chicago: Nelson-Hall, 1973. 249 pp.

Essays on James Wong Howe, Charlie Chaplin, Howard Hawks, George Cukor, George Stevens, Fred Zinnemann, Stanley Kubrick, Carol Reed, David Lean, Joseph Losey, Bryan Forbes, John Schlesinger, and Ken Russell.

3773 Schnitzer, Luda; Schnitzer, Jean; and Martin, Marcel (eds.) Cinema in Revolution: The Heroic Era of the Soviet Film. Translated and with additional material by David Robinson. New York: Hill and Wang, 1973. 208 pp.

Autobiographical essays by Sergei Yutkevitch, Sergei Eisenstein, Grigori Alexandrov, Lev Kuleshov, Dziga Vertov, Grigori Kozintsev, Sergei Gerassimov, Vsevolod Pudovkin, Anatoli Golovnya, Alexander Dovzhenko, Yevgeni Gabrilovitch, and Mikhail Romm.

3774 Shipman, David. The Great Movie Stars: The International Years. New York: St. Martin's, 1973. 568 pp.

Career information on over 150 post-1945 stars.

3775 Slide, Anthony. The Griffith Actresses. South Brunswick, N.J.: A. S. Barnes, 1973. 181 pp.

With material on Lillian and Dorothy Gish, Blanche
Sweet, Carol Dempster, Mary Pickford, Mae Marsh,
Miriam Cooper, Clarine Seymour, and others.

3776 Thomas, Bob (ed.) Directors in Action: Selections From
Action, the Official Magazine of the Director's Guild of
America. Indianapolis: Bobbs-Merrill, 1973. 283 pp.
Includes interviews of or material on Stanley Kubrick,
Orson Welles, Alfred Hitchcock, Roger Corman, Don
Siegel, John Frankenheimer, John Schlesinger, Robert
Altman, George Stevens, Richard Lester, Gordon Parks,
Mel Brooks, John Cassavetes, Paul Newman, Jack Lem-
mon, Carl Reiner, Paul Henreid, Sam Peckinpah, Henry
Hathaway, Burt Kennedy, John Ford, William Friedkin,
Paul Williams, Bill Norton, James Bridges, Cy Howard,
Hal Ashby, Lawrence Turman, Gilbert Cates, Dick
Richards, Michael Ritchie, Richard Colla, and others.

3777 Thomas, Tony. Cads and Cavaliers: The Gentlemen Adven-
turers of the Movies. South Brunswick, N.J.: A. S.
Barnes, 1973. 242 pp.
With material on Douglas Fairbanks, Sr., Douglas
Fairbanks, Jr., John Barrymore, George Sanders, Vincent
Price, David Niven, Basil Rathbone, and Errol Flynn.

3778 Thomas, Tony. Music for the Movies. South Brunswick,
N.J.: A. S. Barnes, 1973. 270 pp.
Material on the careers of Hollywood film composers,
including George Antheil, Elmer Bernstein, Aaron Cop-
land, Hugo Friedhofer, Ernest Gold, Jerry Goldsmith,
John Green, Bernard Herrmann, Bronislau Kaper, Erich
Wolfgang Korngold, Henry Mancini, Alfred Newman, Alex
North, Andre Previn, David Raksin, Leonard Rosenman,
Laurence Rosenthal, Miklos Rozsa, Lalo Schifrin, Max
Steiner, Virgil Thomson, Dimitri Tiomkin, Franz Waxman,
and Victor Young.

3779 Zierold, Norman. Sex Goddesses of the Silent Screen. Chi-
cago: Regnery, 1973. 207 pp.
With material on Theda Bara, Barbara Lamarr, Pola
Negri, Mae Murray, Clara Bow, and others.

3780 Agan, Patrick. Whatever Happened To--. New York: Ace,
1974. 201 pp.
Biographical updates of past stars.

3781 Barris, Alex. Hollywood's Other Men. South Brunswick,
N.J.: A. S. Barnes, 1974. 223 pp.
Survey of actors who played the loser in the proverbial
love triangle, including Ralph Bellamy, Gig Young, Patric
Knowles, Tony Randall, and others.

3782 Baxter, John. Stunt: The Story of the Great Movie Stunt Men.

Garden City, N.Y.: Doubleday, 1974. 320 pp.
With material on the work of Tom Mix, Douglas
Fairbanks, Yakima Canutt, B. Reeves Eason, Carey
Loftin, and others.

3783 Castell, David. Superstars of the '70s. London: Barnden
Castell Williams, 1974. 96 pp.

3784 Corliss, Richard. Talking Pictures: Screenwriters in the
American Cinema. Woodstock, N.Y.: Overlook, 1974.
398 pp.
Includes material on Ben Hecht, Preston Sturges,
Norman Krasna, Frank Tashlin, George Axelrod, Peter
Stone, Howard Koch, Bordon Chase, Abraham Polonsky,
Billy Wilder, Samuel Raphelson, Nunnally Johnson,
Ernest Lehman, Betty Comden, Garson Kanin and Ruth
Gordon, Robert Riskin, Dudley Nichols, Joseph L. Man-
kiewicz, Dalton Trumbo, Jules Furthman, Sidney Buch-
man, Casey Robinson, Morrie Ryskind, Edwin Justus
Mayer, Delmer Daves, Charles Lederer, Charles Brac-
kett, Frank S. Nugent, Ring Lardner, Jr., Terry Southern,
Erich Segal, Buck Henry, Jules Feiffer, and David New-
man and Robert Benton.

3785 Curtis, Anthony (ed.) The Rise and Fall of the Matinee
Idol: Past Deities of Stage and Screen, Their Roles,
Their Magic, and Their Worshippers. New York: St.
Martin's, 1974. 215 pp.

3786 Hochman, Stanley (comp.) A Library of Film Criticism:
American Film Directors. New York: Ungar, 1974.
590 pp.
With film criticism on Frank Borzage, Richard
Brooks, Clarence Brown, Tod Browning, Frank Capra,
John Cassavetes, Charlie Chaplin, James Cruze, George
Cukor, Michael Curtiz, Cecil B. De Mille, William Die-
terle, Allan Dwan, Robert Flaherty, Victor Fleming,
John Ford, John Frankenheimer, D. W. Griffith, Henry
Hathaway, Howard Hawks, Alfred Hitchcock, John Huston,
Thomas Ince, Rex Ingram, Elia Kazan, Buster Keaton,
Henry King, Stanley Kramer, Stanley Kubrick, Gregory
La Cava, Fritz Lang, Mervyn LeRoy, Anatole Litvak,
Frank Lloyd, Pare Lorentz, Ernst Lubitsch, Sidney
Lumet, Leo McCarey, Rouben Mamoulian, Joseph L.
Mankiewicz, Lewis Milestone, Vincente Minnelli, F. W.
Murnau, Mike Nichols, Arthur Penn, Edwin S. Porter,
Otto Preminger, Robert Rossen, Victor Seastrom, Mack
Sennett, Josef von Sternberg, George Stevens, Eric von
Stroheim, John Sturges, Preston Sturges, Maurice Tour-
neur, W. S. Van Dyke, King Vidor, Raoul Walsh, Andy
Warhol, Orson Welles, William Wellman, Billy Wilder,
William Wyler, and Fred Zinnemann.

3787 Kobal, John. 50 Super Stars. New York: Bounty, 1974.
      160 pp.
      Biographies, filmographies, and photographs of over
      50 major Hollywood stars.

3788 Lewis, Grover. Academy All the Way. San Francisco:
      Straight Arrow, distributed by Simon and Schuster, 1974.
      348 pp.
      Material on THE LAST PICTURE SHOW, Robert Red-
      ford, Barbra Streisand, Stacy Keach, John Huston, PLAY
      IT AS IT LAYS, John Cassavetes, Sam Peckinpah, Lee
      Marvin, Paul Newman, Robert Mitchum, and others.

3789 Liehm, Antonin J. Closely Watched Films: The Czechoslovak
      Experience. White Plains, N.Y.: International Arts and
      Sciences Press, 1974. 485 pp.
      With material on Martin Fric, Otakar Vavra, Alfred
      Radok, Jiri Weiss, Jiri Krejcik, Miroslav Hubacek,
      Zbynek Brynych, Ladislav Helge, Vojtech Jasny, Karel
      Kachyna, Vaclav Krska, Oldrich Danek, Frantisek Vlacil,
      Stanislav Barabas, Peter Solan, Stefan Uher, Jaromil
      Jires, Milos Forman, Vera Chytilova, Jaroslav Kucera,
      Evald Schorm, Ester Krumbachova, Jan Nemec, Jiri
      Menzel, Pavel Juracek, Jan Schmidt, Hynek Bocan, Jaro-
      slav Papousek, Juraj Jakubisko, Elo Havetta, Ivan Passer,
      and Jan Kadar.

3790 McClure, Arthur F. and Jones, Ken D. Star Quality: Screen
      Actors From the Golden Age of Films. South Brunswick,
      N.J.: A. S. Barnes, 1974. 285 pp.
      Essay on Errol Flynn and biographical sketches on
      Don Ameche, Evelyn Ankers, William Bendix, Charles
      Bickford, Joan Blondell, Johnny Mack Brown, Bruce
      Cabot, Judy Canova, John Carroll, Jack Carson, Tom
      Conway, Buster Crabbe, Alan Curtis, Joan Davis, Frances
      Dee, Brian Donlevy, Paul Douglas, James Dunn, Dan
      Duryea, Ann Dvorak, Stu Erwin, Frances Farmer, Glenda
      Farrell, Dick Foran, Preston Foster, Kay Francis, Van
      Heflin, Paul Henreid, Irene Hervey, John Hodiak, Judy
      Holliday, Rochelle Hudson, Rita Johnson, Nancy Kelly,
      Paul Kelly, Patric Knowles, Carole Landis, Priscilla
      Lane, Anita Louise, Frank Lovejoy, Edmund Lowe, Diana
      Lynn, Herbert Marshall, Marilyn Maxwell, Joel McCrea,
      Marie McDonald, Ann Miller, Carmen Miranda, Maria
      Montez, Dennis Morgan, Chester Morris, Wayne Morris,
      Jean Muir, Tom Neal, Lloyd Nolan, Jack Oakie, Dennis
      O'Keefe, Eleanor Parker, Jean Parker, Kane Richmond,
      Cesar Romero, Gail Russell, Sabu, Lizabeth Scott,
      Zachary Scott, Ann Sheridan, Milburn Stone, Lyle Talbot,
      Lee Tracy, Claire Trevor, Sonny Tufts, Lupe Velez,
      Helen Walker, Robert Walker, Warren William, Grant
      Withers, and Fay Wray; plus portrait photographs of many
      more stars.

3791 Parish, James Robert. Hollywood's Great Love Teams. New
Rochelle, N.Y.: Arlington, 1974. 828 pp.
With material on Ronald Colman and Vilma Banky,
John Gilbert and Greta Garbo, Charles Farrell and Janet
Gaynor, Clark Gable and Joan Crawford, Clark Gable
and Jean Harlow, Dick Powell and Ruby Keeler, George
Brent and Kay Francis, William Powell and Myrna Loy,
Leslie Howard and Bette Davis, Fred MacMurray and
Claudette Colbert, Nelson Eddy and Jeanette MacDonald,
Errol Flynn and Olivia de Havilland, James Stewart and
Margaret Sullavan, Tyrone Power and Loretta Young,
Mickey Rooney and Judy Garland, James Cagney and Ann
Sheridan, Walter Pidgeon and Greer Garson, Clark Gable
and Lana Turner, Spencer Tracy and Katharine Hepburn,
Alan Ladd and Veronica Lake, Jon Hall and Maria Montez,
Van Johnson and June Allyson, Humphrey Bogart and
Lauren Bacall, Tony Curtis and Janet Leigh, David Niven
and Deborah Kerr, Paul Newman and Joanne Woodward,
Rock Hudson and Doris Day, and Richard Burton and
Elizabeth Taylor.

3792 Parish, James Robert. The RKO Gals. New Rochelle, N.Y.:
Arlington, 1974. 896 pp.
Chapters on Ann Hardy, Constance Bennett, Irene
Dunne, Ginger Rogers, Katharine Hepburn, Ann Shirley,
Lucille Ball, Joan Fontaine, Wendy Barrie, Lupe Velez,
Maureen O'Hara, Jane Russell, Barbara Hale, and Jane
Greer; also material on Pandro S. Berman, Merian C. Cooper,
Ned E. Depinet, William Dozier, Howard Hughes, Charles W.
Koerner, William Lebaron, Kenneth Macgowan, Nathaniel
Peter Rathvon, Sid Rogell, Charles R. Rogers, George I.
Schaefer, Dore Schary, David O. Selznick, and others.

3793 Reed, Rex. People Are Crazy Here. New York: Delacorte,
1974. 306 pp.
With material on Tennessee Williams, Marcello Mas-
troianni, Sally Kellerman, Grace Slick, Merle Oberon,
Kay Thompson, Bette Midler, Carrie Snodgress, Sylvia
Miles, Joan Hackett, Cliff Robertson, Joel Grey, Troy
Donahue, Laurence Olivier, Michael Caine, George C.
Scott, Elia Kazan, Richard Chamberlain, Alice Faye,
Dorothy Malone, Doris Day, Carroll Baker, Tuesday
Weld, Gloria Grahame, Joanne Woodward, Maggie Smith,
Glenda Jackson, Liv Ullmann, Edward Albert, Jacqueline
Susann, Ken Russell, Alfred Hitchcock, Alice Cooper,
Roger Moore, Peter Bogdanovich, Cybill Shepherd, Ann-
Margret, Jack Lemmon, Jack Nicholson, and Adolph Zukor.

3794 Springer, John and Hamilton, Jack. They Had Faces Then:
Super Stars, Stars, and Starlets of the 1930's. Secaucus,
N.J.: Citadel, 1974. 342 pp.
Brief analysis, biography, and photographs of over
400 female stars.

3795 Steen, Mike. Hollywood Speaks: An Oral History. New
York: Putnam, 1974. 379 pp.
Interviews with members of the various Hollywood
professions, including Henry Fonda, Rosalind Russell,
Agnes Moorehead, William Wellman, James Wong Howe,
Edith Head, Busby Berkeley, Hal Roach, Sr., David
Cannon, Pandro S. Berman, James Pratt, Hank Moonjean,
Randell Henderson, Preston Ames, Arthur Krams, Perc
Westmore, Nellie Manley, Arnold Gillespie, Fred Smith,
Bernard Freericks, Catalina Lawrence, and Ruth Burch.

3796 Abbe, James (photographs) and Early, Mary Dawn (text).
Stars of the Twenties: Observed by James Abbe. New
York: Viking, 1975. 105 pp.
Primarily photographic portraits by Abbe.

3797 Agan, Patrick. Is That Who I Think It Is? New York: Ace,
1975. 201 pp.

3798 Barris, Alex. Hollywood's Other Women. South Brunswick,
N.J.: A. S. Barnes, 1975. 212 pp.
Survey of actresses who played "second fiddle" types,
including the classic bitch, mothers, buddies, sirens,
maiden aunts, maids, and so forth; a separate chapter on
Bette Davis.

3799 Bazelon, Irwin. Knowing the Score: Notes on Film Music.
New York: Van Nostrand, 1975. 352 pp.
Includes interviews with Elmer Bernstein, Leonard
Rosenman, Jerry Goldsmith, John Williams, Richard
Rodney Bennett, Alex North, Lalo Schifrin, Bernard
Herrmann, David Raksin, Bernardo Segall, Laurence
Rosenthal, Johnny Mandel, Paul Glass, John Barry, and
Gail Kubik.

3800 Best, Marc. Their Hearts Were Young and Gay. South
Brunswick, N.J.: A. S. Barnes, 1975. 269 pp.
Material on 40 child stars, including Scotty Beckett,
Bobby Blake, Bobby Breen, Jackie Coogan, Frankie
Darro, Patty Duke, Bonita Granville, Darla Hood, Claude
Jarman, Jr., Gloria Jean, Terry Kilburn, the Mauch
Twins, Donald O'Connor, Juanita Quigley, Larry Simms,
Elizabeth Taylor, Ann Todd, and others.

3801 Bowers, Ronald L. The Selznick Players. South Brunswick,
N.J.: A. S. Barnes, c. 1975, 1976. 255 pp.
Includes substantial sections on Ingrid Bergman,
Vivien Leigh, Joan Fontaine, Jennifer Jones, Dorothy
McGuire, Joseph Cotten, Gregory Peck, and Shirley
Temple, as well as material on Rory Calhoun, Rhonda
Fleming, Kim Hunter, Louis Jourdan, Guy Madison,
Hildegarde Knef, Joan Tetzel, and Alida Valli.

3802 Chase, Donald (for the American Film Institute). Filmmaking:
The Collaborative Art. Boston: Little, Brown, 1975.
314 pp.

Interviews with Jack Benny, Lynn Carlin, Leslie Caron,
John Cassavetes, Peter Falk, Nina Foch, Henry Fonda,
Charlton Heston, Robert Stephens, Ingrid Thulin, Jean-
Louis Trintignant, Liv Ullmann, Jon Voight, Conrad Hall,
Winton Hoch, James Wong Howe, Laszlo Kovacs, Hal
Mohr, Joseph Ruttenberg, John Seitz, Haskell Wexler,
Gordon Willis, Elmer Bernstein, Jerry Goldsmith, John
Green, Alex North, Edith Head, Theodora Van Runkle,
Hal Ashby, David Bretherton, Frank Keller, Daniel Man-
dell, Frederic Steinkamp, Peter Bart, Pandro S. Berman,
Bob Christiansen and Rick Rosenberg, Merian C. Cooper,
Roger Corman, Albert S. Ruddy, Gene Allen, Harry
Horner, Polly Platt, Leigh Brackett, Ray Bradbury, Lonne
Elder III, Howard Estabrook, Nunnally Johnson, W. D.
Richter, Alvin Sargent, Budd Schulberg, Leonard Spigel-
gass, Donald Ogden Stewart, Hannah Scheel, and Karen
Wookey.

3803 Cowie, Peter (ed.) 50 Major Film-Makers. South Brunswick,
N.J.: A. S. Barnes, 1975. 287 pp.

Material on Lindsay Anderson, Michelangelo Antonioni,
Ingmar Bergman, Bernardo Bertolucci, Sergey Bondarchuk,
Robert Bresson, Richard Brooks, Luis Buñuel, Claude
Chabrol, Jacques Demy, Jörn Donner, Mark Donskoy,
Federico Fellini, Milos Forman, Georges Franju, John
Frankenheimer, Bert Haanstra, Alfred Hitchcock, Kon
Ichikawa, Joris Ivens, Miklos Jancso, Elia Kazan,
Grigori Kozintsev, Stanley Kubrick, Akira Kurosawa,
Joseph Losey, Sidney Lumet, Dusan Makavejev, Louis
Malle, Jean-Pierre Melville, Jan Nemec, Nagisa Oshima,
Pier Paolo Pasolini, Arthur Penn, Roman Polanski, Sat-
yajit Ray, Alain Resnais, Eric Rohmer, Francesco Rosi,
John Schlesinger, Evald Schorm, Jerzy Skolimowski,
Jacques Tati, Leopoldo Torre Nilsson, Jan Troell,
François Truffaut, Luchino Visconti, Andrzej Wajda,
Orson Welles, Bo Widerberg.

3804 Franklin, Lindy. Hollywood Star Reporter. New York:
Popular Library, 1975. 158 pp.
Interviews with Hollywood personalities.

3805 Fry, William F. and Allen, Melanie. Make 'em Laugh: Life
Studies of Comedy Writers. Palo Alto, Cal.: Science and
Behavior Books, 1975. 202 pp.
With material on Norman Lear, Ruth Flippen, Herbie
Baker, and others.

3806 Grebanier, Bernard D. Then Came Each Actor: Shakespearean Actors, Great and Otherwise, Including Players

and Princes, Rogues, Vagabonds and Actors Motley, From
Will Kempe to Olivier and Gielgud and After. New York:
McKay, 1975. 626 pp.

3807 Guiles, Fred Lawrence. Hanging On In Paradise. New York:
McGraw-Hill, 1975. 412 pp.
An account of writers in Hollywood; with material on
F. Scott Fitzgerald, Ben Hecht, John Howard Lawson,
Charles Lederer, Charles MacArthur, Dorothy Parker,
Robert Sherwood, Donald Ogden Stewart, Preston Sturges,
Lillian Hellman, Christopher Isherwood, Aldous Huxley,
and others.

3808 Hofsess, John. Inner Views: Ten Canadian Film-Makers.
Toronto, New York: McGraw-Hill Ryerson, 1975. 171 pp.
With material on Claude Jutra, Allan King, Donald
Shebib, Jack Darcus, William Fruet, Graeme Ferguson,
Frank Vitale, Paul Almond, Denys Arcand, and Pierre
Berton.

3809 Hyland, Wende and Haynes, Roberta. How to Make It in
Hollywood. Chicago: Nelson-Hall, 1975. 237 pp.
Includes interviews with Jack Lemmon, Walter Mat-
thau, Albert S. Ruddy, Daniel Mann, Renee Valente,
Meyer Mishkin, Milton Katselas, and others.

3810 Manvell, Roger. Love Goddesses of the Movies. London:
Hamlyn, 1975. 176 pp.
Material on Mary Pickford, Theda Bara, Clara Bow,
Gloria Swanson, Greta Garbo, Marlene Dietrich, Jean
Harlow, Joan Crawford, Arletty, Vivien Leigh, Betty
Grable, Rita Hayworth, Marilyn Monroe, Ingrid Bergman,
Brigitte Bardot, Gina Lollobrigida, Sophia Loren, Eliza-
beth Taylor, and Jeanne Moreau.

3811 Mellen, Joan. Voices From the Japanese Cinema. New
York: Liveright, 1975. 295 pp.
Interviews with Daisuke Ito, Akira Kurosawa, Mme.
Kashiko Kawakita, Kaneto Shindo, Tadashi Imai, Kon
Ichikawa, Masaki Kobayashi, Setsu Asakura, Hiroshi
Teshigahara, Susumu Hani, Sachiko Hidari, Toichiro
Narushima, Masahiro Shinoda, Nagisa Oshima, and Shuji
Terayama.

3812 McCarthy, Todd and Flynn, Charles (eds.) Kings of the Bs:
Working Within the Hollywood System; An Anthology of
Film History and Criticism. New York: Dutton, 1975.
561 pp.
With material on Roger Corman, Sam Katzman, Joseph
H. Lewis, Val Lewton, Russ Meyer, Joe Solomon, Edgar
G. Ulmer, Samuel Z. Arkoff, Steve Broidy, William Castle,
Joseph Kane, Phil Karlson, Herschell Gordon Lewis,
Arthur Lubin, Albert Zugsmith, and others.

3813 Mercer, Jane. Great Lovers of the Movies. London, New
      York: Hamlyn, 1975. 176 pp.
          Biographical and filmographic information on Douglas
      Fairbanks, Rudolph Valentino, Ramon Novarro, John
      Barrymore, John Gilbert, Ronald Colman, Leslie Howard,
      Gary Cooper, Clark Gable, Cary Grant, Charles Boyer,
      Errol Flynn, Humphrey Bogart, Robert Taylor, Alan Ladd,
      Tyrone Power, Robert Mitchum, Rock Hudson, Marlon
      Brando, Paul Newman, Steve McQueen, Robert Redford
      and Clint Eastwood.

3814 Parish, James Robert and Stanke, Don E. The Glamour
      Girls. New Rochelle, N.Y.: Arlington, 1975. 752 pp.
          With material on nine stars, including Joan Bennett,
      Yvonne De Carlo, Rita Hayworth, Audrey Hepburn, Maria
      Montez, Kim Novak, and Merle Oberon.

3815 Parish, James Robert. Great Movie Heroes. New York:
      Harper and Row, 1975. 115 pp.
          With material on Humphrey Bogart, Marlon Brando,
      Gary Cooper, James Dean, Clint Eastwood, Errol Flynn,
      Henry Fonda, Clark Gable, Elliott Gould, Cary Grant,
      Dustin Hoffman, Alan Ladd, Steve McQueen, Paul New-
      man, Sidney Poitier, Tyrone Power, Robert Redford,
      Burt Reynolds, George Segal, Jimmy Stewart, Spencer
      Tracy, and John Wayne.

3816 Schickel, Richard. The Men Who Made the Movies: Inter-
      views with Frank Capra, George Cukor, Howard Hawks,
      Alfred Hitchcock, Vincente Minnelli, King Vidor, Raoul
      Walsh, and William A. Wellman. New York: Atheneum,
      1975. 308 pp.

3817 Smith, Sharon. Women Who Make Movies. New York: Hop-
      kinson and Blake, 1975. 307 pp.

3818 Sussex, Elizabeth. The Rise and Fall of British Documentary:
      The Story of the Film Movement Founded by John Grierson.
      Berkeley: University of California Press, 1975. 219 pp.
          Interviews with John Grierson, Basil Wright, John
      Taylor, Paul Rotha, Edgar Anstey, Arthur Elton, Stuart
      Legg, Harry Watt, Alberto Cavalcanti, Pat Jackson, W. H.
      Auden, and Ian Dalrymple.

3819 Taylor, John Russell. Directors and Directions: Cinema for
      the Seventies. New York: Hill and Wang, 1975. 327 pp.
          Essays on Claude Chabrol, Pier Paolo Pasolini, Lind-
      say Anderson, Stanley Kubrick, Andy Warhol/Paul Mor-
      rissey, Satyajit Ray, Miklos Jancso, and Dusan Makavejev.

3820 Wagner, Walter. You Must Remember This. New York:
      Putnam, 1975. 320 pp.

An oral history of Hollywood: interviews with Mary
Pickford, Walter Field, Minita Durfee Arbuckle, Eddie
Le Veque, John Ford, Gaylord Carter, Claire Windsor,
George Jessel, Douglas Fairbanks, Jr., Frances Goldwyn,
Jimmy Fidler, Richard Arlen, Darla Hood, Jesse Lasky,
Jr., Lew Ayres, Ken Murray, Ann Rutherford, Sue Carol,
Edith Head, Martin Rackin, Ward Kimball, Stanley Kramer,
Jack Lemmon, and Mike Medavoy.

3821 Parish, James Robert and Leonard, William T. Hollywood
      Players: The Thirties. New Rochelle, N.Y.: Arlington,
      1976. 576 pp.
         With material on Eddie Albert, Hardie Albright,
      Robert Armstrong, Lynn Bari, Binnie Barnes, John Beal,
      Louise Beavers, Ralph Bellamy, Charles Bickford, John
      Boles, Mary Brian, Bruce Cabot, Helen Chandler, Mae
      Clark, Donald Cook, Larry "Buster" Crabbe, Richard
      Cromwell, Constance Cummings, Frances Dee, Brian Don-
      levy, James Dunn, Ann Dvorak, Sally Eilers, Frances
      Farmer, Glenda Farrell, Stepin Fetchit, Preston Foster,
      Richard "Skeets" Gallagher, William Gargan, Wynne Gib-
      son, Bonita Granville, Mitzi Green, Richard Greene,
      Phillips Holmes, Ian Hunter, Josephine Hutchinson, Kay
      Johnson, Allan Jones, Victor Jory, Arline Judge, Paul
      Kelly, Elissa Landi, Francis Lederer, Eric Linden,
      Margaret Lindsay, Anita Louise, Paul Lukas, David
      Manners, Burgess Meredith, Douglass Montgomery,
      Dickie Moore, Chester Morris, Wayne Morris, Lloyd
      Nolan, Jack Oakie, Gail Patrick, Roger Pryor, Gene
      Raymond, Gilbert Roland, Cesar Romero, Simone Simon,
      Penny Singleton, Anna Sten, Gloria Stuart, Genevieve To-
      bin, Lee Tracy, Helen Twelvetrees, Jane Withers, Anna
      May Wong, Fay Wray, and Jane Wyatt.

3822 Parish, James Robert. The Tough Guys. New Rochelle,
      N.Y.: Arlington, 1976. 635 pp.
         With material on James Cagney, Kirk Douglas, Burt
      Lancaster, Robert Mitchum, Paul Muni, Edward G.
      Robinson, and Robert Ryan.

3823 Tuska, Jon (ed.) Close Up: The Contract Director. Metuchen,
      N.J.: Scarecrow, 1976. 457 pp.
         With material on Walter Lang, H. Bruce Humberstone,
      William Dieterle, Joseph Kane, William Witney, Lesley
      Selander, Yakima Canutt, Lewis Milestone, Edward Dmy-
      tryk, and Howard Hawks.

PART VII

INDIVIDUAL FILMS:
STUDIES, SCRIPTS & CASE HISTORIES

INTRODUCTION

This section includes works which are devoted in whole or in significant part to a particular film; they include screenplays, extended analyses, and case histories/production accounts. We have not included souvenir or program books; the reader should be aware, however, that program books, although often ephemeral, do exist for a great number of films--especially American "A" movies--and can often be obtained from specialty bookstores like Larry Edmunds in Los Angeles or Cinemabilia in New York. Nor have we included books which merely contain script excerpts; both Clifford McCarty's Published Screenplays and G. Howard Poteet's Published Radio, Television, and Film Scripts do include excerpt citations.

If no annotation is given, and the title does not indicate otherwise, the reader should assume that the book is a screenplay. Note that a published screenplay may be the original screenplay, the shooting script, a written transcript of the completed film, or some variation on one of these forms. All the screenplays listed here are published; unpublished screenplays can often be found in film archives or obtained from the various Hollywood studios. In most cases the director as well as the screenwriter(s) have been identified for each film; thus these names will be picked up in the name index, thus facilitating research on the films of a given individual. If a particular film has more than one book devoted to it, the credits have been provided only on the first entry. The directing credit is designated by the initial D followed by a colon. We have not distinguished between the terms screenwriter, scenarist, author of the original treatment, adapter, etc.; these various screenwriting credits are all designated by the initial S followed by a colon. The year of a movie is given only when there exists more than one film with the same title. Foreign films are listed under the title by which they are primarily recognized; however, films whose foreign and English titles are equally recognized have been cross-referenced for the reader's convenience. The word "unproduced" in the citation indicates that to the best of our knowledge the script has not been filmed. (Some of these unproduced scripts, in fact, seem intended for the purpose of experimentation or variation in literary form rather than for the purpose of future film production.) The reader should also note the exclusion here of books about individual Disney films. These books or booklets, usually published by the Disney organization and often intended for children, are so numerous that we feel they require a separate research effort outside the scope of this bibliography.

A NOUS LA LIBERTE

3823a Clair, René. A Nous la Liberté and Entr'Acte. New York:
Simon and Schuster, 1970. 140 pp. D/S: René Clair.

ACCIDENT

3824 Pinter, Harold. Five Screenplays. New York: Grove, 1971.
367 pp. D: Joseph Losey. S: Harold Pinter.

ADAM'S RIB

3825 Gordon, Ruth and Kanin, Garson. Adam's Rib. New York:
Viking, 1972. 118 pp. D: George Cukor. S: Ruth
Gordon and Garson Kanin.

THE ADVENTURERS

3826 Wolfe, Maynard Frank. The Making of The Adventurers.
New York: Paperback Library, 1970. 239 pp. D: Lewis
Gilbert. S: Michael Hastings and Lewis Gilbert.
Production account plus extended interview with Gilbert.

AFRICA ADDIO

3827 Cohen, John (text). Africa Addio. New York: Ballantine,
1966. 320 pp. D/S: Gualtiero Jacopetti and Franco
Prosperi.

THE AFRICAN QUEEN

3828 Agee, James. Agee on Film: Volume Two, Five Film
Scripts. New York: McDowell, Obolensky, 1960. 488 pp.
(Reprinted New York: Grosset and Dunlap, 1969) D: John
Huston. S: James Agee and John Huston.

L'AGE D'OR

3829 Buñuel, Luis. L'Age D'Or and Un Chien Andalou. New York:
Simon and Schuster, 1968. 124 pp. Translated by
Marianne Alexander. D: Luis Buñuel. S: Luis Buñuel
and Salvador Dali.
Screenplays and essays.

ALEXANDER NEVSKY

3830 Eisenstein, Sergei M. The Complete Films of Eisenstein,
Together with an Unpublished Essay by Eisenstein. New
York: Dutton, 1974. 154 pp. Translated by John
Hetherington. D: Sergei Eisenstein assisted by Dimitry
Vassiliev. S: Sergei Eisenstein and Pyotr Pavlenko.

3831 Eisenstein, Sergei M. Eisenstein: Three Films. Edited by

Jay Leyda. New York: Harper and Row, c. 1974.
189 pp. Translated by Diana Matias.
Includes introduction and research commentary by Leyda.

ALICE'S RESTAURANT

3832   Herndon, Venable and Penn, Arthur. Alice's Restaurant.
Garden City, N.Y.: Doubleday, 1970. 141 pp. D:
Arthur Penn. S: Venable Herndon and Arthur Penn.

3833   Giannetti, Louis D. Godard and Others: Essays in Film
Form. Rutherford, N.J.: Fairleigh Dickinson University
Press, 1975. 184 pp.
Includes a detailed analysis of ALICE'S RESTAURANT
as a plotless film.

THE ALIEN CORN   (see QUARTET)

ALL ABOUT EVE

3834   Mankiewicz, Joseph L. All About Eve. New York: Random,
1951. 245 pp. D/S: Joseph L. Mankiewicz.

3835   Carey, Gary with Joseph L. Mankiewicz. More About All
About Eve. New York: Random, 1972. 357 pp.
Screenplay and lengthy interview with Mankiewicz.

THE ALL-AMERICAN BOY

3836   Eastman, Charles. The All-American Boy: A Screenplay.
New York: Farrar, Straus, Giroux, 1973. 183 pp.
D/S: Charles Eastman.

ALL THAT MONEY CAN BUY

3837   Gassner, John and Nicholas, Dudley (eds.) Twenty Best Film
Plays. New York: Crown, 1943. 1112 pp. D: William
Dieterle. S: Dan Totheroh and Stephen Vincent Benet.

3838   Gassner, John and Nichols, Dudley (eds.). Great Film Plays.
New York: Crown, 1959. 334 pp. (Shorter edition of
Twenty Best Film Plays.)

ALL THE KING'S MEN

3839   Rossen, Robert. Three Screenplays: All the King's Men, The
Hustler, Lilith. Edited by Steven Rossen. Garden City,
N.Y.: Doubleday, 1972. 276 pp. D/S: Robert Rossen.
Screenplay and full Rossen filmography.

ALL THE WAY HOME

3840   Mosel, Tad and Reisman, Philip, Jr. All the Way Home.

New York: Avon, 1963. 365 pp. D: Alex Segal. S:
Philip Reisman, Jr.
Screenplay plus text of the stage play by Mosel.

3841 Keisman, Michael E. and Sheratsky, Rodney E. The Creative
Arts: Four Representative Types. New York: Globe,
1968. 572 pp.
Includes screenplay by Reisman.

ALPHAVILLE

3842 Godard, Jean-Luc. Alphaville. London: Lorrimer, 1966.
New York: Simon and Schuster, 1968. 104 pp. Trans-
lated by Peter Whitehead. D/S: Jean-Luc Godard.
Original treatment and screenplay.

AMARCORD

3843 Fellini, Federico with Guerra, Tonino. Amarcord: Portrait
of a Town. New York: Berkley Windhover, 1974. 124
pp. Translated by Nina Rootes. D: Federico Fellini.
S: Federico Fellini and Tonino Guerra.
Novelized format.

AMERICA AMERICA

3844 Kazan, Elia. America America. New York: Stein and Day,
1962. 190 pp. D/S: Elia Kazan.
Novelized format.

AMERICAN GRAFFITI

3845 Lucas, George; Katz, Gloria; and Huyck, Willard. American
Graffiti. New York: Grove, 1973. 189 pp. D: George Lucas. S: George Lucas, Gloria Katz, and Willard Huyck.

AN AMERICAN IN PARIS

3846 Knox, Donald. The Magic Factory: How MGM Made An
American in Paris. New York: Praeger, 1973. 217 pp.
D: Vincente Minnelli. S: Alan Jay Lerner.

AN AMERICAN TRAGEDY (1931)

3847 Baird, James Lee. The Movie in Our Heads: An Analysis of
Three Film Versions of Theodore Dreiser's "An American
Tragedy." University of Washington: Ph.D., 1967. 252 pp.
D: Josef von Sternberg. S: Samuel Hoffenstein.

AN AMERICAN TRAGEDY (Unproduced)

3848 Baird, James Lee. The Movie in Our Heads: An Analysis
of Three Film Versions of Theodore Dreiser's "An

American Tragedy." University of Washington: Ph.D.,
1967. 252 pp. Unproduced. S: Sergei Eisenstein, Grigori Alexandrov, and Ivor Montagu.

3849   Montagu, Ivor. With Eisenstein in Hollywood: A Chapter of
Autobiography. New York: International, 1969. 356 pp.
Includes the complete original scenario.

AMONG THE PATHS TO RUIN   (see TRILOGY)

ANATOMY OF A MURDER

3850   Griffith, Richard. Anatomy of a Motion Picture. New York:
St. Martin's, 1959. 119 pp. D: Otto Preminger. S:
Wendell Mayes.
Production account of ANATOMY OF A MURDER.

AN ANDALUSIAN DOG   (see UN CHIEN ANDALOU)

ANGER

3851   Ionesco, Eugene. Plays, Volume VII. London: Calder and
Boyars, 1968. 172 pp. D: Sylvain Dhome. S: Eugene
Ionesco.
Screenplay of an episode in THE 7 CAPITAL SINS.

ANIMAL CRACKERS

3852   Anobile, Richard J. (comp.) Hooray for Captain Spaulding:
Verbal and Visual Gems From Animal Crackers. New
York: Darien, 1974. 224 pp. D: Victor Heerman.
S: Morrie Ryskind.

ANIMAL FARM

3853   Manvell, Roger. The Animated Film. London: Sylvan, 1954.
63 pp. D: John Halas and Joy Batchelor. S: Lothar
Wolff, Borden Mace, Philip Stapp, John Halas and Joy
Batchelor.
Includes discussion and production account of ANIMAL
FARM.

THE ANT AND THE GRASSHOPPER   (see ENCORE)

ANTOINE AND COLETTE

3854   Truffaut, François. The Adventures of Antoine Doinel: Four
Screenplays. New York: Simon and Schuster, 1971.
320 pp. Translated by Helen G. Scott. D/S: François
Truffaut.
First treatment and final screenplay of an episode from
LOVE AT TWENTY.

APARAJITO   (see THE APU TRILOGY)

THE APARTMENT

3855   Wilder, Billy and Diamond, I. A. L.   The Apartment and
       The Fortune Cookie: Two Screenplays.   New York:
       Praeger, 1971.   191 pp.   D: Billy Wilder.   S: Billy
       Wilder and I. A. L. Diamond.

3856   Garrett, George P.; Hardison, O. B., Jr.; and Gelfman,
       Jane R.   Film Scripts Three.   New York: Appleton-
       Century-Crofts, 1972.   618 pp.

THE APU TRILOGY

3857   Wood, Robin.   The APU Trilogy.   New York: Praeger, 1971.
       96 pp.   D/S: Satyajit Ray.
       Analysis of the three films in the trilogy: PATHER
       PANCHALI, APARAJITO, and THE WORLD OF APU.

APUR SANSAR   (see THE APU TRILOGY)

ARMORED ATTACK   (see THE NORTH STAR)

ARMY IN ACTION

3858   Parker, Norton S.   Audiovisual Scriptwriting.   New Bruns-
       wick, N.J.:   Rutgers University Press, 1968.   330 pp.
       D/S: Norton S. Parker.
       Includes scripts of four episodes from the documentary
       series, ARMY IN ACTION: "Winds of Change," "The
       Three Faces of Evil," "Flames on the Horizon," "The
       Finest Tradition."

ASHES AND DIAMONDS

3859   Wajda, Andrzej.   The Wajda Trilogy.   New York: Simon and
       Schuster, 1973.   239 pp.   D: Andrzej Wajda.   S: Jerry
       Andrzejewski and Andrzej Wajda.

UNE AUSSI LONGUE ABSENCE

3860   Duras, Marguerite.   Hiroshima Mon Amour and Une Aussi
       Longue Absence.   London: Calder and Boyars, 1966.
       191 pp.   Translated by Barbara Wright.   D: Henri Colpi.
       S: Marguerite Duras and Gerard Jarlot.

L'AVVENTURA

3861   Antonioni, Michelangelo.   Screenplays.   New York: Orion,
       1963.   361 pp.   D: Michelangelo Antonioni.   S: Miche-
       langelo Antonioni, Elio Bartolini, and Tonino Guerra.

3862 Antonioni, Michelangelo. L'Avventura. New York: Grove,
      1969. 288 pp.
      Interviews with Antonioni, critical essays, and the
      screenplay, including omitted and variant scenes.

BABY DOLL

3863 Williams, Tennessee. Baby Doll. New York: New Direc-
      tions, 1956. 208 pp. D: Elia Kazan. S: Tennessee
      Williams.

BACHELOR MOTHER

3864 Wald, Jerry and Macaulay, Richard (eds.) The Best Pictures,
      1939-1940, and The Yearbook of Motion Pictures in
      America. New York: Dodd, Mead, 1940. 534 pp. (Re-
      printed New York: Gordon, 1975) D: Garson Kanin. S:
      Norman Krasna.
      Includes condensed screenplay.

THE BACHELOR PARTY

3865 Chayefsky, Paddy. The Bachelor Party. New York: New
      American Library, 1957. 127 pp. D: Delbert Mann.
      S: Paddy Chayefsky.

THE BACK OF BEYOND

3866 Else, Eric. The Back of Beyond: A Compilation for Use in
      Studying John Heyer's Film of Inland Australia. London:
      Longmans Green, 1968. 176 pp. D: John Heyer.

THE BAD SLEEP WELL

3867 Kurosawa, Akira. The Complete Works of Akira Kurosawa,
      Volume 9. Tokyo: Kinema Jumpo Sha, 1971. 247 pp.
      D: Akira Kurosawa. S: Shinobu Hashimoto, Hideo Oguni,
      Ryuzo Kikushima, Eijiro Hisaita, and Akira Kurosawa.
      Text of the screenplay in Japanese and English.

THE BALLAD OF CABLE HOGUE

3868 Evans, Max. Sam Peckinpah, Master of Violence: Being the
      Account of Making a Movie and Other Sundry Things.
      Vermillion, S.D.: Dakota, 1972. 92 pp. D: Sam
      Peckinpah. S: John Crawford and Edmund Penney.

BALLET MECANIQUE

3869 Lawder, Standish D. The Cubist Cinema. New York: New
      York University Press, 1975. 265 pp. D: Fernand
      Leger.

Includes discussion and shot analysis of BALLET MECANIQUE.

THE BANK DICK

3870 Fields, W. C. The Bank Dick. New York: Simon and Schuster, 1973. 88 pp. D: Edward Cline. S: Mahatma Kane Jeeves (pseudonym for Fields).

BARABBAS

3871 Jones, Lon (ed.) Barabbas: The Story of a Motion Picture. Bologna, Italy: Capelli, 1962. 189 pp. D: Richard Fleischer. S: Christopher Fry.
Treatments and excerpts from the screenplay, plus production account essays by various collaborators on the film.

THE BASEMENT

3872 Pinter, Harold. The Lover, Tea Party, The Basement: Two Plays and a Film Script. New York: Grove, 1967. 112 pp. Unproduced. S: Harold Pinter.

THE BATTLE AT ELDERBUSH GULCH

3873 Niver, Kemp R. D. W. Griffith's The Battle at Elderbush Gulch. Edited by Bebe Bergsten. Los Angeles: Locare Research Group, 1972. 65 pp. D: D. W. Griffith.

THE BATTLE OF ALGIERS

3874 Mellen, Joan. Filmguide to The Battle of Algiers. Bloomington: Indiana University Press, 1973. 82 pp. D: Gillo Pontecorvo. S: Franco Solinas and Gillo Pontecorvo.

3875 Solinas, Pier Nico (ed.) The Battle of Algiers. New York: Scribner's, 1973. 206 pp.
Screenplay plus interviews with the director and screenwriter.

THE BATTLE OF BRITAIN

3876 Mosley, Leonard. The Battle of Britain: The Making of a Film. New York: Stein and Day, 1969. 207 pp. D: Guy Hamilton.

BATTLESHIP POTEMKIN

3877 Kuiper, John B. An Analysis of the Four Silent Films of Sergei Eisenstein. University of Iowa: Ph.D., 1960. 436 pp. D: Sergei Eisenstein. S: Nina Agadjanova and Sergei Eisenstein.

3878   Eisenstein, Sergei.   Potemkin.   New York: Simon and
       Schuster, 1968.   100 pp.   Translated by Gillon R. Aitken.
       Screenplay plus an essay by Eisenstein.

3879   Mayer, David.   Sergei M. Eisenstein's Potemkin: A Shot-
       By-Shot Presentation.   New York: Grossman, 1972.
       252 pp.

3880   Eisenstein, Sergei.   The Complete Films of Eisenstein, To-
       gether With an Unpublished Essay by Eisenstein.   New
       York: Dutton, 1974.   154 pp.   Translated by John
       Hetherington.

3881   Eisenstein, Sergei.   Eisenstein: Three Films.   Edited by
       Jay Leyda.   New York: Harper and Row, c. 1974.
       189 pp.   Translated by Diana Matias.
       Introduction and research commentary by Leyda.

THE BEACH AT FALSEA

3882   Thomas, Dylan.   The Beach at Falsea.   New York: Stein
       and Day, 1963.   126 pp.   Unproduced.   S: Dylan Thomas.

BEAUTY AND THE BEAST

3883   Cocteau, Jean.   La Belle et la Bete/Beauty and the Beast.
       Edited by Robert M. Hammond.   New York: New York
       University Press, 1970.   441 pp.   D: Jean Cocteau.   S:
       Jean Cocteau.
       Text of the screenplay in French and English.

3884   Cocteau, Jean.   Beauty and the Beast: Diary of a Film.
       New York: Roy, 1950.   216 pp.   Translated by Ronald
       Duncan.   (Revised with a new introduction by George
       Amberg, New York: Dover, 1972.)
       Production account diary of the 1945-46 making of
       the film.

3885   Cocteau, Jean.   Cocteau: Three Screenplays: L'Eternal
       Retour, Orphee, La Belle et la Bete.   New York: Gross-
       man, 1972.   250 pp.

LA BEAUTE DU DIABLE

3886   Clair, René.   Four Screenplays: Le Silence Est D'Or, La
       Beauté du Diable, Les Belles-de-Nuit and Les Grandes
       Manoeuvres.   New York: Orion, 1970.   439 pp.   Trans-
       lated by Piergiuseppe Bozzetti.   D: René Clair.   S:
       René Clair and Armand Salacrou.

BED AND BOARD

3887   Truffaut, François.   The Adventures of Antoine Doinel: Four

Screenplays. New York: Simon and Schuster, 1971.
320 pp. Translated by Helen G. Scott. D: François
Truffaut. S: François Truffaut, Claude de Givray, and
Bernard Revon.
Outline, work notes, and final screenplay.

THE BEGINNING OR THE END

3888 Miller, Leslie. The Beginning or the End: The Book of the
Film. London: Hollywood Publishers, 1947. Approx.
90 pp. D: Norman Taurog. S: Frank Wead.

BELLE DE JOUR

3889 Buñuel, Luis. Belle de Jour. New York: Simon and
Schuster, 1971. 168 pp. Translation and descriptions
by Robert Adkinson. D: Luis Buñuel. S: Luis Buñuel
and Jean-Claude Carriere.
Screenplay, interviews with Buñuel, and article by
Andrew Sarris.

LA BELLE ET LA BETE   (see BEAUTY AND THE BEAST)

LES BELLES-DE-NUIT

3890 Clair, René. Four Screenplays: Le Silence Est D'Or, La
Beauté du Diable, Les Belles-de-Nuit and Les Grandes
Manoeuvres. New York: Orion, 1970. 439 pp. Trans-
lated by Piergiuseppe Bozzetti. D/S: Rene Clair.

BERLIN WALL

3891 Von Hanwehr, Wolfram H. A Critical Analysis of the Structure of the East German Film, "Berlin Wall." University
of Southern California: Ph.D., 1970. 454 pp.

THE BEST MAN

3892 Garrett, George P.; Hardison, O. B., Jr.; and Gelfman, Jane
R. Film Scripts Four. New York: Appleton-Century-
Crofts, 1972. 500 pp. D: Franklin Schaffner. S: Gore
Vidal.

THE BEST YEARS OF OUR LIVES

3893 Russell, Harold with Rosen, Victor. Victory in My Hands.
New York: Creative Age, 1949. 279 pp. D: William
Wyler. S: Robert E. Sherwood.
Includes lengthy section on the production of THE
BEST YEARS OF OUR LIVES.

BEZHIN MEADOW

3894   Eisenstein, Sergei. The Complete Films of Eisenstein, To-
gether With an Unpublished Essay by Eisenstein. New
York: Dutton, 1974. 154 pp. Translated by John
Hetherington. D: Sergei Eisenstein. S: Alexander
Rzechevsky, Sergei Eisenstein, and Isaac Babel.

THE BIBLE

3895   Fry, Christopher. The Bible: Original Screenplay. New
York: Pocket Books, 1966. 174 pp. D: John Huston.
S: Christopher Fry.

THE BICYCLE THIEF

3896   De Sica, Vittorio. Bicycle Thief. New York: Simon and
Schuster, 1968. 100 pp. Translated by Simon Hartog.
D: Vittorio De Sica. S: Cesare Zavattini.

IL BIDONE

3897   Fellini, Federico. Three Screenplays: I Vitelloni, Il Bidone,
The Temptations of Doctor Antonio. New York: Orion,
1970. 288 pp. Translated by Judith Green. D: Federico
Fellini. S: Federico Fellini, Ennio Flaiano, and Tullio
Pinelli.

THE BIG SLEEP

3898   Garrett, George P.; Hardison, O. B., Jr.; and Gelfman,
Jane R. Film Scripts One. New York: Appleton-
Century-Crofts, 1971. 544 pp. D: Howard Hawks.
S: William Faulkner, Leigh Brackett, and Jules Furthman.

BILLY JACK

3899   Christina, Frank and Teresa. Billy Jack. New York: Avon,
1973. 124 pp. D: T. C. Frank. S: Frank and Teresa
Christina.
Screenplay plus introduction by Tom Laughlin and
Delores Taylor.

THE BIRTH OF A NATION

3900   Huff, Theodore. A Shot Analysis of D. W. Griffith's The
Birth of a Nation. New York: Museum of Modern Art,
1961. 69 pp. D: D. W. Griffith. S: D. W. Griffith,
Frank E. Woods, and Thomas Dixon, Jr.

3901   Aitken, Roy E. (as told to Al P. Nelson). The Birth of a
Nation Story. Middleburg, Va.: William W. Denlinger,

1965. 96 pp.
Production account related by the film's producer.

3902 Silva, Fred (ed.) Focus on The Birth of a Nation. Engle-
wood Cliffs, N.J.: Prentice-Hall, 1971. 184 pp.
Contributors include James Agee, Lillian Gish, Thomas
Dixon, D. W. Griffith, Andrew Sarris, and Lewis Jacobs.

THE BLOOD OF A POET

3903 Cocteau, Jean. The Blood of a Poet. New York: Bodley,
1949. 53 pp. Translated by Lily Pons. D/S: Jean
Cocteau.
Scenario and an address by Cocteau.

3904 Cocteau, Jean. Two Screenplays: The Blood of a Poet and
The Testament of Orpheus. New York: Orion, 1968. 144 pp.
Translated by Carol Martin-Sperry.

BLOW-UP

3905 Antonioni, Michelangelo. Blow-Up. New York: Simon and
Schuster, 1971. 119 pp. D: Michelangelo Antonioni.
S: Michelangelo Antonioni and Tonino Guerra.
Screenplay, interviews and articles by Antonioni.

3906 Huss, Roy (ed.) Focus on Blow-Up. Englewood Cliffs, N.J.:
Prentice-Hall, 1971. 171 pp.
Original story plus essays by Charles Thomas Samuels,
Andrew Sarris, Arthur Knight, Stanley Kauffmann, and
others.

THE BLUE ANGEL

3907 von Sternberg, Josef. The Blue Angel: An Authorized Trans-
lation of the German Continuity. New York: Simon and
Schuster, 1968. 111 pp. D: Josef von Sternberg. S:
Robert Liebmann.
Screenplay plus essay by von Sternberg.

THE BLUE HOTEL

3908 Agee, James. Agee on Film: Volume Two, Five Film
Scripts. New York: McDowell, Obolensky, 1960. 488 pp.
(Reprinted New York: Grosset and Dunlap, 1969.) Un-
produced. S: James Agee.
Never filmed but produced as television play.

BLUE MOVIE

3909 Warhol, Andy. Blue Movie. New York: Grove, 1970.
126 pp. D/S: Andy Warhol.

BLUE WATER, WHITE DEATH

3910 Matthiessen, Peter. Blue Meridian: The Search for the
      Great White Shark. New York: New American Library,
      1971. 175 pp. D: Peter Gimbel.
      Chronicle of the expedition that filmed BLUE WATER,
      WHITE DEATH.

BOCCACCIO '70 (see THE TEMPTATIONS OF DOCTOR
      ANTONIO and THE JOB)

BONNIE AND CLYDE

3911 Wake, Sandra and Hayden, Nicola (eds.) The Bonnie and
      Clyde Book. New York: Simon and Schuster, 1972.
      223 pp. D: Arthur Penn. S: David Newman and
      Robert Benton.
      Screenplay, interviews with Arthur Penn and Warren
      Beatty, and articles by various critics.

3912 Cawelti, John G. (ed.) Focus on Bonnie and Clyde. Engle-
      wood Cliffs, N.J.: Prentice-Hall, 1973. 176 pp.
      Critical essays, interview with Arthur Penn, and
      material on script preparation.

BORN FREE

3913 Foreman, Carl. A Cast of Lions: The Story of the Filming
      of Born Free. Norwich: Collins Fontana, 1966. 128 pp.
      D: James Hill. S: Gerald L. C. Copley.
      Mainly photographs.

3914 Jay, John. Any Old Lion. London: Frewin, 1966. 138 pp.
      Production account.

3915 McKenna, Virginia and Travers, Bill. On Playing With
      Lions. New York: Harcourt, Brace, 1966. 124 pp.
      Production account by the two principal actors in the
      film.

BREWSTER McCLOUD

3916 McClelland, C. Kirk. On Making a Movie: Brewster Mc-
      Cloud, A Day-By-Day Journal of the On-Location Shooting
      of the Film in Houston. New York: New American Li-
      brary, 1971. 359 pp. D: Robert Altman. S: C. Kirk
      McClelland and Doran William Canon.
      Production account, shooting script and original
      screenplay.

THE BRIDE COMES TO YELLOW SKY

3917 Agee, James. Agee on Film: Volume Two, Five Film

Scripts. New York: McDowell, Obolensky, 1960. 488 pp.
(Reprinted, New York: Grosset and Dunlap, 1969.) D:
Bretaigne Windust. S: James Agee.
Part II of the 1952 film FACE TO FACE.

THE BRIDGE (Also titled THE SPY)

3918 Garrett, Gerald R. and Erskine, Thomas L. (comps.) From
      Fiction to Film: Ambrose Bierce's An Occurrence at
      Owl Creek Bridge. Encino, Cal.: Dickenson, 1973.
      216 pp. D/S: Charles Vidor.
      Shot analysis of the film, original story, and critical
      essays.

BRIEF ENCOUNTER

3919 Manvell, Roger (ed.) Three British Screen Plays: Brief
      Encounter, Odd Man Out, Scott of the Antarctic. London:
      Methuen, 1950. 299 pp. D: David Lean. S: Noel
      Coward.

3920 Masterworks of the British Cinema. Introduction by John
      Russell Taylor. New York: Harper and Row, c. 1974.
      352 pp.

BROTHER CARL

3921 Sontag, Susan. Brother Carl: A Filmscript. New York:
      Farrar, Straus and Giroux, 1974. 176 pp. D/S: Susan
      Sontag.
      Screenplay plus essay by Sontag.

BUTCH CASSIDY AND THE SUNDANCE KID

3922 Goldman, William. Butch Cassidy and the Sundance Kid.
      New York: Bantam, 1969. 184 pp. D: George Roy
      Hill. S: William Goldman.

THE CABINET OF DR. CALIGARI

3923 Byrne, Richard B. Films of Tyranny: Shot Analysis of
      The Cabinet of Dr. Caligari, The Golem, Nosferatu.
      Madison, Wisconsin: College Printing and Typing, 1966.
      152 pp. D: Robert Wiene. S: Carl Mayer and Hans
      Janowitz.

3924 Wiene, Robert; Mayer, Carl; and Janowitz, Hans. The
      Cabinet of Dr. Caligari. New York: Simon and Schuster,
      1972. 104 pp. Translation and descriptions by Robert
      V. Adkinson.
      Screenplay plus articles by Siegfried Kracauer, Erich
      Pommer, and Paul Rotha.

CAESAR AND CLEOPATRA

3925 Deans, Marjorie. Meeting at the Sphinx. London: Mac-
Donald, 1946. 146 pp. D: Gabriel Pascal. S: George
Bernard Shaw and Marjorie Deans.
Production account.

THE CANDIDATE

3926 Bahrenberg, Bruce. Filming The Candidate. New York:
Warner Paperback Library, 1972. 254 pp. D: Michael
Ritchie. S: Jeremy Larner.

3927 Maynard, Richard A. (ed.) Literature of the Screen: Power.
New York: Scholastic Book Services, 1974. 224 pp.
Screenplay and supplementary educational material.

CARNAL KNOWLEDGE

3928 Feiffer, Jules. Carnal Knowledge. New York: Farrar,
Straus and Giroux, 1971. 118 pp. D: Mike Nichols.
S: Jules Feiffer.

CASABLANCA

3929 Gassner, John and Nichols, Dudley (eds.) Best Film Plays
of 1943-1944. New York: Crown, 1945. 694 pp. D:
Michael Curtiz. S: Julius J. and Philip G. Epstein and
Howard Koch.

3930 Koch, Howard. Casablanca: Script and Legend. Woodstock,
N.Y.: Overlook, 1973. 223 pp.
Screenplay, production account and essay by Richard
Corliss.

3931 Anobile, Richard J. Casablanca. New York: Darien, 1974.
256 pp.
Shot-by-shot frame enlargements and dialogue.

CAST A GIANT SHADOW

3932 Shavelson, Melville. How to Make a Jewish Movie. Engle-
wood Cliffs, N.J.: Prentice-Hall, 1971. 244 pp. D/S:
Melville Shavelson.
Includes production account material on CAST A
GIANT SHADOW.

CHAFED ELBOWS

3933 Downey, Robert. Chafed Elbows. New York: Lancer,
1967. 144 pp. D/S: Robert Downey.

CHARADE

3934   Garrett, George P.; Hardison, O. B., Jr.; and Gelfman,
       Jane R. Film Scripts Three. New York: Appleton-
       Century-Crofts, 1972. 618 pp. D: Stanley Donen.
       S: Peter Stone.

UN CHIEN ANDALOU

3935   Buñuel, Luis. L'Age D'Or and Un Chien Andalou. New
       York: Simon and Schuster, 1968. 124 pp. Translated
       by Marianne Alexander. D: Luis Buñuel. S: Luis
       Buñuel and Salvador Dali.
       Original shooting script, final screen version and an
       essay by Jean Vigo.

THE CHILDHOOD OF MAXIM GORKY

3936   Erikson, Erik H. Childhood and Society. New York:
       Norton, 1950. 397 pp. (Revised 1963, 445 pp.) D:
       Mark Donskoi. S: I. Gruzdev.
       Includes a lengthy psychological analysis in relation
       to the film.

CHILDREN OF PARADISE

3937   Carné, Marcel. Children of Paradise. New York: Simon
       and Schuster, 1968. 218 pp. Translated by Dinah Brooke.
       D: Marcel Carné. S: Jacques Prevert.
       Screenplay plus short interviews with Carné and
       Prevert.

3938   Warfield, Nancy. Notes on Les Enfants du Paradis. New
       York: Little Film Gazette (?), 1967. 34 pp.

CHINA IS NEAR

3939   Bellocchio, Marco. China Is Near. New York: Orion, 1969.
       160 pp. Translated by Judith Green. D: Marco Belloc-
       chio. S: Elda Tattoli and Marco Bellocchio.
       Screenplay, essay by Tommasco Chiaretti, and inter-
       view with Bellocchio and Tattoli.

A CHRISTMAS MEMORY   (see TRILOGY)

CISCO PIKE

3940   Norton, Bill L. Cisco Pike: Original Screenplay. Edited
       by Norma M. Whittaker and Bob Silverstein. New York:
       Bantam, 1971. 165 pp. D/S: Bill L. Norton.
       Screenplay, interview with Norton and essays.

CITIZEN KANE

3941   Gottesman, Ronald (ed.) Focus on Citizen Kane. Englewood
        Cliffs, N.J.: Prentice-Hall, 1971. 178 pp. D: Orson
        Welles. S: Herman J. Mankiewicz and Orson Welles.
        Contributors include William Johnson, Bernard Herr-
        mann, Gregg Toland, Andrew Sarris, Arthur Knight, and
        François Truffaut.

3942   Kael, Pauline; Mankiewicz, Herman J.; and Welles, Orson. The
        Citizen Kane Book. Boston: Little, Brown, 1971. 440 pp.
        Screenplay and cutting continuity, plus lengthy essay
        by Kael.

CLEOPATRA   (1963)

3943   Brodsky, Jack and Weiss, Nathan. The Cleopatra Papers:
        A Private Correspondence. New York: Simon and
        Schuster, 1963. 175 pp. D: Joseph L. Mankiewicz.
        S: Joseph L. Mankiewicz, Ranald MacDougall, and Sidney
        Buchman.
        Correspondence of the film's publicity managers.

3944   Wanger, Walter and Hyams, Joe. My Life with Cleopatra.
        New York: Bantam, 1963. 182 pp.
        Production account.

A CLOCKWORK ORANGE

3945   Kubrick, Stanley. A Clockwork Orange. New York: Abelard-
        Schuman, 1972. unpaged. D/S: Stanley Kubrick.
        Shot-by-shot photographic reproduction plus dialogue.

CLOSELY WATCHED TRAINS

3946   Menzel, Jiri and Bohumil, Hrabal. Closely Watched Trains.
        New York: Simon and Schuster, 1971. 144 pp. D: Jiri
        Menzel. S: Bohumil Hrabal and Jiri Menzel.
        Screenplay plus essays by Hrabal, Jan Zalman and
        John Simon.

THE COCK CROWS AT MIDNIGHT

3947   The Cock Crows at Midnight. Peking, 1973. 68 pp.
        Stills of a film produced at the Shanghai Animation
        Studio.

THE COLONEL'S LADY   (see QUARTET)

COMING APART

3948   Ginsberg, Milton Moses. Coming Apart. New York: Lancer,
        1969. 208 pp. D/S: Milton Moses Ginsberg.

THE COMMUNICANTS   (see WINTER LIGHT)

COOL HAND LUKE

3949   Maynard, Richard A. (ed.) Literature of the Screen: Identity.
New York: Scholastic Book Services, 1974. 192 pp. D:
Stuart Rosenberg. S: Don Pearce and Frank R. Pierson.
Screenplay and supplementary educational material.

A CORNER IN WHEAT

3950   Petric, Vlada. A Corner in Wheat: A Critical Analysis.
Cambridge, Mass.: University Film Study Center, 1975.
Approx. 30 pp. D/S: D. W. Griffith.

THE COURTSHIP OF THE NEWT

3951   Benchley, Robert. The Reel Benchley: Robert Benchley at
His Hilarious Best in Words and Pictures. Compiled by
George Hornby. New York: A. A. Wyn, 1950. 96 pp.
D: Roy Rowland. S: Robert Benchley.
Narration and stills of the 1938 short.

CRIN BLANC   (see WHITE MANE)

CUL-DE-SAC

3952   Polanski, Roman. Polanski: Three Film Scripts. New
York: Harper and Row, 1975. 214 pp. D: Roman
Polanski. S: Roman Polanski and Gerard Brach.
Screenplay, introduction by Boleslaw Sulik, and inter-
view with Polanski.

CYPRUS IS AN ISLAND

3953   Lee, Laurie and Keene, Ralph. We Made a Film in Cyprus.
London, New York: Longmans Green, 1947. 92 pp.
D: Ralph Keene. S: Laurie Lee.
Screenplay and production account.

DANISH BLUE

3954   Axel, Gabriel. Danish Blue. New York: Grove, 1971.
126 pp. D/S: Gabriel Axel.

DARLING

3955   Garrett, George P.; Hardison, O. B., Jr.; and Gelfman,
Jane R. Film Scripts Four. New York: Appleton-
Century-Crofts, 1971. 500 pp. D: John Schlesinger.
S: Frederic Raphael.

DAVID COPPERFIELD   (1970)

3956   Curry, George. Copperfield '70: The Story of the Making of
the Omnibus 20th Century-Fox Film of Charles Dickens'
David Copperfield. New York: Ballantine, 1970. 210 pp.
D: Delbert Mann. S: Jack Pulman and Frederick Brogger.
Screenplay and production account.

DAVID HOLZMAN'S DIARY

3957   Carson, L. M. Kit and McBride, Jim. David Holzman's
Diary. New York: Farrar, Straus and Giroux, 1970.
126 pp. D: Jim McBride. S: L. M. Kit Carson.

A DAY AT THE RACES

3958   Pirosh, Robert; Seaton, George; and Oppenheimer, George.
A Day at the Races. New York: Viking, 1972. 276 pp.
D: Sam Wood. S: Robert Pirosh, George Seaton, and
George Oppenheimer.

DAY FOR NIGHT

3959   Truffaut, François. Day For Night. New York: Grove,
1975. 173 pp. Translated by Sam Flores. D: François
Truffaut. S: François Truffaut, Jean-Louis Richard, and
Suzanne Shiffman.
Screenplay plus article by Truffaut.

DAY OF WRATH

3960   Dreyer, Carl Theodor. Four Screenplays. Bloomington:
Indiana University Press, 1970. 312 pp. Translated by
Oliver Stallybrass. D: Carl Dreyer. S: Mogens Skot-
Hansen and Poul Knudsen.

DEEP THROAT

3961   The Deep Throat Papers. Introduced by Pete Hamill. New
York: Manor, 1973. 192 pp.
Primarily courtroom testimony from the DEEP
THROAT's obscenity trial; also includes articles by Peter
Wolff, Sally Tramweber, and others.

3962   Smith, Richard. Getting Into Deep Throat. Chicago: Playboy, 1973. 286 pp. D/S: Jerry Gerard.

THE DEFIANT ONES

3963   Garrett, George P.; Hardison, O. B., Jr.; and Gelfman,
Jane R. Film Scripts Two. New York: Appleton-

Century-Crofts, 1971. 548 pp. D: Stanley Kramer.
S: Nathan E. Douglas and Harold Jacob Smith.

DESTROY SHE SAID

3964   Duras, Marguerite. Destroy She Said [and] Destruction and
Language: An Interview with Marguerite Duras. New
York: Grove, 1970. 133 pp. Translated by Barbara
Bray and Helen Lane Cumberford. D/S: Marguerite
Duras.
Novel on which the film is based, plus discussion by
Jacques Rivette, Jean Narboni, and Duras about the two
media and DESTROY SHE SAID.

DESTRY RIDES AGAIN

3965   Wald, Jerry and Macaulay, Richard (eds.) The Best Pictures,
1939-1940, and The Yearbook of Motion Pictures in
America. New York: Dodd, Mead, 1940. 534 pp. (Re-
printed New York: Gordon, 1975.) D: George Marshall.
S: Felix Jackson, Gertrude Purcell, and Henry Myers.
Includes condensed screenplay.

THE DISPOSSESSED

3966   John, Errol. Force Majeure, The Dispossessed, Hasta
Luego: Three Screenplays. London: Faber and Faber,
1967. 194 pp. Unproduced. S: Errol John.

DOC

3967   Hamill, Pete. Doc: The Original Screenplay. New York:
Paperback Library, 1971. 202 pp. D: Frank Perry.
S: Pete Hamill.

THE DOCTOR AND THE DEVILS

3968   Thomas, Dylan. The Doctor and the Devils: From the Story
by Donald Taylor. London: Dent, 1953. 138 pp. (Reprinted New York: Time Incorporated, 1964. 177 pp.)
Unproduced. S: Dylan Thomas.

3969   Thomas, Dylan. The Doctor and the Devils and Other Scripts.
New York: New Directions, 1966. 229 pp.

DR. EHRLICH'S MAGIC BULLET

3970   Wald, Jerry and Macaulay, Richard (eds.) The Best Pictures,
1939-1940, and The Yearbook of Motion Pictures in
America. New York: Dodd, Mead, 1940. 534 pp. (Re-
printed New York: Gordon, 1975) D: William Dieterle.
S: John Huston, Heinz Herald, and Norman Burnside.
Includes condensed screenplay.

DR. JEKYLL AND MR. HYDE

3971 Anobile, Richard J. Rouben Mamoulian's Dr. Jekyll and Mr.
      Hyde. New York: Darien, 1975. 256 pp. D: Rouben
      Mamoulian. S: Samuel Hoffenstein and Percy Heath.
      Shot-by-shot frame enlargements and dialogue.

DOCTOR ZHIVAGO

3972 Bolt, Robert. Doctor Zhivago: The Screenplay. New York:
      Random, 1965. 224 pp. D: David Lean. S: Robert
      Bolt.

DO-DES KA-DEN

3973 Kurosawa, Akira. The Complete Works of Akira Kurosawa:
      Volume 1. Tokyo: Kinema Jumpo Sha, 1971. 138 pp.
      D: Akira Kurosawa. S: Akira Kurosawa, Hideo Oguni,
      and Shinobu Hashimoto.
      Text of screenplay in Japanese and English.

LA DOLCE VITA

3974 Fellini, Federico. La Dolce Vita. New York: Ballantine,
      1961. 276 pp. Translated by Oscar DeLiso and Bernard
      Shir-Cliff. D: Federico Fellini. S: Federico Fellini,
      Tullio Pinelli, Ennio Flaiano, and Brunello Rondi.

3975 Reynolds, Lessie. An Analysis of the Non-Verbal Symbolism
      in Federico Fellini's Film Trilogy, La Dolce Vita, 8½,
      and Juliet of the Spirits. University of Michigan: Ph.D.,
      1969. 207 pp.

DON'T LOOK BACK

3976 Pennebaker, D. A. Bob Dylan: Don't Look Back. New
      York: Ballantine, 1968. 159 pp. D: D. A. Penne-
      baker.
      Transcript of the cinema verite film plus many stills.

DOUBLE INDEMNITY

3977 Gassner, John and Nichols, Dudley (eds.) Best Film Plays--
      1945. New York: Crown, 1946. 648 pp. D: Billy
      Wilder. S: Billy Wilder and Raymond Chandler.

DRAGONSEED

3978 Gassner, John and Nichols, Dudley (eds.) Best Film Plays
      of 1943-1944. New York: Crown, 1945. 694 pp. D:
      Jack Conway and Harold S. Bucquet. S: Marguerite
      Roberts and Jane Murfin.

DRUNKEN ANGEL

3979 Kurosawa, Akira. The Complete Works of Akira Kurosawa:
Volume 3. Tokyo: Kinema Jumpo Sha, 1971. 136 pp.
D: Akira Kurosawa. S: Keinosuke Uegusa and Akira
Kurosawa.
Text of the screenplay in Japanese and English.

DUCK SOUP

3980 Marx Brothers. The Four Marx Brothers in Monkey Business and Duck Soup. New York: Simon and Schuster,
1972. 183 pp. D: Leo McCarey. S: Bert Kalmer and
Harry Ruby.

DUET FOR CANNIBALS

3981 Sontag, Susan. Duet for Cannibals. New York: Farrar,
Straus and Giroux, 1970. 129 pp. D/S: Susan Sontag.

EARTH

3982 Dovzhenko, Alexander. Mother, A Film by V. I. Pudovkin;
Earth, A Film by Alexander Dovzhenko. New York:
Simon and Schuster, 1973. 102 pp. D/S: Alexander
Dovzhenko.

EARTHQUAKE

3983 Fox, George. Earthquake: The Story of the Movie. New
York: New American Library, 1974. 128 pp. D: Mark
Robson. S: George Fox and Mario Puzo.
Transcript of the film plus lengthy production account.

EASY RIDER

3984 Fonda, Peter; Hopper, Dennis; and Southern, Terry. Easy
Rider. Edited by Nancy Hardin and Marilyn Schlossberg.
New York: New American Library, 1969. 191 pp. D:
Dennis Hopper. S: Peter Fonda, Dennis Hopper, and
Terry Southern.
Screenplay plus articles on Hopper, Fonda, and Jack
Nicholson.

THE ECLIPSE (see L'ECLISSE)

L'ECLISSE

3985 Antonioni, Michelangelo. Screenplays. New York: Orion,
1963. 361 pp. D: Michelangelo Antonioni. S: Michelangelo Antonioni, Tonino Guerra, Elio Bartolini, and
Ottiero Ottieri.

3986   Perry, Edward.   A Contextual Study of Michelangelo Antonioni's Film, L'Eclisse.   University of Iowa: Ph.D.,
1968.   560 pp.

$8\frac{1}{2}$

3987   Boyer, Deena.   The Two Hundred Days of $8\frac{1}{2}$.   New York:
Macmillan, 1964.   218 pp.   Translated by Charles Lam
Markmann.   D: Federico Fellini.   S: Federico Fellini,
Tullio Pinelli, Ennio Flaiano, and Brunello Rondi.
Production account.

3988   Reynolds, Lessie.   An Analysis of the Non-Verbal Symbolism
in Federico Fellini's Film Trilogy, La Dolce Vita, $8\frac{1}{2}$,
and Juliet of the Spirits.   University of Michigan: Ph.D.,
1969.   207 pp.

3989   Benderson, Albert Edward.   Critical Approaches to Federico
Fellini's $8\frac{1}{2}$.   New York: Arno, 1974.   235 pp.

3990   Perry, Ted.   Filmguide to $8\frac{1}{2}$.   Bloomington: Indiana University Press, 1975.   89 pp.

THE ELEANOR ROOSEVELT STORY

3991   MacLeish, Archibald.   The Eleanor Roosevelt Story.   New
York: Houghton-Mifflin, 1965.   101 pp.   D: Richard
Kaplan.   S: Archibald MacLeish.
Narration and stills from the 1965 film.

ENCORE

3992   Maugham, W. Somerset.   Encore.   Garden City, N.Y.:
Doubleday, 1952.   156 pp.   "The Ant and the Grass-
hopper"--D: Pat Jackson; S: T. E. B. Clarke.   "Winter
Cruise"--D: Anthony Pelissier; S: Arthur Macrae.
"Gigolo and Gigolette"--D: Harold French; S: Eric
Ambler.
Screenplays of the three parts and the original
Maugham stories on which they are based.

LES ENFANTS DU PARADIS   (see CHILDREN OF PARADISE)

L'ENGRENAGE   (see IN THE MESH)

ENTR'ACTE

3993   Clair, René.   A Nous la Liberte and Entr'Acte.   New York:
Simon and Schuster, 1970.   140 pp.   Translation and
description by Richard Jacques and Nicola Hayden.   D/S:
René Clair.

ESPOIR   (See MAN'S HOPE)

THE ETERNAL RETURN

3994   Cocteau, Jean. Cocteau: Three Screenplays, L'Eternel
       Retour, Orphee, La Belle et la Bete. New York: Gross-
       man, 1972. 250 pp. D: Jean Cocteau. S: Jean Delan-
       noy.

L'ETERNEL RETOUR   (see THE ETERNAL RETURN)

EUROPA

3995   Stern, Anatol. Europa, A Poem. With Photographs from
       the Film Europa Made in 1930 by Stefan and Franciszka
       Themerson. London: Gaberocchus, 1962. 26 pp. D/S:
       Stefan and Franciszka Themerson.
              Photographs and contemporary criticism of an early
       Polish experimental film.

EVENTS

3996   Baker, Fred. Events, 1968-1969: A Film. New York:
       Grove, 1970. 128 pp. D/S: Fred Baker.

THE EXORCIST

3997   Blatty, William Peter. William Peter Blatty on The Exor-
       cist: From Novel to Film. New York: Bantam, 1974.
       375 pp. D: William Friedkin. S: William Peter Blatty.
              First draft screenplay, transcript of final film and
       articles by Blatty.

3998   Newman, Howard. The Exorcist: The Strange Story Behind
       the Film. New York: Pinnacle, 1974. 168 pp.

3999   Travers, Peter and Reiff, Stephanie. The Story Behind the
       Exorcist. New York: Crown, 1974. 245 pp.

THE EXTERMINATING ANGEL

4000   Buñuel, Luis. Three Screenplays: Viridiana, The Exter-
       minating Angel and Simon of the Desert. New York:
       Orion, 1969. 245 pp. D/S: Luis Buñuel.

4001   Buñuel, Luis. The Exterminating Angel, Nazarin, and Los
       Olvidados. New York: Simon and Schuster, 1972.
       299 pp.
              Screenplay plus article on THE EXTERMINATING
       ANGEL by Ado Kyrou.

A FACE IN THE CROWD

4002   Schulberg, Budd. A Face in the Crowd. New York:

Random, 1957. 172 pp. D: Elia Kazan. S: Budd
Schulberg.
Screenplay plus introduction by Kazan.

4003 Maynard, Richard A. (ed.) Literature of the Screen: Power.
New York: Scholastic Book Services, 1974. 224 pp.
Screenplay and supplementary educational material.

FACE TO FACE (see THE BRIDE COMES TO YELLOW SKY)

FACES

4004 Cassavetes, John. Faces. New York: New American Library, 1970. 319 pp. D/S: John Cassavetes.
Original screenplay and final version of the film.

THE FACTS OF LIFE (see QUARTET)

THE FALLEN IDOL

4005 Henrey, Robert. A Film Star in Belgrave Square. London:
Peter Davies, 1948. 186 pp. D: Carol Reed. S:
Graham Greene.
Includes production account material on THE FALLEN
IDOL; by the father of its child star, Bobby Henrey.

THE FAMILY WAY

4006 Maynard, Richard A. (ed.) Literature of the Screen: Men
and Women. New York: Scholastic Book Services, 1974.
Approx. 200 pp. D: Roy Boulting. S: Bill Naughton.
Screenplay and supplementary educational material.

FELLINI SATYRICON

4007 Zanelli, Dario (ed.) Fellini Satyricon. New York: Ballantine, 1970. 280 pp. D: Federico Fellini. S: Federico
Fellini and Bernardino Zapponi.
Original treatment, screenplay, essays, and a dialogue between Alberto Moravia and Fellini.

4008 Hughes, Eileen. On the Set of Fellini Satyricon: A Behind-
the-Scenes Diary. New York: Morrow, 1971. 248 pp.

UNE FEMME EST UNE FEMME (see A WOMAN IS A
WOMAN)

THE FERGANA CANAL

4009 Eisenstein, Sergei. The Complete Films of Eisenstein, Together with an Unpublished Essay by Eisenstein. New
York: Dutton, 1974. 154 pp. Translated by John

Hetherington. D: Sergei Eisenstein. S: Pyotr Pavlenko and Sergei Eisenstein. (Only partially filmed;
footage later edited into a short documentary.)

THE FIGHT FOR LIFE

4010 Gassner, John and Nichols, Dudley (eds.) Twenty Best Film
Plays. New York: Crown, 1943. 1112 pp. D/S: Pare
Lorentz.

FILM

4011 Beckett, Samuel. Film. New York: Grove, 1969. 95 pp.
D: Alan Schneider. S: Samuel Beckett.
Scenario, many stills, and an essay by Alan Schneider.

FORCE MAJEURE

4012 John, Errol. Force Majeure, The Dispossessed, Hasta
Luego: Three Screenplays. London: Faber and Faber,
1967. 194 pp. Unproduced. S: Errol John.

THE FORGOTTEN VILLAGE

4013 Steinbeck, John. The Forgotten Village. New York: Viking,
1941. 143 pp. D: Herbert Kline. S: John Steinbeck.

THE FORTUNE COOKIE

4014 Wilder, Billy and Diamond, I. A. L. The Apartment and
The Fortune Cookie. New York: Praeger, 1971. 191 pp.
D: Billy Wilder. S: Billy Wilder and I. A. L. Diamond.

THE 400 BLOWS

4015 Denby, David (ed.) The 400 Blows. New York: Grove,
1969. 256 pp. D: François Truffaut. S: François
Truffaut and Marcel Moussy.
Screenplay (including omitted scenes), interviews
with Truffaut, and critical essays.

4016 Truffaut, François. The Adventures of Antoine Doinel:
Four Screenplays. New York: Simon and Schuster,
1971. 320 pp.
The first treatment and dialogue excerpts.

FRANKENSTEIN (1931)

4017 Anobile, Richard J. (ed.) Frankenstein. New York: Uni-
verse, 1974. 256 pp. D: James Whale. S: Garrett
Fort and Francis Edward Faragoh.
Shot-by-shot frame enlargements and dialogue.

FREEDOM TO LOVE

4018   Kronhausen, Phyllis and Eberhard. Freedom to Love. New
       York: Grove, 1970. 191 pp. D/S: Phyllis and Eberhard
       Kronhausen.
           Screenplay plus interviews with the Kronhausens,
       Hugh Hefner, Kenneth Tynan, and others.

THE FRESHMAN

4019   McCaffrey, Donald W. Three Classic Silent Screen Comedies
       Starring Harold Lloyd. Rutherford, N.J.: Fairleigh
       Dickinson University Press, 1975. 264 pp. D: Sam
       Taylor and Fred Newmeyer. S: Sam Taylor, Ted Wilde,
       John Grey, and Tim Whelan.
           Detailed analysis of the film's structure and comic
       techniques.

THE FRIENDLY PERSUASION

4020   West, Jessamyn. To See the Dream. New York: Harcourt,
       Brace, 1957. 314 pp. D: William Wyler. S: Jessa-
       myn West, Robert Wyler, and Michael Wilson (uncredited).
           West's journal concerning the film production of her
       novel.

FURY

4021   Gassner, John and Nichols, Dudley (eds.) Twenty Best Film
       Plays. New York: Crown, 1943. 1112 pp. D: Fritz
       Lang. S: Bartlett Cormack and Fritz Lang.

THE GENERAL

4022   Rubenstein, E. Filmguide to The General. Bloomington:
       Indiana University Press, 1973. 83 pp. D/S: Buster
       Keaton and Clyde Bruckman.

4023   Anobile, Richard J. (ed.) The General. New York: Darien,
       1975. 256 pp.
           Shot-by-shot frame enlargements plus intertitles;
       also includes interview with Marion Mack by Raymond
       Rohauer.

GENERAL LINE

4024   Kuiper, John B. An Analysis of the Four Silent Films of
       Sergei Eisenstein. University of Iowa: Ph.D., 1960.
       436 pp. D/S: Sergei Eisenstein and Grigori Alexandrov.

4025   Eisenstein, Sergei. The Complete Films of Eisenstein, To-
       gether with an Unpublished Essay by Eisenstein. New

York: Dutton, 1974. 154 pp. Translated by John
Hetherington.

GENERATION

4026 Wajda, Andrzej. The Wajda Trilogy. New York: Simon and
      Schuster, 1973. 239 pp. D: Andrzej Wajda. S: Bohdan
      Czeszko.

GERMANY--YEAR ZERO

4027 Roncoroni, Stefano (ed.) Rossellini: The War Trilogy:
      Open City, Paisan, Germany--Year Zero. New York:
      Grossman, 1973. 467 pp. Translated by Judith Green.
      D: Roberto Rossellini. S: Roberto Rossellini with Max
      Colpet.

GIGOLO AND GIGOLETTE (see ENCORE)

GLOUMOV'S DIARY

4028 Eisenstein, Sergei. The Complete Films of Eisenstein, To-
      gether with an Unpublished Essay by Eisenstein. New
      York: Dutton, 1974. 154 pp. Translated by John
      Hetherington. D/S: Sergei Eisenstein.

THE GO-BETWEEN

4029 Pinter, Harold. Five Screenplays. New York: Grove, 1971.
      367 pp. D: Joseph Losey. S: Harold Pinter.

THE GODDESS

4030 Chayefsky, Paddy. The Goddess. New York: Simon and
      Schuster, 1958. 167 pp. D: John Cromwell. S: Paddy
      Chayefsky.

THE GODFATHER

4031 Puzo, Mario. The Godfather Papers and Other Confessions.
      New York: Putnam, 1972. 252 pp. D: Francis Ford
      Coppola. S: Mario Puzo and Francis Ford Coppola.
          Includes a chapter entitled "The Making of THE GOD-
      FATHER. "

4032 Zuckerman, Ira. The Godfather Journal. New York: Manor,
      1972. 143 pp.
          Production account.

GOING MY WAY

4033 Gassner, John and Nichols, Dudley (eds.) Best Film Plays

of 1943-1944. New York: Crown, 1945. 694 pp. D:
Leo McCarey. S: Frank Butler and Frank Cavett.

THE GOLDEN AGE (see L'AGE D'OR)

THE GOLEM (1920)

4034 Byrne, Richard B. Films of Tyranny: Shot Analyses of The
Cabinet of Dr. Caligari, The Golem, Nosferatu. Madison,
Wisconsin: College Printing and Typing, 1966. 152 pp.
D: Paul Wegener with Henrik Galeen and Carl Boese.
S: Henrik Galeen.

4035 Masterworks of the German Cinema. Introduction by Roger
Manvell. New York: Harper and Row, 1973. 300 pp.
Screenplays plus brief essay by Lotte Eisner.

GONE WITH THE WIND

4036 Lambert, Gavin. GWTW: The Making of Gone With the
Wind. Boston: Little, Brown, 1973. 238 pp. D: Victor
Fleming. S: Sidney Howard.

4037 Flamini, Roland. Scarlett, Rhett, and a Cast of Thousands:
The Filming of Gone With the Wind. New York: Macmillan, 1975. 355 pp.

THE GOOD EARTH

4038 Gassner, John and Nichols, Dudley (eds.) Twenty Best Film
Plays. New York: Crown, 1943. 1112 pp. D: Sidney
Franklin. S: Talbot Jennings, Tess Slesinger, and
Claudine West.

4039 Gassner, John and Nichols, Dudley (eds.) Great Film Plays.
New York: Crown, 1959. 334 pp. (Shorter edition of
Twenty Best Film Plays.)

GOODBYE, MR. CHIPS

4040 Wald, Jerry and Macaulay, Richard (eds.) The Best Pictures,
1939-1940, and The Year Book of Motion Pictures in
America. New York: Dodd, Mead, 1940. 534 pp. (Re-
printed New York: Gordon, 1975.) D: Sam Wood. S:
R. C. Sherriff, Claudine West, and Eric Maschwitz.
Includes condensed screenplay of the film.

GRAND ILLUSION

4041 Renoir, Jean. Grand Illusion. New York: Simon and
Schuster, 1968. 108 pp. Translated by Marianne Alexandre
and Andrew Sinclair. D: Jean Renoir. S: Charles

Spaak and Jean Renoir.
Screenplay plus brief article by Erich von Stroheim.

4042   Masterworks of the French Cinema. Introduction by John
        Weightman. New York: Harper and Row, 1974.
        350 pp.

4043   Trope, Zipora Sharf. A Critical Application of Andre Bazin's
        "Mise-en-Scène" Theory in: The Last Laugh, Grand
        Illusion, and The Magnificant Ambersons. University of
        Michigan: Ph. D., 1974. 187 pp.

LES GRANDES MANOEUVRES

4044   Clair, René. Four Screenplays: Le Silence est D'Or, La
        Beauté du Diable, Les Belles-de-Nuit and Les Grandes
        Manoeuvres. New York: Orion, 1970. 439 pp. Trans-
        lated by Piergiuseppe Bozzetti. D: René Clair. S:
        René Clair with Jerome Geronimi and Jean Marsan.

GRANDMA'S BOY

4045   McCaffrey, Donald W. Three Classic Silent Screen Come-
        dies Starring Harold Lloyd. Rutherford, N.J.: Fair-
        leigh Dickinson University Press, 1975. 264 pp. D:
        Fred Newmeyer. S: Hal Roach, Sam Taylor, and Jean
        Havez.
            Detailed analysis of the film's structure and comic
        techniques.

THE GRAPES OF WRATH

4046   Gassner, John and Nichols, Dudley (eds.) Twenty Best Film
        Plays. New York: Crown, 1943. 1112 pp. D: John
        Ford. S: Nunnally Johnson.

4047   French, Warren. Filmguide to The Grapes of Wrath. Bloom-
        ington: Indiana University Press, 1973. 87 pp.

THE GREAT GATSBY

4048   Bahrenburg, Bruce. Filming The Great Gatsby. New York:
        Berkley, 1974. 255 pp. D: Jack Clayton. S: Francis
        Ford Coppola.
            Production account.

THE GREAT WALDO PEPPER

4049   Goldman, William. The Great Waldo Pepper. New York:
        Dell, 1975. 224 pp. D: George Roy Hill. S: William
        Goldman.
            Screenplay plus material by George Roy Hill.

GREED

4050 von Stroheim, Erich. Greed. Brussels: Belgian Film Library, 1958. 274 pp. D/S: Erich von Stroheim.

4051 Finler, Joel W. (ed.) Greed. New York: Simon and Schuster, 1972. 352 pp.
Original version and released version, plus articles by von Stroheim, Herman Weinberg, Jean Hersholt, and William Daniels.

4052 Weinberg, Herman G. (comp.) The Complete Greed of Erich von Stroheim. New York: Dutton, 1972. Unpaged.
Reconstruction of the film with frame enlargements and production stills.

IL GRIDO

4053 Antonioni, Michelangelo. Screenplays. New York: Orion, 1963. 361 pp. D: Michelangelo Antonioni. S: Michelangelo Antonioni, Elio Bartolini, and Ennio De Concini.

THE GROUP

4054 Kael, Pauline. Kiss Kiss Bang Bang. Boston: Little, Brown, 1968. 404 pp. D: Sidney Lumet. S: Sidney Buchman.
Includes a lengthy essay on the making of the film.

LA GUERRE EST FINIE

4055 Semprun, Jorge. La Guerre est Finie. New York: Grove, 1967. 192 pp. Translated by Richard Seaver. D: Alain Resnais. S: Jorge Semprun.

GUESS WHO'S COMING TO DINNER

4056 Newquist, Ron. A Special Kind of Magic. Chicago: Rand McNally, 1967. 156 pp. D: Stanley Kramer. S: William Rose.
Extended interviews with Spencer Tracy, Stanley Kramer, Katharine Hepburn, Sidney Poitier, and Katherine Houghton; largely about the making of GUESS WHO'S COMING TO DINNER.

GUILTY OF TREASON

4057 Lavery, Emmet. Guilty of Treason: Shooting Script of the Screenplay. St. Paul, Minn.: Catholic Digest, 1949. 126 pp. D: Felix Feist. S: Emmet Lavery.

HAIL THE CONQUERING HERO

4058 Gassner, John and Nichols, Dudley (eds.) Best Film Plays
      of 1943-1944. New York: Crown, 1945. 694 pp. D/S:
      Preston Sturges.

HAMLET (1948)

4059 Cross, Brenda (ed.) The Film Hamlet: A Record of Its
      Production. London: Saturn, 1948. 76 pp. D: Lau-
      rence Olivier.
      Articles by the film's cast and crew including Olivier,
      Desmond Dickinson, Roger Furse, Stanley Holloway, Jean
      Simmons, William Walton and Muir Mathieson.

4060 Dent, Alan (ed.) Hamlet: The Film and the Play. London:
      World Film Publications, 1948. Approx. 200 pp.
      Text of the play with annotations about the film
      version's omissions, excerpts from the film script,
      photographs, and essays by Olivier, Alan Dent and Roger
      Furse.

HAMLET (1964)

4061 Kozintsev, Grigori. Shakespeare, Time and Conscience.
      New York: Hill and Wang, 1966. 276 pp. D/S: Gri-
      gori Kozintsev.
      Includes lengthy appendix of Kozintsev's diary re-
      lating to the U.S.S.R. film version of HAMLET.

HAND IN HAND

4062 Morgan, Diana. Hand In Hand. Kingswood, Surrey: World's
      Work, 1963. 58 pp. D: Helen Morgan. S: Diana
      Morgan.
      Mainly stills from the 1961 film; juvenile literature.

A HARD DAY'S NIGHT

4063 Garrett, George P.; Hardison, O. B., Jr.; and Gelfman,
      Jane R. Film Scripts Four. New York: Appleton-
      Century-Crofts, 1972. 500 pp. D: Richard Lester.
      S: Alun Owen.

HASTA LUEGO

4064 John, Errol. Force Majeure, The Dispossessed, Hasta
      Luego: Three Screenplays. London: Faber and Faber,
      1967. 194 pp. Unproduced. S: Errol John.

HENRY V

4065 Hutton, Clayton. The Making of Henry V. London: E. J.

Day, 1944. 72 pp. D: Laurence Olivier. S: Laurence Olivier, Reginald Beck, and Alan Dent.

4066 Shakespeare, William. Henry V: With an Introduction and Additional Notes on the Laurence Olivier Film Production. Pickering, Ontario: Global, ca. 1947. 141 pp.

4067 Garrett, George P.; Hardison, O. B., Jr.; and Gelfman, Jane R. Film Scripts One. New York: Appleton-Century-Crofts, 1971. 544 pp.

4068 Geduld, Harry M. Filmguide to Henry V. Bloomington: Indiana University Press, 1973. 82 pp.

HERE COMES MR. JORDAN

4069 Gassner, John and Nichols, Dudley (eds.) Twenty Best Film Plays. New York: Crown, 1943. 1112 pp. D: Alexander Hall. S: Sidney Buchman and Seton I. Miller.

THE HIDDEN FORTRESS (see THREE BAD MEN IN A HIDDEN FORTRESS)

HIGH NOON

4070 Garrett, George P.; Hardison, O. B., Jr.; and Gelfman, Jane R. Film Scripts Two. New York: Appleton-Century-Crofts, 1971. 548 pp. D: Fred Zinnemann. S: Carl Foreman.

4071 Wald, Malvin and Werner, Michael (comps.) Three Major Screenplays. New York: Globe, 1972. 394 pp. Screenplay plus articles.

4072 Maynard, Richard A. (ed.) Literature of the Screen: Values in Conflict. New York: Scholastic Book Services, 1974. Approx. 200 pp. Screenplay and supplementary educational material.

THE HILL

4073 Fast, Howard. The Hill: An Original Screenplay. Garden City, N.Y.: Doubleday, 1964. 123 pp. Unproduced. S: Howard Fast.

HIROSHIMA MON AMOUR

4074 Duras, Marguerite. Hiroshima Mon Amour. New York: Grove, 1961. 112 pp. Translated by Richard Seaver. D: Alain Resnais. S: Marguerite Duras.

4075 Duras, Marguerite. Hiroshima Mon Amour and Une Aussi

Longue Absence. London: Calder and Boyars, 1966.
191 pp. Translated by Richard Seaver.

HOME OF THE BRAVE

4076 Wilner, Daniel M.   Attitude as a Determinant of Perception
in the Mass Media: Reactions to the Motion Picture
"Home of the Brave." University of California: Ph. D.,
1951. D: Mark Robson. S: Carl Foreman.

UN HONNETE HOMME

4077 Kyrou, Ado.   Un Honnête Homme/An Honest Man. London:
Rodney, 1964. 39 pp. English translation by Alan Hull
Walton. D/S: Ado Kyrou.
Text of the screenplay in French and English.

THE HOUSE

4078 Agee, James.   The Collected Short Prose of James Agee.
Edited by Robert Fitzgerald. Boston: Houghton Mifflin,
1968. 243 pp. Unproduced.
Lengthy and detailed film treatment.

THE HOUSEHOLDER

4079 Jhabvala, Ruth Prawer. The Householder: A Screenplay.
Delhi: Ramlochan, ca. 1965. 168 pp. D: James Ivory.
S: Ruth Prawer Jhabvala.

HOW GREEN WAS MY VALLEY

4080 Gassner, John and Nichols, Dudley (eds.) Twenty Best Film
Plays. New York: Crown, 1943. 1112 pp. D: John
Ford. S: Philip Dunne.

HOW TO BE A DETECTIVE

4081 Benchley, Robert. The Reel Benchley: Robert Benchley at
His Hilarious Best in Words and Pictures. Compiled by
George Hornby. New York: A. A. Wyn, 1950. 96 pp.
D: Felix E. Feist. S: Robert Benchley.
Narration and stills of the 1936 short.

HOW TO SLEEP

4082 Benchley, Robert. The Reel Benchley: Robert Benchley at
His Hilarious Best in Words and Pictures. Compiled by
George Hornby. New York: A. A. Wyn, 1950. 96 pp.
D: Nick Grinde. S: Robert Benchley.
Narration and stills of the 1935 short.

HOW TO TRAIN A DOG

4083   Benchley, Robert.   The Reel Benchley: Robert Benchley at
       His Hilarious Best in Words and Pictures.   Compiled by
       George Hornby.   New York: A. A. Wyn, 1950.   96 pp.
       D: Arthur Ripley.   S: Robert Benchley.
       Narration and stills of the 1936 short.

THE HUSTLER

4084   Rossen, Robert.   Three Screenplays: All the King's Men,
       The Hustler, Lilith.   Edited by Steve Rossen.   Garden
       City, N.Y.: Doubleday, 1972.   276 pp.   D: Robert
       Rossen.   S: Robert Rossen and Sidney Carrol.

4085   Maynard, Richard A. (ed.)   Literature of the Screen: Values
       in Conflict.   New York: Scholastic Book Services, 1974.
       Approx. 200 pp.
       Screenplay and supplementary educational materials.

I AM CURIOUS (BLUE)

4086   Sjoman, Vilgot.   I Am Curious (Blue).   New York: Grove,
       1970.   219 pp.   Translated by Martin Minow and Jenny
       Bohman.   D/S: Vilgot Sjoman.

I AM CURIOUS (YELLOW)

4087   Sjoman, Vilgot.   I Am Curious (Yellow).   New York: Grove,
       1968.   254 pp.   Translated by Martin Minow and Jenny
       Bohman.   D/S: Vilgot Sjoman.
       Screenplay plus extensive excerpts from the transcript
       of the film's obscenity trial.

4088   Sjoman, Vilgot.   I Was Curious: Diary of the Making of a
       Film.   New York: Grove, 1968.   217 pp.   Translated
       by Alan Blair.

I NEVER SANG FOR MY FATHER

4089   Anderson, Robert.   I Never Sang For My Father.   New York:
       New American Library, 1970.   159 pp.   D: Gilbert Cates.
       S: Robert Anderson.
       Screenplay plus articles by Anderson and Cates.

THE IDIOT

4090   Kurosawa, Akira.   The Complete Works of Akira Kurosawa:
       Volume 6.   Tokyo: Kinema Jumpo Sha, 1971.   190 pp.
       D: Akira Kurosawa.   S: Eijiro Hisaita and Akira Kuro-
       sawa.
       Text of the screenplay in Japanese and English.

IF....

4091   Anderson, Lindsay and Sherwin, David.   If....   New York:
       Simon and Schuster, 1969.   167 pp.   D: Lindsay Ander-
       son. S: David Sherwin.

IKIRU

4092   Kurosawa, Akira. Ikiru.   Edited and introduced by Donald
       Richie. New York: Simon and Schuster, 1968.   88 pp.
       D: Akira Kurosawa. S: Shinobu Hashimoto, Hideo
       Oguni, and Akira Kurosawa.

4093   Kurosawa, Akira.   The Complete Works of Akira Kurosawa:
       Volume 6. Tokyo: Kinema Jumpo Sha, 1971.   190 pp.
       Text of the screenplay in Japanese and English.

THE IMMORTAL ONE

4094   Robbe-Grillet, Alain.   The Immortal One.   London: Calder
       and Boyars, 1971.   173 pp. Translated by A. M. Sheri-
       dan Smith.   D/S: Alain Robbe-Grillet.

IN THE FRENCH STYLE

4095   Shaw, Irwin.   In the French Style.   New York: Macfadden-
       Bartell, 1963.   207 pp. D: Robert Parrish. S: Irwin
       Shaw.
           Screenplay plus articles and original stories by Shaw.

IN THE MESH

4096   Sartre, Jean-Paul.   In the Mesh.   London: Andrew Dakers,
       1954. 128 pp. Unproduced. S: Jean-Paul Sartre.

THE INFORMER

4097   Hatcher, Harlan (ed.)   Modern British Dramas.   New York:
       Harcourt, Brace, 1941.   374 pp. (Revised as Modern
       Dramas, 1944.   495 pp.) D: John Ford. S: Dudley
       Nichols.
           Includes the cutting continuity of THE INFORMER.

INTOLERANCE

4098   Huff, Theodore.   Intolerance, The Film by David Wark
       Griffith: A Shot-by-Shot Analysis.   New York: Museum
       of Modern Art, 1966.   155 pp. D/S: D. W. Griffith.

THE INVISIBLE WALL

4099   Du Rynn, Sebastian.   The Invisible Wall, Anatomy of a

Camera-Script. London: Arcade Recording Circuit, 1974.
108 pp. Unproduced. S: Sebastian Du Rynn.

IRMA LA DOUCE

4100 Wilder, Billy and Diamond, I. A. L. Irma La Douce: A
      Screenplay. New York: Tower, 1963. 127 pp. D:
      Billy Wilder. S: Billy Wilder and I. A. L. Diamond.

IT ALWAYS RAINS ON SUNDAY

4101 Collier, John W. A Film in the Making. London: World
      Film Publications, 1947. 96 pp. D: Robert Hamer.
      S: Angus MacPhail, Robert Hamer, and Henry Cornelius.
      Production account.

IT HAPPENED HERE

4102 Brownlow, Kevin. How It Happened Here: The Making of a
      Film. Garden City, N.Y.: Doubleday, 1968. 184 pp.
      D/S: Kevin Brownlow.

IT HAPPENED ONE NIGHT

4103 Gassner, John and Nichols, Dudley (eds.) Twenty Best Film
      Plays. New York: Crown, 1943. 1112 pp. D: Frank
      Capra. S: Robert Riskin.

4104 Gassner, John and Nichols, Dudley (eds.) Great Film Plays.
      New York: Crown, 1959. 334 pp. (Shorter edition of
      Twenty Best Film Plays.)

THE ITALIAN STRAW HAT

4105 Masterworks of the French Cinema. Introduction by John
      Weightman. New York: Harper and Row, 1974. 350 pp.
      D/S: Rene Clair.

IVAN THE TERRIBLE

4106 Eisenstein, Sergei. Ivan the Terrible: A Screenplay.
      Edited and translated by Ivor Montagu and Herbert
      Marshall. New York: Simon and Schuster, 1962.
      319 pp. D/S: Sergei Eisenstein.
          Screenplay and various essays including one by
      Eisenstein.

4107 Eisenstein, Sergei. Ivan the Terrible. New York: Simon
      and Schuster, 1970. 264 pp. Translated by A. E. Ellis.
      Screenplays for Parts I, II, and III plus essays.

4108 Eisenstein, Sergei. The Complete Films of Eisenstein,

Together With an Unpublished Essay by Eisenstein. New
York: Dutton, 1974. 154 pp. Translated by John
Hetherington.

JAN HUSS

4109   Kratochvil, Milos V. and Vavra, Otakar. Jan Huss. Prague:
Artia, 1957. 174 pp. D: Otakar Vavra. S: Milos V.
Kratochvil and Otakar Vavra.

JAWS

4110   Blake, Edith. On Location ... On Martha's Vineyard: The
Making of the Movie Jaws. Orleans, Mass.: Lower
Cape, 1975. 133 pp. D: Steven Spielberg. S: Peter
Benchley.

4111   Gottlieb, Carl. The Jaws Log. New York: Dell, 1975.
217 pp.
Production account.

JESUS

4112   Dreyer, Carl Theodor. Jesus. New York: Dell, 1971.
312 pp. Unproduced. S: Carl Theodor Dreyer.
The "film manuscript" plus articles by and about
Dreyer, including tributes by Renoir, Fellini, and
Truffaut.

JESUS CHRIST SUPERSTAR

4113   James, David. Jesus Christ Superstar. New York: Dell,
1973. 112 pp. D: Norman Jewison. S: Melvyn Bragg
and Norman Jewison.
Primarily photographs, plus brief production account.

JOAN OF ARC   (1948)

4114   Anderson, Maxwell and Solt, Andrew. Joan of Arc. New
York: William Sloane, 1948. 172 pp. D: Victor
Fleming. S: Maxwell Anderson and Andrew Solt.

THE JOB

4115   Visconti, Luchino. Three Screenplays: White Nights, Rocco
and His Brothers, and The Job. New York: Orion,
1970. 313 pp. Translated by Judith Green. D: Luchino
Visconti. S: Suso Cecchi d'Amico and Luchino Visconti.
Screenplay of a segment from BOCCACCIO '70.

JOE

4116   Wexler, Norman. Joe: Screenplay. New York: Avon,

1970. 128 pp. D: John G. Avildsen. S: Norman
Wexler.
Screenplay and essay by Judith Crist.

LE JOUR SE LEVE

4117 Carne, Marcel and Prevert, Jacques. Le Jour se Leve.
New York: Simon and Schuster, 1970. 128 pp. Trans-
lation and description by Dinah Brooke and Nicola Hayden.
D: Marcel Carne. S: Jacques Viot and Jacques Prevert.
Screenplay and an essay by Andre Bazin.

JUAREZ

4118 Gassner, John and Nichols, Dudley (eds.) Twenty Best Film
Plays. New York: Crown, 1943. 1112 pp. D: William
Dieterle. S: John Huston, Wolfgang Reinhardt, and
Aeneas MacKenzie.

JUDGMENT AT NUREMBERG

4119 Mann, Abby. Judgment at Nuremberg. London: Cassell,
1961. 182 pp. D: Stanley Kramer. S: Abby Mann.

JULES AND JIM

4120 Truffaut, François. Jules and Jim. New York: Simon and
Schuster, 1968. 104 pp. Translated by Nicholas Fry.
D: François Truffaut. S: François Truffaut and Jean
Gruault.

JULIET OF THE SPIRITS

4121 Kezich, Tullio (ed.) Juliet of the Spirits. New York: Bal-
lantine, 1966. 318 pp. Translated by Howard Greenfeld.
D: Federico Fellini. S: Federico Fellini, Tullio Pinelli,
Ennio Flaiano, and Brunello Rondi.
Screenplay, transcript of the final film, and interview
with Fellini.

4122 Reynolds, Lessie. An Analysis of the Non-Verbal Symbolism
in Federico Fellini's Film Trilogy, La Dolce Vita, 8 ,
and Juliet of the Spirits. University of Michigan: Ph.D.,
1969. 207 pp.

JULIUS CAESAR (1953)

4123 Culkin, John. Julius Caesar: The Complete Text With Notes:
A Case Study of Julius Caesar as a Play and as a Film.
New York: Scholastic Book Services, 1963. 186 pp.
D/S: Joseph L. Mankiewicz.
Includes material from the screenplay.

KANAL

4124 Wajda, Andrzej.   The Wajda Trilogy.   New York: Simon
      and Schuster, 1973. 239 pp. D: Andrzej Wajda. S:
      Jerzy Stefan Stawinski.

KIND HEARTS AND CORONETS

4125 Masterworks of the British Cinema.   Introduction by John
      Russell Taylor. New York: Harper and Row, 1974.
      352 pp. D: Robert Hamer. S: John Dighton.

KING KONG (1933)

4126 Annan, David.   Ape: The Kingdom of Kong.   London: Lor-
      rimer, 1975. 95 pp. D: Ernest B. Schoedsack and
      Merian C. Cooper. S: James A. Creelman and Ruth
      Rose.
      Includes extensive analysis of the 1933 KING
      KONG.

4127 Goldner, Orville and Turner, George E.   The Making of
      King Kong. South Brunswick, N.J.: A. S. Barnes,
      1975. 271 pp.
      Production account plus material on the careers of
      Schoedsack, Cooper, and Willis H. O'Brien, special ef-
      fects creator.

THE KITE   (see QUARTET)

KNIFE IN THE WATER

4128 Polanski, Roman.   Polanski: Three Film Scripts.   New
      York: Harper and Row, 1975. 214 pp. D: Roman
      Polanski. S: Jerzy Skolimowski, Jakub Goldberg, and
      Roman Polanski.
      Screenplay, introduction by Boleslaw Sulik, and inter-
      view with Polanski.

LACOMBE, LUCIEN

4129 Malle, Louis and Modiano, Patrick.   Lacombe, Lucien.
      New York: Viking, 1975. 122 pp. Translated by Sabine
      Destree. D: Louis Malle. S: Louis Malle and Patrick
      Modiano.

THE LAST CHANCE

4130 Schweizer, Richard.   The Last Chance.   London: Secker
      and Warburg and Lindsay Drummond, 1947. 113 pp.
      Translated by Lord Sudley. D: Leopold Lintberg. S:
      Richard Schweizer.
      Novelized format.

THE LAST LAUGH

4131 Trope, Zipora Sharf. A Critical Application of Andre Bazin's
      "Mise-en-Scène" Theory in: The Last Laugh, Grand Il-
      lusion, and The Magnificent Ambersons. University of
      Michigan: Ph. D. , 1974. 187 pp. D: F. W. Murnau.
      S: Carl Mayer.

LAST TANGO IN PARIS

4132 Bertolucci, Bernardo and Arcalli, Franco. Last Tango in
      Paris. New York: Delta, 1973. 224 pp. D: Bernardo
      Bertolucci. S: Bernardo Bertolucci and Franco Arcalli.
      Screenplay and critical essays by Pauline Kael and
      Norman Mailer.

4133 Carroll, Kent E. (ed.) Close-Up: Last Tango in Paris.
      New York: Grove, 1973. 176 pp.
      Includes interviews with Bertolucci and Maria Schneider,
      plus articles on the film by Charles Michener, Parker
      Tyler, Fernando Arrabal, John Simon, Alberto Moravia,
      Stuart Byron, Norman Mailer, and others.

THE LAST WORDS OF DUTCH SCHULTZ

4134 Burroughs, William S. The Last Words of Dutch Schultz:
      A Fiction in the Form of a Film Script. London: Cape
      Goliard, 1970. 81 pp. New York: Viking, 1975. 115 pp.
      Unproduced. S: William S. Burroughs.

LAST YEAR AT MARIENBAD

4135 Robbe-Grillet, Alain. Last Year at Marienbad. New York:
      Grove, 1962. 168 pp. Translated by Richard Howard.
      D: Alain Resnais. S: Alain Robbe-Grillet.
      Screenplay plus essay by Robbe-Grillet.

4136 Blumenberg, Richard Mitchell. The Manipulation of Time
      and Space in the Novels of Alain Robbe-Grillet and in the
      Narrative Films of Alain Resnais, With Particular Refer-
      ence to Last Year at Marienbad. Ohio University: Ph. D. ,
      1969. 197 pp.

IL LAVORO (see THE JOB)

LAWRENCE OF ARABIA

4137 Kent, Howard. Single Bed for Three: A Lawrence of Arabia Note-
      book. London: Hutchinson, 1963. 208 pp. D: David Lean.
      S: Robert Bolt.

LEGEND OF THE WEREWOLF

4138 Buscombe, Edward. Making Legend of the Werewolf. London:

British Film Institute, 1975. 121 pp. D: Freddie
Francis. S: John Elder.

LET THERE BE LIGHT

4139 Hughes, Robert (ed.) Film: Book 2: Films of Peace and
War. New York: Grove, 1962. 255 pp. D: John
Huston. S: Charles Kaufman.

LES LIAISONS DANGEREUSES

4140 Vadim, Roger. Les Liaisons Dangereuses. New York:
Ballantine, 1962. 256 pp. Translated by Bernard Shir-
Cliff. D: Roger Vadim. S: Roger Vailland, Roger
Vadim, and Claude Brule.

THE LICKERISH QUARTET

4141 Metzger, Radley. The Lickerish Quartet. New York: Audo-
bon, 1970. Unpaged. D: Radley Metzger. S: Michael
DeForrest.

THE LIFE AND DEATH OF COLONEL BLIMP

4142 Robson, E. W. and M. M. The Shame and Disgrace of
Colonel Blimp. London: Sidneyan Society, 1944. 31 pp.
D/S: Michael Powell and Emeric Pressburger.
Analysis of the film.

THE LIFE AND TIMES OF JUDGE ROY BEAN

4143 Milius, John. The Life and Times of Judge Roy Bean. New
York: Bantam, 1973. 180 pp. D: John Huston. S:
John Milius.

LIFE IS A SONG

4144 Lustig, Ernst. Life Is a Song: A Script for a Musical Motion Picture or Stage Production. New York: William-
Frederick, 1951. 30 pp. Unproduced. S: Ernst Lustig.

THE LIFE, LOVE, AND DEATH OF SAINT BRENDAN

4145 Moore, David. The Life, Love, and Death of Saint Brendan:
A Movie by David Moore: The Spiritual Pilgrimage of
America's Patron Sinner. New York: Hobson, 1946.
250 pp. Unproduced. S: David Moore.

THE LIFE OF EMILE ZOLA

4146 Gassner, John and Nichols, Dudley (eds.) Twenty Best Film
Plays. New York: Crown, 1943. 1112 pp. D: William

Dieterle. S: Heinz Herald, Geza Herczeg, and Norman
Reilly Raine.

4147   Gassner, John and Nichols, Dudley (eds.) Great Film Plays.
New York: Crown, 1959. 334 pp. (Shorter edition of
Twenty Best Film Plays.)

LILIES OF THE FIELD

4148   Wald, Malvin and Werner, Michael (comps.) Three Major
Screenplays. New York: Globe, 1972. 394 pp. D:
Ralph Nelson. S: James Poe.
Screenplay plus articles.

LILITH

4149   Rossen, Robert. Three Screenplays: All the King's Men,
The Hustler, Lilith. Edited by Steven Rossen. Garden
City, N.Y.: Doubleday, 1972. 276 pp. D: Robert
Rossen. S: Robert Alan Aurthur and Robert Rossen.

THE LION IN WINTER

4150   Goldman, James. The Lion in Winter. New York: Dell,
1968. 139 pp. D: Anthony Harvey. S: James Goldman.

LITTLE CAESAR

4151   Gassner, John and Nichols, Dudley (eds.) Twenty Best Film
Plays. New York: Crown, 1943. 1112 pp. D: Mervyn
LeRoy. S: Frances Edwards Faragoh.

LITTLE FAUSS AND BIG HALSY

4152   Eastman, Charles. Little Fauss and Big Halsy. New York:
Farrar, Straus and Giroux, 1970. 164 pp. D: Sidney
J. Furie. S: Charles Eastman.

LITTLE SISTERS OF THE GRASSLAND

4153   Little Sisters of the Grassland. Peking, 1973. 89 pp.
Stills of a film produced at the Shanghai Animation
Studio.

LIVE AND LET DIE

4154   Moore, Roger. Roger Moore's James Bond Diary. Greenwich, Conn.: Fawcett, 1973. 184 pp. D: Guy Hamilton. S: Tom Mankiewicz.
Includes production account material.

LIVING FREE

4155 Couffer, Jack. The Lions of Living Free. New York:
      Dutton, 1972. 96 pp. D: Jack Couffer. S: Millard
      Kaufman.
      Primarily a production account.

LOLITA

4156 Nabokov, Vladimir. Lolita: A Screenplay. New York:
      McGraw-Hill, 1974. 213 pp. D: Stanley Kubrick. S:
      Vladimir Nabokov.

LONDON CAN TAKE IT

4157 Reynolds, Quentin. Britain Can Take It: Based on the Film.
      New York: Dutton, 1941. 32 pp. D: Humphrey Jen-
      nings and Harry Watt. S: Quentin Reynolds.
      Photographs from LONDON CAN TAKE IT plus narra-
      tion by Reynolds.

THE LONELINESS OF THE LONG-DISTANCE RUNNER

4158 Maynard, Richard A. (ed.) Literature of the Screen:
      Identity. New York: Scholastic Book Services, 1974.
      192 pp. D: Tony Richardson. S: Alan Sillitoe.
      Screenplay and supplementary educational material.

THE LONG ABSENCE (see UNE AUSSIE LONGUE ABSENCE)

THE LOST WEEKEND

4159 Gassner, John and Nichols, Dudley (eds.) Best Film Plays--
      1945. New York: Crown, 1946. 648 pp. D: Billy
      Wilder. S: Charles Brackett and Billy Wilder.

LOVE AT TWENTY (see ANTOINE AND COLETTE)

LOVE STORY

4160 Meyer, Nichols. The Love Story Story. New York: Avon,
      1971. 224 pp. D: Arthur Hiller. S: Erich Segal.
      Production account material.

THE LOVED ONE

4161 Southern, Terry. The Journal of The Loved One: The
      Production Log of a Motion Picture. New York: Random,
      1965. 116 pp. D: Tony Richardson. S: Terry Southern
      and Christopher Isherwood.

LUCIA

4162 Meyerson, Michael (ed.) Memories of Underdevelopment:
The Revolutionary Films of Cuba. New York: Grossman,
1973. 214 pp. D: Humberto Solas. S: Humberto
Solas, Julio Garcia Espinosa, and Nelson Rodriguez.
Includes description of parts I and II ("Lucia 1895"
and "Lucia 1933") and the script of part III ("Lucia 196-").

M (1931)

4163 Lang, Fritz. M. New York: Simon and Schuster, 1968.
112 pp. Translated by Nicholas Garnham. D: Fritz
Lang. S: Thea von Harbou.

4164 Masterworks of the German Cinema. Introduction by Roger
Manvell. New York: Harper and Row, 1973. 300 pp.
Screenplay plus an essay by Paul Jensen about the
film.

MACBETH (1960)

4165 Hutton, Clayton. Macbeth: The Making of a Film. London:
Parrish, 1960. 80 pp. D: George Schaefer. S: William
Shakespeare.

MADE IN U.S.A.

4166 Godard, Jean-Luc. Made in U.S.A. London: Lorrimer,
1967. 87 pp. D/S: Jean-Luc Godard.

THE MAGICIAN

4167 Bergman, Ingmar. Four Screenplays of Ingmar Bergman.
New York: Simon and Schuster, 1960. 330 pp. Trans-
lated by Lars Malmstrom and David Kushner. D/S:
Ingmar Bergman.

THE MAGNIFICENT AMBERSONS

4168 Trope, Zipora Sharf. A Critical Application of Andre Bazin's
"Mise-en-Scène" Theory in: The Last Laugh, Grand Il-
lusion, and The Magnificent Ambersons. University of
Michigan: Ph.D., 1974. 187 pp. D/S: Orson Welles.

MAIDSTONE

4169 Mailer, Norman. Maidstone: A Mystery. New York: New
American Library, 1971. 191 pp. D/S: Norman Mailer.
Screenplay, essay on filmmaking by Mailer, and pro-
duction account by Sally Beauman, J. Anthony Lukas and
James Toback.

MAJOR BARBARA

4170   Shaw, George Bernard.   Major Barbara: A Screen Version.
New York: Penguin, 1946. 154 pp. (Reprinted Balti-
more: Penguin, 1956.) D: Gabriel Pascal. S: George
Bernard Shaw.

MAKE WAY FOR TOMORROW

4171   Gassner, John and Nichols, Dudley (eds.) Twenty Best Film
Plays. New York: Crown, 1943. 1112 pp. D: Leo
McCarey. S: Vina Delmar.

THE MALTESE FALCON

4172   Anobile, Richard J. (ed.) The Maltese Falcon. New York:
Darien, 1974. 256 pp. D/S: John Huston.
Shot-by-shot frame enlargements and dialogue.

A MAN AND A WOMAN

4173   Lelouch, Claude. A Man and A Woman. New York: Simon
and Schuster, 1971. 120 pp. Translation and description
by Nicholas Fry. D: Claude Lelouch. S: Claude Lelouch with Pierre Uytterhoeven.

MAN OF ARAN

4174   Mullen, Pat. Man of Aran. (Originally published 1935.)
Cambridge, Mass.: M.I.T. Press, 1970. 286 pp.
D/S: Robert Flaherty.
Autobiography of one of the collaborators on MAN OF
ARAN; includes a production account of the filming.

MAN'S HOPE

4175   Michalczyk, John Joseph. Malraux's "Espoir": A Critical
and Historical Analysis of the Film. Harvard University:
Ph.D., 1972. D/S: Andre Malraux.

A MARRIED WOMAN

4176   Godard, Jean-Luc. A Married Woman. New York: Berkly
Medallion, 1965. Unpaged. English text by Ursule Moli-
naro. D/S: Jean-Luc Godard.
Dialogue and stills from the film plus an essay by
Tom Milne.

4177   Godard, Jean-Luc. Godard: Three Films. New York:
Harper and Row, 1975. 192 pp.
Screenplay and essays.

MASCULINE FEMININE

4178   Godard, Jean-Luc.   Masculine Feminine.   New York: Grove,
1969.   288 pp.   D/S: Jean-Luc Godard.
Screenplay, documents, two Guy de Maupassant
stories on which the film is based, critical essays and
interviews.

4179   Giannetti, Louis D.   Godard and Others: Essays in Film
Form.   Rutherford, N.J.:   Fairleigh Dickinson University
Press, 1975.   184 pp.
Includes a detailed analysis of MASCULINE FEMININE.

A MEDAL FOR BENNY

4180   Gassner, John and Nichols, Dudley (eds.)   Best Film Plays--
1945.   New York: Crown, 1946.   648 pp.   D: Irving
Pichel.   S: Frank Butler.

MEDICINE BALL CARAVAN

4181   Forcade, Thomas King.   Caravan of Love and Money: Being
a Highly Unauthorized Chronicle of the Filming of Medicine Ball Caravan.   New York: New American Library,
1972.   128 pp.   D: Francois Reichenbach.   S: Christian
Haren.

4182   Grissim, John, Jr.   We Have Come for Your Daughters:
What Went Down on the Medicine Ball Caravan.   New
York: Morrow, 1972.   254 pp.

MEMORIES OF UNDERDEVELOPMENT

4183   Myerson, Michael (ed.)   Memories of Underdevelopment:
The Revolutionary Films of Cuba.   New York: Gross-
man, 1973.   214 pp.   D: Tomas Gutierrez Alea.   S:
Tomas Gutierrez Alea and Edmundo Desnoes.

METROPOLIS

4184   Lang, Fritz.   Metropolis.   New York: Simon and Schuster,
1973.   131 pp.   D: Fritz Lang.   S: Thea von Harbou.
Screenplay plus essays by Paul Jensen and Siegfried
Kracauer.

MINE WARFARE

4185   Mine Warfare.   Peking: Foreign Language Press, 1971.
178 pp.
Description and stills from the film.

MINNIE AND MOSKOWITZ

4186 Cassavetes, John. Minnie and Moskowitz. Los Angeles:
      Black Sparrow, 1973. 116 pp. D/S: John Cassavetes.

MIRACLE IN MILAN

4187 De Sica, Vittorio. Miracle in Milan. New York: Orion,
      1968. 121 pp. D: Vittorio De Sica. S: Cesare
      Zavattini and Vittorio De Sica.
      Screenplay plus articles by De Sica.

THE MIRACLE OF MORGAN'S CREEK

4188 Gassner, John and Nichols, Dudley (eds.) Best Film Plays
      of 1943-1944. New York: Crown, 1945. 694 pp.
      D/S: Preston Sturges.

MIRIAM (see TRILOGY)

THE MISFITS

4189 Miller, Arthur. The Misfits. New York: Viking, 1961.
      132 pp. D: John Huston. S: Arthur Miller.
      Novelized format.

4190 Goode, James. The Story of The Misfits. Indianapolis:
      Bobbs-Merrill, 1963. 331 pp.
      Production account.

4191 Garrett, George P.; Hardison, O. B., Jr.; and Gelfman,
      Jane R. Film Scripts Three. New York: Appleton-
      Century-Crofts, 1972. 618 pp.

MR. KNOW-ALL (see TRIO)

MR. SMITH GOES TO WASHINGTON

4192 Wald, Jerry and Macaulay, Richard (eds.) The Best Pic-
      tures, 1939-1940, and The Year Book of Motion Pictures
      in America. New York: Dodd, Mead, 1940. 534 pp.
      (Reprinted New York: Gordon, 1975.) D: Frank Capra.
      S: Sidney Buchman.

4193 Gassner, John and Nichols, Dudley (eds.) Twenty Best
      Film Plays. New York: Crown, 1943. 1112 pp.

4194 Maynard, Richard A. (ed.) Literature of the Screen:
      Power. New York: Scholastic Book Services, 1974.
      224 pp.
      Screenplay and supplementary educational material.

MRS. MINIVER

4195   Gassner, John and Nichols, Dudley (eds.) Twenty Best Film
       Plays. New York: Crown, 1943. 1112 pp. D: William
       Wyler. S: Arthur Wimperis, George Froeschel, James
       Hilton, and Claudine West.

MONKEY BUSINESS

4196   Marx Brothers. The Four Marx Brothers in Monkey Busi-
       ness and Duck Soup. New York: Simon and Schuster,
       1972. 183 pp. D: Norman McLeod. S: S. J. Perel-
       man and Will B. Johnstone.

MONSIEUR HULOT'S HOLIDAY

4197   Carriere, Jean-Claude. Monsieur Hulot's Holiday. New
       York: Crowell, 1959. 198 pp. Translated by A. E. Ellis.
       D: Jacques Tati. S: Jacques Tati and Henri Marquet.

THE MORE THE MERRIER

4198   Gassner, John and Nichols, Dudley (eds.) Best Film Plays
       of 1943-1944. New York: Crown, 1945. 694 pp. D:
       George Stevens. S: Robert Russel, Frank Ross, Richard
       Flournoy, and Lewis Foster.

MOROCCO

4199   von Sternberg, Josef. Morocco and Shanghai Express. New
       York: Simon and Schuster, 1973. 136 pp. D: Josef von
       Sternberg. S: Jules Furthman.
       Screenplay plus essay by Andrew Sarris.

MOTHER

4200   Pudovkin, V. I. Mother, A Film by V. I. Pudovkin; Earth,
       A Film by Alexander Dovzhenko. New York: Simon and
       Schuster, 1973. 102 pp. D: V. I. Pudovkin. S: N.
       Zarkhi and V. I. Pudovkin.

MURDER IN THE CATHEDRAL

4201   Eliot, T. S. and Hoellering, George. The Film of Murder
       in the Cathedral. New York: Harcourt, Brace, 1952.
       110 pp. D: George Hoellering. S: T. S. Eliot.
       Screenplay and many stills.

MY FAIR LADY

4202   Beaton, Cecil. Cecil Beaton's Fair Lady. New York: Holt,
       Rinehart and Winston, 1964. 128 pp. D: George Cukor.

S: Alan Jay Lerner.
Journal kept by Beaton during his costuming and set
design of MY FAIR LADY.

MY MAN GODFREY

4203   Gassner, John and Nichols, Dudley (eds.) Twenty Best Film
       Plays. New York: Crown, 1943. 1112 pp. D: Gregory
       La Cava. S: Morrie Ryskind and Eric Hatch.

NANOOK OF THE NORTH

4204   Flaherty, Robert. Nanook of the North. Edited by Robert
       Kraus. New York: Windmill, 1971. 32 pp. D/S:
       Robert Flaherty.
       Selected stills from the film, with captions.

NAZARIN

4205   Buñuel, Luis. The Exterminating Angel, Nazarin, and Los
       Olvidados. New York: Simon and Schuster, 1972.
       299 pp. Translated by Nicholas Fry. D: Luis Buñuel.
       S: Luis Buñuel and Julio Alejandro.
       Screenplay plus article about NAZARIN by J. Fran-
       cisco Aranda.

NEVER GIVE A SUCKER AN EVEN BREAK

4206   Fields, W. C. Never Give a Sucker an Even Break and
       Tillie and Gus. New York: Simon and Schuster, 1973.
       124 pp. D: Edward Cline. S: John T. Neville and
       Prescott Chaplin.

THE NEXT VOICE YOU HEAR

4207   Schary, Dore with Palmer, Charles. Case History of a
       Movie. New York: Random, 1950. 242 pp. D: William
       Wellman. S: Charles Schnee.

THE NIGHT   (see LA NOTTE)

NIGHT AND FOG

4208   Hughes, Robert (ed.) Film: Book 2, Films of Peace and
       War. New York: Grove, 1962. 255 pp. D: Alain
       Resnais. S: Jean Cayrol.

A NIGHT AT THE OPERA

4209   Kaufman, George S. and Ryskind, Morrie. A Night at the
       Opera. New York: Viking, 1972. 216 pp. D: Sam
       Wood. S: George S. Kaufman and Morrie Ryskind.
       Original screenplay and transcript of the final film.

THE NIGHT OF THE HUNTER

4210   Agee, James. Agee on Film: Volume Two, Five Film
       Scripts. New York: McDowell, Obolensky, 1960.   488
       pp. (Reprinted New York: Grosset and Dunlap, 1969.)
       D: Charles Laughton. S: James Agee.

NINOTCHKA

4211   Wald, Jerry and Macaulay, Richard (eds.) The Best Pictures,
       1939-1940, and The Year Book of Motion Pictures in
       America. New York: Dodd, Mead, 1940. 534 pp. (Re-
       printed New York: Gordon, 1975.) D: Ernst Lubitsch.
       S: Charles Brackett, Billy Wilder, and Walter Reisch.
       Includes condensed screenplay of the film.

4212   Brackett, Charles; Wilder, Billy; and Reisch, Walter.
       Ninotchka. New York: Viking, 1972.   114 pp.

4213   Anobile, Richard J. (ed.) Ernst Lubitsch's Ninotchka.   New
       York: Darien, 1975.   256 pp.
       Shot-by-shot frame enlargements and dialogue.

NO REGRETS FOR OUR YOUTH

4214   Kurosawa, Akira. The Complete Works of Akira Kurosawa:
       Volume 2. Tokyo: Kinema Jumpo Sha, 1971. 135 pp.
       D: Akira Kurosawa. S: Eijiro Hisaita and Akira Kuro-
       sawa.
       Text of the screenplay in Japanese and English.

NOA NOA

4215   Agee, James. Agee on Film: Volume Two, Five Film
       Scripts. New York: McDowell, Obolensky, 1960.   488
       pp. (Reprinted New York: Grosset and Dunlap, 1969.)
       Unproduced. S: James Agee.

NONE BUT THE LONELY HEART

4216   Gassner, John and Nichols, Dudley (eds.) Best Film Plays--
       1945. New York: Crown, 1946. 648 pp. D/S: Clif-
       ford Odets.

NORTH BY NORTHWEST

4217   Lehman, Ernest. North By Northwest. New York: Viking,
       1972. 148 pp. D: Alfred Hitchcock. S: Ernest Lehman.

THE NORTH STAR

4218   Hellman, Lillian. The North Star: A Motion Picture About

Some Russian People. New York: Viking, 1943. 118 pp.
D: Lewis Milestone. S: Lillian Hellman.
Screenplay of THE NORTH STAR (also titled
ARMORED ATTACK).

NOSFERATU

4219 Byrne, Richard B. Films of Tyranny: Shot Analyses of The
Cabinet of Dr. Caligari, The Golem, Nosferatu. Madison,
Wisconsin: College Printing and Typing, 1966. 152 pp.
D: F. W. Murnau. S: Henrik Galeen.

4220 Masterworks of the German Cinema. Introduction by Roger
Manvell. New York: Harper and Row, 1973. 300 pp.
Screenplay plus essay on NOSFERATU by Lotte
Eisner.

NOT RECONCILED, OR, ONLY VIOLENCE HELPS WHERE
VIOLENCE RULES

4221 Roud, Richard. Jean-Marie Straub. New York: Viking,
1972. 176 pp. D/S: Jean-Marie Straub.
Includes screenplay of NOT RECONCILED.

NOTHING BUT A MAN

4222 Maynard, Richard A. (ed.) Literature of the Screen: Men
and Women. New York: Scholastic Book Services, 1974.
Approx. 200 pp. D: Michael Roemer. S: Michael
Roemer and Robert Young.

LA NOTTE

4223 Antonioni, Michelangelo. Screenplays. New York:
Orion, 1963. 361 pp. D: Michelangelo Antonioni.
S: Michelangelo Antonioni, Ennio Flaiano, and Tonino
Guerra.

4224 [No entry.]

THE NUN

4225 Diderot, Denis. The Nun. Los Angeles: Holloway, 1968.
315 pp. D: Jacques Rivette. S: Jacques Rivette and
Jean Gruault.
Novel on which the film is based; also includes material on the film's production and censorship.

O LUCKY MAN!

4226 Anderson, Lindsay and Sherwin, David. O Lucky Man! New
York: Grove, 1973. 192 pp. D: Lindsay Anderson.
S: David Sherwin.

Screenplay plus essays by Anderson and Sherwin.

OCCURRENCE AT OWL CREEK BRIDGE

4227   Schreivogel, Paul. An Occurrence at Owl Creek Bridge: A
Visual Study. Dayton, Ohio: Pflaum, 1969. 28 pp.
D/S: Robert Enrico.
Analysis of the film juxtaposed to the text of the story
by Ambrose Bierce.

4228   Garrett, Gerald R. and Erskine, Thomas L. (comps.) From
Fiction to Film: Ambrose Bierce's An Occurrence at
Owl Creek Bridge. Encino, Cal.: Dickenson, 1973.
216 pp.
Shot analysis of the film, original story, and critical
essays.

OCTOBER

4229   Kuiper, John B. An Analysis of the Four Silent Films of
Sergei Eisenstein. University of Iowa: Ph.D., 1960.
436 pp. D/S: Sergei Eisenstein and Grigori Alexandrov.

4230   Eisenstein, Sergei. The Complete Films of Eisenstein, To-
gether with an Unpublished Essay by Eisenstein. New
York: Dutton, 1974. 154 pp. Translated by John
Hetherington.
OCTOBER, also known as TEN DAYS THAT SHOOK
THE WORLD.

4231   Eisenstein, Sergei. Eisenstein: Three Films. Edited by
Jay Leyda. New York: Harper and Row, c. 1974.
189 pp. Translated by Diana Matias.
Introduction and research commentary by
Leyda.

ODD MAN OUT

4232   Manvell, Roger (ed.) Three British Screenplays: Brief En-
counter, Odd Man Out, Scott of the Antarctic. London:
Methuen, 1950. 299 pp. D: Carol Reed. S: F. L.
Green and R. C. Sherriff.

4233   DeFelice, James. Filmguide to Odd Man Out. Bloomington:
Indiana University Press, 1975. 85 pp.

OEDIPUS REX

4234   Pasolini, Pier Paolo. Oedipus Rex. New York: Simon
and Schuster, 1971. 150 pp. Translated by John Mathews.
D/S: Pier Paolo Pasolini.
Screenplay, cutting continuity, and essay by Pasolini.

OEDIPUS THE KING

4235 Sophocles. Oedipus the King. New York: New American
      Library, 1968. 92 pp. Translated by Paul Roche. D:
      Philip Saville. S: Michael Luke and Philip Saville.
          Text of the play, stills from the 1968 film version,
      and an essay on the two by Raymond Palmer.

OLD AND NEW (see THE GENERAL LINE)

LOS OLVIDADOS

4236 Buñuel, Luis. The Exterminating Angel, Nazarin, and Los
      Olvidados. New York: Simon and Schuster, 1972. 299 pp.
      Translated by Nicholas Fry. D: Luis Buñuel. S: Luis
      Buñuel and Luis Alcoriza.
          Screenplay plus article about LOS OLVIDADOS by
      Andre Bazin.

ONE DAY IN THE LIFE OF IVAN DENISOVICH

4237 Solzhenitsyn, Alexander. The Making of One Day in the Life
      of Ivan Denisovich. New York: Ballantine, 1971. 271 pp.
      Translated by Gillon Aitken. D: Casper Wrede. S:
      Ronald Harwood.
          Original novel by Solzhenitsyn, the screenplay, and a
      production account of the film by Ronald Harwood.

ONE DAY, WHEN I WAS LOST

4238 Baldwin, James. One Day, When I Was Lost: A Scenario.
      New York: Dial, 1973. 280 pp. Unproduced. S:
      James Baldwin.
          Screenplay of the life of Malcolm X, based on the
      Alex Haley play.

ONE WONDERFUL SUNDAY

4239 Kurosawa, Akira. The Complete Works of Akira Kurosawa:
      Volume 3. Tokyo: Kinema Jumpo Sha, 1971. 136 pp.
      D: Akira Kurosawa. S: Keinosuke Uegusa and Akira
      Kurosawa.
          Text of the screenplay in Japanese and English.

OPEN CITY

4240 Roncoroni, Stefano (ed.) Rossellini: The War Trilogy:
      Open City, Paisan, Germany--Year Zero. New York:
      Grossman, 1973. 467 pp. Translated by Judith Green.
      D: Roberto Rossellini. S: Sergio Amidei with Fede-
      rico Fellini.

ORDET

4241   Dreyer, Carl Theodor. Four Screenplays. Bloomington:
Indiana University Press, 1970. 312 pp. Translated by
Oliver Stallybrass. D/S: Carl Dreyer.

ORPHEUS

4242   Cocteau, Jean. Cocteau: Three Screenplays: L'Eternel
Retour, Orphée, La Belle et la Bete. New York: Grossman, 1972. 250 pp. D/S: Jean Cocteau.

OTHELLO (1952)

4243   MacLiammoir, Micheal. Put Money in Thy Purse: The
Diary of the Film of Othello. London: Methuen, 1952.
258 pp. D/S: Orson Welles.
Written by the actor who played Iago in the film.

THE OUTCRY (see IL GRIDO)

OVER TWENTY-ONE

4244   Gassner, John and Nichols, Dudley (eds.) Best Film Plays--
1945. New York: Crown, 1946. 694 pp. D: Charles
Vidor. S: Sidney Buchman.

THE OX-BOW INCIDENT

4245   Gassner, John and Nichols, Dudley (eds.) Best Film Plays
of 1943-1944. New York: Crown, 1945. 694 pp. D:
William Wellman. S: Lamar Trotti.

4246   Wald, Malvin and Werner, Michael (comps.) Three Major
Screenplays. New York: Globe, 1972. 394 pp.
Screenplay plus articles.

PAISAN

4247   Roncoroni, Stefano (ed.) Rossellini: The War Trilogy:
Open City, Paisan, Germany--Year Zero. New York:
Grossman, 1973. 467 pp. Translated by Judith Green.
D: Roberto Rossellini. S: Sergio Amidei, Federico
Fellini, and Roberto Rossellini.

PALS

4248   Homoki-Nagy, Istvan. Pals. Budapest: Corvina, 1961.
137 pp. Translated by Istvan Farkas and Jozsef Hat-
vany. D: Istvan Homoki-Nagy.
Production account of the film PALS, which opened
the 1958 Edinburgh Festival.

PANDORA'S BOX

4249   Pabst, G. W. Pandora's Box (Lulu). New York: Simon
        and Schuster, 1971. 136 pp. Translated by Christopher
        Holme. D: G. W. Pabst. S: Ladislaus Vajda.
        Shooting script plus essays by Louise Brooks and
        Lotte Eisner.

PARADISE LOST

4250   Collier, John. Milton's Paradise Lost: Screenplay for
        Cinema of the Mind. New York: Knopf, 1973. 143 pp.
        Unproduced. S: John Collier.

PARDON ME, SIR, BUT IS MY EYE HURTING YOUR ELBOW?

4251   Corso, Gregory and others. Pardon Me, Sir, But Is My
        Eye Hurting Your Elbow? New York: Bernard Geis,
        1968. 173 pp. Unproduced. S: Gregory Corso, Bruce
        Jay Friedman, Allen Ginsberg, Herbert Gold, Arthur
        Kopit, Jack Richardson, Philip Roth, Robert Paul Smith,
        Terry Southern, Arnold Weinstein, Bob Booker, and
        George Foster.

THE PASSENGER

4252   Peploe, Mark; Wollen, Peter; and Antonioni, Michelangelo.
        The Passenger. New York: Grove, 1975. 192 pp.
        D: Michelangelo Antonioni. S: Mark Peploe, Peter
        Wollen, and Michelangelo Antonioni.

LA PASSION DE JEANNE D'ARC

4253   Dreyer, Carl Theodor. Four Screenplays. Bloomington:
        Indiana University Press, 1970. 312 pp. Translated by
        Oliver Stallybrass. D/S: Carl Dreyer.

4254   Bordwell, David. Filmguide to La Passion de Jeanne D'Arc.
        Bloomington: Indiana University Press, 1973. 83 pp.

THE PASSION OF JOAN OF ARC (see LA PASSION DE JEANNE D'ARC)

PAT GARRETT AND BILLY THE KID

4255   Wurlitzer, Rudolph. Pat Garrett and Billy the Kid. New
        York: New American Library, 1973. 130 pp. D: Sam
        Peckinpah. S: Rudolph Wurlitzer.

PATHER PANCHALI (see THE APU TRILOGY)

PERSONA

4256   Bergman, Ingmar.   Persona and Shame: The Screenplays of
       Ingmar Bergman.   New York: Grossman, 1972.   191 pp.
       Translated by Keith Bradfield.   D/S: Ingmar Bergman.

4257   Koch, Christian Herbert.   Understanding Film as Process of
       Change: A Metalanguage for the Study of Film Developed
       and Applied to Ingmar Bergman's Persona and Alan J.
       Pakula's The Sterile Cuckoo.   University of Iowa: Ph.D.,
       1970.   281 pp.

LE PETIT SOLDAT

4258   Godard, Jean-Luc.   Le Petit Soldat.   London: Lorrimer,
       1967.   92 pp.   New York: Simon and Schuster, 1970.
       Translation and description by Nicholas Garnham.   D/S:
       Jean-Luc Godard.
           Screenplay plus brief articles, including an interview
       with Godard.

PIERRE LE FOU

4259   Godard, Jean-Luc.   Pierre le Fou: A Screenplay.   New
       York: Simon and Schuster, 1969.   104 pp.   Translated
       by Peter Whitehead.   D/S: Jean-Luc Godard.
           Screenplay and interview with Godard.

A PLACE IN THE SUN

4260   Baird, James Lee.   The Movie in Our Heads: An Analysis
       of Three Film Versions of Theodore Dreiser's "An Ameri-
       can Tragedy."   University of Washington: Ph.D., 1967.
       252 pp.   D: George Stevens.   S: Michael Wilson and
       Harry Brown.

POINT OF ORDER!

4261   de Antonio, Emile and Talbot, Daniel.   Point of Order!: A
       Documentary of the Army-McCarthy Hearings.   New York:
       W. W. Norton, 1964.   108 pp.   D: Emile de Antonio.
       Transcript of the film.

PORT OF SHADOWS   (see QUAI DES BRUMES)

POTEMKIN   (see BATTLESHIP POTEMKIN)

THE PRINCE AND THE SHOWGIRL

4262   Rattigan, Terence.   The Prince and the Showgirl: The Script
       for the Film.   New York: New American Library, 1957.
       127 pp.   D: Laurence Olivier.   S: Terence Rattigan.

PSYCHO

4263 Naremore, James. Filmguide to Psycho. Bloomington:
      Indiana University Press, 1973. 87 pp. D: Alfred
      Hitchcock. S: Joseph Stephano.

4264 Anobile, Richard J. (ed.) Alfred Hitchcock's Psycho. New
      York: Darien, 1974. 256 pp.
      Shot-by-shot frame enlargements and dialogue.

PULL MY DAISY

4265 Kerouac, Jack. Pull My Daisy. New York: Grove, 1961.
      72 pp. D: Robert Frank and Alfred Leslie. S: Jack
      Kerouac.

PUMPKIN EATER

4266 Pinter, Harold. Five Screenplays. New York: Grove, 1971.
      367 pp. D: Jack Clayton. S: Harold Pinter.

THE PURPLE HEART

4267 Gassner, John and Nichols, Dudley (eds.) Best Film Plays
      of 1943-1944. New York: Crown, 1945. 694 pp. D:
      Lewis Milestone. S: Jerome Cady.

PYGMALION

4268 Shaw, George Bernard. Pygmalion. Baltimore: Penguin,
      1951. 125 pp. D: Anthony Asquith and Leslie Howard.
      S: George Bernard Shaw.

QUAI DES BRUMES

4269 Whitaker, Rodney. The Content Analysis of Film: A Survey
      of the Field, an Exhaustive Study of Quai Des Brumes,
      and a Functional Description of the Elements of the Film
      Language. Northwestern University: Ph.D., 1966.
      490 pp. D: Marcel Carné. S: Jacques Prevert.

QUARTET

4270 Maugham, W. Somerset. Quartet. Garden City, N.Y.:
      Doubleday, 1949. 189 pp. "The Facts of Life"--D:
      Ralph Smart; S: R. C. Sherriff. "The Alien Corn"--
      D: Harold French; S: R. C. Sherriff. "The Kite"--
      D: Arthur Crabtree; S: R. C. Sherriff. "The Colonel's
      Lady"--D: Ken Annakin; S: R. C. Sherriff.
          Screenplays of the four parts and the original Maugham
      stories on which they are based.

4271 Jorgensen, Paul A. and Shroyer, Frederick B. A College

Treasury. New York: Scribner's, 1956.
Includes screenplay of "The Colonel's Lady. "

QUE VIVA MEXICO!

4272 Eisenstein, S. M. Que Viva Mexico! London: Vision,
1951. 89 pp. (Revised, with an afterword by Ivor Mon-
tagu, London: Vision, 1972, 93 pp.) Uncompleted.
D/S: Sergei Eisenstein and Grigori Alexandrov.
Treatment, notes, and stills, with an introduction by
Ernest Lindgren. Footage shot for QUE VIVA MEXICO!
eventually utilized in THUNDER OVER MEXICO, by Sol
Lesser; DEATH DAY, by Sol Lesser; EISENSTEIN IN
MEXICO, by Sol Lesser; TIME IN THE SUN, by Marie
Seton; MEXICAN SYMPHONY, by William F. Kruse; and
EISENSTEIN'S MEXICAN PROJECT, by Jay Leyda.

4273 Geduld, Harry M. and Gottesman, Ronald (eds.) Sergei
Eisenstein and Upton Sinclair: The Making and Unmaking
of Que Viva Mexico! Bloomington: Indiana University
Press, 1970. 449 pp.

4274 Eisenstein, Sergei. The Complete Films of Eisenstein, To-
gether With an Unpublished Essay by Eisenstein. New
York: Dutton, 1974. 154 pp. Translated by John
Hetherington.

QUIET DUEL

4275 Kurosawa, Akira. The Complete Works of Akira Kurosawa:
Volume 4. Tokyo: Kinema Jumpo Sha, 1971. 167 pp.
D: Akira Kurosawa. S: Senkichi Taniguchi and Akira
Kurosawa.
Text of the screenplay in Japanese and English.

THE QUIET ONE

4276 Miller, Harry. The Realist Film and Social Attitudes: An
Exploratory Study of "The Quiet One." Columbia Uni-
versity: Ph.D., 1951. 82 pp. D: Sidney Meyers. S:
Helen Levitt, Janice Loeb, and Sidney Meyers.

QUILLER MEMORANDUM

4277 Pinter, Harold. Five Screenplays. New York: Grove, 1971.
367 pp. D: Michael Anderson. S: Harold Pinter.

RAINTREE COUNTY

4278 Fenderson, Julia and Bill. The Other Side of the Screen:
The Story of the Filming of Raintree County. Culver
City: Kerr, 1957. 63 pp. D: Edward Dmytryk. S:
Millard Kaufman.

RASHOMON

4279 Kurosawa, Akira. Rashomon. New York: Grove, 1969.
      256 pp. D: Akira Kurosawa. S: Akira Kurosawa and
      Shinobu Hashimoto.
           Screenplay, original source stories, articles by
      Parker Tyler and Donald Richie, and an excerpt from
      THE OUTRAGE.

4280 Richie, Donald (ed.) Focus on Rashomon. Englewood Cliffs,
      N.J.: Prentice-Hall, 1972. 185 pp.
           Contributors include Curtis Harrington, Vernon Young,
      Parker Tyler, and Akira Iwasaki.

REBECCA

4281 Wald, Jerry and Macaulay, Richard (eds.) The Best Pic-
      tures, 1939-1940, and The Year Book of Motion Pictures
      in America. New York: Dodd, Mead, 1940. 534 pp.
      (Reprinted New York: Gordon, 1975.) D: Alfred Hitch-
      cock. S: Robert E. Sherwood and Joan Harrison.
           Includes condensed screenplay of the film.

4282 Gassner, John and Nichols, Dudley (eds.) Twenty Best Film
      Plays. New York: Crown, 1943. 1112 pp.

4283 Gassner, John and Nichols, Dudley (eds.) Great Film Plays.
      New York: Crown, 1959. 334 pp. (Shorter edition of
      Twenty Best Film Plays.)

REBECCA'S DAUGHTERS

4284 Thomas, Dylan. Rebecca's Daughters. Boston: Little,
      Brown, 1966. 144 pp. Unproduced. S: Dylan Thomas.

THE RED BADGE OF COURAGE

4285 Ross, Lillian. Picture. New York: Rinehart, 1952. 258
      pp. (Reprinted New York: Avon, 1969. 220 pp.) D:
      John Huston. S: John Huston and Albert Band.
           Production account of the film.

THE RED BALLOON

4286 Lamorisse, Albert. The Red Balloon. Garden City, N.Y.:
      Doubleday, 1957. 48 pp. D/S: Albert Lamorisse.
           Primarily stills from the film.

THE RED SHOES

4287 Gibbon, Monk. The Red Shoes Ballet: A Critical Study.
      London: Saturn, 1948. 95 pp. D: Michael Powell and

Emeric Pressburger.   S: Michael Powell, Emeric Pressburger, and Keith Winter.

LA RELIGIEUSE   (see THE NUN)

REPULSION

4288   Polanski, Roman.   Polanski: Three Film Scripts.   New
       York: Harper and Row, 1975.   214 pp.   D: Roman
       Polanski.   S: Roman Polanski and Gerard Brach.
       Screenplay, introduction by Boleslaw Sulik, and inter-
       view with Polanski.

RESCUE

4289   Cross, John E. and Rattenbury, Arnold (eds.)   Film Today
       Books: Screen and Audience, An Occasional Miscellany
       Devoted to the Contemporary Cinema.   London: Saturn,
       ca. 1949.   90 pp.   D: Ken Annakin.   S: Robert Westerby.
       Includes a production account of RESCUE.

ROCCO AND HIS BROTHERS

4290   Visconti, Luchino.   Three Screenplays: White Nights, Rocco
       and His Brothers, and The Job.   New York: Orion,
       1970.   313 pp.   Translated by Judith Green.   D: Luchino
       Visconti.   S: Luchino Visconti, Suso Cecci d'Amico,
       Pasquale Festa Campanile, Massimo Franciosa, and En-
       rico Medioli.

THE ROCKING HORSE WINNER

4291   Barrett, Gerald and Erskine, Thomas L.   From Fiction to
       Film: D. H. Lawrence's The Rocking Horse Winner.
       Encino, Cal.:   Dickenson, 1974.   238 pp.   D/S: Anthony
       Pelissier.
       Screenplay, original story, and analysis.

THE ROMANCE OF DIGESTION

4292   Benchley, Robert.   The Reel Benchley: Robert Benchley at
       His Hilarious Best in Words and Pictures.   Compiled by
       George Hornby.   New York: A. A. Wyn, 1950.   96 pp.
       D: Felix E. Feist.   S: Robert Benchley.
       Narration and stills of the 1937 short.

LA RONDE

4293   Masterworks of the French Cinema.   Introduction by John
       Weightman.   New York: Harper and Row, 1974.   350 pp.
       D: Max Ophuls.   S: Jacques Natanson and Max Ophuls.

RULES OF THE GAME

4294 Renoir, Jean. The Rules of the Game. New York: Simon
      and Schuster, 1970. 172 pp. Translated by John McGrath
      and Maureen Teitelbaum. D: Jean Renoir. S: Jean
      Renoir and Carl Koch.
      Screenplay, interviews with Renoir, and essays.

4295 Mast, Gerald. Filmguide to the Rules of the Game. Bloom-
      ington: Indiana University Press, 1973. 85 pp.

SAFETY LAST

4296 McCaffrey, Donald W. Three Classic Silent Screen Comedies
      Starring Harold Lloyd. Rutherford, N.J.: Fairleigh
      Dickinson University Press, 1975. 264 pp. D: Fred
      Newmeyer and Sam Taylor. S: Hal Roach, Sam Taylor
      and Tim Whelan.
      Detailed analysis of the film's structure and comic
      techniques.

SAINT JOAN

4297 Shaw, George Bernard. Saint Joan: A Screenplay. Edited
      and introduced by Bernard F. Dukore. Seattle: Uni-
      versity of Washington Press, 1968. 162 pp. Unproduced.
      S: George Bernard Shaw.
      A different version of SAINT JOAN was produced in
      1957, directed by Otto Preminger and scripted by Graham
      Greene.

SALT OF THE EARTH

4298 Biberman, Herbert. Salt of the Earth: The Story of a Film.
      Boston: Beacon, 1965. 373 pp. D: Herbert Biberman.
      S: Michael Wilson.
      Production account, screenplay, and account of the
      film's legal and political controversies.

SALT OF VENGEANCE

4299 Phillips, Henry Albert. The Photodrama: The Philosophy of
      Its Principles, the Nature of Its Plot, Its Dramatic Con-
      struction and Technique, Illumined by Copious Examples,
      Together With a Complete Photoplay and a Glossary,
      Making the Work a Practical Treatise. (Originally pub-
      lished 1914.) New York: Arno, 1970. 221 pp.
      Includes the screenplay of SALT OF VENGEANCE.

SALESMAN

4300 Maysles, Albert; Maysles, David; and Zwerin, Charlotte.

Salesman. New York: New American Library, 1969.
128 pp. D/S: Albert and David Maysles and Charlotte
Zwerin.
Transcript of the film, plus production notes.

LE SANG D'UN POETE (see BLOOD OF A POET)

SANITORIUM (see TRIO)

SANSHIRO SUGATA

4301 Kurosawa, Akira. The Complete Works of Akira Kurosawa:
Volume 2. Tokyo: Kinema Jumpo Sha, 1971. 135 pp.
D/S: Akira Kurosawa.
Text of the screenplay in Japanese and English.

SARABAND FOR DEAD LOVERS

4302 Saraband for Dead Lovers: The Film and Its Production at
Ealing Studios. London: Convoy, 1948. 106 pp. D:
Basil Dearden. S: John Dighton and Alexander MacKen-
drick.
Production account, including material by those who
worked on the film.

SATAN McALLISTER'S HEIR

4303 Pratt, George C. Spellbound in Darkness. Rochester, N.Y.:
University of Rochester, 1966. 452 pp. (Revised Green-
wich, Conn.: New York Graphic Society, 1973, 548 pp.)
D: Walter Edwards. S: C. Gardner Sullivan and Thomas
H. Ince.
Includes complete shooting script and production data.

SATURDAY MORNING

4304 MacKenzie, Kent and Goldsmith, Gary. Saturday Morning.
New York: Avon, 1971. 143 pp. D: Kent MacKenzie.

SATURDAY NIGHT AND SUNDAY MORNING

4305 Masterworks of the British Cinema. Introduction by John
Russell Taylor. New York: Harper and Row, 1974.
352 pp. D: Karel Reisz. S: Alan Sillitoe.

SATYRICON (see FELLINI SATYRICON)

THE SAVAGE INNOCENTS

4306 Maynard, Richard A. (ed.) Literature of the Screen: Values
in Conflict. New York: Scholastic Book Services, 1974.
Approx. 200 pp. D/S: Nicholas Ray.
Screenplay and supplementary educational material.

SAVAGES

4307   Ivory, James.   Savages and Shakespeare Wallah.   New York:
       Grove, 1973.   152 pp.   D: James Ivory.   S: George
       Swift Trow and Michael O'Donoghue.
       Treatment and screenplay.

SCENES FROM A MARRIAGE

4308   Bergman, Ingmar.   Scenes From a Marriage: Six Dialogues
       for Television.   New York: Bantam, 1974.   212 pp.
       D/S: Ingmar Bergman.
       Scripts of the six television segments, later released
       in a shortened film version.

SCOTT OF THE ANTARCTIC

4309   James, David.   Scott of the Antarctic: The Film and Its
       Production.   London: Convoy, 1948.   151 pp.   D:
       Charles Frend.   S: Walter Meade and Ivor Montagu.
       Production account.

4310   Manvell, Roger (ed.)   Three British Screenplays: Brief En-
       counter, Odd Man Out, Scott of the Antarctic.   London:
       Methuen, 1950.   299 pp.

SECRET PEOPLE

4311   Anderson, Lindsay (ed.)   Making a Film; The Story of
       Secret People, Together With the Shooting Script of the
       Film.   London: Allen and Unwin, 1952.   223 pp.   D:
       Thorold Dickinson.   S: Thorold Dickinson and Wolfgang
       Wilhelm.

SENSO

4312   Visconti, Luchino.   Two Screenplays: La Terra Trema,
       Senso.   New York: Orion, 1970.   186 pp.   Translated
       by Judith Green.   D: Luchino Visconti.   S: Luchino
       Visconti, Suso Cecchi D'Amico, Giorgio Prosperi, Carlo
       Alianello and Giorgio Bassani.

THE SERVANT

4313   Pinter, Harold.   Five Screenplays.   New York: Grove, 1971.
       367 pp.   D: Joseph Losey.   S: Harold Pinter.

THE 7 CAPITAL SINS   (see ANGER)

THE SEVEN SAMURAI

4314   Kurosawa, Akira.   The Seven Samurai.   Introduction and

translation by Donald Richie. New York: Simon and
Schuster, 1970. 224 pp. D: Akira Kurosawa. S:
Shinobu Hashimoto, Hideo Oguni, and Akira Kurosawa.

THE SEVENTH SEAL

4315   Bergman, Ingmar. Four Screenplays of Ingmar Bergman.
New York: Simon and Schuster, 1960. 330 pp. Trans-
lated by Lars Malmstrom and David Kushner. D/S:
Ingmar Bergman.

4316   Bergman, Ingmar. The Seventh Seal. New York: Simon
and Schuster, ca. 1968. 84 pp. Translated by Lars
Malmstrom and David Kushner.

4317   Steene, Birgitta (ed.) Focus on The Seventh Seal. Engle-
wood Cliffs, N.J.: Prentice-Hall, 1972. 182 pp.
Articles by Marianne Hook, James Scott, Ingmar
Bergman, Bosley Crowther, Andrew Sarris, Peter Cowie,
Amedee Ayfre, among others, and an interview with
Bergman.

SHAKESPEARE WALLAH

4318   Ivory, James. Savages and Shakespeare Wallah. New York:
Grove, 1973. 152 pp. D: James Ivory. S: R. Prawer
Jhabvala and James Ivory.

SHAME

4319   Bergman, Ingmar. Persona and Shame: The Screenplays of
Ingmar Bergman. New York: Grossman, 1972. 191 pp.
Translated by Keith Bradfield. D/S: Ingmar Bergman.

SHANGHAI EXPRESS

4320   von Sternberg, Josef. Morocco and Shanghai Express. New
York: Simon and Schuster, 1973. 136 pp. D: Josef von
Sternberg. S: Jules Furthman.
Screenplay and an essay by Andrew Sarris.

SHOOT THE PIANO PLAYER

4321   Braudy, Leo (ed.) Focus on Shoot the Piano Player. Englewood Cliffs, N.J.: Prentice-Hall, 1972. 182 pp. D/S:
Francois Truffaut.
Interview with Truffaut and articles by Gabriel Pearson
and Eric Rhode, Pauline Kael, Karel Reisz and Gavin Millar, Roger Greenspun, Roy Armes, and Penelope Houston.

[A SHORT LIFE OF DIETRICH BONHOEFFER]

4322   Gill, Theodore A. Memo for a Movie: A Short Life of

Dietrich Bonhoeffer. New York: Macmillan, 1971.
268 pp.
Biographical material written as research treatment
for a potential film on Dietrich Bonhoeffer.

THE SILENCE

4323 Bergman, Ingmar. A Film Trilogy: Through a Glass
Darkly, The Communicants (Winter Light), The Silence.
New York: Orion, 1967. 143 pp. Translated by Paul
Britten Austin. (Reprinted as Three Films by Ingmar
Bergman, New York: Grove, 1970.) D/S: Ingmar
Bergman.

LE SILENCE EST D'OR

4324 Clair, René. Four Screenplays: Le Silence est D'Or, La
Beauté du Diable, Les Belles-de-Nuit and Les Grandes
Manoeuvres. New York: Orion, 1970. 439 pp. Trans-
lated by Piergiuseppe Bozzetti. D/S: René Clair.

SILENT SNOW, SECRET SNOW

4325 Barrett, Gerald R. and Erskine, Thomas L. From Fiction
to Film: Conrad Aiken's Silent Snow, Secret Snow.
Encino, Cal.: Dickenson, 1972. 193 pp. D/S: Gene
Kearney.
Shot analysis, essays, and original story.

SIMON OF THE DESERT

4326 Buñuel, Luis. Three Screenplays: Viridiana, The Exterminating Angel and Simon of the Desert. New York: Orion,
1969. 245 pp. D/S: Luis Buñuel.

SINGIN' IN THE RAIN

4327 Comden, Betty and Green, Adolph. Singin' in the Rain. New
York: Viking, 1972. 75 pp. D: Gene Kelly and Stanley
Donen. S: Betty Comden and Adoph Green.

SMILES OF A SUMMER NIGHT

4328 Bergman, Ingmar. Four Screenplays of Ingmar Bergman.
New York: Simon and Schuster, 1960. 330 pp. Trans-
lated by Lars Malmstrom and David Kushner. D/S:
Ingmar Bergman.

SOME LIKE IT HOT

4329 Wilder, Billy and Diamond, I. A. L. Some Like it Hot: A
Screenplay. New York: New American Library, 1959.

144 pp. D: Billy Wilder. S: Billy Wilder and I. A. L. Diamond.

SONS OF MATTHEW

4330 Dunn, Maxwell. How They Made Sons of Matthew. Sydney: Angus and Robertson, 1949. 209 pp. D: Charles Chauvel.

THE SORROW AND THE PITY

4331 Ophuls, Marcel. The Sorrow and the Pity. New York: Outerbridge and Lazard, 1972. 194 pp. Translated by Mireille Johnston. D: Marcel Ophuls.
Transcript of the film, introduction by Stanley Hoffman, and appendices of historical information relating to the film.

THE SOUTHERNER

4332 Gassner, John and Nichols, Dudley (eds.) Best Film Plays-- 1945. New York: Crown, 1946. 648 pp. D/S: Jean Renoir.

SPELLBOUND

4333 Gassner, John and Nichols, Dudley (eds.) Best Film Plays-- 1945. New York: Crown, 1946. 648 pp. D: Alfred Hitchcock. S: Ben Hecht.

SPLENDOR IN THE GRASS

4334 Inge, William. Splendor in the Grass. New York: Bantam, 1961. 121 pp. D: Elia Kazan. S: William Inge.

4335 Maynard, Richard A. (ed.) Literature of the Screen: Men and Women. New York: Scholastic Book Services, 1974. Approx. 200 pp.
Screenplay and supplementary educational material.

STAGECOACH

4336 Gassner, John and Nichols, Dudley (eds.) Twenty Best Film Plays. New York: Crown, 1943. 1112 pp. D: John Ford. S: Dudley Nichols.

4337 Gassner, John and Nichols, Dudley (eds.) Great Film Plays. New York: Crown, 1959. 334 pp. (Shorter edition of Twenty Best Film Plays.)

4338 Nichols, Dudley and Ford, John. Stagecoach. New York: Simon and Schuster, 1971. 152 pp.
Screenplay and original story.

4339   Anobile, Richard J. (ed.) John Ford's Stagecoach. New
       York: Darien, 1975. 256 pp.
            Shot-by-shot frame enlargements and dialogue.

STATE OF SIEGE

4340   Costa-Gavras and Solinas, Franco. State of Siege. New
       York: Ballantine, 1973. 214 pp. Translated by Brooke
       Leveque and Raymond Rosenthal. D: Costa-Gavras.
       S: Franco Solinas.
            Screenplay, interviews with Solinas and Costa-Gavras,
       and documents relating to the film's subject.

STAVISKY

4341   Semprun, Jorge. Stavisky. New York: Viking, 1975.
       163 pp. Translated by Sabine Destree. D: Alain Res-
       nais. S: Jorge Semprun.
            Screenplay and interview with Resnais.

THE STEAGLE

4342   Sylbert, Paul. Final Cut: The Making and Breaking of a
       Film. New York: Seabury, 1974. 243 pp. D/S: Paul
       Sylbert.

THE STERILE CUCKOO

4343   Koch, Christian Herbert. Understanding Film as Process
       of Change: A Metalanguage for the Study of Film De-
       veloped and Applied to Ingmar Bergman's Persona and
       Alan J. Pakula's The Sterile Cuckoo. University of Iowa:
       Ph.D., 1970. 281 pp.

STOLEN KISSES

4344   Truffaut, François. The Adventures of Antoine Doinel:
       Four Screenplays. New York: Simon and Schuster, 1971.
       320 pp. Translated by Helen G. Scott. D: François
       Truffaut. S: François Truffaut, Claude de Givray, and
       Bernard Revon.
            Work notes, first treatment, and final screenplay.

STORM IN THE WEST

4345   Lewis, Sinclair and Schary, Dore. Storm in the West. New
       York: Stein and Day, 1963. 192 pp. Unproduced. S:
       Sinclair Lewis and Dore Schary.

THE STORY OF G.I. JOE

4346   Gassner, John and Nichols, Dudley (eds.) Best Film Plays--

1945. New York: Crown, 1946. 648 pp. D: William
Wellman. S: Leopold Atlas, Guy Endore, and Philip
Stevenson.

STRAY DOG

4347 Kurosawa, Akira. The Complete Works of Akira Kurosawa:
Volume 4. Tokyo: Kinema Jumpo Sha, 1971. 167 pp.
D: Akira Kurosawa. S: Ryuzo Kikushima and Akira
Kurosawa.
Text of screenplay in Japanese and English.

A STREETCAR NAMED DESIRE

4348 Garrett, George P.; Hardison, O. B., Jr.; and Gelfman,
Jane R. Film Scripts One. New York: Appleton-Century-
Crofts, 1971. 544 pp. D: Elia Kazan. S: Tennessee
Williams.

STRIKE

4349 Kuiper, John B. An Analysis of the Four Silent Films of
Sergei Eisenstein. University of Iowa: Ph. D., 1960.
436 pp. D: Sergei Eisenstein. S: Valeri Pletnyov,
Sergei Eisenstein, I. Kravchunovsky, and Grigori Alexandrov.

4350 Eisenstein, Sergei. The Complete Films of Eisenstein, To-
gether With an Unpublished Essay by Eisenstein. New
York: Dutton, 1974. 154 pp. Translated by John
Hetherington.

SUNDAY BLOODY SUNDAY

4351 Gilliatt, Penelope. Sunday Bloody Sunday. New York:
Viking, 1972. 135 pp. D: John Schlesinger. S:
Penelope Gilliatt.

SUPERFLY

4352 Ward, Francis. Superfly: A Political and Cultural Condem-
nation by the Kuumba Workshop. Chicago: Institute of
Positive Education, 1972. 18 pp. D: Gordon Parks, Jr.
S: Phillip Feny.

SUTTER'S GOLD

4353 Montagu, Ivor. With Eisenstein in Hollywood: A Chapter
of Autobiography. New York: International, 1969.
356 pp. Unproduced. S: Sergei Eisenstein, Grigori
Alexandrov, and Ivor Montagu.
Includes the original scenario.

SWEET SWEETBACK'S BAADASSSSS SONG

4354   Van Peebles, Melvin. Sweet Sweetback's Baadasssss Song.
       New York: Lancer, 1971. 191 pp. (Reprinted as The
       Making of Sweet Sweetback's Baadasssss Song, 1972.)
       D/S: Melvin Van Peebles.

THE SWIMMER

4355   Perry, Eleanor. The Swimmer. New York: Stein and Day,
       1967. 127 pp. D: Frank Perry. S: Eleanor Perry.

THE SWINDLERS   (see IL BIDONE)

TAKING OFF

4356   Forman, Milos; Guare, John; Carriere, Jean-Claude; and
       Klein, John. Taking Off. New York: New American
       Library, 1971. 220 pp. D: Milos Forman. S: Milos
       Forman, John Guare, Jean-Claude Carriere, and John
       Klein.
          Screenplay, interview, and an article by Forman.

TALES OF BEATRIX POTTER

4357   Godden, Rumer. The Tale of the Tales: The Beatrix Potter
       Ballet. London: Frederick Warne, 1971. 208 pp. D:
       Reginald Mills.
          Production account and script of the film.

THE TALES OF HOFFMAN

4358   Gibbon, Monk. The Tales of Hoffman: A Study of the Film.
       London: Saturn, 1951. 96 pp. D/S: Michael Powell
       and Emeric Pressburger.

THE TEMPTATIONS OF DOCTOR ANTONIO

4359   Fellini, Federico. Three Screenplays: I Vitelloni, Il Bidone,
       The Temptations of Doctor Antonio. New York: Orion,
       1970. 288 pp. Translated by Judith Green. D: Federico
       Fellini. S: Federico Fellini, Ennio Flaiano, and Tullio
       Pinelli.
          Screenplay of an episode from BOCCACCIO '70.

THE TEN COMMANDMENTS   (1956)

4360   Noerdlinger, Henry S. Moses and Egypt: The Documentation
       to the Motion Picture The Ten Commandments. Los
       Angeles: University of Southern California Press, 1956.
       202 pp. D: Cecil B. De Mille. S: Aeneas MacKenzie,
       Jesse L. Lasky, Jr., Jack Gariss, and Frederic M. Frank.

Account of pre-production research and preparation for
THE TEN COMMANDMENTS.

TEN DAYS THAT SHOOK THE WORLD   (see OCTOBER)

LA TERRA TREMA

4361   Visconti, Luchino.   Two Screenplays: La Terra Trema,
Senso.   New York: Orion, 1970.   186 pp.   Translated
by Judith Green.   D/S: Luchino Visconti.

THE TESTAMENT OF ORPHEUS

4362   Cocteau, Jean.   Two Screenplays: The Blood of a Poet and
The Testament of Orpheus.   New York: Orion, 1968.
144 pp.   Translated by Carol Martin-Sperry.   D/S: Jean
Cocteau.

THAT'S ME

4363   Maynard, Richard A. (ed.)   Literature of the Screen: Identity.
New York: Scholastic Book Services, 1974.   192 pp.   D:
Walker Stuart.   S: Alan Arkin and Andrew Duncan.
Screenplay and supplementary educational material.

THEY MIGHT BE GIANTS

4364   Goldman, James.   They Might be Giants: The Screenplay.
New York: Lancer, 1970.   152 pp.   D: Anthony Harvey.
S: James Goldman.

THEY SHOOT HORSES, DON'T THEY?

4365   McCoy, Horace.   They Shoot Horses, Don't They?   New York:
Avon, 1969.   319 pp.   D: Sydney Pollack.   S: James
Poe and Robert E. Thompson.
Includes the novel and the screenplay.

THE THIRD MAN

4366   Greene, Graham.   The Third Man.   New York: Simon and
Schuster, 1968.   134 pp.   D: Carol Reed.   S: Graham
Greene.

4367   Masterworks of the British Cinema.   Introduction by John
Russell Taylor.   New York: Harper and Row, 1974.
352 pp.

THIRTY SECONDS OVER TOKYO

4368   Gassner, John and Nichols, Dudley (eds.)   Best Film Plays--
1945.   New York: Crown, 1946.   648 pp.   D: Mervyn
LeRoy.   S: Dalton Trumbo.

THIS IS IT: MARIN COUNTY COURTHOUSE SHOOTOUT

4369 Goodwin, Michael and Marcus, Greil. Double Feature:
      Movies and Politics. New York: Outerbridge and Lazard,
      1972. 128 pp. Unproduced. S: Michael Goodwin and
      Greil Marcus.
      Script about the 1970 George Jackson trial.

THIS LAND IS MINE

4370 Gassner, John and Nichols, Dudley (eds.) Twenty Best Film
      Plays. New York: Crown, 1943. 1112 pp. D: Jean
      Renoir. S: Dudley Nichols.

THOSE MAGNIFICENT MEN IN THEIR FLYING MACHINES

4371 Wheeler, Allen H. Building Aeroplanes for Those Magnificent
      Men. Sun Valley, Cal.: J. W. Caler, 1965. 94 pp.
      D: Ken Annakin. S: Jack Davies and Ken Annakin.

THREE BAD MEN IN A HIDDEN FORTRESS

4372 Kurosawa, Akira. The Complete Works of Akira Kurosawa:
      Volume 9. Tokyo: Kinema Jumpo Sha, 1971. 247 pp.
      D: Akira Kurosawa. S: Shinobu Hashimoto, Ryuzo
      Kikushima, Hideo Oguni, and Akira Kurosawa.
      Text of the screenplay in Japanese and English.

THREE FACES OF CUBA

4373 Truth About Cuba Committee. An Expose of the Insidious
      Film "Three Faces of Cuba." Miami: Truth About Cuba
      Committee, 1965. 104 pp. D: Robert Cohen.
      Transcript plus articles attacking the film on political
      grounds.

THE THREEPENNY OPERA (1931)

4374 Masterworks of the German Cinema. Introduction by Roger
      Manvell. New York: Harper and Row, 1973. 300 pp.
      D: G. W. Pabst. S: Bela Balazs, Leo Lania, and
      Ladislaus Vajda.
      Screenplay, plus an essay by Paul Rotha and an inter-
      view with Jean Oser.

THRESHOLD: THE BLUE ANGELS EXPERIENCE

4375 Herbert, Frank. Threshold: The Blue Angels Experience.
      New York: Ballantine, 1973. 153 pp.
      Text and stills of the film about stunt flying.

THROUGH A GLASS DARKLY

4376 Bergman, Ingmar. A Film Trilogy: Through a Glass Darkly,
      The Communicants (Winter Light), The Silence. New
      York: Orion, 1967. 143 pp. Translated by Paul Britten
      Austin. (Reprinted as Three Films by Ingmar Bergman,
      New York: Grove, 1970.) D/S: Ingmar Bergman.

TILLIE AND GUS

4377 Fields, W. C. Never Give a Sucker an Even Break and
      Tillie and Gus. New York: Simon and Schuster, 1973.
      124 pp. D: Francis Martin. S: Walter Deleon and
      Francis Martin.

TO BE ALIVE

4378 Reid, Alastair. To Be Alive. New York: Macmillan, 1966.
      90 pp. D: Francis Thompson and Alexander Hammid.
      S: Edward Field.
            Photographs from the multi-screen film TO BE ALIVE,
      presented at the 1964-65 World's Fair; book's text by poet
      Alastair Reid.

TO KILL A MOCKINGBIRD

4379 Foote, Horton. The Screenplay of To Kill a Mockingbird.
      New York: Harcourt Brace Jovanovich, 1964. 117 pp.
      D: Robert Mulligan. S: Horton Foote.

TOM JONES

4380 Osborne, John. Tom Jones: A Film Script. New York:
      Grove, 1964. 192 pp. D: Tony Richardson. S: John
      Osborne.

EL TOPO

4381 Jodorowsky, Alexandro. El Topo: A Book of the Film.
      Edited by Ross Firestone. New York: Douglas, 1971.
      173 pp. Translated by Joanne Pottlitzer. D/S: Alexan-
      dro Jodorowsky.
            Screenplay and an extended interview with Jodorowsky.

A TREE GROWS IN BROOKLYN

4382 Gassner, John and Nichols, Dudley (eds.) Best Film Plays--
      1945. New York: Crown, 1946. 648 pp. D: Elia
      Kazan. S: Tess Slesinger and Frank Davis.

THE TRIAL

4383 Welles, Orson. The Trial. New York: Simon and Schuster,

1970. 176 pp. Translation and description by Nicholas
Fry. D/S: Orson Welles.
Screenplay and brief interview with Welles.

TRILOGY

4384 Capote, Truman; Perry, Eleanor; and Perry, Frank. Trilogy:
An Experiment in Multi-Media. New York: Macmillan,
1969. 276 pp. D: Frank Perry. S: Truman Capote
and Eleanor Perry.
Original Capote stories, screenplays, and adaptation
notes for the three segments of TRILOGY: "Miriam,"
"Among the Paths to Eden," and "A Christmas Memory."

TRIO

4385 Maugham, W. Somerset. Trio. Garden City, N.Y.: Double-
day, 1950. 156 pp. "The Verger"--D: Ken Annakin;
S: W. Somerset Maugham. "Mr. Know-all"--D: Ken
Annakin; S: R. C. Sherriff. "Sanitorium"--D: Harold
French; S: Noel Langley.
Screenplays of the three parts plus the original
Maugham stories on which they are based.

TRIP IN A BALLOON

4386 Lamorisse, Albert. Trip in a Balloon. Garden City, N.Y.:
Doubleday, 1960. Unpaged. Translated by Malcolm
Barnes.
Story of the film, with photographs taken during its
production.

TRISTANA

4387 Buñuel, Luis. Tristana. New York: Simon and Schuster,
1971. 144 pp. Translated by Nicholas Fry. D: Luis
Buñuel. S: Luis Buñuel and Julio Alejandro.
Screenplay and essay by J. Francisco Aranda.

TRIUMPH OF THE WILL

4388 Barsam, Richard Meran. Filmguide to Triumph of the Will.
Bloomington: Indiana University Press, 1975. 82 pp.
D: Leni Riefenstahl.

THE TROJAN WOMEN

4389 Cacoyannis, Michael. The Trojan Women. New York:
Bantam, 1971. 116 pp. D/S: Michael Cacoyannis.
Screenplay and the original play by Euripides.

TWELVE ANGRY MEN

4390   Garrett, George P.; Hardison, O. B., Jr.; and Gelfman,
Jane R. Film Scripts Two. New York: Appleton-Century-
Crofts, 1971. 548 pp. D: Sidney Lumet. S: Reginald
Rose.

TWENTY YEARS A-GROWING

4391   Thomas, Dylan. Twenty Years A-Growing. London: J. M.
Dent, 1964. 91 pp. Unproduced. S: Dylan Thomas.
An unfinished screenplay from the story by Maurice
O'Sullivan.

4392   Thomas, Dylan. The Doctor and the Devils, and Other
Scripts. New York: New Directions, 1966. 229 pp.

TWO FOR THE ROAD

4393   Raphael, Frederic. Two for the Road. New York: Holt,
Rinehart and Winston, 1967. 142 pp. D: Stanley Donen.
S: Frederic Raphael.
Screenplay plus introduction by Raphael.

TWO OR THREE THINGS I KNOW ABOUT HER

4394   Godard, Jean-Luc. Godard: Three Films. New York:
Harper and Row, 1975. 192 pp. D/S: Jean-Luc Godard.
Screenplay and articles.

2001: A SPACE ODYSSEY

4395   Agel, Jerome (ed.) The Making of Kubrick's 2001. New
York: New American Library, 1970. 368 pp. D:
Stanley Kubrick. S: Stanley Kubrick and Arthur C.
Clarke.
Original story by Clarke, production accounts, critical
essays, interviews with Kubrick, and many photographs.

4396   Clarke, Arthur C. The Lost Worlds of 2001. New York:
New American Library, 1972. 240 pp.
Includes original story, plus material on Clarke's
collaboration with Kubrick.

4397   Geduld, Carolyn. Filmguide to 2001: A Space Odyssey.
Bloomington: Indiana University Press, 1973. 87 pp.

TWO-LANE BLACKTOP

4398   Wurlitzer, Rudolph and Corry, Will. Two-Lane Blacktop.
New York: Award, 1971. 160 pp. D: Monte Hellman.

S: Rudolph Wurlitzer and Will Corry.
Screenplay, production notes, and lengthy interview
with Hellman.

UNDER MILK WOOD

4399   Sinclair, Andrew. Under Milk Wood by Dylan Thomas;
Screenplay by Andrew Sinclair. New York: Simon and
Schuster, 1972. 95 pp. D/S: Andrew Sinclair.

UP THE DOWN STAIRCASE

4400   Maynard, Richard A. (ed.) Literature of the Screen: Identity.
New York: Scholastic Book Services, 1974. 192 pp. D:
Robert Mulligan. S: Tad Mosel.
Screenplay and supplementary educational material.

LES VACANCES DE MONSIEUR HULOT   (see MONSIEUR
HULOT'S HOLIDAY)

VAMPIRE   (see VAMPYR)

VAMPYR

4401   Dreyer, Carl Theodor. Four Screenplays. Bloomington:
Indiana University Press, 1970. 312 pp. Translated by
Oliver Stallybrass. D: Carl Dreyer. S: Carl Dreyer
and Christen Jul.

VARIETY LIGHTS

4402   Fellini, Federico. Early Screenplays. New York: Gross-
man, 1971. 198 pp. Translated by Judith Green. D:
Federico Fellini and Alberto Lattuada. S: Federico
Fellini, Ennio Flaiano, Alberto Lattuada, and Tullio
Pinelli.

THE VERGER   (see TRIO)

VINLAND THE GOOD

4403   Shute, Nevil. Vinland the Good. New York: Morrow, 1946.
126 pp. Unproduced. S: Nevil Shute.

THE VIRGIN SPRING

4404   Isaksson, Ulla. The Virgin Spring. New York: Ballantine,
1960. 114 pp. Translated by Lars Malmstrom and David
Kushner. D: Ingmar Bergman. S: Ulla Isaksson.

VIRIDIANA

4405   Buñuel, Luis. Three Screenplays: Viridiana, The

Exterminating Angel, and Simon of the Desert. New York: Orion, 1969. 245 pp. D: Luis Buñuel. S: Luis Buñuel and Julio Alejandro.

VISITATION

4406 Buchanan, Andrew. Visitation: The Film Story of the Medical Missionaries of Mary. Louth, Ireland: Catholic Film Society, 1948. 126 pp. (Revised Droghen, Ireland: Medical Missionaries of Mary, 1950, 145 pp.)

I VITELLONI

4407 Fellini, Federico. Three Screenplays, I Vitelloni, Il Bidone, The Temptations of Doctor Antonio. New York: Orion, 1970. 288 pp. Translated by Judith Green. D: Federico Fellini. S: Federico Fellini and Ennio Flaiano.

VIVA ZAPATA!

4408 Steinbeck, John. Viva Zapata! The Original Screenplay. New York: Viking, 1975. 150 pp. D: Elia Kazan. S: John Steinbeck.
Screenplay and essays.

VREDENS DAG (see DAY OF WRATH)

THE WAGES OF FEAR

4409 Masterworks of the French Cinema. Introduction by John Weightman. New York: Harper and Row, 1974. 350 pp. D: Henri-Georges Clouzot. S: Henri-Georges Clouzot and Jerome Geronomi.

A WALK IN THE SPRING RAIN

4410 Maddux, Rachel; Silliphant, Stirling; and Isaccs, Neil D. Fiction Into Film: A Walk in the Spring Rain. Knoxville: University of Tennessee Press, 1970. 239 pp. D: Guy Green. S: Stirling Silliphant.
Original novella, screenplay, and detailed account of adaptation and production.

THE WAR GAME

4411 Watkins, Peter. The War Game. New York: Avon, 1967. 128 pp. D/S: Peter Watkins.
Adaptation of the film, including the narration and many stills.

WATCH ON THE RHINE

4412 Gassner, John and Nichols, Dudley (eds.) Best Film Plays of 1943-1944. New York: Crown, 1945. 694 pp. D: Herman Shumlin. S: Dashiell Hammett.

THE WEDDING MARCH

4413 Weinberg, Herman G. (comp.) The Complete Wedding March of Erich von Stroheim. Boston: Little, Brown, 1974. 330 pp. D: Erich von Stroheim. S: Erich von Stroheim and Harry Carr.
A photographic reconstruction of the film.

WEEKEND

4414 Godard, Jean-Luc. Weekend and Wind From the East. New York: Simon and Schuster, 1972. 188 pp. D/S: Jean-Luc Godard.
Transcript of the film and an essay by Robin Wood.

WESTWORLD

4415 Crichton, Michael. Westworld. New York: Bantam, 1974. 107 pp. D/S: Michael Crichton.

WHITE MANE

4416 Lamorisse, Albert. White Mane: Text by Albert Lamorisse and Denys Colomb de Daunant; Taken From the Film White Mane by Albert Lamorisse. New York: Dutton, 1954. Unpaged. D: Albert Lamorisse.

WHITE NIGHTS

4417 Visconti, Luchino. Three Screenplays: White Nights, Rocco and His Brothers, and The Job. New York: Orion, 1970. 313 pp. Translated by Judith Green. D: Luchino Visconti. S: Suso Cecchi d'Amico and Luchino Visconti.

WHITE SHEIK

4418 Fellini, Federico. Early Screenplays. New York: Grossman, 1971. 198 pp. D: Federico Fellini. S: Federico Fellini and Tullio Pinelli.

WHO IS HARRY KELLERMAN AND WHY IS HE SAYING THOSE TERRIBLE THINGS ABOUT ME?

4419 Gardner, Herb. Who Is Harry Kellerman and Why Is He Saying Those Terrible Things About Me? New York: New American Library, 1971. 156 pp. D: Ulu Grosbard. S: Herb Gardner.

WHO'S AFRAID OF VIRGINIA WOOLF?

4420   Storrer, William Allin. A Comparison of Edward Albee's
       Who's Afraid of Virginia Woolf? as Drama and as Film.
       Ohio University: Ph. D. , 1968.   202 pp.

WHY WE FIGHT

4421   Hovland, Carl; Lumsdaine, Arthur A; and Sheffield, Fred D.
       Experiments on Mass Communication.   Princeton, N. J. :
       Princeton University Press, 1949.   345 pp.   (Reprinted
       New York: John Wiley, 1965.) Various directors, in-
       cluding Frank Capra, Anatole Litvak, and Anthony Veiller.
           WHY WE FIGHT films utilized in audience effects ex-
       periments.

4422   Bohn, Thomas.   An Historical and Descriptive Analysis of
       the "Why We Fight" Series.   University of Wisconsin:
       Ph. D. , 1968.   269 pp.

THE WILD CHILD

4423   Truffaut, François and Gruault, Jean.   The Wild Child.   New
       York: Washington Square, 1973.   189 pp.   Translated
       by Linda Lewin and Christine Lemery.   D: François
       Truffaut.   S: François Truffaut and Jean Gruault.
           Screenplay plus an essay by Truffaut.

WILD STRAWBERRIES

4424   Bergman, Ingmar.   Four Screenplays of Ingmar Bergman.
       New York: Simon and Schuster, 1960.   330 pp.   Trans-
       lated by Lars Malmstrom and David Kushner.   D/S:
       Ingmar Bergman.

4425   Bergman, Ingmar.   Wild Strawberries.   New York: Simon
       and Schuster, 1969, c. 1960.   124 pp.   Translated by
       Lars Malmstrom and David Kushner.
           Screenplay, cutting continuity, and essays by Bergman,
       including his tribute to Victor Sjostrom.

THE WILD WHITE STALLION   (see WHITE MANE)

WILSON

4426   Gassner, John and Nichols, Dudley (eds.) Best Film Plays
       of 1943-1944.   New York: Crown, 1945.   694 pp.   D:
       Henry King.   S: Lamar Trotti.
           Screenplay and brief production account essay by
       Darryl F. Zanuck.

WIND ACROSS THE EVERGLADES

4427 Schulberg, Budd. Across the Everglades: A Play for the
Screen. New York: Random, 1958. 126 pp. D:
Nicholas Ray. S: Budd Schulberg.

WIND FROM THE EAST

4428 Godard, Jean-Luc. Weekend and Wind From the East. New
York: Simon and Schuster, 1972. 188 pp. D/S: Jean-
Luc Godard and Jean-Pierre Gorin.
Screenplay plus an essay by James Roy MacBean.

WINTER CRUISE (see ENCORE)

WINTER LIGHT

4429 Bergman, Ingmar. A Film Trilogy: Through a Glass
Darkly, The Communicants (Winter Light), The Silence.
New York: Orion, 1967. 143 pp. Translated by Paul
Britten Austin. (Reprinted as Three Films by Ingmar
Bergman, New York: Grove, 1970.) D/S: Ingmar
Bergman.

WOMAN IN THE DUNES

4430 Teshigahara, Hiroshi. Woman in the Dunes. New York:
Phaedra, 1966. 95 pp. D: Hiroshi Teshigahara. S:
Kobo Abe.

A WOMAN IS A WOMAN

4431 Godard, Jean-Luc. Godard: Three Films. New York:
Harper and Row, 1975. 192 pp. D/S: Jean-Luc Godard.
Screenplay, articles, and brief interview with Anna
Karina.

THE WOMEN

4432 Gassner, John and Nichols, Dudley (eds.) Twenty Best
Film Plays. New York: Crown, 1943. 1112 pp. D:
George Cukor. S: Anita Loos and Jane Murfin.

THE WORD (see ORDET)

THE WORLD OF APU (see THE APU TRILOGY)

WORLD OF PLENTY

4433 Knight, Eric and Rotha, Paul. World of Plenty: The Book
of the Film. London: Nicholson and Watson, 1945.
62 pp. D: Paul Rotha. S: Eric Knight.
Text and stills from the film.

WR: MYSTERIES OF THE ORGANISM

4434   Makavejev, Dusan. WR: Mysteries of the Organism: A
       Cinematic Testament to the Life and Teachings of Wilhelm
       Reich. New York: Avon, 1972. 144 pp. D/S: Dusan
       Makavejev.
       Screenplay and interview with Makavejev.

WUTHERING HEIGHTS

4435   Gassner, John and Nichols, Dudley (eds.) Twenty Best Film
       Plays. New York: Crown, 1943. 1112 pp. D: William
       Wyler. S: Ben Hecht and Charles MacArthur.

YELLOW JACK

4436   Gassner, John and Nichols, Dudley (eds.) Twenty Best Film
       Plays. New York: Crown, 1943. 1112 pp. D: George
       B. Seitz. S: Edward Chodorov.

YELLOW SUBMARINE

4437   Wilk, Max (ed.) The Beatles in the Yellow Submarine. New
       York: New American Library, 1968. 128 pp. D:
       George Dunning. S: Lee Minoff, Al Brodax, Jack Mendel-
       sohn, and Erich Segal.

YOUNG WINSTON

4438   Foreman, Carl. Young Winston. New York: Ballantine,
       1972. 157 pp. D: Richard Attenborough. S: Carl
       Foreman.

ZUCKERKANDL

4439   Hutchins, Robert Maynard. Zuckerkandl. New York: Grove,
       1968. 64 pp. D: John and Faith Hubley.
       Narration and illustrations from the animated film.

PART VIII

FILM THEORY AND CRITICISM

A. INDIVIDUAL THEORISTS

This section, on individual theorists, lists the works of those writers who have tried to answer the linked questions, "What is film and how can it be characterized as an art?" Some of these works proclaim the primacy of film's photographic and ontological realism; others proclaim the primacy of its formal structure as language. Some provide coherent theories of film art; others offer striking but undeveloped insights. Most of these books, decades after their initial publication, are still provoking thought and discussion. Although many of them contain discussions of particular films, the emphasis is clearly not on the particular films, but on the general film principles these examples illustrate. As with the other sections of the bibliography, the entries are arranged chronologically to make evident the evolution of the film literature.

For related material on film theory, the reader should also see Part II, section A, aesthetics of technique. For books on visual aesthetics with material on film, see Part VIII, section F-3, film and the visual arts.

Two currently popular film methodologies which relate to theoretical conceptions of film are not, unfortunately, well represented here. As yet, few books deal at length with genre theory or structuralism/semiotics. For material on various film genres the reader should consult the genre sections, Part V, sections C-1 through C-10. For a bibliography of books (and periodicals) relating to the theoretical concept of genre, see the bibliographies in Stuart Kaminsky's American Film Genres (in this section) or in John G. Cawelti's Adventure, Mystery, and Romance: Formula Stories as Art and Popular Culture (Chicago: University of Chicago Press, 1976). For material on the theoretical approach of structuralism/ semiotics the reader should consult the periodical Screen, particularly the Spring/Summer 1973 issue, which is dedicated to semiotics and Christian Metz and which includes a bibliography. Another bibliography to be consulted is the one on linguistics, structuralism, and semiology compiled by John G. Hanhardt and Charles Harpole, which appeared in the May-June 1973 issue of Film Comment. See, too, the bibliography in Bill Nichols' Movies and Methods (cited in Part VIII, section D, anthologies of theory and criticism).

4440   Lindsay, Vachel. The Art of the Moving Picture. (Origi-
        nally published 1915. Revised 1922.) New York:

Liveright, 1970. 324 pp.
New edition includes introduction by Stanley Kauffmann.

4441   Munsterberg, Hugo. The Photoplay: A Psychological Study.
(Originally published 1916.) New York: Arno, 1970.
232 pp. (Also reprinted as The Film: A Psychological
Study, New York: Dover, 1970, 100 pp.)

4442   Freeburg, Victor Oscar. The Art of Photoplay Making.
(Originally published 1918.) New York: Arno, 1970.
283 pp.

4443   Freeburg, Victor Oscar. Pictorial Beauty on the Screen.
(Originally published 1923.) New York: Arno, 1970.
191 pp.

4444   Buckle, Gerard Fort. The Mind and the Film: A Treatise
on the Psychological Factors in Film. (Originally published 1926.) New York: Arno, 1970. 119 pp.

4445   Pudovkin, V. I. Film Technique, and Film Acting. (Film
Technique originally published 1929, enlarged 1933; Film
Acting originally published 1933.) New York: Lear,
1949. 204, 153 pp. Introduced by Lewis Jacobs. Trans-
lated by Ivor Montagu. (Enlarged memorial edition New
York: Grove, 1960, 388 pp. Reprinted 1970.)

4446   Arnheim, Rudolf. Film as Art. (Originally published 1933
as Film.) Revised and enlarged Berkeley: University
of California Press, 1957. 230 pp. (Reprinted with a
brief forward 1968.)

4447   Spottiswoode, Raymond. A Grammar of the Film: An
Analysis of Film Technique. (Originally published 1935.)
Berkeley: University of California Press, 1950. 328 pp.
(Reprinted 1969.)

4448   Nilsen, Vladimir S. The Cinema as a Graphic Art (On a
Theory of Representation in the Cinema); with an appre-
ciation by S. M. Eisenstein. (Originally published 1937.)
New York: Hill and Wang, 1959. 227 pp. Translated
by Stephen Gary, with editorial advice from Ivor Montagu.
(Reprinted 1972.)

4449   Eisenstein, Sergei. The Film Sense. Edited and translated
by Jay Leyda. New York: Harcourt, Brace, 1942.
288 pp. (Reprinted in Film Form [and] The Film Sense:
Two Complete and Unabridged Works, New York: Meridian, 1957, 279, 282 pp. The Film Sense reprinted by
itself New York: Harcourt, Brace, 1969.)

4450   Deren, Maya. An Anagram of Ideas on Art, Form and Film.
Yonkers, N.Y.: Alicat Book Shop, 1946. 52 pp.

4451 Eisenstein, Sergei. Film Form: Essays in Film Theory.
      Edited and translated by Jay Leyda. New York: Har-
      court, Brace, 1949. 279 pp. (Reprinted in Film Form
      [and] The Film Sense: Two Complete and Unabridged
      Works, New York: Meridian, 1957, 279, 282 pp. Film
      Form reprinted by itself New York: Harcourt, Brace,
      1969.)

4452 Eisenstein, Sergei. The Ideas and Words of Sergei Eisen-
      stein. Hollywood: American Russian Institute, 1949.
      9 pp.

4453 Balazs, Bela. Theory of the Film: Character and Growth
      of a New Art. New York: Roy, 1953. 291 pp. Trans-
      lated by Edith Bone. (Reprinted New York: Dover, 1970.)

4454 Langer, Susanne K. Feeling and Form: A Theory of Art.
      New York: Scribner's, 1953. 431 pp.
      Includes the brief essay, "A Note on the Film."

4455 Arnheim, Rudolf. Art and Visual Perception: A Psychology
      of the Creative Eye. Berkeley: University of California
      Press, 1954. 408 pp. (Republished 1965, 485 pp.)

4456 Cocteau, Jean. Cocteau on the Film: A Conversation Re-
      corded by Andre Fraigneau. New York: Roy, 1954.
      140 pp. Translated by Vera Traill. (Reprinted New
      York: Dover, 1972.)

4457 Williams, Raymond and Orrom, Michael. Preface to Film.
      London: Film Drama Ltd., 1954. 129 pp.
      Comprised of "Film and the Dramatic Tradition" by
      Williams and "Film and Its Dramatic Techniques" by
      Orrom.

4458 Moholy-Nagy, Laszlo. Vision in Motion. Chicago: Paul
      Theobald, 1956. 371 pp.
      Includes a chapter on film.

4459 Eisenstein, Sergei. Notes of a Film Director. London:
      Lawrence and Wishart, 1959. 207 pp. Translated by
      X. Danko. (Reprinted New York: Dover, 1970.)

4460 Kracauer, Siegfried. Theory of Film: The Redemption of
      Physical Reality. New York: Oxford University Press,
      1960. 364 pp.

4461 Gregory, John Robert. Some Psychological Aspects of Mo-
      tion Picture Montage. University of Illinois: Ph.D.,
      1961. 138 pp.

4462 Nizhny, Vladimir. Lessons With Eisenstein. Edited and
      translated by Ivor Montagu and Jay Leyda. New York:

Hill and Wang, 1962. 182 pp.
Reconstruction of Eisenstein's lectures at the State
Institute of Cinematography in Moscow.

4463 Lawson, John Howard. Film: The Creative Process; The
Search for an Audio-Visual Language and Structure. New
York: Hill and Wang, 1964. 380 pp. (Reprinted with
a new introductory essay by Lawson, 1967.)

4464 Bazin, André. What Is Cinema? Volume I. Selected and
Translated by Hugh Gray. Berkeley: University of California Press, 1967. 183 pp.

4465 Eisenstein, Sergei. Film Essays, With a Lecture. Edited
by Jay Leyda. London: Dobson, 1968. 220 pp. (Also
published as Film Essays and a Lecture, New York:
Praeger, 1970.)

4466 McGuire, Jeremiah C. Cinema and Value Philosophy. New
York: Philosophical Library, 1968. 91 pp.

4467 Sarris, Andrew. The American Cinema: Directors and Directions, 1929-1968. New York: Dutton, 1968. 383 pp.
Includes a pioneering essay on the auteur theory.

4468 Moholy-Nagy, Laszlo. Painting, Photography, Film. Cambridge, Mass.: M.I.T. Press, 1969. 150 pp. Translated by Janet Seligman.

4469 Wollen, Peter. Signs and Meaning in the Cinema. Bloomington: Indiana University Press, 1969. 168 pp. (Revised
1972, 175 pp.)
Discusses Eisenstein's aesthetics, semiology, and the
auteur theory (with emphasis on the work of Howard Hawks
and John Ford.)

4470 Linden, George W. Reflections on the Screen. Belmont,
Cal.: Wadsworth, 1970. 297 pp.
Discusses the dyadic nature of film form.

4471 Youngblood, Gene. Expanded Cinema. Introduction by R.
Buckminster Fuller. New York: Dutton, 1970. 432 pp.
Explores the theoretical ramifications of film's new
technological possibilities.

4472 Bazin, Andre. What Is Cinema? Volume II. Selected and
translated by Hugh Gray. Berkeley: University of California Press, 1971. 200 pp.
Primarily critical essays (see entry 4491), but includes seminal essay on an aesthetic of reality.

4473 Cavell, Stanley. The World Viewed: Reflections on the
Ontology of Film. New York: Viking, 1971. 174 pp.

4474   Marinetti, Filippo Tommaso. Marinetti: Selected Writings.
Edited by R. W. Flint. New York: Farrar, Straus,
and Giroux, 1972. 366 pp. Translated by R. W. Flint
and Arthur A. Coppotelli.
Theoretical writings of Italian futurist, including material on and relevant to cinema.

4475   Tyler, Parker. The Shadow of an Airplane Climbs the
Empire State Building: A World Theory of Film. Garden
City, N.Y.: Doubleday, 1972. 248 pp.

4476   Bettetini, Gianfranco. The Language and Technique of the
Film. The Hague: Mouton, 1973. 202 pp. Translated
by David Osmond-Smith.
An approach to semiotics.

4477   Burch, Noël. Theory of Film Practice. Introduction by
Annette Michelson. New York: Praeger, 1973. 172 pp.
Translated by Helen R. Lane.

4478   Dreyer, Carl. Dreyer in Double Reflection: Translation of
Carl Th. Dreyer's Writings "About the Film" (On Filmen).
Edited and with accompanying commentary and essays by
Donald Skoller. New York: Dutton, 1973. 205 pp.

4479   Pryluck, Calvin Saul. Sources of Meaning in Motion Pictures
and Television. University of Iowa: Ph.D., 1973.
251 pp.

4480   Kaminsky, Stuart M. American Film Genres: Approaches to
a Critical Theory of Popular Film. Dayton, Ohio:
Pflaum, 1974. 232 pp.

4481   Kuleshov, Lev. Kuleshov on Film. Edited, translated, and
introduced by Ronald Levaco. Berkeley: University of
California Press, 1974. 226 pp.

4482   Metz, Christian. Film Language: A Semiotics of the Cinema.
New York: Oxford University Press, 1974. 268 pp.
Translated by Michael Taylor.

4483   Metz, Christian. Language and Cinema. The Hague: Mouton,
1974. 304 pp. Translated by Donna Jean Umiker-Sebeok.
Semiotic methodology.

4484   Weiss, Paul. Cinematics. Carbondale: Southern Illinois
University Press, 1975. 227 pp.
Observations on film grounded in philosophic reflec-
tions; includes running commentary by Eric Sherman,
Arthur Knight, Robert Thom, and others.

B. INDIVIDUAL CRITICS

In general, this category is composed of the collected reviews of individual critics such as Pauline Kael or John Simon.
The pieces in these volumes are reprinted from major periodicals
for which the reviewer has written regularly, and generally take
individual films as their subjects. For this category we have made
an exception to our usual arrangement of entries; by organizing
these books alphabetically according to the critic's name, we hoped
that the material would be more easily accessible to the reader.
Our annotations characterize the various anthologies by providing
the name of the publication(s) from which the essays were collected,
as well as the time-span in which they were originally written--
unless this information is conveyed in the title itself. Thus, the
reader looking for a particular kind of review on a film of a particular year may have some idea as to which books to consult.
For a comprehensive indexing of some of these works, the reader
should refer to Richard Heinzkill's Film Criticism: An Index to
Critics' Anthologies. For critical material of a slightly different
nature, the reader should consult Part VIII, section C, film movements, styles, and special critical approaches. For anthologies of
criticism with a variety of contributors see Part VIII, section D.

4485 Adler, Renata. A Year in the Dark: Journal of a Film
      Critic, 1968-1969. New York: Random, 1969. 354 pp.
      From The New York Times.

4486 Agate, James. Around Cinemas [In Two Volumes]. Volume
      I. London: Home and van Thal, 1946. 280 pp.
      Volume II. 1948. 294 pp.
      Primarily from The Tatler, 1921-1946.

4487 Agee, James. Agee on Film: Reviews and Comments.
      New York: McDowell, Obolensky, 1958. 432 pp. (Re-
      printed New York: Grosset and Dunlap, 1969.)

4488 Alpert, Hollis. The Dreams and the Dreamers. New York:
      Macmillan, 1962. 258 pp.
      Historical/critical essays on various film trends
      and individuals, including Marlon Brando, Jean Seberg,
      Ross Hunter, Alfred Hitchcock, and Ingmar Bergman.

4489 Artaud, Antonin. Collected Works, Volume Three: Scenarios, On the Cinema, Interviews, Letters. London: Calder and Boyars, 1972. 255 pp. Translated by A. Hamilton. Includes seven film treatments and ten brief essays on cinema.

4490 Bazin, Andre. What Is Cinema? Volume I. Selected and translated by Hugh Gray. Berkeley: University of California Press, 1967. 183 pp.
Primarily theoretical essays, but includes material on Robert Bresson and Charlie Chaplin.

4491 Bazin, Andre. What Is Cinema? Volume II. Selected and translated by Hugh Gray. Berkeley: University of California Press, 1971. 200 pp.
Includes essays on Vittorio De Sica, Roberto Rossellini, many neo-realist films, Charlie Chaplin, and the western.

4492 Bogdanovich, Peter. Pieces of Time: Peter Bogdanovich on the Movies. New York: Arbor, 1973. 269 pp. (Also published as Picture Shows: Peter Bogdanovich on the Movies.)
From Esquire, 1962-1973.

4493 Brown, John Mason. Seeing Things. New York: McGraw-Hill, 1946. 341 pp.
From the Saturday Review of Literature, primarily 1945; only two film essays, both on Walt Disney.

4494 Brown, John Mason. Seeing More Things. New York: Whittlesey, 1948. 347 pp.
From the Saturday Review of Literature, ca. 1946-1948.

4495 Brown, John Mason. Still Seeing Things. New York: McGraw-Hill, 1950. 335 pp.
From the Saturday Review of Literature, 1948-1950; includes many essays on film as well as other topics.

4496 Brown, John Mason. As They Appear. New York: McGraw-Hill, 1952. 258 pp.
From The Saturday Review, 1950-1952; only one essay related to film, on Walt Disney.

4497 Crist, Judith. The Private Eye, The Cowboy, and The Very Naked Girl: Movies From Cleo to Clyde. New York: Holt, Rinehart and Winston, 1968. 292 pp.
Primarily from New York Herald and World Journal Tribune, 1963-1968.

4498 Crist, Judith. Judith Crist's TV Guide to the Movies. New

York: Popular Library, 1974. 415 pp.
Short essays on hundreds of films.

Delaney, Marshall, pseudonym (see Fulford, Robert)

4499 Farber, Manny. Negative Space: Manny Farber on the
Movies. New York: Praeger, 1971. 288 pp. (Also
published as The Movies, New York: Hillstone, 1971.)
From various periodicals, primarily Nation and Art-
forum, 1949-1970.

4500 Ferguson, Otis. The Film Criticism of Otis Ferguson.
Edited by Robert Wilson. Philadelphia: Temple Univer-
sity Press, 1971. 475 pp.
From the New Republic, 1934-1942.

4501 Fulford, Robert. Marshall Delaney at the Movies: The Con-
temporary World as Seen on Film. Toronto: Peter
Martin, 1974. 244 pp.
From Saturday Night, ca. 1965-1973; the reviews of
Marshall Delaney, pseudonym for Robert Fulford.

4502 Gilliatt, Penelope. Unholy Fools, Wits, Comics, Disturbers
of the Peace. New York: Viking, 1973. 373 pp.
From various periodicals, 1960-1972.

4503 Godard, Jean-Luc. Godard on Godard: Critical Writings.
Edited by Jean Narboni and Tom Milne. New York:
Viking, 1972. 292 pp.
Primarily from Gazette du Cinéma, Cahiers du
Cinéma, and Arts, 1950-1967.

4504 Greene, Graham. Graham Greene on Film: Collected Film
Criticism, 1935-1940. Edited by John Russell Taylor.
New York: Simon and Schuster, 1972. 284 pp. (Also
published as The Pleasure-Dome: The Collected Film
Criticism of Graham Greene, 1935-1940.)
From The Spectator and Night and Day.

4505 Hills, Janet. Fragments: Janet Hills, 1919-1956. Stroud,
Glos., England: Harold, Margaret, and Clare Hills, ca.
1956. 143 pp.
Film criticism from The Times Educational Supplement, 1949-1956.

4506 Kael, Pauline. I Lost It at the Movies. Boston: Little,
Brown, 1965. 365 pp.
From various periodicals, 1954-1964.

4507 Kael, Pauline. Kiss Kiss Bang Bang. Boston: Little,
Brown, 1968. 404 pp.
From various periodicals, 1965-1967; also includes
commentaries on 280 movies from the past.

4508 Kael, Pauline. Going Steady. Boston: Little, Brown, 1970.
      304 pp.
      Primarily from The New Yorker, 1968-1969.

4509 Kael, Pauline. Deeper Into Movies. Boston: Little, Brown,
      1973. 458 pp.
      From The New Yorker, 1969-1972.

4510 Kael, Pauline. Reeling. Boston: Little, Brown, 1976.
      From The New Yorker, 1972-1975. 497 pp.

4511 Kauffmann, Stanley. A World on Film: Criticism and Com-
      ment. New York: Harper and Row, 1966. 437 pp.
      Primarily from The New Republic, 1958-1965.

4512 Kauffmann, Stanley. Figures of Light: Film Criticism and
      Comment. New York: Harper and Row, 1971. 296 pp.
      Primarily from The New Republic, 1966-1970.

4513 Kauffmann, Stanley. Living Images: Film Comment and
      Criticism. New York: Harper and Row, 1975. 404 pp.
      Primarily from The New Republic and Horizon, 1970-
      1974.

4514 Lejeune, C. A. Chestnuts in Her Lap, 1936-1946. London:
      Phoenix, 1947. 192 pp. (Revised as Chestnuts in Her
      Lap, 1936-1947, London: Phoenix, 1948, 208 pp.)
      From The Observer.

4515 Lorentz, Pare. Lorentz on Film: Movies 1927 to 1941.
      New York: Hopkinson and Blake, 1975. 228 pp.
      From various periodicals.

4516 Macdonald, Dwight. Dwight Macdonald on Movies. Engle-
      wood Cliffs, N.J.: Prentice-Hall, 1969. 492 pp.
      From various periodicals, primarily Esquire; 1929-
      1967.

4517 Mekas, Jonas. Movie Journal: The Rise of the New Ameri-
      can Cinema, 1959-1971. New York: Macmillan, 1972.
      434 pp.
      From The Village Voice.

4518 Pechter, William S. Twenty-Four Times a Second: Films
      and Film-Makers. New York: Harper and Row, 1971.
      324 pp.
      From various periodicals, 1960-1970.

4519 Reed, Rex. Big Screen, Little Screen. New York: Mac-
      millan, 1971. 433 pp.
      Film and television reviews from various periodicals,
      1968-1970; includes a lengthy essay on Cannes Film
      Festival, 1970.

4520   Rotha, Paul. Rotha on the Film: A Selection of Writings
       About the Cinema. Fairlawn, N.J.: Essential Books,
       1958. 338 pp.
            From various periodicals, 1928-1957; includes ma-
       terial on the British film industry, documentary, numerous
       individual films, and other topics.

4521   Sarris, Andrew. The American Cinema: Directors and Di-
       rections, 1929-1968. New York: Dutton, 1968. 383 pp.
            Filmographies, evaluations, and analyses of 200
       directors, with a pioneer essay on the auteur theory.

4522   Sarris, Andrew. Confessions of a Cultist: On the Cinema,
       1955-1969. New York: Simon and Schuster, 1970.
       480 pp.
            Primarily from The Village Voice.

4523   Sarris, Andrew. The Primal Screen: Essays on Film and
       Related Subjects. New York: Simon and Schuster, 1973.
       337 pp.
            From various periodicals, 1962-1972.

4524   Schickel, Richard. Second Sight: Notes on Some Movies,
       1965-1970. New York: Simon and Schuster, 1972.
       351 pp.
            Original reviews from Life magazine, followed by up-
       dated evaluations.

4525   Sheed, Wilfrid. The Morning After: Selected Essays and
       Reviews. New York: Farrar, Straus and Giroux, 1971.
       304 pp.
            Film reviews from Esquire, 1967-1969.

4526   Simon, John. Acid Test. New York: Stein and Day, 1963.
       288 pp.
            From various periodicals; section on film includes
       essays about Billy Wilder, Ingmar Bergman, and Jules
       Dassin.

4527   Simon, John. Private Screenings. New York: Macmillan,
       1967. 316 pp.
            Primarily from New Leader, 1963-1966.

4528   Simon, John. Movies Into Film: Film Criticism, 1967-
       1970. New York: Dial, 1971. 448 pp.
            Primarily from New Leader.

4529   Sontag, Susan. Against Interpretation and Other Essays.
       New York: Farrar, Straus and Giroux, 1966. 304 pp.
            From various periodicals, 1961-1965; section on
       film includes essays about Robert Bresson, Vivre Sa Vie,
       the science fiction film, Flaming Creatures, Muriel, and
       novels and film.

4530   Sontag, Susan. Styles of Radical Will. New York: Farrar,
       Straus and Giroux, 1969. 274 pp.
           From various periodicals, 1966-1968; section on film
       includes essays on theatre and film, Persona, and Godard.

       Tyler, Parker (see Part VIII, section C)

4531   Tynan, Kenneth. Tynan Right and Left: Plays, Films,
       People, Places, and Events. New York: Atheneum,
       1967. 479 pp.
           Film criticism from various periodicals, 1953-1966.

4532   Van Doren, Mark. The Private Reader: Selected Articles
       and Reviews. New York: Holt, 1942. 416 pp.
           Film reviews from Nation, 1935-1938.

4533   Warshow, Robert. The Immediate Experience: Movies,
       Comics, Theatre and Other Aspects of Popular Culture.
       Garden City, N.Y.: Doubleday, 1962. 282 pp.
           Primarily from Commentary and Partisan Review,
       1946-1955.

4534   Weightman, John. The Concept of the Avant-Garde: Explora-
       tions in Modernism. LaSalle, Ill.: Library Press, 1973.
       323 pp.
           Film criticism from Encounter, ca. 1968-1972.

4535   Weinberg, Herman G. Saint Cinema: Selected Writings,
       1929-1970. New York: Drama Book Specialists, 1970.
       354 pp.
           From various periodicals (including much from his
       column in Film Culture), 1929-1970.

4536   Winnington, Richard. Drawn and Quartered: A Selection of
       Weekly Film Reviews and Drawings. London: Saturn,
       ca. 1948. 126 pp.
           Primarily from News Chronicle, 1943-1948.

4537   Winnington, Richard. Film Criticism and Caricatures, 1943-
       1953. Selected and introduced by Paul Rotha. London:
       Elek, 1975. 196 pp.
           Primarily from News Chronicle.

4538   Young, Vernon. On Film: Unpopular Essays on a Popular
       Art. Chicago: Quadrangle, 1972. 428 pp.
           From various periodicals, primarily Hudson Review,
       1954-1969.

C. FILM MOVEMENTS, STYLES AND
SPECIAL CRITICAL APPROACHES

Works of criticism are scattered throughout this bibliography. Part V contains critical studies of particular kinds of film,
including genre criticism; Part VI contains critical studies of particular individuals, including auteur criticism; Part VII contains
critical studies of particular films; Part IX contains sociological
criticism. In general, the books in this section tend to be those
which cannot exclusively or appropriately be categorized elsewhere.
As such, this section contains many different kinds of books, including books which deal with particular film movements--such as
the new wave or neo-realism--and books which deal with particular
film styles--such as the cubist or transcendental styles. Although
books in this category may often deal with a variety of individual
films, they generally operate from a specific critical or aesthetic
perspective; consequently, political, mythological, psychological,
and feminist criticism have been included here.

4539 Hunter, William. Scrutiny of the Cinema. (Originally pub-
lished 1932.) New York: Arno, 1972. 87 pp.
A general assessment of the state of film art, with
some discussion of individual films and brief essays on
Charles Chaplin, Sergei Eisenstein, René Clair, V. I.
Pudovkin, Fritz Lang, and others.

4540 Tyler, Parker. The Hollywood Hallucination. New York:
Creative Age Press, 1944. 246 pp. (Reprinted with
an introduction by Richard Schickel, New York: Simon
and Schuster, 1970.)
Psychological analysis of the movie-going experience,
the films, and the stars of the thirties and forties.

4541 Tyler, Parker. Magic and Myth of the Movies. New York:
Henry Holt, 1947. 283 pp. (Reprinted with an introduction by Richard Schickel, New York: Simon and Schuster,
1970.)
"Psychoanalytic-mythological" criticism of American
films and stars of the late thirties and forties.

4542 Lawson, John Howard. Film in the Battle of Ideas. New
York: Masses and Mainstream, 1953. 126 pp.

Analyzes the ideological function of film, discusses numerous American films, and advocates development of a "people's art."

4543 Tyler, Parker. The Three Faces of the Film: The Art, The Dream, The Cult. New York: Yoseloff, 1960. 150 pp. (Revised South Brunswick, N.J.: A. S. Barnes, 1967, 141 pp.)
      Includes discussion of film as a fine art, the avant-garde film, film as ritual and myth, and contemporary film trends.

4544 Durgnat, Raymond. Nouvelle Vague: The First Decade. Loughton, England: Motion, 1963. 90 pp. (Also published as French Cinema: The A-Z Guide to the "New Wave.")

4545 Taylor, John Russell. Cinema Eye, Cinema Ear: Some Key Filmmakers of the Sixties. New York: Hill and Wang, 1964. 294 pp.
      Includes a chapter on the New Wave and directors François Truffaut, Jean-Luc Godard, and Alain Resnais.

4546 Huaco, George A. The Sociology of Film Art. New York: Basic Books, 1965. 229 pp.
      Includes sociological studies of German expressionism, Soviet expressive realism, and Italian neo-realism.

4547 Durgnat, Raymond. Films and Feelings. Cambridge, Mass.: M.I.T. Press, 1967. 288 pp.
      Discusses various films and filmmakers.

4548 Lovell, Alan. Anarchist Cinema. London: Goodwin, ca. 1967. 40 pp.
      Analyzes the work of Jean Vigo, Georges Franju, and Luis Buñuel in terms of their common elements of anarchist cinema.

4549 Graham, Peter (ed.) The New Wave: Critical Landmarks. Garden City, N.Y.: Doubleday, 1968. 184 pp.
      For description, see entry 4581.

4550 Deming, Barbara. Running Away From Myself: A Dream Portrait of America Drawn From Films of the Forties. New York: Grossman, 1969. 210 pp.
      Psychological analysis of films, heroes, and heroines in terms of dreams, wish fulfillment, and identification.

4551 Tyler, Parker. Sex, Psyche, Etcetera in the Film. New York: Horizon, 1969. 240 pp.
      Includes general essays, analysis of individual films, and material on Andy Warhol, Michelangelo Antonioni, Federico Fellini, Ingmar Bergman, Orson Welles, Charlie Chaplin, and others.

4552   Armes, Roy. Patterns in Realism. South Brunswick, N. J.:
       A. S. Barnes, 1971. 226 pp.
       Study of Italian neo-realism.

4553   Bazin, Andre. What Is Cinema? Volume II. Selected and
       translated by Hugh Gray. Berkeley: University of Cali-
       fornia Press, 1971. 200 pp.
       Includes material on the aesthetic concepts underlying
       Italian neo-realism, as well as essays on several of the
       neo-realist films.

4554   Matthews, J. H. Surrealism and Film. Ann Arbor: Uni-
       versity of Michigan Press, 1971. 198 pp.
       A study of scripts, films, and filmmakers in the
       context of the surrealist vision.

4555   Cinema of the Third World. Auckland: Auckland University
       Students' Association, 1972. 76 pp.
       Includes a lengthy essay entitled, "Toward a Third
       Cinema" by Fernando Solanas and Ottavio Getino, which
       discusses the role of film in achieving revolutionary goals.

4556   Kawin, Bruce F. Telling It Again and Again: Repetition in
       Literature and Film. Ithaca, N. Y.: Cornell University
       Press, 1972. 197 pp.
       A study of repetition as an aesthetic device in litera-
       ture and film, with some emphasis on the work of Alain
       Resnais.

4557   Perkins, V. F. Film as Film: Understanding and Judging
       Movies. Baltimore: Penguin, 1972. 198 pp.
       Develops the concept of an aesthetic of coherence for
       film, utilizing as example the work of Eisenstein, Alfred
       Hitchcock, Nicholas Ray, Otto Preminger, Richard Brooks,
       and others.

4558   Schrader, Paul. Transcendental Style in Film: Ozu, Bresson,
       Dreyer. Los Angeles: University of California Press,
       1972. 194 pp.
       Develops an aesthetic of filmic forms which express
       the Transcendent.

4559   Johnston, Claire (ed.) Notes on Women's Cinema. London:
       Society for Education in Film and Television, 1973.
       40 pp.
       Comprised of "To Be Our Own Muse: The Dialectics
       of a Culture Heroine" by Naome Gilburt; "Women's
       Cinema as Counter-Cinema" by Claire Johnston; "Sub-
       jecting Her Objectification, or Communism Is Not Enough"
       by Barbara Halpern Martineau; and an interview with
       Nelly Kaplan.

4560   Winston, Douglas Garrett.   The Screenplay as Literature.
       Rutherford, N.J.:   Fairleigh Dickinson University Press,
       1973.   240 pp.
          Discusses the artistic development of film, with em-
       phasis on the work of Robert Bresson, Ingmar Bergman,
       Federico Fellini, and Michelangelo Antonioni.

4561   Armes, Roy.   Film and Reality: An Historical Survey.
       Baltimore: Penguin, 1974.   254 pp.
          Divided into major sections on film realism, film
       illusion, and film modernism.

4562   Vogel, Amos.   Film as a Subversive Art.   New York:
       Random, 1974.   336 pp.
          Discusses aesthetic, sexual, and ideological forms
       of subversion in film.

4563   Dorfman, Ariel and Mattelart, Armand.   How to Read Donald
       Duck: Imperialist Ideology in the Disney Comic.   Intro-
       duced and translated by David Kunzle.   New York: Inter-
       national General, 1975.   112 pp.
          A Marxist study of the Disney comic and cultural
       imperialism, with relevance to Disney's film work.

4564   Giannetti, Louis D.   Godard and Others: Essays in Film
       Form.   Rutherford, N.J.:   Fairleigh Dickinson University
       Press, 1975.   184 pp.
          Essays on the mobile camera, the cinematic meta-
       phor, the plotless film, and the cinematic essay.

4565   Greenberg, Harvey R.   The Movies on Your Mind.   New
       York: Saturday Review Press, 1975.   273 pp.
          Applies Freudian analysis as a critical model to films.

4566   Lawder, Standish D.   The Cubist Cinema.   New York: New
       York University Press, 1975.   265 pp.
          Examines the interrelationships between the Cubist
       movement in painting and in film.

4567   MacBean, James Roy.   Film and Revolution.   Bloomington:
       Indiana University Press, 1975.   339 pp.
          Approaches the work of Godard and Gorin, Roberto
       Rossellini, Dusan Makavejev, Marcel Ophuls, Elio Petri,
       Robert Kramer, Fernando Solanas, and Ottavio Getino
       from the perspective of Marxist film criticism.

D. ANTHOLOGIES OF THEORY AND CRITICISM

This section is composed of those anthologies of theory
and criticism which include a number of contributors. In general,
this section includes three kinds of books: collected film society
notes on individual films, directors, or national cinemas; collections
of film reviews from a variety of critics; and wide-ranging historical,
critical, and theoretical anthologies often intended to be used in
introductory film courses or as general surveys of critical issues.
Most of these books have been annotated regarding content and contributors so that the reader may infer their appropriateness for his
or her needs. Most of the essays appearing in these anthologies
can be found in other works in this bibliography; many essays tend
to be anthologized again and again. As a general rule we have not
repeated within the annotation the editor's name as a contributor;
the reader should be aware, however, that most editors have con-
tributed essays to their own anthologies.

4568 Cooke, Alistair (ed.) Garbo and The Night Watchmen: A
      Selection Made in 1937 from the Writings of British and
      American Film Critics. (Originally published 1937.)
      New York: McGraw-Hill, 1971. 285 pp.
          Contributions by Robert Herring, Don Herold, John
      Marks, Meyer Levin, Robert Forsythe, Graham Greene,
      Otis Ferguson, and Cecilia Ager. Variety of reviews but
      one chapter on MODERN TIMES.

4569 Manvell, Roger with Neilson-Baxter, R. K. and Wollenberg,
      H. H. (eds.) The Cinema 1950. Harmondsworth, England:
      Penguin, 1950. 224 pp.
          Contributions by Robert Flaherty, Anthony Asquith,
      Thorold Dickinson, Michael Bell, Richard Winnington,
      Dilys Powell, Basil Wright, Leonard England, Peter Usti-
      nov, Ivor Montagu, Siegfried Kracauer, and others.
      Topics include THE QUEEN OF SPADES, experimentation
      in films, box office success and audience tastes, stereo-
      scopic cinema, television and cinema, and national typage
      in Hollywood films, among others.

4570 Sutro, John (ed.) Diversion: Twenty-Two Authors on the
      Lively Arts. London: Parrish, 1950. 224 pp.

Contributions by Dilys Powell, Cecil Beaton, Thorold
Dickinson, Terence Rattigan, and others. Film topics include screenwriting, film music, publicity, fan letters,
the horror film, and INTOLERANCE.

4571 Anstey, Edgar; Manvell, Roger; Lindgren, Ernest; and Rotha,
Paul (eds.) Shots in the Dark: A Collection of Reviewers'
Opinions of Some of the Leading Films Released Between
January 1949 and February 1951. London: Allan Wingate,
1951. 268 pp.
Contributions by 27 British critics.

4572 Manvell, Roger with Neilson-Baxter, R. K. (eds.) The
Cinema 1951. Harmondsworth, England: Penguin, 1951.
224 pp.
Contributions by Thorold Dickinson and Roger Manvell,
Helen van Dongen, Gavin Lambert, James Monahan, Catherine de la Roche, Basil Wright, Sinclair Road, Henri
Storck and P. E. Sales-Gomes, T. E. B. Clarke, Karel
Reisz, Alexander Knox, Herbert Read, and others. Topics
include the general filmmaking process, editing, the making
of Jean Vigo's ZERO DE CONDUITE, screenwriting, the
producer, film acting, film programming, and television,
among others.

4573 Manvell, Roger with Neilson-Baxter, R. K. (eds.) The
Cinema 1952. Harmondsworth, England: Penguin, 1952.
224 pp.
Contributions by Robert Flaherty, Gavin Lambert,
Jack Beddington, Sergei Eisenstein, Karel Reisz, and
others. Includes screenplay excerpts from CHANCE OF
A LIFETIME, GREAT EXPECTATIONS, THE LAVENDER
HILL MOB, KIND HEARTS AND CORONETS, THE THIRD
MAN, and SECRET PEOPLE, essays on film criticism,
the making of THE BATTLESHIP POTEMKIN, and adapting
novels into films, among other topics.

4574 Talbot, Daniel (ed.) Film: An Anthology. New York:
Simon and Schuster, 1959. 649 pp. (Abridged edition
Berkeley: University of California Press, 1966, 404 pp.)
Contributions by Elie Faure, Erwin Panofsky, Su-
sanne Langer, Parker Tyler, Arnold Hauser, Seymour
Stern, John Grierson, James Agee, Manny Farber,
Pauline Kael, V. I. Pudovkin, Gilbert Seldes, Bela
Balazs, Rudolf Arnheim, Sergei Eisenstein, René Clair,
Jean Cocteau, Paul Rotha, Georges Sadoul, Henry Miller,
Alva Johnston, Lillina Ross, Ben Hecht, and others.
Topics include film theory and aesthetics, screenwriting,
directors of the thirties, comedy, the western, under-
ground film, documentary, D. W. Griffith, THE CABINET
OF DR. CALIGARI, and Chaplin, among others.

4575 Jacobs, Lewis (ed.) Introduction to the Art of the Movies:

An Anthology of Ideas on the Nature of Movie Art. New
York: Noonday, 1960. 302 pp. (Numerous reprintings.)
Contributions by Vachel Lindsay, Alexander Bakshy,
Kenneth Macgowan, Herman G. Weinberg, Fernand Leger,
Dorothy Jones, Evelyn Gerstein, Andre Levinson, Seymour
Stern, Sergei Eisenstein, Harry Alan Potamkin, Dwight
Macdonald, Kirk Bond, James Shelley Hamilton, Siegfried
Kracauer, Andre Sennwald, Maya Deren, Dudley Nichols,
Henry Hart, Hans Richter, Slavko Vorkapich, Hollis Alpert,
and others. Lengthy historical introduction by Lewis
Jacobs. Topics include aesthetics of film, Erich von
Stroheim, SUNRISE, THE PASSION OF JOAN OF ARC,
Eisenstein, Pudovkin, Griffith, Walt Disney, Jean Vigo,
Carl Lakewood's TUESDAY BROWN, CITIZEN KANE,
Henry James, RASHOMON, and Ingmar Bergman, among
others.

4576   Lennig, Arthur (ed.)   Film Notes.   Madison: Wisconsin Film
       Society, 1960.   139 pp.
          Critical/historical notes on over 20 films, primarily
       from German, Russian, Scandinavian, and American Cinema.

4577   Lennig, Arthur (ed.)   Classics of the Film.   Madison: Wis-
       consin Film Society, 1965.   238 pp.
          Critical/historical articles, primarily on films from
       the French, German, American, and Scandinavian cinemas.

4578   MacCann, Richard Dyer (ed.)   Film: A Montage of Theories.
       New York: Dutton, 1966.   384 pp.
          Contributions by V. I. Pudovkin, Sergei Eisenstein,
       Rene Clair, Gavin Lambert, Alfred Hitchcock, Dudley
       Nichols, Vachel Lindsay, Parker Tyler, Hollis Alpert,
       Rudolf Arnheim, Robert Nathan, George Bluestone, Ing-
       mar Bergman, Bela Balazs, Ralph Block, Mack Sennett,
       Herbert Read, Slavko Vorkapich, Hans Richter, Arnold
       Hauser, Susanne Langer, John Grierson, Cesare Zavattini,
       Hugo Mauerhofer, Siegfried Kracauer, Michael Roemer,
       Gideon Bachmann, Robert Drew, Richard Leacock, D. A.
       Pennebaker, Carl Dreyer, Charles Barr, Stan Vanderbeek,
       Jonas Mekas, Pauline Kael, Penelope Houston, François
       Truffaut, Federico Fellini, and others.   Surveys most
       aspects of film; section titles are "The Plastic Material,"
       "Film and the Other Arts," "The Cinematic Essence,"
       "Dream and Reality," and "An Evolving Art."

4579   Pratt, George C. (ed.)   Spellbound in Darkness: A History
       of the Silent Film.   Rochester, N.Y.: University of
       Rochester Press, 1966.   452 pp. (Revised Greenwich,
       Conn.: New York Graphic Society, 1973, 548 pp.)
          Compilation of articles about silent film from con-
       temporary sources.   Includes chapters on Georges Méliès
       and Edwin S. Porter, Griffith, Thomas H. Ince, Mack

Sennett and Charlie Chaplin, Mary Pickford and Theda
Bara, Cecil B. De Mille, Ernst Lubitsch, Erich von Stroheim and Robert J. Flaherty, Carl Dreyer, experimental
film, as well as various national cinemas.

4580   Robinson, W. R. with Garrett, George (eds.) Man and the
       Movies. Baton Rouge: Louisiana State University Press,
       1967. 371 pp.
          Contributions by Larry McMurtry, Walter Korte,
       Leslie Fiedler, and others. Topics include adaptation of
       Osborne's TOM JONES, westerns, the horror film, skin
       flicks, Alfred Hitchcock, D. W. Griffith, Ingmar Berg-
       man, Federico Fellini, Michelangelo Antonioni, Visconti's
       SANDRA, William Faulkner in Hollywood, and film criti-
       cism, among others.

4581   Graham, Peter (ed.) The New Wave: Critical Landmarks.
       Garden City, N.Y.: Doubleday, 1968. 184 pp.
          Contributions by François Truffaut, Alexandre Astruc,
       Andre Bazin, Gerard Gozlan, Claude Chabrol, Jean-Luc
       Godard, and Robert Benayoun. Essays primarily from
       Cahiers du Cinéma and Positif; included are interviews
       with Truffaut, Bazin's essays on the evolution of film
       language and the politique des auteurs, material on the
       Nouvelle Vague, essays about Bazin's writings, and a re-
       view of Astruc's UNE VIE.

4582   Kirstein, Lincoln; Leyda, Jay; Losey, Mary; Stebbins, Robert;
       and Strasberg, Lee (eds.) Films: A Quarterly of Dis-
       cussion and Analysis. New York: Arno, 1968. Various
       pagings.
          Reprint of the four issues of the periodical Films,
       published 1939-1940. Contributions by Alberto Cavalcanti,
       John Grierson, Georges Sadoul, Joris Ivens, James Agee,
       Richard Griffith, Rudolf Arnheim, and others.

4583   McBride, Joseph (ed.) Persistence of Vision: A Collection
       of Film Criticism. Madison: Wisconsin Film Society
       Press, 1968. 222 pp.
          Contributions by Arthur Lennig, Howard Koch, Michael
       Wilmington, Andrew Sarris, Richard Thompson, and others.
       Critical/historical material on both silent and sound films;
       includes a lengthy section on Orson Welles.

4584   Sarris, Andrew (ed.) The Film. Indianapolis: Bobbs-Mer-
       rill, 1968. 64 pp.
          Contributions by Pauline Kael, E. Archer, Hollis
       Alpert, Roger Greenspun, Richard Roud, John Simon,
       Dwight Macdonald, and others. Topics include LOLITA,
       Elia Kazan, Jerry Lewis, Robert Bresson, The New Wave,
       Michelangelo Antonioni, and Federico Fellini, among
       others.

4585   Schickel, Richard and Simon, John (eds.) Film 67/68: An
       Anthology by the National Society of Film Critics. New
       York: Simon and Schuster, 1968. 320 pp.
       Reviews of the films of 1967 by leading critics; also
       documents the Society's annual awards.

4586   Alpert, Hollis and Sarris, Andrew (eds.) Film 68/69: An
       Anthology by the National Society of Film Critics. New
       York: Simon and Schuster, 1969. 281 pp.
       Reviews of the films of 1968 by leading critics; also
       documents the Society's annual awards.

4587   Bowser, Eileen (ed.) Film Notes. New York: Museum of
       Modern Art, 1969. 128 pp.
       Critical notes on films (1894-1950) screened at the
       Museum of Modern Art; contributions by Iris Barry, Gary
       Carey, Alistair Cooke, Richard Griffith, Arthur Knight,
       and Eileen Bowser.

4588   Jacobs, Lewis (ed.) The Emergence of Film Art: The Evo-
       lution and Development of the Motion Picture as an Art,
       From 1900 to the Present. New York: Hopkinson and
       Blake, 1969. 453 pp.
       Contributions by Seymour Stern, Paul Rotha, Harry
       Alan Potamkin, Dwight Macdonald, Sergei Eisenstein,
       Alberto Cavalcanti, John Howard Lawson, Hanns Eisler,
       Len Lye, Robert Flaherty, Lindsay Anderson, Peter
       Cowie, Arthur Knight, Ingmar Bergman, Andrew Sarris,
       Pauline Kael, Donald Richie, Michelangelo Antonioni,
       Geoffrey Nowell-Smith, Jonas Mekas, Stanley Kauffmann,
       and others. Historical introductions by Lewis Jacobs.
       Topics include Georges Méliès, Edwin S. Porter, D. W.
       Griffith, German cinema, the French avant-garde, Eisen-
       stein, V. I. Pudovkin, sound, color, the composer, René
       Clair, John Ford, animation, CITIZEN KANE, Italian
       neorealism, François Truffaut, Alain Resnais, Federico
       Fellini, Richard Lester, Saul Bass, cinema verite, the
       auteur theory, free cinema and the new wave, and others.

4589   Minton, Eric (comp.) American Musicals, 1929-1933. Ot-
       tawa: n.p., 1969. 75 pp.
       Film reviews of musicals from the New York Times,
       1929-1933.

4590   Stern, Seymour; Jacobs, Lewis; and others (eds.) Experi-
       mental Cinema, 1930-1934. Introduction by George Am-
       berg. New York: Arno, 1969. Various pagings.
       Compilation of the five issues of the periodical titled
       Experimental Cinema, which was established to counteract
       tendencies in the capitalist film industry and to stimulate
       a proletarian film movement; special emphasis on Soviet
       and independent cinema. Contributions by Sergei Eisen-
       stein, V. I. Pudovkin, Dziga Vertov, J. Lengyel, V.

Turin, David Platt, Samuel Brody, Leon Moussinac, Bela
Balazs, M. Kaufman, Werner Klingler, Ralph Bond, G.
L. George, V. G. Alexandroff, Kirk Bond, René Clair,
A. Dovzhenko, Conrad Seiler, and many others.

4591   Wollen, Peter (ed.) Working Papers on the Cinema: So-
       ciology and Semiology. London: British Film Institute,
       ca. 1969. 36 pp.
       Contributors include Terry Lovell, Andrew Tudor,
       Frank West, and Paul Filmer.

4592   Bellone, Julius (ed.) Renaissance of the Film. New York:
       Macmillan, 1970. 366 pp.
       Essays by various critics primarily on well-known
       foreign films of the fifties and sixties.

4593   Jacobs, Lewis (ed.) The Movies as Medium. New York:
       Farrar, Straus, and Giroux, 1970. 335 pp.
       Contributions by Arthur Goldsmith, Nicola Chiaro-
       monte, Herbert A. Lightman, Gregg Toland, Ezra Good-
       man, Hilary Harris, Stanley J. Solomon, Irving Pichel,
       Robert Gessner, Maya Deren, John Howard Lawson, Ivor
       Montagu, Carl Dreyer, Sergei Eisenstein, William Johnson,
       Bella Belazs, Henwar Rodakiewicz, Kurt Weill, Alexander
       Bakshy, Arthur Lennig, Jonas Mekas, and others. Sec-
       tions titled "Directors Speak," "Image," "Movement,"
       "Time and Space," "Color," "Sound," etc.

4594   Morgenstern, Joseph and Kanfer, Stephen (eds.) Film 69/70
       An Anthology by the National Society of Film Critics.
       New York: Simon and Schuster, 1970. 286 pp.
       Reviews of the films of 1969 by leading critics; also
       documents the Society's annual awards.

4595   The New York Times Film Reviews, 1913-1968 [in Six
       Volumes]. Volume I, 1913-1931; Volume II, 1932-1938;
       Volume III, 1939-1948; Volume IV, 1949-1957; Volume V,
       1959-1968; Volume VI, Appendix, Index. New York:
       The New York Times and Arno, 1970. 4961 pp. (Supple-
       ments published biennially. The New York Times Film
       Reviews, 1969-1970 published 1971, 333 pp. The New
       York Times Film Reviews, 1971-1972 published 1973, 435
       pp. The New York Times Film Reviews, 1973-1974, pub-
       lished 1975, 383 pp.)
       See entry 137.

4596   Ross, T. J. (ed.) Film and the Liberal Arts. New York:
       Holt, Rinehart and Winston, 1970. 419 pp.
       Contributions by Andre Bazin, James Agee, Dwight
       Macdonald, Sergei Eisenstein, Luis Buñuel, Robert
       Warshow, Susan Sontag, William K. Everson, David
       Reisman, Marshall McLuhan, and others. Divided into
       sections which discuss film's relationship to other areas,

such as literature, music, society, visual arts, aesthetics, etc.

4597   Samuels, Charles Thomas (ed.) A Casebook on Film. New York: Van Nostrand Reinhold, 1970. 250 pp.
Contributions by Erwin Panofsky, Arnold Hauser, Michael Roemer, Maya Deren, Nicola Chiaromonte, Andrew Sarris, Dudley Nichols, V. I. Pudovkin, Basil Wright, Irving Pichel, John Simon, Penelope Houston, Robert Brustein, and others. Includes sections on film theory, the filmmaking process, and film criticism, as well as focusing on THE GRADUATE, BONNIE AND CLYDE, and BLOW-UP.

4598   Screen Monographs I. New York: Arno, 1970. Various pagings.
Comprised of "The Art of Cineplastics" (1923) by Elie Faure; "The Technique of the Film" (1937) by Bernard Gordon and Julian Zimet; and "Parnassus to Let" (1928) by Eric Walter White.

4599   Screen Monographs II. New York: Arno, 1970. Various pagings.
Comprised of "The Crisis of the Film" (1929) by John Gould Fletcher; "The Photo Drama" (1915) by William Morgan Hannon; "See and Hear" (1929) by Will H. Hays; and "The American Influence in France" (1930) by Philippe Soupault.

4600   Sitney, P. Adams (ed.) Film Culture Reader. New York: Praeger, 1970. 438 pp.
Compilation of articles from the periodical Film Culture. Contributions by Hans Richter, Jonas Mekas, Andrew Sarris, Walter S. Michel, Parker Tyler, Rudolf Arnheim, Herman G. Weinberg, Richard Leacock, Ken Kelman, Michael McClure, Maya Deren, Arthur Miller, Dylan Thomas, Jane and Stan Brakhage, Gene Youngblood, Dziga Vertov, Sidney Peterson, Annette Michelson, and others. Topics include CITIZEN KANE, Dimitri Kirsanov, Erich von Stroheim, the New American Cinema, the auteur theory, Carl Dreyer, Jane Mansfield, Stan Brakhage, Harry Smith, Kenneth Anger, Peter Kubelka, Jordan Belson, structural film, Orson Welles, and much more particularly related to the avant-garde in America.

4601   Amberg, George (comp.) The New York Times Film Reviews: A One-Volume Selection, 1913-1970. New York: Arno, 1971. 495 pp.
Selected reviews from the complete seven-volume set (see entry 137); introductory essays by Amberg.

4602   Boyum, Jay Gould and Scott, Adrienne (comps.) Film as

Film: Critical Responses to Film Art. Boston: Allyn
and Bacon, 1971. 397 pp.
    Primarily consists of reviews by leading critics on
25 well-known films, ranging from von Sternberg's THE
BLUE ANGEL to Antonioni's BLOW-UP.

4603 Denby, David (ed.) Film 70/71: An Anthology by the Na-
     tional Society of Film Critics. New York: Simon and
     Schuster, 1971. 319 pp.
        Reviews of the films of 1970 by leading critics; also
     documents the Society's annual awards.

4604 Kirschner, Allen and Linda (eds.) Film: Readings in the
     Mass Media. New York: Odyssey, 1971. 315 pp.
        Contributions by Marshall McLuhan, Mack Sennett,
     D. W. Griffith, Irving Thalberg, H. L. Mencken, Rudolf
     Arnheim, Alfred Hitchcock, Michelangelo Antonioni, Ing-
     mar Bergman, Ken Kelman, Mervyn LeRoy, Richard
     Schickel, Walter Kerr, Stanley Kauffmann, Arthur Knight,
     Judith Crist, Anthony Schillaci, Tom Wolfe, William Fadi-
     man, Ernest Callenbach, Renata Adler, Parker Tyler,
     and others. Sections are titled "Form and Technique,"
     "Audience and Effect," and "Critics and Criticism"; the
     latter includes several articles on THE GRADUATE and
     a questionnaire symposium, "The Future of the Film,"
     with members of the National Society of Film Critics.

4605 MacPherson, Kenneth and others (eds.) Close Up ... Devoted
     to the Art of Films [in Ten Volumes]. Introduced by
     Herman Weinberg. New York: Arno, 1971.
        Reprint of film periodical published 1927-1933; contri-
     butions by Dorothy Richardson, Robert Herring, Oswell
     Blakeston, Ernest Betts, Harry Alan Potamkin, Winifred
     Bryher, and others. Includes material on history, theory,
     criticism, and aesthetics of film.

4606 The Art of Cinema: Selected Essays. With a foreword by
     George Amberg. New York: Arno, 1972. Various
     pagings.
        Comprised of "The Ambivalence of Realism" by
     George Amberg; "An Anagram of Ideas on Art, Form and
     Film" by Maya Deren; "Cinematography: The Creative
     Use of Reality" by Maya Deren, "Psychology of Film Ex-
     perience" by Hugo Mauerhofer; "Towards a Film Aesthetic"
     by Herbert Read; and "The Witness Point: Definitions of
     Film Art" by Vernon Young.

4607 Cameron, Ian (ed.) Movie Reader. New York: Praeger,
     1972. 120 pp.
        Collected articles from the British periodical Movie,
     1962-1965. Contributions by V. F. Perkins, Paul Mayers-
     berg, Robin Wood, Charles Barr, and Raymond Durgnat.

Includes material on Alfred Hitchcock, Otto Preminger, Howard Hawks, Nicholas Ray, Joseph Losey, Michael Powell, Claude Chabrol, Frank Tashlin, and Josef von Sternberg.

4608   Denby, David (ed.) Film 71/72: An Anthology by the National Society of Film Critics. New York: Simon and Schuster, 1972. 299 pp.
Reviews of the films of 1971 by leading critics; also documents the Society's annual awards.

4609   Geduld, Harry M. (ed.) Authors on Film. Bloomington: Indiana University Press, 1972. 303 pp.
Articles about film (particularly the silent period, screenwriting, and the Hollywood milieu) by well-known authors: Maxim Gorky, Frank Norris, Leo Tolstoy, Upton Sinclair, Jean-Paul Sartre, Carl Sandburg, Jack Kerouac, Bertolt Brecht, H. G. Wells, Aldous Huxley, Virginia Woolf, H. L. Mencken, G. K. Chesterton, G. B. Shaw, Heinrich Mann, W. Somerset Maugham, T. S. Eliot, Graham Greene, William Faulkner, Theodore Dreiser, F. Scott Fitzgerald, E. M. Forster, Jean Cocteau, John Dos Passos, Ernest Hemingway, James Baldwin, and others.

4610   Hound and Horn: Essays on Cinema. New York: Arno and The New York Times, 1972. Various pagings.
Compilation of essays on film selected from the periodical Hound and Horn, 1928-1934. Contributions by Jere Abbott, Alfred H. Barr, Jr., Kirk Bond, Sergei Eisenstein, Lincoln Kirstein, Harry Alan Potamkin, Kenneth White, and others. Topics include Eisenstein, German cinema, QUE VIVA MEXICO!, transition to sound, contemporary film magazines, James Cagney, G. W. Pabst, Pudovkin, animation, F. W. Murnau, Ernst Lubitsch, and others.

4611   Kauffmann, Stanley with Henstell, Bruce (eds.) American Film Criticism: From the Beginnings to Citizen Kane: Reviews of Significant Films at the Time They First Appeared. New York: Liveright, 1972. 443 pp.
Over 180 articles. Contributions by Frank E. Woods, W. Stephen Bush, Louis Reeves Harrison, Francis Hackett, Robert E. Sherwood, Evelyn Gerstein, Alexander Bakshy, Harry Alan Potamkin, Pare Lorentz, Richard Watts, Jr., William Troy, Gilbert Seldes, Otis Ferguson, Paul Goodman, Andre Sennwald, Frank S. Nugent, Lincoln Kirstein, Howard Barnes, and many others.

4612   Shales, Tom; Brownlow, Kevin; and others. American Film Heritage: Impressions From the American Film Institute Archives. Washington, D.C.: Acropolis, 1972. 184 pp.

Essays on various directors, films, and genres in
American film history, particularly the pre-1940 years; for
list of individuals discussed, see entry 3759.

4613 Denby, David (ed.) Film 72/73: An Anthology by the National
Society of Film Critics. Indianapolis: Bobbs-Merrill,
1973. 266 pp.
Reviews of the films of 1972 by leading critics; also
documents the Society's annual awards.

4614 Nobile, Philip (ed.) Favorite Movies: Critics' Choice. New
York: Macmillan, 1973. 301 pp.
Articles by Dwight Macdonald, Peter Bogdanovich,
Jay Cocks, Joseph McBride, John Simon, Andrew Sarris,
William Pechter, Stephen Farber, David Denby, Richard
Roud, Roger Greenspun, Richard Schickel, Jonas Mekas,
Molly Haskell, Peter Harcourt, Robin Wood, Charles
Thomas Samuels, Richard Gilman, Ellen Willis, Judith
Crist, Francis X. J. Coleman, Richard Corliss, Colin L.
Westerbeck, Jr., Parker Tyler, Howard Thompson, Stuart
Byron, and Martin Rubin.

4615 Solomon, Stanley J. The Classic Cinema: Essays in Criti-
cism. New York: Harcourt Brace Jovanovich, 1973.
354 pp.
Articles on 14 classic films from INTOLERANCE to
FELLINI SATYRICON. With contributions by Lillian Gish,
Paul O'Dell, Siegfried Kracauer, Lotte Eisner, Arthur
Lennig, Jay Leyda, Sergei Eisenstein, A. R. Fulton,
Robert Payne, Ernest Callenbach, Tom Milne, Paul Jen-
sen, Jacques Joly, Charles Higham, David Bordwell,
André Bazin, Gian-Lorenzo Darretta, Norman N. Holland,
Jorn Donner, Robin Wood, Donald M. Spoto, John S.
Bragin, Elliot Stein, Federico Fellini, and many others.

4616 Cocks, Jay and Denby, David (eds.) Film 73/74: An Anthology by the National Society of Film Critics. Indianapolis: Bobbs-Merrill, 1974. 369 pp.
Reviews of the films of 1973 by leading critics; also
documents the Society's annual awards.

4617 Hochman, Stanley (ed.) A Library of Film Criticism: American Film Directors. New York: Ungar, 1974. 590 pp.
Excerpts from reviews of the films of 60 directors; for
list of names, see entry 3786.

4618 Mast, Gerald and Cohen, Marshall (eds.) Film Theory and
Criticism: Introductory Readings. New York: Oxford
University Press, 1974. 639 pp.
Contributions by Siegfried Kracauer, André Bazin,
Rudolf Arnheim, William Earle, Parker Tyler, V. I.
Pudovkin, Sergei Eisenstein, Christian Metz, Charles

Barr, Erwin Panofsky, Bela Balazs, Robert Warshow, F.
E. Sparshott, Hugo Munsterberg, Susan Sontag, Geoffrey
Reeves, Frank Kermode, J. Blumenthal, Stanley Cavell,
Richard Meram Barsam, Gilbert Seldes, Joe Adamson,
Annette Michelson, Otis Ferguson, Andrew Sarris, Pauline
Kael, Peter Wollen, Richard Corliss, Richard Koszarski,
Roland Barthes, Kenneth Tynan, Gene Youngblood, Walter
Benjamin, and others. Sections titled "Film and Reality, "
"Film Image and Film Language, " "The Film Medium, "
"Film, Theater, and Literature, " "Kinds of Films, " "The
Film Artist, " and "The Film Audience. "

4619 Scaramazza, Paul A. (ed.) Ten Years in Paradise. Arling-
      ton, Va.: Pleasant Press, 1974. 289 pp.
      Film reviews published in Photoplay, 1921-1930.

4620 Brode, Douglas (ed.) Crossroads to the Cinema. Boston:
      Holbrook, 1975. 480 pp.
          Contributions by Marshall McLuhan, Pauline Kael,
      Parker Tyler, Dore Schary, Anthony Schillaci, Andrew
      Sarris, William Goldman, Richard Schickel, Andre Bazin,
      Ernest Lindgren, Harriet Parsons, Elmer Bernstein, Judy
      Tucker, Robert Steele, Hollis Alpert, Raymond Durgnat,
      Allegra Fuller Snyder, Rudolf Arnheim, Hans Richter,
      William K. Everson, John Baxter, Brian Murphy, John
      Russell Taylor and Arthur Jackson, Gerald Mast, James
      M. Wall, Larry L. King, Peter Bogdanovich, Robin Wood,
      Robert Vas, Marjorie Rosen, and others. Sections titled
      "The Movie Medium, " "The Makeup of the Movies, " "Film
      and the Arts, " "Film Genres, " and "Themes, Trends, and
      Transitions. "

4621 Sitney, P. Adams (ed.) The Essential Cinema: Essays on
      Films in the Collection of the Anthology Film Archives.
      New York: Anthology Film Archives and New York Uni-
      versity Press, 1975. 380 pp.
          Contributions by Seymour Stern, Standish D. Lawder,
      Annette Michelson, Ken Kelman, Donald Weinstein, and P.
      Adams Sitney. Topics include INTOLERANCE, Sergei
      Eisenstein, Dovzhenko's ARSENAL, Vertov's THE MAN
      WITH A MOVIE CAMERA, Luis Buñuel, Jean Vigo, Robert
      Bresson, Michael Snow, Markopoulos' SWAIN, Stan Brak-
      hage's ANTICIPATION OF THE NIGHT, and Bruce Conner's
      REPORT, among others.

4622 Nichols, Bill (ed.) Movies and Methods. Berkeley: Univer-
      sity of California Press, 1976. 640 pp.
          Contributions by O. Brik and V. Shklovsky, Jean-Luc
      Comolli and Jean Narboni, Susan Sontag, Fernando Solanas
      and Ottavio Getino, James Roy Macbean, Andrew Tudor,
      Richard Griffith, André Bazin, Richard Collins, Alan
      Lovell, Claire Johnston, Siew Hwa Beh, François Truffaut,

Andrew Sarris, V. F. Perkins, Raymond Durgnat, David
Bordwell, Robin Wood, Brian Henderson, Geoffrey Nowell-
Smith, Regina Cornwell, Sergei Eisenstein, Sam Rohdie,
Peter Wollen, Pier Paolo Pasolini, Christian Metz, Um-
berto Eco, and the editors of Cahiers du Cinéma. Includes material on political criticism, genre criticism,
auteur criticism, mise-en-scene criticism, film theory,
and structuralism-semiology.

E. ANALYSIS AND SURVEY OF
THEORY AND CRITICISM

This section contains those works which do not primarily put forward original theory as much as they survey and/or analyze existing theory and criticism. For works exclusively devoted to one particular critic or theorist, the reader should consult the name in Part VI, section A, individual biography, analysis, and interview.

4623 Davy, Charles (ed.) Footnotes to the Film. (Originally published 1938.) New York: Arno, 1970. 334 pp.
Includes a lengthy essay entitled "The Critic in Film History" by Alistair Cooke.

4624 British Film Institute. The Elements of Film Criticism. London: British Film Institute, 1944. 27 pp.

4625 Keller, Hans Heinrich. The Need for Competent Film Music Criticism: A Pamphlet for Those Who Care for Film as Art, with a Final Section for Those Who Do Not. London: British Film Institute, 1947. 22 pp.

4626 Lindgren, Ernest. The Art of the Film: An Introduction to Film Appreciation. London: Allen and Unwin, 1948. 242 pp. (Revised without subtitle New York: Macmillan, 1963, 258 pp.)
Includes a section on film criticism.

4627 Bobker, Lee R. Elements of Film. New York: Harcourt, Brace, 1969. 303. pp. (Revised New York: Harcourt Brace Jovanovich, 1974, 272 pp.)
Includes a section on film criticism which analyzes the work of James Agee, Penelope Gilliatt, John Russell Taylor, Dwight Macdonald, Renata Adler, Wilfrid Sheed, Stanley Kauffmann, Andrew Sarris, and Pauline Kael.

4628 Hunt, Todd. Reviewing for the Mass Media. Philadelphia: Chilton, 1972. 190 pp.

4629 Perkins, V. F. Film as Film: Understanding and Judging Movies. Baltimore: Penguin, 1972. 198 pp.

Includes a lengthy analysis of several film theorists: Rudolf Arnheim, Sergei Eisenstein, André Bazin, V. I. Pudovkin, and Siegfried Kracauer.

4630 Lounsbury, Myron Osborn. The Origins of American Film Criticism, 1909-1939. New York: Arno, 1973. 547 pp.
Includes study of the work of Alexander Bakshy, Welford Beaton, Kirk Bond, Barnet Braverman, James Dugan, Otis Ferguson, Robert Forsythe, Victor Freeburg, Paul Goodman, Lewis Jacobs, Lincoln Kirstein, Vachel Lindsay, Kenneth Macgowan, Meyer Levin, Hugo Munsterberg, Harry Alan Potamkin, Gilbert Seldes, Robert Stebbins, Seymour Stern, William Troy, and others.

4631 Tudor, Andrew. Theories of Film. New York: Viking, 1973. 168 pp.
Discusses and evaluates the theories of Eisenstein, John Grierson, André Bazin, and Siegfried Kracauer as well as the auteur and genre critical methods.

4632 Bywater, Timothy Robert. Critical Approaches to Film.
University of Utah: Ph.D., 1974. 219 pp.
Discusses journalistic, genre, behavioral, theoretical, historical-biographical, auteur, personal, and structural approaches to film.

4633 Murray, Edward. Nine American Film Critics: A Study of Theory and Practice. New York: Ungar, 1975. 248 pp.
Critics analyzed are James Agee, Robert Warshow, Andrew Sarris, Parker Tyler, John Simon, Pauline Kael, Stanley Kauffmann, Vernon Young, and Dwight Macdonald.

4634 Andrew, J. Dudley. The Major Film Theories: An Introduction. London, New York: Oxford University Press, 1976. 278 pp.
Analyzes theories of Hugo Munsterberg, Rudolf Arnheim, Sergei Eisenstein, Bela Balazs, Siegfried Kracauer, André Bazin, Jean Mitry, Christian Metz, and Amedee Ayfre and Henri Agel.

F. FILM AND THE OTHER ARTS

1. Film and Literature

In general the film and literature section contains two
kinds of books: those that deal with the similarities, differences,
and influences existing between the two forms, and those that deal
with the process of adaptation from literature to film. The reader
should note, however, that Part VII is composed of many books
that contain both the screenplay and the original literary source
from which it was adapted; unless a comparison between the two
forms is absolutely explicit, such books have not been listed again
here. The reader should also be aware that many of the critics in
Part VIII, section B often deal with adaptation questions in their
reviews of films adapted from other mediums. Some books in
Part II, section C-10, screenwriting, may also have material pertinent to adaptation.

4635 Asheim, Lester E. From Book to Film: A Comparative
      Analysis of the Content of Novels and the Motion Pictures
      Based Upon Them. University of Chicago Ph.D., 1950.
      188 pp.

4636 Runden, Charity E. Film and Poetry: Some Interrelation-
      ships. Indiana University: Ph.D., 1951. 134 pp.

4637 Bluestone, George. Novels Into Film. Baltimore: Johns
      Hopkins University Press, 1957. 237 pp. (Reprinted
      Berkeley: University of California Press, 1971.)
          Includes lengthy analyses of THE INFORMER,
      WUTHERING HEIGHTS, GRAPES OF WRATH, PRIDE
      AND PREJUDICE, THE OXBOW INCIDENT, and MADAME
      BOVARY.

4638 Van Nostrand, Albert D. The Denatured Novel. Indianapolis:
      Bobbs-Merrill, 1960. 224 pp.
          A study of the influence of cinema on the form of the
      novel.

4639 Gollub, Judith Podselver. Nouveau Roman et Nouveau
      Cinema/New Novel and New Cinema. University of Cali-
      fornia, Los Angeles: Ph.D., 1966. 174 pp.

4640 Baird, James Lee. The Movie in Our Heads: An Analysis
      of Three Film Versions of Theodore Dreiser's "An Ameri-
      can Tragedy." University of Washington: Ph.D., 1967.
      252 pp.
      Analyzes Eisenstein's scenario; AN AMERICAN TRAG-
      EDY (1931); and A PLACE IN THE SUN (1951).

4641 Capote, Truman; Perry, Eleanor; and Perry, Frank. Trilogy:
      An Experiment in Multi-Media. New York: Macmillan,
      1969. 276 pp.
      Includes original Capote stories, adaptation notes, and
      the screenplays for the three segments of TRILOGY.

4642 Richardson, Robert. Literature and Film. Bloomington:
      Indiana University Press, 1969. 149 pp.

4643 Cawelti, John. The Six Gun Mystique. Bowling Green, Ohio:
      Bowling Green University Popular Press, ca. 1970.
      138 pp.
      An interdisciplinary interpretation of popular artistic
      forms utilizing the western in literature and film as pri-
      mary example.

4644 Eidsvik, Charles Vernon. Cinema and Literature. University
      of Illinois, Urbana-Champaign: Ph.D., 1970. 119 pp.

4645 Laurence, Frank. The Film Adaptations of Hemingway:
      Hollywood and the Hemingway Myth. University of Penn-
      sylvania: Ph.D., 1970. 418 pp.

4646 Marcus, Fred H. (ed.) Film and Literature: Contrasts in
      Media. Scranton, Pa.: Chandler, 1971. 283 pp.
      Contributions by Bela Balazs, V. I. Pudovkin, Lee
      Bobker, Raymond Durgnat, Stanley Kauffmann, George
      Bluestone, Pauline Kael, Robert Richardson, Allardyce
      Nicoll, and others.

4647 Barrett, Gerald R. and Erskine, Thomas L. From Fiction
      to Film: Conrad Aiken's "Silent Snow, Secret Snow."
      Encino, Cal.: Dickenson, 1972. 193 pp.
      Lengthy essay on concept of adaptation, original story,
      shot analysis of the film, and critical essays on each
      medium.

4648 Kawin, Bruce F. Telling It Again and Again: Repetition in
      Literature and Film. Ithaca, N.Y.: Cornell University
      Press, 1972. 197 pp.

4649 MacDonald, George Buchanan. An Application of New Critical

Methodology to the Study of the Narrative Fictional Film.
Lehigh University: Ph.D., 1972. 244 pp.
Discusses the analytical methods of literary New Criticism in relation to specific films.

4650   Magny, Claude Edmonde. The Age of the American Novel:
The Film Aesthetic of Fiction Between the Two Wars.
New York: Ungar, 1972. 239 pp. Translated by Eleanor
Hochman.

4651   Murray, Edward. The Cinematic Imagination: Writers and
the Motion Picture. New York: Ungar, 1972. 330 pp.
Novelists discussed include Theodore Dreiser, James
Joyce, Virginia Woolf, William Faulkner, John Dos Passos,
F. Scott Fitzgerald, Nathanael West, Ernest Hemingway,
Graham Green, John Steinbeck, and Alain Robbe-Grillet.

4652   Savarese, Paul. Cinematic Techniques in the Novels of William Faulkner. St. Louis University: Ph.D., 1972.
162 pp.

4653   Vogel, Amos (comp.) Poetry and Film. New York: Gotham
Book Mart, 1972. 28 pp.

4654   Barrett, Gerald R. and Erskine, Thomas L. From Fiction
to Film: Ambrose Bierce's "An Occurrence at Owl Creek
Bridge." Encino, Cal.: Dickenson, 1973. 216 pp.
Lengthy essay on concept of adaptation, original story,
shot analysis of the films (THE BRIDGE and OCCURRENCE
AT OWL CREEK BRIDGE), and critical essays on each
medium.

4655   Pirie, David. A Heritage of Horror: The English Gothic
Cinema, 1946-1972. London: Gordon Fraser, 1973.
192 pp.
Traces the horror genre from the Gothic novel.

4656   Appel, Alfred, Jr. Nabokov's Dark Cinema. New York:
Oxford University Press, 1974. 324 pp.
Study of the influence of popular films on Nabokov's
writing.

4657   Barrett, Gerald R. and Erskin, Thomas L. From Fiction to
Film: D. H. Lawrence's "The Rocking Horse Winner."
Encino, Cal.: Dickenson, 1974. 238 pp.
Lengthy essays on concept of adaptation, original story,
shot analysis of the film, and critical essays on each
medium.

4658   Fell, John L. Film and the Narrative Tradition. Norman:
University of Oklahoma Press, 1974. 284 pp.

4659   McConnell, Frank D. The Spoken Seen: Film and the

Romantic Imagination. Baltimore: Johns Hopkins University Press, 1975. 195 pp.
Analyzes cinema's use of the Romantic literary tradition.

4660 Wagner, Geoffrey. The Novel and the Cinema. Rutherford,
N. J.: Fairleigh Dickinson University Press, 1975.
394 pp.

2. Film and Theatre

The books in this section deal with the relationship between film and theatre and the influences of each upon the other.
For additional material see the writings of critics and theorists
such as André Bazin, Bela Balazs, and Susan Sontag, whose collected works include material on film and theatre. For material
on films adapted from the plays of Shakespeare, see Part V, section C-9. See, also, many of the books on screenwriting in Part
II, section C-10 which often discuss the differences between screenwriting and playwriting.

4661 Carter, Huntly. The New Spirit in the Russian Theatre,
1917-1928; and a Sketch of the Russian Kinema and
Radio, 1919-1928, Showing the New Communal Relationship Between the Three. (Originally published 1929.)
New York: Blom, 1970. 348 pp. (Also published with
abridged title, The New Spirit in the Russian Theatre,
1917-1928, New York: Arno, 1970.)

4662 Nicoll, Allardyce. Film and Theatre. (Originally published
1936.) New York: Arno, 1972. 255 pp.

4663 Gorelik, Mordecai. New Theatres for Old. New York:
French, 1940. 553 pp. (Reprinted 1952 and 1962.)
Primarily history and analysis of various theatrical
movements and styles, with references to cinema.

4664 Vardac, Nicholas. Stage to Screen: Theatrical Method From
Garrick to Griffith. Cambridge, Mass.: Harvard Uni-
versity Press, 1949. 283 pp. (Reprinted New York:
Blom, 1968.)
Traces the influence of nineteenth-century theatre on
early film practices.

4665 Gaupp, Charles John. A Comparative Study of the Changes
in Fifteen Film Plays Adapted From Stage Plays. University of Iowa: Ph.D., 1950.

4666 Williams, Raymond and Orrom, Michael. Preface to Film.
London: Film Drama Ltd., 1954. 129 pp.

Comprised of "Film and the Dramatic Tradition" by Williams and "Film and Its Dramatic Techniques" by Orrom.

4667 Chenoweth, Stuart Curran. A Study of the Adaptation of Acting Technique From Stage to Film, Radio and Television in the United States, 1900-1951. Northwestern University: Ph.D., 1957. 393 pp.

4668 Costello, Donald P. The Serpent's Eye: Shaw and the Cinema. Notre Dame, Ind.: University of Notre Dame Press, 1965. 209 pp.

4669 Skoller, Donald S. Problems of Transformation in the Adaptation of Shakespeare's Tragedies From Play-Script to Cinema. New York University: Ph.D., 1968. 459 pp.

4670 Storrer, William Allin. A Comparison of Edward Albee's "Who's Afraid of Virginia Woolfe?" as Drama and as Film. Ohio University: Ph.D., 1968. 202 pp.

4671 Eisner, Lotte H. The Haunted Screen: Expressionism in the German Cinema and the Influence of Max Reinhardt. Berkeley: University of California Press, 1969. 360 pp. Translated by Roger Greaves.

4672 Nulf, Frank Allen, Jr. Luigi Pirandello and the Cinema: A Study of His Relationship to Motion Pictures and the Significance of that Relationship to Selected Examples of His Prose and Drama. Ohio University: Ph.D., 1969. 253 pp.

4673 Embler, Jeffrey Brown. A Historical Study of the Use of Film to Provide Additional Content to Theatrical Productions on the Legitimate Stage. University of Pittsburgh: Ph.D., 1971. 214 pp.

4674 Olf, Julian M. The Play as a Moving Picture: Toward a Phenomenology of Theatre. New York University: Ph.D., 1971. 292 pp.

4675 Murray, Edward. The Cinematic Imagination: Writers and the Motion Picture. New York: Ungar, 1972. 330 pp. Dramatists discussed include George Bernard Shaw, Luigi Pirandello, Eugene O'Neill, Bertolt Brecht, Tennessee Williams, Arthur Miller, Eugene Ionesco, and Samuel Beckett.

4676 Hurt, James (ed.) Focus on Film and Theatre. Englewood Cliffs, N.J.: Prentice-Hall, 1974. 188 pp. Contributions by Vachel Lindsay, Allardyce Nicoll, Eric Bentley, Richard Gilman, Stanley Kauffmann, Josef von Sternberg, Lillian and Helen Ross, Sergei Eisenstein,

Peter Handke, George Bernard Shaw, Harold Pinter, and Elia Kazan.

3. Film and the Visual Arts

This section includes works which deal with film's relationships to the visual arts. For the most part we have not included books which present general aesthetics for all visual media without specific mention of film. Thus, the reader will not find here any of the important works of aestheticians like Monroe Beardsley, Stephen C. Pepper, David W. Prall, DeWitt Parker, Clive Bell, Roger Bell, et al., even though the works of these men certainly have relevance to film. For listings of these works the reader should consult bibliographies of aesthetics or of painting.

4677 Kepes, Gyorgy. Language of Vision. Chicago: Paul Theobald, 1944. 228 pp. (Reprinted 1967.)
      Examination of the fundamentals of visual language, with relevance to the various media of visual expression.

4678 Arnheim, Rudolf. Art and Visual Perception: A Psychology of the Creative Eye. Berkeley: University of California Press, 1954. 408 pp. (Republished 1965, 485 pp.)

4679 Moholy-Nagy, Laszlo. Vision in Motion. Chicago: Paul Theobald, 1956. 371 pp.
      Includes a chapter on film.

4680 Baldinger, Wallace S. with Green, Harry B. The Visual Arts. New York: Holt, Rinehart and Winston, 1960. 308 pp.

4681 Kepes, Gyorgy (ed.) The Visual Arts Today. Middletown, Conn.: Wesleyan University Press, 1960. 272 pp.
      Includes essays on film by Boris Kaufman, Robert Gardner, Maya Deren, and George Amberg.

4682 Kepes, Gyorgy (ed.) The Nature and Art of Motion. New York: Braziller, 1965. 195 pp.
      Includes essays on film by Hans Richter and Robert Gessner.

4683 Feldman, Edmund Burke. Art as Image and Idea. Englewood Cliffs, N.J.: Prentice-Hall, 1967. 511 pp. (Revised as Varieties of Visual Experience: Art as Image and Idea, 1972, 680 pp. Abridged as Varieties of Visual Experience, 1973, 504 pp.)
      Includes a chapter on film.

4684 Noxon, Gerald. Pictorial Origins of Cinema Narrative: The

Birth and Development of the Scene in Pre-Historic and Ancient Art. Bridgewater, Mass.: Experiment Press, 1968. 56 pp.

4685 Arnheim, Rudolf. Visual Thinking. Berkeley: University of California Press, 1969. 345 pp.

4686 Eisner, Lotte H. The Haunted Screen: Expressionism in the German Cinema and the Influence of Max Reinhardt. Berkeley: University of California Press, 1969. 360 pp. Translated by Roger Greaves.

4687 Moholy-Nagy, Laszlo. Painting, Photography, Film. Cambridge, Mass.: M.I.T. Press, 1969. 150 pp. Translated by Janet Seligman.

4688 Matthews, J. H. Surrealism and Film. Ann Arbor: University of Michigan Press, 1971. 198 pp.

4689 Fell, John L. Film and the Narrative Tradition. Norman: University of Oklahoma Press, 1974. 284 pp.
Includes a lengthy section on film and the visual arts.

4690 Lawder, Standish D. The Cubist Cinema. New York: New York University Press, 1975. 265 pp.
Examines the interrelationships between the Cubist movement in painting and in film.

4. Film and Popular Culture/Mass Media

This category contains books which deal with film's relationships to popular culture or mass media. These books take a variety of approaches: some attack popular culture, some defend it, some take a historical approach, others a sociological or analytic one, etc. This part of the bibliography is not at all exhaustive; we have included, for instance, only those mass media books which explicitly deal with film, and have excluded those which define mass media primarily in terms of television, radio, and the press.
This category has been divided into two sections: a) those books which are individual studies; and b) those books which are anthologies. In general the anthologies tend to have a variety of essays, often on the various arts, the film articles frequently being general introductions to various aspects of film. In fact, many of the film articles in the mass media anthologies can also be found in the various books listed in Part VIII, section D, anthologies of theory and criticism. Although we have annotated only the articles specifically on film, both the anthologies and the individual studies also contain material on general popular culture/mass media concepts relevant to film as an aspect of contemporary culture.

a) Individual Studies

4691 Seldes, Gilbert. The 7 Lively Arts. (Originally published
      1924.) Revised New York: Sagamore, 1957. 306 pp.

4692 Austrian, Ralph B. Film and Television: The Perfect Com-
      bination. Hollywood: Affiliated Committee for Television,
      1945. 8 ℓ.
      Speech delivered by Ralph Austrian with counterviews
      by Sgt. Carl Beier.

4693 Seldes, Gilbert. The Great Audience. New York: Viking,
      1950. 299 pp.
      Analyzes radio, television, and film.

4694 Wagner, Geoffrey. Parade of Pleasure: A Study of Popular
      Iconography in the USA. New York: Library, 1955.
      192 pp.
      Includes a lengthy chapter which criticizes aspects of
      American movies.

4695 Barnouw, Eric. Mass Communication: Television, Radio,
      Film, Press; The Media and Their Practice in the United
      States of America. New York: Rinehart, 1956. 280 pp.

4696 Seldes, Gilbert. The Public Arts. New York: Simon and
      Schuster, 1956. 303 pp.
      Discusses radio, television, and film.

4697 Schramm, Wilbur. Responsibility in Mass Communications.
      New York: Harper, 1957. 391 pp.

4698 Seldes, Gilbert. You and the Mass Media [in Two Volumes].
      White Plains, N.Y.: Fund for Adult Education, 1957.
      (Republished as The New Mass Media: Challenge to a
      Free Society, Washington, D.C.: Public Affairs Press,
      1968, 100 pp.)

4699 Wright, Charles R. Mass Communications: A Sociological
      Perspective. New York: Random, 1959. 124 pp. (Re-
      vised 1975, 179 pp.)

4700 Emery, Edwin; Ault, Phillip H.; and Agee, Warren K. Intro-
      duction to Mass Communications. New York: Dodd, Mead,
      1960. (Revised 1970, 444 pp.)

4701 Jacobs, Norman (ed.) for the Tamiment Institute. Culture
      for the Millions? Mass Media in Modern Society.
      Princeton, N.J.: Van Nostrand, 1961. 200 pp.
      Based on papers presented at a Tamiment Institute
      seminar, June 1959.

4702 Warshow, Robert. The Immediate Experience: Movies,
      Comics, Theatre, and Other Aspects of Popular Culture.
      Garden City, N.Y.: Doubleday, 1962. 282 pp. (Re-
      printed New York: Atheneum, 1970.)

4703 Beaumont, Charles. Remember? Remember? New York:
      Macmillan, 1963. 248 pp.
        Informal history of popular culture, including material
      on film.

4704 International Edinburgh Film Festival, 1963. Film and Tele-
      vision: Basic Principles and Definitions; Report of a
      Conference. Edinburgh: Contrast, 1964. 47 pp.
        Cover title: "What is a television film?"

4705 McLuhan, Marshall. Understanding Media: The Extensions
      of Man. New York: McGraw-Hill, 1964. 364 pp.

4706 Hall, Stuart and Whannel, Paddy. The Popular Arts. New
      York: Pantheon, 1965. 480 pp.

4707 Ulanov, Barry. The Two Worlds of American Art: The
      Private and the Popular. New York: Macmillan, 1965.
      528 pp.

4708 Manvell, Roger. This Age of Communication: Press,
      Books, Films, Radio, TV. Glasgow: Blackie, 1966.
      166 pp.

4709 Mendelsohn, Harold A. Mass Entertainment. New Haven,
      Conn.: College and University Press, 1966. 203 pp.

4710 Peterson, Theodore; Jensen, Jay W.; and Rivers, William L.
      The Mass Media and Modern Society. New York: Holt,
      Rinehart and Winston, 1966. 259 pp.

4711 McLuhan, Marshall and Fiore, Quentin. The Medium is the
      Massage: An Inventory of Effects. New York: Bantam,
      1967. Unpaged.

4712 Casty, Alan. Mass Media and Mass Man. New York: Holt,
      Rinehart and Winston, 1968. 260 pp.

4713 Nye, Russel. The Unembarrassed Muse: The Popular Arts
      in America. New York: Dial, 1970. 497 pp.

4714 Slade, Mark. Language of Change. Toronto: Holt, Rine-
      hart and Winston, 1970. 186 pp.
        Proposes that the image in motion is the "new lan-
      guage" of our times.

4715 Steinberg, Charles S. The Communicative Arts: An

Introduction to Mass Media. New York: Hastings, 1970.
371 pp.

4716 Buscombe, Edward. Films on TV: A Report on the Trans-
mission of Cinematographic Films on Television and on
Television Programmes About the Cinema, in the United
Kingdom and Eire. London: Society for Education in Film
and Television, c. 1973, 64 pp.

4717 Clark, David G. and Blankenburg, William B. You and
Media: Mass Communication and Society. San Francisco:
Canfield, 1973. 275 pp.

4718 Valdes, Joan and Crow, Jeanne. The Media Works. Dayton,
Ohio: Pflaum, 1973. 282 pp.

4719 Hiebert, Ray Eldon; Ungurait, Donald F.; and Bohn, Thomas
W. Mass Media: An Introduction to Modern Communication. New York: David McKay, 1974. 495 pp.

4720 Gordon, George N. Communications and Media: Constructing
a Cross-Discipline. New York: Hastings, 1975. 209 pp.

4721 Whitney, Frederick C. Mass Media and Mass Communications
in Society. Dubuque, Iowa: William C. Brown, 1975.
474 pp.

b) Anthologies

4722 Laws, Frederick (ed.) Made for Millions: A Critical Study
of the New Media of Information and Entertainment. London: Contact, 1947. 116 pp.
Includes essays on film by G. W. Stonier and Adrian
Brunel.

4723 Schramm, Wilbur (ed.) Mass Communications: A Book of
Readings. Urbana: University of Illinois Press, 1949.
552 pp. (Revised 1960, 695 pp.)
Includes essays on film by Terry Ramsaye, Robert
A. Brady, and Martha Wolfenstein and Nathan Leites.

4724 Rosenberg, Bernard and White, David Manning (eds.) Mass
Culture: The Popular Arts in America. Glencoe, Ill.:
Free Press, 1957. 561 pp.
Includes essays on film by Siegfried Kracauer, Hor-
tense Powdermaker, E. Larrabee, David Riesman, and
others.

4725 Irving, John A. (ed.) Mass Media in Canada. Toronto:
Ryerson, 1962. 236 pp.

4726   Steinberg, Charles S. (ed.) Mass Media and Communication.
       New York: Hastings, 1966. 530 pp. (Revised 1972,
       686 pp.)
             Includes essays on film by Ruth Inglis and Hortense
       Powdermaker, plus an appendix reprinting the Motion Pic-
       ture Production Code.

4727   Deer, Irving and Harriet A. (eds.) The Popular Arts: A
       Critical Reader. New York: Scribner's, 1967. 356 pp.
             Includes essays on film by Robert Warshow, Gilbert
       Highet, Albert Hunt, Vernon Young, James Agee, and
       others.

4728   White, David Manning and Averson, Richard (eds.) Sight,
       Sound, and Society: Motion Pictures and Television in
       America. Boston: Beacon, 1968. 466 pp.
             Includes essays on film by Robert Steele, Norman N.
       Holland, William Fadiman, Robert Vas, David T. Bazelon,
       Paul Mayersberg, Philip French, Clifford Odets, Andrew
       Sarris, Michael Blankfort, and John M. Culkin.

4729   Agee, Warren K. Mass Media in a Free Society. Lawrence:
       The University Press of Kansas, 1969. 96 pp.
             Includes an essay on film by Bosley Crowther.

4730   Dorfles, Gillo (ed.) Kitsch: The World of Bad Taste. New
       York: Universe, 1969. 313 pp.
             Includes material on film by Lotte Eisner.

4731   Rissover, Fredric and Birch, David C. (eds.) Mass Media
       and the Popular Arts. New York: McGraw-Hill, 1971.
       348 pp.
             Brief articles on film by Larry Cohen, Edward Arthur,
       Pauline Kael, and Lawrence DeVine.

4732   Rosenberg, Bernard and White, David Manning (eds.) Mass
       Culture Revisited. New York: Van Nostrand Reinhold,
       1971. 473 pp.
             Includes essays on film by Robert Steele and Diana
       Trilling.

4733   Burke, John Gordon (ed.) Print, Image and Sound: Essays
       on Media. Chicago: American Library Association, 1972.
       181 pp.
             Includes an essay on film by Charles T. Samuels.

4734   Hammel, William M. (ed.) The Popular Arts in America:
       A Reader. New York: Harcourt Brace Jovanovich, 1972.
       436 pp.
             Essays on film by Leo Rosten, James Baldwin,
       Stanley Kauffmann, Roy Huss, Norman Silverstein, Ingo
       Preminger, Robert Warshow, James Agee, and Ingmar
       Bergman.

4735 Wells, Alan (ed.) Mass Media and Society. New York: May-
      field, 1972. 412 pp.
          Essays on film by Edwin Emery, Phillip H. Ault and
      Warren K. Agee, David G. Clark and William B. Blanken-
      burg, Lewis Lapham, and Gregg Kilday.

4736 Allen, Don (ed.) The Electric Anthology: Probes into Mass
      Media and Popular Culture. Dayton, Ohio: Pflaum,
      1975. 198 pp.
          Includes contributions by Marshall McLuhan, Tom
      Wolfe, Pauline Kael, and Richard Schickel.

4737 Valdes, Joan and Crow, Jeanne (eds.) The Media Reader.
      Dayton, Ohio: Pflaum, 1975. 390 pp.
          Essays on film by Pauline Kael, Ivor Montagu, Stanley
      Kauffmann, René Clair, Lillian Ross, and others.

4738 White, David Manning (advisory ed.) Popular Culture. New
      York: The New York Times and Arno, 1975. 415 pp.
          Compilation of articles from The New York Times on
      the various popular arts. Includes a lengthy section on
      the movies with material on film history, genres, box
      office and the stars. Contributors include John Ford,
      Louis Mayer, Mordaunt Hall, Thomas M. Pryor, Bosley
      Crowther, Vincent Canby, Mack Sennett, Paul Gardner,
      Harold Lloyd, Humphrey Bogart, and Alfred Hitchcock,
      among many others.

PART IX

FILM AND SOCIETY

INTRODUCTION

This classification, film and society, contains a variety of works, most of which have the relationship of film to societal structure and behavior as their primary concern. Some of these works deal with society at large, some with the entity of the audience, some with the Hollywood community. Other sections treat historical situations such as blacklisting and censorship which have particular sociological significance. The reader should note that many of the books in the history sections as well as in the film classification sections deal implicitly, if not explicitly, with sociological issues; these sections should not be overlooked as potential sources of information on film's relationship to society. Works dealing with various aspects of film violence can be found in several places: Part IX, section B, film in society: reflection and influence; Part IX, section C-2, films and children; Part V, section C-10, miscellaneous genres and recurrent themes and iconography; and Part IX, section D-1, censorship, obscenity, self-regulation, and pressure groups. Many other studies on the effects of visual violence deal with television rather than film; although relevant, works about television have not been included in this bibliography.

A. TYPES AND GROUPS

This section, types and groups, deals with the presentation of certain national, racial, or personality types in film. Additional material on national types can also be found in some of the books in Part IX, section B, reflection and influence. The books in the section on minorities, Part IX, section A-2, deal with the image of blacks and Indians. The reader should note that we have included in Part IX, section A-3, Men and Women, only those books with an explicit analysis of sexual roles or individual stereotypes. Thus, books such as James Robert Parish's The Glamour Girls have been classified only in Part VI, section B, collective biography, analysis, and interview. For additional material on sexuality, see Part V, section F, sexual films and sexual themes. For listings of films by or about women or catalogs showing these films' availability, see the reference sections, Part I, sections C-3 and C-4 and the education section, Part X, section B-3.

1. National Types

4739 Wilson, Norman. Presenting Scotland: A Film Survey.
        Edinburgh: Edinburgh Film Guild, 1945. 36 pp.
        Includes a survey of the presentation of Scotland in
        documentaries.

4740 Jones, Dorothy B. The Portrayal of China and India on the
        American Screen, 1896-1955: The Evolution of Chinese
        and Indian Themes, Locales, and Characters as Portrayed
        on the American Screen. Cambridge: Center for Inter-
        national Studies, Massachusetts Institute of Technology,
        1955. 129 pp.

4741 Madsen, Roy Paul. A Critical Interpretation of China in
        American Educational Films, 1936-1963: A Historical
        and Statistical Analysis. University of Southern Cali-
        fornia: Ph.D., 1966. 499 pp.

4742 Richards, Jeffrey. Visions of Yesterday. London: Routledge,
        1973. 391 pp.

Includes material on film typage in relation to American populism, British imperialism, and German Nazism.

4743   Maynard, Richard (ed.)   Africa on Film: Myth and Reality. Rochelle Park, N.J.: Hayden, 1974. 84 pp.

4744   Burton, Pierre. Hollywood's Canada: The Americanization of Our National Image. Toronto: McClelland and Stewart, 1975. 303 pp.

2. Minorities

4745   Noble, Peter. The Negro in Films. London: Skelton Robinson, ca. 1948. 288 pp. (Reprinted New York: Arno, 1970.)

4746   Jerome, V. J. The Negro in Hollywood Films. New York: Masses and Mainstream, 1950. 64 pp.

4747   Bloom, Samuel William. A Social Psychological Study of Motion Picture Audience Behavior: A Case Study of the Negro Image in Mass Communication. University of Wisconsin: Ph.D., 1956. 439 pp.

4748   Burke, William Lee. The Presentation of the American Negro in Hollywood Films 1946-1961: Analysis of a Selected Sample of Feature Films. Northwestern University: Ph.D., 1965. 379 pp.

4749   Hughes, Langston and Meltzer, Milton. Black Magic: A Pictorial History of the Negro in American Entertainment. Englewood Cliffs, N.J.: Prentice-Hall, 1967. 375 pp.

4750   Rollins, Charlemae. Famous Negro Entertainers of Stage, Screen & TV. New York: Dodd, Mead, 1967. 127 pp.
          For the young reader; for list of names, see entry 3692.

4751   Buchanan, Singer Alfred. A Study of the Attitudes of the Writers of the Negro Press Toward the Depiction of the Negro in Plays and Films, 1930-1965. University of Michigan: Ph.D., 1968. 319 pp.

4752   Pines, Jim. Blacks in the Cinema: The Changing Image. London: British Film Institute, 1971. 24 pp.

4753   Friar, Ralph E. and Natasha A. The Only Good Indian: The Hollywood Gospel. New York: Drama Book Specialists, 1972. 332 pp.

4754 Mapp, Edward. Blacks in American Films: Today and
      Yesterday. Metuchen, N.J.: Scarecrow, 1972. 278 pp.

4755 Worth, Sol and Adair, John. Through Navajo Eyes: An
      Exploration in Film Communication and Anthropology.
      Bloomington: Indiana University Press, 1972. 286 pp.

4756 Archer, Leonard C. Black Images in the American Theatre:
      NAACP Protest Campaigns--Stage, Screen, Radio & Tele-
      vision. Brooklyn, N.Y.: Pageant-Poseidon, 1973. 351 pp.

4757 Bogle, Donald. Toms, Coons, Mulattoes, Mammies, and
      Bucks: An Interpretive History of Blacks in American
      Films. New York: Viking, 1973. 260 pp.

4758 Landay, Eileen. Black Film Stars. New York: Drake,
      1973. 194 pp.
      For list of names, see entry 3767.

4759 Murray, James P. To Find an Image: Black Films From
      Uncle Tom to Super Fly. Indianapolis: Bobbs-Merrill,
      1973. 205 pp.

4760 Maynard, Richard (ed.) The Black Man on Film: Racial
      Stereotyping. Rochelle Park, N.J.: Hayden, 1974.
      134 pp.
      Also includes brief sections on the Indian and the Jew.

4761 Leab, Daniel J. From Sambo to Superspade: The Black Ex-
      perience in Motion Pictures. Boston: Houghton Mifflin,
      1975. 301 pp.

4762 Null, Gary. Black Hollywood: The Negro in Motion Pictures.
      Secaucus, N.J.: Citadel, 1975. 254 pp.

4763 Patterson, Lindsay (ed.) Black Films and Film-Makers: A
      Comprehensive Anthology From Stereotype to Superhero.
      New York: Dodd, Mead, 1975. 298 pp.
      Contributions by James Baldwin, Bosley Crowther,
      Lena Horne, Richard Schickel, Pauline Kael, and others.

4764 Pines, Jim. Blacks in Films: A Survey of Racial Themes
      and Images in the American Film. London: Studio Vista,
      1975. 143 pp.

                    3. Men and Women

4765 Flora, Paul. Viva Vamp! A Book of Photographs in Praise
      of Vamps From Mae West to Marilyn Monroe, From
      Marlene Dietrich to Brigitte Bardot. Commentary by

Paul Flora. Poetical salute by Ogden Nash. New York:
David McKay, 1959. Unpaged.

4766 Beauvoir, Simone de. Brigitte Bardot and the Lolita Syn-
      drome. New York: Reynal, 1960. 37 pp. Translated
      by Bernard Fretchman. (Reprinted New York: Arno,
      1972.)

4767 Everson, William K. The Bad Guys: A Pictorial History of
      the Movie Villain. New York: Citadel, 1964. 241 pp.

4768 Walker, Alexander. The Celluloid Sacrifice: Aspects of Sex
      in the Movies. New York: Hawthorn, 1967. 241 pp.
      ____ Includes analysis of female stars' images; for list of
      individuals discussed, see entry 3694.

4769 Bruno, Michael. Venus in Hollywood: The Continental En-
      chantress From Garbo to Loren. New York: Lyle Stuart,
      1970. 257 pp.

4770 Morella, Joe and Epstein, Edward Z. Rebels: The Rebel
      Hero in Films. New York: Citadel, 1971. 210 pp.

4771 Johnston, Claire (ed.) Notes on Women's Cinema. London:
      Society for Education in Film and Television, 1973.
      40 pp.
      ____ Includes material on women's images in film; see
      entry 4559.

4772 Mellen, Joan. Women and Their Sexuality in the New Film.
      New York: Horizon, 1973. 255 pp.
      ____ Includes chapters on the work of Ingmar Bergman,
      Eric Rohmer, and Mae West and on the films LAST
      TANGO IN PARIS, WR: MYSTERIES OF THE ORGANISM,
      TRISTANA, DEATH IN VENICE, THE FOX, and UP THE
      SANDBOX.

4773 Rosen, Marjorie. Popcorn Venus: Women, Movies & the
      American Dream. New York: Coward, McCann, Geog-
      hegan, 1973. 416 pp.

4774 Kobal, John. Gods and Goddesses of the Movies. New York:
      Crescent, 1973. 152 pp. (Also titled Romance and the
      Cinema.)

4775 Betancourt, Jeanne. Women in Focus. Dayton, Ohio:
      Pflaum, 1974. 186 pp.
      ____ Discusses films relating to feminine consciousness-
      raising.

4776 Haskell, Molly. From Reverence to Rape: The Treatment
      of Women in the Movies. New York: Holt, Rinehart and
      Winston, 1974. 388 pp.

4777 Manvell, Roger. Love Goddesses of the Movies. London:
      Hamlyn, 1975. 176 pp.

4778 Saxton, Martha. Jayne Mansfield and the American Fifties.
      Boston: Houghton Mifflin, 1975. 223 pp.

4779 Welsch, Janice Rita. An Analysis of the Film Images of
      Hollywood's Most Popular Post-World War II Female
      Stars. Northwestern University: Ph. D., 1975. 372 pp.

B. FILM IN SOCIETY:
REFLECTION AND INFLUENCE

This section, Film in Society: Reflection and Influence, is perhaps one of the most wide-ranging categories in this bibliography. The books in this section deal with some aspect of the complex and reciprocal relationships between film and society: film's responsibilities, its influence and use as propaganda, its sociological or anthropological meaning to its audience, analysis of its content in relationship to the society this content reveals, etc. For related material, the reader should refer to the genre sections in Part V, C-1 through C-10, since much genre criticism is implicitly or explicitly sociological in approach. Section C-10 in Part V, especially, contains much material surveying various recurrent themes to be found in the cinema. For psychological, mythological, and political approaches to film, see the theory and criticism section, Part VIII, section C.

4780   Young, Donald Ramsey. Motion Pictures: A Study in Social
         Legislation. (Originally published 1922.) New York:
         Ozer, 1971. 109 pp.
              Study of film in relation to social standards.

4781   King, Clyde L. and Tichenor, Frank A. (eds.) The Motion
         Picture in Its Economic and Social Aspects. (Originally
         published 1926, 195 pp.) Reprinted in The Motion Picture
         in Its Economic and Social Aspects [and] The Motion Pic-
         ture Industry. New York: Arno, 1970. 195, 236 pp.

4782   Seabury, William Marston. The Public and the Motion Pic-
         ture Industry. (Originally published 1926.) New York:
         Ozer, 1971. 340 pp.
              Proposes the conversion of the film industry into a
         public utility.

4783   National Conference on Motion Pictures, New York, 1929.
         The Community and the Motion Picture: Report. (Origi-
         nally published 1929 by the Motion Picture Producers and
         Distributors of America.) New York: Ozer, 1971. 96 pp.
              Report of conference, organized by Will Hays, at
         which various community leaders discuss the cinema.

511

4784   Peters, Charles C. Motion Pictures and Standards of
       Morality. (Originally published 1933.) New York: Arno,
       1970.   285 pp.
       One of the Payne Fund studies.

4785   Dale, Edgar. The Content of Motion Pictures. (Originally
       published 1935.) New York: Arno, 1970.   234 pp.
       One of the Payne Fund studies; analyzes various
       themes, types, locales, etc. in films.

4786   Perlman, William J. (ed.) The Movies on Trial: The Views
       and Opinions of Outstanding Personalities Anent Screen
       Entertainment Past and Present. (Originally published
       1936.) New York: Ozer, 1971.   254 pp.
       Essays on the moral responsibilities and social in-
       fluence of film; contributors include Edward G. Robinson,
       Seymour Stern, and Upton Sinclair, among others.

4787   Robson, E. W. and M. M. The Film Answers Back: An
       Historical Appreciation of the Cinema. (Originally pub-
       lished 1939.) London: Bodley Head, 1947.   336 pp.
       (Reprinted New York: Arno, 1972.)
       Cultural analysis of American and European films.

4788   Thorp, Margaret Farrand. America at the Movies. (Origi-
       nally published 1939, 313 pp.) London: Faber and
       Faber, 1946.   184 pp. (Reprinted New York: Arno,
       1970.   313 pp.)
       Discusses the American movie-going audience, both
       the effect of film on the audience and the influence of
       audience taste on film content.

4789   Stewart, Donald Ogden (ed.) Fighting Words. New York:
       Harcourt, Brace, 1940.   168 pp.
       Transcripts of speeches made at the 1939 Congress
       of the League of American Writers which primarily dealt
       with writers' problems in the cultural milieu; includes a
       section on the "Hollywood Brigade."

4790   Johnston, Winifred. Visual "Education"?   The Serious Stu-
       dent's Guide to Social Misinformation. (The Movies and
       Public Opinion, No. 2). Norman: Cooperative Books,
       1941.   55 pp.
       Discusses film propaganda.

4791   Kracauer, Siegfried. Propaganda and the Nazi War Film.
       New York: Museum of Modern Art Film Library, 1942.
       90 pp. (Reprinted as a supplement in From Caligari
       to Hitler: A Psychological History of the German Film--
       See entry 4802.)

4792   U.S. Senate Committee on Interstate Commerce. Propaganda
       in Motion Pictures: Hearings Before a Subcommittee of

the Committee on Interstate Commerce, United States
Senate, Seventy-Seventh Congress, First Session, on S.
Res., 152, A Resolution Authorizing an Investigation of
War Propaganda Disseminated by the Motion-Picture
Industry and of any Monopoly in the Production, Distribu-
tion, or Exhibition of Motion Pictures. Washington, D.C.:
Government Printing Office, 1942. 449 pp.

4793   Waples, Douglas (ed.) Print, Radio, and Film in a Democracy: Ten Papers on the Administration of Mass Communications in the Public Interest. Chicago: University
of Chicago Press, 1942. 197 pp.
Includes "The Film and Public Opinion" by Donald
Slesinger.

4794   British Film Institute. The Film in National Life: Being the
Proceedings of a Conference Held by the British Film
Institute in Exeter, April, 1943. London: British Film
Institute, 1943. 39 pp.
Includes material on children and the cinema, the
psychology of cinema-going, and other topics.

4795   Harmon, Francis S. The Command Is Forward: Selections
From Addresses on the Motion Picture Industry in War
and Peace. New York: Richard R. Smith, 1944. 56 pp.

4796   Manvell, Roger. Film. Harmondsworth: Penguin, 1944.
191 pp. (Revised 1946, 240 pp. Revised again 1950,
287 pp.)
Includes a lengthy section entitled "The Influence of
Film on Present-Day Society."

4797   U.S. Office of Strategic Services, Research and Analysis
Branch. Japanese Films: A Phase of Psychological War-
fare; An Analysis of the Themes, Psychological Content,
Technical Quality, and Propaganda Value of Twenty Recent
Japanese Films. Washington, D.C.: U.S. Office of
Strategic Services, 1944. 19 pp.

4798   Writers' Congress, University of California at Los Angeles.
Writers' Congress: The Proceedings of the Conference
Held in October 1943 Under the Sponsorship of the Holly-
wood Writers' Mobilization and the University of California.
Berkeley: University of California Press, 1944. 663 pp.
Material on the role of writers from various media,
including film, in aiding the war effort; includes sections
on documentary, animation, and the feature film. Contri-
butions by Darryl F. Zanuck, William Dozier, Edward
Dmytryk, Philip K. Scheuer, Talbot Jennings, Robert
Rossen, Arthur L. Mayer, Joris Ivens, Thomas Baird,
James Wong Howe, John Hubley, Karl Van Leuven, Adolph
Deutsch, Gail Kubick, Dudley Nichols, Dalton Trumbo,

John Howard Lawson, Howard Estabrook, Harry Kurnitz,
Ben Maddow, Kenneth Macgowan, and others.

4799   Farrell, James T.   The League of Frightened Philistines
       and Other Papers.   New York: Vanguard, 1945.   210 pp.
       Includes chapters on the relationship between Holly-
       wood's film content and the public.

4800   Gutsche, Thelma.   The History and Social Significance of
       Motion Pictures in South Africa, 1895-1940.   (Originally
       University of Cape Town: Dissertation, 1946.)   Cape
       Town: Timmins, 1972.   404 pp.

4801   Mayer, J. P.   Sociology of Film: Studies and Documents.
       London: Faber and Faber, 1946.   328 pp.   (Reprinted
       with new introduction by Mayer, New York: Arno, 1972.)
       Includes extensive audience questionnaires and inter-
       views, plus analysis of film's impact on general and child
       audiences.

4802   Kracauer, Siegfried.   From Caligari to Hitler: A Psycho-
       logical History of the German Film.   Princeton, N.J.:
       Princeton University Press, 1947.   361 pp.   (Reprinted
       1969.)

4803   Robson, E. W. and M. M.   The World Is My Cinema.
       London: Sidneyan Society, 1947.   207 pp.
       Cultural analysis of films and film trends in many
       countries.

4804   Watkins, Gordon S. (ed.)   The Motion Picture Industry.
       Philadelphia: American Academy of Political and Social
       Sciences, 1947.   236 pp.   (Reprinted in The Motion
       Picture in Its Economic and Social Aspects [and] The
       Motion Picture Industry, New York: Arno, 1970, 195,
       236 pp.)
       Includes material on censorship, self-regulation, the
       public, and effects of film; contributions by Terry Ram-
       saye, William Fadiman, Martha Wolfenstein and Nathan
       Leites, Martin Quigley, Hortense Powdermaker, Leo
       Rosten, Paul Lazarsfeld, Robert W. Chambers, and
       others.

4805   Mayer, J. P.   British Cinemas and Their Audiences: So-
       ciological Studies.   London: Dobson, 1948.   280 pp.
       Includes extensive material from audience question-
       naires.

4806   Berelson, Bernard and Janowitz, Morris (eds.)   Reader in
       Public Opinion and Communication.   Glencoe, Ill.:   The
       Free Press, 1950.   505 pp.   (Revised 1953, 611 pp.
       Revised again New York: The Free Press, 1966, 788 pp.)

Comprehensive survey of communications research; includes essays on film by Lester Asheim and W. W. Charters.

4807   Handel, Leo A. Hollywood Looks at Its Audience: A Report of Film Audience Research. Urbana: University of Illinois Press, 1950. 240 pp.

4808   Seldes, Gilbert. The Great Audience. New York: Viking, 1950. 299 pp.
Includes analysis of film as a medium of mass entertainment and its effect on the public.

4809   Wolfenstein, Martha and Leites, Nathan. Movies: A Psychological Study. Glencoe, Ill.: The Free Press, 1950. 316 pp. (Reprinted New York: Hafner, 1971.)

4810   Lawson, John Howard. Film in the Battle of Ideas. New York: Masses and Mainstream, 1953. 126 pp.
Discusses the ideological function of film, analyzes the patterns in Hollywood films, and advocates the development of a "people's film art."

4811   Cunningham, Robert P. A Sociological Approach to Esthetics: An Analysis of Attitudes Toward the Motion Picture. University of Iowa: Ph.D., 1954. 180 pp.

4812   Krutch, Joseph Wood, and others. Is the Common Man Too Common? An Informal Survey of Our Cultural Resources and What We are Doing About Them. Norman: University of Oklahoma Press, 1954. 146 pp.
Includes "Hollywood verdict: gilt but not guilty" by Arthur Mayer.

4813   Honigmann, John and van Doorslaer, Marguerite. Some Themes From Indian Film Reviews. Chapel Hill: Institute for Research in Social Science, University of North Carolina, 1955. 28 ℓ.

4814   Manvell, Roger. The Film and the Public. Harmondsworth: Penguin, 1955. 352 pp.
Includes a lengthy section entitled "The Cinema and Society."

4815   Riesman, David. The Oral Tradition, The Written Word, and The Screen Image. Yellow Springs, Ohio: Antioch Press, 1956. 40 pp.
Discusses the impact of modes of communication on culture and society.

4816   Seldes, Gilbert. The Public Arts. New York: Simon and Schuster, 1956. 303 pp.

Discusses television, radio, and film and their effect on the public.

4817 Wickham, Glynne and Gladstone, William. The Relation Between Universities and Films, Radio and Television. London: Butterworths, published for the University of Bristol, 1956. 55 pp.

4818 Opinion Research Corporation. The Public Appraises Movies: Highlights of a Survey Conducted in June and July 1957 for Motion Picture Association of America. Princeton, N.J.: Opinion Research Corporation, 1957. 23 pp.

4819 Hughes, Robert (ed.) Film: Book 1--The Audience and the Filmmaker. New York: Grove, 1959. 184 pp.
       Emphasizes problems encountered by the "serious" filmmaker. Includes material on Robert Flaherty, George Stoney, and Federico Fellini; commentary on the filmmaker and the audience by various directors; and articles on unproduced scripts by James Agee and Cesare Zavattini.

4820 Hughes, Robert (ed.) Film: Book 2--Films of Peace and War. New York: Grove, 1962. 255 pp.
       Examines the relationship between film and society's survival. Articles by John Huston, Norman McLaren, Alain Resnais, Donald Richie, Colin Young, Thorold Dickinson, and others. Symposium participants include Noel Burch, Andre Cayette, Samuel Fuller, Sergei Gerasimov, Len Lye, Roger Manvell, Louis Marcorelles, Marshall McLuhan, Tony Richardson, Jean Renoir, Paul Rotha, Dore Schary, George Stoney, François Truffaut, and Robert Wise, among others.

4821 MacCann, Richard Dyer (ed.) Film and Society. New York: Scribner's, 1964. 182 pp.
       With contributions by Irving Thalberg, Ernie Pyle, James Agee, Leo Rosten, Upton Sinclair, Mortimer Adler, Bosley Crowther, Joe Hyams, Norman Cousins, and G. B. Shaw.

4822 McLuhan, Marshall. Understanding Media: The Extensions of Man. New York: McGraw-Hill, 1964. 364 pp.

4823 Huaco, George A. The Sociology of Film Art. New York: Basic Books, 1965. 229 pp.
       Applies a sociological model to German expressionism, Soviet expressive realism, and Italian neo-realism.

4824 Whitaker, Rodney. The Content Analysis of Film: A Survey of the Field, An Exhaustive Study of Quai Des Brumes, and A Functional Description of the Elements of the Film Language. Northwestern University: Ph.D., 1966. 490 pp.

4825 McLuhan, Marshall and Fiore, Quentin. The Medium is the
      Massage: An Inventory of Effects. New York: Bantam,
      1967. Unpaged.

4826 Thomson, David. Movie Man. New York: Stein and Day,
      1967. 234 pp.
      Examines the all-pervasiveness of film in modern
      culture and society.

4827 Larsen, Otto N. (ed.) Violence and the Mass Media. New
      York: Harper and Row, 1968. 310 pp.
      Discusses the effects and regulation of media violence;
      articles on film include "Violence in the Cinema" by
      Philip French and "The Morality Seekers: A Study of
      Organized Film Criticism in the United States" by Jack
      Schwartz.

4828 Quinn, James. The Film and Television as an Aspect of
      European Culture. Leyden, Netherlands: A. W. Sijthoff,
      1968. 168 pp.
      Surveys the relationship of film and television to
      various sectors such as government, the church, and the
      public.

4829 White, David Manning and Averson, Richard (eds.) Sight,
      Sound, and Society: Motion Pictures and Television in
      America. Boston: Beacon, 1968. 466 pp.
      Essays which examine the relationship between film
      and television and American social institutions; for list of
      contributors, see entry 4728.

4830 Deming, Barbara. Running Away From Myself: A Dream
      Portrait of America Drawn From Films of the Forties.
      New York: Grossman, 1969. 210 pp.

4831 Wollen, Peter (ed.) Working Papers on the Cinema: So-
      ciology and Semiology. London: British Film Institute,
      ca. 1969. 36 pp.
      For list of contributors, see entry 4591.

4832 Jarvie, I. C. Movies and Society. New York: Basic Books,
      1970. 394 pp. (Also published as Towards a Sociology
      of the Cinema: A Comparative Essay on the Structure
      and Functioning of a Major Entertainment Industry.)

4833 Lowe, Clayton Kent. Image Making and Integrity: An His-
      torical Survey and Analysis of the Priorities and Value
      Systems of Image Makers and Image Viewers in American
      Society. Ohio State University: Ph.D., 1970. 367 pp.
      Utilizes 25 case histories to explore value system
      conflicts; includes material on theatrical and documentary
      films.

4834   Merritt, Russell Lamonte.   The Impact of D. W. Griffith's
       Motion Pictures From 1908 to 1914 on Contemporary
       American Culture.   Harvard University: Ph.D., 1970.

4835   Bergman, Andrew.   We're in the Money: Depression America
       and Its Films.   New York: New York University Press,
       1971.   200 pp.

4836   Durgnat, Raymond.   A Mirror for England: British Movies
       From Austerity to Affluence.   New York: Praeger, 1971.
       336 pp.

4837   Furhammar, Leif and Folke, Isaksson.   Politics and Film.
       New York: Praeger, 1971.   257 pp.   Translated by
       Kersti French.

4838   McClure, Arthur F. (ed.)   The Movies: An American Idiom;
       Readings in the Social History of the American Motion
       Picture.   Rutherford, N.J.:   Fairleigh Dickinson Uni-
       versity Press, 1971.   435 pp.
            Contributions by Terry Ramsaye, Louise Tanner,
       Lewis Jacobs, Siegfried Kracauer, John Howard
       Lawson, Richard Schickel, John C. Holmes, and
       others.

4839   Paine, Jeffrey Morton.   The Simplification of American Life:
       Hollywood Films of the 1930's.   Princeton University:
       Ph.D., 1971.   311 pp.

4840   Savary, Louis M. and Carrico, J. Paul (eds.)   Contemporary
       Film and the New Generation.   New York: Association
       Press, 1971.   159 pp.
            Articles which discuss the conflicts of young people
       and their culture as expressed in popular film.

4841   Jowett, Garth Samuel.   Media Power and Social Control:
       The Motion Picture in America, 1894-1936.   University
       of Pennsylvania: Ph.D., 1972.   499 pp.

4842   White, David Manning and Averson, Richard.   The Celluloid
       Weapon: Social Comment in the American Film.   Boston:
       Beacon, 1972.   271 pp.

4843   Worth, Sol and Adair, John.   Through Navajo Eyes: An
       Exploration in Film Communication and Anthropology.
       Bloomington: Indiana University Press, 1972.   286 pp.
            Account of an experiment in ethnographic filmmaking.

4844   Dowdy, Andrew.   Movies are Better Than Ever: Wide-
       Screen Memories of the Fifties.   New York: Morrow,
       1973.   242 pp.   (Reprinted as The Films of the Fifties:
       The American State of Mind, 1975.)

4845 Richards, Jeffrey. Visions of Yesterday. London: Routledge
      and Kegan Paul, 1973. 391 pp.
      Analyzes films in relation to American populism,
      British imperialism, and German Nazism; includes sec-
      tions on John Ford, Frank Capra, Leo McCarey, and
      Leni Riefenstahl.

4846 Rimberg, John David. The Motion Picture in the Soviet
      Union, 1918-1952: A Sociological Analysis. New York:
      Arno, 1973. 238 pp.

4847 Field, Audrey. The Picture Palace: A Social History of
      the Cinema. London: Gentry, 1974. 160 pp.
      Primarily deals with British cinema.

4848 Stoil, Michael Jon. Cinema Beyond the Danube: The Camera
      and Politics. Metuchen, N.J.: Scarecrow, 1974. 198 pp.
      Emphasizes the social significance of films in the
      U.S.S.R. and Eastern Europe.

4849 Strebel, Elizabeth Grottle. French Social Cinema of the
      Nineteen-Thirties: A Cinematographic Expression of
      Popular Front Consciousness. Princeton University:
      Ph.D., 1974. 299 pp.

4850 Tudor, Andrew. Image and Influence: Studies in the Sociology
      of Film. London: Allen and Unwin, 1974. 260 pp.
      Analyzes the structure and pattern of film/audience
      communication, as well as examining film language, popu-
      lar genres, and film movements (particularly German ex-
      pressionism).

4851 Burns, E. Bradford. Latin American Cinema: Film and
      History. Los Angeles: UCLA Latin American Center,
      1975. 137 pp.

4852 Hockings, Paul (ed.) Principles of Visual Anthropology. The
      Hague: Mouton, distributed by Aldine, Chicago, 1975.
      521 pp.
      Discusses various aspects of the ethnographic film;
      for list of contributors, see entry 1782.

4853 Maynard, Richard A. (ed.) Propaganda on Film: A Nation
      at War. Rochelle Park, N.J.: Hayden, 1975. 147 pp.
      Explores the relationship between commercial films
      and political propaganda.

4854 Sklar, Robert. Movie-Made America: A Social History of
      American Movies. New York: Random, 1975. 340 pp.
      (Also titled Movie-Made America: a Cultural History of
      American Movies.)

4855 Smith, Julian. Looking Away: Hollywood and Vietnam. New
York: Scribner's, 1975. 236 pp.
Analyzes the psychological influence of Vietnam on
American films.

4856 Wood, Michael. America in the Movies: Or "Santa Maria,
It Had Slipped My Mind." New York: Basic Books, 1975.
206 pp.
Discusses the images and myths of America as reflected in Hollywood films, primarily of the forties and
fifties.

C. AUDIENCE AND EFFECTS RESEARCH

1. General Studies and Experiments

This section, general studies and experiments, includes those books which try to study the effects of film on general audiences, as well as books dealing with the various issues involved in an individual's perceptual response to film. For books dealing with propaganda, see Part IX, section B, reflection and influence.

4857   Gibson, James J. (ed.) Motion Picture Testing and Research. Washington, D.C.: U.S. Government Printing Office, 1947. 267 pp.
Army Air Forces Aviation Psychology Program Research Reports.

4858   Hovland, Carl I; Lumsdaine, Arthur A; and Sheffield, Fred D. Experiments on Mass Communication. Princeton, N.J.: Princeton University Press, 1949. 345 pp. (Reprinted New York: John Wiley, 1965.)
Part of the "Studies in Social Psychology in World War II" series; deals with the ideological effects of the "Why We Fight" series on men in service.

4859   Fearing, Franklin. Motion Pictures as a Medium of Instruction and Communication: An Experimental Analysis of the Effects of Two Films. Berkeley: University of California Press, 1950. 100 pp.
A study of the effects of two educational films produced by the Air Force.

4860   Hoban, Charles F. and Van Ormer, Edward B. Instructional Film Research 1918-1950: Rapid Mass Learning. Port Washington, N.Y.: Special Devices Center, 1950. Various pagings. (Reprinted New York: Arno, 1970.)
Surveys film effects and audience response studies in America from 1918-1950, including a section on the Payne Fund studies.

4861 Rose, Nicholas. A Psychological Study of Motion Picture
      Audience Behavior. University of California, Los Angeles:
      Ph.D., 1951.

4862 Wilner, Daniel M. Attitude as a Determinant of Perception
      in the Mass Media of Communication: Reactions to the
      Motion Picture "Home of the Brave." University of Cali-
      fornia, Los Angeles: Ph.D., 1951.

4863 Spiegelman, J. Marvin. Ambiguity and Personality in the
      Perception of a Motion Picture. University of California,
      Los Angeles: Ph.D., 1952.

4864 Mercer, John. Optical Effects and Film Literacy. Univer-
      sity of Nebraska: Ph.D., 1953. 323 pp.

4865 Arnheim, Rudolf. Art and Visual Perception: A Psychology
      of the Creative Eye. Berkeley: University of California
      Press, 1954. 408 pp. (Republished 1965, 485 pp.)

4866 Millard, William John, Jr. A Study in the Sociology of
      Communications: Determinants and Consequences of Ex-
      posure to American Motion Picture Films in the Near
      and Middle East. Columbia University: Ph.D., 1955.
      224 pp.

4867 Bloom, Samuel William. A Social Psychological Study of
      Motion Picture Audience Behavior: A Case Study of the
      Negro Image in Mass Communication. University of
      Wisconsin: Ph.D., 1956. 439 pp.

4868 Goldberg, Albert. The Effects of Two Types of Sound Motion
      Pictures on Attitudes of Adults Towards Minority Groups.
      Indiana University: Ed.D., 1956. 142 pp.

4869 Fritz, John Otto. Film Persuasion in Education and Social
      Controversies: A Theoretical Analysis of the Components
      Manifest in Viewer-Film Involvement as They Affect the
      Viewer's Urge to Further Inquiry into Social Controversies.
      Indiana University: Ed.D., 1957. 426 pp.

4870 Evans, Ralph M. Eye, Film, and Camera in Color Photog-
      raphy. New York: John Wiley, 1959. 410 pp.
      Relates the psychology of vision and theories of human
      perception to photography and photographic aesthetics, par-
      ticularly in terms of color factors.

4871 Thayer, David Lewis. A Study of the Influence of Conven-
      tional Film Lighting on Audience Response. University
      of Iowa: Ph.D., 1960. 163 pp.

4872 Gregory, John Robert. Some Psychological Aspects of Motion

Picture Montage. University of Illinois, Urbana-Champaign, 1961. 138 pp.

4873   Furhammar, Leif. Motion Pictures--Attitude Influence--Advance Preparation. Uppsala: Institute of Education, Uppsala University, 1965. 24 ℓ.

4874   Post, Gene Leroy. A Study of the Effect of a Subliminal Stimulus Upon Attitudes Developed Toward a Character Portrayed in a Motion Picture Film. Oklahoma State University: Ed.D., 1965. 102 pp.

4875   Gregory, R. L. Eye and Brain: The Psychology of Seeing. New York: McGraw-Hill, 1966. 255 pp.

4876   Chittock, John. Film and Effect. London: Financial Times, 1967. 28 pp.
          Cover subtitle: A Pilot Experiment to Assess the Effectiveness of Sponsored Documentary Films in Changing Public Attitudes.

4877   Miller, William C., III. An Experimental Study of the Relationship of Film Movement and Emotional Involvement Response, and Its Effect on Learning and Attitude Formation. University of Southern California: Ph.D., 1967. 245 pp.

4878   Penn, Roger. An Experimental Study of the Meaning of Cutting-Rate Variables in Motion Pictures. University of Iowa: Ph.D., 1967. 138 pp.

4879   Ritze, Frederick Henry. Responses of Pakistani College Students to a Selected American Film. Columbia University: Ed.D., 1967. 166 pp.

4880   Moakley, Francis Xavier. The Effects on Learning From a Motion Picture Film of Selective Changes in Sound Track Loudness Levels. Indiana University: Ed.D., 1968. 132 pp.

4881   Reynolds, James Conrad. The Effect of Viewer Distance on Film Induced Anxiety. Indiana University: Ph.D., 1968. 80 pp.

4882   Utz, Walter Julius, Jr. The Comparative Effect of Color and Black and White Film Clips Upon Related Perception of Reality. University of Illinois, Urbana-Champaign, Ph.D., 1968. 101 pp.

4883   Gerrero, Richard Henry. Music as a Film Variable. Michigan State University: Ph.D., 1969. 110 pp.

4884   Gregory, R. L. The Intelligent Eye. New York: McGraw-

Hill, 1970. 191 pp.
Discusses cultural traditions in terms of concepts of perception.

4885 Hoover, William. Replicating Photographic Lighting Effects to Elicit Certain Conditioned Responses in Motion Picture Audiences. Wayne State University: Ed. D., 1970. 154 pp.

4886 Wight, Warland Davis. The Relevance of Selected Theories for Developing Systematic Research of Film Communications. University of Washington: Ph. D., 1970. 221 pp.

4887 Rosene, James Melvin. The Effects of Violent and Sexually Arousing Film Content: An Experimental Study. Ohio University: Ph. D., 1971. 129 pp.

4888 Troth, Marilyn Mumma. The Relative Effectiveness of the Motion Picture and the Single Still Picture Presenting Modes in Facilitating the Perception of Dynamic Action Concepts. East Texas University: Ph. D., 1971. 184 pp.

4889 Lynch, Francis Dennis. Clozentropy: A Technique for Studying Audience Response to Films. University of Iowa: Ph. D., 1972. 136 pp.
Deals with audience prediction patterns, film complexity, and audience sophistication.

4890 Ruhly, Sharon Kay. The Communication of Cultures Through Film. Ohio State University: Ph. D., 1972. 474 pp.
Comparison of four ethnological films, revealing differences in perception between members within and members outside the culture.

4891 Bacal, Jeffrey. The Effect of Image Iconicity on Film Interpretation. University of Iowa: Ph. D., 1973. 267 pp.

4892 Connolly, Patrick Joseph. Content Analysis of the Persuasive Principles of the Documentary Film "Which Way America?" University of Southern California: Ph. D., 1973. 350 pp.

4893 Weber, Alan Melchior. The Responses of College Students to Film. University of Illinois, Urbana-Champaign: Ph. D., 1973. 172 pp.
Results of an experiment in classifying verbal responses to film.

4894 Ryan, Steve Staszak. Recognition of Film Techniques Related to Selected Characteristics of Film Sophistication: A Pilot Study. Ohio State University: Ph. D., 1974. 199 pp.

4895 Tudor, Andrew. Image and Influence: Studies in the

Sociology of the Film.   London: Allen and Unwin, 1974.
260 pp.
Includes analysis of the structure and pattern of film/
audience communication.

2.   Film and Children

This section contains those books dealing specifically with
the effects of film on children or, occasionally, the film tastes of
children, including the many Payne Fund studies.   For material on
entertainment films for children, see the children's genre category,
Part V,   section E.

4896   Mitchell, Alice Miller.   Children and Movies.   (Originally
published 1929.)   New York: Ozer, 1971.   181 pp.

4897   Blumer, Herbert.   Movies and Conduct.   (Originally published
1933.)   New York: Arno, 1970.   257 pp.
A Payne Fund study, primarily composed of essays
by adolescents and young people describing how movies
affect their lives.

4898   Blumer, Herbert and Hauser, Philip M.   Movies, Delinquency,
and Crime.   (Originally published 1933.)   New York: Arno,
1970.   233 pp.
A Payne Fund Study.

4899   Charters, W. W.   Motion Pictures and Youth: A Summary.
(Originally published 1933.)   New York: Arno, 1970.   66 pp.
An overview and summary of the various Payne Fund
studies.

4900   Dysinger, Wendell S. and Ruckmick, Christian A.   The Emo-
tional Responses of Children to the Motion Picture Situa-
tion.   (Originally published 1933.)   Reprinted with Edgar
Dale's Children's Attendance at Motion Pictures, New York:
Arno, 1970.   122, 81 pp.
A Payne Fund study.

4901   Forman, Henry James.   Our Movie Made Children.   (Originally published 1933.)   New York: Arno, 1970.   288 pp.
A Payne Fund study.

4902   Holaday, Perry W. and Stoddard, George D.   Getting Ideas
from the Movies.   (Originally published 1933.)   New
York: Arno, 1970.   102 pp.
A Payne Fund study.

4903   Peterson, Ruth C. and Thurstone, L. L.   Motion Pictures
and Social Attitudes of Children.   (Originally published

1933.) Reprinted with Frank K. Shuttleworth and Mark A.
May's The Social Conduct and Attitudes of Movie Fans.
New York: Arno, 1970. 75, 142 pp.
A Payne Fund study.

4904 Renshaw, Samuel; Miller, Vernon L.; and Marquis, Dorothy
P. Children's Sleep. (Originally published 1933.) New
York: Arno, 1970. 242 pp.
A Payne Fund study.

4905 Shuttleworth, Frank K. and May, Mark A. The Social Con-
duct and Attitudes of Movie Fans. (Originally published
1933.) Reprinted with Ruth C. Peterson and L. L.
Thurstone's Motion Pictures and the Social Attitudes of
Children. New York: Arno, 1970. 142, 75 pp.
A Payne Fund study.

4906 Dale, Edgar. Children's Attendance at Motion Pictures.
(Originally published 1935.) Reprinted with Wendell S.
Dysinger and Christian A. Ruckmick's The Emotional
Responses of Children to the Motion Picture Situation.
New York: Arno, 1970. 81, 122 pp.
A Payne Fund study.

4907 Ford, Richard. Children in the Cinema. (Originally published
in London 1939.) New York: Ozer, 1971. 232 pp.

4908 British Film Institute. Children and the Cinema: A Report
of a Conference Organized by the British Film Institute
and the National Council of Women. London: British Film
Institute, 1946. 31 pp.

4909 Mayer, J. P. Sociology of Film: Studies in Documents.
London: Faber and Faber, 1946. 328 pp. (Reprinted
with new introduction by Mayer, New York: Arno, 1971.)
Includes material on the effects of film on children
and adults.

4910 Scott, Walter J. Reading, Film and Radio Tastes of High
School Boys and Girls. London: Oxford University Press,
for the New Zealand Council for Educational Research,
1947. 207 pp.

4911 Sterner, Alice P. Radio, Motion Picture, and Reading
Interests: A Study of High School Pupils. New York:
Bureau of Publications, Teachers College, Columbia
University, 1947. 102 pp.

4912 Frank, Josette. Comics, Radio, Movies--and Children.
New York: Public Affairs Committee, 1949. 32 pp.

4913 Henne, Frances; Brooks, Alice; and Ersted, Ruth (eds.)

Youth, Communication and Libraries.   Chicago: American
Library Association, 1949.   233 pp.
   Includes essay entitled "Motion Pictures, Radio Pro-
   grams, and Youth" by Paul F. Lazarsfeld.

4914   Report of the Departmental Committee on Children and the
   Cinema.   Chairman, K.C. Wheare.   London: His
   Majesty's Stationery Office, 1950.   108 pp.

4915   Bauchard, Philippe.   The Child Audience: A Report on Press,
   Film and Radio for Children.   Paris: UNESCO, 1952.
   198 pp.

4916   Field, Mary.   Children and Films: A Study of Boys and
   Girls in the Cinema: A Report to the Carnegie United
   Kingdom Trustees on an Enquiry Into Children's Responses
   to Films.   Dunfermline, Fife: Carnegie United Kingdom
   Trust, 1954.   56 pp.

4917   U.S. Senate, Committee on the Judiciary.   Motion Pictures
   and Juvenile Delinquency: Report of the Committee on the
   Judiciary Containing an Interim Report of the Subcommittee
   to Investigate Juvenile Delinquency, Pursuant to S. Res.
   173 (84th Congress, 2nd Session) Relative to the Investigation of Juvenile Delinquency in the United States.   Washington, D.C.:   Government Printing Office, 1956.   122 pp.

4918   Denny, Earl Walter.   A Study of the Effectiveness of Selected
   Motion Pictures for Reducing Frustration in Children.
   University of Washington: Ed.D., 1958.   111 pp.

4919   Bailyn, Lotte.   Mass Media and Children: A Study of Exposure Habits and Cognitive Effects.   Washington, D.C.:
   American Psychological Association, 1959.   48 pp.

4920   Hills, Janet.   Are They Safe at the Cinema?   London: British
   Film Institute, 1960.   24 pp.
   "A considered answer to critics of the cinema."

4921   Barclay, J. B.   Viewing Tastes of Adolescents in Cinema
   and Television.   Glasgow: Scottish Educational Film Association and Scottish Film Council, 1961.   73 pp.

4922   Levinson, Elias.   Effects of Motion Pictures on the Response
   to Narrative: A Study of the Effects of Film Versions of
   Certain Short Stories on the Responses of Junior High
   School Students.   New York University: Ph.D., 1963.
   225 pp.

4923   Redclay, Lillian Bilkey.   Adolescent Reactions to a Film Regarding Pre-Marital Sex Experiences.   Pennsylvania State
   University: Ed.D., 1964.   275 pp.

4924 Sennton, Olena. Exposure to Films and School Adjustment:
        Studies in Cinema Attendance and Film Violence Prefer-
        ence as Related to Emotional Adjustment and School
        Achievement. Stockholm: Almquist and Wiksell, 1965.
        287 pp.

4925 Hirsch, Kenneth William. Children's Discrimination Between
        and Reaction to Actuality and Make-Believe in Violent
        Television/Film Messages. University of Oregon: Ph. D.,
        1967. 176 pp.

4926 European Committee on Crime Problems. The Cinema and
        the Protection of Youth. Strasbourg, France: Council
        of Europe, 1968. 167 pp.

4927 Chittister, Joan. The Perception of Prose and Filmic Fiction.
        Pennsylvania State University: Ph. D., 1971. 187 pp.
        An experiment comparing perception of literature and
        film, using high school students as subjects.

4928 Glucksmann, Andre. Violence on the Screen: A Report on
        Research into the Effects on Young People of Scenes of
        Violence in Films and Television. London: British Film
        Institute, 1971. 78 pp. Translated by Susan Bennett.

4929 Moore, Douglas. A Study in the Influence of the Film "The
        Birth of a Nation" on the Attitudes of Selected High School
        White Students Toward Negroes. University of Illinois,
        Urbana-Champaign: Ph. D., 1971. 140 pp.

4930 Rheinish, Robert. A Study of the Development of Children's
        Perceptions of Selected Filmic Conventions. Indiana Uni-
        versity: Ph. D., 1971. 292 pp.

D. SOCIAL AND POLITICAL RESTRAINTS

1. Censorship, Obscenity, Self-Regulation, and Pressure Groups

4931 Griffith, D. W. The Rise and Fall of Free Speech in America. (Originally published 1916.) Hollywood: Larry Edmunds Book Shop, 1967. 59 pp.
Includes material on the controversy surrounding THE BIRTH OF A NATION.

4932 Oberholtzer, Ellis Paxson. The Morals of the Movie. (Originally published 1922.) New York: Ozer, 1971. 251 pp.
Written by a member of the Pennsylvania State Board of Censors, who discusses various types of films and censorship.

4933 Young, Donald Ramsey. Motion Pictures: A Study in Social Legislation. (Originally published 1922.) New York: Ozer, 1971. 109 pp.
Discusses moral standards in motion pictures and advocates state censorship.

4934 Ernst, Morris L. and Lorentz, Pare. Censored: The Private Life of the Movies. (Originally published 1930.) New York: Ozer, 1971. 199 pp.
Anecdotal survey of censorship in various regions of America.

4935 Beman, Lamar T. (comp.) Selected Articles on Censorship of the Theatre and Moving Pictures. (Originally published 1931.) New York: Ozer, 1971. 385 pp.
Material on film censorship arranged in the form of a pro and con debate.

4936 Nizer, Louis. New Courts of Industry: Self-Regulation Under the Motion Picture Production Code; Including an Analysis of the Code. (Originally published 1935.) New York: Ozer, 1971. 344 pp.

4937 Martin, Olga J. Hollywood's Movie Commandments: A Handbook for Motion Picture Writers and Reviewers. (Originally published 1937.) New York: Arno, 1970. 301 pp. Explains the Production Code.

4938 Ernst, Morris L. and Lindey, Alexander. The Censor Marches On: Recent Milestones in the Administration of the Obscenity Law in the United States. New York: Doubleday, Doran, 1940. 346 pp.

4939 Harley, John Eugene. World-Wide Influence of the Cinema: A Study of Official Censorship and the International Cultural Aspects of Motion Pictures. Los Angeles: University of Southern California, 1940. 320 pp. (Reprinted New York: Ozer, 1971.)

4940 Elliot, Paul with Quintanilla, Luis. With a Hays Nonny Nonny. New York: Random, 1942. 188 pp. Includes the Production Code and a satirical look at its implications.

4941 Facey, Paul W. The Legion of Decency: A Sociological Analysis of the Emergence and Development of a Social Pressure Group. Fordham University: Ph.D., 1945. (Reprinted New York: Arno, 1974, 206 pp.)

4942 Inglis, Ruth Ardel. The Hays Office Control of Motion Picture Content. Bryn Mawr College: Ph.D., 1945. 201 pp.

4943 Moley, Raymond. The Hays Office. Indianapolis: Bobbs-Merrill, 1945. 266 pp. (Reprinted New York: Ozer, 1971, 266 pp.)

4944 Commission on Freedom of the Press. A Free and Responsible Press: A General Report on Mass Communication: Newspapers, Radio, Motion Pictures, Magazines, and Books. Chicago: University of Chicago Press, 1947. 138 pp.

4945 Inglis, Ruth A. Freedom of the Movies. Chicago: University of Chicago Press, 1947. 242 pp. A report on self-regulation from the Commission on Freedom of the Press.

4946 Salemson, Harold J. (ed.) Thought Control in U.S.A.: Complete Proceedings of the Conference on Thought Control, Hollywood ASP-PCA. Hollywood: Hollywood A.S.P. Council, P.C.A., 1947. 432 pp. Transcripts of the conference speeches and panels; participants include John Cromwell, John Howard Lawson, Norman Corwin, Albert Maltz, Philip Stevenson, Irving Pichel, Howard Da Silva, Carey McWilliams, Adrian Scott,

Richard Collins, Paul Draper, Frank Tuttle, Lee J. Cobb,
Anne Revere, Morris Carnovsky, Larry Parks, Shepperd
Strudwick, and others.

4947 Turner, Max W. State Regulation of the Motion Picture In-
      dustry. University of Iowa: Ph.D., 1947. 293 pp.

4948 Litsky, Leo. Censorship of Motion Pictures in the United
      States: A History of Motion Picture Censorship and an
      Analysis of Its Most Important Aspects. New York Uni-
      versity: Ph.D., 1948.

4949 Terrou, Fernand and Solal, Lucien. Legislation for Press,
      Film and Radio: Comparative Study of the Main Types of
      Regulations Governing the Information Media. Paris:
      UNESCO, 1951. 420 pp.

4950 Kerr, Walter. Criticism and Censorship. Milwaukee: Bruce,
      1954. 86 pp.

4951 Motion Picture Association of America. A Code to Govern
      the Making of Motion Pictures; The Reasons Supporting It
      and The Resolution for Uniform Interpretation. Washing-
      ton, D.C.: Motion Picture Association of America, 1955.
      16 pp.

4952 Paul, Elliot. Film Flam. London: Muller, 1956. 160 pp.
      Includes discussion of censorship as well as sundry
      other film topics.

4953 Wirt, Frederick Marshall. State Film Censorship with Par-
      ticular Reference to Ohio. Ohio State University: Ph.D.,
      1956. 492 pp.

4954 Haney, Robert W. Comstockery in America: Patterns of
      Censorship and Control. Boston: Beacon, 1960. 199 pp.

4955 Crowther, Bosley. Movies and Censorship. New York:
      Public Affairs Committee, 1962. 28 pp.

4956 Roeburt, John. The Wicked and the Banned. New York:
      Macfadden, 1963. 159 pp.
      Includes lengthy chapter on motion picture censorship.

4957 Sargent, John A. Self-Regulation: The Motion Picture Pro-
      duction Code, 1930-1961. University of Michigan: Ph.D.,
      1963. 277 pp.

4958 Carmen, Ira Harris. State and Local Motion Picture Censor-
      ship and Constitutional Liberties with Special Emphasis
      on the Communal Acceptance of Supreme Court Decision-
      Making. University of Michigan: Ph.D., 1964. 458 pp.

4959   Ernst, Morris L. and Schwartz, Allan U. Censorship: The
       Search for the Obscene. New York: Macmillan, 1964.
       288 pp.
       Including material on film cases, particularly from
       the DON JUAN court decision.

4960   Milner, Michael. Sex on Celluloid. New York: Macfadden,
       1964. 224 pp.

4961   Schumach, Murray. The Face on the Cutting Room Floor:
       The Story of Movie and Television Censorship. New
       York: Morrow, 1964. 305 pp.

4962   Carmen, Ira H. Movies, Censorship and the Law. Ann
       Arbor: University of Michigan Press, 1966. 339 pp.

4963   McCraw, William. Political Sponsorship of the Arts: Sub-
       sidization and Censorship of Motion Pictures and the Per-
       forming Arts by the Italian National Government, 1943-
       1962. Stanford University: Ph.D., 1966. 398 pp.

4964   Hunnings, Neville March. Film Censors and the Law. Lon-
       don: Allen and Unwin, 1967. 474 pp.

4965   European Committee on Crime Problems. The Cinema and
       the Protection of Youth. Strasbourg, France: Council of
       Europe, 1968. 167 pp.
       Includes discussion of European censorship.

4966   Lloyd, Peter. Not for Publication. London: Bow, 1968.
       80 pp.
       Includes material on movie censorship in Great
       Britain.

4967   Phelan, John. The National Catholic Office for Motion Pic-
       tures: An Investigation of the Policy and Practice of Film
       Classification. New York University: Ph.D., 1968.
       364 pp.

4968   Randall, Richard S. Censorship of the Movies: The Social
       and Political Control of a Mass Medium. Madison: Uni-
       versity of Wisconsin Press, 1968. 280 pp.

4969   Sjöman, Vilgot. I Am Curious (Yellow). New York: Grove,
       1968. 254 pp. Translated by Martin Minow and Jenny
       Gohman.
       Includes extensive excerpts from the transcript of the
       film's obscenity trial.

4970   De Grazia, Edward. Censorship Landmarks. New York:
       Bowker, 1969. 657 pp.
       Includes many film-related cases.

4971   Friedman, Leon (ed.) Obscenity: The Complete Oral Argu-
       ments Before the Supreme Court in the Major Obscenity
       Cases. New York: Chelsea, 1970. 342 pp.
            Contains film censorship cases, including those over
       LADY CHATTERLY'S LOVER and THE LOVERS.

4972   The Obscenity Report: The Report to the Task Force on
       Pornography and Obscenity. New York: distributed by
       Stein and Day, 1970. 130 pp.

4973   Vizzard, Jack. See No Evil: Life Inside a Hollywood Censor.
       New York: Simon and Schuster, 1970. 381 pp.

4974   Censorship: For and Against. Introduction by Harold H.
       Hart. New York: Hart Publishing, 1971. 255 pp.
            Contributors include Hollis Alpert and Judith Crist.

4975   Devol, Kenneth S. (ed.) Mass Media and the Supreme Court:
       The Legacy of the Warren Years. New York: Hastings,
       1971. 369 pp.
            Includes material on film censorship.

4976   Farber, Stephen. The Movie Rating Game. Washington,
       D.C.: Public Affairs Press, 1972. 128 pp.
            Deals with the Motion Picture Association of America
       Code and Rating Administration.

4977   Linden, Kathryn Bertha. The Film Censorship Struggle in
       the United States From 1926 to 1957, and the Social
       Values Involved. New York University: Ph.D., 1972.
       513 pp.

4978   McClelland, Doug. The Unkindest Cuts: The Scissors and
       the Cinema. South Brunswick, N.J.: A. S. Barnes,
       1972. 220 pp.

4979   Trevelyan, John. What the Censor Saw. London: Joseph,
       1973. 276 pp.
            Primarily on film censorship in Great Britain.

4980   Cline, Victor B. (ed.) Where Do You Draw the Line? An
       Exploration Into Media Violence, Pornography, and Censor-
       ship. Provo, Utah: Brigham Young University Press,
       1974. 365 pp.

4981   Leach, Michael. I Know It When I See It: Pornography,
       Violence, and Public Sensitivity. Philadelphia: West-
       minster, 1975. 153 pp.

4982   Phelps, Guy. Film Censorship. London: Gollancz, 1975.
       319 pp.
            Primarily on British censorship.

4983 Phillips, Baxter. Cut: The Unseen Cinema. New York:
      Crown, 1975.

      2. Hollywood Politics and Blacklisting

4984 Antonious (pseudonym). The Hollywood "Trial." London:
      Notable, 1948. 32 pp.

4985 Fagan, Myron C. Moscow Over Hollywood. Los Angeles:
      Cary, 1948. 107 pp.

4986 Kahn, Gordon. Hollywood on Trial: The Story of the Ten
      Who Were Indicted. New York: Boni and Gaer, 1948.
      229 pp. (Reprinted New York: Arno, 1972.)
          With material on Alvah Bessie, Herbert Biberman,
      Lester Cole, Edward Dmytryk, Ring Lardner, Jr., John
      Howard Lawson, Albert Maltz, Samuel Ornitz, Adrian
      Scott, and Dalton Trumbo.

4987 Fagan, Myron C. Red Treason in Hollywood. Hollywood
      Cinema Educational Guild, 1949. 121 pp.

4988 Fagan, Myron C. Documentation of the Red Stars in Holly-
      wood. Hollywood: Cinema Educational Guild, 1950.
      110 pp.

4989 Trumbo, Dalton. The Time of the Toad: A Study of Inquisi-
      tion in America by One of the Hollywood Ten. Hollywood:
      n.p., ca. 1950. 38 pp. (Reprinted and revised as The
      Time of the Toad: A Study of Inquisition in America, and
      Two Related Pamphlets, New York: Harper and Row,
      1972, 161 pp.)
          1972 version includes The Devil in the Book (originally
      published 1956) and Honor Bright and All That Jazz.

4990 Kempton, M. Part of Our Time: Some Ruins and Monuments
      of the Thirties. New York: Simon and Schuster, 1955.
      334 pp.
          Includes material on John Howard Lawson, Paul Robe-
      son, and the Communist movement in Hollywood.

4991 Cogley, John. Report on Blacklisting: Volume I, Movies.
      New York: Fund for the Republic, 1956. 312 pp. (Re-
      printed New York: Arno, 1972.)

4992 Trumbo, Dalton. The Devil in the Book. Los Angeles:
      California Emergency Defense Committee, 1956. 42 pp.
      (Reprinted in The Time of the Toad: A Study of Inquisi-
      tion in America, and Two Related Pamphlets, New York:
      Harper and Row, 1972, 161 pp.)

4993   U.S. House Committee on Un-American Activities. Investigation of So-Called "Blacklisting" in Entertainment Industry;
Report of the Fund for the Republic, Inc. Hearings Before
the Committee on Un-American Activities, House of Representatives, Eighty-Fourth Congress, Second Session.
Washington, D.C.: U.S. Government Printing Office, 1956.
Three volumes.

4994   Bessie, Alvah. Inquisition in Eden. New York: Macmillan,
1965. 278 pp.
   Deals with the House Committee on Un-American Activities (HUAC) investigation of Hollywood.

4995   Biberman, Herbert. Salt of the Earth: The Story of a Film.
Boston: Beacon, 1965. 373 pp.
   Production account, complete screenplay, and account
of the corresponding legal and political controversies.

4996   Goodman, Walter. The Committee. New York: Farrar,
Straus and Giroux, 1968. 564 pp.
   An account of the House Committee on Un-American
Activities.

4997   Bentley, Eric (ed.) Thirty Years of Treason: Excerpts
from Hearings Before the House Committee on Un-American Activities 1938-1968. New York: Viking, 1971.
991 pp.
   Includes testimony of over 50 witnesses.

4998   Bentley, Eric (ed.) Are You Now or Have You Ever Been?
The Investigation of Show Business by the Un-American
Activities Committee 1947-1958. New York: Harper and
Row, 1972. 160 pp.
   Transcripts of the testimony of Sterling Hayden, Larry
Parks, Lionel Stander, Elia Kazan, Edward Dmytryk, Sam
G. Wood, Ring Lardner, Jr., Jose Ferrer, Abe Burrows,
Tony Kraber, Jerome Robbins, Elliott Sullivan, Martin
Berkeley, Lillian Hellman, Marc Lawrence, Zero Mostel,
Arthur Miller, and Paul Robeson.

4999   Vaughn, Robert. Only Victims: A Study of Show Business
Blacklisting. New York: Putnam, 1972. 355 pp.

5000   Kanfer, Stefan. A Journal of the Plague Years. New York:
Atheneum, 1973. 306 pp.
   Material on blacklisting and the Hollywood Ten.

E. RELIGIOUS AND MORAL APPROACHES

This section contains those books which adopt a religious or moral approach to film. Most of these books attack the "immorality" of cinema, although some take a more enlightened approach, proclaiming film's potential as a reflector of social mores and moral values. Often the authors of the works in this section not only examine film and its relationship to society as this relationship exists, but also argue or propose what that relationship should be in the future.

5001 Cinema Commission of Inquiry. The Cinema: Its Present Position and Future Possibilities: Being the Report of and Chief Evidence Taken by the Cinema Commission of Inquiry Instituted by the National Council of Public Morals. (Originally published London, 1917.) New York: Arno, 1970, 471 pp.

5002 Quigley, Martin. Decency in Motion Pictures. New York: Macmillan, 1937. 100 pp. (Reprinted New York: Ozer, 1971.)
    Written by one of the drafters of the Production Code of 1930.

5003 Sumrall, Lester F. Worshippers of the Silver Screen. Grand Rapids, Mich.: Zondervan, 1940. 64 pp.
    A religious/moral attack on Hollywood.

5004 Harding, Ulla Earl. Movie Mad America: An Utterly Frank and Revealing Expose of the American Movie. Grand Rapids, Mich.: Zondervan, 1942. 55 pp.

5005 Miles, Herbert J. Movies and Morals. Grand Rapids, Mich.: Zondervan, 1947. 121 pp.

5006 Upson, Wilfrid. Movies and Monasteries in U.S.A. Gloucester: Prinknash Abbey, 1950. 91 pp.

5007 National Legion of Decency. Motion Pictures Classified. New York: National Legion of Decency, 1951. 184 pp.
    Catholic moral classifications of films from 1936 to 1950.

5008 Paine, Stephen William. The Christian and the Movies.
      Grand Rapids, Mich.: Eerdmans, 1957. 79 pp.

5009 Pius XII, Pope. Miranda Prorsus: Encyclical Letter of His
      Holiness Pius XII ... Concerning the Cinema, Sound
      Broadcasting and Television. London: Catholic Trust
      Society, 1957. 44 pp.

5010 Boyd, Malcolm. Christ and Celebrity Gods: The Church in
      Mass Culture. Greenwich, Conn.: Seabury, 1958.
      145 pp.

5011 Gardiner, Harold C. Catholic Viewpoint on Censorship.
      Garden City, N.Y.: Hanover, 1958. 192 pp.

5012 Lynch, William F. The Image Industries. New York:
      Sheed and Ward, 1959. 159 pp.
      Offers a Catholic oriented aesthetic of film.

5013 Getlein, Frank and Gardiner, Harold C. Movies, Morals
      and Art. New York: Sheed and Ward, 1961. 179 pp.
      Catholic viewpoint on morality and aesthetic judge-
      ments.

5014 Gardiner, Harold C. and Walsh, Moira. Tenets for Movie
      Viewers. New York: America Press, 1962. 56 pp.
      From a Catholic viewpoint.

5015 Koenigil, Mark. Movies in Society: Sex, Crime and
      Censorship. New York: Speller, 1962. 214 pp.

5016 Worden, James William. The Portrayal of the Protestant
      Minister in American Motion Pictures, 1951-1960, and
      Its Implications for the Church Today. Boston University:
      Ph.D., 1962. 400 pp.

5017 Fitzgerald, John E. Film Classification: The Bishop Speaks
      Again. Notre Dame, Ind.: Our Sunday Visitor Press,
      1966. 23 pp.

5018 Daughters of St. Paul (ed.) Mass Means of Communication.
      Boston: St. Paul Editions, 1967. 202 pp.
      Includes statements and addresses on the motion
      picture by Pope Paul VI, Pius XI ("Vigilanti Cura"),
      and Pope Pius XII ("Miranda Prorsus").

5019 Klausler, Alfred P. Censorship, Obscenity and Sex. St.
      Louis: Concordia, 1967. 104 pp.
      A Christian perspective; includes material on film.

5020 Haselden, Kyle. Morality and the Mass Media. Nashville,
      Tenn: Broadman, 1968. 192 pp.

A Christian approach to moral issues in various
media, including film.

5021 Phelan, John. The National Catholic Office for Motion Pic-
      tures: An Investigation of the Policy and Practice of
      Film Classification. New York University: Ph. D. , 1968.
      364 pp.

5022 Schillaci, Anthony. Movies and Morals. Notre Dame, Ind.:
      Fides Press, 1968. 181 pp.
      A defense of film as a source of emotional maturity
      and moral sensitivity.

5023 Kuhns, William. The Electronic Gospel: Religion and Media.
      New York: Herder and Herder, 1969. 173 pp.

5024 Cooper, John C. and Skrade, Carl (eds.) Celluloid and
      Symbols. Philadelphia: Fortress, 1970. 143 pp.
      Theological approach to contemporary films, including
      essays on Ingmar Bergman, Roman Polanski, and Fede-
      rico Fellini.

5025 Hurley, Neil P. Theology Through Film. New York: Harper
      and Row, 1970. 212 pp. (Reprinted as Toward a Film
      Humanism, New York: Dell, 1975.)

5026 Reile, Father Louis. Films in Focus. St. Meinrad, Ind.:
      Abbey Press, 1970. 107 pp.
      An introduction to various aspects of film from a
      Catholic viewpoint.

5027 Kahle, Roger and Lee, Robert E. A. Popcorn and Parable:
      A New Look at the Movies. Minneapolis: Augsburg,
      1971. 128 pp.

5028 Wall, James M. Church and Cinema: A Way of Viewing
      Film. Grand Rapids, Mich.: Eerdmans, 1971. 135 pp.

5029 Williams, Larry. A Comparative Study of the Views of Man
      in Christian Thought and in Contemporary Film Art.
      Southwest Baptist Theological Seminary: Ph. D. , 1971.

5030 Arnold, James W. "Seen Any Good Dirty Movies Lately?"
      A Christian Critic Looks at Contemporary Films. Cin-
      cinnati, Ohio: St. Anthony Messenger Press, 1972. 118 pp.

5031 Konzelman, Robert G. Marquee Ministry: The Movie Theatre
      as Church and Community Forum. New York: Harper and
      Row, 1972. 123 pp.

5032 Drew, Donald J. Images of Man: A Critique of the Contem-
      porary Cinema. Downers Grove, Ill.: InterVarsity Press,
      1974. 121 pp.

F. THE HOLLYWOOD COMMUNITY

This classification, the Hollywood community, is a problematic one. In one sense, books on Hollywood could be considered a sub-section of United States film history. Since most of these books, however, do not discuss particular films, film movements, or inventions, but instead elucidate various aspects of the complex Hollywood social community, we have classified them under film and society. We have divided this section into four sub-sections: 1, historical and pictorial perspectives; 2, sociological studies of Hollywood and its image; 3, the star phenomenon; and 4, anecdotal views of Hollywood and Hollywood personalities. Since the distinctions among these sub-sections cannot be sharply defined and many of the books defy perfect classification, the reader is advised to consult all these sub-sections for relevant material.

1. Historical and Pictorial Perspectives

This section includes formal and informal histories of Hollywood, histories of particular aspects of Hollywood, picture books which are implicitly historical, as well as those works which attempt to communicate the Hollywood lifestyle. For additional material, the reader might also consult many of the books dealing with California and Southern California, which often have material on Hollywood, but which in general have not been included here. For related material, see the studio histories in Part IV, section D-2.

5033 Editors of Look. Movie Lot to Beachhead: The Motion Picture Goes to War and Prepares for the Future. Garden City, N.Y.: Doubleday, Doran, 1945. 291 pp.
    Includes material on the Hollywood community's participation in the war effort, with a particular section on Jimmy Stewart.

5034 McWilliams, Carey. Southern California Country: An Island on the Land. New York: Duell, Sloan, and Pearce, 1945. 387 pp.

Includes a chapter entitled "The Island of Hollywood."

5035 Hollywood Reporter. Facts About Hollywood, U.S.A.: Information for the Nation. Hollywood: Hollywood Reporter,
1947. 28 pp.

5036 Hancock, Ralph. Fabulous Boulevard. New York: Funk and
Wagnalls, 1949. 322 pp.
History of Wilshire Boulevard in Los Angeles and
Hollywood.

5037 Harris, Weejee and Mel. Naked Hollywood. New York:
Pellegrini and Cudahy, 1953. 120 pp. (Reprinted New
York: DaCapo, 1975.)
Photographs of Hollywood inhabitants and locales.

5038 Clymer, Floyd. Cars of the Stars and Movie Memories.
Los Angeles: Clymer, 1954. 152 pp.
Primarily photographs of early stars and their auto-
mobiles.

5039 Orr, Edwin J. The Inside Story of the Hollywood Christian
Group. Grand Rapids, Mich.: Zondervan, 1955.
134 pp.

5040 Halliday, Ruth S. Stars on the Crosswalks: An Intimate
Guide to Hollywood, Including Restaurants, Motels, Traf-
fic Regulations, Vegetation, Important Addresses, Tourist
Information and Nearby Points of Interest. Sherman Oaks,
Cal.: Mitock, 1958. 100 pp.

5041 Day, Beth. This Was Hollywood: An Affectionate History of
Filmland's Golden Years. Garden City, N.Y.: Doubleday, 1960. 287 pp.

5042 Lindsay, Cynthia. The Natives are Restless. Philadelphia:
Lippincott, 1960. 223 pp.
Study of the Southern California community, with ma-
terial on Beverly Hills and Hollywood.

5043 Canfield, Alyce. God in Hollywood. New York: Wisdom
House, 1961. 160 pp.
Discusses religious groups and stars in Hollywood
with material on Jane Russell, June Haver, Pat Boone,
and others.

5044 Goodman, Ezra. The Fifty-Year Decline and Fall of Hollywood. New York: Simon and Schuster, 1961. 465 pp.

5045 Rivkin, Allen and Kerr, Laura (eds.) Hello, Hollywood! A
Book About the Movies by the People Who Make Them.

Garden City, N.Y.: Doubleday, 1962. 571 pp.
Kaleidoscopic anthology on Hollywood and the movies,
with contributions by over 100 members of the Hollywood
community.

5046 Regan, Michael. Stars, Moguls, Magnates: The Mansions
of Beverly Hills. Los Angeles: Regan, 1966. 79 pp.
Primarily photographs; includes the homes of Mary
Pickford, Buster Keaton, Conrad Veidt, Richard Bathel-
mess, Marion Davies, Harold Lloyd, William Powell,
Thomas Ince, Harry Cohn, Samuel Goldwyn, David O.
Selznick, and others.

5047 Knight, Arthur (text) and Elisofon, Eliot (photographs). The
Hollywood Style. New York: Macmillan, 1969. 216 pp.
Account of the homes and life styles of Hollywood
personalities.

5048 Graham, Sheilah. The Garden of Allah. New York: Crown,
1970. 258 pp.
Account of the Hollywood apartment complex and the
celebrities who lived there, including Robert Benchley,
F. Scott Fitzgerald, Marc Connelly, Dorothy Parker, John
O'Hara, Greta Garbo, Donald Ogden Stewart, and Errol
Flynn.

5049 Thorpe, Edward. The Other Hollywood. London: Michael
Joseph, 1970. 174 pp.
Discusses various aspects of contemporary Hollywood.

5050 Thomas, Bob. The Heart of Hollywood: A 50-Year Pictorial
History of the Film Capital and the Famed Motion Picture
and Television Relief Fund. Los Angeles: Price, Stern,
Sloan, 1971. 110 pp.

5051 Marion, Frances. Off With Their Heads! A Serio-Comic
Tale of Hollywood. New York: Macmillan, 1972. 356 pp.
Reminiscences about Hollywood's history and personali-
ties by a noted screenwriter.

5052 Scott, Evelyn F. Hollywood When Silents Were Golden. New
York: McGraw-Hill, 1972. 223 pp.
Reminiscences of early Hollywood life, with emphasis
on scenarist Beulah Marie Dix and the De Mille family.

5053 Lewis, Arthur H. It Was Fun While It Lasted. New York:
Trident, 1973. 320 pp.
Discussion of Hollywood's past glory, supplemented
by informally conducted interviews with many Hollywood
personalities.

5054 Schultheiss, John Edward. A Study of the "Eastern" Writer

in Hollywood in the 1930's.   University of Southern California: Ph.D., 1973.   566 pp.

5055   Barris, George (photographer) and Scagnetti, Jack (text).
        Cars of the Stars.   Middle Village, N.Y.:   Jonathan David,
        1974.   243 pp.

5056   Cary, Diana Serra.   The Hollywood Posse: The Story of a
        Gallant Band of Horsemen Who Made Movie History.
        Boston: Houghton Mifflin, 1975.   268 pp.
            Account of the Hollywood milieu in which cowboy
        stuntmen and extras worked, written by silent child-star
        "Baby Peggy."

5057   Guiles, Fred Lawrence.   Hanging on in Paradise.   New York:
        McGraw-Hill, 1975.   412 pp.
            Account of writers within the Hollywood milieu; for
        list of individuals discussed, see entry 3807.

5058   Wagner, Walter.   You Must Remember This.   New York:
        Putnam, 1975.   320 pp.
            Oral reminiscences of Hollywood by many Hollywood
        personalities; for list of names, see entry 3820.

2.   Sociological Studies of
Hollywood and Its Image

5059   Rosten, Leo C.   Hollywood: The Movie Colony, The Movie
        Makers.   New York: Harcourt, Brace, 1941.   436 pp.
        (Reprinted New York: Arno, 1970.)

5060   Powdermaker, Hortense.   Hollywood: The Dream Factory:
        An Anthropologist Looks at the Movie-Makers.   Boston:
        Little, Brown, 1950.   342 pp.

5061   Lokke, Virgil L.   The Literary Image of Hollywood.   Uni-
        versity of Iowa: Ph.D., 1955.   249 pp.

5062   Dunne, John Gregory.   The Studio.   New York: Farrar,
        Straus, and Giroux, 1968.   255 pp.
            A study of the workings of Twentieth-Century Fox in
        1967-68.

5063   Mayersberg, Paul.   Hollywood: The Haunted House.   New
        York: Stein and Day, 1968.   188 pp.
            Analysis of the Hollywood system, including interview
        material with Richard Brooks, Delmer Daves, John
        Sturges, Stanley Cortez, George Cukor, Daniel Taradash,
        Don Siegel, Stanley Kramer, and others.

5064   Spatz, Jonas.   Hollywood in Fiction: Some Versions of the
       American Myth.   The Hague: Mouton, 1969.   148 pp.

5065   Faulkner, Robert R.   Hollywood Studio Musicians: Their
       Work and Careers in the Recording Industry.   Chicago:
       Aldine, Atherton, 1971.   218 pp.
       Sociological study of the musician's role within the
       Hollywood work structure.

5066   Wells, Walter.   Tycoons and Locusts: A Regional Look at
       Hollywood Fiction of the Thirties.   Carbondale: Southern
       Illinois University Press, 1973.   139 pp.

3.   The Star Phenomenon

       The books in this section examine the phenomenon of
stardom and "celebrity." For books which use the concept of
stardom primarily as a basis for the presentation of biographical
material (such as Richard Schickel's The Stars), see Part VI, section B, collective biography, analysis, and interview.   Many of the
books in the biography sections do contain material on the phenomenon of stardom as well.

5067   Freeman, William M.   The Big Name.   New York: Printers'
       Ink Books, 1957.   230 pp.
       Study of celebrity endorsements in advertising.

5068   Morin, Edgar.   The Stars: An Account of the Star-System
       in Motion Pictures.   New York: Grove, 1960.   192 pp.
       Analyzes the star system in terms of the relationship
       between star and audience; particularly includes material
       on Charlie Chaplin and James Dean.

5069   Klapp, Orrin E.   Symbolic leaders: Public Dramas and Public
       Men.   Chicago: Aldine, 1964.   272 pp.
       Study of the concept of celebrity, which uses stars
       among its examples.

5070   Walker, Alexander.   The Celluloid Sacrifice: Aspects of
       Sex in the Movies.   New York: Hawthorn, 1967.   241 pp.
       Includes a chapter analyzing Elizabeth Taylor and the
       phenomenon of stardom.

5071   Griffith, Richard.   The Movie Stars.   Garden City, N.Y.:
       Doubleday, 1970.   498 pp.
       Many photographs, plus historical/analytical discussion
       of the star system.

5072   Walker, Alexander.   Stardom: The Hollywood Phenomenon.

New York: Stein and Day, 1970. 392 pp.
Historical/analytical study of stardom; includes ma-
terial on Florence Lawrence, D. W. Griffith, Lillian Gish,
Richard Barthelmess, Mack Sennett, Charlie Chaplin,
Douglas Fairbanks, Gloria Swanson, Pola Negri, Greta
Garbo, Rudolph Valentino, John Gilbert, Bette Davis, Joan
Crawford, Clark Gable, and John Wayne.

5073 Wertham, Fredric. The World of Fanzines: A Special Form
of Communication. Carbondale: Southern Illinois University Press, 1973. 144 pp.

5074 Kobal, John (ed.) 50 Super Stars. New York: Bounty, 1974.
160 pp.
Primarily photographs, with an essay on star quality
and stardom by John Russell Taylor.

4. Anecdotal Views of Hollywood
and Hollywood Personalities

        This section, Anecdotal Views of Hollywood and Hollywood
Personalities, lists a wide variety of works including reminiscences,
anecdotes, books by gossip columnists on the colorful lives of the
most popular stars, personal and subjective views of the Hollywood
community, and books dealing with the major Hollywood scandals.
Some are written by insiders, others are written by those on the
peripheries of the Hollywood community. For material on individual
columnists, see Part VI, section A, individual biography, analysis,
and interview.

5075 Partridge, Helen. A Lady Goes to Hollywood: Being the
Casual Adventures of an Author's Wife in the Much Misunderstood Capitol of Filmland. New York: Macmillan,
1941. 259 pp.
A screenwriter's wife discusses her Hollywood stay.

5076 Ilf, Ilya and Petrov, Eugene. Little Golden America: Two
Famous Soviet Humourists Survey the United States.
London: Routledge, 1944. 296 pp.
Includes a humorous view of Hollywood.

5077 Wilson, Earl. I Am Gazing Into My 8-Ball. Garden City,
N.Y.: Doubleday, Doran, 1945. 182 pp.
Gossip column anecdotes with material on many
Hollywood personalities.

5078 Hecht, Andrew. Hollywood Merry-Go-Round. New York:
Grosset and Dunlap, 1947. 212 pp.

5079 Martin, Pete. Hollywood Without Makeup. Philadelphia:

Lippincott, 1948. 255 pp.
Includes material on Greer Garson, Ava Gardner,
Maria Montez, Nunnally Johnson, Mark Hellinger, Leo
McCarey, Michael Curtiz, John Carradine, Dan Duryea,
Francis X. Bushman, Gregory Peck, Burt Lancaster,
Hoagy Carmicheal, Shirley Temple, and others.

5080　Life and Death in Hollywood: The Sensational Picture Document of Hollywood's Most Turbulent Years. Cincinnati:
Zebra Picture Books, 1950. 96 pp.
Primarily photographs of scandal-related film personalities.

5081　Rosenstein, Jaik. Hollywood Leg Man. Los Angeles: Madison, 1950. 212 pp.
Anecdotes written by an associate of Hedda Hopper.

5082　Haskin, Dorothy. Behind the Scenes in Hollywood. Grand
Rapids, Mich.: Zondervan, 1951. 77 pp.
Includes material on religious aspects of Hollywood.

5083　Duncan, Peter. In Hollywood Tonight. London: Laurie,
1952. 144 pp.

5084　Myers, Denis (ed.) Secrets of the Stars. London: Odhams,
1952. 143 pp.
Many photographs; biographical/anecdotal material on
various stars.

5085　Gardner, Hy. Champagne Before Breakfast. New York:
Henry Holt, 1954. 304 pp.
Anecdotes by a columnist, with material on film
personalities including chapter entitled "So This Is Hollywood."

5086　Sumner, Robert L. Hollywood Cesspool: A Startling Survey
of Movieland Lives and Morals, Pictures and Results.
Wheaton, Ill.: Sword of the Lord, 1955. 284 pp.
An evangelist's view of Hollywood.

5087　Zinsser, William K. Seen Any Good Movies Lately? Garden
City, N.Y.: Doubleday, 1958. 239 pp.
Anecdotal essays by a former critic of the New York
Herald Tribune.

5088　Anderson, Clinton. Beverly Hills Is My Beat. Englewood
Cliffs, N.J.: Prentice-Hall, 1960. 218 pp.
Material on Hollywood personalities by Beverly Hills'
chief-of-police.

5089　Golden, Milton M. Hollywood Lawyer. New York: New
American Library, 1960. 192 pp.

Relates "Hollywood" court cases, but rarely mentions
actual names.

5090 Davidson, Bill. The Real and the Unreal. New York:
      Harper, 1961. 275 pp.
      Essays by a Hollywood reporter on Hollywood milieu
      and personalities, including chapters on Frank Sinatra,
      Kim Novak, Dick Clark, Clark Gable, Elizabeth Taylor,
      Ingrid Bergman, Fred Astaire, and Joshua Logan.

5091 Parsons, Louella. Tell It To Louella. New York: Putnam,
      1961. 316 pp.
      Material by a gossip columnist about Clark Gable,
      Ingrid Bergman, Rita Hayworth, William Randolph Hearst,
      Joan Crawford, Frank Sinatra, Lana Turner, Howard
      Hughes, Grace Kelly, Marilyn Monroe, Marlon Brando,
      Elizabeth Taylor, Judy Garland, Janet Leigh, and Tony
      Curtis.

5092 Carr, William A. Hollywood Tragedy. New York: Lancer,
      1962. 159 pp.
      Primarily material on scandals related to Marilyn
      Monroe, Fatty Arbuckle, William Desmond Taylor, Thelma
      Todd, Errol Flynn, Jean Harlow and Paul Bern, Charlie
      Chaplin, Lupe Velez, Ingrid Bergman, Lana Turner, and
      Elizabeth Taylor.

5093 Evans, Charles. The Reverend Goes to Hollywood. New
      York: Crowell-Collier, 1962. 222 pp.
      Reminiscences by a minister who went to Hollywood
      to become an actor.

5094 Guild, Leo. Hollywood Screwballs. Los Angeles: Holloway,
      1962. 223 pp.
      Discusses "screwball" behavior of Hollywood personali-
      ties.

5095 Edmonds, I. G. Hollywood R. I. P. Evanston, Ill.: Re-
      gency, 1963. 158 pp.
      Deals with scandals and trials in the Hollywood com-
      munity.

5096 Hopper, Hedda and Brough, James. The Whole Truth and
      Nothing But. Garden City, N.Y.: Doubleday, 1963.
      331 pp.
      Material on Hollywood personalities, based on Hopper's
      years as a gossip columnist.

5097 Moger, Art. Some of My Best Friends are People. Boston:
      Challenge Press, 1964. 156 pp.
      Anecdotes by a Hollywood press agent.

5098 Anger, Kenneth. Hollywood Babylon. Phoenix: Associated

Professional Services, 1965. 272 pp. (Reprinted San
Francisco: Straight Arrow Books, 1975. 305 pp.)
Scandal and gossip about a wide variety of Hollywood
personalities.

5099   Nuetzel, Charles. Whodunit? Hollywood Style. Beverly
Hills: Book Company of America, 1965. 169 pp.
Scandal material on the usual Hollywood figures.

5100   Hamblett, Charles. Who Killed Marilyn Monroe? Or Cage
to Catch Our Dreams. London: Leslie Frewin, 1966.
175 pp. (Republished as The Hollywood Cage, New York:
Hart, 1969. 437 pp.)
Material based on conversations and interviews with
various Hollywood stars; some emphasis on Marilyn
Monroe and Kim Novak.

5101   Graham, Sheilah. Confessions of a Hollywood Columnist.
New York: Morrow, 1969. 309 pp.

5102   Austin, John. Hollywood's Unsolved Mysteries. New York:
Ace, 1970. 190 pp.
Primarily discusses the familiar Hollywood scandals.

5103   Wilk, Max (ed.) The Wit and Wisdom of Hollywood: From
the Squaw Man to the Hatchet Man. New York: Atheneum,
1971. 330 pp.
Various humorous quotations and stories about Hollywood.

5104   Wilson, Earl. The Show Business Nobody Knows. Chicago:
Cowles, 1971. 428 pp.
Includes material on film personalities as well as
other show business branches.

5105   Zeltner, Irwin. What the Stars Told Me: Hollywood in Its
Heydey. New York: Exposition, 1971. 182 pp.
Reminiscences of a press agent.

5106   Beck, Marilyn. Marilyn Beck's Hollywood. New York:
Hawthorn, 1973. 258 pp.
Anecdotal material by a columnist.

5107   Eder, Shirley. Not This Time, Cary Grant! and Other
Stories About Hollywood. Garden City, N.Y.: Doubleday,
1973. 295 pp.
Observations by a Hollywood columnist.

5108   Messick, Hank. The Beauties and the Beasts: The Mob in
Show Business. New York: McKay, 1973. 256 pp.
(Also published as The Mob in Show Business.)
With material on Jean Harlow, Fanny Brice, Jill St.
John, George Raft, Joe E. Lewis, Frank Sinatra, and others.

5109   Hagen, John. Holly-Would. New Rochelle, N.Y.: Arlington,
       1974. 254 pp.
            Primarily gossip and caricature.

5110   Halliwell, Leslie. The Filmgoer's Book of Quotes. New
       Rochelle, N.Y.: Arlington, 1974. 222 pp.
            Quotations from films and by and about film people.

5111   Holzer, Hans. Haunted Hollywood: Ghostly Encounters.
       Indianapolis: Bobbs-Merrill, 1974. 133 pp.
            Study of ghosts and psychic phenomena in the Holly-
       wood community.

5112   Kanin, Garson. Hollywood: Stars and Starlets, Tycoons and
       Flesh-Peddlers, Moviemakers and Moneymakers, Frauds
       and Geniuses, Hopefuls and Has-Beens, Great Lovers and
       Sex Symbols. New York: Viking, 1974. 393 pp.

5113   Wilson, Earl. Show Business Laid Bare. New York: Put-
       nam, 1974. 336 pp.
            Primarily about the sexual behavior of entertainers,
       including film personalities.

5114   Marchak, Alice and Hunter, Linda. The Supersecs: Behind
       the Scenes With the Secretaries of the Superstars! North
       Hollywood: Charles, 1975.
            Written by the secretaries of Marlon Brando and
       Julie Andrews.

PART X

FILM AND EDUCATION

A. FILM AS ART

In general, the relationship of film to education can be divided into two different concepts: the study of film itself as an art form, and the use of film as an educational resource toward the study of other subjects. The film and education category, therefore, has been dichotomized to reflect this distinction. Users of this book interested in the study of film as art will find all related materials in the first of the two major classifications, section A. We have further divided this film-as-art classification into three sub-sections: A-1, which is composed of all works dealing with the teaching of film history, film appreciation, and film production; A-2, which is composed of all those works which serve as very general texts and introductions to film study and appreciation; and A-3, which is composed of those works which deal with the formation and running of film societies. Note that we have included in A-2 those books intended for use in the English or art course, since they tend to deal more with film as art than with film as resource. The reader should also be aware that there are many books and pamphlets on film education published by the British Film Institute which are not included here; for these works, the reader should consult the Catalogue of the Book Library of the British Film Institute. The emphasis in this section, as elsewhere, is on those works that have been most readily available in the United States. The user of this bibliography should also note that books intended for children or intended to be used as textbooks have not necessarily been classified in education, but have been classified according to their subject matter. Thus, a children's book on film production would be classified in Part II, section B, general filmmaking guides; a juvenile biography of Walt Disney would be classified in Part VI, section A (individual biography, analysis, and interview) under Disney; an international history text would be classified in Part IV, section C, world cinema surveys. Books intended for the young reader can be recognized throughout this bibliography by the annotation "For the young reader." In general, we have not tried to differentiate the exact age group for which these books are intended, and this annotation can imply an intended readership anywhere from the first grade up through early high school. And further, teacher's manuals for textbooks have not been classified separately in section A-1, but rather have been added to the citation of the original text for which the manual was created. A teacher looking for a book to be used as a text on a particular subject should consult the classification for that particular subject area. The reader searching for educationally appropriate texts is especially referred to Part VIII, section D, anthologies of theory and criticism, for many books designed to be used in an educational context, as well as to Part II, section A for aesthetic texts of technique and to Part VIII, section F-4-b for anthologies of mass media and popular culture.

1. The Study and Teaching
of Film as Art

5115 Brooker, Floyde E. and Herrington, Eugene H. Students Make Motion Pictures: A Report on Film Production in the Denver Schools. Washington, D.C.: American Council on Education, 1941. 142 pp.

5116 Spearman, Walter. The Film Yesterday, Today and Tomorrow. Chapel Hill: University of North Carolina Press, 1941. 36 pp.
       Outline material for a general course on motion pictures.

5117 British Film Institute. Film Appreciation and Visual Education: A Summary of Some of the Speeches Delivered at the BFI's Summer School at Bangor, August, 1944. London: British Film Institute, ca. 1944. 91 pp.

5118 Eisenstein, Sergei. Programme for Teaching the Theory and Practice of Film Direction. Hollywood: Larry Edmunds Bookshop, 1944. 20 pp. Translated by Stephen Garry with Ivor Montagu.

5119 Hills, Janet. Films and Children: The Positive Approach. London: British Film Institute, ca. 1951. 59 pp.

5120 Lods, Jean. Professional Training of Film Technicians. Paris: UNESCO, 1951. 155 pp.
       Survey of available training institutions.

5121 Mitchell, John W. A Survey of the Motion Picture Production Activities of Selected Universities. Indiana University: Ph.D., 1952.

5122 Rosenthal, Newman Hirsch. Films in Our Lives: An Approach to Film Appreciation. Melbourne: Cheshire, 1953. 68 pp.

5123 Ellis, Jack C. Approaches to Film as an Art Form: A Handbook for College Teachers. Columbia University: Ed.D., 1955. 355 pp.

5124 Greiner, Grace. Teaching Film: A Guide to Classroom
      Method. London: British Film Institute, 1955. 29 pp.

5125 Wickham, Glynne William Gladstone (ed.) The Relation Be-
      tween Universities and Films, Radio and Television.
      London: Butterworths, published for the University of
      Bristol, 1956. 55 pp.

5126 Reed, Stanley. The Film: United Kingdom: An Account of
      the Work Which is Being Done in English Schools to
      Raise Standards of Film Appreciation. London: British
      Film Institute, 1960. 15 pp.

5127 Rees, Sidney and Waters, Don. Film Making in School: A
      Primer on the Organization of Children's Film Making.
      London: Society of Education in Film and Television,
      1960. 16 pp. (Revised as Young Film Makers, 1963,
      20 pp.)

5128 Peters, J. M. L. Teaching About the Film. New York:
      International Documents Service, distributed by Columbia
      University Press by arrangement with UNESCO, 1961.
      120 pp.

5129 Reed, Stanley. A Guide to Good Viewing. London: Educa-
      tional Supply Association, 1961. 122 pp.

5130 Nizhny, Vladimir. Lessons With Eisenstein. Edited and
      translated by Ivor Montagu and Jay Leyda. New York:
      Hill and Wang, 1962. 182 pp.
          A reconstruction of Eisenstein's lectures at the State
      Institute of Cinematography in Moscow.

5131 Selby, Stuart. The Study of Film as an Art Form in Ameri-
      can Secondary Schools. Columbia University: Ed.D.,
      1963. 271 pp.

5132 University Film Foundation. Motion Picture Production Facili-
      ties of Selected Colleges and Universities: A Survey Re-
      ported by Don G. Williams and Louella V. Snyder. Wash-
      ington, D.C.: U.S. Department of Health, Education, and
      Welfare, Office of Education, 1963. 345 pp.

5133 Hall, Stuart; Knight, Roy; Hunt, Albert; and Lovell, Alan.
      Studies in the Teaching of Film Within Formal Education:
      Four Courses Described. Edited by Paddy Whannel and
      Peter Harcourt. London: British Film Institute, Educa-
      tion Department, 1964. 107 pp. (Republished 1968.)

5134 Hodgkinson, A. W. Screen Education: Teaching a Critical
      Approach to Cinema and Television: A Study, Deriving
      from the International Meeting on Film and Television

Teaching, Organized at Leangkollen, Oslo, Norway, in Oct. 1962 by the International Centre of Films (Cinema and Television) for Children. New York: UNESCO, 1964. 99 pp.

5135 Mallery, David. The School and the Art of Motion Pictures: A Challenge to Teachers. Boston: National Association of Independent Schools, 1964, 101 pp. (Revised as The School and the Art of Motion Pictures: A Discussion of Practices and Possibilities, 1966, 147 pp.)

5136 Culkin, John Michael. Film Study in the High School. New York: Fordham Film Study Center, Fordham University, ca. 1965. 35 pp.

5137 Culkin, John Michael. The Planning, Organization, and Teaching of a Course in the Moving Picture as an Art Form: A Project in Curriculum Development and Implementation. Harvard University: Ph.D., 1965.

5138 Limbacher, James L. The Movies Before 1920: A Guide to the Study of the History and Appreciation of the Motion Picture. Dearborn, Mich.: Dearborn Public Library(?), 1965. 57 ℓ.

5139 National Council of Teachers of English. The Motion Picture and the Teaching of English. New York: Appleton-Century-Crofts, 1965. 168 pp.
       Contributors include Marion C. Sheridan, Harold H. Owen, Jr., Ken Macrorie, and Fred Marcus.

5140 Harcourt, Peter and Theobald, Peter (eds.) Film Making in Schools and Colleges. London: British Film Institute, 1966. 79 pp.

5141 Kitses, Jim with Mercer, Ann. Talking About the Cinema: Film Studies for Young People. London: British Film Institute, 1966. 98 pp.

5142 Stewart, David C. (ed.) Film Study in Higher Education. Washington, D.C.: American Council on Education, 1966. 174 pp.
       Contributors include Jack Ellis, George Stoney, Arthur Knight, Pauline Kael, Hugh Gray, and others.

5143 Tucker, Nicholas. Understanding the Mass Media: A Practical Approach for Teaching. Cambridge: Cambridge University Press, 1966. 198 pp.

5144 Great Britain. Committee to Consider the Need for a National Film School. National Film School: Report. London: Her Majesty's Stationery Office, 1967. 49 pp.

5145 Sullivan, Bede. Movies: Universal Language; Film Study in
      High School. Notre Dame, Ind.: Fides Press, 1967.
      160 pp.

5146 Larson, Rodger. A Guide for Film Teachers to Filmmaking
      by Teenagers. New York: Cultural Affairs Foundation,
      1968. 48 pp.

5147 Lowndes, Douglas. Film Making in Schools. New York:
      Watson-Guptill, 1968. 128 pp.

5148 Sohn, David A. Film Study and the English Teacher.
      Bloomington: Indiana University Audio-Visual Center,
      1968. 13 pp.

5149 Amelio, Ralph J. with Own, Anita and Schaefer, Susan.
      Willowbrook Cinema Study Project: A Two-Semester
      Course on Film as a Medium for Intellectual and Aes-
      thetic Experience. Dayton, Ohio: Pflaum, 1969. 84 pp.

5150 American Film Institute. Guide to College Film Courses
      1969-70. Washington, D.C.: The American Film Insti-
      tute, 1969. 44 pp. (Fifth edition published as Guide to
      College Courses in Film and Television, Washington,
      D.C.: Acropolis, 1975, 286 pp.)
      Includes a section on foreign film programs.

5151 Feyen, Sharon and Wigal, Donald (eds.) Screen Experience:
      An Approach to Film. Dayton, Ohio: Pflaum, 1969.
      273 pp.

5152 Sohn, David A. and Stucker, Melinda. Film Study in the
      Elementary School, Grades Kindergarten Through Eight:
      A Curriculum Report to the American Film Institute.
      Washington, D.C.: American Film Institute, ca. 1969.
      281 pp.

5153 Andersen, Yvonne. Teaching Film Animation to Children.
      New York: Van Nostrand Reinhold, 1970. 112 pp.

5154 Bryne-Daniel, J. Grafilm: An Approach to a New Medium.
      New York: Van Nostrand Reinhold, 1970. 96 pp.
          A curriculum of six projects toward the production
      of "grafilms," films which combine graphic and illustrative
      techniques with film techniques; written primarily for de-
      signers and art students.

5155 Fensch, Thomas. Films on the Campus. South Brunswick,
      N.J.: A. S. Barnes, 1970. 534 pp.
          Surveys the various orientations of film programs
      and productions at U.S. colleges and universities.

5156 Lidstone, John and McIntosh, Don. Children as Film Makers.
      New York: Van Nostrand Reinhold, 1970. 111 pp.

5157 Ross, T. J. (ed.) Film and the Liberal Arts. New York:
      Holt, Rinehart and Winston, 1970. 419 pp.

5158 Schreivogel, Paul A. Films in Depth: A Series of Twelve
      Film Studies. Dayton, Ohio: Pflaum, 1970.
            A series of student/teacher booklets to accompany
      the study of twelve short films: FLAVIO, LANGUAGE
      OF FACES, LITTLE ISLAND, NIGHT AND FOG, NO
      REASON TO STAY, AN OCCURRENCE AT OWL CREEK
      BRIDGE, OVERTURE--OVERTURE NYITANY, STAIN ON
      HIS CONSCIENCE, SUNDAY LARK, TIME PIECE, TOYS,
      and ORANGE AND BLUE.

5159 Weiss, Gene Stephen. The Establishment of a Rationale and
      a Set of Criteria for the Use of Art Films in the Educa-
      tional Curriculum. Ohio State University: Ph.D., 1970.
      243 pp.

5160 Allen, Don. The Electric Humanities: Patterns for Teaching
      Mass Media and Popular Culture. Dayton, Ohio: Pflaum,
      1971. 276 pp.

5161 Amelio, Ralph J. Film in the Classroom: Why Use It, How
      to Use It. Dayton, Ohio: Pflaum/Standard, 1971. 181 pp.

5162 Goldman, Frederick and Burnett, Linda R. Need Johnny
      Read? Practical Methods to Enrich Humanities Courses
      Using Films and Film Study. Dayton, Ohio: Pflaum/
      Standard, 1971. 238 pp.

5163 Katz, John Stuart (comp.) Perspectives on the Study of Film.
      Boston: Little, Brown, 1971. 339 pp.
            Contributors include Aldous Huxley, Marshall McLuhan,
      Stanley Kauffmann, Bela Balazs, Erwin Panofsky, Susan
      Sontag, Slavko Vorkapich, Andrew Sarris, Pauline Kael,
      Jonas Mekas, Sol Worth, Stan Vanderbeek, and Peter Har-
      court.

5164 McGregor, Edgar Russell. A Design for a Mediated First
      Course in Film Production. University of Southern Cali-
      fornia: Ph.D., 1971. 323 pp.

5165 Rynew, Arden. Filmmaking for Children; Including Motion
      Picture Production Handbook. Dayton, Ohio: Pflaum/
      Standard, 1971. 85, 59 pp.

5166 Samples, Gordon. How to Locate Criticism and Reviews of
      Plays and Films. San Diego: San Diego State, Malcolm
      A. Love Library, 1971. 23 ℓ. (Revised as How to

Locate Reviews of Plays and Films: A Bibliography of
Criticism From the Beginnings to the Present, Metuchen,
N.J.: Scarecrow, 1976, 114 pp.)

5167 Sweeting, Charles (ed.) A Film Course Manual. Berkeley:
      McCutchan, 1971. 58 pp.

5168 Brown, Roland G. A Bookless Curriculum. Dayton, Ohio:
      Pflaum/Standard, 1972. 134 pp.

5169 Clare, Warren L. and Ericksen, Kenneth J. Multimmediate:
      Multi Media and the Art of Writing. New York: Random,
      1972. 257 pp.

5170 Giblin, Thomas R. (ed.) Popular Media and the Teaching of
      English. Pacific Palisades, Cal.: Goodyear, 1972.
      276 pp.

5171 Katz, John Stuart with Oliver, Curt and Aird, Forbes. A
      Curriculum in Film. Toronto: Ontario Institute for
      Studies in Education, 1972. 130 pp.

5172 Kennedy, Keith. Film Making in Creative Teaching. New
      York: Watson-Guptill, 1972. 128 pp.

5173 Knight, Roy (ed.) Film in English Teaching. London:
      Hutchinson Educational, 1972. 248 pp.

5174 Lacey, Richard A. Seeing With Feeling: Film in the Class-
      room. Philadelphia: Saunders, 1972. 118 pp.

5175 Poteet, G. Howard (ed.) The Compleat Guide to Film Study.
      Urbana, Ill.: National Council of Teachers of English,
      1972. 242 pp.

5176 Walz, Eugene P.; Harrington, John; and DiMarco, Vincent
      (eds.) Frames of Reference: Essays on the Rhetoric of
      Film. Dubuque, Iowa: Kendall/Hunt, 1972. 145 pp.

5177 Manchel, Frank. Film Study: A Resource Guide. Ruther-
      ford, N.J.: Fairleigh Dickinson University Press, 1973.
      422 pp.

5178 Morrison, Jack. The Rise of the Arts on the American
      Campus. New York: McGraw-Hill, 1973. 223 pp.
      Material on all the arts, including film.

5179 Rice, Susan and Mukerji, Rose (eds.) Children Are Centers
      for Understanding Media. Washington, D.C.: Associa-
      tion for Childhood Education International, 1973. 89 pp.
      Includes description of techniques for teaching various
      types of filmmaking to children.

5180   Amelio, Ralph J. (ed.) Hal in the Classroom: Science Fic-
       tion Films. Dayton, Ohio: Pflaum, 1974. 153 pp.
       Includes articles and annotated filmography and bib-
       liography on the science fiction genre.

5181   Anderson, Albert Arthur, Jr. Film Study as Aesthetic Edu-
       cation: A Foundation for Curriculum. Ohio State Uni-
       versity: Ph.D., 1974. 143 pp.

5182   Coynik, David. Moviemaking: A Worktext for Super 8 Film
       Production. Chicago: Loyola University Press, 1974.
       240 pp.
       A curriculum with units on the various aspects of
       film production.

5183   Rose, Ernest D. World Film and TV Study Resources: A
       Reference Guide to Major Training Centers and Archives.
       Bonn-Bad Godesberg, Federal Republic of Germany:
       Friedrich-Ebert-Stiftung, 1974. 421 pp.

5184   Amelio, Ralph J. The Filmic Moment: Teaching American
       Genre Film Through Extracts. Dayton, Ohio: Pflaum,
       1975. 164 pp.

5185   Bryan, Margaret B. and Davis, Boyd H. Writing About
       Literature and Film. New York: Harcourt Brace
       Jovanovich, 1975. 192 pp.

5186   Gidley, M. and Wicks, Stephen. Film Education: A Collec-
       tion of Experiences and Ideas. Exeter: University of
       Exeter, School of Education, 1975. 96 pp.

5187   Goldfield, Dave (ed.) A Guide to Film and Television
       Courses in Canada/Un Guide des Cours de Cinema et
       Television Offerts au Canada 1975-76. Ottawa: National
       Film Board of Canada, 1975. 209 pp.

2.   General Texts for Film Study and Appreciation

       For material on finding other books which can be used as
textbooks, see the explanation after Part X, section A, film as art.

5188   Lescarboura, Austin C. Behind the Motion-Picture Screen.
       (Originally published 1919.) New York: Blom, 1971.
       420 pp.

5189   Lane, Tamar. What's Wrong with the Movies? (Originally
       published 1923.) New York: Ozer, 1971. 254 pp.
       Explains and evaluates all aspects of filmmaking in
       America.

5190 Barry, Iris. Let's Go to the Movies. (Originally published
      1926.) New York: Arno, 1972. 278 pp.

5191 Dale, Edgar. How to Appreciate Motion-Pictures. (Origi-
      nally published with subtitle A Manual of Motion-Picture
      Criticism Prepared for High School Students, 1933.)
      New York: Arno, 1970. 243 pp.

5192 Davy, Charles (ed.) Footnotes to the Film. (Originally
      published 1938.) New York: Arno, 1970. 334 pp.
      With contributions by Forsyth Hardy, Elizabeth Bowen,
      Alberto Cavalcanti, Robert Donat, Basil Wright, Graham
      Greene, Alexander Korda, Alfred Hitchcock, Alistair
      Cooke, John Grierson, Maurice Jaubert, Basil Dean,
      John Betjeman, and others.

5193 British Film Institute. The Elements of Film Criticism.
      London: British Film Institute, 1944. 27 pp.

5194 Lindgren, Ernest. The Cinema. London: English Univer-
      sities Press, published for the Association for Education
      in Citizenship, 1944. 23 pp.

5195 Manvell, Roger. Film. Harmondsworth: Penguin, 1944.
      191 pp. (Revised 1946, 240 pp. Revised again 1950,
      287 pp.)

5196 Buchanan, Andrew. Film and the Future. London: Allen
      and Unwin, 1945. 104 pp.
      Discusses various aspects of film and its potential
      future development.

5197 O'Laoghaire, Liam. Invitation to the Film. Tralee, Ireland:
      Kerryman, 1945. 203 pp.

5198 Harman, Jympson. Good Films: How to Appreciate Them.
      London: Daily Mail, 1946. 30 pp.
      For the young reader.

5199 Buchanan, Andrew. Going to the Cinema. London: Phoenix,
      1947. 160 pp.
      For the young reader.

5200 Field, Mary and Miller, Maud. The Boys' and Girls' Film
      Book. London: Burke, 1947. 192 pp.
      For the young reader.

5201 Wollenberg, H. H. Anatomy of the Film: An Illustrated
      Guide to Film Appreciation. London: Marsland, 1947.
      104 pp. (Reprinted New York: Arno, 1972.)

5202 Wood, Leslie. The Miracle of the Movies. London: Burke,
      1947. 352 pp.

5203 Allen, Kenneth S. The Silver Screen. London: Gifford,
      1948. 66 pp.
      For the young reader.

5204 Schmidt, Georg; Schmalenbach, Werner; and Bächlin, Peter.
      The Film: Its Economic, Social, and Artistic Problems.
      English language version: Hugo Weber and Roger Manvell.
      London: Falcon, 1948. 132 pp.

5205 Sproxton, Vernon. Watching Films. London: SCM Press,
      1948. 56 pp.

5206 Wright, Basil. The Use of the Film. London: Bodley Head,
      1948. 72 pp. (Reprinted New York: Arno, 1972.)

5207 Daugherty, Charles Michael. Let 'em Roll. New York:
      Viking, 1950. 189 pp.
      For the young reader.

5208 Ommanney, Katherine Anne and Pierce C. The Stage and
      the School. New York: Harper, 1950. 571 pp. (Re-
      vised New York: McGraw-Hill, 1960, 530 pp.)
      Revision includes limited material on film.

5209 Manvell, Roger. A Seat at the Cinema. London: Evans,
      1951. 192 pp.

5210 Le Harivel, Jean Philippe. Focus on Films. London:
      C. A. Watts, 1952. 90 pp.

5211 Beckoff, Samuel. Motion Pictures. New York: Oxford
      Book Company, 1953. 114 pp. (Published with a
      teacher's manual.)
      For the high school audience.

5212 Callenbach, Ernest. Our Modern Art: The Movies. Chicago:
      Center for the Study of Liberal Education for Adults, 1955.
      116 pp.
      An introduction to critical viewing, utilizing specific
      films.

5213 Harrison, Richard M. The True Book About Films. Lon-
      don: Muller, 1956. 142 pp.
      For the young reader.

5214 Lewin, William and Frazier, Alexander. Standards of Photo-
      play Appreciation Including a Photoplay Approach to
      Shakespeare. Summit, N.J.: Educational and Recrea-
      tional Guides, 1957. 160 pp.
      Primarily for the junior and senior high school
      audience.

5215 Wright, Edward A. A Primer for Playgoers: An Introduction

to the Understanding and Appreciation of Cinema, Stage,
Television. Englewood Cliffs, N.J.: Prentice-Hall,
1958. 270 pp.

5216 Wright, Edward A. Understanding Today's Theatre: Cinema,
Stage, Television. Englewood Cliffs, N.J.: Prentice-
Hall, 1959. 178 pp.

5217 Yurka, Blanche. Dear Audience: A Guide to the Enjoyment
of Theatre. Englewood Cliffs, N.J.: Prentice-Hall,
1959. 167 pp.
Includes material on film.

5218 Fischer, Edward. The Screen Arts: A Guide to Film and
Television Appreciation. New York: Sheed and Ward,
1960. 184 pp.

5219 Manvell, Roger. The Living Screen: Background to the
Film and Television. London: Harrap, 1961. 192 pp.

5220 Reed, Stanley. A Guide to Good Viewing. London: Educational Supply Association, 1961. 122 pp.
For the young reader.

5221 Vereker, Barbara. The Story of Films. London: Hutchinson, 1961. 128 pp.
For the young reader.

5222 Field, Mary and Miller, Maud with Manvell, Roger. The
Boys' and Girls' Book of Films and Television. New
York: Roy, 1962. 143 pp.
For the young reader.

5223 Jennings, Gary. The Movie Book. New York: Dial, 1963.
212 pp.
For the young reader.

5224 Minney, R. J. The Film Maker and His World: A Young
Person's Guide. London: Gollancz, 1964. 160 pp.
For the young reader.

5225 Montagu, Ivor. Film World: A Guide to Cinema. Baltimore:
Penguin, 1964. 327 pp.

5226 Barry, Sir Gerald; Bronowski, J.; Huxley, Sir Julian; and
others (eds.) The Doubleday Pictorial Library of the
Arts: Man's Creative Imagination. Garden City, N.Y.:
Doubleday, 1965. 367 pp. (Also published as Man the
Artist: His Creative Imagination.)
Includes a section on film by Basil Wright.

5227 Manvell, Roger. What Is a Film? London: MacDonald,

1965. 184 pp.

5228   Altshuler, Thelma and Janaro, Richard Paul. Responses to Drama: An Introduction to Plays and Movies. Boston: Houghton Mifflin, 1967. 351 pp.

5229   Kernodle, George R. Invitation to the Theatre. New York: Harcourt, Brace, 1967. 677 pp.
Includes a section on the motion picture.

5230   Kuhns, William and Stanley, Robert. Exploring the Film. Dayton, Ohio: Pflaum, 1968. 190 pp. (Published with Teaching Program: Exploring the Film, 94 pp.)

5231   Bobker, Lee R. Elements of Film. New York: Harcourt, Brace, 1969. 303 pp. (Revised New York: Harcourt, Brace, Jovanovich, 1974, 272 pp.)

5232   Feyen, Sharon and Wigal, Donald (eds.) Screen Experience: An Approach to Film. Dayton, Ohio: Pflaum, 1969. 273 pp.

5233   Lignell, E. E. The Mobile Image, Film as Environment. New York: Herder and Herder, 1970. 32 pp.

5234   Linden, George W. Reflections on the Screen. Belmont, Cal.: Wadsworth, 1970. 297 pp.

5235   Sohn, David A. Film: The Creative Eye. Dayton, Ohio: Pflaum, 1970. 176 pp.
Discussion of film aesthetics via analysis of 17 short films; includes material on Saul Bass, Fred Hudson, Dan McLaughlin, Charles Braverman, David Adams, Greg MacGillivray, and Jim Freeman.

5236   Fischer, Edward. Film as Insight. Notre Dame, Ind.: Fides Press, 1971. 208 pp.

5237   Garrett, George P; Hardison, O. B., Jr.; and Gelfman, Jane R. (eds.) Film Scripts [In Four Volumes].
Volume I, Film Scripts One. New York: Appleton-Century-Crofts, 1971. 544 pp. Volume II, Film Scripts Two. 1971. 548 pp. Volume III, Film Scripts Three. 1972. 618 pp. Volume IV, Film Scripts Four. 1972. 500 pp. (Published with Suggestions for Instructors to Accompany Film Scripts One and Film Scripts Two, 1971, 95 pp.)
An introduction to film through the study of 12 scripts: HENRY V, THE BIG SLEEP, A STREETCAR NAMED DESIRE, HIGH NOON, TWELVE ANGRY MEN, THE DEFIANT ONES, THE APARTMENT, THE MISFITS, CHARADE, A HARD DAY'S NIGHT, THE BEST MAN, and DARLING.

5238 Jinks, William. The Celluloid Literature: Film in the Humanities. Beverly Hills, Cal.: Glencoe Press, 1971. 164 pp.

5239 Wlaschin, Ken. The Bluffer's Guide to the Cinema. New York: Crown, 1971. 64 pp.
A guide to critical consensus on directors, actors, and genres.

5240 Coynik, David. Film: Real to Reel. Winona, Minn.: St. Mary's College Press, 1972. 274 pp. (Published with Teaching Guide for Film: Real to Reel.)

5241 Giannetti, Louis D. Understanding Movies. Englewood Cliffs, N.J.: Prentice-Hall, 1972. 217 pp.

5242 Kinder, Marsha and Houston, Beverle. Close-Up: A Critical Perspective on Film. New York: Harcourt Brace Jovanovich, 1972. 395 pp.
Deals with a variety of films from different aesthetic contexts.

5243 Kuhns, William. Movies in America. Dayton, Ohio: Pflaum/ Standard, 1972. 248 pp. (Published with Teaching in the Dark: Resource Guide for Movies in America, by William Kuhns and John Carr, 1973, 110 pp.)

5244 McKowen, Clark and Sparke, William. It's Only a Movie. Designed by Mel Byars. Englewood Cliffs, N.J.: Prentice-Hall, 1972. 188 pp.
Wide ranging visual-verbal anthology on films and filmmaking.

5245 Perkins, William H. Learning the Liveliest Arts: The Critical Enjoyment of Film and Television. Sydney: Angus and Robertson, 1972. 319 pp.

5246 Solomon, Stanley J. The Film Idea. New York: Harcourt Brace Jovanovich, 1972. 403 pp.

5247 Starr, Cecile. Discovering the Movies: An Illustrated Introduction to the Motion Picture. New York: Van Nostrand Reinhold, 1972. 144 pp.

5248 Stewart, Bruce. The World of Film: An Introduction to the Cinema. Richmond, Va.: John Knox, 1972. 75 pp.

5249 Harrington, John. The Rhetoric of Film. New York: Holt, Rinehart and Winston, 1973. 175 pp.

5250 Madsen, Roy Paul. The Impact of Film: How Ideas Are

Communicated Through Cinema and Television. New
York: Macmillan, 1973. 571 pp.

5251 Wald, Malvin and Werner, Michael (comps.) Three Major
Screenplays. New York: Globe, 1973. 394 pp. (Published with a teacher's manual.)
Screenplays of THE OXBOW INCIDENT, HIGH NOON,
and LILIES OF THE FIELD; articles about the films; and
general film education material.

5252 Roberge, Gaston. Chitra Bani: A Book on Film Appreciation. Calcutta: Chitra Bani, 1974. 274 pp.

5253 Blumenberg, Richard M. Critical Focus: An Introduction to
Film. Belmont, Cal.: Wadsworth, 1975. 315 pp.

5254 DeNitto, Dennis and Herman, William. Film and the Critical
Eye. New York: Macmillan, 1975. 543 pp.
Includes analysis of THE LAST LAUGH, THE GOLD
RUSH, M, GRAND ILLUSION, THE RULES OF THE GAME,
BEAUTY AND THE BEAST, RASHOMON, LA RONDE, THE
SEVENTH SEAL, WILD STRAWBERRIES, ASHES AND
DIAMONDS, L'AVVENTURA, IL POSTO, and JULES AND
JIM; intended to be used as an introductory text.

5255 Fell, John L. Film: An Introduction. New York: Praeger,
1975. 274 pp.

5256 Halliwell, Leslie and Murray, Graham. The Clapperboard
Book of the Cinema. London: Hart-Davis, 1975. 126 pp.
For the young reader.

5257 Kuhns, William with Groetsch, Raymond and McJimsey, Joe.
The Moving Picture Book. Dayton, Ohio: Pflaum, 1975.
292 pp.

5258 Scott, James F. Film, The Medium and the Maker. New
York: Holt, Rinehart and Winston, 1975. 340 pp.

3. Film Societies

        This section is composed of books dealing with the forming
and running of film societies. For rental information on full-length,
non-educational motion pictures, see James Limbacher's Feature
Films on 8mm and 16mm and Linda Artel and Kathleen Weaver's
Film Programmer's Guide to 16mm Rentals in Part X, section B-3.
For material on the use of film in the community, the church, the
study group, and in other educational contexts, see Part X, section
B-1, the use of film as an educational resource.

5259   Parnaby, Mary C. and Woodhouse, Maurice T. (eds.)   Children's Cinema Clubs. London: British Film Institute, 1947. 9 pp.

5260   Federation of Film Societies and the British Film Institute. Forming and Running a Film Society. London: Federation of Film Societies and the British Film Institute, 1950. 36 pp. (Revised 1961, 24 pp.)

5261   Hodgkinson, A. W. (ed.)   Twenty Films to Use in Junior Film Societies. London: British Film Institute and the Society of Film Teachers, 1953. 65 pp.

5262   Starr, Cecile with Henig, Carolyn (eds.)   Film Society Primer: A Compilation of Twenty-Two Articles About and For Film Societies. Forest Hills, N.Y.: American Federation of Film Societies, 1956. 84 pp.

5263   Kidd, J. Roby and Storr, Carter B.   Film Utilization: A Handbook for Leaders in Community Groups, Film Councils, Home and School Associations, Parent Teacher Groups, Women's Clubs and Service Clubs, Farm and Labour Organizations, Schools, Colleges, Church Organizations. New York: Educational Film Library Association, ca. 1957. 47 pp.

5264   Smith, Jack. Running a School Film Society. London: Society of Film Teachers, 1958.

5265   Beauvais, Jean and Cote, Guy-L.   Handbook for Canadian Film Societies. Ottawa: Canadian Federation of Film Societies, 1959. 116 pp.

5266   Limbacher, James L. A Handbook for Film Societies. Dearborn, Mich.: Dearborn Public Library(?), 1965. 10 ℓ.

5267   McAnany, Emile G. and Williams, Robert. The Filmviewer's Handbook. Glen Rock, N.J.: Paulist, 1965. 208 pp.
       Primarily about organizing a film society, but includes introductory historical and aesthetic material as well.

5268   Vannoey, R. C. (ed.) A Film Society Handbook. London: Society for Education in Film and Television, ca. 1965. 53 pp.

5269   Limbacher, James L. (ed.) Using Films: A Handbook for the Program Planner. New York: Educational Film Library Association, 1967. 130 pp.

5270   Weiner, Janet. How to Organize and Run a Film Society. New York: Macmillan, 1973. 210 pp.

B. FILM AS RESOURCE

This classification includes those books which deal with film as an educational resource. It has been divided into three sub-sections: B-1, which is composed of those books which discuss ways in which film can be used as an educational resource toward study in other disciplines; B-2, which is composed of those books which serve as general guides to the use of audio-visual materials, including film; and B-3, those books which are primarily 16mm film and audio-visual catalogs intended as reference resources for the teacher planning to integrate educational films into his/her curriculum. For further material, outside the scope of this bibliography, the reader should consult bibliographies of education.

1. The Use of Film as an Educational Resource

5271 Dale, Edgar and others (eds.) Motion Pictures in Education: A Summary of the Literature. (Originally published 1937.) New York: Arno, 1970. 472 pp.
Surveys aspects of teaching with visual aids.

5272 Adam, T. R. Motion Pictures in Adult Education. New York: American Association for Adult Education, 1940. 94 pp.

5273 Cochran, Blake. Films on War and American Policy. Washington, D.C.: American Council of Education, 1940. 63 pp.
Using film to teach an understanding of the war situation.

5274 The Staff of the Tower Hill School. A School Uses Motion Pictures. Washington, D.C.: American Council on Education, 1940. 114 pp.

5275 Bell, Reginald; Cain, Leo F.; Lamoreaux, Lillian A.; and others. Motion Pictures in a Modern Curriculum: A Report on the Use of Films in the Santa Barbara Schools.

Washington, D.C.: American Council on Education, 1941.
179 pp.

5276 Hoban, Charles F., Jr. Focus on Learning: Motion Pictures
in the School. Washington, D.C.: American Council on
Education, 1942. 172 pp.

5277 McDonald, Gerald Doan. Educational Motion Pictures and
Libraries. Chicago: American Library Association,
1942. 184 pp.

5278 Carter, S. B. The Films. London: Workers' Educational
Association, 1945. 20 pp. (Revised as Ourselves and
the Cinema, 1948, 44 pp.)
      Suggested film discussion topics for Workers' Educa-
tional Association groups.

5279 Rosenthal, Newman Hirsch. Films in Instruction [in Two
Volumes]. Volume I, Films, Their Use and Misuse.
Melbourne: Robertson and Mullens, 1945. 36 pp.
Volume II, The Teacher's Manual. 1947.

5280 Wenger, Roy Emerson. Motion Pictures in Teacher Education at the Ohio State University. Ohio State University:
Ph.D., 1945. 224 pp.

5281 Benoit-Levy, Jean Albert. The Art of the Motion Picture.
New York: Coward-McCann, 1946. 263 pp. Translated
by Theodore R. Jaeckel. (Reprinted New York: Arno,
1970.)
      Includes a major section on the educational role of
films.

5282 Educational Film Library Association, Committee on Community Use of Film. Making Films Work for Your Community: A Project of the Educational Film Library Association. New York: Educational Film Library Association,
1946. 71 pp. (Also titled A Handbook on How to Use
Educational Films in the Community.)

5283 Fern, George H. and Robbins, Eldon. Teaching With Films.
Milwaukee: Bruce, 1946. 146 pp.

5284 Hoban, Charles F., Jr. Movies That Teach. New York:
Dryden, 1946. 189 pp.

5285 Wittich, Walter Arno and Fowlkes, John Guy. Audio-Visual
Paths to Learning: A Comparison of Three Classroom
Methods of Using Educational Sound Films. New York,
London: Harper, 1946. 135 pp.

5286 British Film Institute. The Film in Colonial Development:

A Report of a Conference. London: British Film Institute, 1948. 53 pp.
Deals with the film's educational use, particularly its effects on illiterates.

5287   Elliott, Godfrey M. Film and Education: A Symposium on the Role of Film in the Field of Education. New York: Philosophical Library, 1948. 597 pp.

5288   American Council on Education, Commission on Motion Pictures: Mark A. May, chairman. Planning Films for Schools: The Final Report of the Commission on Motion Pictures. Washington, D.C.: American Council on Education, 1949. 34 pp.

5289   Greenhill, Leslie P. and Tyo, John. Instructional Film Production, Utilization, and Research in Great Britain, Canada, and Australia. Port Washington, New York: Office of Naval Research, Special Devices Center, 1949. 27 ℓ.

5290   Waldron, Gloria with Starr, Cecile. The Information Film: A Report of the Public Library Inquiry. New York: Columbia University Press, 1949. 281 pp.
Material on the educational use and distribution of the documentary film as well as on library film services.

5291   Buchanan, Andrew. The Film in Education. London: Phoenix, 1951. 256 pp.

5292   Starr, Cecile (ed.) Ideas on Film: A Handbook for the 16mm Film User. New York: Funk and Wagnalls, 1951. 251 pp.
With contributions by Rudolph Arnheim, Willard Van Dyke, Irving Jacoby, Arthur Knight, Amos Vogel, Pearl S. Buck, Arthur Mayer, and others.

5293   Davidson, Arthur O. Deterrents to Film Use in School. Harvard University: Ph.D., 1952.

5294   Guss, Carolyn. A Study of Film Evaluation and Selection Practices in Twelve Universities and Colleges with Recommendations for Improvements. Indiana University: Ph.D., 1952.

5295   Kidd, J. Roby. Pictures with a Purpose: The Distribution of Non-Theatrical Films in Canada. Toronto: Canadian Association for Adult Education, 1953. 72 pp.

5296   Meierhenry, Wesley C. Enriching the Curriculum Through Motion Pictures: Final Report. Lincoln: University of Nebraska Press, 1953. 255 pp.

Report of the Nebraska Program of Education Enrichment Through the Use of Motion Pictures.

5297   Smith, R. A. N. The Loop Film: A Practical Manual for Teachers, Sports Coaches, Research Workers and Managers in Industry. London: Current Affairs, 1953. 109 pp.

5298   Alter, Forrest and others. Sixty Years of 16mm Film 1923-1983: A Symposium. Evanston, Ill.: Film Council of America, 1954. 220 pp.
Anthology providing overview of 16mm production, distribution, and usage in educational institutions, government, industry, church, etc.

5299   Morton-Williams, P. Cinema in Rural Nigeria: A Field Study of the Impact of Fundamental-Educational Films on Rural Audiences in Nigeria. Lagos(?): Federal Information Service, ca. 1955. 195 pp.

5300   Kidd, J. Roby and Storr, Carter B. Film Utilization: A Handbook for Leaders in Community Groups, Film Councils, Home and School Associations, Parent Teacher Groups, Women's Clubs and Service Clubs, Farm and Labour Organizations, Schools, Colleges, Church Organizations. New York: Educational Film Library Association, ca. 1957. 47 pp.

5301   May, Mark A. and Lumsdaine, Arthur A. Learning From Films. New Haven: Yale University Press, 1958. 357 pp.

5302   British Film Institute and the Association of Teachers in Colleges and Departments of Education. Film and Television in Education for Teaching: A Report of a Joint Working Party. London: British Film Institute, 1959. 66 pp.

5303   Hefzallah, Ibrahim Mikhail Hanna. Adaptation of Educational Films. Ohio State University: Ph.D., 1959. 228 pp.
Adapting educational films of one language to another.

5304   Forsdale, Louis (ed.) 8mm Sound Film and Education. New York: Bureau of Publications, Teachers College, Columbia University, 1962. 166 pp.
Proceedings of a conference held at Teachers College on November 8, 9, and 10, 1961.

5305   Friedlander, Madeline S. Leading Film Discussions: A Handbook for Discussion Leaders to Use Films Effectively to Conduct Film Discussion Workshops. New York: League of Women Voters of the City of New York, 1963. 59 pp. (Revised with subtitle A Guide to Using Films for Discussion, Training Leaders, Planning Effective Programs, 1972, 42 pp.)

5306   Judd, R. Stephen. Teaching by Projection. London: Focal, 1963. 170 pp.

5307   UNESCO, Mass Communication Techniques Division. The Teaching Film in Primary Education. Paris: UNESCO, 1963. 51 pp.

5308   Chamberlin, Ray Philip. Cinema in Adult Education: A Study of the Feature Film Series in America. University of California, Los Angeles: Ed.D., 1965. 259 pp.

5309   Groves, Peter D. (ed.) Film in Higher Education and Research. Elmsford, N.Y.: Pergamon, 1966. 332 pp.

5310   Jones, George William. Sunday Night at the Movies. Richmond, Va.: John Knox, 1967. 127 pp.
The use of film in the church.

5311   Limbacher, James L. (ed.) Using Films: A Handbook for the Program Planner. New York: Educational Film Library Association, 1967. 130 pp.

5312   Beeler, Duane and McCallister, Frank. Creative Use of Films in Education: A Case Study of an Adult Educational Program for Union Leaders. Chicago: Roosevelt University, Labor Education Division, 1968. 86 pp.

5313   Eastman Kodak Company. Movies with a Purpose: A Teacher's Guide to Planning and Producing Super 8 Movies for Classroom Use. Rochester, New York: Eastman Kodak Company, ca. 1968. 27 pp.

5314   Mallery, David. Film in the Life of the School: Programs, Practices, and New Directions. Boston: National Association of Independent Schools, 1968. 53 pp.

5315   Heyer, Robert and Meyer, Anthony. Discovery in Film. Paramus, N.J.: Paulist-Newman, 1969. 220 pp.
Discusses the use of the short film for educational purposes: for sourcebook, see entry 5433.

5316   Jackson, B. F., Jr. (ed.) Television-Radio-Film for Churchmen. Nashville, Tenn.: Abingdon, 1969. 317 pp.

5317   Jones, G. William and others (eds.) Dialogue with the World: A Modern Approach to the Humanities. Wilmette, Ill.: Films Inc., ca. 1969. 206 pp.
Reviews and discussion questions for 100 motion pictures.

5318   Pryluck, Calvin. Structure and Function in Educational
       Cinema. Washington, D.C.: U.S. Office of Education,
       Bureau of Research, 1969. 74 ℓ.

5319   Summers, Stanford. Secular Films and the Church's Ministry.
       New York: Seabury, 1969. 64 pp.

5320   Yeamans, George Thomas. Projectionists' Programmed
       Primer. Muncie, Ind.: Ball State Bookstore, 1969.
       Various pagings. (Revised 1973.)
       The use of film in programmed instruction.

5321   Schillaci, Anthony and Culkin, John M. (eds.) Films Deliver:
       Teaching Creatively with Film. New York: Citation,
       1970. 348 pp.

5322   Goldman, Frederick and Burnett, Linda R. Need Johnny
       Read? Practical Methods to Enrich Humanities Courses
       Using Films and Film Study. Dayton, Ohio: Pflaum /
       Standard, 1971. 238 pp.

5323   Hopkinson, Peter. The Role of Film in Development. Paris:
       UNESCO, Department of Mass Communication, 1971.
       51 pp.

5324   Maynard, Richard A. The Celluloid Curriculum: How to Use
       Movies in the Classroom. New York: Hayden, 1971.
       276 pp.

5325   Brown, Roland G. A Bookless Curriculum. Dayton, Ohio:
       Pflaum /Standard, 1972. 134 pp.

5326   Elson, Stewart Leslie. A Model for Film Education in the
       Local Church. School of Theology at Claremont: Ph.D.,
       1972.

5327   Konzelman, Robert G. Marquee Ministry: The Movie
       Theatre as Church and Community Forum. New York:
       Harper and Row, 1972. 123 pp.
       The use of film in religious education.

5328   Jones, George William. Landing Rightside Up in TV and
       Film: An Unusual Experience in Screen Media Readiness
       for Teachers, Churchmen, and Youth-Serving Agencies.
       Nashville, Tenn.: Abingdon, 1973. 128 pp.

5329   O'Connor, John E. and Jackson, Martin A. Teaching History
       with Film. Washington, D.C.: American Historical As-
       sociation, 1974. 74 pp.

5330   Burns, E. Bradford. Latin American Cinema: Film and
       History. Los Angeles: UCLA Latin American Center,

1975. 137 pp.
Discusses the use of film for historical research and
teaching.

2. General Guides to Audio-Visual Materials

5331 Dent, Ellsworth C. The Audio-Visual Handbook. (Originally
published as A Handbook of Visual Instruction, 1934.)
Chicago: Society for Visual Education, 1946. 226 pp.

5332 McClusky, Frederick Dean. Visual-Sensory Instruction in the
Modern School. Ann Arbor, Mich.: Brumfield and Brum-
field, 1940. 101 pp. (Revised as Audio-Visual Teaching
Techniques, Dubuque, Iowa: Brown, 1949, 118 pp.)

5333 McKown, Harry C. and Roberts, Alvin B. Audio-Visual Aids
to Instruction. New York: McGraw-Hill, 1940. 385 pp.

5334 Dale, Edgar. Audio-Visual Methods in Teaching. New York:
Dryden, 1946. 546 pp. (Revised 1954, 534 pp.)

5335 Mannino, Philip. ABC's of Visual Aids and Projectionist's
Manual. Ypsilanti, Mich.: n.p., 1946. 83 pp. (Re-
vised 1948, 110 pp. Revised again as ABC's of Audio-
Visual Equipment and the School Projectionist's Manual,
State College, Pa., 1958, 80 pp.)

5336 Noel, Elizabeth Goudy and Leonard, J. Paul. Foundations
for Teacher Education in Audio-Visual Instruction. Washington, D.C.: American Council on Education, 1947.
60 pp.

5337 Chandler, Anna Curtis and Cypher, Irene F. Audio-Visual
Techniques for Enrichment of the Curriculum. New York:
Noble and Noble, 1948. 252 pp.

5338 Strauss, L. Harry and Kidd, J. Roby. Look, Listen and
Learn: A Manual on the Use of Audio-Visual Materials
in Informal Education. New York: Association Press,
1948. 235 pp.

5339 Henne, Frances; Brooks, Alice; and Ersted, Ruth (eds.)
Youth, Communication and Libraries. Chicago: Ameri-
can Library Association, 1949. 233 pp.
Includes an essay entitled "Audio-Visual Material and
Libraries for Children and Young People" by Margaret I.
Rufsvold.

5340 Kinder, James S. Audio-Visual Materials and Techniques.
New York: American Book Company, 1950. 624 pp.
(Revised 1959, 592 pp.)

5341 Wittich, Walter Arno and Schuller, Charles Francis. Audio-
      Visual Materials: Their Nature and Use. New York:
      Harper, 1953. 564 pp. (Revised 1957, 570 pp.; 1962,
      500 pp; and 1967, 554 pp.)

5342 Freedman, Florence B. and Berg, Esther L. Classroom
      Teacher's Guide to Audio-Visual Materials. Philadelphia:
      Chilton, 1961. 240 pp.

5343 Kemp, Jerrold E. National Workshop on Educational Media
      Demonstrations: Final Report. San Jose, Cal.: San
      Jose State College, 1962. 27 pp.

5344 Kemp, Jerrold E. and others. Planning and Producing
      Audiovisual Materials. San Francisco: Chandler, 1963.
      169 pp. (Revised Scranton, Pa.: Chandler, 1968, 251 pp.)

5345 Eastman Kodak Company. Kodak AV Handbook. Rochester,
      New York: Eastman Kodak Company, ca. 1967. 16
      pamphlets.

5346 Schramm, Wilbur and others. The New Media: Memo to
      Educational Planners. Paris: UNESCO, 1967. 175 pp.
      The educational use of media, including film.

5347 Davis, Harold S. (ed.) Instructional Media Center: Bold
      New Venture. Bloomington: Indiana University Press,
      1971. 237 pp.

5348 Linton, Dolores and David. Practical Guide to Classroom
      Media. Dayton, Ohio: Pflaum/Standard, 1971. 118 pp.

5349 Sedlik, Jay M. Systems Techniques for Pretesting Mediated
      Instructional Materials. Los Angeles: Education and
      Training Consultants, 1971. 110 pp.

5350 Laybourne, Kit. Doing the Media: A Portfolio of Activities
      and Resources. New York: Center for Understanding
      Media, 1972. 219 pp.

5351 Tindall, Kevin; Collins, Bill; and Reid, David. The Elective
      Classroom: Audio Visual Methods in Teaching. Sydney:
      McGraw-Hill, 1973. 188 pp.

5352 Zelmer, A. C. Lynn. Community Media Handbook. Metuchen,
      N.J.: Scarecrow, 1973. 241 pp.

5353 Sive, Mary Robinson. Educator's Guide to Media Lists.
      Littleton, Co.: Libraries Unlimited, 1975. 234 pp.

3.   16mm Film and Audio-Visual Catalogs

This section is composed primarily of 16mm film and
audio-visual catalogs intended as reference resources. The reader
is particularly directed to the Library of Congress Catalog: Motion
Pictures and Filmstrips for the most comprehensive, continuing
listing of educational and instructive films. Although we have not
included distributors' catalogs, because they are issued with such
frequency, they are available from the distributors themselves;
addresses may be found in James Limbacher's Feature Films on
8mm and 16mm and in Linda Artel and Kathleen Weaver's Film
Programmer's Guide to 16mm Rentals, among other sources. For
annual audio-visual references or directories to audio-visual services, the reader is directed to the reference sections, Part I,
sections A-3 and A-4. For discussion and listings of films for
children see also the children's genre category, Part V, section E.

5354   Cochran, Blake. Films on War and American Policy. Wash-
          ington, D.C.: American Council on Education, 1940.
          63 pp.

5355   American Council on Education, Committee on Motion Pictures
          in Education. Selected Educational Motion Pictures: A
          Descriptive Encyclopedia. Washington, D.C.: American
          Council on Education, 1942. 372 pp.

5356   Losey, Mary. Films for the Community in Wartime. New
          York: National Board of Review of Motion Pictures, 1943.
          78 pp.

5357   U.S. Employment Service. Industrial Films: A Source of
          Occupational Information. Washington, D.C.: U.S. Em-
          ployment Service, Occupational Analysis and Industrial
          Services Division, 1946. 72 pp.

5358   U.S. Library of Congress, Motion Picture Division. Guide
          to United States Government Motion Pictures. Edited by
          Henrietta B. Perry. Washington, D.C.: U.S. Govern-
          ment Printing Office, 1947. 104 pp.

5359   Gilbert, Dorothy B. (ed.) Guide to Art Films. Washington,
          D.C.: American Federation of Arts, 1949. 28 pp.
          (Revised 1950, 40 pp.)

5360   International Council of Religious Education. AVRG: Audio-
          Visual Resource Guide for Use in Religious Education.
          New York: International Council of Religious Education,
          Department of Audio-Visual and Radio Education, 1949.
          (Ninth edition 1972, 477 pp.)

5361 Reid, Seerley. Motion Pictures on Democracy: A Selective
      Bibliography of 16mm Sound Films Selected and Recom-
      mended by an Office of Education Advisory Committee.
      Washington, D.C.: Federal Security Agency, Office of
      Education, 1949. 39 pp. (Revised as 102 Motion Pic-
      tures on Democracy: 16mm Sound Films Selected and
      Recommended by an Office of Education Advisory Com-
      mittee, 1950, 51 pp.)

5362 UNESCO. Films on Art: A Specialized Study. Paris:
      UNESCO, 1949. 72 pp.

5363 The Editors of Business Screen Magazine. The Index of
      Training Films. Chicago: Business Screen Magazine,
      ca. 1950. 86 pp.

5364 McClusky, Frederick D. The A.-V. Bibliography. Dubuque,
      Iowa: Brown, 1950. 185 pp. (Revised 1955, 218 pp.)

5365 Reid, Seerley. United States Government and Pan American
      Union Motion Pictures on the Other American Republics.
      Washington, D.C.: U.S. Government Printing Office,
      1950. 16 pp.

5366 UNESCO. An International Index of Films on the Conserva-
      tion and Utilization of Resources. Lake Success, United
      Nations: UNESCO, 1950. 175 pp.

5367 UNESCO-WHO. Child Welfare Films: An International Index
      of Films and Filmstrips on the Health and Welfare of
      Children. Geneva: UNESCO-WHO, 1950. 213 pp.

5368 Association of American Medical Colleges, Medical Audio-
      Visual Institute. Reviews of Films in Atomic Medicine,
      Prepared by Medical Film Institute of the American
      Medical Colleges. Raleigh, N.C.: Health Publications
      Institute, 1951. 65 pp.

5369 Association of American Medical Colleges, Medical Audio-
      Visual Institute. Reviews of Films in Medicine and Re-
      lated Sciences. Edited by Adolf Nichtenhauser and John
      L. Meyer, II. New York(?): n.p., 1951.

5370 Reid, Seerley and Wilkins, Virginia. 3434 U.S. Government
      Films. Washington, D.C.: Federal Security Agency,
      Office of Education, 1951. 329 pp.

5371 British Film Institute. Films From Britain: 1,000 Films
      on Educational, Scientific and Cultural Subjects, Available
      for Sale Abroad. London: Her Majesty's Stationery
      Office, 1952. 158 pp.

5372 Chapman, William McKissack. Films on Art 1952. New

York: American Federation of Arts, printed in Kingsport, Tenn.:   Kingsport Press, 1952.   160 pp.

5373   Jones, Emily Strange (ed.)   Films and People: A Descriptive
Catalog of Selected Films on United Nations and UNESCO
Topics, With Purchase and Rental Sources.   New York:
Educational Film Library Association, 1952.   31 pp.

5374   Notarius, Nanette and Larson, Allan S. (comps.)   The Handbook of Free Films.   New York: Allanan Associates,
1952.   237 pp.
Includes over 2000 films.

5375   Scientific Film Association, London.   List of Distributors of
Industrial Films.   London: Scientific Film Association,
1952.   23 ℓ.

5376   Scientific Film Association, London.   List of Films on
Farming, Gardening, Forestry, Beekeeping.   London:
Scientific Film Association, 1952.   33 pp.

5377   Association of American Medical Colleges, Medical Audio-
Visual Institute.   Films in Psychiatry, Psychology and
Mental Health.   New York: Health Education Council,
1953.   269 pp.
With contributions by Adolf Nichtenhauser, Marie L.
Coleman, and David S. Ruhe.

5378   Ruhe, David S. and others.   Films in the Cardiovascular
Diseases: Survey, Analysis, and Conclusions [in Two
Volumes].   Volume I.   New York: Association of Ameri-
can Medical Colleges, Medical Audio-Visual Institute and
the American Heart Association, 1953.   Volume II, Survey
Conclusion.   1954.

5379   U.S. Library of Congress.   Library of Congress Catalog:
Motion Pictures and Filmstrips: A Cumulative List of
Works Represented by Library of Congress Printed Cards.
1953-1957 reference work published as Volume 28 of The
National Union Catalog.   1958-1962 reference work published as Volumes 53 and 54 of The National Union Catalog.
1963-1967 reference work published as two volumes of
The National Union Catalog.   1968-1972 reference work
published as four volumes of The National Union Catalog.
1973 reference work published as Library of Congress
Catalog: Films and Other Materials for Projection.   1974
reference work published as Library of Congress Catalog:
Films and Other Materials for Projection.   1975 reference
work published as Library of Congress Catalog: Films and
Other Materials for Projection.
A comprehensive listing of films especially of educational or instructive value released in the United States
or Canada; provides credits and synopses.

5380   Lavastida, A. (ed.) Motion Pictures Produced by Members
       of the University Film Producers Association. New York:
       Educational Film Library Association, 1954. 84 pp.

5381   American Library Association, Audio-Visual Board. Films
       for Public Libraries, Selected by a Committee of the
       American Library Association Audio-Visual Board. Chi-
       cago: American Library Association, 1955. 60 pp.

5382   Reid, Seerley with Carpenter, Anita and Daugherty, Annie
       Rose. U.S. Government Films for Public Educational
       Use. Washington, D.C.: U.S. Department of Health,
       Education, and Welfare, 1955. 651 pp. (Revised with
       Katharine W. Clugston, 1961, 502 pp.)

5383   UNESCO, Department of Mass Communications. Catalogues
       of Short Films and Filmstrips: Selected List. Paris:
       UNESCO, Clearing House, Department of Mass Communi-
       cations, 1955. 25 pp. (Revised as Selected List of
       Catalogues for Short Films and Filmstrips, 1965, 36 pp.)

5384   Scientific Film Association, London. Films on Anaesthesia
       and Related Subjects. London: Scientific Film Associa-
       tion, 1956. 40 pp.

5385   Scientific Film Association, London. Films on Education:
       A Catalogue Prepared in Collaboration with the University
       of London Institute of Education. London: Scientific Film
       Association, 1957. 43 pp.

5386   Scientific Film Association, London. Films on Psychology
       and Psychiatry: A Catalogue Prepared in Collaboration
       with the University of London Institute of Education.
       London: Scientific Film Association, 1957. 64 pp.

5387   U.S. Department of Health, Education, and Welfare. Motion
       Pictures and Recordings on Aging: A Selected Listing of
       Visual and Auditory Presentations Compiled by the Special
       Staff on Aging. Washington, D.C.: U.S. Department of
       Health, Education, and Welfare, 1957. 31 pp.

5388   Joint Council on Economic Education. 100 Selected Films in
       Economic Education. New York: Joint Council on Eco-
       nomic Education, 1960. 34 pp.

5389   Shetler, Donald J. Film Guide for Music Educators. Wash-
       ington, D.C.: Music Educators National Conference,
       1961. 119 pp.

5390   American Library Association, Audio-Visual Committee.
       Films for Libraries: Selected by a Subcommittee of the
       American Library Association Audio-Visual Committee.
       Chicago: American Library Association, 1962. 81 pp.

5391   U.S. Government Films.   Washington, D.C.:   Norwood Films,
       1962.   87 pp.

5392   Bell, Violet M. and others (eds.)   A Guide to Films, Film-
       strips, Maps and Globes, Records on Asia.   New York:
       Asia Society, 1964.   87 pp.

5393   Educational Media Council.   Educational Media Index [in 14
       Volumes].   New York: McGraw-Hill, 1964--.
       Audio-visual index, including film, to various educa-
       tional subjects.

5394   Educational Film Library Association.   Film Evaluation Guide
       1946-1964.   New York: Educational Film Library Asso-
       ciation, 1965.   528 pp.   (Supplement [to] Film Evaluation
       Guide published 1968, 157 pp.   Supplement Two [to] Film
       Evaluation Guide published 1972, 131 pp.)
       Synopsis, limited credits, and evaluation of 5000
       films altogether.

5395   Limbacher, James L. (comp.)   A Directory of 16mm Sound
       Feature Films Available for Rental in the United States.
       New York: Continental 16, distributed by the Educational
       Film Library Association, 1966.   102 pp.   (Revised as
       Feature Films on 8mm and 16mm: A Directory of
       Feature Films Available for Rental, Sale and Lease in
       the United States.   New York: Educational Film Library
       Association, 1969.   Third edition New York: Bowker,
       1971, 269 pp.   Fourth edition published as Feature Films
       on 8mm and 16mm: A Directory of Feature Films Avail-
       able for Rental, Sale, and Lease in the United States,
       with Serials and Director's Indexes, 1974, 368 pp.)

5396   Stevens, Warren D. (ed.)   African Film Bibliography, 1965.
       Bloomington, Ind.:   African Studies Association, 1966.
       31 pp.
       Descriptions of films about sub-Saharan Africa.

5397   Ackermann, Jean Marie.   Guide to Films on International
       Development.   Beverly Hills, Cal.:   Film Sense, 1967.
       53 pp.   (Revised as Films of a Changing World: A
       Critical International Guide, Washington: Society for
       International Development, 1972, 106 pp.)

5398   Kuhns, William.   Short Films in Religious Education.   Day-
       ton, Ohio: Pflaum, 1967.   129 pp.

5399   McCaffrey, Patrick J.   A Guide to Short Films for Religious
       Education Programs.   Notre Dame, Ind.:   Fides Press,
       1967.   106 pp.

5400   Powell, G. H. and L. S.   A Guide to the 8mm Loop Film.

London: British Association for Commercial and Industrial Education, 1967. 43 pp.

5401   Scottish Central Film Library, Glasgow. Catalogue of 16mm. Silent Educational, Documentary and Classic Films. Glasgow: Scottish Film Office, 1967. 95 pp.

5402   Scottish Central Film Library, Glasgow. Visual Aids: Films, Filmstrips, Loop Films, Produced by Educational Films of Scotland. Glasgow: Scottish Central Film Library, ca. 1967. 19 pp.

5403   Solomon, Martin B., Jr. and Lovan, Nora G. Annotated Bibliography of Films in Automation, Data Processing and Computer Science. Lexington: University of Kentucky Press, 1967. 38 pp.

5404   Kingdon, J. M. (ed.) A Classified Guide to Sources of Educational Film Material. London(?): Educational Foundation for Visual Aids and National Committee for Audio-Visual Aids in Education, 1968. 48 pp.

5405   McCaffrey, Patrick J. A Guide to Short Films for Religious Education, II, Including Some Experiences with Use of Films. Notre Dame, Ind.: Fides Press, 1968. 108 pp.

5406   UNESCO. Ten Years of Films on Ballet and Classical Dance, 1956-1965. Paris: UNESCO, 1968. 105 pp.

5407   American Association of Industrial Management. Film Guide for Industrial Training. Philadelphia: American Association of Industrial Management, 1969. 187 pp.

5408   Cushing, Jane. 101 Films for Character Growth. Notre Dame, Ind.: Fides Press, 1969. 110 pp.

5409   Goodman, Louis S. Films for Personnel Management: An Annotated Directory of 16mm Films, Filmstrips, and Videotapes. New York: Educational Film Library Association, 1969. 116 pp.

5410   Kone, Grace (comp.) 8mm Film Directory 1969-1970. New York: Educational Film Library Association, 1969. 532 pp.
          Information on over 8000 films.

5411   National Audiovisual Center. U.S. Government Films: A Catalog of Motion Pictures and Filmstrips for Sale by the National Audiovisual Center. Washington, D.C.: National Archives and Records Service, General Services Administration, 1969. 165 pp.

5412   National Information Center for Educational Media. Index to

8mm Motion Cartridges. New York: Bowker, 1969.
402 pp. (Second edition Los Angeles: University of
Southern California Press, 1971, 210 pp. Third edition
1973, 689 pp.)
   Guide to commercially produced educational 8mm
cartridges.

5413 National Information Center For Educational Media. Index
      to 16mm Educational Films. New York: Bowker, 1969.
      1111 pp. (Third edition Los Angeles: University of
      Southern California Press, 1971, 729 pp. Fourth edition
      1973.)

5414 Sprecher, Daniel. Guide to Films (16mm) About Famous
      People. Alexandria, Va.: Serina, 1969. 206 pp.
      Contains synopses of over 1400 films.

5415 Sprecher, Daniel. Guide to Foreign Government Loan Film,
      16mm. Alexandria, Va.: Serina, 1969. 136 pp. (Re-
      vised 1970, 205 pp.)
        Catalogue of 3000 films available from 66 foreign
      countries.

5416 Sprecher, Daniel. Guide to Government-Loan Film (16mm).
      Alexandria, Va.: Serina, 1969. 130 pp.

5417 Sprecher, Daniel. Guide to Military-Loan Film (16mm).
      Alexandria, Va.: Serina, 1969. 148 pp.

5418 Sprecher, Daniel. Guide to State-Loan Film (16mm).
      Alexandria, Va.: Serina, 1969. 56 pp.

5419 Dougal, Lucy. The War/Peace Film Guide. Berkeley, Ca.:
      World Without War Council, 1970. 50 pp. (Revised
      Chicago: World Without War, 1973, 123 pp.)

5420 Kennedy, Peter (ed.) Films on Traditional Music and Dance:
      A First International Catalogue Compiled by the Inter-
      national Folk Music Council. Paris: UNESCO, 1970.
      261 pp.

5421 Kuhns, William. Themes: Short Films for Discussion.
      Dayton, Ohio: Pflaum, 1970. Loose-leaf.

5422 New York Library Association; Esther Helfand, Chairman.
      Films for Young Adults: A Selected List and Guide to
      Programming. New York: Educational Film Library
      Association, 1970. 34 pp.

5423 Sprecher, Daniel. Guide to Films (16mm) About Negroes.
      Alexandria, Va.: Serina, 1970. 87 pp.

5424   Sprecher, Daniel. Guide to Free-Loan Training Films
        (16mm). Alexandria: Serina, 1970. 205 pp.

5425   Turner, D. John (ed.) 800 Films for Film Study. Ottawa:
        Canadian Film Institute, 1970. 112 pp.

5426   Jones, Emily S. (ed.) The College Film Library Collection:
        A Selected Annotated List of Films for Use in College
        and Advanced High School Courses [in Two Volumes].
        Williamsport, Pa.: Bro-Dart, 1971.

5427   Sprecher, Daniel. Guide to Films (16mm) About Ecology,
        Adaptation, and Pollution. Alexandria, Va.: Serina,
        1971. 55 pp.

5428   Sprecher, Daniel. Guide to Films (16mm) About the Use of
        Dangerous Drugs, Narcotics, Alcohol, and Tobacco.
        Alexandria, Va.: Serina, 1971. 61 pp.

5429   Sprecher, Daniel. Guide to Personal Guidance Films
        (16mm). Alexandria, Va.: Serina, 1971. 36 pp.

5430   Artel, Linda J. and Weaver, Kathleen (eds.) Film Program-
        mer's Guide to 16mm Rentals. San Francisco: San
        Francisco Community Press, 1972. 164 pp.

5431   Parlato, Salvatore J., Jr. Films--Too Good for Words: A
        Directory of Nonnarrated 16mm Films. New York:
        Bowker, 1972. 209 pp.

5432   Women's History Research Center. Films by and/or About
        Women 1972: Directory of Filmmakers, Films, and
        Distributors, Internationally, Past and Present. Berkeley:
        Cal.: Women's History Research Center, 1973. 72 pp.

5433   Gordon, Malcolm W. Discovery in Film: Book 2, A Teacher
        Sourcebook. Paramus, N.J.: Paulist-Newman, 1973.
        162 pp.
        For Book 1, see entry 5315.

5434   Minus, Johnny and Hale, William Storm (comps.) Film
        Superlist: Twenty Thousand Motion Pictures in the Public
        Domain [in Ten Volumes]. New York: 7 Arts, 1973.

5435   Winick, Mariann P. Films for Early Childhood: A Selected
        Annotated Bibliography. New York: Early Childhood
        Education Council of New York City, 1973. 124 pp.
        Descriptions of several hundred films.

5436   Kuhns, William. Themes Two: One Hundred Short Films
        for Discussion. Dayton, Ohio: Pflaum, 1974. 193 pp.

5437   Raab, Ernest L. and Perry, Nancy. 16mm Film Resources:
       A Handbook for 16mm Film Programmers in the United
       States and Canada. Stanford, Cal.: Association of Col-
       lege Unions, 1974. 36 pp.

5438   Dawson, Bonnie. Women's Films in Print: An Annotated
       Guide to 800 16mm Films by Women. San Francisco:
       Booklegger Press, 1975. 165 pp.

5439   Langman, Larry and Fajans, Milt. Cinema and the School:
       A Guide to 101 Major American Films. Dayton, Ohio:
       Pflaum, 1975. 157 pp.

5440   Morrison, James and Blue, Richard. Political Change: A
       Film Guide. Minneapolis, Minn.: Audio Visual Library
       Service, University of Minnesota, 1975. 87 pp.
       Material on films dealing with political change and
       economic development.

5441   Rehrauer, George. The Short Film: An Evaluative Selection
       of 500 Recommended Films. New York: Macmillan,
       1975. 199 pp.

5442   Women's Films: A Critical Guide. Bloomington: Audio-
       Visual Center, Indiana University, 1975. 121 pp.
       A guide to films by and about women.

TITLE INDEX

New Courts of Industry: Self-
Regulation Under the Mo-
tion Picture Code; Including
an Analysis of the Code
1251, 4936
New Directions in Documentary:
Report of the International
Conference Held at Edin-
burgh, August 25-26, 1952
1757
The New Documentary in Action:
A Casebook in Film-Making
1772, 3743
New Face of the Czechoslovak
Cinema 1677
The New Film Index: A Bib-
liography of Magazine
Articles in English, 1930-
70 421
New Forms in Film 1802
The New Hollywood: American
Movies in the '70s 1507
The New Mass Media: Challenge
to a Free Society 4698
The New Media: Memo to Edu-
cational Planners 5346
New Novel and New Cinema
1606, 4639
A New Pictorial History of the
Talkies 1406, 1411
New Screen Techniques 1045
New Singer, New Song: The
Cliff Richard Story 3314
The New Spirit in the Cinema
1393
The New Spirit in the Russian
Theatre, 1917-1928; and
a Sketch of the Russian
Kinema and Radio, 1919-
1928 ... 1352, 1610,
4661
The New Swedish Cinema 1664
The New Theatre and Cinema
of Soviet Russia 1350,
1609
New Theatres for Old 790,
4663
The New Wave: Critical Land-
marks 4549, 4581
The New York Times Direc-
tory of the Film 304, 412
The New York Times Film
Reviews: A One-Volume

Selection, 1913-1970
4601
The New York Times Film
Reviews, 1971-1972 137,
4595
The New York Times Film
Reviews, 1973-1974 137,
4595
The New York Times Film
Reviews, 1969-1970 137,
4595
The New York Times Film
Reviews, 1913-1968 137,
196, 385, 4595
The New York Times Guide to
Movies on TV 138
Newsreels Across the World
1755
Next Time Drive Off the Cliff!
1517
Nice Work: The Story of
Thirty Years in British
Film Production 2266
A Night at the Opera 4209
Nine American Film Critics:
A Study of Theory and
Practice 4633
The Nine Lives of Billy Rose
3367
The Nine Lives of Michael
Todd 3486
Ninotchka 4212
No Case for Compulsion 1587,
1766
No Chip on My Shoulder 3088
No People Like Show People
3643
No Star Nonsense 2398
Noel 2403
Noel Coward 2401
Non-Book Materials and the
Librarian: A Select Bib-
liography 387
Nonfiction Film: A Critical
History 1775
Norma Jean: The Life of
Marilyn Monroe 3144
Norman McLaren 3042
North by Northwest 4217
The North Star: A Motion
Picture About Some
Russian People 4218
Not by a Long Shot: Adventures

NAME INDEX

685

Barrett, Gillian 496
Barrett, Rona 2151, 3704
Barrie, Wendy 3792
Barrios, Gregg 1789
Barrios, Jaime 782
Barris, Alex 3781, 3798
Barris, George 5055
Barron, Arthur 3738, 3743
Barrot, Jean-Pierre 2002
Barry, Donald 3766
Barry, Sir Gerald 5226
Barry, Iris 363, 1396, 1957,
    2752, 3537, 4587, 5190
Barry, John 3799
Barrymore, Blanche Oelrichs
    2152
Barrymore, Diana 2153, 3657
Barrymore, Elaine 2162
Barrymore, Ethel 2154, 2155,
    2156, 2157, 3646, 3690
Barrymore, John 2152, 2158,
    2159, 2160, 2161, 2162,
    2627, 3682, 3748, 3752,
    3777, 3813
Barrymore, Lionel 2163, 2164,
    3771
Barsam, Richard Meran 1775,
    4388, 4618
Barson, Alfred T. 2077
Bart, Peter 3802
Barthelmess, Richard 3690,
    5046, 5072
Barthes, Roland 4618
Bartholomew, Freddie 3676,
    3732
Bartok, Eva 2165
Bartolini, Elio 3861, 3985,
    4053
Barton, Buzz 3723
Barton, C. H. 763
Barton, Jack 764
Basinger, Jeanine 2896, 3475
Baskakov, Vladimir 1617
Bass, Saul 4588, 5235
Bassani, Giorgio 4312
Bast, William 2444
Basti, Abdul Zaher 1206
Batchelor, Joy 1986
Bateman, Robert 599, 621, 632,
    637
Battcock, Gregory 1790
Battison, John H. 569
Battle, Barbara Helen 2419

Batty, Linda 416
Bau, Nicolas 547
Bauchard, Philippe 1999
Baumgarten, Paul A. 1215,
    1294
Bawden, Liz-Anne 11
Baxter, Anne 3740
Baxter, Brian 2827
Baxter, John 1473, 1488, 1496,
    1734, 1862, 1920, 2028,
    2618, 3378, 3534, 3782,
    4620
Bay, Howard 797
Bayer, Michael 3580
Bayer, William S. 1319, 1439
Bayne, Beverly 3737
Bazelon, David T. 4728
Bazelon, Irwin 946, 3799
Bazin, Andre 428, 1954, 2166,
    2222, 2257, 2834, 3302,
    4043, 4117, 4236, 4490,
    4491, 4581, 4596, 4615,
    4618, 4620, 4622, 4629,
    4631, 4634
Beal, J. D. 638, 687
Beal, John 3821
Beale, Kenneth 2886
Bean, Robin 1950
Beasley, Rex 2521
Beatles 2167, 2168, 2169, 2170,
    2171, 2172, 2173, 2174,
    2175, 4437
Beaton, Cecil 2176, 2177, 2178,
    2179, 3145, 3628, 3642,
    3650, 3656, 4202, 4570
Beattie, Eleanor 180
Beatty, Warren 3911, 3699
Beauchamp, Anthony 2180
Beaudine, William 3759
Beauman, Sally 4169
Beaumont, Charles 4702
Beauvais, Jean 5265
Beauvoir, Simone de 2145
Beaver, Frank Eugene 2417
Beavers, Louise 3767, 3821
Beavers, Robert 2181
Bebb, Richard 1905
Beck, Bernard 1878
Beck, Calvin Thomas 1890
Beck, Marilyn 5106
Beck, Reginald 4065, 4066,
    4067, 4068
Becker, Jacques 1604

Bronowski, J. 5226
Bronson, Charles 2260, 2261,
    3684
Brook, Peter 3693
Brooke, Dinah 3937, 4117
Brooker, Floyde E. 5115
Brooks, Alice 4913
Brooks, Louise 3737, 4249
Brooks, Mel 3776
Brooks, Richard 3646, 3720,
    3786, 3803, 4557, 5063
Brosnan, John 1030, 1929
Brough, James 2609, 2773,
    2993, 3605, 5096
Brown, Catherine Hayes 2798
Brown, Clarence 3695, 3786
Brown, Curtis F. 2208
Brown, Frederick 2375
Brown, H. G. 1108
Brown, Harry 4260
Brown, James W. 96
Brown, Jim 2262, 3767
Brown, Joe E. 2263
Brown, John Mason 2264, 3411,
    4493, 4494, 4495, 4496
Brown, Johnny Mack 3766, 3790
Brown, Karl 2265
Brown, Lewis S. 1325
Brown, Roland G. 5168
Brown, Royal S. 2716
Brown, William 659, 2957
Brown, William R. 3358
Browning, Norma Lee 3113
Browning, Tod 3786
Brownlow, Kevin 1378, 3759,
    4102
Broz, Jaroslav 1679
Bruccoli, Matthew J. 2585,
    2586, 2590
Bruckman, Clyde 4022
Brule, Claude 4140
Brunel, Adrian 975, 2266, 4722
Bruno, Michael 3713
Brusendorff, Ove 2008
Brustein, Robert 4597
Bryan, John 3635
Bryan, Julien 1754, 2267
Bryan, Margaret B. 5185
Bryer, Jackson R. 2585
Bryher, Winifred 4605
Bryne-Daniel, J. 5154
Brynych, Zbynek 3789
Buache, Freddy 465, 2275

Buchanan, Andrew 545, 4406,
    5196, 5199, 5291
Buchanan, Donald William 1541
Buchanan, Edgar 3769
Buchanan, Jack 3690
Buchanan, Singer Alfred 4751
Bucher, Felix 170
Buchman, Herman 882
Buchman, Sidney 3943, 3784,
    4054, 4069, 4192, 4244
Buck, Frank 2268
Buck, Pearl S. 1754
Buckle, Gerard Fort 4444
Bucquet, Harold S. 3978
Budgen, Suzanne 2555
Bukalski, Peter J. 392
Bull, Clarence Sinclair 2269,
    3696
Bull, Peter 2270
Bulleid, Henry Anthony Vaughan
    584, 1015
Buñuel, Luis 1785, 2271, 2272,
    2273, 2274, 2275, 2276,
    2277, 2278, 2279, 3685,
    3693, 3803, 3829, 3889,
    3935, 4000, 4001, 4205,
    4236, 4326, 4387, 4405,
    4548, 4596, 4621
Buono, Victor 3684
Buranelli, Prosper 3485
Burch, Noel 676, 4820
Burch, Ruth 3795
Burder, John 913, 1081
Burdick, Loraine 3476
Burford, Roger 1306
Burger, Chester 105
Burgess, Muriel 3094
Burke, Billie 2280, 2281, 3690
Burke, John 3129
Burke, John Gordon 4733
Burke, William Lee 4748
Burnett, Carol 2282
Burnett, Linda R. 5162
Burnett, Ruth 2458
Burnford, Paul 551
Burnley, Fred 3743
Burns, E. Bradford 1730, 1731
Burns, George 2283, 3636,
    3711, 3726
Burnside, Norman 3970
Burr, Raymond 3684
Burroughs, Edgar Rice 1945,
    1946

Carr, Harry 4413
Carr, Larry 2408
Carr, William A. 5092
Carradine, John 5079
Carrick, Edward 557, 791,
    792, 794
Carrico, J. Paul 4840
Carrier, Rick 668
Carriere, Jean-Claude 3889,
    4197, 4356
Carrillo, Leo 2306
Carrol, Sidney 4084
Carroll, David 668, 3748
Carroll, Diahann 3767
Carroll, Joan 3732
Carroll, John 3790
Carroll, John S. 871
Carroll, Kent E. 4133
Carroll, Nancy 2307
Carson, Jack 3790
Carson, L. M. Kit 3957
Carson, Sunset 3766
Carson, William 2861
Carstairs, John Paddy 2308,
    2309, 2919
Carter, Ann 3732
Carter, Donald 1834
Carter, Gaylord 3820
Carter, Huntly 1350, 1352,
    1393
Carter, Jack 3731
Carter, Maurice 3635
Carter, S. B. 5278
Carter, Tasile 1270
Caruso, Dorothy 2310
Caruso, Enrico 2310
Cary, Diana Serra 5056
Cary, John 1976
Carynnyk, Marco 2495
Casey, Ralph D. 364
Cashin, Fergus 2286
Casper, Joseph Andrew 3121
Cassady, Ralph, Jr. 1274, 1284
Cassady, Ralph, III 1284
Cassavetes, John 2312, 3718,
    3776, 3786, 3788, 3802,
    4004, 4186
Cassidy, Hopalong 2056
Cassyd, Syd 61
Castell, David 3783
Castle, Charles 2403
Castle, Irene and Vernon 2313
Castle, William 3812

Casty, Alan 527, 1440, 3369,
    4712
Cates, Gilbert 3776, 4089
Catling, Gordon 622
Caulfield, Joan 3756
Caunter, Julien 1016, 1018,
    1024
Cavalcanti, Alberto 1306, 2130,
    3818, 4582, 4588, 5192
Cavell, Stanley 4473, 4618
Cavender, Kenneth 152
Cavett, Frank 4033
Cawelti, John 1837, 1847, 3912
Cawkwell, Tim 9
Cawston, Richard 3738, 3743
Cayette, Andre 4820
Cayrol, Jean 4208
Cazacu, Matei 1892
Cendrars, Blaise 1806
Ceram, C. W. 1341
Chabot, Jean 3714
Chabrol, Claude 1605, 2314,
    2834, 3693, 3803, 3819,
    4581, 4607
Chadwick, Stanley 1581
Chamberlain, Richard 3793
Chamberlin, Ray Philip 5308
Chambers, Marilyn 2315
Chambers, Robert W. 1035,
    4804
Champion, Gower 3699
Chan, Charlie 1919, 2056
Chandler, Anna Curtis 5337
Chandler, David 3230
Chandler, Helen 3821
Chandler, Raymond 2316, 2317,
    3674, 3741, 3977
Chaneles, Sol 301
Chaney, Lon 2318, 2319
Chaney, Lon, Jr. 1898, 2320
Chang, Kuang-nien 2363
Chapin, Billy 3732
Chaplin, Charles 2321, 2322,
    2323, 2324, 2325, 2326,
    2327, 2328, 2329, 2330,
    2331, 2332, 2333, 2334,
    2335, 2336, 2337, 2338,
    2339, 2340, 2341, 2342,
    2343, 2344, 2345, 2346,
    2347, 2348, 2699, 2700,
    3623, 3661, 3662, 3682,
    3685, 3690, 3693, 3695,
    3745, 3772, 3786, 4490,

Curran, Charles W. 577
Current, Ira B. 842
Currie, Hector 533, 1793
Curry, George 3956
Curti, Carlo 3426
Curtis, Alan 3790
Curtis, Anthony 3785
Curtis, David 1798
Curtis, Tony 3672, 3791, 5091
Curtiss, Thomas Quinn 3539
Curtiz, Michael 2422, 3759,
    3786, 3929
Cushing, Jane 5408
Cushing, Peter 1898, 2423
Cushman, George W. 661, 908,
    1000, 1054
Cushman, Robert B. 3244
Cussler, Margaret 2424
Custer, Bob 3723
Cypher, Irene F. 5337
Czeszko, Bohdan 4026

-D-

Daborn, John 1058
Dache, Lilly 2425
Daguerre, L. J. M. 2426
Dahl, Arlene 3701
Dahl, David 2685
Dahl, Roald 3181
Dahn, Maurice 1263
Daisne, Johan 200
Dale, Edgar 366, 370, 506,
    4785, 4906, 5271, 5334
Dale, R. C. 1878
Daley, Cass 3770
Dali, Salvador 3657, 3688,
    3829, 3935
Dalrymple, Ian 2867, 3818
Dalton, David 2448
Daly, Marsha 3386
d'Amico, Suso Cecchi 4115,
    4290, 4312, 4417
Dandridge, Dorothy 2427, 2428,
    3767
Danek, Oldrich 3789
Daniels, Bebe 2429, 3690
Daniels, Douglas 3635
Daniels, William 2430, 4051
Danischewsky, Monja 2130, 2431
Danko, X. 2527
Dante, Michael 3684
Danton, Ray 3684

Darcus, Jack 3808
d'Arcy, Susan 2225
Darin, Bobby 3691
Darling, Brian 2714
Darlington, William Aubrey 3209
Darmenberg, Joseph 33
Darnell, Linda 1308, 3701, 3740
Darretta, Gian-Lorenzo 4615
Darro, Frankie 3800
Dart, Peter 3274
Da Silva, Howard 4946
Dassin, Jules 3753, 4526
Daudelin, Robert 3714
Daugherty, Annie Rose 5382
Daugherty, Charles Michael 5207
Daves, Delmer 3784, 5063
Davidson, Arthur O. 5293
Davidson, Bill 5090
Davies, Brenda 2411, 2491
Davies, Hunter 2172
Davies, Jack 4371
Davies, Marion 2432, 2433,
    3737, 5046
Davies, Mary 1448
Davis, Bette 2434, 2435, 2436,
    2437, 2438, 3632, 3698,
    3707, 3791, 3798, 5072
Davis, Boyd H. 5185
Davis, Brian 1931
Davis, Christopher 2536
Davis, Denys 578, 601
Davis, Edward E. 2174
Davis, Elise Miller 3344
Davis, Frank 4382
Davis, Harold S. 5347
Davis, Joan 2439, 3790
Davis, Ossie 3767
Davis, Owen 2440
Davis, Sammy, Jr. 2441, 3681,
    3692, 3697, 3767
Davy, Charles 5192
Dawe, Cedric 3635
Dawn, Norman O. 1425
Dawson, Bonnie 307
Day, Barry 3046
Day, Beth 3353, 5041
Day, Donald 3352, 3353, 3355
Day, Doris 2442, 3704, 3747,
    3791, 3793
de Antonio, Emile 4261
De Blasio, Edward 2167
de Brigard, Emilie 1782
De Broca, Philip 3739

Fischer, Soren 2827
Fischinger, Oskar 1785
Fisher, J. David 863
Fisher, Terence 1877
Fitzgerald, Edward 3438
Fitzgerald, Ella 3747
Fitzgerald, F. Scott 2578, 2579,
    2580, 2581, 2582, 2583,
    2584, 2585, 2586, 2587,
    2588, 2589, 2590, 3660,
    3741, 3758, 3807, 4609,
    4651, 5048
Fitzgerald, John E. 5017
Fitzgerald, Robert 4078
Fitzgerald, Zelda (see Fitzger-
    ald, F. Scott)
Fitz-Richard, Helen 363
Flagg, James Montgomery 2591
Flaherty, Frances Hubbard 2595
Flaherty, Robert 2592, 2593,
    2594, 2595, 2596, 2597,
    2598, 3685, 3764, 3786,
    4174, 4204, 4569, 4573,
    4579, 4588, 4819
Flaiano, Ennio 3897, 3974,
    3987, 4121, 4223, 4359,
    4402, 4407
Flamini, Roland 4037
Flanders, Mark 2075
Fleischer, Richard 3871
Fleming, Ian 3674
Fleming, Rhonda 3701, 3801
Fleming, Victor 3786, 4036,
    4114
Fletcher, John Gould 4599
Flint, Leslie 3513
Flint, R. W. 4474
Flippen, Ruth 3805
Flipper 2599
Flora, Paul 4765
Flores, Sam 3959
Florescu, Radu 1870, 1892
Florey, Robert 3086, 3745
Flournoy, Richard 4198
Flowers, Bess 3769
Flye, Father 2071
Flynn, Charles 2039
Flynn, Errol 2600, 2601, 2602,
    2603, 2604, 2605, 2606,
    2700, 3633, 3777, 3790,
    3791, 3813, 3815, 5048,
    5092
Foch, Nina 3802

Fonda, Henry 2607, 2608,
    2609, 2610, 2611, 3647,
    3709, 3795, 3802, 3815
Fonda, Jane 2607, 2608, 2609,
    2610, 2611
Fonda, Peter 2607, 2608,
    2609, 2610, 2611, 3699,
    3717, 3736, 3984
Font, Jose Luis 1648
Fontaine, Joan 3792, 3801
Fontanne, Lynn 3029, 3030,
    3620
Fontnouvelle, Pierre de 3662
Foort, Reginald 921
Foote, Horton 4379
Foran, Dick 3790
Forbes, Bryan 2612, 3772
Forcade, Thomas King 4181
Ford, Glenn 2613
Ford, John 1979, 2614, 2615,
    2616, 2617, 2618, 2619,
    2620, 2621, 3693, 3763,
    3764, 3776, 3786, 3820,
    4046, 4047, 4080, 4097,
    4336, 4337, 4338, 4339,
    4469, 4588, 4738, 4845
Ford, Richard 4907
Fordin, Hugh 1537
Foreman, Carl 3733, 3913,
    4070, 4076, 4438
Forman, Denis 1576, 1580
Forman, Harrison 2622
Forman, Henry James 4901
Forman, Milos 2623, 2624,
    3718, 3789, 3803, 4356
Formby, George 2625
Forsdale, Louis 5304
Forster, E. M. 4609
Forsythe, Robert 4568, 4630
Fort, Garrett 4017
Foster, Dianne 3701
Foster, George 4251
Foster, Lewis 4198
Foster, Preston 3790, 3821
Foster, Walter T. 759
Foulke, Adrienne 2271
Fowler, Gene 2160, 2508, 2626,
    2627, 2628, 2629, 3403
Fowler, Roy 1600, 3567
Fowler, Will 2629
Fowlie, Wallace 2370, 2373
Fowlkes, John Guy 5285
Fox, George 3983

Meeker, Ralph 3684
Meierhenry, Wesley C. 5296
Meighan, Thomas 3690
Meisner, Sanford 745
Mekas, Jonas 525, 1790, 1793, 1799, 1802, 1911, 3549, 3688, 4578, 4588, 4593, 4600, 4614, 5163
Melies, Georges 3100, 3101, 3102, 4579, 4588
Mellen, Joan 1699, 3148, 3874, 4772
Mellor, G. J. 1592
Melnitz, William C. 375
Melton, David 2681
Meltzer, Milton 4749
Melville, Jean-Pierre 1605, 3103, 3753, 3803
Mencken, H. L. 4604, 4609
Mendelsohn, Harold A. 4709
Mendelsohn, Jack 4437
Menjou, Adolphe 3104
Menville, Douglas 1894
Menzel, Jiri 3789, 3946
Mercer, Ann 5141
Mercer, John 636, 4864
Mercouri, Melina 3105, 3699, 3704
Meredith, Burgess 3620, 3821
Meredith, Scott 2892
Merkel, Una 3769
Merman, Ethel 3106, 3643
Merrill, Gary 3684
Merritt, Russell LaMonte 2758
Merwin, Sam 3216
Merz, Irena 1671
Messel, Oliver 3635
Messick, Hank 5108
Messter, Oskar 1425
Mesta, Perle 3107
Metz, Christian 4482, 4483, 4618, 4622, 4634
Metzger, Radley 4141
Meyer, Anthony 5315
Meyer, Emile 3684
Meyer, Nicholas 4160
Meyer, Richard 2760
Meyer, Russ 1212, 3812
Meyers, Sidney 4276
Meyers, Warren B. 192
Meyerson, Michael 4162
Meyerson, Peter 2445
Michael, Maurice 2662

Michael, Paul 5, 434, 2229
Michaelis, Anthony R. 1090
Michaels, Delores 3701
Michalczyk, John Joseph 4175
Michalek, Boleslaw 3543
Micheaux, Oscar 3767
Michel, Walter S. 4600
Michelson, Annette 1790, 1800, 1802, 4477, 4600, 4618, 4621
Michener, Charles 4133
Middleton, George 3108
Middleton, Robert 3684
Midler, Bette 3793
Miles, Herbert J. 5005
Miles, Peter 3732
Miles, Sylvia 3793
Miles, Vera 3701
Milestone, Lewis 3109, 3110, 3705, 3786, 3823, 4218, 4267
Milford, Nancy 2584
Milgrom, Al 3530
Milius, John 4143
Milland, Ray 1567, 3111, 3112
Millar, Daniel 2257
Millar, Gavin 4321
Millard, William John, Jr. 4866
Miller, Ann 3113, 3790
Miller, Arthur 3741, 4189, 4600, 4675, 4998
Miller, Arthur C. 834, 3114, 3115, 3116
Miller, Diane Disney 2476
Miller, Don 2038
Miller, Edwin 3727
Miller, George 466
Miller, Harry 4276
Miller, Henry 1785, 4574
Miller, Jonathan 3049
Miller, Leslie 3888
Miller, Maud M. 2, 5222
Miller, Patricia George 27
Miller, Ruby 3117
Miller, Seton I. 4069
Miller, Tony 27
Miller, Vernon L. 4904
Miller, Virgil E. 3118
Miller, William C. III 4877
Millerson, Gerald 872
Mills, Earl 2428
Mills, Hayley 2185, 3699
Mills, Jack 3715

Mills, John 1567, 2185
Mills, Juliet 2185
Mills, Reginald 4357
Mills, Robert 3290
Milne, Tom 2502, 2716, 2719,
  3020, 3056, 4176, 4615
Milner, Michael 2011
Milton, John 4250
Mineo, Sal 3691
Minnelli, Liza 3119
Minnelli, Vincente 3120, 3121,
  3122, 3705, 3786, 3816,
  3846
Minney, R. J. 1147, 2114,
  2329, 5224
Minoff, Lee 4437
Minott, Rodney G. 3474
Minow, Martin 4086, 4087
Minter, L. F. 586, 1056
Minter, Mary Miles 3737
Minton, Eric 1906
Minus, Johnny 1209, 1211,
  1296, 5434
Mirams, Gordon 1732
Miranda, Carmen 3740, 3790
Mirisch, Walter M. 910
Mishkin, Meyer 3809
Mitchell and Durant 3726
Mitchell, Alice Miller 4896
Mitchell, George 1970
Mitchell, Grant 3123
Mitchell, John W. 5121
Mitchell, Leslie 1564
Mitchell, Robert A. 962
Mitchum, Robert 2699, 2700,
  3124, 3686, 3788, 3813,
  3822
Mitry, Jean 4634
Mix, Olive Stokes 3125
Mix, Paul E. 3126
Mix, Tom 3125, 3126, 3723,
  3748, 3782
Mizener, Arthur 2578
Mizner, Addison 3127
Mizner, Wilson 3128, 3129
Mizoguchi, Kenji 3130
Moakley, Francis Xavier 4880
Modiano, Patrick 4129
Moen, Lars 572
Moffett, Sharyn 3732
Moger, Art 5097
Moholy-Nagy, Laszlo 3132, 3133,
  4458, 4468

Moholy-Nagy, Sibyl 3132
Mohr, Hal 3134, 3742, 3802
Moisio, Mikki 421
Moley, Raymond 4943
Molinaro, Ursule 4176
Molloy, Edward 953
Momand, A. B. 1235
Monaco, James 29, 403
Monaghan, John P. 3089
Monahan, James 4572
Monett, Negley 3135
Monier, Pierre 590
Monroe, Marilyn 3136, 3137,
  3138, 3139, 3140, 3141,
  3142, 3143, 3144, 3145,
  3146, 3147, 3148, 3149,
  3150, 3151, 3152, 3153,
  3655, 3665, 3671, 3694,
  3740, 3810, 3811, 4765,
  5091, 5092, 5100
Montagu, Ivor 508, 519, 525,
  884, 888, 2528, 2529, 3848,
  3849, 4106, 4272, 4309,
  4445, 4569, 4593, 4737
Montez, Maria 3698, 3790,
  3791, 3814, 5079
Montgomery, Douglass 3821
Montgomery, Elizabeth R. 2482
Montgomery, John 1808
Montgomery, Robert 3154, 3637
Monti, Carlotta 2572
Monty, Ib 2500
Moody, Richard 2814
Moonjean, Hank 3795
Moore, Colleen 3155, 3690,
  3745
Moore, David 4145
Moore, Dick 1313
Moore, Dickie 3732, 3821
Moore, Douglas 4929
Moore, Grace 3156, 3690
Moore, James Whitney 1057
Moore, Joanna 3701
Moore, Roger 3793, 4154
Moore, Sonia 740, 746
Moorehead, Agnes 3157, 3795
Morahan, Tom 3635
Moran and Mack 3726
Moravia, Alberto 4007, 4133
More, Kenneth 3158
Moreau, Jeanne 3697, 3810
Morehouse, Ward 2381
Morella, Joe 1247, 2134, 2249,

London, Kurt 922
Lone Ranger 3494
Longstreet, Stephen 2304
Lonsdale, Freddy 3009
Lonstein, Albert I. 3420
Loos, Anita 3010, 3011, 3690,
    3742, 3749, 4432
Loren, Sophia 3012, 3013,
    3014, 3015, 3810
Lorentz, Pare 3016, 3017,
    3786, 4010, 4515, 4611,
    4934
Lorenz, Denis 463
Lorre, Peter 3018, 3633
Losey, Joseph 3019, 3020,
    3693, 3698, 3707, 3744,
    3772, 3803, 3824, 4029,
    4313, 4607
Losey, Mary 1749, 1754, 4582,
    5356
Louise, Anita 3790, 3821
Lounsbury, Myron Osborn 4630
Lovan, Nora G. 5403
Love, Bessie 3737
Lovejoy, Frank 3790
Lovelace, Linda 3021, 3022
Lovell, Alan 1548, 1774, 3412,
    4548, 4622, 5133
Lovell, Hugh 1270
Lovell, Terry 4591
Low, Rachel 1357, 1358, 1362,
    1386
Lowe, Clayton Kent 4833
Lowe, Edmund 3790
Lowndes, Douglas 5147
Loy, Myrna 3690, 3707, 3791
Lubin, Arthur 3812
Lubitsch, Ernst 3023, 3024,
    3693, 3763, 3764, 3786,
    4211, 4579, 4610
Luboviski, Git 384
Lucas, George 3845
Luce, Clare Booth 3751
Ludlum, Barbara 2006
Lugosi, Bela 3025, 3026, 3027
Lukas, J. Anthony 4169
Lukas, Paul 3821
Luke, Keye 3770
Luke, Michael 4235
Lumet, Sidney 3733, 3762,
    3786, 3803, 4054, 4390
Lumiere, Louis 1425, 3028,
    3685

Lumsdaine, Arthur A. 4858,
    5301
Lundbergh, Holger 2194
Lung, Ti 1978
Lunt, Alfred 3029, 3030, 3620
Lustig, Ernst 4144
Luther, Rodney 1166
Lutz, Edwin George 800
Lye, Len 1911, 4588, 4820
Lynch, Francis Dennis 4889
Lynch, William F. 5012
Lynn, Diana 3756, 3790
Lynx, J. J. 3638
Lyon, Ben 3031
Lyons, Timothy J. 1221

-M-

McAllister, Frank 5312
McAnany, Emile G. 5267
MacArthur, Charles 3032, 3033,
    3807, 4435
McArthur, Colin 1923, 3542
MacArthur, Mary 2798
Macartney-Filgate, Terence
    3034
Macauley, Richard 42
MacBean, James Roy 4428,
    4567, 4622
McBride, Jim 3718, 3957
McBride, Joseph 2621, 2793,
    3574, 4583, 4614
McCabe, John 2958, 2962,
    2964
McCabe, Peter 2175
McCaffrey, Donald W. 1814,
    1822, 2341, 4019
McCaffrey, Patrick J. 5399,
    5405
McCallum, David 3691
McCallum, John 2386, 2911
McCambridge, Mercedes 3035,
    3701
MacCann, Richard Dyer 374,
    421, 1191, 1776, 4578, 4821
McCarey, Leo 1308, 3763,
    3786, 3980, 4033, 4171,
    4845, 5079
McCarthy, Joe 2084
McCarthy, Joseph 4261
McCarthy, Todd 2039
McCarty, Clifford 188, 388,
    2228, 2605, 3421

Salemson, Harold J.   4946
Sales-Gomes, P. E.   4572
Salkin, Leo 592
Salter, James 3762
Salumbides, Vicente 1715
Samples, Gordon 390, 415
Samuels, Charles 2649, 2899,
    3557, 3757, 3906, 4597,
    4614, 4733
Sandburg, Carl 4609
Sanders, George 3384, 3707,
    3777
Sanderson, Richard Arlo 1369
Sandford, Jeremy 3743
Sandro, Paul Denney 2278
Sands, Diana 3767
Sands, Pierre Norman 493
Santaniello, A. E.   379
Sargeant, Winthrop 3639
Sargent, Alvin 3802
Sargent, John A.   4957
Sarkar, Kobita 1714
Saroyan, William 3758
Sarris, Andrew   1790, 2039,
    2222, 2793, 2834, 3532,
    3693, 3744, 3762, 3889,
    3902, 3906, 3941, 4199,
    4317, 4320, 4521, 4522,
    4523, 4583, 4584, 4586,
    4588, 4597, 4600, 4614,
    4618, 4620, 4622, 4627,
    4633, 4728, 5163
Sartre, Jean-Paul 4096, 4609
Sassoon, Vidal 3385
Satariano, Cecil 683
Saunders, Richard Drake 39
Savage, Ann 3701
Savage, Nadine Dormoy 596
Savalas, Telly 3386
Savarese, Paul 2549
Savary, Louis M.   4840
Saville, Philip 4235
Saville, Victor 3387
Saxton, Martha 4778
Scagnetti, Jack 1983, 3516,
    5055
Scaramazza, Paul A.   4619
Schaefer, George 3792, 4165
Schaefer, Susan 5149
Schaffner, Franklin 3892
Schary, Dore 3388, 3613, 3703,
    3742, 3792, 4207, 4345,
    4620, 4820

Scheel, Hannah 3802
Schenck, Hilbert, Jr.   820
Schenk, Joseph 3703, 3712
Schenk, Nicholas 3712
Schenker, Susan 403
Scherer, Kees 432
Scheuer, Philip K.   4798
Scheuer, Steven H.   131, 1445
Schiaparelli, Elsa 3389
Schickel, Richard 1420, 1504,
    2479, 2542, 2543, 2851,
    3000, 3669, 3816, 4524,
    4540, 4541, 4585, 4604,
    4614, 4620, 4736, 4763,
    4838
Schiffman, Suzanne 3959
Schifrin, Lalo 3778, 3799
Schildkraut, Joseph 3390
Schildkraut, Rudolf 3391
Schillaci, Anthony 4604, 4620,
    5022, 5321
Schillaci, Peter 2276
Schlesinger, John 3733, 3739,
    3772, 3776, 3803, 3955,
    4351
Schlossberg, Marilyn 3984
Schlosser, Anatol I.   3328
Schmalenbach, Werner 513
Schmidt, Georg 513
Schmidt, Jan 3789
Schnee, Charles 4207
Schneider, Alan 4011
Schneider, Maria 4133
Schnitzer, Jean 1625
Schnitzer, Luda 1625
Schoedsack, Ernest B.   4126,
    4127
Scholz, Charles B.   692
Schonberg, Michael 1686
Schonfeld, Robert D.   2175
Schoolcraft, Ralph Newman 404
Schorm, Evald 3789, 3803
Schrader, Paul 2258
Schramm, Wilbur 4697, 4723,
    5346
Schreck, Everett M.   752
Schreiber, Robert Edwin 959
Schreivogel, Paul 4227, 5158
Schulberg, Budd 3712, 3741,
    3758, 3802, 4002, 4427
Schuller, Charles Francis 5341
Schultheiss, John E.   308, 5054
Schultz, Ed and Dodi 673

Storck, Henri 1088, 3738, 4572
Stork, Leopold 1077
Storr, Carter B. 5263, 5300
Storrer, William Allin 4420
Stote, Helen M. 1033
Stout, Wesley W. 2997
Stovin, P. D. 2902
Strait, Raymond 3063, 3240
Strange, Michael 2152
Strasberg, Lee 741, 745, 3145, 4582
Strasser, Alex 546, 970, 1106
Straub, Jean-Marie 3446, 3714, 4221
Strauss, L. Harry 5338
Strebble, Elizabeth Grottle 1608
Streisand, Barbra 3447, 3448, 3449, 3699, 3704, 3788
Strenge, Walter 834
Strenkovsky, Serge 878
Strick, Marv 2033
Strick, Philip 2097
Strickland, Francis Cowles 726
Stringer, Michael 798
Strode, R. 60
Stroheim, Erich von (see von Stroheim, Erich)
Stromgren, Richard L. 1447
Strong, Harry Hotchkiss 1398
Strudwick, Shepperd 4946
Struss, Karl 3450
Stuart, Frederic 1467
Stuart, Gloria 3821
Stuart, John 3451
Stuart, Ray 3675
Stuart, Walker 4363
Stucker, Melinda 5152
Stulberg, Gordon 1212
Sturges, John 910, 3786, 5063
Sturges, Preston 3452, 3693, 3741, 3744, 3749, 3763, 3784, 3786, 3807, 4058, 4188
Sucksdorff, Arne 3453
Sudley, Lord 3576, 4130
Suid, Murray 682
Sulik, Boleslaw 1227, 3542, 3952
Sullavan, Margaret 3454, 3647, 3791
Sullivan, Bede 5145
Sullivan, C. Gardner 4303
Sullivan, Ed 2336

Sullivan, Elliott 4998
Sullivan, John 58
Sullivan, Scott 2096
Summers, Hope 3769
Summers, Stanford 5319
Sumner, Robert L. 5086
Sumrall, Lester F. 5003
Sundgren, Nils Petter 1664
Surgenor, Alexander John 844
Susann, Jacqueline 3716, 3793
Suschitzky, Wolfgang 3715
Sussex, Elizabeth 1783, 2091
Sutherland, Duncan 3635
Sutro, John 4570
Sutton, Grady 3769
Svensson, Arne 178
Swallow, Norman 1764
Swanberg, W. A. 2805
Swanson, Gloria 3455, 3456, 3537, 3657, 3690, 3695, 3737, 3756, 3810, 5072
Sweeney, Russell C. 1249
Sweet, Blanche 3737, 3742, 3775
Sweeting, Charles 5167
Sweny, Karen 432
Swindell, Larry 2675, 3008, 3488
Switzer, Carl "Alfalfa" 3732
Sylbert, Paul 4342

-T-

Taber, Elizabeth S. 878
Tabori, Paul 2929, 3383
Taft, Robert 1326
Tailleur, Roger 3458
Talbot, Daniel 4261, 4574
Talbot, Frederick A. 541
Talbot, Lyle 3790
Talbot, William Henry Fox 3457
Talese, Gay 3730
Tall, Joel 1001
Talmadge, Constance 3690
Talmadge, Norma 3690, 3737, 3745
Tandy, Jessica 3594, 3681
Taniguchi, Senkichi 4275
Tanner, Louise 3660, 4838
Taradash, Daniel 5063
Taranow, Gerda 2217
Tarshis, Barry 753

Tarzan 1943, 1944, 1945, 1946,
  2056
Tashlin, Frank 3458, 3784,
  4607
Tati, Jacques 1604, 3803, 4197
Tattoli, Elda 3939
Taubman, Joseph 1288
Taurog, Norman 3888
Taylor, Deems 1458, 3334
Taylor, Delores 3899
Taylor, Donald 3968
Taylor, Dwight 3459
Taylor, Elizabeth 3460, 3461,
  3462, 3463, 3464, 3465,
  3466, 3467, 3694, 3791,
  3800, 3810, 5070, 5090,
  5091, 5092
Taylor, Frank E. 786
Taylor, Jackie Lynn 3468
Taylor, John Russell 1909,
  3059, 3818, 3819, 3920,
  4504, 4545, 4620, 4627,
  5074
Taylor, Laurette 3469
Taylor, Michael 4482
Taylor, Michael M. 2563
Taylor, Robert 3470, 3471, 3813
Taylor, Robert Lewis 2564
Taylor, Sam 4019, 4045, 4296
Taylor, T. Allan 1527, 1535
Taylor, Theodore 1201
Taylor, William Desmond 5092
Teal, Ray 3684
Teichmann, Howard 2891
Teitelbaum, Maureen 4294
Telberg, Val 21
Tell, Pincus W. 1309
Tellegren, Lou 3748
Temple, Shirley 3472, 3473,
  3474, 3475, 3476, 3660,
  3676, 3732, 3740, 3801,
  5079
Terayama, Shuji 3811
Terrou, Fernand 1266
Terry, Alice 3737
Terry, Ellen 3671
Terry, Jim 2212
Terry-Thomas 3477, 3478
Teshigahara, Hiroshi 3811, 4430
Tetzel, Joan 3801
Tewkesbury, Joan 3479
Thalberg, Irving 3480, 3481,
  3661, 3695, 3703, 3712,
  4604, 4821

Thayer, David Lewis 4871
Themerson, Franciszka 3995
Themerson, Stefan 3995
Theobald, Peter 5140
Theodorakis, Mikis 3482
Thin Man, The 2056
Thom, Robert 4484
Thomas, Bob 2251, 2382, 2477,
  2478, 2860, 3312, 3400,
  3480, 3776, 5050
Thomas, D. B. 859, 1340
Thomas, Dylan 3882, 3968,
  3969, 4284, 4391, 4392,
  4399, 4600
Thomas, Lawrence B. 1528
Thomas, T. T. 2446
Thomas, Tony 1509, 1917, 1982,
  2212, 2252, 2492, 2605,
  2908, 2924, 2942, 3509,
  3777
Thomey, Tedd 2602, 2603, 3731
Thompson, Charles 2416
Thompson, Charles Victor 984
Thompson, Francis 4378
Thompson, Howard 138, 2117,
  3442, 4614
Thompson, Kay 3793
Thompson, Morton 3483
Thompson, Richard 4583
Thompson, Robert E. 4365
Thomson, David 312, 4826
Thomson, Fred 3723
Thomson, Virgil 3778
Thorndike, Sybil 744, 3484
Thornton, Michael 3093
Thorp, Margaret Farrand 4788
Thorpe, Edward 5049
Thorpe, Frances 427
Thrasher, Frederic M. 1462
Three Stooges, The 3726, 3755
Thulin, Ingrid 3802
Thurstone, L. L. 4903
Tichenor, Frank A. 1133
Tierney, Gene 2920, 3740
Tindall, Kevin 5351
Tiomkin, Dimitri 945, 1308,
  3485, 3778
Tizzo, Romano 2863
Toback, James 2262, 4169
Tobin, Genevieve 3821
Todd, Ann 3800
Todd, Michael 3486
Todd, Thelma 3726, 3755, 5092

-U-

Uegusa, Keinosuke 3979, 4239
Uggams, Leslie 3692
Uher, Stefan 3789
Ulanov, Barry 2413, 4707
Ullmann, Liv 3793, 3802
Ulm, Gerith von 2322
Ulmer, Edgar G. 3507, 3812
Umiker-Sebeok, Donna Jean
    4483
Underhill, Frederic 3045
Underwood, Peter 2883
Unger, Ivan 3677
Ungurait, Donald F. 4719
Unwin, Mary 1938
Upson, Wilfrid 5006
Ursini, James 1897, 2968, 3452
Ussher, Bruno 39
Ustinov, Peter 3508, 3509,
    3631, 3657, 4569
Utz, Walter Julius, Jr. 4882
Uytterhoeven, Pierre 4173

-V-

Vadim, Roger 1605, 4140
Vailland, Roger 4140
Vajda, Ladislaus 4249, 4374
Valdes, Joan 4718, 4737
Vale, Eugene 973
Valente, Renee 3809
Valentino, Rudolph 3510, 3511,
    3512, 3513, 3514, 3515,
    3516, 3517, 3661, 3682,
    3748, 3813, 5072
Valenzuela, Louis 91
Vallance, Tom 331, 1832
Vallee, Rudy 3518, 3519, 3657
Valli, Alida 3801
Van Cleef, Lee 3684
Van Dongen, Helen 4572
Van Doorslaer, Marguerite 1704
Van Doren, Mark 4532
Van Dyke, W. S. 3520, 3786
Van Dyke, Willard 1754, 3738
Van Fleet, Jo 3701
Van Hecke, B. C. 1921
Van Leuven, Karl 4798
Van Nostrand, Albert D. 4638
Van Ormer, Edward B. 4860
Van Peebles, Melvin 3767, 4354
Van Runkle, Theadora 3802

Van Vooren, Monique 3657
Vance, Philo 2051
Vanderbeek, Stan 1790, 1793,
    1911, 4578, 5163
Vannoey, R. C. 5268
Varda, Agnes 1605
Vardac, Nicholas 1361, 2760,
    4664
Vas, Robert 4620, 4728
Vassiliev, Dimitry 3830
Vaughn, Ciba 2377, 2715, 3573
Vaughn, Robert 4999
Vaughn, Robert (actor) 3672,
    3691
Vavra, Otakar 3789, 4109
Veidt, Conrad 5046
Veiller, Anthony 4421
Veinstein, Andre 466
Velez, Lupe 3790, 3792, 5092
Velguth, Paul 1785
Venturini, Franco 371
Verdon, Gwen 3699
Verdone, Mario 428
Vereker, Barbara 5221
Vermilye, Jerry 2437, 2740,
    2941, 3434
Verneuil, Louis 2215
Vertov, Dziga 1620, 3685, 3773,
    4590, 4600, 4621
Vesselinova, Liliana 1683
Vetchinsky, Alec 3635
Vidal, Gore 3892
Vidor, Charles 3918, 4244
Vidor, Florence 3737
Vidor, King 900, 903, 3521,
    3522, 3705, 3786, 3816
Viertel, Salka 3523
Vigo, Jean 3524, 3525, 3526,
    3683, 3935, 4548, 4572,
    4575, 4621
Vincent, Carl 371, 428
Viot, Jacques 4117
Visconti, Luchino 3527, 3803,
    4115, 4290, 4312, 4361,
    4417, 4580
Vitale, Frank 3808
Vivienne 3654
Vizcaino Casas, Fernando 1647
Vizzard, Jack 4973
Vlacil, Frantisek 3789
Vogel, Amos 1790, 1804, 4652,
    5292
Voight, Jon 3707, 3717, 3802

Wayne, Jane Ellen 3470
Wayne, John 3559, 3560, 3561,
  3562, 3563, 3564, 3565,
  3672, 3673, 3763, 3815,
  5072
Wead, Frank 3888
Wead, George Adam 2905
Weatherwax, Rudd B. 2954
Weaver, John T. 198, 201
Weaver, Kathleen 5430
Weaver, Randolph and Dorothy
  3298
Weaver, William 3611
Webb, Clifton 3684, 3690
Webber, Robert 3684
Weber, Alan Melchior 4893
Weber, Hugo 513
Wegener, Paul 4034
Weidler, Virginia 3732
Weightman, John 1801, 4042,
  4534
Weill, Kurt 525, 4593
Weinberg, Herman G. 428,
  1640, 2592, 3024, 3316,
  3524, 3529, 3533, 3535,
  3537, 3540, 4051, 4052,
  4413, 4535, 4575, 4600
Weiner, Janet 5270
Weinstein, Arnold 4251
Weinstein, Donald 4621
Weintraub, Joseph 3578
Weisbart, David 910
Weiss, Gene Stephen 5159
Weiss, Harvey 684
Weiss, Jiri 3789
Weiss, Ken 338
Weiss, Nathan 1241
Weiss, Paul 4484
Weissmuller, Johnny 3566,
  3698
Welch, Raquel 3704, 3717,
  3740
Weld, Tuesday 3672, 3701,
  3793
Weldon, Don 2952
Welles, Orson 2433, 2853,
  3567, 3568, 3569, 3570,
  3571, 3572, 3573, 3574,
  3655, 3674, 3685, 3693,
  3717, 3744, 3776, 3786,
  3803, 3941, 3942, 4168,
  4243, 4383, 4551, 4583,
  4600

Wellman, William 903, 3575,
  3695, 3786, 3795, 3816,
  4207, 4245, 4346
Wellman, William, Jr. 2793
Wells, Alan 4735
Wells, H. G. 4609
Wells, Ingeborg 3576
Wells, John Warren 2027
Wells, Ted 3723
Wells, Walter 5066
Wells, Zetta and Carveth 3277,
  3278
Welsch, Janice Rita 4779
Welsh, Paul 1898
Weltman, Manuel 3585
Wenden, D. J. 1390
Wenger, Roy Emerson 5280
Werner, Gösta 428
Werner, Michael 5251
Werner, Oskar 3707
Wertham, Fredric 5073
West, Claudine 4038, 4195
West, Frank 4591
West, George 918
West, Jessamyn 4020
West, Mae 3577, 3578, 3579,
  3580, 3694, 3756, 4772,
  4765
West, Nathanael 3581, 3582,
  3583, 3584, 3758, 4651
Westerbeck, Colin L., Jr. 4614
Westerby, Robert 4289
Westmore, Michael G. 883
Westmore, Perc 3795
Wexler, Haskell 3802
Wexler, Norman 4116
Whale, James 4017
Whannel, Paddy 4706, 5133
Wheare, K. C. 4914
Wheaton, Christopher D. 502,
  1298
Wheeler, Allen H. 4371
Wheeler, Dennis 1800
Wheeler, Leslie J. 580, 812,
  840, 841
Wheeler and Woolsey 3726
Whelan, Tim 4019, 4296
Whitaker, Rod 526, 4824
Whitaker, Sheila 3319
White, Carol 3707
White, David Manning 1972,
  4724, 4728, 4732, 4738
White, Eric Walter 4598

Winquist, Sven G.   161, 162, 169
Winslow, George "Foghorn"   3732
Winston, Douglas Garrett   4560
Winston, Richard   1341
Winter, David   3314
Winter, Keith   4287
Winter, Myrtle   1094
Winters, Shelley   3594, 3663, 3698, 3701
Wirt, Frederick Marshall   4953
Wise, Arthur   1028
Wise, Robert   910, 3596, 3720, 4820
Wiseman, Frederick   1781, 3738, 3743
Wiseman, Thomas   1423, 3655
Witcombe, Rick Trader   1984
Withers, Grant   3790
Withers, Jane   3676, 3732, 3821
Witney, William   3823
Wittek, Jerzy   1689
Wittenberg, Philip   1272
Wittich, Walter Arno   5285, 5341
Wlaschin, Ken   5239
Wodehouse, P. G.   3597
Wolf, Leonard   1874, 1885
Wolf Man, The   2056
Wolf, William   3087
Wolfe, Glenn J.   2995
Wolfe, Halley   997
Wolfe, Maynard Frank   3826
Wolfe, Tom   4604, 4736
Wolfenstein, Martha   4723, 4804, 4809
Wolff, Lothar   3853
Wolff, Peter   3961
Wolheim, Louis   3691
Wollen, Peter   2222, 2641, 3571, 4252, 4469, 4591, 4618, 4622
Wollenberg, H. H.   1632, 5201
Wolper, David L.   3598
Wolsky, Albert   301
Wong, Anna May   3821
Wood, Alan   2742, 3281
Wood, Joan   3599
Wood, Leslie   1400
Wood, Mary   2742
Wood, Michael   4856
Wood, Natalie   3732
Wood, Peggy   3600
Wood, Robert   1310

Wood, Robin   2100, 2199, 2314, 2711, 2792, 2793, 2832, 2834, 3235, 3714, 3857, 4414, 4607, 4614, 4615, 4620, 4622
Wood, Sam   1308, 3601, 3958, 4040, 4209, 4998
Wood, Tom   3588
Woodhouse, Bruce   1155
Woodhouse, Maurice T.   5259
Woods, Frank E.   3900, 4611
Woodward, Joanne   3704, 3707, 3791, 3793
Wookey, Karen   3802
Woolf, Virginia   4609, 4651
Woollcott, Alexander   3086
Wooten, William Patrick   2614
Worden, James William   5016
Worth, Fred L.   10
Worth, Sol   4843
Worthington, Clifford   1036
Wortley, Richard   2034
Wray, Fay   3790, 3821
Wrede, Casper   4237
Wright, Barbara   3860
Wright, Basil   1446, 1576, 1577, 1747, 1748, 1750, 2596, 2867, 3738, 3818, 4569, 4572, 4597, 5192, 5206, 5226
Wright, Charles R.   4699
Wright, Cobina   3602
Wright, Edward A.   5215, 5216
Wright, Jacqueline   3503
Wright, Will   1853
Wurlitzer, Rudolph   4255, 4398
Wyatt, Jane   3821
Wyckoff, Robert   686
Wyler, Robert   4020
Wyler, William   3211, 3603, 3604, 3656, 3720, 3786, 3893, 4020, 4195, 4435
Wyman, Jane   3707
Wynn, Ed   3605, 3711
Wynn, Keenan   3605, 3606, 3672
Wysotsky, Michael Z.   1008

-Y-

Yablonsky, Lewis   3280
Yanni, Nicholas   2576, 3379
Yeamans, George Thomas   5320
Yellin, David G.   2638